THE
MATRIX
OF RACE

Sara Miller McCune founded SAGE Publishing in 1965 to support the dissemination of usable knowledge and educate a global community. SAGE publishes more than 1000 journals and over 800 new books each year, spanning a wide range of subject areas. Our growing selection of library products includes archives, data, case studies and video. SAGE remains majority owned by our founder and after her lifetime will become owned by a charitable trust that secures the company's continued independence.

Los Angeles | London | New Delhi | Singapore | Washington DC | Melbourne

THE MATRIX OF RACE

Social Construction, Intersectionality, and Inequality

Rodney D. Coates
Miami University of Ohio

Abby L. Ferber
University of Colorado, Colorado Springs

David L. Brunsma
Virginia Tech

SAGE

Los Angeles | London | New Delhi
Singapore | Washington DC | Melbourne

FOR INFORMATION:

SAGE Publications, Inc.
2455 Teller Road
Thousand Oaks, California 91320
E-mail: order@sagepub.com

SAGE Publications Ltd.
1 Oliver's Yard
55 City Road
London EC1Y 1SP
United Kingdom

SAGE Publications India Pvt. Ltd.
B 1/I 1 Mohan Cooperative Industrial Area
Mathura Road, New Delhi 110 044
India

SAGE Publications Asia-Pacific Pte. Ltd.
3 Church Street
#10-04 Samsung Hub
Singapore 049483

Printed in Canada

ISBN 978-1-4522-0269-3

Acquisitions Editor: Jeff Lasser
Editorial Assistant: Adeline Wilson
Content Development Editor: Sarah Dillard
Production Editor: Andrew Olson
Copy Editor: Judy Selhorst
Typesetter: C&M Digitals (P) Ltd.
Proofreader: Caryne Brown
Indexer: Teddy Diggs
Cover Designer: Gail Buschman
Marketing Manager: Kara Kindstrom

This book is printed on acid-free paper.

17 18 19 20 21 10 9 8 7 6 5 4 3 2 1

■ ■ BRIEF CONTENTS

■ ■ ■ ■ DETAILED CONTENTS

Almost 16 years ago, the three of us (Rodney, Abby, and Dave) began a series of conversations that led ultimately to the production of this volume, *The Matrix of Race: Social Construction, Intersectionality, and Inequality*. Two events, separated by more than 7 years, served as stimuli for these conversations. These events, not quite bookends, but rather landmarks, served to highlight the need for such conversations. The first of these events was 9/11, with all of its associated terror; the second was the election, in November 2008, of the first African American to the presidency of the United States. Collectively, these landmarks and the events surrounding them challenged our notions of race, its relevance, and its continual transformation. Scholarship on race and ethnicity exists to help humanity think through collective events such as these and how they move us forward or further entrench us. As we considered contemporary and classic work on race and ethnic relations along with the prominent textbooks on race and ethnicity, we began to question whether a better approach was needed.

Our review of these works identified a significant group of texts that provide a plethora of theoretical expositions of race in the United States. Most provide syntheses of theory, histories, and structures that present cross-cultural analyses of race and ethnicity involving multiple groups—opting, often, for approaches that offer voyeuristic walks through the "races" and "ethnicities," as if readers were walking through a museum. Some of these texts highlight a concern for hate crimes, racial conflict, structural and systemic patterns of animosity, segregation, and inequality that duplicates racial and ethnic hierarchies across histories and societies. We also note the

prevailing logic that racism and ethnic discrimination are bad, and multiculturalism, diversity, and integration are good. Since the terrorist attacks on New York City and the Pentagon on September 11, 2001, there has also been increased attention given to the changing nature of racism, particularly as many additional groups have now become racialized, such as Muslims and other Middle Easterners. Similarly, increased attention has been paid post-9/11 to issues such as immigration, assimilation, racial profiling, terrorism, domestic security, and globalization. The election of Barack Obama was heralded by many as evidence that we, the United States, had made a significant step toward, if not actually arrived at, a postracial society. Such reactions were not only naive but also harmful, as they served to marginalize and minimize ongoing racial and ethnic problems that have developed over centuries, as seen in wealth gaps, education gaps, entrenched poverty, and inequities in criminal sanctioning and policing. Once again, as we were writing this textbook, we began witnessing protests and riots, charges of police brutality and political indifference, and the killing of people of color. These events and realities, then and now, convinced us that what we were witnessing was not limited to a simplistic concern for race and ethnicity—it was something far deeper, more complex, and nuanced.

We began envisioning a different approach: one of increased breadth and scope; one that would more closely reflect people's personal and lived experiences; and one that would dispense with the static categories of race and ethnicity, looking instead at the intersecting, multilayered identities of contemporary society. Not only are racial and ethnic groups socially constructed, but they also intersect with other aspects of identity (including gender and sexuality, age, and social class) that vary across both temporal and geographical spaces. We decided to use the core concept of *the matrix* to capture these complex intersections. Many texts concerned with race and ethnic relations are written by academics who provide excellent scholarly treatments of the subject, but all too often students perceive such treatments as removed from their own lives, or sterile. We decided to also add a concern for the reader's personal identity and its intersection with society. It is our view that such an approach will not only stir emotion but also compel self-appraisal. We believe that this approach will enable our discussion to be closer to the reader's lived experiences. We have deliberately tied our text not only to current research but also to a wide array of media and other supplements, making it more dynamic than what is typically offered. In the process, we have discovered that our identities are not separate from the various social settings and structures that occupy us from birth to death. These social settings and structures, which govern our personal and lived experiences, are typically associated with the major institutions of our society.

The Matrix of Race is a textbook that helps instructors navigate the diversity of students in their race/ethnic relations courses—both members of minority groups who have experienced the impact of race in their own lives and members of dominant groups who might believe that we now live in a "color-blind" society, in which race and racism are relics of the past. Our goal is to make race and racial inequality "visible" in new ways to all students, regardless of their backgrounds.

The "matrix" in the title refers to a way of thinking about race that can help readers get beyond the familiar "us versus them" arguments that can lead to resistance and hostility. This framework incorporates a number of important theories and perspectives from contemporary sociologists who study this subject: (a) Race is socially constructed—it changes from one place to another and across time. (b) When talking about racial inequality, it is more useful to focus on the structures of society (institutions) than to blame individuals. (c) Race is intersectional—it is embedded in other socially constructed categories of difference (like gender, social class, ethnicity, and sexuality). And (d) there are two sides to race: oppression and privilege. Both are harmful, and both can be experienced simultaneously.

We are sure that as you work through this text while considering your own story, you will come to the same conclusions that we have: We are all active agents in maintaining or challenging the matrix of race. How successful have we been? Tell us your story.

■ DIGITAL RESOURCES

SAGE edge offers a robust online environment featuring an impressive array of tools and resources for review, study, and further exploration, keeping both instructors and students on the cutting edge of teaching and learning. SAGE edge content is open access and available on demand. Learning and teaching has never been easier! We gratefully acknowledge Jamie Chapman, Westminster College; Benjamin Drury, Indiana University; and Brittne Lunniss, University of Massachusetts, for developing the digital resources on this site.

SAGE EDGE FOR STUDENTS
https://edge.sagepub.com/coates

SAGE edge enhances learning in an easy-to-use environment that offers:

- Mobile-friendly **flashcards** that strengthen understanding of key terms and concepts, and make it easy to maximize your study time, anywhere, anytime

- Mobile-friendly practice **quizzes** that allow you to assess how much you've learned and where you need to focus your attention

- **Multimedia links** to open web video and audio resources that allow students to dive deeper into topics with a click of the mouse

- Exclusive access to influential **SAGE journal and reference content** that ties important research and scholarship to chapter concepts to strengthen learning

SAGE COURSEPACKS FOR INSTRUCTORS

makes it easy to import our quality content into your school's LMS.
sagepub.com/coursepacks

For use in: Blackboard, Canvas, Brightspace by Desire2Learn (D2L), and Moodle

Don't use an LMS platform? No problem, you can still access many of the online resources for your text via SAGE edge.

SAGE coursepacks include:

- Our content delivered directly into your LMS

- Intuitive, simple format makes it easy to integrate the material into your course with minimal effort

- Pedagogically robust assessment tools foster review, practice, and critical thinking, and offer a more complete way to measure student engagement, including:

  o Diagnostic chapter **pre-tests and post-tests** identify opportunities for improvement, track student progress, and ensure mastery of key learning objectives

  o **Test banks** built on Bloom's Taxonomy provide a diverse range of test items with ExamView test generation

  o **Activity and quiz options** allow you to choose only the assignments and tests you want

  o Instructions on how to use and integrate the comprehensive assessments and resources provided

  o EXCLUSIVE, influential **SAGE journal and reference** content, built into course materials and assessment tools, that ties important research and scholarship to chapter concepts to strengthen learning

  o Editable, chapter-specific **PowerPoint®** **slides** offer flexibility when creating multimedia lectures so you don't have to start from scratch but you can customize to your exact needs

  o All tables and figures from the textbook

■■■■ ACKNOWLEDGMENTS

■ RODNEY'S ACKNOWLEDGMENTS

I honor the ancestors of all races, ethnicities, genders, and periods who not only survived but also challenged, transformed, and thrived in spite of the racial matrix. I stand on the shoulders of these giants. There are many whose names, input, and insights go unmentioned here, but not forgotten. Throughout my life I have been blessed to have a continual stream of teachers, mentors, colleagues, and heroes who refused to let me be mediocre. So I must thank Clifford Harper, Judith Blau, William J. Wilson, Eduardo Bonilla-Silva, Darnell Hawkins, Douglas Parker, Corey W. Dolgan, Joe Feagin, Al Long, and C. Lee Harrington for always being there. Where would I be without the constant support, love, and companionship of my family? I could not, nor would I want to, make it without you, Sherrill, Angela, Chris, and Avery. And to the hundreds of students who read, studied, asked critical questions about, and reflected on multiple drafts of these chapters—you have my thanks and sympathies. Some of those early drafts were truly murder. My coauthors, Abby and David, what can I say, no words, no tributes can equal your devotion and faith in this project. Thanks, my friends.

■ ABBY'S ACKNOWLEDGMENTS

I was honored and humbled when Rodney Coates invited me to join this project. I have learned and grown, both personally and professionally, working with Rodney and David. None of us expected that we would still be writing this text in 2017, and it is due to Rodney's persistence and brilliant leadership that we have continued on this journey. I am incredibly grateful for the many colleagues and mentors who have touched my life and strengthened and supported both my professional and personal growth. A few of the people I want to especially acknowledge are Donald Cunnigen, Joe Feagin, Andrea Herrera, Elizabeth Higginbotham, Michael Kimmel, Peggy McIntosh, Eddie Moore Jr., Wanda Rushing, and Diane Wysocki. Personally, I dedicate this book to the late Joan Acker, Miriam Johnson, and Sandra Morgen. When I was a graduate student at the University of Oregon, each of these faculty mentors changed the course of my life as a scholar/teacher, along with Mary Romero, Rose Brewer, and John Lie. I am grateful for my teammates and coconspirators at the Matrix Center (and especially the Knapsack Institute), who have contributed to building the matrix model over the past 18 years; to the many folks I have had the honor of building relationships with in my service to the White Privilege Conference and the Privilege Institute; and to the many people who have invested their time and passion in creating, nurturing, and growing Sociologists for Women in Society. I do not take for granted the gift of this wide community of social justice activists and academics, both those who have preceded me and those I work and grow beside. Finally, and most important, I thank my husband, Joel, and daughter, Sydney, for their patience, support and boundless love. I love you more than words can tell.

DAVID'S ACKNOWLEDGMENTS

I would like to thank my longtime brother Rodney Coates for reaching out to me in the summer of 2011 to ask if I wanted to join him in creating a unique, critical, and intersectional race textbook. Our early discussions centered on changing the way we teach race and ethnicity to undergraduate students and inspired this textbook. I was equally enthralled when Abby Ferber agreed to join us on this journey. The journey has been a long one, with many twists and turns. Along the way several people have been there to lean on, to discuss with, to commiserate with, and to bounce ideas off of. No list is ever complete, but I would like to acknowledge my deeply supportive partner, Rachel, and my three wonderful children, Karina, Thomas, and Henry—I love you all more than you will ever know. I also must acknowledge the following people for their support along the way: David Embrick, Jennifer Wyse, James Michael Thomas, John Ryan, Sarah Ovink, Jaber Gubrium, Ellington Graves, Minjeong Kim, Petra Rivera-Rideau, Kerry Ann Rockquemore, Slade Lellock, Nate Chapman, Hephzibah Strmic-Pawl, Megan Nanney, Carson Byrd, and Anthony Peguero. All of these people, and many, many graduate students and undergraduate students, have heard me discuss "the textbook" that I am writing—well, here it is. I also want to thank my inspirations, among many: Gloria Anzaldúa, Charles Mills, Patricia Hill Collins, Immortal Technique, Eduardo Bonilla-Silva, Lauryn Hill, Michael Omi, Paulo Freire, Joey Sprague, J. R. R. Tolkien, and my grandfather, Wilbur Nachtigall.

FROM ALL THREE AUTHORS

Jointly, we thank the SAGE crew—Jeff Lasser, Jessica Carlisle, and a host of others—thanks for being there, pushing us, and walking with us down this path. We would also like to thank the reviewers who contributed their many suggestions, critiques, and insights that helped us write *The Matrix of Race*:

Thea S. Alvarado, Pasadena City College

Steven L. Arxer, University of North Texas at Dallas

Celeste Atkins, Cochise College

Laura Barnes, Lenoir Community College

Joyce Bell, University of Pittsburgh

Michelle Bentz, Central Community College Nebraska, Columbus Campus

Jacqueline Bergdahl, Wright State University

Latrica Best, University of Louisville

Devonia Cage, University of Memphis

Elizabeth E. Chute, Carroll College

James A. Curiel, Norfolk State University

Melanie Deffendall, Delgado Community College

Sherry Edwards, University of North Carolina at Pembroke

David G. Embrick, Loyola University Chicago

Katherine Everhart, Northern Arizona University

Amy Foerster, Pace University

Joan Gettert Gilbreth, Nebraska Wesleyan University

Robert W. Greene, Marquette University

Denise A. Isom, California Polytechnic State University San Luis Obispo

Shanae Jefferies, University of North Texas

Shelly Jeffy, University of North Carolina Greensboro

Hortencia Jimenez, Hartnell College

Gary Jones, University of Winchester

Tony S. Jugé, Pasadena City College

Henry Kim, Wheaton College

Jeanne E. Kimpel, Hofstra University

Phil Lewis, Queens College

David Luke, University of Kentucky

Ying Ma, Austin Peay State University

Keith Mann, Cardinal Stritch University

Lynda Mercer, University of Louisville

Dan Monti, Saint Louis University

Sarah Morrison, Lindenwood University and Southern Illinois University Edwardsville

Kaitlyne A. Motl, University of Kentucky

Zabedia Nazim, Wilfrid Laurier University

Mytoan Nguyen-Akbar, University of Washington

Godpower O. Okereke, Texas A&M University-Texarkana

Mary Kay Park, Biola University

Chavella T. Pittman, Dominican University

Jennifer Pizio, Mercy College

Janis Prince, Saint Leo University

Allan Rachlin, Franklin Pierce University

Heather Rodriguez, Central Connecticut State University

Penny J. Rosenthal, Minnesota State University, Mankato

Enrique Salmon, California State University East Bay

Allison Sinanan, Stockton University

Don Stewart, College of Southern Nevada,

Mary Frances Stuck, State University of New York Oswego

Paul Sturgis, William Woods University

Rita Takahashi, San Francisco State University

Michelle Tellez, Northern Arizona University

Santos Torres Jr., California State University, Sacramento

Kathryn Tillman, Florida State University

Gerald Titchener, De Moines Area Community College

Catherine Turcotte, Colby-Sawyer College

Curt Van Guison, St. Charles Community College

Rodney D. Coates is a professor in the Department of Global and Intercultural Studies at Miami University (Ohio). He specializes in the study of race and ethnic relations, inequality, critical race theory, and social justice. He has served on the editorial boards of the *American Sociological Review, Social Forces,* and *Race, Class and Gender*; on the executive boards of the Southern Sociological Society and Sociologists without Borders; and as chair of the American Sociological Association's Section on Race and Ethnic Minorities. Rodney has published dozens of articles and several edited books, and he writes frequently on issues of race and ethnicity, education and public policy, civil rights, and social justice. His 2004 edited book, *Race and Ethnicity: Across Time, Space, and Discipline,* won the Choice Award from the American Library Association. He is also a recipient of the Joseph Himes Career Award in Scholarship and Activism from the Association of Black Sociologists.

Abby L. Ferber is Professor of Sociology and Women's and Ethnic Studies at the University of Colorado, Colorado Springs, where she teaches both undergraduate and graduate courses on privilege, race, gender, and sexuality, all from an intersectional perspective. She is the author of *White Man Falling: Race, Gender, and White Supremacy* (Rowman & Littlefield) and coauthor of *Hate Crime in America: What Do We Know?* (American Sociological Association) and *Making a Difference: University Students of Color Speak Out* (Rowman & Littlefield). She is

the coeditor, with Michael Kimmel, of *Privilege: A Reader* (Westview Press), and also coedited *The Matrix Reader* (McGraw-Hill) and *Sex, Gender, and Sexuality: The New Basics* (Oxford University Press). Abby is the associate director of the university's Matrix Center for the Advancement of Social Equity and Inclusion and has served as cofacilitator of the Matrix Center's Knapsack Institute: Transforming Teaching and Learning. She is also the founding coeditor of the journal *Understanding and Dismantling Privilege,* a joint publication of the Matrix Center and The Privilege Institute (TPI), the nonprofit organization that is the home of the annual White Privilege Conference (WPC). She is a founding board member of TPI and on the national planning team for the WPC.

David L. Brunsma is professor of sociology at Virginia Tech, where he teaches and researches in the areas of race, racism, multiracial identity, and human rights. He is the author of *Beyond Black: Biracial Identity in America* (Rowman & Littlefield), *A Symbolic Crusade: The School Uniform Movement and What It Tells Us about American Education* (Rowman & Littlefield Education), and *The Handbook of Sociology and Human Rights* (Routledge). His work has appeared in *American Teacher Magazine, Principal Magazine,* and the *Audio Journal of Education.* David is the founding coeditor of the journal *Sociology of Race and Ethnicity* and executive officer of the Southern Sociological Society. He is also a recipient of the W. E. B. Du Bois Award from Sociologists without Borders.

PART I

INTRODUCTION TO RACE AND THE SOCIAL MATRIX

RACE AND THE SOCIAL CONSTRUCTION OF DIFFERENCE

David Rae Morris / Polaris/Newscom

The city of New Orleans's decision to remove this statue of Robert E. Lee, and three others celebrating Confederate figures, led to protests, with some celebrating the removal and others claiming the move was disrespectful of the heritage of the South.

CHAPTER OUTLINE

LEARNING OBJECTIVES

LO 1.1   Explain how race and ethnicity are socially constructed.

LO 1.2   Evaluate the relationship between social contexts and race.

LO 1.3   Identify the concepts and operation of racism.

LO 1.4   Examine the link between our personal narratives and the broader "story" of race.

Our country has a history of memorializing wars and the people who fought them with medals, holidays, and monuments. The Civil War (1861–65) between the North and the South was quite possibly the bloodiest and subsequently the most commemorated four years in U.S. history. After the final shot was fired, some 1,500 memorials and monuments were created, including many commemorating the heroes of the Confederacy, the seven slaveholding Southern states that formally seceded from the Union in 1861 (Graham 2016). Over the past few years, protests around the appropriateness of these monuments have highlighted the racial fault lines in America.

In 2016, New Orleans, Louisiana, became a racial seismic epicenter as protests rocked the city. At issue was the city's decision to remove four landmark Civil War–related monuments: a statue of Jefferson Davis, president of the Confederacy;

statues of Confederate generals P. G. T. Beauregard and Robert E. Lee; and a monument memorializing a White supremacist uprising during the Reconstruction era.

As the city pondered how and what to rebuild after the devastation of Hurricane Katrina in 2005, anti-Confederate sentiment began to simmer. It reached a boiling point in June 2015 when nine Black churchgoers in Charleston, South Carolina, were killed by a gunman waving a Confederate flag (Wootson 2017). To many, these monuments represented not only the racially-based terrorism of groups like the Ku Klux Klan but also a sanitized history that "whitewashed" the Confederacy cause and glorified slavery and White supremacy (Landrieu 2017). After the monuments were successfully removed, under the cover of darkness and with snipers stationed nearby to protect the workers, lawmakers in Louisiana and Alabama immediately responded by passing laws to make it more difficult to remove Confederate monuments in the future (Park 2017).

Confederate monuments are a symptom of a much deeper set of issues that mark our nation's troubled history with race. The mayor of New Orleans, Mitch Landrieu (2017), remarked that we as a nation continue to confuse the "difference between remembrance of history and reverence of it." Our collective memories often reflect this same distortion as we attempt to reconcile our democratic principles of freedom, justice, and equality with the racial realities of prejudice, bigotry, and discrimination. Landrieu's statement and the controversy surrounding the removal of Confederate monuments mirror concerns that are deeply rooted within the social fabric of our country. They highlight the promises and the problems associated with race in the United States. What is race, and how has it become so central to our experiences? Is race so ingrained in our basic identities that it is now a permanent fixture of our social landscape? Alternatively, if race is a social invention, with a set of origins, purposes, and realities, then is it within our ability to influence, change, or eliminate it? The answers to these questions drive the purpose of this book.

■ THE SOCIAL CONSTRUCTION OF RACE

Nothing better demonstrates the complexity and social dynamics of race than performing an Internet image search using the term "biracial twins." When most children are born, they are assumed to belong to particular races because of the color of their skin. But race is not so simple. Even twins can have very different skin colors, and this can raise some interesting questions. Some twins who have one Black parent and one White parent are routinely asked to produce their birth certificates to prove that they are not only related but also twins. So are they White, or are they Black? It depends. In some cases, the twins self-identify according to their perceived racial identities (Perez 2015).

Defining Race

The term **race** refers to a social and cultural system by which we categorize people based on presumed biological differences. An examination of genetic patterns across the major world population groups reveals that while Africans have some genes unique to them as a group, all other groups share genetic patterns with Africans. This leads to the conclusion, held by most geneticists, anthropologists, and sociologists, that all humans are derived from Africans and that Africa is the cradle of humanity. Geneticists go further, declaring that the differences we observe between various groups are the results of geographical and social isolation, and that if such populations were to mix freely, then even these differences would disappear (Yudell, Roberts, DeSalle, and Tishkoff 2016).

Lucy and Maria Aylmer are twins, born to a half-Jamaican mother and a white father. Lucy identifies as white and Maria as black, despite their shared parentage.

Since human genes have changed, or mutated, over time, we must question if race is either natural or static. If race were indeed a fact of nature, it would be simple to identify who falls into which racial category, and we would expect racial categories to remain static across history and societies. Differences in physical features, such as skin color, hair color, eye color, and height, exist both within and between groups. And as we've seen, physical features can vary even within families. However, these differences are not due to an underlying biological basis of race. There is more biological variation within our so-called racial groups than there is between them. Race must derive from human interventions. These interventions reflect the social construction of race.

Racial classifications have persisted as a means of advancing specific hierarchies through attention to the reputed differences in behaviors, skill sets, and inherent intelligence attributed to people according to their classifications. As a consequence, what social scientists and geneticists alike have come to understand is that race and **racial categorizations** are uniquely social creations that have been purposefully constructed. Specific rewards, privileges, and sanctions have been used to support and legitimate race. The systematic distribution of these rewards, privileges, and sanctions across populations through time has produced and reproduced social hierarchies that reflect our racial categorizations. We collectively refer to these systematic processes as the **social construction of race**.

Constructing Race around the World

If we examine the social construction of race across geographical spaces and historical periods, then an interesting range of constructions is immediately apparent.

South Africa

Many countries have historically instituted laws that dictated where the members of different racial groups could live and work, and how they must behave. Once such system, known as apartheid, existed in South Africa until 1994. One of the measures of determining race in South Africa was the so-called pencil test. If a pencil pushed through the hair stayed put, the person was deemed to have Afro-textured hair and might be classified as Black or Colored (of mixed racial heritage). If the pencil fell to the floor, the person was classified as White. A Colored classification allowed a person to have significantly more rights than those who were considered Black, but still fewer rights and responsibilities than those considered White. Given the multiple products and processes used to "straighten" Black hair, and the social benefits associated with enhanced social status, is it any wonder that many Black South Africans sought to have their identify changed to Colored? Apartheid allowed a racial hierarchy to be reified into law—an illustration of how race was socially constructed in South Africa. While technically illegal, these racial hierarchies are still a part of South African cultural identity and heritage, and the legacies of apartheid still haunt South Africa more than 20 years after the system officially ended.

South America

The Southern Cone of South America is a geographic region composed of the southernmost areas of the continent, including the countries of Argentina, Brazil, Chile, Paraguay, and Uruguay (see Figure 1.1). Among these Latin American countries, **phenotypical traits**—physical traits such as skin color, hair texture, and facial features typically used to characterize people into racial groups—are linked to socioeconomic status.

At the top of the hierarchy are White Hispanics and others with light skin. Mixed indigenous and African ancestry, often referred to as *mulatto,* is associated with less opportunity, higher levels of poverty, and lower social status. Those individuals who claim both indigenous and Hispanic ancestry, called *mestizos,* occupy a middle position and tend to have slightly more opportunities for social and economic advancement than do mulattos.

There are also nation-specific racial categorizations. The Brazilian census identifies six racial categories: *Brancos* (White), *Pardos* (Brown), *Pretos* (Black), *Amarelos* (East Asian), indigenous, and undeclared. Such categories and their links to the social and economic hierarchies in Latin American countries exist to this day in what scholars

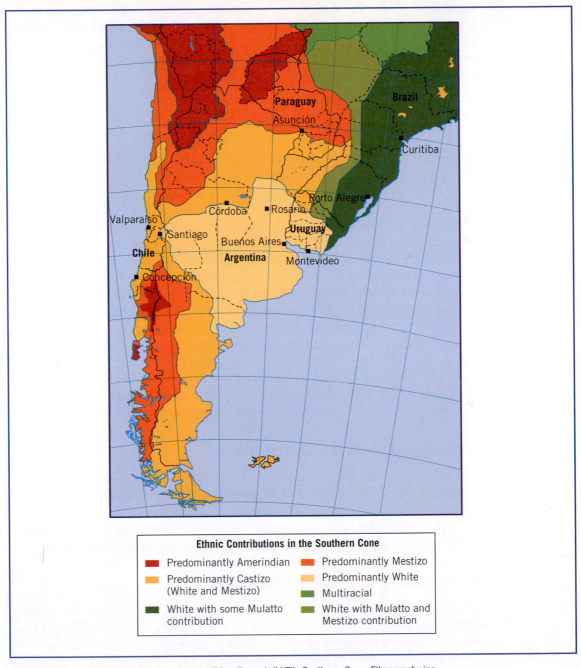

Ethnic Contributions in the Southern Cone

- ■ Predominantly Amerindian
- ■ Predominantly Castizo (White and Mestizo)
- ■ White with some Mulatto contribution
- ■ Predominantly Mestizo
- ■ Predominantly White
- ■ Multiracial
- ■ White with Mulatto and Mestizo contribution

Source: Wikimedia Commons, https://commons.wikimedia.org/wiki/File:Southern_Cone_Ethnography.jpg.

refer to as **pigmentocracies**—governments and other social structures that grant political power based on a hierarchy defined by skin tone, regardless of race or social status (Telles and the Project on Ethnicity and Race in Latin America 2014). But these are not exclusive categorizations. One study conducted by the Brazilian Institute of Geography and Statistics, the governmental entity responsible for the census, asked people what racial categories they would place themselves in, and the researchers received 134 different answers (Fish 2011).

Australia

Race was similarly constructed in Australia when Britain began to colonize and marginalize the indigenous population in 1791. In the early phase of colonization, Britain declared much of Australia's most valuable land to be *terra nullius,* or "empty land." Under this determination, all of the natives, or Aboriginals, saw their rights to land revoked, as the Europeans declared the indigenous population's 50,000 years of residency null. Thus began an apartheid-like social structure, where Europeans were accorded all the rights, privileges, and status, while Aborigines were reduced to living in poverty on settlements. This segregated racial structure has been successfully challenged only in the last 20 years, as courts have begun to grant rights and privileges to Australia's Aborigines. The historical legacy of such a racialized structure has not been limited to Australia. Of note, several European nations used the declaration of *terra nullius* as a means of justifying colonial expansion and the subsequent racialization of indigenous peoples in many places, including, but not limited to, New Zealand, Grenada, Singapore, South Rhodesia, Tobago, Trinidad, Guano Islands, Burkina Faso, and Niger. In each case, a racial hierarchy favoring Europeans was socially constructed. Indigenous populations were subject to subjugation, isolation, or genocide. The United States is another one of these cases.

Constructing Race in the United States

Whiteness came into being as a way for European colonists to explain and justify imperialism, genocide, slavery, and exploitation. In Chapter 2, we will discuss the extent to which the construction of race in the United States follows the pattern of European settler colonialism and imperialism. For now, we present a brief explanation of how racial categorizations became significant within the United States.

The Significance of Where and When

The United States has its roots in three separate colonial settlements. These settlements, associated with the Spanish, French, and English, developed different types of racial classification structures. While all of them reserved the highest category for Europeans, they varied in how they accommodated other groups. This variability accounts for the slight differences we can still often observe between the former

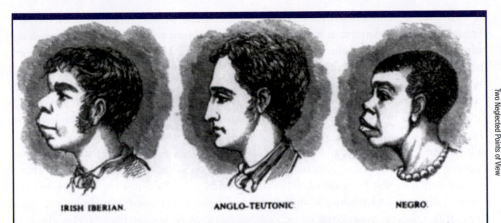

Drawing by: H. Strickland Constable, 1899, Ireland from One or Two Neglected Points of View

IRISH IBERIAN.   ANGLO-TEUTONIC.   NEGRO.

The Iberians are believed to have been originally an African race, who thousands of years ago spread themselves through Spain over Western Europe. Their remains are found in the barrows, or burying places, in sundry parts of these countries. The skulls are of low prognathous type. They came to Ireland, and mixed with the natives of the South and West, who themselves are supposed to have been of low type and descendants of savages of the Stone Age, who, in consequence of isolation from the rest of the world, had never been out-competed in the healthy struggle of life, and thus made way, according to the laws of nature, for superior races.

Constructing race in 1899. The caption that appeared with this image in an 1899 edition of *Harper's Weekly* reads: "The Iberians are believed to have been originally an African race, who thousands of years ago spread themselves through Spain over Western Europe. Their remains are found in the barrows, or burying places, in sundry parts of these countries. The skulls are of low prognathous type. They came to Ireland and mixed with the natives of the South and West, who themselves are supposed to have been of low type and descendants of savages of the Stone Age, who, in consequence of isolation from the rest of the world, had never been out-competed in the healthy struggle of life, and thus made way, according to the laws of nature, for superior races."

Spanish and French colonial regions (e.g., in California and Louisiana) and the former English colonial areas. These differences are most reflected in the heightened status of Creoles (people of mixed race, European and indigenous) in the former Spanish and French colonies and the more rigidly defined racial categories within the English. The reasons for these differences, as we will discover, are associated with the differences in settlement types. Here, it is important simply to note that these differences were real and that they further demonstrate the processes of the social construction of race.

The social construction of race also varies across time, as the sets of descriptors used to create racial categories have varied in different historical periods. At an earlier time in U.S. history, for example, the Irish were considered to be of African descent. The "Iberian hypothesis" purported that the "Black Irish" were descendants of Africans and those from the Gaelic island. Although the Iberian hypothesis has since been discredited (Radford 2015), in 1899 it was considered fact. Irish immigrants experienced a tremendous amount of prejudice in the United States and were not considered to be among the country's elite White ethnics. In Chapter 2 we shall see that these biases underscored many of our attitudes toward race and how Whiteness came into being.

In 1924, the Racial Integrity Act defined a "colored person" as anyone with any African or Native American ancestry at all; this is often referred to as the **one-drop rule**. The rules for defining who falls into what racial categories have long been inconsistent across the United States. Over time and in different states, the amount of ancestry required to make someone Black has variously been defined as one drop (of Black blood) and by fractions ranging from $\frac{1}{4}$ to $\frac{1}{8}$ to $\frac{1}{32}$. A person could "change" races by simply stepping over a state line. Why did having $\frac{1}{32}$ Black ancestry make someone Black, yet having $\frac{31}{32}$ of White ancestry not make someone White? And why have such clear-cut rules never been established for other racial groups? How many Asian ancestors are required to define someone as Asian? These inconsistencies exist because racial classifications are based not on biology but on social, political, and economic dynamics and power relationships. Under the one-drop rule, Native Americans of mixed ancestry were systematically classified as Negro (or Black) and denied tribal rights, and those who crossed the color line were subject to criminal punishments.

Race in the Contemporary United States

So what does this racially constructed system look like in the contemporary United States? Try this exercise: First, create a list of the racial groups in the United States. Then, write down your estimate of the percentage of the U.S. population that is accounted for by each group.

When we ask our students to attempt this exercise, the answers we get are varied. Some list four races; some list ten. Some include Hispanics/Latinos, and some do not. Some include Middle Easterners, while some do not. Some include a category for multiracial identity. Race is something we assume we all know when we see it, but we may in fact be "seeing" different things. Race cannot be reduced to physical features like skin color—in fact, while skin tone is often the first item we "check off" on our racial checklist, we then move to other social and visual clues.

The U.S. Constitution requires that a counting of the nation's population be conducted every 10 years—a national census (see Figure 1.2). The purposes and uses of the census have both changed and expanded across the years. The census was originally necessary to determine voting representation, including the numbers of representatives states could elect to Congress, the allocation of federal and state funds, and more. Over time, the census categories of race and other cultural and language groups have changed to reflect the nation's evolving population as well as, importantly, the political interests and power relations of the time.

So what have we discovered? Race is a social construction that artificially divides people into distinct groups based on characteristics such as physical appearance, ancestry, culture, ethnic classification, and the social, economic, and political needs, desires, and relations of a society at a given historical moment (Adams, Bell, and

Griffin 1997; Ferrante and Brown 2001). The U.S. Census Bureau, for instance, currently recognizes five racial categories, along with a "some other race" option (which was added in 2000 in response to public pressure). The five categories are as follows:

1. American Indian or Alaska Native

2. Asian

3. Black or African American

4. Native Hawaiian or other Pacific Islander

5. White

Not only have our official designations for race and ethnic groups differed over time, but how people identify themselves has also shown a great deal of variability. For example, from the 2000 census to that of 2010, almost 10 million U.S. residents changed how they identified their race when asked by the Census Bureau (Linshi 2014). This clearly demonstrates the fluidity of racial groups.

People often associate an elaborate array of behaviors, attitudes, and values with particular racial groups, presuming that these reflect innate or culturally specific traits. As one observer has noted: "What is called 'race' today is chiefly an outcome of intergroup struggles, marking the boundaries, and thus the identities, of 'us' and 'them' along with attendant ideas of social worth or stigma. As such, 'race' is an ideological construct that links supposedly innate traits of individuals to their place in the social order" (Rumbaut 2011).

We often assume that racial differences have existed throughout history, but race is a relatively new concept. Human differences exist along a continuum, and racial classifications have been arbitrarily imposed on that continuum, separating people into seemingly distinct groups, much as we separate the color spectrum into distinct categories that we have selected to label red, orange, yellow, green, and so on—though there is only one spectrum of color.

Recent genetic evidence presents a much more varied set of human identities. For example, most of us derive from multiple ancestries. Genomes reveal that the average African American can identify not only with African ancestry (about 73.2%) but also with European (24%) and Native American (0.8%). Latinos average about 18% Native American ancestry, 65% European ancestry (mostly from the Iberian Peninsula), and 6.2% African ancestry. And about 3.5% of European Americans carry African ancestry. These are more likely to be in southern states, such as South Carolina and Louisiana (where 12% of European Americans have at least 1% African ancestry). In Louisiana, about 8% of Europeans derive at least 1% of their ancestries from Native Americans (Wade 2014).

1790	1850	1890	1910	1930	1960
		Indian	Indian	Indian	Aleut; American Indian; Eskimo
		Chinese; Japanese	Chinese; Japanese	Chinese; Filipino; Hindu; Japanese; Korean	Chinese; Filipino; Japanese
Slaves	Black; Mulatto	Black; Mulatto; Quadroon; Octoroon	Black (Negro); Mulatto	Negro	Negro
				Mexican	
					Hawaiian; Part-Hawaiian
Free White Females and Males	White	White	White	White	White
All Other Free Persons			Other	Other	

1820	1860	1900	1920	1950
	Indian	Indian	Indian	American Indian
	Chinese	Chinese; Japanese	Chinese; Filipino; Hindu; Japanese; Korean	Chinese; Filipino; Japanese
Slaves; Free Colored Persons	Black; Mulatto	Black (Negro or of Negro Descent)	Black (Negro); Mulatto	Negro
Free White Females and Males	White	White	White	White
All Other Free Persons			Other	Other

Source: U.S. Census Bureau, "Measuring Race and Ethnicity across the Decades: 1790–2010," http://www.census.gov/population/race/data/MREAD_1790_2010.html.

1970

Indian (Amer.)

Chinese; Filipino; Japanese; Korean

Negro or Black

Origin or Descent: Mexican; Puerto Rican; Cuban; Central or South American; Other Spanish

Hawaiian

White

Other

1990

Aleut; Eskimo; Indian (Amer.)

Asian or Pacific Islander: Chinese; Filipino; Korean; Vietnamese; Japanese; Asian Indian; Other API

Black or Negro

Spanish/Hispanic Origin: Mexican, Mexican-Am., Chicano; Puerto Rican; Cuban; Other Spanish/Hispanic

Hawaiian; Samoan; Guamanian; Other API

White

Other Race

2010

American Indian or Alaska Native

Asian Indian; Chinese; Filipino; Japanese; Korean; Vietnamese; Other Asian

Black, African Am., or Negro

Hispanic, Latino, or Spanish Origin: Mexican, Mexican Am., Chicano; Puerto Rican; Cuban; Another Hispanic, Latino, or Spanish Origin

Native Hawaiian; Guamanian or Chamorro; Samoan; Other Pacific Islander

White

Some Other Race

1980

Aleut; Eskimo; Indian (Amer.)

Asian Indian; Chinese; Filipino; Japanese; Korean; Vietnamese

Black or Negro

Spanish/Hispanic Origin or Descent: Mexican, Mexican-Amer., Chicano; Puerto Rican; Cuban; Other Spanish/Hispanic

Hawaiian; Guamanian; Samoan

White

Other

2000

American Indian or Alaska Native

Asian Indian; Chinese; Filipino; Japanese; Korean; Vietnamese; Other Asian

Black, African Am., or Negro

Spanish/Hispanic/Latino: Mexican, Mexican Am., Chicano; Puerto Rican; Cuban; Other Spanish/Hispanic/Latino

Native Hawaiian; Guamanian or Chamorro; Samoan; Other Pacific Islander

White

Some Other Race

Note: According to the 2000 Census, as the 2010 Census did not ask questions about ancestry. Please note that respondents may have selected more than one ancestry group.

The Role of Ethnicity

While race has been imposed on physical bodies, **ethnicity** encompasses cultural aspects of individuals' lives, including religion, tradition, language, ancestry, nation, geography, history, beliefs, and practice. Ethnic groups often see themselves, and are seen by others, as having distinct cultural identities. Physical characteristics are not usually tied to definitions of ethnicity. For example, Blacks in the United States come from many different ethnic backgrounds, including African Americans whose ancestors arrived enslaved generations ago and recent immigrants from Ethiopia, Jamaica, and other parts of the world. Often we confuse ancestry with ethnicity and race. The term **ancestry** typically refers to point of origin, lineage, or descent. For instance, Abby, one of the authors of this text, is racially White, ethnically Jewish, and of Eastern European ancestry. Ancestry is often one characteristic in definitions of ethnicity or race (see Figure 1.3).

Figure 1.3 ■ The Nine Largest Ancestry Groups in The United States

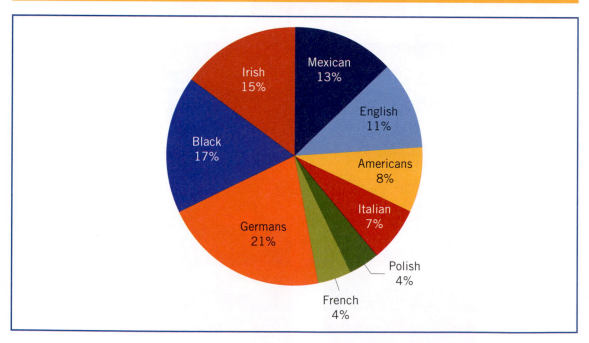

Source: Derived from data in Liz O'Connor, Gus Lubin, and Dina Spector, "The Largest Ancestry Groups in the United States," *Business Insider,* August 13, 2013, http://www.businessinsider.com/largest-ethnic-groups-in-america-2013-8.

Often when we concentrate on large racial groups in the United States, we tend to ignore just how diverse we are as a nation. Although the most recent census, in 2010, did not ask a question regarding ancestry, the Census Bureau's American Community Survey tracks most major ancestry groups on an ongoing basis. The data collected by that survey reveal that Germans and Blacks make up the largest single ancestry groups within the United States.

When we focus on racial groups as distinct groups whose members supposedly have much in common while ignoring the ethnic and ancestral diversity within the socially constructed categories, we further exaggerate the significance of racial designations. Furthermore, we erase the differences among the various and diverse ethnic peoples grouped into these racial categories. The only thing that people grouped together under a racial designation share is a history of oppression based on their racialization. Other than that, racial categories themselves tell us very little about the people classified into them.

Native Americans

The original, indigenous inhabitants of the Americas, Native Americans (or American Indians) and Alaska Natives, do not constitute one single race. As of the 2010 census, members of these groups made up 2% of the total U.S. population. Of these, about 49% exclusively defined themselves as either American Indians or Alaska Natives. The remaining 51% identified as some combination of American Indian or Alaska Native and one or more other races (U.S. Census Bureau 2012). A total of 630 separate federally recognized American Indian and Alaska Native reservations existed in 2012, excluding the Hawaiian Home Lands. There are 566 federally recognized American Indian and Alaska Native tribes, with the five largest tribal groupings being the Cherokee, Navajo, Choctaw, Mexican American Indian, and Chippewa groupings (see Figure 1.4). At the time of the 2010 census, the majority of Native Americans were living in 10 states: California, Oklahoma, Arizona, Texas, New York, New Mexico, Washington, North Carolina, Florida, and Michigan (U.S. Census Bureau 2012).

Asian Americans

All racial categories can be described as "panethnic." Yen Le Espiritu coined the term **panethnicity** in 1992 in reference to Asian Americans (see Espiritu 1994). It is generally applied to regional groups who are placed into a large category. As Espiritu points out, many Asian groups—including Chinese, Hmong, Japanese, Korean, Bangladeshi, Asian Indian, and Vietnamese—have been lumped together and viewed as an artificial whole.

Asians make up 5.8% of the total U.S. population. While many Americans are aware of the increasing presence of Hispanic-origin immigrants, Asians actually now make up an even larger share of immigrants to the United States. In 2014, the Asian share of the U.S. foreign-born population increased to 30% of the nation's 42.4 million immigrants (Zong and Batalova 2014). In that year, most of the 4.2 million Asians entering the United States came from Southeast Asia, followed by East Asia, South Central Asia, and Western Asia. India and China accounted for the largest share of these immigrants (17% each), followed by the Philippines (15%), Vietnam (10%), and Korea (9%). Asian immigrants also come from dozens of other countries in the Far East, Southeast Asia, and the Indian continent (Zong and Batalova 2016).

Figure 1.4 ■ American Indians and Alaskan Natives Identify Across Different Tribal Groupings

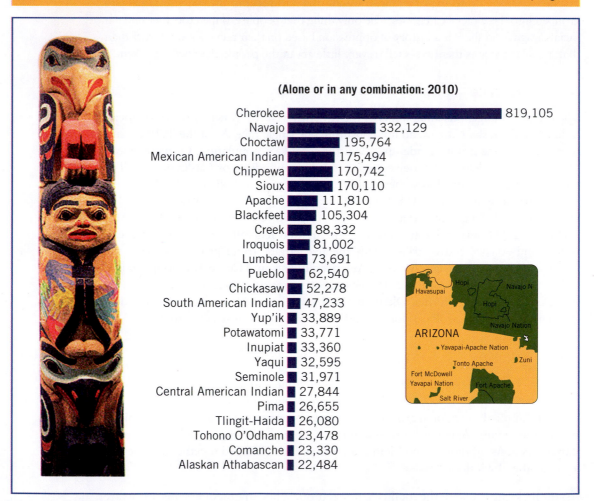

(Alone or in any combination: 2010)

Tribal Grouping	Population
Cherokee	819,105
Navajo	332,129
Choctaw	195,764
Mexican American Indian	175,494
Chippewa	170,742
Sioux	170,110
Apache	111,810
Blackfeet	105,304
Creek	88,332
Iroquois	81,002
Lumbee	73,691
Pueblo	62,540
Chickasaw	52,278
South American Indian	47,233
Yup'ik	33,889
Potawatomi	33,771
Inupiat	33,360
Yaqui	32,595
Seminole	31,971
Central American Indian	27,844
Pima	26,655
Tlingit-Haida	26,080
Tohono O'Odham	23,478
Comanche	23,330
Alaskan Athabascan	22,484

Source: U.S. Census Bureau, "25 Largest Tribal Groupings among American Indians and Alaska Natives," 2010, https://www.census.gov/content/dam/Census/newsroom/facts-for-features/2014/cb14-ff26_aian_graphic.jpg.

Black Americans

Historically, scholars have rarely discussed ethnicity among Blacks. This further highlights racial designations while marginalizing the differences among various ethnic groups. Some Blacks in the United States can trace their roots back to slavery, while others are recent immigrants from Africa. People defined as Black may have African, Caribbean, Haitian, Filipino, and other diverse ancestries. In fact, racial designations based on geography become meaningless as we attempt to apply them to North Africans, such as Egyptians, Moroccans, and Algerians (groups frequently defined by the U.S. Census Bureau as White). According to the U.S. Census Bureau (2015), in 2014 Blacks constituted an estimated 13% of the U.S. population.

As of 2015, 2.1 million African immigrants were living in the United States, accounting for 4.8% of the U.S. population, compared to just 0.8% in 1970. While typically these immigrants are lumped into the racial category of Black, Figure 1.5 shows that such racial homogenization hides much of the ethnic diversity among them (Anderson 2017).

White Ethnic Groups

White ethnics, who have until recently provided the largest share of immigration to these shores, derive mostly from European countries. Many of these today simply refer to themselves as "American." In fact, major streams of European immigration can be identified during the colonial era, the first portion of the 19th century, and the period from the 1880s to 1920. European immigrants were granted increased access to the United States as stipulated in the 1882 Chinese Exclusion Act. This quota system was not effectively ended until the passage of the Immigration and Nationality Act of 1965. White ethnic groups include people of British, Greek, Russian, German, and Norwegian ancestry, as well as many others. Figure 1.6 shows that European immigration has been relatively stable over the past 20 years. In 2010, the top five countries of origin for European immigrants were the United Kingdom (670,000, or 14%), Germany (605,000, or 13%), Poland (476,000, or 10%), Russia (383,000, or 8%), and Italy (365,000, or 8%) (Russell and Batalova 2012).

Hispanics

If an individual identifies with an ethnic group that speaks Spanish, then the U.S. Census Bureau labels that person as Hispanic. Hispanics may have families that came to the United States from Spain, Mexico, Guatemala, Cuba, or one of many other Spanish-speaking countries (see Figure 1.7). They may be White, Black, or some other race. Other than language, they may have nothing in common. Hispanic is a category created by the government, and many people classified as Hispanic prefer to define themselves as Latino/a, Chicano/a, or Mexican American, Cuban

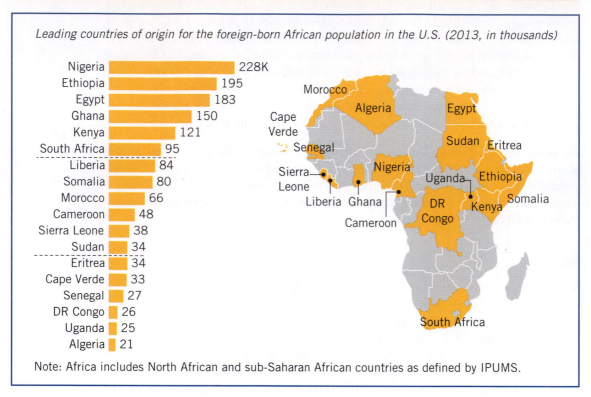

Leading countries of origin for the foreign-born African population in the U.S. (2013, in thousands)

Nigeria	228K
Ethiopia	195
Egypt	183
Ghana	150
Kenya	121
South Africa	95
Liberia	84
Somalia	80
Morocco	66
Cameroon	48
Sierra Leone	38
Sudan	34
Eritrea	34
Cape Verde	33
Senegal	27
DR Congo	26
Uganda	25
Algeria	21

Note: Africa includes North African and sub-Saharan African countries as defined by IPUMS.

Source: Chart and Map: "Nigeria, Ethiopia, Egypt are top birthplaces for African immigrants in the U.S." From African immigrant population in U.S. steadily climbs by Monica Anderson, Pew Research Center Fact Tank, February 14, 2017.

American, or the like. Some sociologists argue that Latino/as have been historically racialized and defined as inferior by Whites and should be classified as a race rather than an ethnic group. Much of the rich contemporary literature on racial inequality in the United States adopts this definition of Hispanics/Latino/as as a racialized group (Feagin and Cobas 2013; Ortiz and Telles 2012). We also generally treat them as a racial group in this book, and, indeed, many Hispanics have recently organized to push for categorization as a racial group in the next census, in 2020. Throughout this text, we will frequently use the terminology adopted by the research under discussion, thus referring at times to Hispanics and at other times to Latino/as (also, at times we will refer to Blacks and at other times to African Americans).

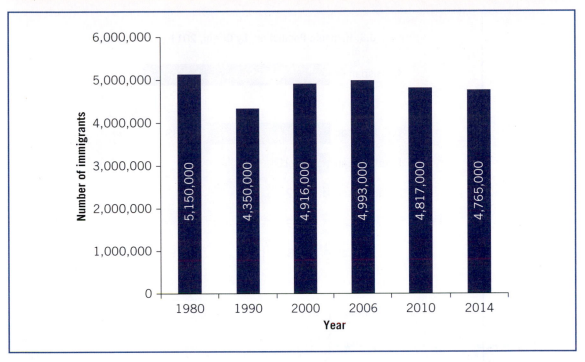

Source: Jie Zong and Jeanne Batalova, "European Immigrants in the United States," Migration Policy Institute, December 1, 2015, http://www.migrationpolicy.org/article/european-immigrants-united-states. Data from U.S. Census Bureau, American Community Surveys, 2006, 2010, and 2014; and Campbell J. Gibson and Kay Jung, "Historical Census Statistics on the Foreign-Born Population of the United States: 1850–2000," Working Paper 81, U.S. Census Bureau, February 2006.

Although it is surprising to many, the U.S. Census Bureau does not currently list Hispanic as a race, instead defining Hispanics as an ethnic group. The census includes a separate question specifically about Hispanic origin, asking self-identified Hispanics to select Mexican, Puerto Rican, Cuban, or other. The census form then asks them to identify their race.

Racial and Ethnic Compositions in the Future

So what will our country look like in the next 50 years? Projections of population growth indicate that minorities (including Hispanics, Blacks, Asian Americans, and Native Hawaiians and other Pacific Islanders) will make up slightly more than 50%

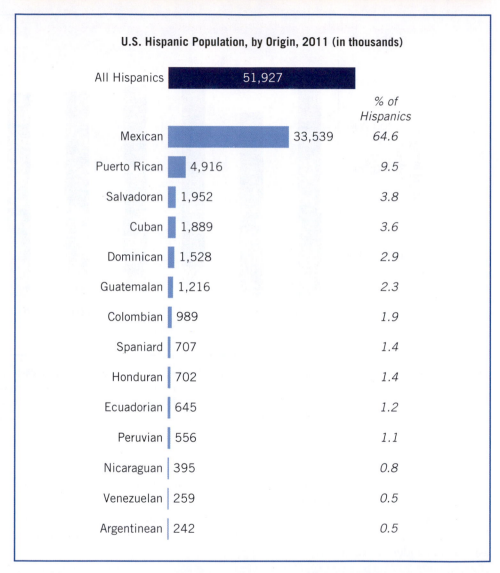

U.S. Hispanic Population, by Origin, 2011 (in thousands)

	(in thousands)	% of Hispanics
All Hispanics	51,927	
Mexican	33,539	64.6
Puerto Rican	4,916	9.5
Salvadoran	1,952	3.8
Cuban	1,889	3.6
Dominican	1,528	2.9
Guatemalan	1,216	2.3
Colombian	989	1.9
Spaniard	707	1.4
Honduran	702	1.4
Ecuadorian	645	1.2
Peruvian	556	1.1
Nicaraguan	395	0.8
Venezuelan	259	0.5
Argentinean	242	0.5

Source: Figure 2, "U.S. Hispanic Origin Groups, by Population, 2013. In The Impact of Slowing Immigration: Foreign-Born Share Falls Among 14 Largest U.S. Hispanic Origin Groups, by Gustavo Lopez and Eileen Patten, Pew Research Center Hispanic Trends, September 15, 2015.

of the U.S. population. The most significant changes will be seen in the reduced numbers of Whites and the almost doubling of the numbers of Hispanics and other minorities. We often read headlines predicting that Whites will become a minority. However, these are misleading. Whites will still be the single largest group in the United States, constituting 49.4% of the population in 2060 (Figure 1.8). The United States will become a minority-majority nation, which means that the total of all minority groups combined will make up the majority of the population. We may see little change in the dynamics of power and race relations, however, as the proportion of Whites will still be nearly twice that of any individual minority group.

Figure 1.8 ■ Population Growth Projections Over the Next Fifty Years Predict a Minority-Majority Nation

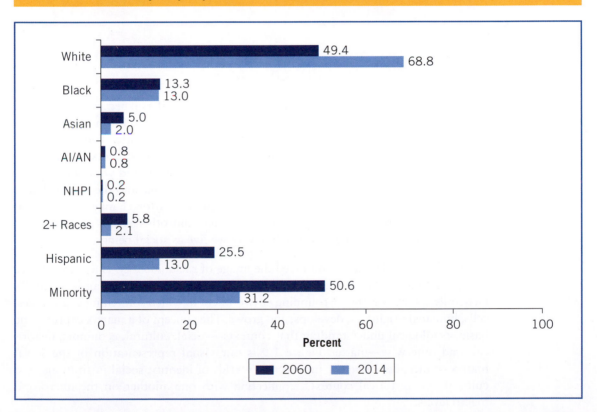

Source: U.S. Census Bureau, "Projections of the Size and Composition of the U.S. Population: 2014–2060," Population Estimates and Projections, Current Population Reports, March 2015.

1. History has shown that race and ethnicity are socially constructed. What do current trends suggest about how these social constructions may change in the future?

2. How might these changes affect social institutions such as marriage and family, education, and the military?

3. In what ways might these changes affect how we, as Americans, view ourselves? How might this affect how individuals categorize others and how they self-identify?

4. Can you trace your roots? What different racial and ethnic groups are in your family tree? What does this say about how we define racial and ethnic groups?

■ THE SOCIAL MATRIX OF RACE

Our goal in this book is to provide you with historical perspectives, theoretical frameworks, and diverse views of race and racial ideologies so that you can intelligently participate and contribute to such dialogues. We will offer you a variety of ways in which you can understand your identity, your environments, the relationships between those, and the ways you can change yourself and your society with dignity and self-determination. We focus particularly on race and the way it shapes our identities, society and its institutions, and prospects for change. But we also examine race within the context of gender, class, and other social identities that interact with one another and reflect the way we live as social beings.

A number of scholars have embraced the image of racial identity as a matrix (Case 2013; Collins 2000; Ferber, Jiménez, O'Reilly Herrera, and Samuels 2009). Generally, a **matrix** is the surrounding environment in which something (e.g., values, cells, humans) originates, develops, and grows. The concept of a matrix captures the basic sociological understanding that contexts—social, cultural, economic, historical, and otherwise—matter. Figure 1.9 is our visual representation of the social matrix of race, depicting the intersecting worlds of identity, social institutions, and cultural and historical contexts, connecting with one another on the micro and macro levels.

If our primary focus were gender, we could center the gendered self in such a matrix. In this text we center the concepts and experiences of race within the context of our many shifting social identities and systems of inequality. Our social identities are the ways in which our group memberships, in such things as races, classes, and genders,

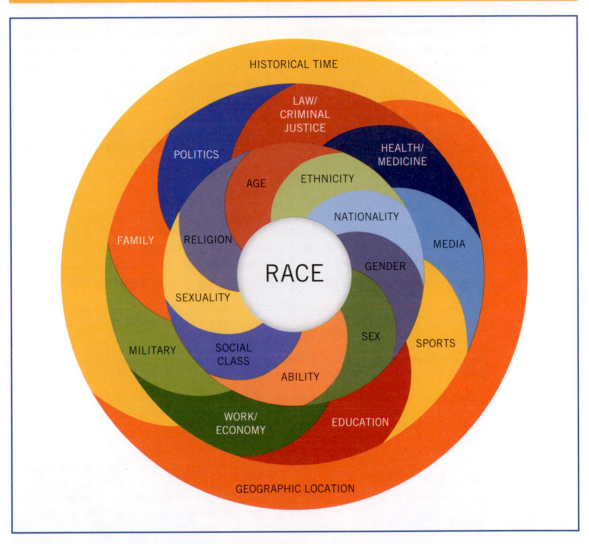

Source: Copyright Rodney D. Coates, Abby L. Ferber, and David L. Brunsma.

help define our sense of self. While we often assume a concrete or single group identity, the reality is that identity is seldom so simple. For example, while many of us identify as being White, Black, Hispanic, Asian, or Native American, few of us are racially or ethnically homogeneous. Consequently, how we derive our racial identity is actually a result of both historical and contemporary social constructions.

The same can be said regarding our social status, class, gender, and other identities. We also recognize that these identities interact in ways that produce extremely nuanced and complex, dynamic identities. The third ring of the social matrix of race consists of the social institutions in which we live and interact. **Social institutions** are patterned and structured sets of roles and behaviors centered on the performance of important social tasks within any given society. These institutions help order and facilitate social interactions. That being so, many of our activities happen within social institutions such as marriage and family, education, sports, the military, and the economy. In Figure 1.9 we have included only the social institutions we examine in this text; this is not an exhaustive list. Finally, all of these systems are shaped by place and time.

To support an understanding of race within the context of a social matrix, in the following sections we introduce the five key insights about race that we will develop throughout this text (see Table 1.1).

Race Is Inherently Social

We have already introduced the argument that race is a social construction. As race theorists Matthew Desmond and Mustafa Emirbayer (2010, 51) put it, "You do not come into this world African or European or Asian; rather, this world comes into you." If races are constructed, it makes sense then to ask: When does this happen,

Table 1.1 ■ Five Key Insights about Race	
Race is inherently social.	Race has no biological basis, and it varies both cross-culturally and historically.
Race is a narrative.	We learn narrative story lines that we draw upon to interpret what we see and experience, and these stories become embedded in our minds as truth, closing off other ways of seeing and sense making.
Racial identity is relational and intersectional.	Our racial identity is defined in our relationships to others, based on interactions with them and our reactions to our experiences and socialization. Further, our racial identity is shaped by, and experienced in the context of, our other social identities, such as gender, class, sexuality, ability, and age.
Race is institutional and structural.	Independently and together, various institutional structures, including family, school, community, and religion, influence our actions and beliefs about race.
We are active agents in the matrix.	We move among a variety of social institutions, and as we do, we contribute to their reproduction. We make choices every day, often unconsciously, that either maintain or subvert racial power dynamics and inequality.

and why? The creation of "races" occurred at a specific point in time to advance specific relations of inequality. The classifications were invented by those they were created to serve, not by those who came to be defined as "Others" by Whites. We will examine this history in Chapter 2.

Race Is a Narrative

As we have established, race is not real; it is a fiction with very real consequences. Because it is fictional, scholars across many disciplines have used the language of storytelling to discuss race. For example, perhaps one of the most dominant stories we hear today is that race is a taboo topic. When children ask their parents about racial differences, they are often hushed and told not to talk about such things in public. Perhaps the most significant racial narrative is the story that races exist in nature. We have just shown that this is not true. Yet until we are taught otherwise, most of us go through life assuming that biological racial differences exist. This is the power of narrative in our lives as social beings.

Anthropologist Audrey Smedley (2007) has identified some of the key features of this narrative. In it, racial classifications are constructed as follows:

1. They are exclusive, discrete classifications.
2. They involve visible physical differences that reflect inherent internal ones (such as intelligence, disposition, morals).
3. They are inherited.
4. They are unchanging, determined by nature and/or God.
5. They are valued differently and ranked hierarchically (in terms of superiority, beauty, degree of civilization, capacity for moral reasoning, and more).

This narrative makes clear that the ideology of race privileges some groups by dividing people into artificial, hierarchical categories to justify inequitable access to resources.

The ideology of race is part of what Joe Feagin (2010) identifies as the "white racial frame." In societies characterized by racial hierarchies, **racial frames** are constructed from the ideological justifications, processes, procedures, and institutions that define and structure society. They are the "comprehensive orienting structure or tool kit by which dominant racial groups and others are understood," and their actions are interpreted within social settings (Feagin 2010, 13). According to Feagin (2010, 10–11), a racial frame consists of the following:

1. racial stereotypes (a beliefs aspect);
2. racial narratives and interpretations (integrating cognitive aspects);

3. racial images (a visual aspect) and language accents (an auditory aspect);

4. racialized emotions (a "feelings" aspect); and

5. inclinations to discriminatory action.

The repetition of the White racial frame over generations, in fact since the founding of the United States, is the key to its power. When the same messages are repeated over and over, they appear to be part of our social being; they become "natural" to us.

In her popular book *Storytelling for Social Justice* (2010), educator and activist Lee Anne Bell provides a model for analyzing stories about race. She argues that there are essentially four different kinds of stories that we encounter in our lives: **stock stories, concealed stories, resistance stories,** and **transforming stories**.

- *Stock stories:* "Stock stories are the tales told by the dominant group," but they are often embraced by those whose oppression they reinforce (Bell 2010, 23). They inform and organize the practices of social institutions and are encoded in law, public policy, public space, history, and culture. Stock stories are shaped by the White racial frame.

- *Concealed stories:* We can always find concealed stories if we look closely enough. These consist of the data and voices that stock stories ignore and often convey a very different understanding of identity and inequity. In the case of concealed stories, "we explore such questions as: What are the stories about race and racism that we don't hear? Why don't we hear them? How are such stories lost/left out? How do we recover these stories? What do these stories show us about racism that stock stories do not?" (24).

- *Resistance stories:* Narratives that directly challenge stock stories are resistance stories. They speak of defying domination and actively struggling for racial justice and social change. "Guiding questions for discovering/uncovering resistance stories include: What stories exist (historical or contemporary) that serve as examples of resistance? What role does resistance play in challenging the stock stories about racism? What can we learn about antiracist action and perseverance against the odds by looking at these stories?" (25).

- *Transforming stories:* Once we examine concealed and resistance stories, we can use them to write transforming stories that guide our actions as we work toward a more just society. "Guiding questions include: What would it look like if we transformed the stock stories? What can we draw from resistance stories to create new stories about what ought to be? What kinds of stories can support our ability to speak out and act where instances of racism occur?" (26).

Many people claim **color blindness** in regard to race and ethnicity—that is, they assert that they do not see race or ethnicity, only humans—and the idea of color blindness informs many of our most prevalent stock stories today. According to this ideology, if we were all to embrace a color-blind attitude and just stop "seeing" race, race and its issues would finally become relics of the past. This approach argues that we should treat people simply as human beings, rather than as racialized beings (Plaut 2010). In fact, White people in the United States generally believe that "we have achieved racial equality," and about half believe that African Americans are doing as well as, or even better than, Whites (Bush 2011, 4). But pretending race does not exist is not the same as creating equality.

Just when the blatantly discriminatory policies and practices of **Jim Crow racism,** the laws and practices that originated in the American South to enforce racial segregation, were finally crumbling under attack, the early foundations of a "new racism" were taking form (Irons 2010). This new racism is much less overt, avoiding the use of blatantly racist terminology. Sociologist Eduardo Bonilla-Silva (2010) has labeled this ideology **color-blind racism.** According to Bonilla-Silva, color-blind ideology has four components:

- *Abstract liberalism:* Abstract concepts of equal opportunity, rationality, free choice, and individualism are used to argue that discrimination is no longer a problem, and any individual who works hard can succeed.

- *Naturalization:* Ongoing inequality is reframed as the result of natural processes rather than social relations. Segregation is explained, for example, as the result of people's natural inclination to live near others of the same race.

- *Cultural racism:* It is claimed that inherent cultural differences serve to separate racialized groups.

- *Minimization of racism:* It is argued that we now have a fairly level playing field, everyone has equal opportunities to succeed, and racism is no longer a real problem.

While many embrace color blindness as nonracist, by ignoring the extent to which race still shapes people's life chances and opportunities, this view actually reinforces and reproduces the subtle and institutional racial inequality that shapes our lives. Throughout this text, we will examine the extent to which racial inequality is still pervasive, as well as many stock stories in circulation today that make it difficult for us to see this reality. We will challenge many stock stories by exploring concealed

Saul Loeb / AFP / Getty Images

Color-blind ideology leads to the conclusion that we've done all we can in regard to racial inequality. Many Whites invoke the election of Barack Obama to the presidency as confirmation of their assumptions of a color-blind nation (Bonilla-Silva 2010; Cunnigen and Bruce 2010). The concealed story revealed by sociology, however, is that racial inequality has been and remains entrenched in the United States.

and resistance stories, and by considering the possibilities for constructing transformative stories.

Racial Identity Is Relational and Intersectional

As philosopher Elizabeth Spelman (1988) points out, we often think about our various identities—race, gender, sexuality, class, ability—as though they are connected like the beads of a necklace. But unlike the beads of the necklace, our separate identities can't just be popped apart. They intersect and shape each other; they are relational and intersectional (Crenshaw 1991).

The **relational aspects of race** are demonstrated by the fact that categories of race are often defined in opposition to each other (for example, to be White means one is not Black, Asian, Hispanic, or Native American) and according to where they fall along the continuum of hierarchy. Race is also relational in its intersections with other social identities, such as gender and class.

Intersectional theories argue that race, gender, and other salient social identities are intertwined and inseparable, and cannot be comprehended on their own. Sociologist Ivy Ken offers a useful metaphor. If we think about race as sugar, gender as flour, and class as baking soda, what happens when we mix them and a few other ingredients together? If we are lucky, we end up with cookies; we "produce something new—something that would not exist if that mixing had not occurred" (Ken 2008, 156). When these ingredients are combined, they are changed in the process.

David J. Connor (2006), a special education teacher in New York City, provides an example. He wondered why his classes were filled overwhelmingly with African American and Latino males despite the fact that learning disabilities occur in both males and females across class and race. Connor found that he needed an intersectional perspective to understand: "I noticed that the label [learning disabled] signified different outcomes for different people. What seemed to be a beneficial category of disability to middle-class, white students, by triggering various supports and services—served to disadvantage black and/or Latino/a urban youngsters, who were more likely to be placed in restrictive, segregated settings" (154). Here, race, class, and gender intersect to produce different consequences for differently situated youth.

As this example demonstrates, sources of oppression are related, and interrelated, in varied ways. There is no single formula for understanding how they work together. We are all shaped by all of these significant constructs, whether they privilege us or contribute to our oppression; we all experience specific configurations of race, class, and gender that affect our subjectivities, opportunities, and life chances.

Although its name is new, intersectional theory has a long history. Early theorists like Maria Stewart, Sojourner Truth, Frederick Douglass, Ida B. Wells, and Anna

Julia Cooper struggled with the ways race divided the women's suffrage movement, and gender limited Black women's participation in the antislavery movement. Decades later, women of color waged battles for full inclusion within the civil rights and women's movements. African American sociologists like Belinda Robnett (1999) and Bernice McNair Barnett (1995) have examined the ways in which the foundational leadership activities of Black women in many civil rights organizations have been ignored or written out of history (becoming concealed stories). Vicki Ruiz (1999) has examined similar dynamics in her research on the work of Chicanas in the Chicano movement. We can find many resistance stories in the lives of women of color who have refused to direct their energies toward just one form of oppression, arguing that their lives are shaped by their race and their gender simultaneously.

An intersectional approach does not require that we always examine every form of inequality. Instead, we need to recognize that intersectionality permeates every subject we study, and that even when we choose to focus on a single system of inequality, such as race, we must bring an intersectional lens to the work or we will never get a full picture of the experiences and dynamics of race.

Over the past few decades, research involving explicitly intersectional analysis has accelerated. Sociologists and others have examined the ways our various social locations intersect and interact in shaping our lives and society at every level. These represent interconnected axes of oppression and privilege that shape all of our lived experiences (Collins 2000).

Race Is Institutional and Structural

To say that race is institutional is to recognize that it operates alongside and in tandem with our dominant social institutions. For instance, education is a social institution in which there are roles (e.g., teachers and students) and expected behaviors (e.g., teaching and learning) that come together as a social structure to educate. But schools also contribute to other important social tasks, including socialization and social control (Spade and Ballantine 2011).

From the perspective of an individual in a human community, we might think about an institution by completing the following statement: "In this society/community, there is a *way* to do [fill in the blank]." In a society, like the United States, there is a *way* to do marriage, for example. When we mention the word *marriage* we are invoking a cultural script as well as a social structure—certain bodies come to mind, certain expectations, certain relationships, certain beginnings and outcomes. This is, perhaps, why gaining the right to marry has been such an amazing uphill battle for same-sex couples—as "same-sex marriage" runs counter to the prevailing sense of the institution of "marriage" (Baunach 2012). All of our dominant social institutions organize our lives, and they do so in deeply powerful ways that are intimately tied to how race (as well as gender, class, and sexuality) fundamentally structures and organizes our lives within society.

We Are Active Agents in the Matrix

While constructs of race and ethnicity shape us, we also shape them. Stories are often simply internalized, processed and made sense of by individuals and groups. Human beings, as active agents, have the potential to question inherited stories. Throughout this text we will examine various kinds of stories so that each of us may be better educated and informed in order to develop and support the stories by which we want to live our lives. It is only in this way that we can contribute to the construction of transformative stories that might produce a more equitable society.

Once we realize that race is socially constructed, it follows that we recognize our role as active agents in reconstructing it—through our actions and through the stories we construct that inform our actions (Markus and Moya 2010, 4). Emphasizing the concept of agency is also essential to creating social change. If race is something we *do*, then we can begin to do it differently. Yet many people believe that race is biological, and so they believe it is inevitable. If people believe that they can make changes, then they inherently understand the complex factors that shape their own possibilities (Bush 2011). Such agency empowers people to resist and transform the economic, political, and social realities associated with racial frames and other forms of inequality.

It is because we, too, embrace the concept of agency that we have written this text. We hope to make visible the stock stories that perpetuate racial inequality, and to examine the ways in which those narratives govern the operations of organizations and institutions. All of us, as individuals, play a role in reproducing or subverting the dominant narratives, whether we choose to or not. While we inherit stories about race that help us to explain the world around us, we can also seek out alternative stories. All of us, as individuals, play a role in the reproduction of institutional structures, from our workplaces to our places of worship to our schools and our homes.

Each of the key insights that inform our framework, discussed above, is essential. Each provides just one piece of the puzzle. Further, these elements interact and work together, constantly influencing one another from moment to moment, so that it is often difficult to look at any one piece in isolation. Racial attitudes and racialized social structures need to be examined in relationship to one another. For example, many scholars have argued that economic insecurity and resource scarcity often fan the flames of race prejudice. Critical knowledge is gained when we understand how dominant discourses and ideology preserve and perpetuate the status quo. Understanding how these dominant discourses are framed and how they are buttressed by our institutional practices, policies, and mechanisms allows us to see not only how these patterns are replicated and reproduced but also how they can be replaced (Bush 2011, 37).

CRITICAL THINKING

1. If race is a social construction, how might different institutions affect how race is perceived? How might these perceptions vary across time and place?

2. Using yourself as an example, how has your identity changed as you shifted from being a preteen to a teen to a college student? Do these changes remain constant across different institutions? (Think about the various clubs, committees, and groups to which you belong.)

3. What kinds of impacts can you have in the various groups to which you belong? In what ways do your possible impacts reflect your various identities?

4. Are there some groups to which you have greater or lesser access? What does your degree of access suggest about your level of agency?

■ THE OPERATION OF RACISM

In the first half of this chapter, we have examined what race is, how it is constructed, and how it is reproduced. We now shift our focus to the concept and operation of racism.

Prejudice and Discrimination

Anyone can be the victim of prejudice. **Prejudice** is a judgment of an individual or group, often based on race, ethnicity, religion, gender, class, or other social identities. It is often shaped by, and also leads to, the promotion of **stereotypes**, which are assumptions or generalizations applied to an entire group. Even seemingly positive stereotypes put people in boxes, like the myth of Asian Americans as the "model minority," which includes the stereotype that all Asian Americans are gifted in math and science. How might this stereotype affect Asian American students who are not doing well in school? How does it prevent us from seeing the poverty that specific Asian American groups, such as the Hmong, Cambodians, and Thais, are more likely to experience (Takei and Sakamoto 2011)?

Prejudices and stereotypes are beliefs that often provide foundations for action in the form of **discrimination**—that is, the differential allocation of goods, resources, and services, and the limitation of access to full participation in society, based on an individual's membership in a particular social category (Adams et al. 1997). Prejudices and stereotypes exist in the realm of beliefs, and when these beliefs guide the ways in which we treat each other, they produce discrimination. Anyone can be the victim of prejudice, stereotyping, or discrimination, including White people, and for a wide variety of reasons, such as clothing, appearance, accent, and membership in clubs or gangs. Put simply, discrimination is prejudice plus power.

Prejudice, stereotypes, and discrimination are probably what first come to mind when we think about racism. But the study of racism goes far beyond these. Like sexism, racism is a system of oppression. **Oppression** is more than simply individual beliefs and actions—it involves the systematic devaluing, undermining, marginalizing, and disadvantaging of certain social identity groups in contrast to a privileged norm (Ferber and Samuels 2010). Oppression is based on membership in socially constructed identity categories; it is *not* based on individual characteristics.

One sociologist describes racial oppression as a birdcage: an interlocking network of institutional barriers that prevents escape (Frye 2007). Alternatively, others point out the **systemic nature of racial oppression**. This view posits that core racist realities, values, and ideologies are manifested in all of the major institutions within society (Feagin 2001, 6). Throughout this text we will demonstrate how race exists both historically and contextually as an ongoing form of inequality that pervades every major social institution, including education, employment, government, health care, family, criminal justice, sports, and leisure. Thinking about oppression as a birdcage helps us to understand how it limits people's lives. For example, the gendered wage gap is just one wire in the birdcage that constrains women. If it were the only wire, women could fly around it and escape. However, women face inequality in the home (in domestic labor, child care, elder care, and more), in education, in health care, in the workplace, in the criminal justice system, and more. They are trapped by an entire system of wires that form a cage.

Racism

Racism is a system of oppression by which those groups with relatively more social power subordinate members of targeted racial groups who have relatively little social power. This subordination is supported by individual actions, cultural values, and norms embedded in stock stories, as well as in the institutional structures and practices of society (National Education Association 2015). It is inscribed in codes of conduct, legal sanctions, and organizational rules and practices. Specifically, racism is the subordination of people of color by those who consider themselves White; by implication, the practice of racism defines Whites as superior and all non-Whites as inferior.

The Sociology of Racism

Racism is systemic. It is not about isolated individual actions; individual actions take place within a broader, systemic, cross-institutional context. People of color may themselves harbor prejudices and discriminate on the basis of race; however, without the larger social and historical context of systemic, systematic differences in power, these individual actions do not constitute racism. While this may seem counterintuitive, keep in mind that we are looking at racism from a sociological perspective, focusing on the importance of social context, research, and group experience, rather than on individual behavior. Individual experiences of race and racism will vary. We find it less important to focus on "racists" than on the social matrix of racism in which we live. Additionally, while White people do not experience racism, they may face oppression based on sexual orientation, class, or other social identities.

Who Practices Racism?

Racism in the United States is directed primarily against Blacks, Asian Americans, Latino/as, and Native Americans. Some argue that Muslims may also be considered targets of racism, as they are becoming a racialized group. Racism is the basis of conflict and violence in societies throughout the world, and the forms it takes are varied. Racism is practiced by Whites against Blacks, Coloreds, and Indians in South Africa; by Islamic Arabs against Black Christians in the Sudan; by East Indians against Blacks in Guyana; by those of Spanish descent against those of African and Indian descent in Brazil and Paraguay; by White "Aryans" against Jews and the Romani (Gypsies) in Germany; by the Japanese against the Eta, or Burakumin, in Japan; and by Whites against Africans, Sikhs, Muslims, and Hindus in Great Britain. Racism can take many forms, and it changes over time.

Types of Racism

Formal or overt racism occurs when discriminatory practices and behaviors are sanctioned by official rules, codes, or laws of an organization, institution, or society. Many of the most obvious forms of racism are no longer legally or openly accepted in U.S. society. Such racist practices as slavery, Jim Crow laws, the Black codes, the Indian Removal Act, the internment of Japanese residents during World War II, and the Chinese Exclusion Act are now condemned (but also too conveniently forgotten). Debate is ongoing regarding whether or not other practices—such as immigration policy, the display of the Confederate flag, and the use of American Indian sports mascots—are racist in intent or impact.

Informal or covert racism is subtle in its application, and often ignored or misdiagnosed. It acts informally in that it is assumed to be part of the natural, legitimate, and normal workings of society and its institutions. Thus, when we discuss student learning outcomes we may talk about poor motivation, inadequate schools, or broken homes. We ignore that these characteristics are also typically associated with poor Black and Latino/a neighborhoods (Coates 2011). Microaggressions are subtle insults (verbal, nonverbal, and/or visual) directed toward individuals

The subtle insults known as microaggressions are common in everyday interactions, like at the post office, even when things seem fine on the surface.

of oppressed social groups, sometimes made unconsciously. Research on college campuses finds that even when things look fine on the surface, inequality and discrimination still manifest themselves in "subtle and hidden forms" that shape interactions and experiences in dorms, class-rooms, dining halls, and student health centers. Over time, these can affect students' performance, and even their mental and physi-cal health (we discuss micro-aggressions in more depth in Chapter 5).

Understanding Privilege

When we study racism, we most often study the experiences of marginalized and oppressed groups. However, everyone's life is shaped by race. **Privilege** is the flip side of oppression—it involves the systemic favoring, valuing, validating, and including of certain social identities over others. Whiteness is a privileged status.

The Privilege of Whiteness

To be White is to have greater access to rewards and valued resources simply because of group membership. Because they exist in relationship to each other, oppression and privilege operate hand in hand; one cannot exist without the other. Just like oppression, privilege is based on group memberships, not individual factors. We do not choose to be the recipients of oppression or privilege, and we cannot opt out of either one. A White person driving down the street cannot ask the police to pull her over because of her race. Experiences of racism can affect some people and not oth-ers independent of their desires and behaviors.

Making Whiteness visible by acknowledging privilege allows us to examine the ways in which all White people, not just those we identify as "racist," benefit from their racial categorization. Accepting the fact that we live in a society that is immersed in systems of oppression can be difficult, because it means that despite our best intentions, we all participate in perpetuating inequality. In fact, privilege is usually invisible to the people who experience it until it is pointed out. The reality is that White people do not need to think about race very often. Their social location becomes both invisible and the assumed norm.

Research on White privilege has grown over the past three decades, along with the interdisciplinary subfield of **Whiteness studies**. Works by literary theorists, legal scholars, anthropologists, historians, psychologists, and sociologists alike have contributed to this burgeoning field (Brodkin 1998; Case 2013; Jacobson 1998; Haney López 2006; Moore, Penick-Parks, and Michael 2015; Morrison 1992). However, people of color have been writing about White privilege for a long time. Discussions of White privilege are found in the works of writers such as W. E. B. Du Bois, Anna Julia Cooper, and Ida B. Wells.

Whites are seen as the average, normal, universal human: the "mythical norm" (Lorde [1984] 2007). Descriptions in newspapers and books assume that subjects are White unless other racial identities are made clear. Some were outraged when Noma Dumezweni was cast as Hermione Granger in *Harry Potter and the Cursed Child*, despite the character's race being neither relevant nor specified in the Harry Potter series.

Peggy McIntosh's (1988) classic article "White Privilege and Male Privilege" was one of the first attempts by a White person to document the unearned advantages that Whites experience on a daily basis. For example, White privilege means being able to assume that most of the people you or your children study with in school will be of the same race; being able to go shopping without being followed around in the store; never being called a credit to your race; and being able to find "flesh-colored" bandages to match your skin color. McIntosh also identifies a second type of privilege that gives one group power over another. This conferred dominance legitimates privileges that no one should have in a society that values social justice and equity, such as the right to "own" another human being.

Most of us are the beneficiaries of at least one form of privilege, and often many more. Recognizing this often leads people to feel guilt and shame. However, privilege is derived from group membership; it is not the result of anything we have done as individuals. We are born into these systems of privilege and oppression; we did not create them. Once we become aware of them, though, we must be accountable and work to create change. We can choose whether to acknowledge privilege as it operates in our lives, and whether to use it as a means of creating social change. As Shelly Tochluk (2008, 249–50) notes, this requires that we "begin with personal investigation. . . . If we are going to take a stand, we need to feel prepared to deal with our own sense of discomfort and potential resistance or rejection from others."

The Impact of Stock Stories

The enduring stock story of the United States as a meritocracy makes it very difficult for us to see inequality as institutionalized (McNamee and Miller 2014). An "oppression-blind" belief system ignores the reality of inequality based on social group memberships and sees the United States as the land of equal opportunity, where anyone who works hard can succeed (Ferber 2012).

It is no wonder that individuals, especially those who are most privileged, often resist acknowledging the reality of ongoing inequality. We are immersed in a culture where the ideology of oppression blindness is pervasive. The news and entertainment media bombard us with color-blind "depictions of race relations that suggest that discriminatory racial barriers have been dismantled" (Gallagher 2009, 548). However, these institutionalized barriers still exist. Individuals often experience some cognitive dissonance when confronted with the concept of privilege. We often turn to our familiar stock stories to explain how we feel, countering with responses like "The United States is a meritocracy!" or "Racism is a thing of the past!" Table 1.2 lists some common responses, informed by our stock stories, to learning about privilege (Ferber and Samuels 2010). Do you share any of these feelings?

While our stock stories serve the interests of the dominant group, they are a part of our socialization and social fabric and become perceived as natural, normal, and the way of the world. It is easy to forget that these stories were created at specific moments to justify specific sets of interactions. Race, as part of our structured social system, has become realized as residential segregation, differential educational outcomes, income gaps, racially stratified training and occupational outcomes, social stigmas, and restrictions on social relationships (Smedley 2007, 21–22).

It is only through a deliberate process of critical inquiry that we can deconstruct these seemingly normal relationships to reveal the intentional and unintentional processes of construction and their underlying context. Critical sociological inquiry into the creation and maintenance of difference helps make the familiar strange, the natural unnatural, and the obvious not so obvious, and, in a world where things are often not what they seem, it allows us to see more clearly and deeply.

■ OUR STORIES

As we learn to understand ourselves and others, we can break down the divisions between us and build a foundation for transformative stories and new relationships. That is our goal for you, and we have designed this textbook to guide you through that

Table 1.2 ■ Feeling Race: Understanding Privilege

"I don't feel privileged, my life is hard too!"	This is an example of minimizing or denying privilege (Johnson 2006). We often focus on our oppressed identities as a means of ignoring our privilege.
"My family didn't own slaves!"	As historians have documented, "Into the mid-nineteenth century, the majority of whites—in the elites and among ordinary folk—either participated directly in slavery or in the trade around slavery, or did not object to those who did so" (Feagin 2000, 15). The economies of many northern cities were based almost entirely on the slave trade, and generations of Whites have reaped "undeserved enrichment" from the forced labor of slaves, the cheap labor of other minority group members, and the land and resources taken, often violently, from Native Americans and Mexicans. These practices contribute directly to today's tremendous racial wealth gap.
"I treat everyone the same!"	This type of response shifts the focus to prejudiced and bigoted individuals and allows us to ignore systemic oppression and privilege, and our own role in their reproduction.
"Anyone could succeed if they would just try harder!"	This adherence to the myth of meritocracy attributes the failures of an individual solely to that individual without taking into account systemic inequalities that create an unfair system. It is a form of blaming the victim (Johnson 2006).
"We need to move on! If we would just stop talking about it, it wouldn't be such a big problem!"	Systemic inequalities exist, and ignoring them will not make them go away. As Justice Harry Blackmun stated in his opinion in the U.S. Supreme Court case of *University of California v. Bakke* (1978) some 40 years ago, "In order to get beyond racism, we must first take account of race. There is no other way" (para. 14).
"Stop being so sensitive! I didn't mean it."	Speaking in a derogatory manner about a person or group of people based on social group memberships can have a devastating impact (Sue 2010). Disconnecting our own language or actions is another form of resistance because it minimizes the indiscretion and sends the message that anyone who challenges the language or behavior is simply being overly sensitive.
"I am just one person, I can't change anything!"	Seeing ourselves as incapable of creating change is a means of excusing ourselves from accepting any responsibility and denies agency.

CRITICAL THINKING

1. Racism is dynamic across geographic and social places and across historical periods. Consider some recent events either in the news or at your university: How do they reflect these dynamic processes? (*Hint:* Do you believe that the same types of events would have taken place, say, 50 years ago?)

2. Consider some common stereotypes about athletes, academics, or other professionals. Can you identify any racial stereotypes about which groups might be better at certain sports, disciplines, or professions? What might account for the prevalence of these stereotypes? Do you believe that they have changed over time, or that they would be similar to those in, say, England or Nigeria? What may account for either the similarities or the differences you observe?

3. At your institution are there any student groups that appear to have greater access to rewards and resources than other groups do? If so, what might account for their privilege?

4. Are there any common features (racial or gender or class) among the privileged student groups that you can identify? If so, what does this suggest about privilege?

process. We will journey together to see ourselves, each other, and our society at a deeper level. Our goal is not only to share information and knowledge about the dynamics of race and racism but also to connect this knowledge with our individual lives.

Now, we want to share some of our own stories. Race is deeply personal for each one of us, yet, as sociologists, we have learned much more about ourselves by situating our own lives within a broader context. We hope to help you do the same. We are all situated somewhere in the matrix, so this text is about each of us. We are all in this together.

Rodney

My grandfather was a sharecropper from Yazoo, Mississippi. In 1917, he arrived in East St. Louis, Illinois, a city with a robust industrial base that benefited significantly from World War I, and where much of the mostly White labor force was either in the military or on strike. Many Black men were migrating to East St. Louis at the time, looking for work.

White organized labor, fearful of losing job security, became hostile and targeted the new arrivals. On May 28, at a White union meeting, rumors began circulating that Black men were forcibly seducing and raping White women. A mob of more than 3,000 White men left this meeting and began beating random Black men on the street. The violence claimed the life of a 14-year-old boy, his mother was scalped, and 244 buildings were destroyed—all before the governor called in the National Guard. Rumors continued to circulate, and Blacks were selectively attacked by roving groups of White vigilantes.

But it wasn't over. On July 1, 1917, a Black man attacked a White man. The retaliatory response by Whites was massive, and an entire section of the Black community was destroyed while the police and fire departments refused to respond. My grandfather said that "blood ran like water through the streets." Many residents were lynched, and the entire Black section of the city was burned. No Whites have ever been charged with or convicted of any of these crimes. For the next 50 years, segregation maintained an uneasy peace in this troubled city.

Rodney Coates

Racial segregation, not only in housing but also in hospitals, dictated that I could not be born in the city where my parents resided (East St. Louis, Illinois), because the only hospital that would allow Negro women access was in St. Louis, Missouri. I grew up in a segregated city and went to all-Black elementary, middle, and high schools. Since mainstream educational institutions tended not to hire Black professionals, many of my English, math, and science teachers had advanced degrees, so I received the equivalent of a private education. Given my Blackness and the presumption that I would be a laborer and not a scholar, I also was equally trained in carpentry and sheet metal work. A system designed to keep the races separate provided an outstanding education—one that I was more than ready to take advantage of during the height of the civil rights movement.

The landmark U.S. Supreme Court decision in *Brown v. Board of Education* (1954) had desegregated the schools, and suddenly places like Southern Illinois University, the University of Illinois, and the University of Chicago were open to someone like me, a kid from a city that would soon become

After the first wave of racial violence in East St. Louis in 1917, in which hundreds of buildings were burned and a boy was killed, the governor called in the National Guard, seen here escorting a Black citizen through the rubble.

Bettmann / Bettmann / Getty Images

defined as a ghetto. As Blacks asserted their rights and the courts supported them, more doors opened to Blacks, and many Whites began to flee to the suburbs. This **White flight,** and the loss of business and industries, served to create ghettos where just a few short years before there had been thriving urban centers. I eventually obtained a bachelor's degree, two master's degrees, and a PhD from some of the best educational institutions in this country. My story has sensitized me to the ways in which race, class, and gender are intertwined in the great American narrative. I specialize in critical pedagogy, critical race theory, race and ethnic relations, stratification, human rights and social justice, educational sociology, political processes, urban sociology, political sociology, and public sociology.

Abby

I never had reason to think about race, or my own racial identity as White, until I became a graduate student. Instead, throughout my childhood, my Jewish identity was much more salient. My family was not very religious, but we were "cultural Jews." Growing up in a White, Jewish, upper-middle-class suburb of Cleveland, Ohio (one of the most segregated U.S. cities), I attended religious school on Sunday mornings and services at the synagogue on the High Holy Days. I learned about the Holocaust, the Inquisition, and the long history of pogroms. When I was in elementary school, the school building was bombed one night, and anti-Semitic epithets were scrawled on the walls. The message I internalized was that Jews were the universal scapegoat, and even when they were fully assimilated and successful, their safety was never secure. So even though I have never considered myself religious, I learned that what often matters more is whether other people see me as Jewish.

Abby Ferber

My great-grandmother fled her small Russian village when she was 16 years old to avoid an arranged marriage. Her parents disowned her, and she never spoke to them again. After she immigrated to the United States, she learned that her entire family had perished in concentration camps. My grandmother grew up in a Catholic community where her Jewish family was ostracized. At Ohio State University in the 1960s, my mother's roommate asked to see her horns. Last year, on a family vacation with my adolescent daughter, another member of our tour group took the guide's microphone and entertained the group with anti-Semitic jokes.

Yet I am also the beneficiary of White privilege, and this has had a greater impact on my life. I have never had to worry about being pulled over by police, not getting a job, or not being able to rent or purchase a home because of my race. I did not have to teach my daughter how to behave around the police for her own security. As Jews became defined as White, my grandparents were able to take out loans and start a small business. My parents were both able to attend college. Today, Jews are accepted as White in the United States.

In the years before and after World War II, many Jews fled their homes in Russia and Europe. These Jewish immigrants from Eastern Europe sought visas at the U.S. embassy in Paris, hoping to reach the United States.

My dissertation research examined the construction of race and gender in the context of the organized White supremacist movement. My research made my White privilege much more visible and real to me, ironically, because for White supremacists I am *not* White. Their ideology lumps Jews into the broad category of non-Whites, along with African Americans, Latinos, and Asian Americans. Studying this movement was the first time I really became aware of my White privilege, as I finally understood that it could be taken away. Privilege and oppression are not the result of anything a person has done as an individual. For instance, I have no control over who recognizes me as White or non-White, or when.

I also grew up acutely aware of gender oppression, even if I did not have the language to name it. I experienced sexual harassment at every job I held between middle school and graduate school, experienced numerous attempted rapes, and have received unequal pay compared to men doing the same job as me.

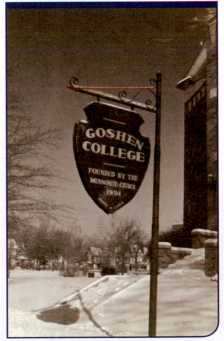

Goshen College is a Mennonite institution that focuses on outreach, study abroad, and missionary and/or "development" work.

As a graduate student, I first learned about privilege and intersectionality, and this provided a framework that allowed me to better understand the complexity of who I am, not only a Jewish female, but a White, heterosexual, middle-class, temporarily able-bodied and -minded, Jewish woman. I now have a greater understanding of

David Brunsma

how all of those identities intersect in shaping my life experience. And I now realize, as a person who benefits from White privilege, that it is my responsibility to work to reduce racial inequality. I never experienced guilt or shame when I learned of my privilege, but instead started asking how I could be a part of the solution.

Dave

I was born in Des Moines, Iowa, to a Puerto Rican mother and a largely unknown White father. My mother and her brothers and sisters had been adopted and raised by my solidly White, privileged, Christian grandparents in mostly White neighborhoods. While there were some variations in the degree of Puerto Rican identity felt among my family members, by and large they were White. I too was raised White. I have come to embrace my Puerto Rican identity, but I did not really know about it until the stories and structures of my life were already quite fully built along White lines.

As I grew up, although I delved into critical literatures, music, and film outside the scope of public school and family, it was expected that I would be White—talk White, dress White, and, ultimately, think and live White. I was also destined to reproduce the structures of White privilege and racism, despite the fact that I could see them then, and can see them even more clearly now. My life as a White American preordained my complacency and tacit agreement with the exploitative racial contract in White America, even while I fully disagree with it.

I went to a Mennonite college that preaches a kind of liberation theology, from which many go on to serve in missionary or "development" capacities all around the world—with good intentions but often ending up as color-blind extensions of American (or Jesus) imperialism. There were few people of color there, or in graduate school. Meanwhile, my critical, social justice lenses were becoming more sharply focused. I am still learning to "see" myself, my story, my place in the matrix; this is an important step in seeing others deeply as well. My research is focused on (multi)racial identity, race and ethnicity, human rights, sociology of education, and the sociology of culture.

CRITICAL THINKING

1. Each of us has a story. In what ways does your story reflect a particular narrative? How might your story be different from the stories of your parents or grandparents, or from those of your peers?

2. Are you a first-generation college student or did your parents also attend college? How are your college experiences different from their experiences (either as students or not)?

3. In what ways might your race, class, and gender affect your experiences? What does this suggest about how time and space interact with identity?

4. What changes do you envision for your children or the next generation? What stories do you think they will tell? And how might they interpret your story?

KEY TERMS

LO 1.1 Explain how race and ethnicity are socially constructed.

Race changes over time and across geographical spaces. It is an unstable and shifting concept. The U.S. Census Bureau attempts to identify the major racial groups in the United States, but it changes its definitions often. Defining a race is an example of the process of "Othering." Ethnicity and panethnicity are much more nuanced and layered concepts than those reflected in typical race categories. Within the United States, White ethnics have consistently been dominant, in terms of power as well as in numbers. This dominance owes its origins to practices, ideologies, and institutions that derive from our colonial past. And these practices, ideologies, and institutions have served to reinforce racial categorizations while obscuring the fluidity of race and ethnicity. Race definitions, structures, and practices are not applied consistently across the globe.

LO 1.2 Evaluate the relationship between social contexts and race.

The social context of race illustrates the reality of race in our society. Our focus on race helps us to understand how it shapes our identities, institutions, societies, and prospects for change. We use the concept of the matrix of race to help us see how the social construction of race is realized within our society. Our identities intersect along race, gender, and other axes, and these intersectional identities operate across various institutional and geographical spaces and historical periods. Looking at race in the social matrix highlights it as a social construct, as narrative, as relational and intersectional, and as institutional and structural, and it also emphasizes the role of humans as active agents in the process of racialization.

LO 1.3 Identify the concepts and operation of racism.

We use a variety of narrative types to highlight the operation and potential for transformation of race and racial structures. Our stock stories narrate how reality works. These stories often obscure or legitimate various types of oppression. Concealed stories are uncovered as we attempt to understand the actual ways in which race operates. By uncovering these narratives we often become aware of stories of resistance (where individuals or groups have attempted to circumvent or overcome racial structures) and/or stories of transformation (where individuals or groups have actually facilitated changes to race and racial structures). Prejudice, stereotyping, and discrimination, which anyone may encounter, are part of racism, but racism reaches beyond those practices and is systematic and institutional. Racism is a system of oppression.

LO 1.4 Examine the link between our personal narratives and the broader "story" of race.

We all have stories. Understanding our own narratives helps us examine how race, the matrix, and intersectionality operate within our lives.

THE SHAPING OF A NATION

The Social Construction of Race in America

John Moore / Getty Images News / Getty Images

Hundreds of Sudanese refugees have fled civil war and settled in the U.S., where they have a great deal to learn. Many cities have nonprofit organizations dedicated to helping these refugees acclimate to their new home towns.

CHAPTER OUTLINE

LEARNING OBJECTIVES

LO 2.1 Explore how recent events have affected how we experience race.

LO 2.2 Describe the Americas before Columbus.

LO 2.3 Examine the patterns of Spanish, French, and British colonialism in the Americas.

LO 2.4 Evaluate the intersections of race, identities, institutions, and resistance.

Thon Marial Maker was born in the midst of the Sudanese civil war in 1997. He fled the turmoil, along with some family members, and escaped into Uganda. From there he immigrated as a refugee into Australia. At the age of 14, Maker was discovered by Edward Smith, an Australian basketball coach who works with children from immigrant backgrounds to help them excel in the sport. Smith had previously worked with Ater Majok and Mathiang Muo, who went on to become professional basketball players, Majok for the Los Angeles Lakers and Muo for the Perth Wildcats in Western Australia. Smith offered Maker and his family the same opportunities, providing food, clothing, and education. In 2011, Maker and

Smith traveled to Texas to attend a basketball talent camp, where he was recruited to play. Maker played high school basketball first in Louisiana, then at Carlisle High School in Martinsville, Virginia. He was named the Gatorade Virginia Boys Basketball Player of the Year in 2014. The following year, cable sports channel ESPN ranked him as the top high school basketball player in the United States (Biancardi 2015). He was drafted by the Milwaukee Bucks in 2016. As a pro, Maker has averaged 9.6 rebounds and 14.2 points per game (Gardner 2017).

Maker was one of the almost 20,000 Sudanese boys uprooted because of civil war over the past three decades. Of this group, who have come to be known as the Lost Boys of Sudan, some 4,000 came to the United States. Hundreds would eventually settle in areas such as Atlanta, Boston, Dallas, Phoenix, Salt Lake City, San Diego, Seattle, and Tucson. Maker and the Lost Boys joined millions of immigrants who have come to the United States seeking peace, justice, freedom, and the American Dream. Their story is at the heart of our story and the shaping of a nation. As we will see, it is a story that has defined the racial matrix, created intersectionality, and set us on the path that we continue to walk to this day.

■ RACE TODAY: ADAPTING AND EVOLVING

Turn on a television, scroll your social media feed, or watch any movie, and you will discover that it is almost impossible to avoid the conclusion that race is intricately involved in most current events and issues. In fact, it often seems that our nation is consumed with race. How did we get here, and what does this obsession suggest about who we are as a people? In this chapter we will discuss the unique set of circumstances that started us down this path. But first, let's take a look at the current realities of race. While race seems both elusive and static, it is continually adapting and evolving.

Changing Demographics

The United States, as a nation of immigrants, has historically been defined by racial and ethnic diversity. Close to 60 million immigrants have arrived in the United States over the past 50 years. In 2016, nearly 14% of U.S. residents were foreign-born, most hailing from Latin America and Asia (Cohn and Caumont 2016).

The U.S. population is projected to grow from 422 million to 458 million in the next 40 years. During this period, as the baby boomers—that is, those who are part of the demographic group born right after World War II—age, our nation will also become slightly older. The proportion of the population made up of people age 65 and older will increase from 13% to about 20%. During this same period, total births will reach their highest level, with an estimated 4.3 million births. Much of this increase will be due to recent immigrants, who average higher fertility rates than the general population. The proportion of the population ages 15 to 64 is also expected to increase by 42% (Kotkin 2010).

Figure 2.1 ■ The Face of America is Changing

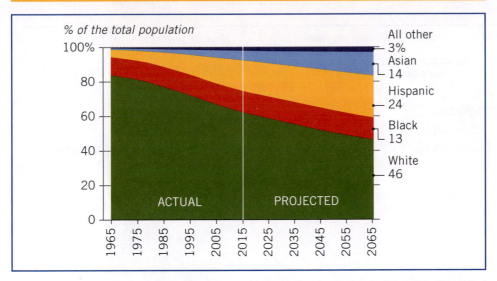

% of the total population

All other
3%
Asian
14
Hispanic
24
Black
13
White
46

ACTUAL PROJECTED

Source: D'Vera Cohn and Andrea Caumont, "10 Demographic Trends That Are Shaping the U.S. and the World," Fact Tank, Pew Research Center, March 31, 2016, http://www.pewresearch.org/fact-tank/2016/03/31/10-demographic-trends-that-are-shaping-the-u-s-and-the-world.

These demographic changes will have significant impacts on most of our institutions. As we will see in Chapter 10, the 2016 electorate was the most diverse in U.S. history, and it was the increasing growth in the numbers of racial minority voters that gave Barack Obama victories in both 2008 and 2012. But while younger voters are becoming increasingly diverse, one of the fastest-growing voting groups consists of the older Americans of the baby boomer generation. Donald Trump's 2016 election victory was a result of these older voters supporting him with 53% of their votes (Tyson and Maniam 2016).

These demographic changes will also have an immediate impact on colleges and universities across the nation. We can forecast these trends by examining the current racial makeup of grade school classrooms. In 2014, for the first time, the number of Latinos, African Americans, Asian Americans, Pacific Islanders, and Native Americans combined exceeded the number of Whites in public grade school classrooms (Williams 2014). Non-Hispanic Whites are currently in the minority in the populations of four states: California (which has a 61% minority population), Hawaii (77% minority), New Mexico (61% minority), and Texas (56% minority). And Nevada (48.5% minority), Maryland (47.4% minority), and Georgia (45% minority) are not that far behind (Maciag 2015).

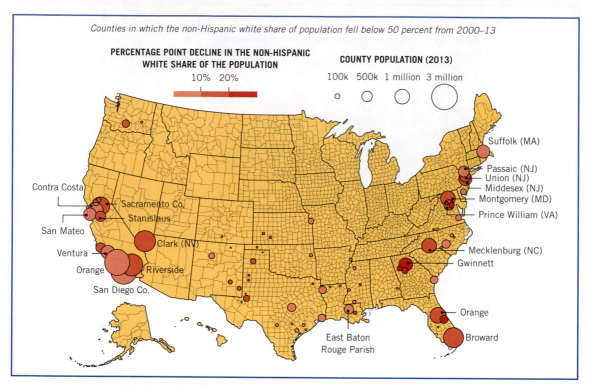

Counties in which the non-Hispanic white share of population fell below 50 percent from 2000–13

PERCENTAGE POINT DECLINE IN THE NON-HISPANIC WHITE SHARE OF THE POPULATION

COUNTY POPULATION (2013)

Source: "Where Minorities Became the Majority Between 2000 and 2013." In "Reflecting a Racial Shift, 78 Counties Turned Majority-Minority since 2000," by Jens Manuel Krogstad, Pew Research Center Fact Tank, April 8, 2015. http://www.pewresearch.org/fact-tank/2015/04/08/reflecting-a-racial-shift-78-counties-turned-majority-minority-since-2000.

Figure 2.2 shows that since 2000, 78 counties in 19 U.S. states became majority-minority. Of these, 14 had been at least 60% White (Krogstad 2015).

The most diverse counties are concentrated in California, in the South, and on the East Coast. And in 19 of the 25 largest U.S. counties (measured by population), Whites made up less than half of the population. Six of these that were majority White in 2000 are no longer so. These are San Diego, Orange, Riverside, and Sacramento Counties in California; Clark County, Nevada; Broward County, Florida (Krogstad 2015). As such changes take place, they will have impacts on everything from work and the economy to family structures to who serves in the military. Our media and other forms of entertainment, including sports, will also be affected. Some impacts are even now becoming apparent.

The Influence of a Changing World

The United States has been experiencing a particularly turbulent period since the September 11, 2001, terrorist attacks that resulted in the deaths of more than 3,000 people. This single event has fundamentally altered the experiences of everyone in this country and in the world. During this period we have also witnessed four separate wars, as well as countless other military operations from Haiti to Libya, Afghanistan to Iraq—many of them rooted in notions of "the Other" and difference.

During the past few decades, ethnic violence has erupted into **genocide**—the large-scale, systematic destruction of a people or nation—among the Tutsis and Hutus in Rwanda and among the Serbs, Croats, and Muslims in Bosnia. **Racial violence**, violence that pits one racial group against another, has occurred around the world, including in places like Australia, India, Belgium, France, and the United Kingdom. Closer to home, riots and civil unrest stemming from issues of race have disrupted a number of U.S. cities, including Cincinnati, Ohio (2001);

Benton Harbor, Michigan (2003); Oakland, California (2009); Hempstead, New York (2010); Ferguson, Missouri (2014–15); and Baltimore, Maryland (2015). And we have witnessed the public reactions to violence between police forces and people of color, reactions that reveal our anxieties and frustrations about race.

After Freddie Gray, a 25-year-old Black Baltimorean, died from injuries he sustained while in police custody in 2015, the city erupted in protests.

Not all of the change has been violent. We have also witnessed several firsts for women and persons of color. Many of you may have experienced the euphoria of the 2003 launch of the space shuttle *Columbia,* carrying possibly the most diverse flight crew ever seen, and also experienced the tragedy of that crew's loss as the shuttle disintegrated during reentry. We celebrated the fall of the Berlin Wall in 1989, and the election of the first Black president of the United States in 2008. In 2005, the deadly force of Hurricane Katrina revealed the ugly underbelly of race, class, and gender as thousands of New Orleans residents were displaced—the largest internal displacement in American history (Kromm and Sturgis 2008). America has discovered new phrases such as "racial profiling," "subprime loans," and "dining while Black"—all of which demonstrate our continued obsession and problems associated with difference and solidify the idea that each of us experiences the world from our own position within the matrix (Goyette and Scheller 2016). Compared to Americans living in previous periods, we are generally more fashion conscious, upbeat, diverse, liberal, confident, self-expressive, and open to change (Taylor and Keeter 2010). As we learned earlier, Latinos are quickly emerging as a population that is significantly altering what it means to be American, and college enrollment among Hispanics is now the largest and fastest growing of all student groups (Fry 2011).

Revising the Experience of Work, Gender, and Race

Women currently make up only about 4% of CEOs in Fortune 500 firms, and Asians, Hispanics, and Blacks account for slightly more than 1% (Zarya 2016). Alongside some gains, women of all social groups have on average lost ground over the past few years due to the **triple glass ceiling**, or three-pronged workplace discrimination based on race, gender, and class (Gutiérrez, Meléndez, and Noyola 2007). This and other disparities have been aggravated by the financial recession that began in 2008.

Wage disparities affect all women, but Hispanic, African American, American Indian, Native Hawaiian, and other native women are the lowest paid. For the women in these groups, however, the gender gap—the difference between their wages and those of men in the same groups—is not as great as the gap for White non-Hispanic women, who experience the largest gender gap.

Closer examination reveals that among all groups, Hispanic women, followed by African American women, have the largest earning gap when compared to White men (54% and 63%, respectively). These gaps increase with age: Median earnings of women ages 16–19 are 89% of the earnings of their male counterparts, compared to 74% for those 65 and older. Finally, while education does improve the earnings of women of all races and ethnicities, racial and gendered differences remain. Among educated women, Asian Americans lead all other women in median annual earnings regardless of education.

Sources of Change and Diversity

Although Americans as a nation are more diverse than ever before, many of us find our realities still structured by race. For instance, White students are only slightly less likely than students of previous generations to attend nearly all-White primary and secondary schools, while minority students, including Latino and Black students, are actually more likely to attend nearly all-minority schools (Childress 2014). In fact, some researchers have documented that American primary and secondary schools are even more segregated by race and class today than they were in the late 1950s after the landmark Supreme Court desegregation case *Brown v. Board of*

Education of Topeka, Kansas (Orfield 2009). This apparent contradiction is a by-product of the civil rights movement, which led more affluent families of color to move from the cities to the suburbs, while urban schools became increasingly less diverse. As middle-class women and women of color have, on average, reversed the achievement gap for college completion and graduate school admissions, among lower-class women and men of color these gaps have become even more entrenched. As a result of these shifts, young Latinos for the first time now outnumber young Blacks on campus, even though Black college enrollment has also grown steadily for decades, and it, too, has surged in recent years (Fry 2011).

The Evolving Narrative of Popular Culture

Two recent popular book series, J. K. Rowling's *Harry Potter* series and Stephenie Meyer's *Twilight* saga, demonstrate how race, class, and gender issues prevail even in fictional universes (Moje, Young, Readence, and Moore 2000; Strommen and Mates 2004). Some of the allure of the *Twilight* series might be that it weaves together concerns about sex, race, and class as the human protagonist violates racial-like norms and falls in love with a vampire. The story suggests that our society can overcome both racism and sexism in this fictionalized world where vampires, werewolves, and humans get along and battle for gender equality (Wilson 2011). Unfortunately, this fictionalized social reality is just that—fictionalized (Bonilla-Silva 2008). Other popular books feature worlds where race, power, oppression, and liberation are clearly etched into the narratives. Take the case of the *Harry Potter* books, which present a strikingly racialized narrative where the world is divided among the "pure-blood" wizarding families; the "half-bloods," or wizards born of nonwizarding families, and the "Muggles," or nonmagical humans.

The Impact of Social Media and Technology

About 7 out of 10 Americans now use online social networks (Perrin 2015). You might assume that our online experiences would reflect society's increasingly diverse demographic structure. However, research shows that even online, our experiences are structured by race, class, and gender. Facebook friendships among college students are not only more likely to be among those living in the same dorm

In recent years the international phenomenon of the *Hunger Games* trilogy has brought the topics of the structures of inequality, the excesses of power, and the promises of liberation struggles and uprisings back into the popular discourse.

and studying the same subject but also self-segregated by gender, race, class, and even hometown (Lewis, Gonzalez, and Kaufman 2011). Rather than challenging the racial status quo, the online world has ultimately reproduced it. Perhaps it is not so strange that this is so; human beings have been grappling with issues of difference since the dawn of civilization.

With more than 316 million residents and a history of immigration that goes back more than 500 years, to long before the founding of the nation, the United States is one of the most ethnically and racially diverse countries in the world. We are a nation of immigrants. While English is the dominant language, more than 300 other languages are spoken here (Shin and Kominski 2010). In fact, the United States has no official language. Examining the nation's story helps us understand why.

CRITICAL THINKING QUESTIONS

1. Why do current demographic shifts define us as a nation? How might these changes differ across different geographical areas?

2. How do demographic shifts affect various social institutions?

3. How might future demographic changes affect different areas and institutions? How can social media become an instrument of change?

4. How will the demographic evolution affect you? Are you ready for the changes that are coming?

■ INDIGENOUS PEOPLES: THE AMERICAS BEFORE COLUMBUS

As a nation, we rely on certain stories to bind us together, the most central of which has to do with the founding and discovery of our country—our own "stock story":

> In fourteen hundred and ninety-two, Columbus sailed the ocean blue.

According to this story, a brave and daring Christopher Columbus set off from Europe with three ships to find a shorter route to Asia. Columbus, often portrayed as a scientific and astronomical genius, proved not only that the world is round but also that its circumnavigation was feasible.

Figure 2.3 ■ European Colonization Began with Viking Exploration in 986

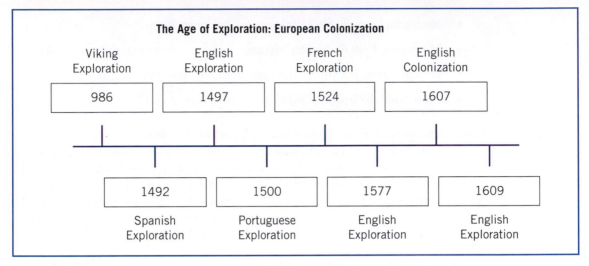

The Age of Exploration: European Colonization

Source: Kimberly Burgess, "The Age of Discovery," http://theageofdiscoverykbsp14.weebly.com/european-colonization-timeline.html.

Recent historical revisions have challenged this story, suggesting that this "discovery" was more like an invasion. Though vastly outnumbered by the natives of the Americas, the Europeans benefited greatly from "guns, germs, and steel"—the superior weaponry and disease-causing microbes they brought from Europe that allowed them to impose their wills on the indigenous Americans (Diamond 1999).

The Earliest Americans

Prior to Columbus, the Americas was inhabited by Native Americans. From the Abenakis of Maine to the Zunis of New Mexico, Native Americans are descendants of an even earlier group of immigrants to the Americas. These Asian immigrants were the first Americans, arriving more than 20,000 years ago. There is a good chance that they came via two different routes:

1. People on foot, traversing the glacial land bridge between Siberia and Alaska, were mostly hunters and gatherers who followed the mastodon and long-horned bison, and might have been responsible for their eventual extinction.

2. Fishers and hunters utilizing boats from the Pacific Islands allowed the currents to guide them to these shores (Arnaiz-Villena et al. 2010).

Many geographical place names help identify the first peoples of the Americas. More than half of U.S. state names are representative of the original inhabitants of those areas. The following are just a few:

- Michigan, from the Allegany language, meaning "big water"

- Minnesota, from the Siouan language, meaning "water that reflects the sky"

- Missouri, from the Siouan language, meaning "water flowing along"

- Ohio, from the Iroquois language, meaning "good river"

Many state names reflect the dominance of particular tribes, such as Massachusetts, Connecticut, Illinois, and Dakota. While Native Americans rarely gave a single name to an entire river or mountain, they typically gave names to specific features, such as the mouth or bend of a particular river. They tended to name each peak or crag rather than the whole mountain. We have many of these names still with us today, such as Potomac (Iroquois, meaning "the place to which tribute is brought") or Allegheny (Iroquois derived from *monongahela,* which means "falling banks").

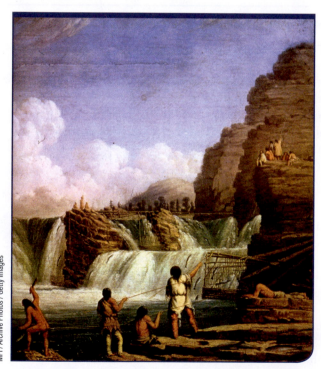

MPI / Archive Photos / Getty Images

Native Americans typically gave specific names to each feature of a river or mountain. Many of these names are still in use today.

Many of the early Native American communities were urban, with populations reaching the tens of thousands. Archaeologists and anthropologists have identified several towns, with temples and evidence of a priestly class, along with nobles, merchants, and artisans, demonstrating highly stratified, hierarchical, and technologically sophisticated civilizations.

A Rich History

Hundreds of years before Columbus, North America was home to millions of people and hundreds of population groups, tribes, and linguistic and cultural systems. These people called themselves Iroquois and Mohawk, Miami and Illini, Lakota and Apache, and hundreds of other names. As noted above, many areas in our country retain the names of this rich history. In the Northeast, the Iroquois and the Algonquin, two major language and cultural groups, occupied a region now known as the Northeastern Woodlands. The Algonquin controlled two major areas, one encompassing the Great Lakes and the other near the Atlantic Ocean. Several tribes constituted the Algonquin. The Wampanoag were the first tribe in this region encountered by the Europeans. Both the Illini and the Potawatomi occupied the Illinois region. The League of the Iroquois, formed as early as 1090, comprised five tribes who lived in the areas today known as New York State and the Southeastern Woodlands (which stretched from the Atlantic Ocean to the Mississippi River and from the Gulf of Mexico to the Ohio River). The largest northern groups in the confederation were the Cherokee, the Chickasaw, and the Creek. The southern regions were dominated by the Natchez, Biloxi, and Seminole—known as the Mound Builders (Lord and Burke 1991).

Their histories are reflected in the many names they gave this land—such as the Lakota and Mohawk's Anowarkowa (Turtle Island), the Powhatan's Tsenacommacah (densely inhabited area), and the Shawnee's Kantukee (the great meadow, or the dark and bloody ground). They lived in teepees and huts, cities and villages; they built burial mounds, temples, and multistory buildings. And they routinely and systematically planted and harvested more than 100 kinds of crops (including tomatoes, quinoa, and peaches) using crop-rotation techniques and an understanding of the importance of seasonal flooding for the enrichment of nutrient-poor soil (Mann 2005).

In their farming, these original Americans added charcoal and broken pottery to the tropical red clays—an agricultural method recognized today. Skilled at metallurgy, they examined metals for their malleability and toughness (Mendoza 1997).

The earliest Americans hunted buffalo, boar, turkey, rabbit, and deer. Their diet also included perch, catfish, oysters, and salmon. They mastered carving, weaving, tanning, and pot making. Not only did they develop highly sophisticated artistry in jewelry, weaving, and textiles, but they also created pictorial art on cave walls and rocks. Their works are displayed in some of the finest museums across the world today. These peoples had highly developed written, oral, and symbolic languages; math and calendar systems; religions; political systems; and constitutions. Their civilizations were hundreds of years older than the oldest European nation, richer than we will ever know, and more varied than has ever been captured in the stock stories of "cowboys and Indians."

These Native Americans were neither brutes nor savages, neither pagans nor infidels. They were not prototypical environmentalists or solitary figures in contest with the forces of progress—they were humans, with all of the creative and marvelous social inventions we have come to recognize as human, such as democratic governance and constitutional bodies, federations and confederations, family and community. They had both philosophies and mythologies, prophecies and paradigms, educational systems and beliefs about the cosmos, hopes and dreams. They had wars and civil unrest, and military, political, civil, and religious leaders.

They bartered and traded and had many types of coinage and economies. Ultimately, they lived full, expansive, rich, and complete lives long before Columbus and the Europeans discovered them and entered their matrix to create a new one.

◼ DISCOVERY AND ENCOUNTERS: THE SHAPING OF OUR STORIED PAST

European colonization of the Americas actually began in the 10th to 11th centuries, when Viking sailors explored what is currently Canada (Figure 2.3). In their explorations, they settled Greenland, sailed up the Arctic region of North America, and engaged in violent conflict with several indigenous populations. More extensive European colonization began in 1492, when Spanish ships captained by Christopher Columbus inadvertently landed on the northern tip of Cuba. In all instances, colonial adventures were particularly nationalistic, as evidenced by the names of Nueva Española, Nouvelle-France, and New England. Settlement of this so-called New World centered on transplanting, cloning, and grafting European institutions into the Americas. These particularities were aggravated by competition over control of land, ports, raw resources, and native peoples.

Understanding Colonialism

Colonialism is a set of hierarchical relationships in which groups are defined culturally, ethnically, and/or racially, and these relationships serve to guarantee the political, social, and economic interests of the dominant group (Barrera 1976, 3). Under the guise of advancing the "kingdom of God," the Spanish, French, and English pursuit of colonies was more closely aligned with greed and fame.

Religious ideology was used to justify wars of aggression, exploitation, subjugation, extermination, enslavement, and colonization. The structures, ideologies, and actions that form patterns of colonialism shape groups' interrelated experiences in profound ways—the realities behind colonialism are complex, and usually structurally and culturally catastrophic for the colonized. We can view colonialism through three primary lenses:

1. As a structure of domination subjugating one group of people to another across political entities

2. As "internal" or "domestic" colonialism, a similar structure occurring within a given nation-state, typically against socially marked groups

3. As a "colonialism of the mind," wherein the colonized are institutionally, pedagogically, linguistically, and cognitively conquered by the colonizer

The colonies that developed within the Americas are best classified as settler colonies. **Settler colonies** are distinguished by the colonizing nation's control of political, economic, social, and cultural mechanisms in the colonies, which creates a colonial elite. The European elite who migrated to the settler colonies in the Americas were intent on settlement, creation of a self-sustaining independent political/economic system, and domination of both geography and indigenous populations. Even while settler colonies maintained dependency relationships with their respective European nations, they nevertheless achieved significant autonomy (Stasiulis and Yuval-Davis 1995).

European settlements and population dynamics varied considerably both across different European groups and compared with those established by Native Americans. Pre-Columbian population estimates suggest that Native Americans were generally distributed throughout the Americas, with most occupying the areas that are now Mexico and Central America (47%), followed by South America (35%) and the Caribbean (10%). The remainder were scattered across what would become the United States and Canada. The first groups of colonizers, the Spanish and Portuguese, settled in the most densely populated areas. Later colonizing efforts by both the French and the English created settlements in the less densely populated areas primarily in North America and Canada (Figure 2.4). Such dynamics produced very different sets of opportunities and issues for both the colonizers and the colonized.

Spanish Colonialism (1492)

We must be willing to confront the history of the Americas in terms that are more complex and nuanced than those often provided by simple historical accounts. At no time were the colonies ever fully independent of or politically isolated from what was happening in Europe or among the various Native American nations. In 1492, when Columbus stumbled on a set of islands off the coast of Florida, he named them Hispana, the Latin name for Spain. Despite the fact that this land was home to a significant population, Columbus declared it *terra nullius* (empty land), revealing much about how explorers and, later, colonists saw themselves in relation to others and the world around them.

Constructing a Racial Ideology

The Spanish encountered a significantly different people with specific cultural, political, and gender systems. Native American gender systems varied across tribal groups. Gender relations within the Taino tribes, for example, were both egalitarian and nonexclusive. Women were able to own property and often served as ritual leaders and organized most of the subsistence work (Deagan and Cruxent 2002, 31–32; Deagan 2004).

Figure 2.4 ■ European Colonizers Settled in Distinct Geographic Areas

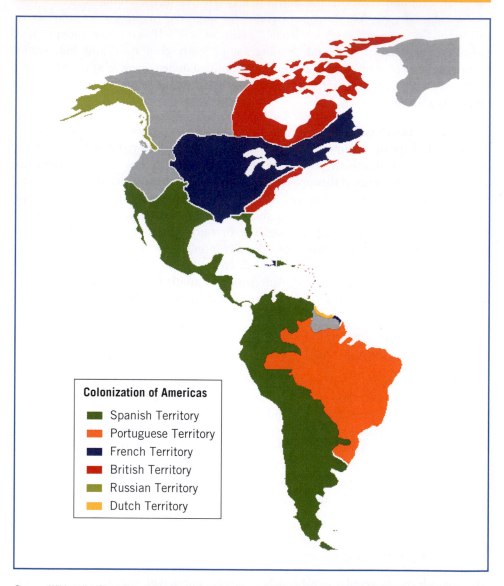

Colonization of Americas

■ Spanish Territory
■ Portuguese Territory
■ French Territory
■ British Territory
■ Russian Territory
■ Dutch Territory

Source: Wikimedia Commons, https://upload.wikimedia.org/wikipedia/commons/thumb/b/b0/Colonization_of_the_Americas_1750.PNG/300px-Colonization_of_the_Americas_1750.PNG.

By 1570, the Spanish colonies were utilizing two racial distinctions:

1. *Spanish-born or –descended:* This group consisted of those born in either Spain or the colonies and included both those of mixed heritage and those considered to be "purebloods."

2. *Native-born or –descended:* This group consisted of all Native Americans, who were considered vassals of the king.

Each of these groups had different rights, obligations, and privileges. Natives, under Spanish laws, were obliged to provide labor for both government and private enterprises deemed vital to colonial interests, and to pay special poll taxes or tributes. While these laws were intended to create two distinct classes, the flexible laws of both marriage and residence allowed many Native Americans to adopt European-style dress and "pass" as purebloods (Jackson 2006, 902).

The Catholic Church, notably through the Spanish Inquisition and the Franciscan order, used purity certifications to impose barriers on some Spaniards who sought to immigrate to the Americas. The church would use these same purity levels to label both Africans and Native Americans as "New Christians" and mark both as "impure" (Martinez 2004, 483). Any offspring of interracial unions involving New Christians would thus be less valued. Put simply, Blacks, Native Americans, and others could be redeemed and baptized, but they still could not mix with "purebloods."

Grounded in vague notions of purity and supposed biological differences, these rules would later become the basis for the **racial caste system,** a permanent hierarchy based on race, that developed in Spanish America (Martinez 2008). These laws also reveal the centrality of gender relations to the construction of culture and race. In order to distinguish one culture from another and define one as superior, societies must maintain borders. These borders are inscribed onto women's bodies and then policed by regulating sexual relationships. The bodies and wombs of White women were considered sacred—they were the only source of future generations of Whites (Martinez 2008, 483–84). European men, on the other hand, maintained for themselves access to all women's bodies. Ultimately, this racial caste system would be linked to the social and economic hierarchies that exist today in Latin American countries in what scholars refer to as pigmentocracies, as discussed in Chapter 1 (Telles and the Project on Ethnicity and Race in Latin America 2014).

The Slave System

Columbus was the first to employ slavery in the colonies. Two days after he "discovered" America, Columbus wrote in his journal that with 50 men he could order that "the entire population be taken to Castile, or held captive." On his second voyage in December 1494, Columbus captured 1,500 Tainos on the island of Hispaniola and selected 550 of "the best males and females" to be presented to the Spanish queen,

Isabella, and sold in the slave markets of Seville, Spain (Beal 2008, 60). In 1525 a total of 5,271 slaves appeared on the notarial records of Seville; almost 400 were listed as Blacks or mulattoes (Phillips 1985, 161).

The Spanish colonies were considered lenient with regard to racial classification, for multiple reasons:

- The colonial laws accorded protections to Native Americans and to slaves.

- Slaves' rights were protected by both judicial and ecclesiastical authority.

- Spanish slave laws were derived from Roman legal traditions.

- Manumission (the freeing of slaves) did not require prior approval from the crown.

- Slaves could purchase their own freedom.

- Slaves had legal recourse through the Spanish courts, even for grievances against their masters. (Parise 2008, 13–14)

Ultimately, the supply of Native American labor in the Spanish colonies was decimated by continual warfare, disease, and sheer overwork. Under the licensing system established by King Ferdinand in 1513, an estimated 75,000 to 90,000 African slaves were sent to Spanish America by 1600. This figure would more than triple by the end of the 17th century, accounting for approximately 350,000 enslaved Africans (Landers 1997, 85). With these massive increases in the labor force, the Spanish colonies shifted to plantation economies, which also fundamentally altered Spanish slavery. Blacks began to outnumber Whites in Hispaniola and Mexico by an estimated ratio of 10 to 1 by the early to mid-16th century. Many of the medieval slave protections were stripped away, and Spanish officials' worst nightmares were realized as slave insurrections repeatedly threatened one colonial settlement after another.

Black slaves were the major source of labor on sugar plantations in Spanish America, particularly after Native American populations were decimated.

© British Library Board / Robana / Art Resource, NY

French Colonialism (1534)

New France, the first site colonized by France in North America, was created by the 1534 expedition headed by Jacques Cartier along the Saint Lawrence River in what is now Quebec (Figure 2.5). Cartier's explorations allowed France to claim the land that would later become Canada. The French sought gold along the Saint Lawrence River, but settled for fishing and fur trading instead. And it was here, in 1608, that Quebec was established as the first French colony (Greer 1997, 6).

The French attempted to colonize a large chunk of the Americas with an extremely small and mostly male colonial force. The fact that the Frenchmen were outnumbered and unable to establish cultural dominance and stable communities helps explain their eventual failure.

Among financiers and merchants, the French colonial expansion into the Americas was conceived of as a business venture, and profits were often seen as more important than colonial development. Officially, the primary goal of these ventures was the Christianization of the natives, but it was not until after the first successful

Figure 2.5 ■ France Claimed Much of the Land that Would Later Become Canada

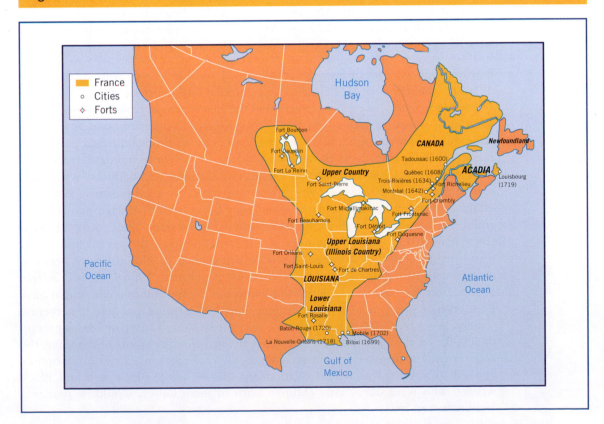

settlements were established that this royal rhetoric was given serious consideration. The thrust of the efforts, inspired by the fur trade, provided the motivation to integrate the indigenous population into the French colonial policy, as governors and foreign missionaries were determined to save the "savages" (Belmessous 2005).

Labor Crisis and Slavery

The French, like the Spanish, soon discovered that Native American slaves could not provide sufficient labor. As the plantations and economies expanded, so did labor needs. French colonies like Louisiana encountered labor crises as they attempted to shift their economies to tobacco and sugar production. On May 1, 1689, King Louis XIV gave royal approval for the trade and use of Africans as slaves. Twenty years later, in 1709, slavery was declared legal in New France.

The first groups of imported slaves came from both France and Africa between 1717 and 1720. The group from France consisted of more than 1,400 White men and women who had been convicted as thieves and deported to New France. Riots by these French slaves caused a sudden halt to this form of slavery. Ultimately, it was Africans who filled the labor needs of New France, particularly in Louisiana. During this period close to 4,000 Africans were forcefully brought to the colony (Hall 1992). As this history demonstrates, Africans did not become slaves because they were Black; many other cultural groups were also forced into slavery (Pitts 2012).

France produced a set of laws governing slaves and Blacks that were qualitatively different from the laws of Spain. France's Colonial Ordinance of 1685, also known as the **Black Code** (Code Noir), legislated the life, death, purchase, marriage, and religion of slaves, as well as the treatment of slaves by their masters. It formally required all slaves to be baptized and educated in the Catholic faith and prohibited masters from forcing slaves to work on Sundays and religious holidays. It required masters to provide slaves with food, shelter, and clothing, and with care when sick. It held that slaves could not own property or have any legal recourse. It further established when they could marry, where they could be buried, what punishments could be meted out to them, and under what conditions they could be freed (Buchanan 2011). These laws were an attempt to curtail the sexual and moral problems generated by frontier society, which tended to blur the lines between groups with differing status. The Black Code prohibited Whites, as well as free Blacks, from having sexual relationships with slaves. Any children who might have been born of such unions were to become wards of the state and held in perpetual slavery. In other words, a slave's status could not be altered based on marriage, and the child of a slave would become a slave. In legalizing the status of the slave, the code created a firm border between slaves and free persons. The only loophole applied to any existing sexual relationships between free Black men and Black women who were slaves. Any children born of these unions would be rendered legitimate and free.

Left-Handed Marriages and Plaçage

Within these frontier situations, "social relations were more fluid and social hierarchies less established than they would become with the entrenchment of plantation agriculture" (Spear 2003, 90). Under these circumstances, a strange norm developed whereby men often formed alliances with Creole women in what were termed **left-handed marriages**. These "marriages," temporary in nature, often resulted in children who served as interpreters and mediators (Shippen 2004, 358). While such relationships were equivalent to common-law marriages, the women were not legally recognized as wives; among free people of color, these social arrangements were referred to as *plaçage*.

Plaçage flourished throughout both French and Spanish colonies. Such relationships were celebrated as part of high society in New Orleans during what became known as the city's "quadroon balls." **Quadroon** literally means one-quarter Black by descent. These balls provided a carnival atmosphere where elite White males could make their selections from a collection of light-skinned free women of color. A woman selected was accorded a household, typically with servants, where her status was slightly less than that of a wife and greater than that of a concubine. *Plaçage* therefore constituted a socially sanctioned form of **miscegenation**, or

Under the plaçage system, white men would take light skinned free women of color as their common law wives and establish them in household, often with servants.

the mixing of different racial groups, often lasting even after the man was legally married to a White woman. While technically free, the women involved in *plaçage* were both economically and socially dependent on their sexual objectification, availability, attractiveness, and ability to satisfy the fantasies of elite White men (Li 2007, 86). Eventually, the large number of free people of color and their relationships to others of mixed heritage caused the Louisiana Supreme Court to declare all such mixed-race people to be free (Hall 1992). This group had greater access to education and wealth and used both to become advocates for racial reform and freedom.

British Colonialism (1587)

After some failed attempts, the Plymouth Company's *Mayflower* finally reached the New World in 1620, where the ship's passengers established the next set of English colonies in a place they declared to be Plymouth in Massachusetts (Figure 2.6).

These settlers shared the European rationalization for imperial expansion by declaring the indigenous peoples barbaric—and saving these pagans via Christian civilization was the goal.

Building a Tradition of Slavery

The first group of non–Native Americans to wear chains in New England were poor Whites, primarily from Ireland. These slaves began arriving in New England in the early 1600s. English slave masters looked upon the Irish as backward, lazy, unscrupulous, and fit to be enslaved (Beckles 1990, 510–11). Upwards of 50,000 Irish people, mostly women and children, were forcibly deported to the Americas. Harsh treatment, hostility, and degradation led Irish and Black slaves to engage frequently in collaborative rebellions (Bernhard 1999, 89–91).

In all likelihood, the first Blacks entered Jamestown, in the colony of Virginia, in 1619 as indentured servants, but by 1661 they were legislated servants for life. In the next year, a revised statute linked slavery to maternity by declaring that all children would be free or slave according to the status of their mothers. This Virginia law was a

Figure 2.6 ■ There Were 13 Original English Colonies

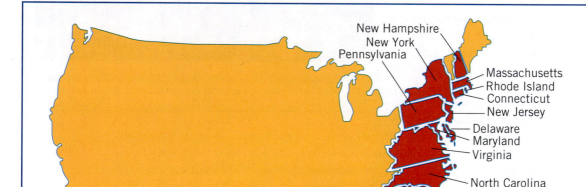

Source: U.S. Geological Survey, *National Atlas of the United States of America* (Washington, DC: U.S. Department of the Interior, 1970).

significant departure from previous British laws, which traced the status of children to their fathers. The lucrative commerce in Native American slaves commenced among the English with the founding of Carolina in 1670 and lasted through 1717. What emerged was a distinct racial hierarchy in which male European landowners dominated both Native American and African slaves (Gallay 2002). Thus, on the backs of African slaves, a racial hierarchy was constructed.

Like the Spanish and French, the English manipulated the ethnic conflicts among the various Native American groups. The English encouraged the Native Americans to avoid slavery by enslaving their adversaries and selling them to the English for trifles of cloth and beads, and, of course, guns (Gallay 2002, 6).

This new racial system finally gave birth to racial classification and defined race relations throughout the nation until the dawn of the Civil War. These new laws and new hierarchies were also motivated by attempts to divide those who otherwise might be inclined to join together in revolt.

Slave Rebellions: Voices of Resistance

Slave rebellions represented a continual and persistent source of both strain and stress for the White planter class. The response was the continual evolution of racial hierarchies buttressed by laws, sanctions, and privileges that pervaded the entire colonial social structure. Throughout this text, we will show how these resistance stories have become an integral part of Americans' national identity.

The first significant slave rebellion against the English occurred in Gloucester County, Virginia, in 1663. This conspiracy, which included both White indentured servants and slaves, aimed to overthrow the White masters. The plot was exposed by an informant, which led to the execution of several of the plotters and the passage of a series of laws that began to emphasize the ineradicable distinctions between slave masters and slaves.

Bacon's Rebellion of 1676 was the most significant challenge to the class structure (Breen 1973). The elite response to Bacon's Rebellion was to create new identities of color and race to usurp divisions of class and status. In order to understand this threat, we must understand the labor situation in 17th-century Virginia. In this revolt, Black, Irish, Scottish, and English bond servants were pitted against a small and nervous group of planter elites. Bacon, a member of displaced White labor, found himself and his group literally between a rock and a hard place. The real issue was that the increasing use of Africans as bonded labor had forced a large number of White laborers out of their positions. The irony of this is that while the members of the planter class were gaining land grants with each new allotment of workers, no such provisions were being made for those displaced by the increasing numbers of cheaper laborers.

Crop failures in 1676 provided the fuel for the violence that followed. The revolt quickly became a mass rebellion of bond servants who aimed to level the government and the entire class structure. More than 6,000 European Americans and 2,000 African Americans took up arms and fought against a tiny Anglo-American slave-owning planter class. They marched to West Point, where they took over the garrisons and military arsenal. They forced the military governor to flee and shut down all tobacco production for the next 14 months.

The rebellion threatened the very heart of the British colonial system by challenging the power of the Anglo-American slave-owning planter elite. The members of the planter class responded by solidifying slavery into a racial caste system. In the process, Whiteness was created.

Bacon's Rebellion, in Virginia in 1676, remade class and status distinctions and hardened slavery into a racial caste system.

Borderlands and Frontiers

At the time of European colonization, most of the land in the Americas was formally under the control of various Native American federations. Europeans purposefully defined these lands as frontiers or borderlands. This designation, often preserved and presented as historical fact, fails to appreciate the reality of these contested spaces (Haan 1973). Under the guise of protecting the interests of weaker states, the Europeans placed the Native Americans and their lands into "protectorate" relationships, in which the stronger European nations took on the responsibility of protectors (Haan 1973, 146). Concurrently, these same "protected" spaces became universally known as **frontiers** or borderlands. This designation also provided convenient camouflage for the more aggressive actions of the various European colonial systems.

These contested spaces between the Spanish, French, and English colonies provided the colonial powers with three important benefits:

- They created the illusion of Native American national sovereignty.

- They served as an outlet or safety valve for excess and displaced colonial labor and capital accumulation.

- They served as spaces where the European powers could wage imperialistic wars against each other. These wars, in which the Europeans typically encouraged or manipulated Native American tribal differences, can be viewed as proxy wars.

In this section we shall explore how frontiers and borderlands came to fulfill these functions.

The Turner Thesis—Our First Stock Story

Perhaps no single idea has so captured the American imagination, summarized and serialized the nation's official story, and misrepresented U.S. imperialistic ambitions as what is euphemistically called the **Turner thesis**. What makes historian Frederick J. Turner's argument so important to our narrative is that it became the dominant narrative of the United States. It represents our first stock story. Turner's basic thesis, developed in 1893, was that the American identity, which included democratic governance, rugged individualism, innovative thinking, and egalitarian viewpoints, was forged in the American frontier experience. According to Turner, the American frontier provided not only the encouragement but also the spaces to unleash the progressive spirit of freedom envisioned by various European revolutionary systems (i.e., specifically the French and English Revolutions). As significant as the Turner thesis was to the "official" narrative, it took more than 70 years for the nondominant counternarratives to be heard again. These voices told a different story, one that rejected the idea of a frontier and all of its presumptions. Rather than a blank slate of free land that was just waiting to be settled, developed, and occupied, the "frontier" was made up of sovereign lands controlled by other nations and protected by treaties. In this counternarrative, we learn of deceit and corruption, broken treaties and forgotten promises. This is the story of the frontier.

Understanding Contested Spaces

The rhetorical and political designation of the spaces between European colonies as frontiers or borderlands is central to an understanding of what and how these areas and their peoples were viewed. The crossing of frontiers and the loss of their people are typically viewed as some kind of cosmic inevitability or evolutionary truth. Such a truth positions the Native Americans as victims who passively accepted their fate. Their fate, viewed as irreversible, was that the exotic, yet inferior, native cultures would lose against the more powerful forces of civilization. While appropriately and passively sorrowful, we are left believing that these events were necessary and the natural consequences of nature, evolution, and/or civilization (Jennings 1975, 15–16). The idea of borderlands helps clarify how the three European colonial powers constructed race and space as conflicting rivalries. These conflicting rivalries not only shaped our nation but also started us on our troubled path toward a racial state (Adelman and Aron 1999, 815–16).

It is strange that our myths regarding these spaces often bring to mind such people as Daniel Boone, Davy Crockett, and James Bowie. As defenders of all

The images conjured up by the names Daniel Boone, Davy Crockett, and James Bowie—memorialized, serialized, and fantasized in both film and school curricula—capture the essence of Turner's thesis. These men are depicted as rugged individualists and noble warriors, honest and fiercely independent. And just as typically, they are juxtaposed against a prideful, ignoble, band of savages hell-bent on destruction.

that we hold dear, these men are the only forces of civilization holding back the frontier. Reality rarely lives up to such hyperbole. The Boones, Crocketts, and Bowies—as we have seen—were often displaced Whites forced into the "frontier." In this scenario, the Native Americans, defined as weak savages, are characterized as expendable and secondary to the interests of frontier survival. This feat is accomplished through the extension of the racial categories developed over time within the colonies and, by virtue of this extension, the necessity to continually extend the boundaries of civilization.

CRITICAL THINKING QUESTIONS

1. How might the racial matrix developed by the Spanish colonies have affected the racial matrices of the French and English colonial powers? What does this suggest about the social construction of race in the Americas?

2. Many institutions were created along with the American colonial systems. List some that were born during this early period.

3. What does the idea of borders as contested spaces in which race and conflict were orchestrated by European colonial elites suggest about the nature of these spaces and racial dynamics? What current events might reflect some of those same racial dynamics in the interaction of race and geography?

4. Neither Native Americans nor African slaves were passive during the colonial era, and they often worked together to challenge the racial matrix even as it was being constructed. What does this agency suggest about the racial matrix, identity, and the likelihood of change?

■ THE U.S. MATRIX AND INTERSECTIONALITY—WHERE DO WE GO FROM HERE?

In this chapter we have explored how the matrix of race and the intersecting realities of race, identities, institutions, and space are the products of European colonialism. Race is not only socially constructed, but in many ways it is also woven into the fabric of our nation. As we have examined the three original colonial roots associated with the founding of the United States, we have also seen how several of the earliest institutions—family, community, the military, the legal system, and the political system—were created within this matrix of race. In the chapters that follow we will continue to explore how race influences other major identities, such as gender, sexuality, ethnicity, and class, by examining our dominant social institutions.

Investigating Institutions and Their Narratives

In the following chapters, we will present the dominant narratives around particular social institutions in the United States. Just as the institutions of gender and race have prominent, legitimated, and powerful institutional narratives that determine bodies, identities, practices, and interactions, so too do the central institutions of social life have their own orienting stories, myths, and cultural blueprints. For instance, a dominant narrative of the institution of education is that schools are great equalizers—that education can equalize life opportunities and life chances, regardless of students' social and economic station. Similarly, the dominant narrative of American sports is that it provides a level playing field where the only factor that merits attention is an individual's talent.

Examining Intersecting Identities

It is important to gain a picture of the contemporary realities for individuals within the matrix as related to each institution. To that end, in each chapter we will provide the most recent data available—for instance, data on how Black women experience the family, on how Whites compare to Latinos within the housing sector, and on the disparities between gays and lesbians within the educational institutions of the United States. This data-rich section of each chapter will give you a glimpse into the ways in which institutional life is experienced differently depending on a person's place in the matrix, with a particular emphasis on the institution of race within each. For example, when we consider sports we identify a history of Black, Hispanic, and female athletes who have overcome both racial and gender stereotypes to dominate the sports from which they were once excluded.

Analyzing Historical Roots and Geographic Differences

Once we have established a picture of the contemporary situation faced by individuals and communities in the matrix of experience, and an understanding the nature of institutions, we can analyze the historical roots and trajectories of each. In each of the following chapters we will investigate how we as a society arrived at this contemporary moment and identify key historical moments that helped define, for instance, the shape of families and the shape of the intersectional experience within them. In our investigation of the institution of education we learn about the role of boarding schools in the cultural genocide of the indigenous communities in the United States. In contrast, we also learn about the role played by historically Black and Hispanic colleges and other institutions in helping to preserve culture and identity.

Appraising Difference, Resistance, and Transformation

Since we know that institutions construct identities, we will be looking closely at the social construction of difference within each institutional realm. How is difference constructed and utilized in the military, or in sports, or in the institution of health care? Furthermore, how do these institutions build the "perfect" soldier, athlete, or patient in order to most effectively do their work and, perhaps, in the process, support the logic of White supremacy and race? We shall repeatedly show how Blacks, Hispanics, and women have found ways to creatively engage and construct identities and cultural institutions that counteract these identities and provide integral spaces for agency. We will explore some of these sites of resistance, including the various slave rebellions and civil rights movements that have helped shape our American story.

It is important to remember that while multiple people may occupy the same position within the matrix, they still may experience it differentially. Experiences and how people perceive events are made up of a complex array of histories, geographies, and influences of family, school, friends, and other social institutions, affecting how they are viewed or remembered. People and groups are not monoliths; rather, they are varied and highly complex wholes that do not equal the sum of their parts. Thus, in the following chapters we will also pursue these variations as well as the commonalities within each institution. While institutions seem to prefer constancy, consistency, and predictability to continue doing their work, individuals and communities do not always follow suit. Both institutions and the people within them can, and often do, present new, inconsistent, and chaotic elements. For example, while Asian Americans

Boston Globe / Boston Globe / Getty Images

American sporting events, like professional football games, regularly feature the military and often allow service members to bring their families to "Military Appreciation" events.

are considered the "model minority" in the U.S. context, in schools and the institution of education, *how* this racialization is experienced varies. Similarly, we will consider who gets to have crimes and other forms of deviance excused and who gets accused—a difference that often reflects race, gender, sexuality, and class.

Following from this discussion, we will also look at a couple of key examples of social movements and collective expressions of agency aimed toward changing the way that particular institutions are experienced within the matrix. Although the logic of race has encouraged certain forms of institutionalization of the family, and schools, and the media, those who suffer from these structures often demand change, both individually and collectively. We will explore the hidden and emergent resistance stories that detail the many Black, Hispanic, Asian, and female veterans who have not only survived but also excelled in times of both war and peace.

Institutions exert a considerable amount of power within society. Most of our daily activities are governed by these institutions—it would be difficult to identify any regular activities or societal functions that are not involved in some way or another with institutions. This is equally true for groups that we identify with, such as racial, ethnic, class, and gender groups. Institutions not only regulate racial groups but also differentially reward them. In this way, institutions become the vehicles by which racial structures and processes are reproduced and the sites through which marginalized groups can transform the system.

Finally, following each chapter's critical walk-through of a central institution, we will briefly discuss the possible futures for that institution, given what we now know.

CRITICAL THINKING QUESTIONS

(We do not expect you to be able to answer these questions now, but you should consider them as you go through the rest of this volume.)

1. How does knowing that race is socially constructed inform us regarding our everyday lives? What might this suggest about how race operates? How might we change these realities?

2. Race and institutions occur both historically and geographically. How might these differences be perceived?

3. How have changes in institutions historically affected the significance or perception of race? What does this suggest about the permanence of race?

4. Agency has been and continues to be seen among various individuals and groups. What key changes have the actions of individuals and groups made in how race operates? What does this suggest regarding your ability to change these same structures?

KEY TERMS

Bacon's Rebellion of 1676, p. 67

Black Code, p. 64

colonialism, p. 58

frontiers, p. 68

genocide, p. 51

left-handed marriages, p. 65

miscegenation, p. 65

plaçage, p. 65

quadroon, p. 65

racial caste system, p. 61

racial violence, p. 51

settler colonies, p. 59

triple glass ceiling, p. 52

Turner thesis, p. 69

CHAPTER SUMMARY

LO 2.1   **Explore how recent events have affected how we experience race.**

The United States is a nation that has historically been defined by racial and ethnic diversity. As the U.S. population increases to an estimated 458 million by 2065, we expect immigrant births and diversity to increasingly define who we are. As much of the world, including the United States, has repeatedly been traumatized by racial and ethnic violence, our continued struggle toward equality remains a dream for some. This is especially true as we look at the triple glass ceiling and other disparities that women, especially those of color, must grapple with continuously. While Asian American women lead all other U.S. women in education, all women experience income gaps relative to White men. More than half of all Americans use online social networks and media like Facebook, and the Internet, and the racial status quo is preserved.

LO 2.2   **Describe the Americas before Columbus.**

Before Columbus sailed the seas, the continents now known as the Americas were home to millions of indigenous peoples whose cultures spanned 12,000 to 20,000 years. The first immigrants to the Americas possibly arrived on foot from Siberia and Alaska or on boats following the currents from the Pacific Islands. More than half of U.S. state names (including Michigan, Minnesota, and Missouri) reflect these rich histories, cultures, and peoples. Contrary to both myth and Hollywood, these original Americans were skilled, knowledgeable, and sophisticated, with highly advanced agricultural and animal husbandry skills, metallurgy knowledge, and a rich tradition of pottery, weaving, and textiles. Their art decorates caves and can be found in museums all over the world.

LO 2.3   **Examine the patterns of Spanish, French, and British colonialism in the Americas.**

European colonization of the Americas was most intense after the Spanish explorations of Christopher Columbus that began in 1492. Each of the major European colonial systems produced unique racial structures that ultimately blended to shape the racial fabric of the United States. Each colonial power was concerned with re-creating an image of the home country within the colonies, and each failed in its attempts. The colonizing Europeans encountered significantly different peoples with different cultural, political, and gendered systems. Their responses to these account for the variability in racial structures and the racial conflict that came to define borders and frontiers. Slave rebellions occurred in all of the colonial lands. Bacon's Rebellion of 1676 linked White and Black bond servants and almost spelled the doom of the English colonies. The racial structures that came into being in reaction to this were intended to preclude labor organizing and revolt across racial lines. In fact, Whiteness was created as a result of this rebellion. Other racial strife was associated with frontiers, or the areas that bordered the various European colonies. Three separate European colonial powers used these borderlands to extend and expand their land and power bases. The conflicting rivalries not only shaped our nation but also started us down the troubled path toward a racial state.

LO 2.4   **Evaluate the intersections of race, identities, institutions, and resistance.**

The matrix of race and the intersecting realities of race, identities, institutions, and space are by-products of European colonialism. All of the social institutions that followed have been infused with the matrix of race. Our goals in this text are to explore several key institutions through the lens of the matrix and the experiences of intersecting identities, and to understand how space and time have influenced both the matrix and identities across these institutions.

THE MATRIX PERSPECTIVE ON SOCIAL INSTITUTIONS

THE SOCIAL CONSTRUCTION AND REGULATION OF FAMILIES

Design Pics Inc / Alamy Stock Photo

Interracial families and those with same-sex parents face additional challenges as they rebut the idea of the traditional or ideal family.

LEARNING OBJECTIVES

LO 3.1 Describe the historical forces that have influenced the intersection of race and family in the United States.

LO 3.2 Examine the current stock theories that explain family inequalities across racial and ethnic lines.

LO 3.3 Apply the matrix lens to an understanding of family inequality.

LO 3.4 Identify alternatives to the current matrix of inequality among families.

Interracial couple Don and Joey always knew they wanted to have children. They contacted a private Black adoption agency, and were thrilled when they learned that a 3-year-old boy in county custody needed a home. They prepared for his arrival by decorating a nursery and purchasing toddler gear. But their dreams were crushed when the county agency refused to place the boy in their home because they could not provide him with a mother.

Eventually the private adoption agency identified a birth mother who was thrilled to find two loving parents for her infant. Don and Joey welcomed 4-month-old Brent into their home, but it took 2 years of navigating a state legal system and bureaucracy ill equipped to handle adoptions by gay or lesbian couples for them to adopt him legally. When Brent was 3, the couple adopted a second son, 14-month-old Jorian, who had been born to an addict and faced a number of health issues as a result.

Brent and Jorian are Black. The family has had to maneuver through a society imbued with racial and sexual inequality, prejudice, and discrimination. Don and Joey realized the importance of providing a strong family support system, so they committed themselves to starting a nonprofit organization to address this need, not only for themselves and their boys but also for their community as a whole. "It's a combination support group, babysitting co-op, and community organization. It's made up of some 70 families 'who value diversity.' . . . The group has become an extended family for all the adults and children in it" (Strah 2003, 128).

In this chapter we explore the stock story of the ideal family, its historical development, and the ways in which the concept has been used as an instrument of power and social control.

■ HISTORICAL REGULATION OF THE FAMILY

When you hear the word *family*, what image comes to mind? In American society's idealized family, the father is the head of household and breadwinner, and the mother is comfortably enshrined in the domestic sphere, where she nurtures the couple's biological children and socializes them for middle-class adulthood. This stock story depicts the family as a private haven, separate from the public sphere. We tend to think of this family form as having a long history and being somehow natural. However, the specific family form of a married couple and their children did not rise to prominence until the mid-1800s (Coontz 2010a). Families are, in fact, in flux and constantly changing. A brief look at history demonstrates not only the wide diversity of successful family forms over time but also the pace and direction of change.

Early Families

In 1500, an estimated 10 to 20 million indigenous people lived on the land we now call the United States, and even greater numbers ranged across the rest of the Americas (Vizenor 1995; Feagin 2000). Historians have documented great variation both in family forms and in the division of labor and power within the family. The Iroquois Confederacy's 1390 constitution gave all members of the confederacy's participating nations, including women, the right to vote (Amott and Matthaei 1996, 33). Many tribes were fairly egalitarian. In some tribes women were recognized as warriors, and in others they served as peacemakers.

Families themselves played various roles within each community. Among many North American indigenous tribes, kin groups—groups of people related by blood or marriage—were a central means of community organization. Most economic production and distribution, political structures, disputes, conflicts, and battles were handled by extended kin groups.

When European settlers, overwhelmingly men, began colonizing the Americas, they encountered a wide range of Native American nations with diverse family formations. Beginning in the 1600s, European women who immigrated to the Americas generally entered their new homeland with their families, while some single women came as indentured servants. The newcomers gradually became more stable and successful as they stole Native American lands and began food and crafts production and home building. The theft of these lands and other resources was justified by an ideology that defined Native Americans as not fully human (Drinnon, cited in Vizenor 1995). As one researcher has observed: "The European families that came to North America were products of a developing market economy and international mercantile system. The way they organized production, exchange, land ownership, and social control put Europeans on a collision course with Indian patterns of existence" (Coontz 2010a, 34).

For the European colonists, marriage was an economic relationship, and wives and children were essential family workers. On average, a White woman in colonial America gave birth to five to eight children, and it was not uncommon for women to have eleven or twelve children (Hill 2005; Hymowitz and Weissman 1978; MacLean 2014). A woman's risk of dying in childbirth could be as high as one in eight, and most families experienced the death of one to two children (MacLean 2014). The definition of family at this time was not based on blood ties but included all those living in the same household under a male household leader.

Those who could not support multiple dependents often sent their children to live with other families as apprentices. Mothers performed essential labor, meeting families' basic needs. Husbands and wives often worked side by side, and both engaged in child rearing and training their children in gender-appropriate skills (Amott and Matthaei 1996, 98–99). Some women worked outside the home in various trades,

The colonists in the Americas interpreted the cultures they encountered through their own ethnocentric lens, viewing their own ways of life as natural and commanded by God. Many were offended to see the difficult work many Native American women did, which conflicted sharply with their own ideals about appropriate work for women and men. Upper-class Europeans also thought of hunting and fishing as leisure activities and stereotyped the Native American men who performed this sustenance work as lazy and effeminate.

and many lived very public lives. Nevertheless, a gendered division of labor prevailed (Hymowitz and Weissman 1978).

White women had no legal rights to property. English common law prevailed, and upon marriage wives lost all legal status and all rights to their belongings, property, and income. They could not sign contracts or file lawsuits. If widowed, they could not be legal guardians to their own minor children. The notion that women literally disappeared as individuals is perhaps best demonstrated by the law's failure to recognize marital rape (Zaher 2002).

Resistance and Assimilation

After the American Revolution, settlers pushed west, and Native Americans were forced to give up lands in the Midwest in exchange for promises that they could retain their remaining lands. By the late 1800s, however, Native Americans had largely been forced to reside on reservations located in barren lands the Europeans saw as the least valuable.

Surviving Native Americans were expected to assimilate—to adopt European lifestyles and modes of organization in their communities and families, and to abandon their own cultural traditions and practices. They resisted at every stage.

Missionaries also played a key role in destroying indigenous culture and family formations. In the 1870s, the reservations were divided among 13 Christian denominations, and a federal boarding school system was created to fully assimilate the next generation of Native Americans. Children were taken from their families and cultures, forced to abandon their native languages and religious beliefs, and given new names (Vizenor 1995). This policy of forced assimilation destroyed many families and future generations' family relationships. Many Native Americans resisted attempts to force them to assimilate into European cultural roles, while others saw their boarding school experiences as a path to becoming successful among the Whites.

In 1887, Congress passed the **Dawes Act**, requiring Native American nations to divide their communal reservations into individual plots of 160 acres, with each assigned to a family head. The remaining land was given to White homesteaders and various corporations, such as railroads and ranching companies. In response to strong Native American resistance, one compromise was made: The allotments would be made to each person, rather than only to male family heads, in acknowledgment of the fact that native cultures recognized the rights of native women to own property (Amott and Matthaei 1996).

Colonial practices and Eurocentric notions of family had negative impacts on every minority racial and ethnic group. The culture and practice of slavery tore apart many African families, beginning with the separation of individuals from their families in Africa and the common experiences of loss on slave ships. Pregnant women and infants born on the transatlantic voyage were often thrown overboard so as not to be a burden to the captain. Further, every African was insured as property, so that a dead African could be more profitable than an unhealthy living one. For slave owners, each slave was a commodity, and husbands and wives were often separated when sold; children were taken away from parents to be sold for the slave owner's profit. Slave owners often raped women slaves to produce children to be sold. The institution of slavery made it nearly impossible for Africans to maintain family relationships, yet many tried as best they could. Slaves resisted their torment in many ways. Slavery was so inhuman and horrific that some mothers would go so far as to kill their infants before they could be taken away, to protect the children from life as slaves. Patterns of intermixing produced lighter-skinned Africans, which created new economic and status dynamics that continue into the present. The impact of the slave trade, slavery itself, and then hundreds of years of continued oppression have had far-reaching, even unimaginable effects on the formation of Black families in the United States.

Domesticity: The Emergence of the Ideology of Separate Spheres

In the early 1800s, the numbers of jobs outside the home were growing, and men began moving out of the domestic sphere, which became defined as women's realm, and into the public sphere to sell their labor. White women's lives became sharply defined by an **ideology of domesticity** and the creation of a public/private dichotomy. Ironically, however, "at the same time as the new ideal of the domestic middle-class family became enshrined in the dominant culture, diversity in family life actually increased" (Coontz 2010a, 39). In working-class families, children and mothers had no choice but to work to help support their families. In the emerging middle class, woman's role was seen as that of housewife and mother, responsible for the home and children, while work and politics became defined as men's sphere. Privileged White women led this "cult of domesticity," arguing in books and lectures that women's natural place was in the home and economically dependent on their husbands. Thus, the ideology of domesticity rationalized White middle- and upper-class privilege as a result of these classes' ability to achieve and maintain the new ideal family formation. This model was actually the result of specific changes in the economy and the organization of work, and it was short-lived. It rose to prominence between 1860 and 1920, after which women began to enter the paid workforce in greater numbers. Family sociologist Kingsley Davis (1984, 404) concludes, "Clearly, the division of labor that arose historically from the separation of the workplace and the home is not the 'normal' or 'traditional' pattern." Why, then, has this particular family formation remained the ideal?

The Legacy of Immigration

While we often refer to the United States as a nation of immigrants, neither African American nor indigenous communities are immigrant populations. Native Americans were here long before Europeans arrived, and, excluding later populations of Blacks who chose to emigrate from Africa and the Caribbean, the African American community is the historical product of slavery. Both populations, and many Mexicans, were forced to largely abandon their own cultures and family traditions. However, they were not the only racial and ethnic groups to face government regulation and intervention in their formation of families.

The Irish constituted the first significant influx of non–Western European immigrants in the 1840s, followed by Eastern and Southern Europeans and Jews. These new arrivals prompted a crisis in how Whiteness was defined. Through the end of the 19th century, being legally defined as White was critical to gaining the rights of citizenship and property ownership, so the racial classification of new immigrant groups was key to their future success in the United States. The Irish were referred to as the "Blacks of Europe" and encountered blatant discrimination by employers (Tehranian 2009, 22). Italians were also linked to Blacks by means of the common nickname "guinea," which had its origins in the European term for the western coast of Africa.

The Expanding Category of Whiteness

Different paths to assimilation were carved out for these new arrivals. For Jewish immigrants, marriage was a step in the direction of Americanization but also a form of resistance. In the United States, marriages could be freely chosen and based on love, a practice that was a rejection of traditional Jewish authority regarding the arrangement of marriages. In adopting American values of freedom, love, and pleasure, Jews modeled modern American families. At the same time, they resisted Americanization through marriage by overwhelmingly marrying other Jews (Prell 1999).

Eventually, European American ethnic immigrant groups were seen as assimilated enough to be defined as White, and the boundaries of Whiteness expanded (we look at some of the economic reasons for this shift in Chapter 4). Marriage and family formation were signs of Americanization (Prell 1999). At the same time the children of immigrants were being encouraged to assimilate through intermarriage, interracial intermarriage was illegal. The line between Blacks and the expanding group of Whites was being more firmly drawn.

Immigration Policy and Family Formation

In contrast with European immigrants, Asian American immigrants were excluded from the expanding category of Whiteness. The first wave of Asian immigrants came from China in the mid-1800s, primarily men who came to work in the California gold rush, in agriculture, or in railroad construction. Labor recruiters sought married men willing to leave their families in China, because they could be paid less (Yang 2011) and would eventually go back to China. Initially many Chinese women immigrated, working as prostitutes to support themselves, until the U.S. government enacted the 1875 Page Law, a landmark attempt to limit the immigration of "undesirables" (Luibhéid 2002, 277). The predominant view, however, was that Chinese prostitutes spread disease and debauchery among both Chinese and White men, threatening the integrity of the White family.

The scarcity of Chinese women did not mean that male Chinese laborers had no families in the United States, however. Many created family formations by establishing clans, associations based on kinship and lineage and open to people with the same last name. Following the anti-immigration Chinese Exclusion Act of 1882, Chinese continued to arrive but at a slower rate. Many petitioned to bring "paper sons," young men from China posing as their U.S.-born sons, a relationship that could not be denied after all birth records were destroyed in the San Francisco earthquake and fire of 1906. It was not until 1943 that Chinese people could again immigrate to the United States (although only 105 Chinese were allowed to enter per year) and finally apply to become U.S. citizens.

After the supply of Chinese labor was cut off in the late 1800s, the first large groups of Japanese laborers were recruited to work in agriculture, lumber, and mining on the West Coast and in Hawaii. As the numbers of Japanese increased on the mainland, so did racism against them. Japanese were barred from joining workers' unions, and various stereotypes arose as they were scapegoated by White labor. Eventually, in 1907–8, the so-called Gentlemen's Agreement was reached, whereby Japan agreed to stop allowing Japanese men to emigrate and the United States agreed to admit the family members of those men who had already immigrated. Approximately 100,000 Japanese joined their husbands, fathers, and sons in the United States, as did about 20,000 "picture brides" of arranged marriages, who often had nothing but photos or letters from the unknown husbands they were about to meet. Julie Otsuka's novel *The Buddha in the Attic* (2011, 18) brings

Leonard McCombe / The LIFE Images Collection / Getty Images

The gender balance in Chinese immigration shifted after World War II, when the War Brides Act permitted Chinese wives and children of U.S. soldiers into the United States, followed by other laws that allowed American soldiers' fiancées to enter. Eventually the McCarran-Walter Act (1952) permitted Chinese wives of Chinese men in the United States to join them here, bringing the "bachelors' society" to an end and allowing Chinese people to play a greater role in shaping their own families in the United States.

together the voices of these women, drawing from collected historical documents and interviews:

> On the boat we could not have known that when we first saw our husbands we would have no idea who they were. That the crowd of men in knit caps and shabby black coats waiting for us down below on the dock would bear no resemblance to the handsome young men in the photographs. That the photographs we had been sent were twenty years old. That the letters we had been written had been written to us by people other than our husbands, professional people with beautiful handwriting whose job it was to tell lies and win hearts. That when we first heard our names being called out across the water one of us would cover her eyes and turn away—I want to go home—but the rest of us would lower our heads and smooth down the skirts of our kimonos and walk down the gangplank and step out into the still warm day. This is America, we would say to ourselves, there is no need to worry. And we would be wrong.

Japanese families became moderately successful in agriculture and family farming and worked hard to keep their cultural traditions alive, turning to schools, religious organizations, and Japanese-language newspapers. Between 1913 and 1920, however, despite resistance, a series of "alien land laws" were passed, banning noncitizens from purchasing land. When Japan bombed Pearl Harbor in 1941, all Japanese Americans were immediately suspect. While not one charge of espionage was ever reported, more than 110,000 first- and second-generation Japanese Americans were forced to abandon their homes, property, possessions, and businesses and were relocated to 10 internment camps in various western states. There, surrounded by barbed wire and armed guards, they faced harsh weather, low-wage labor, and lack of privacy. Family life changed dramatically. Some scholars note that internment led to some increased liberty for women, who were freed from much housework and cooking, and many young women were allowed to leave the camps for college. Nevertheless, internment was devastating for the community, and by the time they were freed in 1945, many Japanese Americans had nothing left to return to.

Both Chinese and Japanese immigrants faced a paradox when it came to the subject of assimilation. Mary Tsukamoto, in conveying her life story to an anthropologist, succinctly identifies this dilemma:

> You see, we were accused of not being assimilated into our American life, but we were always kept in limbo because every time we turned around there was some group trying to agitate to send us back to Japan or send us away from California, so we never knew for sure whether we should sink our roots deeply. And we never knew for sure if we should spend our profits building a new home and living in nice homes like we wanted. So we endured living in shacks that weren't painted because any day we might be driven out. (quoted in Buss 1985, 91–92)

RESISTANCE / STORIES

Art as Resistance

Literature and the arts have frequently been embraced as tools for challenging and resisting oppression. These two works are examples.

This 2001 painting connects many of the most virulently racist stereotypes of racial and ethnic minorities in the United States. The biography on the artist's website states: "Roger Shimomura's paintings, prints, and theatre pieces address sociopolitical issues of ethnicity. He was born in Seattle, Washington, and spent two early years of his childhood in Minidoka (Idaho), one of 10 concentration camps for Japanese Americans during WWII" (http://www.rshim.com).

On her website, artist Margaret Kasahara says: "As an Asian American of Japanese descent, that identity crosses two disparate cultures. I don't view it as a negative or a positive reality; it simply is. . . . I often appropriate cultural symbols and the traditional iconography of Japan and America, and place them in a personal and contemporary context. . . . One person's 'exotic' was my 'everyday,' and I was left with the feeling of not quite being allowed to belong" (http://margaret kasahara.com).

Mr. Wong's Theatre Company, by Roger Shimomura

Americanese: 180 Degrees, by Margaret Kasahara

Changing Families, Changing Attitudes

The **nuclear family** is defined as a mother, a father, and children (biological or adopted), living together. The number of nuclear families in the United States has declined consistently since 1970, and today such families account for only 20% of all families. The idea of the "ideal" and "traditional" nuclear family usually assumes a working father and a stay-at-home mother. Today, less than 25% of two-parent families with children under 15 years old have a stay-at-home mother. In addition to women's increased labor market participation, the number of adult men and women who are not married declined by almost 20% between 1950 and 2016. Families today are increasingly diverse: We see growing numbers of single parents (divorced, widowed, and never married), blended families (families with children from the adult partners' previous relationships), multigenerational families (families with three or more generations residing together), and interracial and same-sex marriages. In addition cohabitation and postponed parenthood are increasingly common, and people are having fewer children (Coles 2009; Martin 2008; Moses 2012; Risman 2010; Proctor, Semega, and Kollar 2016). Abortion rates are also declining, in part because of increased reliance on a variety of birth control methods (Jones and Jerman 2017). Families today are more likely than their counterparts in the past to be caring for elderly relatives at home, and close to 50% of marriages end in divorce. Americans are also less likely to be married: The number of adult individuals living alone has almost doubled since 1960, and in 2016 adults living alone accounted for more than one in four households.

Our definitions of family life and our attitudes toward it are changing along with the lived reality, especially among younger generations. Young adults (ages 18 to 29) are the group most likely to hold positive views about new forms of family, to see one parent as sufficient for healthy child rearing, and to believe both partners in a marriage should help take care of the home (Pew Research Center 2010). Some of these beliefs may be slow to translate into reality, however. Research finds that wives still do considerably more housework than husbands, and while stay-at-home dads are increasing in number, the burden of child care still falls disproportionately on mothers (Pew Research Center, n.d.).

The range of family forms that exists today is fluid and shifting, and statistics often provide an incomplete picture. For example, the U.S. Census Bureau is faced with the challenge of taking a wealth of data about household arrangements and fitting those data into a limited number of categories that define specific "family" formations. These categories, however, cannot tell us much about the reality of people's living arrangements or the relationships among family members. For example, when the census documented an increase in single motherhood in the 1990s, the reality was that "most of the growth . . . was due to an increase in births to women who, while not married, were living with the children's father" (Coontz 2010b, 25). The lives of such mothers and children are very different from the lives of families where mothers are raising children on their own.

CRITICAL THINKING

1. Have you witnessed attitudes about families changing during your lifetime? Provide examples. How do you think the prevailing attitudes about families in the city where you grew up may have differed from those in other cities? Explain.

2. Can you trace your family history back to its roots in what is now the of the United States? How do you think those earlier generations were shaped by the practices, policies, and formation of the United States?

3. How do you think your family life was shaped by race, class, and other social identities?

4. What kind of family structure did you grow up in? Did your family or your parents' families face any stigma?

■ FAMILY INEQUALITY THEORIES

Existing sociological theories approach the family as an institution implicated in the system of race relations. Next we look at the common stock stories as well as counternarratives and critiques based on concealed and resistance stories.

Stock Stories and Assimilation

Recall that stock stories are the predominant, seemingly commonsense narratives circulating in society that naturalize inequality. The functionalist perspective sees society as an ordered system that the family helps to reproduce through the processes of assimilation and socialization. Many functionalist scholars have pointed to **assimilation** to argue that new racial and ethnic groups entering the United States follow specific paths of integration, gradually accepting and adapting to the cultural patterns of the dominant group. In 1964, sociologist Milton Gordon identified seven stages of assimilation, beginning with adoption of the dominant language and cultural patterns and advancing to increased interaction with and relationships among minority and majority group members, reduced levels of prejudice and discrimination, intermarriage, and eventually full integration and acceptance. This model, called assimilation theory, is based largely on the experiences of European American ethnic groups, who were provided with a path to assimilation while other groups faced economic and legal barriers.

Assimilation theory also contains a number of problematic assumptions: First, it assumes that minority groups should and can follow the same path as European immigrants; second, it assumes that non-Whites want to abandon their own cultures and become fully "Americanized"; and third, it assumes that the dominant White culture is ideal and superior to all other cultures (Myers 2005, 10).

Conflict theorists highlight these unspoken assumptions and bring issues of power into the picture, emphasizing that the dominant group seeks to protect its economic and political interests by controlling minority groups' labor and resources. Research from a conflict perspective emphasizes that minority groups have not all been equally welcome to assimilate and asks us to consider who benefits from the smooth functioning of an unequal society. In reviewing the research on families and race relations, scholars often draw from both functionalist and conflict perspectives, asking questions about the context of initial contact and exposing the ways in which minority groups have been both included in and excluded from the dominant group (Myers 2005).

The symbolic interactionist perspective shifts our focus to a micro level of analysis, examining how individuals and families give meaning to cultural phenomena and family relationships and interactions, and how families struggle to pass on their own cultural values and traditions in the face of demands for socialization and assimilation. Families may do this by eating traditional foods, listening to music, carrying out religious and spiritual practices, or dressing in ways that reflect the traditions of their culture. At times the conflict between maintaining cultural practices and assumptions about assimilation becomes politicized—for example, in ongoing debates in the United States over English-only rules, and in many European countries regarding the banning of burkas.

Our current stock stories about the Ideal Traditional Family are rooted in the concept of **separate spheres**, or domesticity ideology. They are informed by a functionalist perspective that assumes this is the best family model for a well-functioning society—an essential unit that fulfills a particular function in a particular way. From this perspective, any families not fitting the ideal are defined as dysfunctional.

This logic also underlies research and public discourse about Black and Latino families that blames them for their own presumed failure to assimilate. Here, we see how family and nation are intertwined—the ideal nuclear family is emblematic of the national family. To belong in the United States, we must accept the traditional nuclear family model as the ideal. To culturally assimilate and become Americans requires giving up other cultural models and accepting the dominant cultural pattern.

From a conflict perspective, this family model operates explicitly to benefit some more than others. It not only reproduces inequality among racial and class groups but also reproduces gender and sexual inequality, valuing hierarchical gender roles, patriarchy, and heterosexuality. For example, consider the phrase "the African American family." What images come to mind? Do you picture a single mother raising numerous children alone and on welfare? While African American families in reality are quite diverse, this image of the dysfunctional Black family has been especially predominant since the 1950s, when the "culture of poverty" thesis was advanced, and many politicians still rely on it to explain the high rates of African American poverty.

This stock story argues that Black families are "pathological" because they do not replicate the traditional nuclear family model, and it blames poverty and other social problems on Black families themselves (Hattery and Smith 2007; Hill 2005). Single mothers are depicted as overbearing, and fathers as weak or absent. The stock story claims that these "dysfunctional" family forms are a part of U.S. Black culture, passed down over generations and firmly entrenched. Black families are often compared to other racial and ethnic groups and are faulted for not "pulling themselves up by their bootstraps" as other immigrant groups have.

Poverty is one of the most significant problems facing African American families (see Table 3.1). Single-female-headed families have significantly higher poverty rates than other family types, and the percentage of single-female-headed families is much higher in the African American community than it is among Whites and other racial groups (U.S. Census Bureau 2015, 2016). Nevertheless, the poverty rate for children in Native American and Latino families is only a few points lower. While marriage is frequently offered as the solution for Black poverty, Black males face such high unemployment, underemployment, and imprisonment rates that marriage to Black men is not likely to raise women and their children out of poverty.

Table 3.1 ■ Percentages of Children in Poverty by Race in the United States, 2015

Race	Percentage in Poverty
American Indian	34
Asian and Pacific Islander	13
Black or African American	36
Hispanic or Latino	31
Non-Hispanic White	12
Two or more races	21

Source: Copyright © 2017 The Annie E. Casey Foundation. Kids Count Data Center, "Children in Poverty by Race and Ethnicity," 2015, http://datacenter.kidscount.org/data/tables/44-children-in-poverty-by-race-and-ethnicity#detailed/1/any/false/573/10,11,9,12,1,185,13/323.

Concealed Stories: The Legacy of Slavery

At least two sociological counternarratives, the legacy of slavery thesis and the revisionist thesis, have emerged to critique the assumption that African Americans are inherently inferior and incapable of sustaining proper families. Each focuses on different historical facts—or different concealed stories—to support its arguments. Concealed stories here consist of missing or ignored history, experiences, and data, as well as alternative theoretical perspectives. Contemporary scholars have leveled critiques at both theories, pointing out that they generally accept the assumption that the traditional nuclear family is indeed ideal and try only to explain why Black families have had a difficult time replicating that ideal. One scholar argues that even social scientists attempting to refute racist assumptions about Black families have themselves taken for granted many of the Eurocentric and race-based assumptions embedded in U.S. culture about what a family is (Dodson 2007). These theories have implications that extend far beyond the level of abstract theorizing; they inform public policy and have real impacts on people's lives.

The Legacy of Slavery Thesis

The **legacy of slavery thesis** attempts to shift the focus from Black people themselves as pathological to the argument that pathological family structures are the result of a long history of structural inequality. The thesis begins with the fact that slavery entailed the capture of Africans who were torn from their families and communities and thrown into a foreign culture where they had little control over their lives. E. Franklin Frazier, an African American sociologist, published two groundbreaking books in the 1930s about Black families. He was one of the strongest advocates of this approach. He embraced the "race relations cycle" proposed by W. Lloyd Warner and Ezra Parks, which posited that all racial and ethnic minority groups would eventually assimilate into U.S. society and values.

Frazier argued that the legacy of slavery had previously made assimilation impossible for Blacks, but that it would eventually become a reality (Hattery and Smith 2007; Hill 2005). According to this perspective, Black single-female-headed families have their roots in the history of slavery, which forced Black women to become strong and independent, without husbands to rely on. Black men were denied the privileges of patriarchy and the role of head of household assumed to be men's natural position in the family. This violation of the gender roles at the heart of the traditional nuclear family ideal became the basis for defining Black families as a problem.

With the end of slavery, opportunities for African Americans to form stable families did not improve. In the South, Black men were largely forced to become sharecroppers and faced lynching and imprisonment. Many children were taken from their families and forced into labor or placed in orphanages if their parents were not married or working. During the 20th century's **Great Migration,** as millions of Blacks moved to cities in the North from the rural South, many women found jobs as live-in domestics, which prevented them from forming or maintaining their own family relations. They remained vulnerable to sexual assaults by White men and cultivated skills of resistance and resilience. Black men did not find the opportunities they sought in the North either, taking low-wage jobs instead and facing disproportionately rising rates of imprisonment for insignificant crimes. Black women often had no economic incentive to marry, because marriage could not provide a path out of poverty.

During the Great Migration, many Black women found work as live-in domestic servants for white families, which made forming their own families difficult.

In sum, the legislation, ongoing discrimination, and high unemployment all continued to undermine Black families (Hill 2005). With the rise of the "cult of domesticity," they became increasingly defined as pathological for failing to fit the ideal.

The legacy of slavery theory was repackaged in 1965 in a controversial report on the state of the Black family by sociologist and Assistant Secretary of Labor (and later U.S. senator) Daniel Patrick Moynihan. Single-women-headed families were increasingly in the public eye as a result of the high concentration of African Americans in impoverished urban centers and the increased access of Black women to welfare programs from which they had previously been excluded. Moynihan argued that single-women-headed families were keeping the Black community trapped in poverty and attributed a host of other problems to "dysfunctional" Black families, including crime, delinquency, and dependence on the government for financial support (Hattery and Smith 2007; Hill 2005).

The Revisionist Thesis

Scholars applying the **revisionist thesis,** including John Blassingame, Eugene Genovese, Robert Hill, and Andrew Billingsley, have responded directly to the legacy of slavery theorists by arguing for the strength and resilience of Black families (Hattery and Smith 2007; Hill 2005). These theorists have provided evidence to counter the dire stereotypes of a Black community racked by poverty and with few intact nuclear families. For example, Billingsley has pointed out that in metropolitan neighborhoods, two out of three Black families include both a husband and a wife, half of the families are middle-class, and nine out of ten are self-sufficient and have no need for welfare (cited in Dodson 2007, 57).

Revisionist scholars have drawn upon concealed stories to argue that slave families were "functional adaptations" to the conditions of slavery. Families and extended kin were viable sources of strength and support, and essential to survival. Revisionist research also has demonstrated the extent to which Black fathers during slavery tried to protect their wives and children and keep their families together at any cost. Renowned historian John Hope Franklin (1947) documented the many efforts of runaway slaves to return to their families and argued that the institution of the family was central to slaves, who were denied access to other social institutions for support (see also Hill 2005). Revisionist research has drawn upon basic precepts of both functionalism and conflict theory, redefining Black families as functional and as a refuge, given the context of oppression and White supremacy. Other scholars, like Carol Stack, have sought to explore the value in multiple family forms by highlighting the ways that low-income Black single mothers often join with extended kin and other households, creating functional family formations to better meet their needs. Joining to share resources, these families demonstrate that isolated nuclear families are not always the best option (Marks 2000, 610).

Revisionist scholars restore agency to African Americans, seeing their family structures not merely as the unfortunate results of slavery and inequality but as viable alternatives formed to improve their quality of life and enable them to maintain kin connections that serve them. As revisionist theories demonstrate, it is possible to construct various stories about the past depending on which facts we highlight and which we ignore.

Applying the Pathology Narrative to Latino/a Families

The stock story of pathology was also applied to Latino/as, currently the largest minority population in the United States. Latino/as were pathologized and criticized for failing to assimilate, and Latino/a culture was blamed for poverty and other social problems. In challenging these assumptions, some scholars critiqued the functionalists' application of assimilationist models to non-European-American groups. According to Calderon (2005), the basic assumptions of assimilation are problematic because they imply that Chicanos have faced a history similar to that experienced by European immigrants and can therefore follow the same path to success. Chicanos, however, had much of their lands stolen and were forced into wage labor that was dangerous and low paying. Their failure to achieve the levels of success reached by European Americans has led some to blame the Chicano community itself (Calderon 2005, 107). Calderon (2005, 110) argues that American schools teach children that the United States purchased the Southwest from Mexico, and that they do not learn "about the many that resisted lynching, murders, theft of land, and resources."

Before 1970, the majority of Latino/as in the United States were from Cuba or Puerto Rico. Since 1990, large numbers of Mexicans have arrived, and smaller numbers of immigrants from El Salvador, the Dominican Republic, Guatemala, Colombia, Honduras, and elsewhere. This diversity makes it problematic to talk about Latino/a families in generalized terms. Different family formations are products not only of groups' cultures of origin but also of the specific time periods in which people immigrated, the communities in which they settled, the immigration laws and restrictions in place at the time, and the work opportunities available.

The Latino/a population in the United States is quite diverse. The largest populations are Mexican American and Puerto Rican, groups that were both colonized and deprived of lands they had occupied for centuries. With the 1848 Treaty of Guadalupe Hidalgo, the United States annexed the Southwest region and guaranteed resident Mexicans property rights and the right to maintain their own culture through language, law, and other means. Nevertheless, the terms of the treaty were ignored. The glossing over of this history allows us to accept the myth that any problems the Mexican American community has stem from culture. It is worth noting that one important custom that Mexican Americans (and a number of other Latino/a groups) have held on to in the United States is that of the **quinceañera**, a celebration of a girl's transformation from a child to an adult at age 15. This tradition, which is practiced across social classes, is also about celebrating the family (Gharib 2016).

The experiences of Latino/a families overall can vary greatly depending on where they reside. The support networks, kin networks, social services, and cultural opportunities available to these families in, say, Los Angeles are worlds apart from those available in a small midwestern town with a slim minority of recent Latino/a immigrants. Family formations are affected by all of the factors noted above (Zambrana 2011). Nevertheless, the typical Latino/a family has been stereotyped as highly patriarchal, devoutly Catholic, committed to rigid gender roles for children, and valuing family over education. Some of these characteristics are more common among low-income Mexican Americans, the primary population that has been studied over the past 40 years, than among other Latino/a groups. However, findings from the research are often generalized to all Latino/a families, portraying them as static and unchanging and reinforcing the notion that they are all the same.

Many policy makers, service providers, and educators have accepted these stereotypes and the assimilationist ideal (Zambrana 2011). The resulting expectations are problematic because they lead to demands that Latino/as abandon the cultures, traditions, and language that for many are sources of pride and identity. However, Latino/as' most significant obstacles to advancement are not their cultures but economic inequality, the criminalization of Latino men in many regions, racial profiling to identify undocumented immigrants, ongoing discrimination and racism, and barriers to opportunities in education, health care, and other institutions. For example, the Southern Poverty Law Center (2102) recently won a lawsuit challenging "tuition policies that treat Florida students who are U.S. citizens and residents of Florida as nonresidents solely because their parents are undocumented residents." Assimilation theorists ignore the reality of ongoing racism and inequality embedded in U.S. culture and institutions and blame people of color for not following the same path as Eastern and Southern European immigrants.

CRITICAL THINKING

1. Historically, why has assimilation been emphasized so strongly in the application of stock sociological theories to immigrant families? What do you see as the costs and benefits of assimilation?

2. What might the policy results have looked like if the theories applied to various racial and ethnic groups had instead highlighted the value of maintaining diversity among families?

3. What role has racial ideology played in shaping the structures of families historically?

4. How are views about individual families depicted in the stock and concealed stories?

■ FAMILY INEQUALITY THROUGH THE MATRIX LENS

Our application of the matrix perspective to stock and concealed stories reveals that ideologies about the family, as well as policies affecting real families' daily lives, "work to naturalize U.S. hierarchies" of race, gender, class, and sexuality, while at the same time "constructing U.S. national identity" (Collins 1998, 65). The family becomes a metaphor for both race and nation, with borders that require policing to prevent the invasion of "outsiders." In addition to allowing us to examine the constructions of race as it intersects with other social identities, the matrix framework asks that we consider culture, ideology, institutions, and structures as they interact with and shape each other. Finally, we also must examine resistance and agency, and all within specific social, historical, economic, and geographical contexts.

Through the matrix lens, a different narrative of family formations emerges. Families are social constructs, and there is no single, "natural" family form.

- A diversity of family forms has always existed.

- Families are not static. They change over time, across generations, and across geographical spaces and local contexts, and they are constantly being rearticulated in new ways.

- What is considered the "ideal" family form varies historically and cross-culturally.

- Stock stories promoting hegemonic family ideals reproduce racial and other forms of inequality, privileging some families over others, and some family members over others.

- Research presents a narrative about families that is often influenced by the culture and values of the researcher and the broader dominant culture, reproducing relationships of power, privilege, and oppression.

- Family formations are shaped by many structural factors, including material and economic, historical, and public policy and legal factors (such as immigration law and welfare policy) and other social institutions (such as criminal justice, education, and health).

- The traditional ideal family of our stock stories will not solve structural problems such as unemployment and poverty (and our focus on it as the answer prevents us from discussing real solutions).

- Gender is central to an understanding of different family formations across history and cultures, and gendered power relations influence our definitions of acceptable and dysfunctional families.

- Racism and other systems of inequality shape family formations as well as the experiences of individual families.

- The family, as an institution, is central to the construction of definitions of both nation and race.

- Families socialize the next generation into hierarchical systems of nation, race, gender, sexuality, and age, among others. They also can, and often do, resist such hierarchies.

The matrix approach directs us to look at recent research that challenges the simplistic stock stories about families head-on and highlights new concealed and resistance stories that add greatly to our understanding of families.

Women's Concealed Stories

As more women have become sociologists and their research has been accepted as legitimate, we have learned more about the importance of gender and other identities in examining Black families. Sociologist Shirley Hill's work on Black families dismisses the functionalist assimilation approach we examined earlier in this chapter. Hill (2005, 10–11) argues that "race and class oppression has left most [African American families] at odds with dominant societal ideals about the appropriate roles of men and women and the proper formation of families." At the same time, the results of this oppression have been blamed on African Americans themselves, rather than on the true underlying causes.

The legacy of slavery and revisionist scholars also debated the extent to which African culture was decimated or maintained by slaves. However, family formations and culture are dynamic and are constantly re-created within specific contexts. Accumulating research provides insight into the diverse contexts that shaped the transmission of African culture over time, for instance. Josephine Beoku-Betts studied the African American Gullah community (descended from slaves) on the Georgia and South Carolina Sea Islands. The Gullah were isolated on these islands, and they did not face the conditions of African Americans on the mainland. Thus, they were able to maintain cohesive communities that preserved important features of African culture. For example, they spoke their own language and passed on to successive generations traditional crafts, African birthing and naming traditions, folktales, religious beliefs, cooking techniques, and more (Beoku-Betts 2000; Joyner 2000). Beoku-Betts (2000, 415) argues that because most of these tasks have been seen as part of women's natural role in the family, they were not studied in the past. Her research uncovers a previously concealed story about what are only now being recognized as practices significant to the "maintenance of tradition."

Many women scholars have continued to make women's experiences visible, revealing further concealed stories and examples of resistance. Donna Franklin (2010) examines the Victorian era, when married Black women were largely working outside the home, often in professional careers. Many White women, in contrast, were relegated to the domestic sphere and believed they could not be successful and advance in professional careers if they were married. As Franklin observes, "Black women seemed to have an easier time juggling the role of activist with the role of mother and wife. . . . Historian Linda Gordon found that 85 percent of black women activists were married, compared to only 34 percent of white women activists" (64).

Black women who were both activists and working professionals were often married to professional men. Work was not stigmatized for Black women as it was for White women; rather, it was seen as contributing to the common cause of advancing the Black community. Further, because slavery had "rendered black men and women equally powerless," it had "leveled the gender 'playing field'" (Franklin 2010, 65). Among married adults today, Black women are more likely than White women to have higher salaries than their husbands, and Black husbands contribute slightly more to household chores than do White husbands (Franklin 2010).

Beginning in the second half of the 20th century, the Black community began facing what has been called a **marriage squeeze**—that is, a change in marriage patterns leading to fewer marriages and fewer suitable partners for Black women (Franklin 2010, 71). Important structural factors creating this situation include the high rates of Black male incarceration and unemployment, both discussed in other chapters. For educated, professional Black women, the problem of low numbers of suitable Black partners is compounded by the increasing rates of marriage between professional Black men and White women. This trend also sends the message that Black women cannot live up to White beauty standards and definitions of femininity as White (Rockquemore and Henderson 2010). As a result, a large pool of single African American women are left with a small number of marriageable Black men.

Recent research on Black families aims to shift the focus away from single motherhood as the problem to be solved and toward the economic hardship Black families face. Socioeconomic and class differences play the most important role in determining outcomes for children, whether they have one, two, or more parents or guardians.

Coontz and Folbre (2010, 186) highlight a number of reasons it does not make sense to define single motherhood as the problem. First, poverty is often an impetus for women to choose not to marry when marriage will not improve their economic security:

> Two-parent families are not immune from the economic stresses that put children at risk. More than one-third of all impoverished young children in the United States today live with two parents [and] single parenthood does not inevitably lead to poverty. In countries with a more adequate social safety net than the United States, single-parent families are much less likely to live in poverty. Even within the United States, single mothers with high levels of education fare relatively well.

Invisible Fathers

There is a common myth that the absence of Black fathers is responsible for the poverty of Black families, and we see all around us stereotypes of the irresponsible Black father. We know that Black fathers are less likely to be married due to high rates of incarceration and unemployment (Smith 2017). However, while Black fathers are less likely to marry the mothers of their children than are other fathers, this fact alone does not support the common assumption that they are not good fathers. The stereotype of the absent Black father that looms so large in our culture has kept us from recognizing and studying those fathers who are actually present in their children's lives (Coles 2009; Edin, Tach, and Mincy 2009).

The little research that exists reveals another concealed story: Single, noncustodial Black fathers are more engaged in their children's lives than are their White counterparts. Multiple studies have found that among nonresidential fathers, African Americans have higher rates of parental involvement than do Whites or Hispanics (McLanahan and Carlson 2002; Edin et al. 2009). Other research has found that unmarried African American fathers are more likely than their White or Hispanic counterparts to contribute to costs during pregnancy and to offer in-kind support and care for their children (Coles 2009).

The myth of the absent Black father is so pervasive, it can prevent us from seeing the reality of Black families.

These findings are especially meaningful given the unique challenges these fathers face. They are more likely than White fathers to reside in poor communities with fewer resources available to support parents, they experience lower rates of education and employment, and they are more likely to be employed in part-time and low-paying jobs that offer fewer benefits. Coles (2009) conducted one of the first major studies of Black single fathers with custody of their children and found that in addition to these challenges, many experienced obstacles dealing with legal and social services, including suspicion and assumptions that they could not be good fathers. Coles concludes that these men can be successful fathers even when they are not married to their children's mothers. She implores us to see that "these are caring fathers: as good, loving, and motivated as any other father. Their existence and their experiences deserve public articulation . . . their stories provide a counterweight to the predominant image of black fathers" (14).

Oppression and Privilege: Support for White Families

The state's part in shaping family and reproduction practices is clearly a racialized and gendered process. It is almost always women's bodies that are targeted for control by courts and legislatures, despite the fact that men play a role in reproduction as well (Flavin 2009). Race, class, and age all influence how the state treats women's reproductive capacity, with effects on family formation.

By the 1950s, every U.S. state had passed laws preventing pregnant women from working, while at the same time withholding unemployment benefits from them (Solinger 2007). Prior to increased women's activism and the sexual liberation movement in the late 1960s, few options were available to single women who became pregnant. There was a strong culture of punishment at the time, which saw women's sexual behavior as unacceptable and unfeminine, and as breaking the hallowed bounds of the ideal nuclear family. A woman facing an unwanted pregnancy could petition the medical community for a "therapeutic" abortion based on psychiatric grounds; however, approval was hard to obtain, and if it was granted, the woman was usually also sterilized at the same time. Other alternatives varied by race. To avoid the shame of out-of-wedlock pregnancy and preserve their daughters' marriageability, White families that could afford it would hide their single pregnant daughters in maternity homes and put their babies up for adoption. Single Black women who became pregnant were barred from Whites-only maternity homes and were more often embraced and accepted by their families and extended kin. Nevertheless, they were stigmatized and seen as examples of broken Black families and communities. They faced prejudices as well as policies that were not designed to help them (Solinger 2013).

While the public in general viewed both White and Black unmarried mothers negatively, the White women were nonetheless seen as producing a valuable commodity for which there was high demand among White married couples unable to have children. In the 1960s, welfare programs began linking the receipt of benefits to compulsory sterilization for many women, especially women of color. African American and Puerto Rican community activists fought these abuses, which were not brought to the public's attention until the mid-1970s (Flavin 2009). In 1968, more than one-third of women in Puerto Rico between the ages of 15 and 45 had been surgically sterilized, often without their knowledge, as a means of controlling the population (Lopez 1987). Figure 3.1 shows the changes in birthrates among unmarried women over time. It is noteworthy that since 1990, the number of births to single teens has been declining steadily.

In the 1950s and 1960s, numerous U.S. states passed "man in the house" laws, which gave welfare agencies the ability to cut off payments to single women who were suspected of engaging in sexual relations. The assumption was that if a woman was involved with a man, he should be "man of the house" and support her and her children, even if they were not his. In essence this law allowed the state to control women's sexual activity in a punitive fashion. This and other welfare and social programs were unevenly applied based on race, and racism often shaped the forms these policies took (Kohler-Hausmann 2007; Lefkovitz 2011). Such uneven enforcement fostered the image of the promiscuous "welfare queen" living on the public dole while indulging her own pleasures (Kohler-Hausmann 2007). This stereotype became increasingly useful in the backlash against welfare among many political conservatives.

From its beginnings, the welfare system has treated families differently based on race. The Social Security Act of 1935 established the Aid to Dependent Children (ADC) program, which became known as "welfare." ADC was not written to benefit

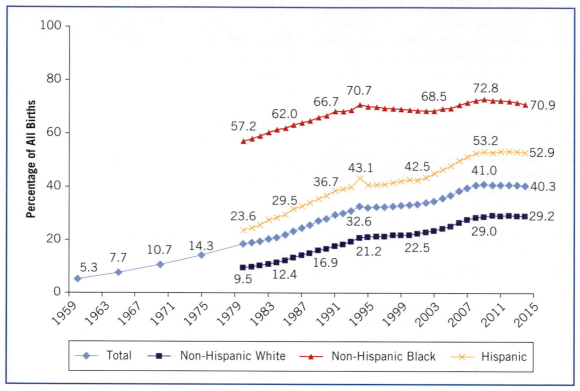

Source: Child Trends Databank. (2015). Births to unmarried women. Available at: http://www.childtrends.org/?indicators=births-to-unmarried-women.

all families equitably, however. Entire categories of workers (domestic workers, agricultural workers), those with high representations of people of color, were excluded from the benefits of the program. As a result, Whites were the primary beneficiaries of welfare. White women were often encouraged to stay at home and focus on raising their children, while women of color were strongly urged to work in the fields or as domestics (Solinger 2010).

Beginning with President George W. Bush and continuing through the Obama administration, so-called **marriage promotion programs**—programs that aim to encourage marriage by teaching relationship and communication skills—were offered as a solution to poverty for single mothers (at the time of this writing, it is not known whether the Trump administration will maintain such programs). More than $800 million in federal money and additional funds at the state level have been poured into marriage promotion advocacy, on the continuing assumption that single parenting is a primary cause of poverty and marriage is the solution (Heath, Randles, and Avishai 2016). Marriage promotion programs are not based on any research evidence, however, and they reproduce the myth of the ideal family. They ignore structural causes of inequality and social, historical, and economic context, instead reinforcing the belief that poverty is simply the result of individuals' poor choices. However, research finds that "the most important predictors of marriage and divorce are not whether an individual has mastered good communication skills but whether he or she has a stable job and a college education" (Avishai, Heath, and Randles 2012, 37).

The Socialization of Children

A large study of mothers and their children found that when mothers had experienced racism (including verbal insults and discrimination), children struggled in school and faced more social and emotional problems (MSN News 2012). Families are a key site of future generations' socialization into the hierarchies of oppression and privilege. As groundbreaking sociologist Patricia Hill Collins (1998, 64) observes, "Individuals typically learn their assigned place in hierarchies of race, gender, ethnicity, sexuality, nation and social class in their families of origin." In communities of color, parents are forced to prepare their children to enter a world that is often hostile toward them and thus dangerous, or at best simply biased against them. James Baldwin writes eloquently about this issue in his 1963 book *The Fire Next Time*:

> [The child] must be "good" not only in order to please his parents and not only to avoid being punished by them; behind their authority stands another, nameless and impersonal, infinitely harder to please, and bottomlessly cruel. And this filters into the child's consciousness through his parents' tone of voice as he is being exhorted, punished, or loved; in the sudden, uncontrollable note of fear heard in his mother's or his father's voice when he has strayed beyond some particular boundary. (40–41)

Chicana mothers engage in "psychological protection" of their children but also teach their daughters "how to resist their subordination" (Hurtado 2003, 78–79). Hurtado (2003, 77, 81) reports that the Chicana women she interviewed described the importance their mothers placed on the safety net of education, while still assuming that their daughters would eventually get married. The young women developed the "ability to 'see' freedom within restriction and the commitment to 'struggle' within 'constraint' . . . [learning that] in a racist, sexist, classist, heterosexist society personal virtue is not enough—the structural scaffolding cannot be climbed by will and talent alone."

White parents need not confront the challenging topic of race with their children, and often do not even consider it. Three-fourths of White parents report that they almost never talk about race with their children (Bronson and Merryman 2009). Many embrace a color-blind perspective, assuming that if they do not talk about race, their children will grow up to see everyone as equal and the same. However, children as young as 6 months old recognize differences in skin color, and by the age of 7 they have already formed conclusions about race, with White children identifying Black children as more likely to be "mean." Further, living in a diverse community or attending a diverse school does not reduce these effects. The only thing that does is White parents' talking to their children about race: "This period of our children's lives, when we imagine it's most important to not talk about race, is the very developmental period when children's minds are forming their first conclusions about race" (Bronson and Merryman 2009). White parents (especially those with White children) have the privilege to choose whether they will talk to their children about race. There are currently many books and other resources available to help parents in addressing race with their children at any age.

CRITICAL THINKING

1. Have any of the historical factors that we have examined in this section surprised you? Which points do you think are most important for people to know?

2. How have social institutions (e.g., the criminal justice system, economics, government policies) created obstacles for some families while providing a hand up for others?

3. Do you believe that the mythical "ideal" family formation should remain the ideal for all families? Explain.

4. What did you learn about race as a child? Did your family talk about race often? If so, what kinds of issues and messages do you remember?

■ TRANSFORMING THE IDEAL FAMILY NARRATIVE

The myth of the ideal family obscures the reality of the diverse family formations in which most of us actually live. Further, our family formations change over the course of our lives. As we live longer, we are more likely to need family assistance. Some 30% of Americans engage in providing assistance to elderly parents, grandparents, disabled children, or other family members who require aid to meet all of their basic needs (Barber and Vega 2011, 20). Among Hispanic families, 36% of households care for elderly family members (Barber and Vega 2011). While caregiving for elderly members means some families are getting larger, others are getting smaller as women have fewer children.

When the Ideal Family Is Not Ideal

Rather than asking why certain families do not conform to the ideal nuclear family model, many researchers are reframing the question, asking whether the nuclear family is necessarily the best model for all families at all times (Coontz 2010a; Hill 2005; Risman 2010). Examining family violence challenges the myth of the ideal family. Research has found that one of two women will be battered at some point in their lives (Hattery and Smith 2016), and 30% of women globally have experienced intimate partner violence (Devries et al. 2013). Close to one-third of women who are murdered are killed by their partners (National Coalition Against Domestic Violence 2015). Until the 1980s, marital rape was not a crime in many states (Hattery and Smith 2016). Domestic violence is a leading cause of the health problems and complications faced by pregnant women (Pan American Health Organization, n.d.).

More than five children die every day as a result of child abuse, most often at the hands of family members (Hattery and Smith 2016). Children with disabilities are at greater risk, and all children suffer higher risks when living in foster care. African American, Hispanic, Asian American, and Native American children are far more likely than White children to be removed from their homes and placed in foster care, putting them at greater risk (Hattery and Smith 2016).

Girls and women are more likely than their male counterparts to experience child sexual abuse and elder abuse, and African American girls and elderly women face much higher rates of abuse than do their White counterparts (Hattery and Smith 2016). The ideology of the family as a private sphere has kept violence within families hidden from public view. Intimate partner violence often remains unreported and undetected. Hattery and Smith's (2007) research has shown that forcing poor women to find mates to escape poverty locks many into a cycle of abusive relationships. Abused women often feel they cannot leave their abusers, and those who do leave still face challenges. Many end up homeless or in other abusive relationships.

Transmigration

The ancestors of many Chicano/as lived in regions that were once part of Mexico but today fall within the United States. National borders in these areas have been fluid over time, and for many Chicano/as, they remain so today. Many Latino/as are **transmigrants**, people who "live their lives across borders, participating simultaneously in social relations that embed them in more than one nation-state" (Glick-Schiller 2003, 105–6). Soehl and Waldinger (2010, 1496) found that the majority of Latino/a transmigrants maintain activities of connectivity with their home countries, making phone calls, visiting, and sending remittances back home. Those with children or assets in their home countries engage in these activities more frequently (1505).

Across the United States, some 5 million children live with one or more undocumented immigrant parents, and many live in families where some family members are U.S. citizens while others are not (American Psychological Association, n.d.). Children born in the United States are legally U.S. citizens. Undocumented parents are sometimes deported, and many leave their children in the United States to be cared for by other relatives or older siblings, in the hope that they will have more opportunities and a better life than they would have in their parents' home countries. One ironic consequence of this is that children with U.S. citizenship often cross to Mexico to visit family members and so maintain ties to Mexican culture, while children who are not citizens cannot risk crossing and thus grow up entirely in the United States, knowing nothing but U.S. culture. As these children become adults seeking jobs or college educations, they increasingly face the risk of deportation to a homeland of which they have no memory (Thorpe 2011).

Undocumented immigrant parents must make difficult decisions based on their desire to do what is best for their families given their circumstances. Researchers are only now beginning to explore the impacts on the children in such families of multiple family separations, changes in caregivers and places of residency, and life under the threat that a parent or other family member could be deported at any time. Some scholars are also looking at the strategies that lead to family resilience in the face of such vulnerability and risk. As the legal landscape changes under the Trump presidential administration, the future for all immigrants and their families is even more uncertain than in the past.

Many Latino residents of the area around the U.S.-Mexico border are transmigrants, living their lives in both countries. Many cross into the U.S. to work, often in agriculture.

inga spence / Alamy Stock Photo

New Reproductive Technologies

New technologies have changed the reproductive possibilities available to families, and innovations in this area will continue into the future. These technologies further destabilize our stock story that the ideal traditional family is rooted in nature.

The United States is one of only a few countries in the world that allow **gestational surrogacy**, in which a woman carries an implanted embryo to term for another couple or mother but has no genetic tie to the child herself. In essence, a gestational surrogate rents out her womb according to the terms of a contract. The demand for gestational surrogates has been increasing for many reasons, including the availability of abortion and birth control, which has limited the number of White babies available for adoption. At the same time, women are marrying later and delaying attempts to get pregnant.

France Winddance Twine (2011) examines gestational surrogacy as a form of labor deeply imbued with hierarchies of race, class, and gender. She finds that it is predominantly White middle- and upper-class women and couples who are able to afford to hire surrogates, while surrogates are most often poor White women and women of color in the United States and poor women in developing nations. As Twine points out, while "contemporary gestational surrogates 'voluntarily' enter into these commercial contracts and willingly sell their 'reproductive' labor, their agency occurs within a context of a stratified system of reproduction" (15). Medical and reproductive tourism is a growing industry in India, and surrogacy is the fastest-growing sector, with more than 1,000 clinics in 2013. According to the World Bank, the surrogacy industry in India will be valued at $2.5 billion by 2020. While it can cost $100,000 for gestational surrogacy in the United States, the price in India is less than half that. At the same time, India has world-class medical facilities and English-speaking practitioners. Most important, India has a huge number of very poor women willing to serve as surrogates. An Indian surrogate is paid approximately $6,000 and receives food and medical care while pregnant (James 2013). This contrasts sharply with the situation of pregnant Indian women who are not surrogates, who have some of the world's highest rates of maternal morbidity and mortality. Research finds that most surrogates are driven by financial need, using surrogacy as "a basic survival strategy for obtaining access to food, shelter, clean water, and healthcare" (Hamm 2013).

Mint / Hindustan Times / Getty Images

Gestational surrogacy is deeply entwined with race and class. Hiring a surrogate in India can cost less than half what it does in the United States.

Interracial Marriage

Laws against interracial marriage were not declared unconstitutional in the United States until 1967. Since then, rates of interracial marriage have been climbing, most quickly in recent years. In 1970, only 1% of all U.S. marriages were interracial. By 2013 the numbers had grown to 6.3% of all marriages and 12% of new marriages (Wang 2015; Pew Research Center 2015).

American Indians, Asian Americans, and Hispanics are most likely to marry outside their racial groups. Figure 3.2 shows the intersections of interracial marriage with race and gender for Whites, Blacks, Asians, and American Indians. Hispanics are not included in this chart, but their rates, like those for Whites, show very little difference between men and women (Pew Research Center 2012).

These patterns reflect the racial hierarchy we live in today. Blacks continue to be characterized as least likely to assimilate, while Latinos and Asians are seen as lying somewhere on the continuum between Blacks and Whites. These rates also reveal something about the way in which gender stereotypes pervade our narratives about Black and Asian families. While Black women have been defined in largely negative terms as unfeminine, stern, and independent, Asian women have been depicted as exotic, erotic, and submissive. The stock story tells us that we reside in a color-blind nation today, but intermarriage rates reveal that this is not the case; more than eight out of ten people marrying today still choose to marry someone of the same race,

Figure 3.2 ■ Race and Gender Affects Patterns of Interracial Marriage

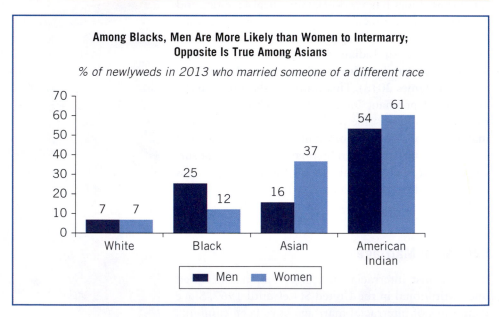

Among Blacks, Men Are More Likely than Women to Intermarry; Opposite Is True Among Asians

% of newlyweds in 2013 who married someone of a different race

Source: Wendy Wang, "Interracial Marriage: Who Is 'Marrying Out'?," Pew Research Center Fact Tank, June 12, 2015, http://www.pewresearch.org/fact-tank/2015/06/12/interracial-marriage-who-is-marrying-out.

and bias against interracial marriage persists (Skinner and Hudac 2017). Nevertheless, the numbers continue to rise.

LGBT Families

Just as our stock stories depict the family as a couple with children, they also tend to assume that the couple is heterosexual. Perhaps one of the most visible ways in which the family is changing is in the growth in numbers of openly gay and lesbian families. All the stock stories about the family that we have examined are predicated on the assumption of heterosexuality. We actively construct heterosexuality as normative, just as we construct patriarchy and Whiteness as normative (Ingraham 2013). The notion of the ideal traditional nuclear family is one of the most important sites of this construction. Same-sex desire and sexual behavior that fall outside our definition of heterosexuality have always existed. These concealed stories have often been ignored or written out of history, as heterosexuality became defined as the only "natural" and legitimate form of relationship on which to base a family. As a result, heterosexuality has been reinforced as the invisible, privileged norm.

Since the U.S. Supreme Court's decision in *Obergefell v. Hodges* (2015), the fundamental right of same-sex couples to marry has been protected in the United States, and valid same-sex marriages sealed in other jurisdictions are recognized. A Gallup poll in June 2016 found that about 123,000 same-sex couples had married since the Court's decision, bringing the national total to about 491,000. About one in ten LGBT adults is now married to a same-sex partner, and gay men are marrying at higher rates than lesbians (Jones 2016). Marriage comes with many rights, including the right to make medical decisions for one's spouse, to inherit from one's spouse, to qualify for spousal Social Security and veteran's and other benefits, and to jointly adopt or foster children. However, many states have passed laws denying married same-sex couples some of these benefits, and allowing religious and state officials to refuse to officiate at weddings for same-sex couples. Battles over many of these issues are currently taking place in the courts (Movement Advancement Project 2017). For all racial groups, the proportion of LGBT people is roughly the same as their representation in the U.S. population as a whole (Pew Research Center 2013b). We see variation by race when we look at same-sex couples, however. Whites represent a disproportionately higher percentage of gay male marriages(Moore 2011). When it comes to same-sex marriage, White and class privilege may make the transition to marriage and parenthood a little bit easier. While they still face homophobia, discrimination, and structural barriers, White gays and lesbians have had the privilege of not having their loyalty to their racial community challenged (Moore 2011). Interestingly, marriages between LGBT persons are more than twice as likely as heterosexual marriages to be interracial (Gates 2012).

RESISTANCE / STORY

Nancy Mezey, 2015

I grew up in an upper-middle-class White suburb of New York City. My family had progressive and openly gay friends, providing me with White, economically successful role models who crossed sexual boundaries. So when I came out as a lesbian in the mid-1990s, my family and friends were neither surprised nor disappointed. Years later, I met my partner, also a White middle-class professional, who shared my desire to have children. Our White middle-class status helped us find other lesbians who were birthing and adopting children, a privilege to which Black working-class lesbians in the area did not have access.

Indeed, networking through a lesbian mothers group, we found a fertility specialist who helped us have two children. Until that point, my partner and I had felt largely unscathed by homophobia and heterosexism. Our first real experience with individual discrimination occurred when we tried to find child care for our oldest child. I called day-care centers in our midwestern town and explained that my son had two mothers (careful not to use the word *lesbian*), only to have the providers explain that "other parents would be uncomfortable" and they could not accept our child.

Later, we experienced institutional discrimination in our [pre-2015] effort to both become legal parents to our children. That process required going through a second-parent adoption in which we paid thousands of dollars for a home study, even though I was our children's biological mother and my partner and I had raised the children together in our home from birth. This was followed by my giving up my legal rights to our children in court, only to adopt them back with my partner.

When we moved to New Jersey, we found a much more welcoming environment. Our privileged statuses allowed us to move into a largely White middle-class town with a strong public school system. In two obvious instances, our children lost friends after their parents realized our children had two mothers. But for the most part, my partner and I buffered our children by having proactive meetings with teachers and screening parents at social events. I often wondered if the few homophobic parents we met knew that we were protecting our children from them as much as they thought they were protecting their children from us. In my personal life, transformation comes through the interactions my family and I have with others on a daily basis that create a new normal of wider acceptance.

Because of the importance of social context in family formation, the experiences of gay and lesbian families themselves differ across race and class lines. On the one hand, "Black cultures, ideologies, and the historical experiences of Black women structure lesbian identities" (Moore 2011, 3). At the same time, Black lesbians exert influence over their own family formations and family lives. For example, Moore (2011) found that "respectability" was a strong theme for the Black lesbian women she studied. Consistently defined by the dominant culture as lazy, poor, hypersexual, and immoral, Black women have employed numerous strategies to present themselves as "respectable" while at the same time asserting their own sexual autonomy.

Recent critical intersectional research is beginning to encompass the full range of family formations. As we broaden our understanding of what counts as a family, we must reassess historical narratives that have excluded certain family formations. Researchers are not exempt from the prejudices and assumptions of the broader culture. As family researcher Stephen Marks (2000, 611) reflects: "Most family scholars continue to be White, heterosexual, married persons such as myself. The research published . . . reflects the interests of those who do the studies." However, as more and more research is conducted by scholars previously excluded—men and women of color, White women, LGBT people, and working-class people, for example—the kinds of subjects that are being studied, the questions that are being asked, and the concealed stories and voices of resistance that are being brought in are changing the field. As Marks goes on, "These scholars have challenged their exclusion . . . and some of us from the dominant groups who earlier saw families in a White, male, middle-class image have been listening and learning" (611).

Thus, we see broadening recognition and research on a wide array of family formations and experiences. At the same time, we need to cultivate more curious citizens who will ask the unasked questions and challenge narratives that distort the realities we see all around us.

CRITICAL THINKING

1. How have technological changes opened up new family formations? What changes do you foresee in the future owing to technology, especially in regard to social identities including race, gender, and dis/ability?

2. How have very recently enacted government policies and laws affected families, including those formations discussed in this last section of this chapter?

3. How does the history of slavery, genocide, immigration, and inequitable access to resources help explain contemporary interracial marriage rates? How do you think future race relations will be affected by rising rates of intermarriage?

4. What other significant changes do you see taking place among families today or in the future?

KEY TERMS

assimilation, p. 89

Dawes Act, p. 82

gestational surrogacy, p. 106

Great Migration, p. 93

ideology of domesticity, p. 83

legacy of slavery thesis, p. 92

marriage promotion programs, p. 102

marriage squeeze, p. 98

nuclear family, p. 88

quinceañera, p. 95

revisionist thesis, p. 93

separate spheres, p. 90

transmigrants, p. 105

CHAPTER SUMMARY

LO 3.1 **Describe the historical forces that have influenced the intersection of race and family in the United States.**

Family formations were inextricably shaped by culture and race in the American colonial era. Native Americans had diverse family structures that were greatly affected by colonization, and African family structures were disrupted when Africans were ripped from their families, transported overseas, and subjected to a system of slavery that consistently broke up families, as each individual was viewed as a commodity. Various immigrating European ethnic groups and Asians were restricted in their family formation by shifting immigration laws that often dictated who could enter the United States. Today family formations continue to shift and remain diverse.

LO 3.2 **Examine the current stock theories that explain family inequalities across racial and ethnic lines.**

A variety of social theories have emerged to explain inequality among families. Stock stories include the functionalist, conflict, and symbolic interactionist perspectives. The primary stock story has revolved around theories of assimilation. In order to explain the less prevalent assimilation of Africans and African Americans, other theories have revealed concealed stories examining the impact of slavery. Some of these same theories and debates have been applies to Chicanos/Latinos.

LO 3.3 **Apply the matrix lens to an understanding of family inequality.**

More recent theorizing has taken an approach that explicitly addresses issues raised by the matrix perspective. Assimilation theories have been reinterpreted as maintaining inequality. Theories that have posited low rates of marriage among African Americans as the leading cause of Black poverty have been directly challenged by examinations of women's lives in particular, as well as by research into the realities facing Black men and their roles as fathers. Government funds that could contribute to decreasing family poverty have instead been directed to programs encouraging marriage, which primarily benefit White families. Some scholars have challenged the notion that the mythical ideal family is ideal at all. Inequality inevitably shapes relationships within families.

LO 3.4   **Identify alternatives to the current matrix of inequality among families.**

Contemporary trends are changing the face of families. Rates of interracial marriage are increasing, and the legalization of same-sex marriage has expanded the rights of people to marry whom they choose. The phenomenon of transmigration and the explosive rise of new reproductive technologies are complicating the lives of families and will continue to do so. Our very definitions of family are shifting, as they always have.

WORK AND WEALTH INEQUALITY

Bob Chamberlain / Los Angeles Times / Getty Images

With high expenses for healthcare and housing, many families have little money saved. A job loss, even with unemployment benefits, can be economically devastating. Eligible Californians, like those seen here, can apply for cash aid on a short term basis.

LEARNING OBJECTIVES

LO 4.1   Describe the current patterns of income and wealth inequality in the United States.

LO 4.2   Compare various stock stories about economic inequality.

LO 4.3   Apply the matrix perspective to the historical foundations of economic inequality.

LO 4.4   Analyze potential solutions to the problem of economic inequality.

Katherine Hackett did everything right. A hardworking, educated professional with 17 years in the health care industry, she paid her taxes, volunteered in her community, and, as a single mother, raised two sons who served in the military. Then, without warning, she was suddenly laid off from work with just a month's severance pay. Her life was turned upside down. Unemployment benefits allowed her to pay her mortgage and the premium for her COBRA health benefits (that is, the benefits available to her through her former employer's group insurance under provisions of the Consolidated Omnibus Budget Reconciliation Act), but that left her only $230 a month, or just over $8 a day, for food, utilities, and everything else.

Like Hackett, about half the U.S. population lives from paycheck to paycheck in a state of "persistent economic insecurity." Nearly half of all families have less than

$5,887 in savings to fall back on in an emergency such as a job loss (Corporation for Enterprise Development 2014).

Scholars who have analyzed social identities such as class, race, gender, sexual orientation, ability/disability, and age have identified economic inequality and the organization of work as key locations where inequality originates and is reproduced in our society. In this chapter we will examine economic inequality across racial groups and how other social identities, like gender and class, intersect with race, which in turn leads to different life outcomes for people within the same racial categories. Income and wealth inequality and the various factors that contribute to it, including economic shifts and social policy, are also key to understanding how and why economic inequality exists. We will also examine the stories we tell about work, wealth, and inequality that obstruct or support social change to reduce these gaps.

■ RECENT TRENDS IN WORK AND WEALTH

The U.S. economy is usually described as being ruled by **capitalism**—that is, it is an economy in which the means of production are held and controlled by private owners, not the government, and in which prices are set by the forces of supply and demand with minimal government interference. In practice, U.S. capitalism is modified by government regulation, and some resources are under public ownership (although this is on the decline). Capitalism produces class inequality, with large numbers of working poor like Katherine Hackett. Despite being one of the wealthiest nations in the world, the United States is also one of the most unequal (Sherman 2015; Tasch 2015). According to a recent report from the Organisation for Economic Co-operation and Development (OECD), this inequality is unhealthy for the nation. Looking over time, the researchers found that increasing inequality produces lower economic growth. Starting around the 1920s and 1930s, economic inequality began declining in the United States and in many European nations, but in the 1970s and 1980s, it sharply increased again (OECD 2015).

Increasing Inequality

Social scientists use two factors to measure economic inequality: income and wealth. **Income** consists of the flow of all incoming funds: earnings from work, profit from items sold, and returns on investments. While estimates vary depending on the sources, it is generally reported that the top 1% of the U.S. population makes between 18% and 33% of the nation's income, and the top 0.1% earns 8% to 12% (Bricker, Henriques, Krimmel, and Sabelhaus 2015; Piketty and Saez 2014). Between 1980 and 2012, the share of the national income made by the top 1% more than tripled (Monaghan 2014). By 2013, income inequality had grown to its highest levels since 1928 (DeSilver 2013).

Wealth (or capital), in contrast to income, consists of the market value of all assets owned, such as a home, a car, artwork, jewelry, a business, and savings and retirement accounts, minus any debts owed, such as credit card debt, mortgages, and college loans (Saez and Zucman 2016). You probably already know that the top 1% of the U.S. population owns a very large proportion of the nation's wealth—that was the key focus of the Occupy Wall Street movement. Estimates of the proportion of total U.S. wealth owned by the top 1% over the past few years have ranged from 30% to 42%, depending on the data sources used. Estimates of

The Occupy movement began in 2011 to protest rising inequality, particularly targeting Wall Street financial firms. The group's slogan is "We are the 99%" to highlight the vast disparities in wealth and income in the U.S.

the proportion of wealth owned by the top 0.1% range from 15% to 22% (Bricker et al. 2015; Ingraham 2015; OECD 2015; Piketty and Saez 2014). Those Americans in the bottom 40% of the population actually have no wealth, and are likely in debt (Ingraham 2015; OECD 2015). Since the late 1970s, the wealth gap has been growing, with the top 0.01% seeing the greatest gains in their wealth. In other words, wealth is increasingly being consolidated into fewer and fewer hands (Piketty and Saez 2014).

These data paint a picture of class inequality. We employ a broad definition of **class** here, referring to "enduring and systematic differences in access to and control over resources for provisioning and survival" (Acker 2006, 444). When we bring in race, we see another dimension of income and wealth inequality.

The racial wealth gap is much wider than the racial income gap, reflecting the fact that wealth is transmitted over generations (see Figures 4.1 and 4.2; note that very few data on wealth and income are available for Native Americans). Wealth can be transmitted in many ways. It can be passed down through inheritance of money, property, stocks, and bonds, or in the form of access to education and paid tuition. Passing a family business on to the next generation is another form of wealth transmittal (Conley 2009; Lareau 2011). In addition, the racial wealth gap grows much larger over the average person's life span. As the saying goes, "It takes money to make money!" Those with more to begin with have the resources (education, financial support) to accumulate more wealth during their lifetimes. Wealth has a far greater overall impact than income on an individual's life, because wealth also provides the

Figure 4.1 ■ Median Household from 1967 to 2015 Differed By Race

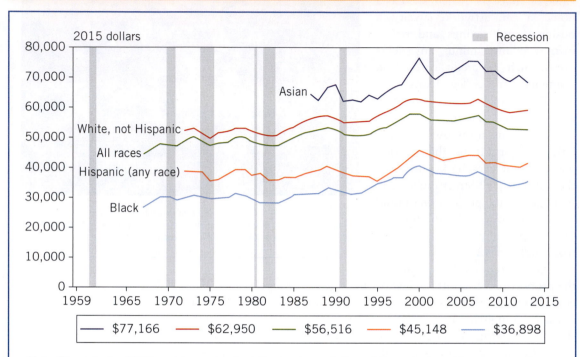

Note: The data for 2013 and beyond reflect the implementation of the redesigned income questions. The data points are placed at the midpoints of the respective years. Median household income data are not available prior to 1967. For more information on recessions, see Appendix A. For more information on confidentiality protection, sampling error, nonsampling error, and definitons, see www2.census.gov/programs-surveys-cps/techdocs/cpsmar16.pdf.

Source: Bernadette D. Proctor, Jessica L. Semega, and Melissa A. Kollar, *Income and Poverty in the United States: 2015,* U.S. Census Bureau, Current Population Reports, P60-256(RV) (Washington, DC: Government Printing Office, 2016), fig. 1, https://www.census.gov/content/dam/Census/library/publications/2016/demo/p60-256.pdf.

opportunities that make a higher income possible. Wealth can pay for a better education, a home that may appreciate in value, and better and more accessible health care; it gives families opportunities to invest and allows them to accumulate savings that can help them make it through rough times, job changes, and retirement. Wealth allows parents to give their children a significant head start in life.

Figure 4.2 ■ Racial Wealth Gaps Have Grown Over the Years

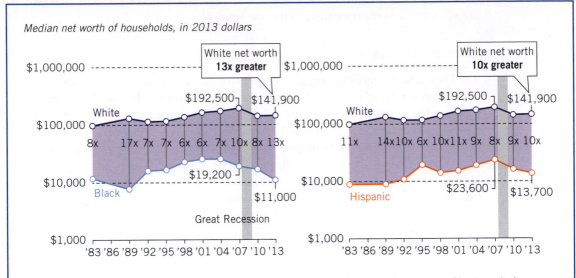

Median net worth of households, in 2013 dollars

Notes: Blacks and Whites include only non-Hispanics. Hispanics are of any race. Chart scale is logarithmic; each gridline is ten times greater than the gridline below it. Great Recession began Dec.'07 and ended June '09.

Source: Rakesh Kochhar and Richard Fry, "Wealth Inequality Has Widened along Racial, Ethnic Lines since End of Great Recession," Fact Tank, Pew Research Center, December 12, 2014, http://www.pewresearch.org/fact-tank/2014/12/12/racial-wealth-gaps-great-recession.

The poverty levels in the United States are another demonstration of the nation's inequitable distribution of income and wealth. Approximately 17% of all children residing in the United States live in poverty (and children are more likely to live in poverty than adults of any age). Proportionally, children of color are over-represented in this group, which is approximately one-third White, one-third Latino, one-fourth Black, and 9% Native American and Asian American (Madrick 2016). The federal poverty line is $24,230 for a family of four per year. The official poverty line for one individual comes out to $16.50 per day. Yet 1.5 million households with children survive (barely) on just $2.00 per person per day, significantly below the government's definition of "deep poverty." The number of households in deep poverty has more than doubled since the mid-1990s (Edin and Shaefer 2015).

Economic Restructuring and Changing Occupations

Today's global capitalist economy is different from the agrarian, rural economy of the past, and as it continues to change, it is altering the ways we work and live. As the economy has transformed, so has the workplace.

Economic Change

The United States faces strong global competition for jobs and ever-increasing levels of international trade. For evidence, just take a look at the labels in your clothes that indicate the countries where they were made. It's unlikely that you'll find many items that were made in the United States. Both globalization and advances in communications and other technologies have contributed to the shift in the United States from a manufacturing economy that produced physical goods like computers, furniture, and clothing to a service economy that provides services such as banking, health care, retail sales, and entertainment. Cheap labor overseas, especially in developing countries, has motivated many American manufacturing companies to move their production activities abroad, closing tens of thousands of U.S. factories and eliminating millions of jobs (Alderson 2015; Dunn 2012; Forbes 2004). The result is that most U.S. job growth in recent years has been in the service sector, where work is lower paying, often part-time and temporary, and much less likely to provide benefits (see Figure 4.3). Sociologists refer to this broad historical shift as economic restructuring, and it has been accompanied by growing wealth and income inequality (Andersen 2001; Dunn 2012).

Occupational Change

While the service sector also includes higher-paying, skilled jobs in fields such as information technology, growth has been far greater in more labor-intensive service-sector jobs (Collins and Mayer 2010, 7). The three largest occupational categories today—health care and social assistance, retail trade, and accommodation and food services—all pay significantly less than manufacturing jobs. These sectors employ large numbers of White women and people of color (U.S. Bureau of Labor Statistics 2015, 2016).

With the rise in joblessness starting with the recession of 2008–9, many more people are now forced to work part-time or temporary jobs, sometimes multiple part-time jobs at once. Today the two largest employers in the United States are Walmart (which hires large numbers of part-time and temporary workers) and Kelly Services, a temp service (Grabell 2013; Making Change at Walmart 2014; Schow 2013). Neither part-time nor temporary work provides health care benefits, paid sick leave or vacation time, pensions, or workers' compensation. Today's workers face limited wage growth in any given job and usually have to move to new jobs to receive higher wages (Iversen and Armstrong 2006).

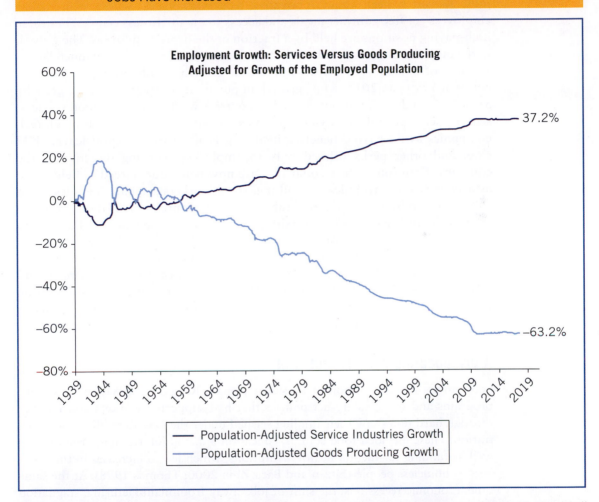

Employment Growth: Services Versus Goods Producing Adjusted for Growth of the Employed Population

37.2%

−63.2%

Population-Adjusted Service Industries Growth
Population-Adjusted Goods Producing Growth

Source: Doug Short, "Charting the Incredible Shift from Manufacturing to Services in America," *Business Insider*, September 5, 2011, http://www.businessinsider.com/charting-the-incredible-shift-from-manufacturing-to-services-in-america-2011-9

Types of jobs are often categorized as blue-collar, white-collar, or pink-collar. Blue-collar jobs traditionally are those involving manual labor, such as in manufacturing and farming. White-collar jobs are professional as well as administrative positions, in offices or cubicles, that involve more mental than physical labor. Pink-collar jobs, so named because of the predominance of women in these occupations, are primarily sales, service, and entertainment positions that involve interaction with customers. While the growth of jobs in the high-tech industry has been assumed to be providing better, higher-paying positions, the fact is that it has also contributed to growth in the lowest-paying jobs. We often hear about innovative tech workplaces, where white-collar employees get free gourmet meals and access to on-site fitness centers, but these high-paying positions are held by a fraction of the firms' employees. The growth in the numbers of outsourced workers in the tech industry has been much larger. A study of Silicon Valley firms found that growth in jobs increased by 18% between 1990 and 2014, while growth in potential contract industries grew by 54%. The kinds of labor outsourced to contract workers include food services, security services, and employment services. By outsourcing these jobs, high-tech companies avoid paying benefits, including health care, parental leave, child care, and other perks offered only to employees working directly for the company. Even some white-collar jobs are now being outsourced in fields such as accounting and technical consulting; these workers are paid 35% less than tech firm employees doing comparable work. Outsourcing this labor also exacerbates the tech industry's "diversity problem." The proportion of Blacks and Latinos working directly for tech firms is only 10%, whereas Blacks and Latinos make up 26% of contracted white-collar employees and 58% of blue-collar contract workers, whose average annual pay is just $19,000 (Benner and Neering 2016; Silicon Valley Rising 2016). Outsourcing as a means of cutting labor costs is not limited to technology industries; it is a growing practice among all kinds of employers.

A Disappearing Social Safety Net

Soon after the inauguration of President Ronald Reagan in 1981, social benefit programs and social safety net policies that had supported workers and families through hard times saw their funding slashed under the new Republican administration. These included food stamps, education aid, and job training programs, as well as funding for mental health institutions, which led to increases in the numbers of homeless people (Eitzen and Baca Zinn 2000; Thomas 1998). At the same time, economic recessions, the shift of jobs away from manufacturing, stagnation of wages (including the minimum wage), and other structural factors led to a predicted increase in poverty. Under the Reagan presidency, from 1981 to 1989, as stable, well-paying manufacturing jobs disappeared, urban areas declined and became more poverty-ridden. Federal funds for public housing and rent assistance were cut in half, and 60% of federal financial support for cities was lost. Public services like hospitals, schools, libraries, and parks faced drastic funding cuts (Cohen 2014).

The Evolution of Welfare

Welfare is a general term used to refer to policies and programs designed to support people in great financial need. Food stamps, Social Security and Medicare benefits, and Medicaid are all examples of welfare. Welfare is meant to provide a safety net for those who would otherwise be unable to meet their basic needs for survival. Today, the safety-net social policies established in the 20th century remain under attack, and many more programs are being slowly dismantled. Changes to welfare under the 1996 Personal Responsibility and Work Opportunity Reconciliation Act (PRWORA) replaced the Aid to Families with Dependent Children (AFDC) program with a new program: Temporary Assistance for Needy Families (TANF). For 61 years, very poor women and children received assistance from the government under AFDC (Eitzen and Baca Zinn 2000; Neubeck and Cazenave 2001). AFDC benefits were not generous, and only succeeded in raising 10% of children out of poverty in the 1990s prior to the program's elimination. One of the greatest problems with AFDC was that mothers lost all benefits if they started working, even if their work income could not cover the costs of child care and basic life necessities. A result was that welfare recipients were portrayed as people who could not take personal responsibility for their own well-being. The stereotype of the African American "welfare queen" having children in order to collect benefits became entrenched in the popular consciousness (Neubeck and Cazenave 2001; Foster 2008). The racialization of the image of the welfare recipient and the defining of welfare as a "Black problem" reduced resistance to the program's overhaul and the change to TANF in 1996, but the reality is that while a higher proportion of the Black population receives assistance, the majority of those on welfare are White (Morin, Taylor, and Patten 2012).

TANF has helped even fewer people than did AFDC. The often-concealed story is that welfare recipients now receive less aid and for a shorter period of time, and they are required to work 30 to 40 hours a week outside the home. Pursuing further education in order to get a better job is no longer an option for women receiving TANF, making it very difficult for them to improve their future opportunities. States now determine who is eligible for benefits, how much they can receive, and what work requirements are imposed, and states may limit the number of months families may receive benefits. Unlike in the past, today many people receiving TANF benefits are already working when they apply. However, their jobs pay such low wages that they cannot make ends meet.

Collins and Mayer's (2010) research has found that even as the funding for government programs for the needy has been cut, such programs have also increasingly been expected to subsidize the income of the working poor and provide other safety

Corporations like Walmart now benefit from government aid to their employees, which supplements the workers' meager salaries and allows companies to keep wages low.

nets once provided by employers, such as maternity leave and unemployment and disability insurance. Many costs have been transferred to taxpayers, while attitudes about the role of public supports have also shifted, leaving U.S. workers with none of the protections once guaranteed by both the private (industry) and public (government) sectors.

Private corporations, rather than private citizens, therefore, are now benefiting from welfare. Taxpayers are in effect supporting the corporate payrolls of the nation's growing number of low-wage service-sector employers (Badger 2015; Picchi 2015). For example, taxpayers pay an estimated $2.6 billion to support Walmart employees. Because Walmart pays employees so little and avoids offering employee benefits, taxpayers are financially supporting these employees with public assistance in the form of food stamps, subsidized housing, Medicaid, and more (O'Connor 2014). Local governments have required other aid recipients to work as strike breakers, taking jobs formerly held by unionized workers (Piven 2002, 26). These people are defined as "welfare recipients" rather than as workers, and in this way they are denied the rights other workers have while their efforts subsidize the labor costs of private business. They cannot choose their jobs and must find their own child care while they are at "work."

Welfare, renamed "workfare" under President Clinton, now benefits private industry, not just workers. In addition, despite the stock story that welfare is an unfair assistance or "entitlement" program costing our nation too much money, it is actually the smallest slice of the public assistance pie.

The Demographics of Welfare

When we look at the concealed story of who receives public assistance, we find that the majority of people in the United States (55%) receive benefits from at least one of the following government programs at some point in their lives: Social Security, Medicare, Medicaid, TANF, unemployment insurance, and food stamps (Morin et al. 2012).

Census data are collected on only a limited number of direct government benefits, however. When other public assistance programs are taken into consideration, it is clear that we *all* benefit from government assistance. Some examples of forms of assistance in addition to those listed above are veterans' benefits, government-subsidized college loans, tax subsidies, and business subsidies.

Did you know that tax breaks such as the Child Tax Credit and the Earned Income Tax Credit together cost the government $116 billion annually, while TANF costs $26.5 billion?

Race, Recession, and Recovery

As workers find themselves increasingly on their own, the payoffs for hard work continue to vary by race, despite attempts to curb racial and gender inequities in the workplace.

Historically, women and workers of color have been disproportionately disadvantaged by downward shifts in the economy while continuing to face outright discrimination (Engemann and Wall 2009; Wilson 1991–92). Over the past three decades, people of color have lost more economic ground than White people, especially during the Great Recession of 2008–9 (Farber 2011; Hoynes, Miller, and Schaller 2012; Sierminska and Takhtamanova 2011). For instance, African Americans' unemployment levels were disproportionately affected by the recession, as Figure 4.4 demonstrates.

From 2005 to 2009, the household median wealth of Whites decreased 16%, while Blacks lost 53%, and Hispanics 66%. At the same time, class inequality grew within each racial group, as the wealth of the top 10% of each demographic increased. The greatest increase was found among Hispanics, where the wealth of the top 10% increased from 56% to 72%. The proportion of households with zero or negative wealth grew from 23% to 31% among Hispanics; 12% to 19% among Asians; 29% to 35% among Blacks; and 11% to 15% among Whites

(Kochhar, Fry, and Taylor 2011). While Asian Americans seem to be the least affected, once unemployed they endure longer periods of unemployment than either Whites or Hispanics, and at levels comparable to those of Blacks (U.S. Department of Labor 2011).

Examining the data intersectionally provides us with a more nuanced understanding of this number, and which people are affected the most.

- *Age is important.* The highest unemployment rates are found across the board among those ages 16 to 19. Young adults are facing greater job losses than those in other age groups and are increasingly living at home with their parents or other family members as they become less likely to support themselves (Engemann and Wall 2009; Qian 2012).

Figure 4.4 ■ African Americans' Unemployment Levels Increased from 2003 to 2010

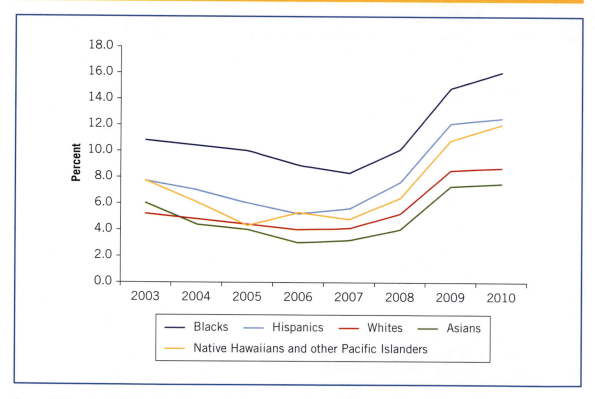

Source: U.S. Department of Labor, "The Asian-American Labor Force in Recovery," July 22, 2011, http://www.dol.gov/_sec/media/reports/asianlaborforce.

- *Gender also matters.* Men are more likely to lose their jobs during recessions, for various reasons, including the fact that women are more likely to be employed in jobs more immune to cutbacks, such as education and nursing, and are also paid less than men (Engemann and Wall 2009). As the economy has recovered, however, men have been quicker to recover their losses than women have (Kochhar 2011).

- *Class also plays a role.* The gains generated by the recovery have further exacerbated economic inequality: the percentage of people living below the poverty line remains worse than it was prior to the recession, and economic gains have overwhelmingly benefited the wealthiest 1% (Kneebone and Holmes, 2015; Saez and Zucman 2016; Wolfers 2015). In the past few years the United States has begun to recover from the Great Recession, but the recovery has not been shared equally by all families. Fully 100% of the wealth increase between 2009 and 2011 went to the richest 7%, while everyone else continued to lose wealth. The ratio of the amount of wealth owned by the top 7% in comparison to the other 93% of households grew from 18:1 to 24:1 (Fry and Taylor 2013).

The effects of both the income gap and the wealth gap are worsened by the fact that people of color face higher costs of living. Data consistently show that people of color and poor Whites actually pay higher prices for essential goods and services, including cars, car insurance, car loans, gasoline, and groceries. Middle- and upper-class Whites have greater access to mainstream financial institutions, so they do not have to rely on "payday lenders" or check-cashing services that charge exorbitantly high interest rates. Further, recent government policy changes leading to the privatization or defunding of many services, including schools and institutions of higher education, have resulted in costs increasingly being passed on to consumers, further exacerbating disparities. For example, families must now pay for many after-school and sports programs previously paid for by education funds (Oliver and Shapiro 2006).

Payday loan and check cashing businesses charge high fees and interest rates but are often the only option for people living paycheck to paycheck.

Bloomberg / Bloomberg / Getty Images

The Wage Gap and Occupational Segregation

The wage gap between men and women in the United States has hovered between 76 cents and 79 cents on the dollar since 2001—that is, on average, a woman is paid 76–79 cents for every dollar a man is paid. Among working women and men with professional degrees, the gap is 67% (Council of Economic Advisers 2015). Gender and race both affect what people can expect to earn. Figure 4.5 depicts the wage gap as it is shaped by the intersections of gender and race.

Occupational Segregation

Industry and occupation account for about 20% of the gender wage gap (Council of Economic Advisers 2015). One reason for the pay gap between races and genders is occupational segregation. Figure 4.5 illustrates the occupations of U.S. men and women by race and ethnicity. As this graph reveals, both White and Asian American men and women are more likely than members of other racial groups to be employed in management and professional occupations. Women in every racial category are more likely than men of the same race to be employed in service jobs, while African Americans and Hispanics have the highest rates. There are also race and gender income gaps *within* occupational categories. In occupations dominated by men as well as occupations dominated by women, there are wage gaps benefiting men.

Figure 4.5 highlights the intersection of race and gender within occupational categories, as well as the wage gap for each group, telling us more than we could learn by focusing on race or gender alone. The inequality we find within occupational categories tells us that occupation is only one factor affecting wage inequality. One source of inequality within an occupation is what is commonly referred to as the "glass ceiling." The metaphor of the glass ceiling represents the limit to women's advancement within their occupations. They can see the top levels of management above them, but rarely can they break through the glass to join them. Considering the ways in which women's experiences further differ by race: Women of color are said to encounter a nearly impenetrable "concrete ceiling," barring them not only from the upper echelons of power but from middle management as well. One barrier most women of color encounter is a lack of mentoring and access to role models and influential people (Moore and Jones 2001; West 1999). As noted in Chapter 2, some scholars have expanded the metaphor of the glass ceiling to argue that many women face a "triple glass ceiling" as a result of discrimination based on gender, race, and class. Another factor that has a negative impact on women is wage discrimination related to parenthood; women with children often earn less than childless women, whereas income tends to increase for men who have children. Further, the lack of paid parental leave has a negative impact on women's long-term salaries and careers (Council of Economic Advisers 2015).

Figure 4.5 ■ Occupations are Segregated by Gender, Race, and Ethnicity

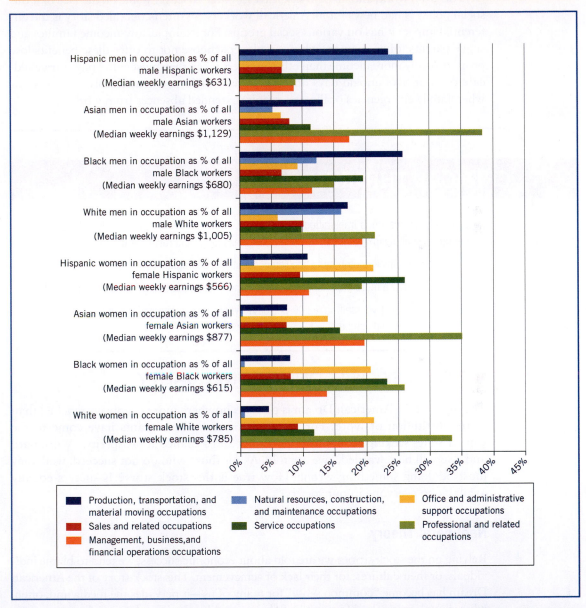

Hispanic men in occupation as % of all
male Hispanic workers
(Median weekly earnings $631)

Asian men in occupation as % of all
male Asian workers
(Median weekly earnings $1,129)

Black men in occupation as % of all
male Black workers
(Median weekly earnings $680)

White men in occupation as % of all
male White workers
(Median weekly earnings $1,005)

Hispanic women in occupation as % of all
female Hispanic workers
(Median weekly earnings $566)

Asian women in occupation as % of all
female Asian workers
(Median weekly earnings $877)

Black women in occupation as % of all
female Black workers
(Median weekly earnings $615)

White women in occupation as % of all
female White workers
(Median weekly earnings $785)

Legend:
- Production, transportation, and material moving occupations
- Sales and related occupations
- Management, business, and financial operations occupations
- Natural resources, construction, and maintenance occupations
- Service occupations
- Office and administrative support occupations
- Professional and related occupations

Source: Table 3, p. 6 in Institute for Women's Policy Research, "The Gender Wage Gap by Occupation 2015 and by Race and Ethnicity." Fact Sheet, IWPR #C440. April 2016. https://iwpr.org/wp-content/uploads/wpallimport/files/iwpr-export/publications/C440.pdf. Reprinted with permission from Institute for Women's Policy Research.

Note: Data for White workers are for Whites alone, non-Hispanic; data for Black and Asian workers may include Hispanics. Hispanics may be of any race.

When we compare the United States with other developed nations, it ranks last in terms of workers' benefits. The United States guarantees workers no paid holidays or other days off from work, and no paid sick leave or parental leave. While on the face of it this social policy is bad news for all American workers, an often-concealed story is the differential impact it has on various social groups. For example, low-income families and single parents (often women) whose employers choose not to offer these benefits lose proportionally more income than other workers when they must either pay extra child-care costs or take unpaid days off on national holidays, when schools are closed, or when family emergencies or illnesses require extended absences from work.

CRITICAL THINKING

1. Consider the ways wealth is transmitted over generations. How does this process contribute to the growing racial wealth gap? What can be done to decrease persistent racial wealth inequality?

2. What factors do you think contribute to ongoing occupational segregation?

3. Why does wealth play a more important role than income in the perpetuation of racial inequality?

4. How would you support yourself on $2.00 per day? Where would you live? Where would you get food? Health care? Would you be able to remain in school?

■ THEORIES OF ECONOMIC INEQUALITY

The myth of the American Dream is perhaps nowhere more deeply entrenched than in the institution of work. For hundreds of years, immigrants have come to the United States seeking economic opportunity and a chance at prosperity. "Work hard and you will be rewarded," we are told. As for those who do not succeed, well, they must be doing something wrong. How true is this stock story? Is success equally available to everyone in our society?

Neoliberal Theory

Relying on the stock stories we are told about economic success, we tend to blame individuals, or their cultures, for their lack of achievement. This stock story of the American Dream has become "common sense" for many of us—it pervades the media and, often, educational curricula. However, it fails to consider the broader social context.

This stock story is based on **neoliberal theory** (sometimes referred to as market fundamentalism), which is a foundational perspective that shapes global economic policy today. According to the World Health Organization, neoliberal theory embraces individualism, free markets, free trade, and limited government intervention or regulation. This approach assumes the following:

- Corporations and businesses (including banking) should be free from national and global governmental intervention and policy in order to pursue maximum growth and profit.

- Free trade benefits everyone, including all nations and their peoples.

- Privatization of many government institutions can save money and increase efficiency.

- Individual behavior is the cause of economic inequality, and redistributionist policies and taxes are unfair.

Neoliberal thinking has pervaded U.S. politics, affecting both Republicans and Democrats to varying degrees. The pervasive narratives that result from neoliberal theory include the following assumptions:

- The United States is a meritocracy, and wealth is the product of an individual's hard work and savings; consequently, those who are poor are lazy, don't want to work, or make poor choices. For example, a neoliberal theorist might argue that women make choices that lead to their lower pay, such as choosing not to pursue higher education, taking lower-paying jobs, and seeking time off to raise children.

- Discrimination on the basis of race or sex is now illegal, so poverty and inequitable employment outcomes are blamed on individual or cultural characteristics (Tilbury and Colic-Peisker 2006).

- The fact that some racial and ethnic minority groups have achieved success and assimilated into the dominant U.S. culture demonstrates that certain cultures value education and hard work while others do not (Chua and Rubenfeld 2014).

- There may be lingering individual prejudices and discrimination, but these will decrease with time.

Neoliberal theory is an oppression-blind approach in that it sees the world in terms of individual choice and a level playing field, and it assumes that the market is objective. It assumes that the economy and work institutions do not operate to the benefit or detriment of any specific groups, and that upturns and downturns affect everyone equally, independent of social identities such as race, gender, age, and sexual or gender identity (Ferber 2014). We know from our review of recent trends that this is not the case. Yet so long as people believe that inequality is a result more of individual behavior than of entrenched social structures, they are unlikely to support the implementation of policy solutions.

Marxist Theories

The other major stock story about economic inequality is rooted in **Marxist theories,** which emphasize class inequality. Karl Marx (1818–83) examined the impact of economic change, such as the shift from land-based feudalism to manufacturing-based industrialization, on class relations and social conditions. He famously declared, "The history of all hitherto existing society is the history of class struggles" (Marx [1848] 2001, 91). Industrialization introduced factory and machinery work, and the rise of the working class, a social group whose members became ever-cheaper commodities themselves. Workers became interchangeable and devalued. The products of the worker's labor were no longer her or his own, but were sold by factory owners in the marketplace for their own profit.

A plethora of Marxist approaches have been developed over the years, offering explanations of class inequality—the growing gap between the wealthy and the poor, and the decreasing wealth and power of the middle class. Some scholars have used Marxist, class-based approaches to explain racial economic inequality. However, in these explanations class relations are always seen as primary and foundational. For example, later scholars influenced by Marx have argued that economic institutions and competition produce racial and ethnic conflict and inequity. Bonacich (1972) asserts that prejudice and discrimination are not responsible for economic inequity; rather, such inequity is a result of the priority of paying less and less for labor. This leads to a **split labor market**, where racial and ethnic minority workers compete for jobs and higher-paid earners, largely White, protect their jobs and wages (often through unions) by excluding new groups (often minorities) entering the labor market from the higher-paying jobs. In their analyses, Marxist approaches prioritize class relations and inequality as most central to understanding all forms of inequality (including racial and gender inequality). This has been critiqued as a limited way to view race and gender relations. However, Marxist theorists importantly emphasize the role of economic production and restructuring in producing inequality, explaining some of the data we have examined above.

While many sociological theories of inequality exist, these two popular analytical approaches—neoliberal and Marxist—provide examples of two stock stories that differ in significant ways. One focuses on individual behaviors and cultural values. The other instead emphasizes the role of the economy in class conflict to explain economic inequality. Based on the tenets of the matrix framework, we would argue that both stock stories are insufficient for explaining the recent trend of growing racial inequality. We turn now to an application of the matrix approach and examine this theory's contributions.

CRITICAL THINKING

1. Based on the recent trends examined earlier in this chapter, critique both of the stock stories we have reviewed. What limitations do you see in each theoretical approach?

2. Provide at least four examples of where and how neoliberal theory is reinforced in American society. Be specific.

3. Which of the two stock stories, that of neoliberal theory or that of Marxist theory, do you think provides more insight into the phenomenon of economic racial inequality? Why?

4. Do you believe the United States is a meritocracy? Defend your answer.

■ APPLYING THE MATRIX TO THE HISTORY OF ECONOMIC INEQUALITY IN THE UNITED STATES

Throughout this chapter, we are implementing a matrix approach to understanding economic inequality. This approach assumes the following:

1. *Race is inherently social.* The processes that are reproducing racial inequities are at the same time reproducing racial classifications as meaningful categories into which people are divided. Every time a policy is applied inequitably or employers or lenders invoke stereotypes and biases and discriminate against people of color, these acts are actively giving meaning to racial classifications.

2. *Race is institutional and structural.* We have seen how changes in the economy and occupations contribute to racial inequality, whether intentional or not. As we move on to examine history, we will see the foundational structures that have shaped racial inequality over time.

3. *Race is a narrative.* We have just reviewed the two prominent stock theoretical stories that shape the way most people interpret economic inequality. We have also glimpsed some of the concealed stories in our look at recent trends. For example, while we may celebrate the economic recovery from the Great Recession, one concealed story is that it is only the very wealthy who have benefited. In the following sections, we will discuss further concealed and resistance stories that have informed the creation of emerging transformative stories.

4. *Racial identity is relational and intersectional.* Throughout this chapter we examine many examples of the ways in which race is intersected and complicated by other social identity positions, such as gender and age. We are seeing that data on race can always be broken down further to reveal more detail and nuance.

5. *We are active agents in the matrix.* As we enter the workforce we play a role, whether we want to or not, in reproducing or challenging assumptions about constructed racial differences that reproduce inequality. For example, gender and racial wage gaps can be found among faculty on many college and university campuses. Students can play a role in highlighting and finding solutions to this problem.

From a matrix perspective, the historical context is essential to any understanding of how we got to where we are today. Historical trends inform recent trends. An intersectional examination of history provides a more nuanced and complex picture of the experiences of racialized groups. Not every member of a racialized group has experienced economic inequality in the same ways, especially when other significant social identities are taken into account.

The Shifting Organization of Work and Wealth

In the 17th-century American colonies, wealthy landholding Whites built plantations on which nonwealthy people began to work for others rather than for themselves, sometimes for limited periods, and sometimes for life. **Indentured servants,** brought from Europe, were legally bound to work for their masters for a set number of years. Slaves, brought forcefully from Africa, were initially indentured servants, but soon became legally defined as property, or chattel, owned by their masters for life. **Chattel slavery** defined the children of slaves as their owners' property as well (Amott and Matthaei 1996, 292).

Slavery and the Colonial Economy

As the colonies were established, slavery was widespread. Smaller numbers of Native Americans were forced into slavery, and some even owned slaves themselves, but the vast majority of slave owners were White, and most slaves were Africans.

Both slave owners and entire towns and cities profited from the use of slave labor on southern sugar, tobacco, rice, and cotton plantations. Slavery was also closely linked to economic development in the northern states, even when the practice itself was banned. Northern banking, finance, insurance, and other industries helped fund and insure the importation and sale of slaves and the products of slave labor. Northern shipbuilders made ships to carry slaves and the commodities they produced. Before it became home to the stock market, New York City held major slave auctions, and in the early 18th century, almost 40% of European American households in New York owned slaves. There were about 40,000 slaves in the United States in the 1770s, and by 1865, that number had increased to 4 million. Between 1770 and 1850, slaves were as large a source of capital as agricultural land in the United States (Piketty 2014).

Slave labor, and the wealth it generated, also fueled the Industrial Revolution in Europe and the Americas. The textile industry, for example, depended on the low-cost cotton grown on slave plantations (Feagin 2000). The wealth of the nation, and of its White citizens, grew as a result of slavery and was passed from one generation to the next. African Americans were denied the opportunity to earn any income or wealth from their own labor for hundreds of years. This provides one clue to the origins of the current dramatic White/Black racial wealth gap.

From Slavery to Sharecropping

Following the Civil War, poor Whites in the South feared job competition from newly freed Blacks, and landowners balked at paying wages to former slaves. These concerns led to the development of Jim Crow segregation and legalized discrimination, which allowed Blacks to be barred from many jobs and to be paid much less than Whites for the jobs they were able to get. Former slaves took on contract labor as sharecroppers or domestic workers (Conrad 1982). In the South, poor Whites also had few options but to become sharecroppers.

Western Expansion and Economic Inequality

The western lands taken from Mexico and Native American tribes were offered in parcels to White homesteaders, but over time these lands became concentrated in the hands of elite Whites, and small family farmers were pushed into working for large landowners (Conrad 1982). Mexicans dispossessed of their lands were also reduced to sharecropping, tenant farming, and migrant farming. Native Americans who lost their lands engaged in subsistence farming, or farming for self-sufficiency, and ranching on the small areas to which they were removed. In the West, Asians

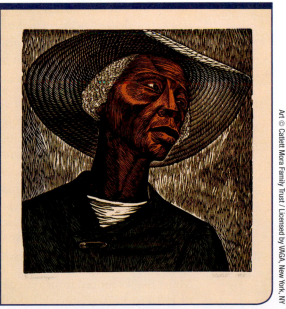

Art © Catlett Mora Family Trust / Licensed by VAGA, New York, NY

African American artist Elizabeth Catlett's 1970 painting captures this anonymous sharecropper's difficult life in the lines of her face, but also her strength and dignity. Throughout history, many oppressed peoples have turned to art as a means of revealing concealed stories and actively resisting the dominant stock stories.

were imported to work on plantations, mines, and the transcontinental railroad, but it was illegal for them to own land. They were often contract workers sent back to their countries of origin once their contracts were up.

The Industrial Revolution and the Shifting Economy

Throughout the 1800s, in Europe and the United States, the Industrial Revolution gained momentum, advancing the transition to a wage-based economy and capitalism. Jobs slowly shifted out of agriculture and into the rapidly growing and better-paying manufacturing sector in the cities. The majority of men and women of color, however, remained in agriculture and domestic labor, the lowest-paying and least secure jobs (Amott and Matthaei 1996). In 1890, half of all African American women (and one-third of African American men) worked in domestic labor and personal service (Amott and Matthaei 1996).

People worked largely in segregated workplaces, among others whose race, gender, and class status were similar to their own. Better-paying jobs in textile mills, as opposed to garment work done at home, were monopolized by White women and men, most often recent immigrants. In the 1800s and early 1900s, the earliest urban factories employed the daughters of poor White families and European immigrants fleeing poverty and political persecution. While these were opportunities often denied to African Americans and other people of color already in the United States, that does not mean the work was easy. Indeed, it was unregulated and extremely dangerous; long hours, health and safety risks, and very low wages were the norm.

Mining conditions were just as dismal. The families of mine workers lived in shanties in "company towns" and were allowed to shop only at the company store, which they became indebted to. Many miners were killed in accidents, and the injured were often fired. Workers fought for the right to organize into labor unions, but mine owners had huge amounts of wealth to invest in antiunion activity and to influence policy makers, lawmakers, and law enforcement. In 1931, one of the bloodiest battles between miners and mine owners ever seen in the United States took place in Harlan County, Kentucky; these events have come to be memorialized as the "Harlan County War." In addition to poor Whites, there were large numbers of Chinese immigrant miners (who were charged a special "foreigner tax").

Many Blacks moved from agriculture into mining as well during the Great Migration of 1910 to 1970 (Fishback 1984), when approximately 6 million African Americans left the South for jobs and other opportunities in the Northeast, the Midwest, and the West (Wilkerson 2010). Factory jobs also began to open up to African Americans during World War I. White workers in the North thus increasingly faced competition not only from European immigrants but also from African Americans leaving the rural South in search of jobs. Many feared their privileged access to work would be undercut by cheaper labor. In the late 1910s and the 1920s, White mobs started race riots in many cities, trying to push African Americans out of town (Amott and Matthaei 1996).

The Rise of Labor Unions

Some early labor unions welcomed both White and Black workers, including the Congress of Industrial Organizations (CIO), but many embraced discriminatory practices. Whites-only unions strove to exclude all people of color to protect their White members' privileged access to jobs and to expand the unions' ranks and power (Hill 1985; Kolchin 2002). Arriving immigrants worked to differentiate themselves from African

During the Great Migration, millions of Blacks moved out of the South in pursuit of better jobs and opportunities, like those offered in the auto factories in Detroit.

Americans in order to gain acceptance as Whites, and the labor movement played a central role in this process (Brodkin 1998; Ignatiev 2008). W. E. B. Du Bois (1918) fought the American Federation of Labor's (AFL) practice of excluding Black workers, arguing that the union was reinforcing employer practices that pitted White and Black workers against one another.

History is replete with stories of resistance among workers. Excluded from the AFL, many Blacks built their own labor organizations. One of the best known and most successful was the Brotherhood of Sleeping Car Porters, founded in 1925 under the leadership of A. Philip Randolph. The porters worked as attendants on overnight trains, in servile roles attending to the personal needs of White passengers, for as many as 100 hours a week, until the Brotherhood eventually won shorter hours and higher pay.

While the location and organization of work have shifted from farms to cities and from mercantilism to capitalism through the course of U.S. history, race, class, and gender inequality has remained a constant. To combat the extent of inequality, especially based on class, various government policies have attempted to intervene in these dynamics. We now turn to an examination of some of these policies and their results.

The Effects of Social Policy

From colonial days to the 20th century, most people toiled in deplorable working conditions just to survive. Largely thanks to union organizing in the 20th century, the United States, along with most other Western nations, instituted child labor laws, health and safety standards, a minimum wage, welfare programs, income protection in case of work-related injuries and disabilities, unemployment benefits, and other safety nets (Collins and Mayer 2010). Race and racial discrimination had become so ingrained in our nation, however, that many of the new policy solutions did not benefit all workers equally.

The New Deal

In response to the Great Depression (1929–39), the U.S. Congress, at the urging of President Franklin Roosevelt, passed a series of laws in the mid-1930s to provide economic relief and institute banking reform. Among other programs, this **New Deal** created a federal minimum wage, Social Security, and Aid to Families with Dependent Children. In the late 1940s and early 1950s, President Harry Truman's **Fair Deal** sought to protect workers from unfair employment practices, raised the minimum wage, provided housing assistance, and more. Both the New Deal and the Fair Deal, however, were not created to serve Whites and people of color equally, and benefits were commonly distributed in a discriminatory manner (Katznelson 2005, 17). For example, in identifying categories of workers to be protected by New Deal legislation, legislators excluded farmworkers and domestic laborers, two groups that together accounted for more than 60% of working African Americans. Further, the administration of AFDC was put into the hands of local officers, who could choose who was "worthy" of aid and who was capable of working. Thus White women were more likely than women of color to receive aid (Amott and Matthaei 1996).

The GI Bill of Rights

The Servicemen's Readjustment Act, commonly known as the **GI Bill of Rights** or simply the GI Bill, passed by Congress in 1944, was perhaps the most far-reaching social welfare program in U.S. history. This legislation included provisions for low-cost guaranteed loans for college degrees, new homes, and businesses; job training; and unemployment benefits. It had an enormous impact on education and economic mobility and was to a great extent responsible for the development of a large American middle class. On the eve of World War II, the United States was producing approximately 160,000 college graduates per year. By 1955, some 2.25 million veterans alone had received higher education under the GI Bill (Katznelson 2005, 116).

While it was touted as an egalitarian plan and did help to create a new Black middle class, the GI Bill also failed to challenge discrimination and in fact increased the wealth gap. Battles over the racial distribution of benefits were waged in the drafting of the legislation, and those arguing for federal administration of the plan, which would ensure equal distribution, lost to those who wanted to place the distribution of federal funds in the hands of state and local governments. Benefits had to be approved by the mostly White-staffed local Veterans Administration centers. In the context of Jim Crow segregation and discrimination, southern Black veterans did not receive the same benefits as White veterans (Katznelson 2005, 128).

Numerous other obstacles to equity existed as well. Within a segregated school system, there were not enough Black colleges to serve all the Black veterans seeking a higher education. Job training programs required that applicants have employers willing to provide them with jobs after the training, but legal job discrimination made this almost impossible for the majority of Blacks. And housing loans for veterans were administered by banks, the majority of which refused to make loans to African Americans. So while in theory the benefits of the GI Bill were available to all veterans, in practice many were largely accessible only by Whites. It is frequently the case that well-intentioned programs designed to benefit everyone can end up reproducing racial or gender inequality, especially when those who design the programs ignore widespread, ongoing discrimination.

The Civil Rights Act

It was not until the passage of the Civil Rights Act of 1964, which also established the Equal Employment Opportunity Commission (EEOC), that discrimination in

New Orleans, Louisiana
SALARY SCHEDULE -- SEPTEMBER 1942
(NOTE: Salaries of white and colored will be equal September, 1943)

WHITE TEACHERS

Years	Without Degree	With B.A.	With M.A.
1	$ 980.00	$1,100.00	$1,100.00
2	1,047.00	1,182.50	1,232.00
3	1,114.00	1,292.50	1,364.00
4	1,181.00	1,402.50	1,496.00
5	1,248.00	1,512.50	1,628.00
6	1,350.00	1,650.00	1,782.00
7	1,490.00	1,804.00	1,936.00
8	1,630.00	1,958.00	2,090.00
9	1,770.00	2,112.00	2,244.00
10	1,910.00	2,266.00	2,398.00
11	2,050.00	2,420.00	2,552.00

Substitutes -- $3.50 per day

COLORED TEACHERS

Years	Without Degree	With B.A.	With M.A.
1	$ 900.00	$1,004.50	$1,007.50
2	1,008.50	1,116.25	1,146.00
3	1,062.00	1,196.25	1,237.00
4	1,120.50	1,276.25	1,328.50
5	1,179.00	1,356.25	1,419.00
6	1,250.00	1,445.00	1,516.00
7	1,345.00	1,542.00	1,628.00
8	1,415.00	1,619.00	1,715.00
9	1,485.00	1,696.00	1,837.00
10	1,600.00	1,823.00	1,939.00
11	1,675.00	1,930.00	2,058.00

Substitutes -- $3.00 per day

WHITE PRINCIPALS -- FORMULA

2495 + M + 20Y + H + 5P = Salary in Dollars
Where 2495 is a constant which represents $75 more than the maximum salary for the teacher with a B.A. Degree:
M = $120 additional amount for possession of Master's Degree
Y = Years of service as principal (Maximum 10)
H = $120 additional amount for principal of a high school
P = Average number of pupils belonging (1200 maximum)

COLORED PRINCIPALS

Calculate on same formula as for white principals, but for session 1942-1943 last year's salary + ½ difference between formula and last year's salary will be paid.

SECRETARIES -- WHITE

Years	Elementary, Asst. High and Study Hall	High
1	$ 880.00	$ 990.00
2	946.00	1,056.00
3	1,012.00	1,120.00
4	1,078.00	1,188.00
5	1,144.00	1,254.00
6	1,210.00	1,320.00
7	1,276.00	1,386.00
8	1,342.00	1,452.00
9	1,408.00	1,518.00
10	1,474.00	1,584.00
11	1,540.00	1,650.00

New Orleans, Louisiana. -- September 11, 1942.

SECRETARIES -- COLORED

Years	Elementary	High
1	$ 740.00	$ 795.00
2	803.00	858.00
3	866.00	920.00
4	929.00	984.00
5	992.00	1,047.00
6	1,055.00	1,110.00
7	1,118.00	1,173.00
8	1,181.00	1,236.00
9	1,244.00	1,299.00
10	1,307.00	1,362.00
11	1,370.00	1,425.00

This pay chart used by a New Orleans school district in 1942 documents the widespread overt and legal pay discrimination practiced before the Civil Rights Act of 1964.

employment became illegal if based on race, color, national origin, sex, or religion. As part of a compromise to get the Civil Rights Act passed, the EEOC was given no power to enforce antidiscrimination laws. For example, one-third of the complaints filed with the EEOC in the agency's first year involved sex discrimination; the EEOC's lack of action on these complaints inspired the formation of the National Organization for Women (NOW) (Freeman 1991). This act also challenged the notion of the man as the family's sole breadwinner. Prior to this time, employers assumed that their male employees were married, with families to support, and a middle-class White man was generally paid enough to support a family. Labor unions pushed strongly for this approach. However, with the Civil Rights Act's elimination of many barriers, there was a shift away from the notion that the father alone was responsible for supporting the family and toward a model of the "solitary wage." This meant a drop in wages, the increasing necessity for both parents in two-parent families to work, and more challenges for single parents.

In 1964, President Lyndon Johnson launched the War on Poverty, prompting the creation of the Office of Economic Opportunity, the initiation of Medicare and Medicaid, the expansion of food aid with the Food Stamp Act, and more. This period made clear that the government does have the ability to improve the welfare of its citizens, and to decrease the tremendous wealth gap (Cohen 2014). Many of these policies were later eliminated, ensuring that poverty remained the reality for millions in the United States, especially children.

The Americans with Disabilities Act

While the Civil Rights Act of 1964 banned some forms of discrimination, it did not protect everyone. In 1990, the passage of the Americans with Disabilities Act (ADA) for the first time extended that protection to those with disabilities, making it possible for them to have access to jobs and participate more fully in public life. The ADA "prohibits discrimination and ensures equal opportunity for persons with disabilities in employment, State and local government services, public accommodations, commercial facilities, and transportation" (U.S. Department of Justice 2010). Under President Trump, the White House has removed all information about the ADA from its website, leaving many people with disabilities fearing that their rights could be curtailed in the future.

Lesbian, gay, bisexual, and transgender people of every race are still fighting for this same level of protection. In most states it is still legal to fire an employee based on sexual or gender identity, and many companies refuse to hire gay or lesbian employees (Bernard 2013). New challenges to protecting LGBT people from discrimination have arisen in the past few years. Those opposing equal rights for LGBT people are framing their opposition as a religious right. They argue that the religious freedom guaranteed by the U.S. Constitution includes the right to discriminate on religious grounds, not only in employment but also in sales and services to LGBT people. Some states, like

North Carolina and Mississippi, have recently passed laws allowing businesses to refuse, on religious grounds, to sell products or provide basic services—such as apartment rentals, counseling, and service in restaurants and shops—to LGBT people.

This very brief overview highlights the importance of historical context for an understanding of contemporary inequality, especially when it comes to wealth. We have seen the tremendous race, class, and gender wealth gaps that exist today. Many are perplexed when it comes to the causes of these gaps and resort to blaming the victims. The more we learn about our nation's racial history, however, the better we can understand the origins of these gaps and how they have been reproduced and even widened over time, and the less likely we are to see wealth inequality as an individual problem. It is essential that we have this full picture before we can come up with solutions.

CRITICAL THINKING

1. How does the brief overview of history above inform your views of neoliberal, Marxist, and matrix theories? Be specific.

2. How do you think the racial inequality examined in this chapter has contributed to building the wealth and development of our nation?

3. What stock stories persist today about early immigrants representing specific minority groups? Provide examples.

4. In our application of the matrix perspective to the history of economic inequality, can you find insights that apply to your own family history? (You may need to talk with older family members to learn more about your family history.)

■ TRANSFORMING THE STORY OF RACE AND ECONOMIC INEQUALITY

Emergent and transformative stories grow out of a deeper examination of the versions of reality depicted in stock stories. We will begin this final section by examining two concealed stories that add another dimension to the history and recent trends in income and wealth inequality discussed above.

None of the stock stories discuss the role of discrimination in reproducing economic inequality. While neoliberalism refers to individual discrimination, in the sense that there are still a few bad apples to be dealt with, the concealed story is much larger. Marxist theories also do not explain ongoing racial discrimination, unless it is in the service of addressing class inequality. The matrix approach, however, brings this piece of the picture into focus. Our discussion of discrimination here will treat racial discrimination as an institutional problem actively reproduced on an ongoing basis, and an issue that should be approached intersectionally.

Workplace Discrimination

We have already examined numerous pieces of the puzzle, including shifts in the organization of the economy, occupational segregation, policy, and history. However, these factors do not fully account for the racial income and wealth gaps. Researchers conclude that the concealed story of continuing discrimination must also be examined (American Association of University Women 2014).

The Civil Rights Act of 1964 made discrimination based on race, color, religion, sex, or national origin illegal, and also banned formal, public segregation. Nevertheless, racial discrimination in housing and employment remain widespread social problems. Many studies have documented continuing discrimination in the housing market (Flippen and Parrado 2015; Freiberg and Squires 2015; Oliveri 2009; Pager and Shepherd 2008). Homeownership has traditionally led to the accumulation of wealth and was long denied to many groups of people of color, especially African Americans. Further, the increase in housing costs since the 1960s has hit the lower class, and people of color, disproportionally. When the housing bubble burst in the 2000s, millions of families lost their homes, and it is estimated that less than a third of them will become homeowners again (Kusisto 2015). We know that homeownership is important to the wealth gap (Foster and Kleit 2015). Overt discrimination in lending and housing segregation still remain widespread. Large numbers of White neighborhoods seek to keep their communities White (Rahill 2015). Continuing segregation not only decreases wealth accumulation by the groups most affected but also affects job availability and income (Moore 2016). For example, many African Americans remain stuck in urban ghettos, where jobs have disappeared (Moore 2016; Wilson 1996).

Not all discrimination is conscious or blatant; much of it is very subtle, covert, and institutionalized. Some scholars have identified what they call the "minority vulnerability thesis," suggesting "that segregation, job networks, and ostensibly race-neutral employer decision making continue to put minority workers in situations of vulnerability when it comes to hiring, mobility, and firing" (Roscigno, Williams, and Byron 2012, 697; see also Pager, Western, and Bonikowski 2009; Roscigno 2007).

What happens when someone enters the job market? Most jobs are not advertised; in fact, approximately 80% are filled without being advertised, as employers rely on their own social networks and those of people they know for their candidate pools (Dickler 2009; Kaufman 2011). Thus, employers in occupations where people of color are already underrepresented effectively (even if inadvertently) limit the number of people of color who apply, making it particularly difficult for them to move into these fields. Other employers practice selective recruitment by placing job ads (when they advertise at all) not in major metropolitan newspapers but in White neighborhood, suburban, or White ethnic newspapers, or by choosing specific organizations, schools, or neighborhoods from which to recruit. Many employers avoid state employment services, welfare offices, and schools in certain neighborhoods when looking for job candidates (Roscigno et al. 2012).

What happens when job applicants are screened? Research finds especially strong anti-Black and anti-Hispanic attitudes among employers (Bertrand and Mullainathan 2003; Doob 2005; Pager 2007, 2008; Pager et al. 2009; Pager and Western 2012). Employers often focus their recruitment efforts on White neighborhoods (Neckerman and Kirschenman 1991). Kirschenman and Neckerman (1991) and Pager (2008) found that employers have many biased attitudes about young inner-city Black males, assuming they will be difficult and unstable workers. Many employers engage in statistical discrimination, relying on stereotypes about race, ethnicity, and class in judging applicants' likely productivity (Wilson 1991–92; Pager and Western 2012). Research in the Netherlands found similar results: Employers valued candidates who were young, healthy, male, and native Dutch, independent of level of education or experience. Further, employers at times choose to invoke soft skills (personality traits) in hiring and promotion decisions as a means of masking prejudice and discrimination (Ortiz and Roscigno 2009; Roscigno et al. 2012). In recent years, access to images and other information about job candidates online has also led to discrimination in the hiring process (McDonald 2015).

Many experimental studies, or audits, have been conducted using testers, where people of various races are recruited to pose as applicants for jobs and are given near-identical résumés to present to prospective employers (Pager and Western 2012). Similar studies have been conducted to document discrimination in other practices, such as mortgage lending. These studies consistently reveal discriminatory practices. Let's examine a few examples.

Pager and her colleagues (2009) conducted a field experiment with White, Black, and Latino job applicants seeking low-wage work in New York City. Equivalent résumés were created for each set of three testers, White, Black, and Latino, who were also matched on demographic characteristics as well as interpersonal skills. The researchers found that White testers were twice as likely as equally qualified Blacks to receive either a callback or a job offer. White applicants whose résumés said they had just been released from prison were just as likely to be hired as Black and Latino applicants with no criminal records.

In another well-known controlled experimental study, researchers sent out fictitious résumés that were identical except for the names on top. The invented applicants with White-sounding names (Emily and Greg) needed to send about 10 résumés for each callback they received, while those with African American–sounding names (Lakisha and Jamal) needed to send 15. The authors concluded that a White-sounding name yields as many additional callbacks as does an additional 8 years of experience, and they found the same statistically significant level of differences across all occupational categories and industries. They also found that race shapes the returns on other qualifications. For example, a higher-quality résumé, additional years of education, and an address in a wealthier neighborhood led to higher percentages of callbacks for those with White names than it did for those with stereotypically African American–sounding names (Bertrand and Mullainathan 2003). Other research has found that, like having an ethnic name, having a Spanish accent reduces an applicant's chances on the job market (Hosoda, Nguyen, and Stone-Romero 2012).

Since the terrorist attacks of September 11, 2001, negative attitudes toward and discrimination against Muslims (and others who are mistaken as Muslim) have dramatically increased, including in the workplace (Greenhouse 2010; Greenberg 2013). In two experiments conducted in Sweden, résumés with stereotypically Muslim-sounding names were significantly less likely to receive callbacks than those with White-sounding names (Rooth 2010). Researchers have found similar patterns of prejudice and discrimination among employers in many Western nations today, often involving applicants who are non-European, Muslim, or Jewish (Eriksson, Johansson, and Langenskiöld 2012, King and Ahmad 2010). Experimental studies like these have also been used to document discrimination against gay men (Tilcsik 2011).

Imagine that someone has finally made it past all barriers and landed a job. For people of color, mistakes at work are more likely to be attributed to individual deficiency and taken as confirmation of stereotypes, whereas for Whites, mistakes are more often attributed to the situational context ("He was having a bad day"). People of color may be seen as tokens and assumed to be the beneficiaries of affirmative action policies established to meet government funding requirements (U.S. Department of Labor 2001; we discuss affirmative action in more depth later in this chapter). Those seen as tokens are more likely to experience sexual and racial harassment, a hostile or unwelcoming climate, and increased levels of stress on the job. They have fewer opportunities to develop the social networks that help people advance through the ranks, often face different expectations, and have fewer opportunities to be mentored (Ortiz and Roscigno 2009; Roscigno et al. 2012; Wingfield 2012).

Nor have demographics at the top levels of corporations changed very much. Even among middle- and upper-class people of color, barriers persist. Today there is a larger Black middle class than ever before, but its members are more likely than their White counterparts to encounter job ceilings, slowed job mobility, and discrimination (Higginbotham 2001; Mong and Roscigno 2010; Roscigno et al. 2012; Wingfield 2012).

Finally, firing is the most frequently reported form of racial discrimination in the workplace (Roscigno et al. 2012; Couch and Fairlie 2010). Seemingly neutral policies such as "last hired, first fired" are more likely to affect women and people of color because they have only recently made inroads into many occupations.

Immigration Stories

While data are extremely important, there are other kinds of concealed stories as well. It can be difficult to see the nuance and complexity behind the numbers. In many of the charts and figures we have examined in this chapter, Asian Americans seem to be doing as well as, if not better than, Whites. Why? According to the stock story, Asian Americans are a "model minority"; they work hard, value education, and have been able to "pull themselves up by their bootstraps." This stock story is often pointed to as evidence that minority group success is based on culture and work ethic, and that the greatest problems African Americans and Latino/as face stem from their cultures.

However, the picture is more complicated than the stock story suggests. First, among Asian Americans, a "household" often includes more workers than the average White household does. Further, many Asians own family businesses where teens and other relatives work, thus contributing the labor of additional workers to the total household income and wealth. Even more important, we must keep in mind that the category of "Asian American" is a social construct, encompassing a very diverse group of cultures with origins in many different nations. The overarching category conceals tremendous diversity within, including inequality in employment, income, and wealth. For example, 76% of Indian Americans have a college degree, a much higher proportion than is found in any other Asian American ethnic group. Hawaiians and Pacific Islanders have a college graduation rate of only 26%. Similarly, employment and poverty rates vary greatly among Asian American ethnic groups (U.S. Department of Labor 2014).

The concealed story reveals that various contextual factors can help explain these differences, especially year of immigration and levels of education and assets accumulated before immigration. After the Immigration Act of 1965 opened the doors to immigrants from more varied countries, the United States put in place occupational preferences, making it easier for immigrants with high levels of education and skills in desired fields to become U.S. citizens. These immigrants, coming from specific countries like India, are able to move into relatively high-paying jobs upon arrival, and they have also brought more education and resources with them (Pew Research Center 2012;

Many Asian American families own businesses, like restaurants, where relatives can find jobs.

Zong and Batalova 2015). The Immigration Act of 1990 furthered these preferences. It is largely social and structural factors, not cultural ones, that explain economic success (Zong and Batalova 2015). The situation for recent Asian immigrants contrasts sharply with conditions faced by Mexican immigrants, also drawn here by the prospects of immediate, but low-skilled, employment, yet facing many obstacles to the achievement of legal status and permanent citizenship. There is no single pathway by which immigrants can gain work visas or become U.S. citizens; immigration policies and their implementation vary based on nationality, class,

RESISTANCE / STORY

PaKou Her and 18 Million Rising

PaKou Her is the campaign director for 18 Million Rising, an organization of activists, artists, and print and social media outlets founded to promote the civic engagement and influence of Asian Americans and Pacific Islanders (AAPI) using the power of technology and social media. In response to our request for her story, she writes:

I entered the world of racial justice organizing in the hopes of being useful, and to challenge the ways in which Asian Americans are socialized into being the Model Minority. I desired to have utility and service to other People of Color in leadership given the relative power and privilege of being Asian American in the white supremacist racial strata. Of being both profiled as "other" while simultaneously not having to wear the same dehumanized dark face at the end of a police officer's gun. Of not having to carry the multigenerational legacy and body memory of enslavement and genocide. Of . . . so much.

The questions I carry about how to show up, be useful, and build solidarity exist beyond single protests or fleeting moments of political action. In the story of race in this nation, there is an Asian American narrative to disrupt: the one that frames Asians as the "model minority," the actors in a play that leverages us as a wedge against other People of Color that invisiblizes our racial reality while negating those of others. Participating in anti-racism organizing is an opportunity to engage in what ChangeLab's Soya Jung and Scot Nakagawa call a "Model Minority Mutiny."

But among progressive Asian Americans I often see an earnestness that borders on the sharp edge of trying too hard. I begin to see what appears to be an exaggerated AAPI performance of allyship that is as much about the unspoken shame surrounding the power and privilege granted on us as the Model Minority as it is about a true, deep desire for solidarity with other folks of color.

I see this performative solidarity and have to ask myself, "Am I doing this, too?" I'm not always sure of the answer. But I stay in the fight despite my fears of misstepping because—irrespective of the preassigned racial script—Asians are here for the struggle, too, and it's our obligation to be Model Minority Mutineers.

refugee status, and other factors. It is important to understand this in order to make sense of current debates over immigration policy.

While immigrants themselves often face discrimination and criticism, we are much less likely to hear criticism of the corporations that hire undocumented labor to avoid paying minimum wage and benefits and to avoid complying with labor laws that limit the numbers of hours employees can work. Undocumented immigrants come to the United States because there are plentiful jobs awaiting them.

Immigration to the United States has always been limited by various factors, including skill level and country of origin. Currently, having an immediate family member who is a U.S. citizen is one category under which a prospective immigrant may apply for a visa; another category is that of refugee. Temporary work visas may also be granted to some immigrants; these are generally set aside for highly skilled workers. Some immigrants may be granted the status of permanent employment-based residence (these individuals are given the right to live here permanently without becoming U.S. citizens).

Permanent Immigration

For the first 100 years of U.S. history, the nation set no limits on immigration; anyone could enter the United States. Today, the number of visas granted for permanent employment-based residency is set at 140,000 per year, and these are divided into five preferences based on skill, profession, and money to invest in the United States (American Immigration Council 2016). Further, there are caps on the numbers of immigrants accepted from individual countries. These requirements make it extremely difficult for uneducated poor people to immigrate to the United States, as our coauthor Abby's own great-grandparents did, and likely many of yours as well.

In addition to being stereotyped as lawbreakers who simply ignored legal opportunities to immigrate, Latino immigrants are often mistakenly blamed for stealing jobs from U.S. citizens, especially minority Americans. One often-cited explanation for minority joblessness is employers' willingness to hire undocumented immigrants at lower wages. While this might sounds like a simple, commonsense assumption, this stock story is unsupported by the research. Rather, minority joblessness is the result of the economic restructuring and ongoing discrimination we have already examined. Generally speaking, undocumented workers are not competing for the same jobs as other low-wage workers. There is no correlation between the presence of undocumented workers and unemployment rates. In an analysis of the impact of immigration on urban centers, Strauss (2013) reveals an interesting concealed story: In cities with high levels of Latino/a immigration, African Americans experience lower levels of unemployment and poverty and higher wages than elsewhere. A longitudinal study in Denmark has documented the same phenomenon, finding that the presence of immigrant workers "pushes" low-wage native workers into jobs requiring less manual labor and higher wages (Foged and Peri 2016). A recent study by the National

Academies of Sciences, Engineering, and Medicine (2016) found that the presence of immigrant workers had only small impacts on job loss among existing workers, and these were largely at the expense of other immigrant workers who had arrived earlier. The researchers also found numerous benefits; however, they were not immediate. For example, after about 10 years, there was an overall positive economic impact on communities as a result of an influx of immigrants. And while communities bear the immediate costs of educating immigrant children, those children grow up to be "among the strongest economic and fiscal contributors in the U.S. population, contributing more in taxes than either their parents or the rest of the native-born population." The researchers conclude that immigrants have an overall positive impact on the long-term economic growth of the nation and that there is little evidence that immigrant workers have a negative impact on the employment of American-born workers.

In other words, it is not a zero-sum game in which one group can win only at the expense of another. The presence of immigrants, both legal and undocumented, can reenergize an aging community by providing an influx of young workers and consumers, which in turn can lead to new jobs and economic growth. Facts are too often ignored in political debates. President Trump is committed to deporting immigrants and migrant workers from Mexico and other parts of Latin and South America who do not have permanent residency status, and to building a wall on the border between the United States and Mexico. The potential economic impacts of these efforts are unknown. At the same time, many sociologists argue that, instead of deporting undocumented workers, we would be much better off providing mechanisms for those working and living in the United States to become permanent residents.

Many undocumented and migrant workers are clustered in agricultural labor, where conditions and wages have changed little since the days of slavery and sharecropping. In Florida, the U.S. attorney's office has prosecuted numerous cases of human trafficking, freeing more than 1,200 workers from captivity and forced labor. Farmworkers in Florida commonly work 10 to 12 hours a day for below-poverty wages. Today a farmworker must pick twice as many tomatoes as 30 years ago in order to receive the minimum wage (Coalition of Immokalee Workers 2012).

We don't need to look far to find stories of resistance. Many workers continue to organize to protect themselves and fight to be treated fairly. The Coalition of Immokalee Workers is a good example. This is a community-based organization of low-wage-earning Latino, Mayan Indian, and Haitian immigrants in Florida organizing for,

> among other things: a fair wage for the work we do, more respect on the part of our bosses and the industries where we work, better and cheaper housing, stronger laws and stronger enforcement against those who would violate workers' rights, the right to organize on our jobs without fear of retaliation, and an end to forced labor in the fields. (Coalition of Immokalee Workers 2012)

Many Stories Lead to Many Solutions

Looking through the lens of the matrix at concealed and resistance stories, we can conclude that the United States has been built upon and nourished by a foundation of wealth inequity. Despite modest attempts to eliminate specific symptoms, such as poverty and discrimination, both continue to exist. Countless suggestions have been offered to address the problem, and many can have modest impacts in specific areas. These include adopting family-friendly policies; building the pipeline of people of color to increase their numbers in higher-paying positions, and increasing EEOC enforcement of the laws concerning employer discrimination (Council of Economic Advisers 2015; Kantor, Fuller, and Scheiber 2016). In the following sections we discuss some large-scale attempts and proposals to significantly decrease racial and economic inequality.

Affirmative Action

One of the more contentious policies ever implemented to eliminate job discrimination in the United States is **affirmative action**. Put in place more than 50 years ago, it was intended to curb discrimination and create a more level playing field. Affirmative action originated in the creation of the Committee on Equal Employment Opportunity (CEEO) by President John F. Kennedy in 1961, through Executive Order 10925. That order created the CEEO in part to "recommend additional *affirmative steps* which should be taken by executive departments and agencies to realize more fully the national policy of nondiscrimination." It also ordered government contractors to "take *affirmative action* to ensure that applicants are employed, and that employees are treated during employment, without regard to their race, creed, color, or national origin" (Kennedy 1961). Under President Richard Nixon, what we today call "affirmative action" was developed further. Current affirmative action programs often establish goals, plans, and timetables in workplaces and schools where discrimination has been historically documented, and where White women and people of color continue to be excluded in numbers disproportional to their representation in the population (Barnes, Chemerinsky, and Onwuachi-Willig 2015). The CEEO was the predecessor of the Equal Employment Opportunity Commission, which is charged with enforcing antidiscrimination laws. Today, EEOC enforcement of antidiscrimination statutes is weak. In 2016, the EEOC had a backlog of 76,000 unresolved cases (Gurrieri 2016).

There are many myths about affirmative action. Many people assume that the policy translates into racial quotas, but quotas are illegal and have been since the 1972 U.S. Supreme Court case *Regents of the University of California v. Bakke*. Another myth is that every workplace is required to implement affirmative action policies. In reality, most private workplaces are not affected by affirmative action guidelines; only those that receive government contracts of $50,000 or more and that employ more than 50 workers must comply (as specified in 1965 by President Lyndon Johnson's Executive

Order 11246). Since 1972, however, affirmative action has continued to face legal and political attacks that have slowly whittled away its effectiveness.

Arguments against affirmative action are generally justified from a neoliberal perspective, with the stock story that discrimination is a thing of the past and that poor individual choices and negative cultural characteristics are the reasons people of color and women have not had more success in the workplace. However, as we have seen throughout this chapter, discrimination continues unabated. More than 300 years of legal, government-sanctioned race and gender discrimination cannot be remedied so easily. The battles over affirmative action reveal just how difficult it is to challenge our deeply entrenched system of discrimination and inequality, as well as deeply entrenched beliefs that discrimination has ended.

Reparations

A clear understanding of the extent to which African American lives, labor, and wealth have been plundered over the course of hundreds of years of slavery and discrimination should lead to a serious national dialogue about reparations (Coates 2014). While the sufficiency of the amounts can be debated, there is much precedent supporting a case for reparations. In 1971, the U.S. government agreed to give $1 billion and 44 million acres of land to Native American tribes in Alaska. Other Native American tribes have received reparations for their stolen lands more recently (CNN 2012). In 1988, Congress allocated $20,000 for each Japanese American survivor of the internment camps established during World War II. History is full of examples of Black individuals and groups demanding reparations for African Americans, and efforts toward reparations have been supported by a United Nations working group 2001 (R. Coates 2004; T. Coates 2014; McCarthy 2004; Zack 2003). More recently, the Movement for Black Lives has made reparations its central concern, supporting its demands with a long list of reasons linking historical inequality to ongoing inequity and wealth disparity today (see Movement for Black Lives, n.d.).

Asset-Based Policies

Oliver and Shapiro (2006) suggest the implementation of the following specific asset-based social policies—that is, policies that focus on wealth rather than jobs and income—many of which have been tested and implemented on a small scale:

- *Match savings.* By matching deposits to savings accounts by low-income adults and children, government could encourage and reward asset building. Historically, society has helped members of the White middle class and the upper class to build wealth, so why not help those living in poverty?

- *Integrate the poor into the formal banking system.* About 22% of low-income families are not connected to formal financial institutions, and they pay more for the financial services they use (such as check cashing). There are many ways government can help bring these families into the banking system—for example, by offering incentives to major banks to open offices in poor and minority neighborhoods.

- *Encourage regional equity and asset building.* Reducing regional inequalities in affordable housing, wage differences, and transportation, and broadening the tax base, would produce fair distribution of resources to schools and other public services.

- *Provide per-child cash allowances.* Social scientists have argued that providing each child under age 6 with a cash allowance of $2,500 a year would cut in half the number of children in poverty, at a price tag of one-fourth the cost of Social Security (not a needs-based benefit). Programs of this type have been widely tested and shown to be successful in other Western developed nations (Garfinkel, Harris, Waldfogel, and Wimer 2016; Madrick 2016). According to Madrick (2016), "If America makes cutting childhood poverty a priority, it can afford to do so."

Revision of the Tax Code

Many economists and sociologists recommend revisions to the tax code, including increasing the estate tax, to help level the playing field for those just starting out in the world. Currently, heirs may inherit up to $5.45 million without paying any estate tax. The estate tax for those inheriting more than this amount is 40%. While this may seem like a significant tax burden, bear in mind that inheritances provide descendants with funds they did not earn themselves. Most Americans never inherit enough to have to pay estate taxes. Inheritance is one significant way that wealth and privilege are passed on over generations. For example, the wealthiest 0.1% of Americans (160,000 families) have an average of $72.8 million. Should this wealth be inherited, more than $67 million would not be taxed (some states also levy inheritance taxes). If the inheritance tax were to be increased, the result would be a decrease in the inequity that begins at birth, and the revenues collected could be used to initiate and fund programs such as a per-child cash allowance (as discussed above). This is unlikely to happen in the near future, however, given that President Trump has proposed eliminating the estate tax altogether, giving billions of dollars per year back to millionaires and billionaires.

Researchers have also argued strongly for a more progressive tax code (Garfinkel et al. 2016; Piketty 2014; Piketty and Saez 2014). Along with the historically proven methods for decreasing the income and wealth gaps discussed above, researchers have suggested the use of incentives to encourage the nonwealthy to save and decrease their debt through more regulation. Garfinkel et al. (2016) advise increasing the Child Tax Credit (the amount of money a family can deduct from the taxes they owe for each child they have), although they note that this option would have less impact than a per-child cash allowance at roughly the same cost.

Transforming a History of Wealth Inequality

It is important that policy makers consider potential solutions that are tested and supported by research evidence, rather than relying on ideological opinions. The solutions described above have all grown out of the work of scholars who have studied the concealed stories about income and wealth in our nation. They are responses to direct resistance to inequality by those most affected by it. Resistance stories provide us with a fuller understanding of the severe consequences of deep poverty. Can you imagine living on $2.00 a day? It is only after consideration of a wide range of stories that we can begin to develop stories that will have the power to transform the 400-year American history of wealth inequality.

The workplace and the economy, like other institutions, are structured by, and actively reproduce, racial inequality. Historical inequality, occupational segregation, discrimination, inequitable application of social policy, immigration policy, and economic restructuring are some of the significant factors contributing to racial inequality in the workplace and the economy. While the impact of income inequality on families today should not be underestimated, it is essential that we also understand the concept of wealth inequality. Wealth inequality reveals the lasting impact of our history of state-sponsored racism. These factors are concealed by stock stories that blame individuals or cultures for their own lack of economic success. Finding solutions that will work is not the primary problem we face, however; rather, the problem is changing attitudes. Our stock stories about American meritocracy and color blindness must be challenged. Scholar Margaret Andersen (2001, 190) identifies the difficulty we face when she asks:

> How do we explain the fact that the intersections of race, class, and gender are so fundamental to the shaping of inequality, power, and privilege—yet members of the dominant group so firmly assert that race no longer matters and that the gender revolution is over? There is increased recognition of "diversity in American society," and yet there is also a persistent belief among privileged groups that race does not matter. This belief keeps people blind to the continuing differences in power and privilege that characterize U.S. society, making it difficult to generate public support for programs designed to reduce inequality.

Until we acknowledge the full extent to which people of color have experienced unearned disadvantage and Whites have benefited from unearned advantage, we will not have the courage to implement solutions. A transformational story can arise only out of an understanding of the dangers of our stock stories and a more complex knowledge of the many concealed stories and histories of resistance. A transformational story recognizes historical and ongoing patterns that reproduce inequality and is committed to taking the necessary structural steps to redress the damage done by that history of privilege and oppression. As Piketty and Saez (2014, 4) sum it up: "In democracies, policies reflect society's view. Therefore, the ultimate driver of inequality and policy might well be social norms regarding fairness of the distribution of income and wealth."

CRITICAL THINKING

1. Compare and contrast current immigration policies and debates with those of the past (delineated in Chapter 3). Do you see any ways we can avoid repeating history?

2. Why do you think the ideas of both affirmative action and reparations to African Americans have faced so much resistance over the years?

3. What role does White privilege play in perpetuating economic inequality?

4. Of all the proposed solutions to wealth inequality, which do you feel have the greatest chances of being implemented? Why?

KEY TERMS

affirmative action, p. 149

capitalism, p. 116

chattel slavery, p. 134

class, p. 117

economic restructuring, p. 120

Fair Deal, p. 138

GI Bill of Rights, p. 138

income, p. 116

indentured servants, p. 134

Marxist theories, p. 132

neoliberal theory, p. 130

New Deal, p. 138

split labor market, p. 132

wealth, p. 117

welfare, p. 123

CHAPTER SUMMARY

LO 4.1 **Describe the current patterns of income and wealth inequality in the United States.**

Since the 1960s the income gaps between Whites and Blacks and between Whites and Hispanics have increased. Even more significant, however, is that the wealth gap separating Whites from Blacks and Hispanics has also increased. Data on economic restructuring and changes in occupations provide more insight into the extent of this gap and the forms it takes. Wealth inequality is also affected by the disappearance of social safety-net programs and by economic cycles such as upturns and downturns. Further, significant wage gaps exist between men and women and between and within racial and ethnic groups.

LO 4.2   **Compare various stock stories about economic inequality.**

Neoliberalism and Marxism are two of the most impactful social theories, or stock stories, that attempt to explain economic inequality. The neoliberal narrative sees the United States as a meritocracy and blames individuals, or their cultures, for their lack of success. Marxist theories, in contrast, focus on groups based on social class. Rather than addressing individuals, they examine the dynamics of the owning class's goal of constantly increasing profit at the expense of labor.

LO 4.3   **Apply the matrix perspective to the historical foundations of economic inequality.**

Today's racial wealth gap has been significantly shaped by historical patterns of racial inequality. The expansion of the category of Whiteness was shaped by competition for jobs. The ability of minority groups to accumulate wealth has been limited by the theft of land and resources from these groups, slavery, sharecropping, Jim Crow laws, immigration policies, occupational segregation, and the inequitable application of social policies. Policy has the potential to move us in the direction of equity, but too often it has upheld and reinforced economic racial inequality.

LO 4.4   **Analyze potential solutions to the problem of economic inequality.**

The United States has the ability to end the great income and wealth inequalities that have been increasing with time. Various solutions have been proffered, and many have been proven effective in other nations. However, key to real change is that we embrace a transformational story that arises out of an understanding of the dangers of our stock stories and a more complex knowledge of the many concealed stories and histories of resistance. Without this knowledge, it is unlikely that our nation will embrace change to increase equity.

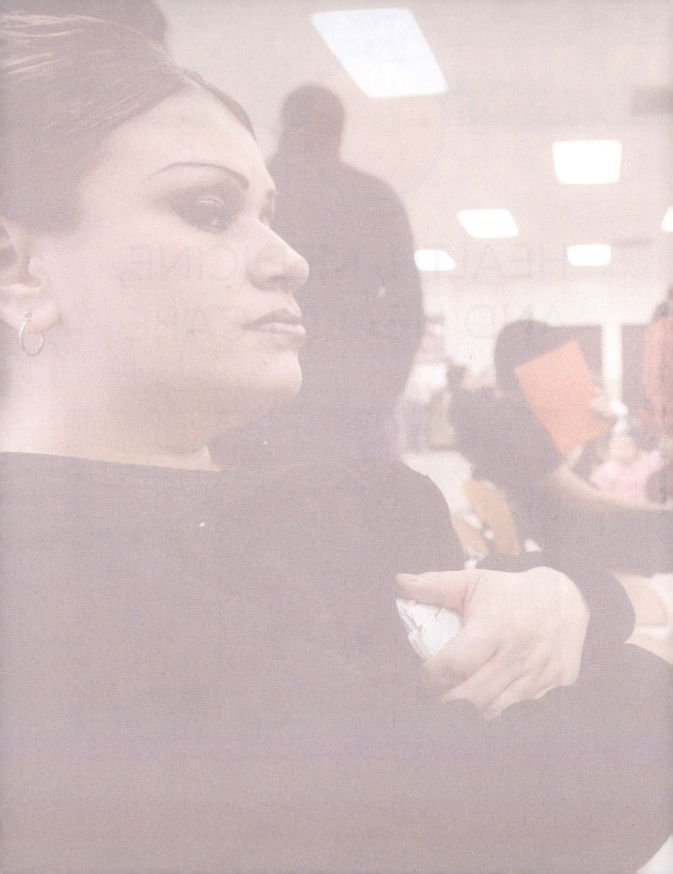

CHAPTER 5

HEALTH, MEDICINE, AND HEALTH CARE

Jim West / Alamy Stock Photo

The Affordable Care Act helped many Americans get health insurance, including 8.9 million White, 4 million Hispanic, and 3 million Black adults.

LEARNING OBJECTIVES

LO 5.1 Describe contemporary inequality in health and health care.

LO 5.2 Examine various stock narratives of inequality in health and medicine.

LO 5.3 Apply the matrix lens to the link between race and health care.

LO 5.4 Explore alternatives to the current matrix of inequality in health and medicine.

We are surrounded by health and wellness information. Our social media feeds are saturated with advice about the latest "superfoods" we should eat for optimal health, how to start and maintain an exercise regimen, and other tips to help us live longer and healthier lives. And we all know the risks involved in the various activities we engage in on a daily basis, like riding in a car, texting while driving, or crossing the street. Close to 40,000 people died in car accidents in the United States in 2016 (Korosec 2017). But how often do we consider our risk of dying because of our race or ethnicity? For those who are White, the answer is likely never. The risk of African Americans dying as the result of race-based factors is about twice as high as the risk of Americans as a whole dying from car, motorcycle, plane, train, and bicycle accidents combined. In fact, the number of race-related deaths is the "equivalent of a Boeing 767 shot out of the sky and killing everyone on board every day, 365 days a year" (Smedley, Jeffries, Adelman, and Cheng 2008, 2). And yet this issue rarely makes the headlines.

In this chapter, we will rely on the matrix framework to explore the role that health and health care narratives play in the construction of "normal" bodies and examine how the definition of normal has been used as an instrument of power and social control. We will briefly examine some key moments in the history of medicine in the United States as it pertains to race, analyze the stock stories about health and medicine and their consequences, and then shift our attention to a matrix-informed sociological approach that highlights concealed and resistance stories.

■ PATTERNS OF INEQUALITY IN HEALTH AND HEALTH CARE

Sociologists argue that examining disparities in health and mortality reveals clear evidence of the long-term effects of structural racism (Feagin and McKinney 2003). For example, researchers who investigated the impacts of both race and years of education (one indicator of class) on life expectancies found that "white U.S. men and women with 16 years or more of schooling had life expectancies far greater than black Americans with fewer than 12 years of education—14.2 years more for white men than black men, and 10.3 years more for white women than black women" (Olshansky et al. 2012, 1803). *The National Healthcare Disparities Report,* an annual report mandated by Congress, compares populations on a wide range of health and health care measures. The most recent report, on data from 2015, shows that African Americans, Hispanics, Asian Americans, and American Indians and Alaska Natives all received significantly worse health care than Whites. Similar results are found when poor populations are compared with high-income populations. Researchers have documented disparities across racial and ethnic groups in access to health care, quality of health care received, health care safety, sickness and death rates, and communication and care coordination. Nevertheless, small improvements were seen in 2015 compared to previous years. This may be linked to the implementation of the Affordable Care Act of 2010. From 2013, when ACA health insurance marketplaces began operating, to early 2016, 8.9 million White, 4 million Hispanic, and 3 million Black adults gained health insurance (Agency for Healthcare Research and Quality 2016).

African Americans, Hispanics, and American Indians and Alaska Natives all have higher rates than Whites of many of the deadliest diseases, such as stroke and type 2 diabetes (Centers for Disease Control and Prevention 2017; Spanakis and Golden 2013). Understanding health inequities and inequalities requires a nuanced examination of the range of factors involved. For example, while disease rates may be the same across racial groups, mortality rates—that is, death rates—may differ. Recent research has found that Black women are much more likely to die from breast cancer than are White women, and this gap has actually increased over the past four decades. While rates of screening have increased and treatments have improved, not all women have benefited from these advancements (Parker-Pope 2013).

Health inequities in the United States are one consequence of a long history of structural racism. As noted above, researchers have found that White men with 16 years or more of education live slightly more than 14 years longer than Black men with less than 12 years of education. At these levels of education, White women live slightly more than 13 years longer than Black women (Olshansky et al. 2012, 1803). Such racial health inequalities are significant, and while some gaps are narrowing, others are actually growing. A wide range of factors are involved, including access to care and early screenings, access to high-quality care, the nature of patient–provider relationships, class inequality, and environmental racism. To some extent, in addition to being outcomes of the long history of systemic racism in the United States, current disparities in health and health care are the results of historical events and the development of the professionalized field of medicine.

Traditional Healing

Traditional medicine consists of indigenous knowledge, skills, and practices that have been passed down over generations. Practitioners of traditional medicine use these tools to prevent and diagnose illness and disease and to improve physical, mental, and spiritual health. Many forms of traditional medicine were practiced throughout the Americas prior to colonization. One example is *curanderismo*, popular among indigenous cultures throughout Latin America and parts of the United States, and still practiced today. *Curandero/as*—traditional healers—tend to specialize in specific forms of medicine, such as midwifery, bone and muscle treatment, and herbalism. Many practitioners of traditional medicine recognize a relationship between people and nature, and may focus on healing the person rather than just the illness.

Traditional healing methods were not valued by modern medicine in the past, as medical practice became defined as the province of physicians who had graduated from medical schools (which limited admission to White men). Nevertheless, many people continued to rely on these methods, and they have played an important role in U.S. Latino culture, among other cultures.

Much of our current knowledge about the medicinal qualities of specific plants and herbs comes from traditional medicine. Researchers are finding that traditional practices continue to offer insights for modern medicine and pharmacology, yet much of this knowledge is being lost as modern practices displace traditional healing and traditional cultures around the world disappear. In the past few decades, a wide range of health professionals have shifted their focus to capturing the insights of traditional medicine. Even the World Health Organization recognizes that traditional healers are

Latina author and poet Pat Mora explores the work of Curanderas and the importance of social and cultural context: "listen to voices from the past and present, who evolve from their culture . . . definitions of illness are culture bound. We might consider it essential to stay in our comfortable homes or apartments if the soles of our feet were covered with blisters. The migrant worker, however, might sigh, apply a salve, and trudge from field to field. Illness is both a biological and social reality, and our reactions are learned" (Mora 1984, 126).

an important part of the provision of health care services in many countries, given the high respect they are usually accorded in their communities, local cultural beliefs that value them, and the very limited access many populations have to physicians and other health professionals. Traditional medicinal practices remain a widespread option around the world today, especially in rural areas and developing nations.

Modern Medicine and Discrimination

Prior to the middle of the 19th century, medicine did not exist in the United States as an organized and institutionalized discipline. Around that time, a small group of established physicians began to organize conventions designed to "defend their profession against the 'unprofessional[s]'" (Charatz-Litt 1992, 718). Facing competition from traditional healers, midwives, and self-proclaimed healers, they created the **American Medical Association** (AMA), a formal organization through which they would define themselves as the only authentic and legitimate practitioners of medicine.

The rise of modern medical practice in the United States was both shaped and reinforced by the broader culture of racism. Modern medicine was developed during the era of slavery, and slaves were frequently used for medical experimentation (Charatz-Litt 1992; Savitt 1982; Washington 2008). After the end of the Civil War, White doctors refused to treat Black patients, and segregation became the law. In fact, the institution of medicine played a prominent role in justifying Jim Crow laws. According to southern physicians, "Blacks were pathologically different from whites, unfit for freedom, and uneducable in the ways of better hygiene" (Charatz-Litt 1992, 719).

Denied access to White medical institutions, members of the African American community mobilized to establish their own, with assistance from White philanthropists and limited government funds. By 1900, 11 medical schools had been founded to train Black doctors. Since Black physicians were excluded from the AMA, in 1895 they created their own professional organization, the National Medical Association (NMA) (see National Medical Association, n.d.). A number of the medical schools for Black doctors did not survive, and many were shut down (Olakanmi, n.d.; Sullivan and

Excluded from the American Medical Association, Black doctors formed the National Medical Association and held annual conventions, like this one in Boston in 1909. The group, which still exists, is dedicated to promoting the interests of patients and doctors of African descent.

Mittman 2010). "Consequently, until World War II, fewer than 20 Black physicians graduated from [medical] programs each year" (Charatz-Litt 1992, 719).

Few hospitals allowed Black doctors to practice and admit patients. African Americans in the South were dramatically more likely to die due to lack of medical care than were Whites; hospitals in the South were segregated, and disproportionately fewer beds were reserved for Black patients. Black physicians and patients in the North encountered similar problems. Black patients could be admitted to only 19 of 29 hospitals in New York City, and only 3 of those allowed Black doctors to treat their patients on the premises (National Medical Association, n.d.). In 1910, life expectancy for White women was 54 years, and for White men it was 50. In stark contrast, African American women, on average, lived to age 38, and African American men to only 34 (Pollitt 1996, 401–2). The NMA was literally fighting for the lives of African Americans across the country.

The story of the NMA is an often-concealed story of resistance. From the NMA came the National Hospital Association, a lobbying arm that pushed for the right of African American doctors to treat their patients in southern hospitals. The NMA founded the *Journal of the National Medical Association,* which published not only medical research but political updates as well. The NMA continued its battles for decades, but hospitals were not desegregated until the passage of the Civil Rights Act of 1964. This very recent history still affects families today. The NMA remains an active organization, committed to addressing inequality in the medical professions and the provision of health care. We have not seen a great increase in the numbers of people of color applying to medical schools or becoming doctors. In 2014, of the total population of physicians in the United States, only about 4% were Black, and Blacks, American Indians and Alaska Natives, and Hispanics/Latinos totaled only 8.9% of all physicians (Association of American Medical Colleges 2014).

The Social Construction of "Fit" and "Unfit" Bodies

Medical institutions not only contributed to the system of White supremacy and supported legal and educational boundaries separating Blacks from Whites, but they also played a central role in racializing other groups and defining where they fell within the racial hierarchy. The stock story of race as a biological reality is one of the most significant narratives justifying health disparities by locating physical differences within the body.

Debates on how the races originated characterized the early stages of the science of race, and they were not resolved until the publication of naturalist Charles Darwin's text on the theory of evolution in 1859. Darwin asserted that all races evolved from the same organisms and thus were part of the same species (Ferber 1998). He also described a process of natural selection, in which those individuals best suited to their environments were more likely to survive and reproduce, furthering their species.

Social Darwinism and the Rise of Eugenics

Darwin's theories, and the discoveries about genetics and inheritance published by scientist and Augustinian friar Gregor Mendel in 1866, sparked a new way of thinking

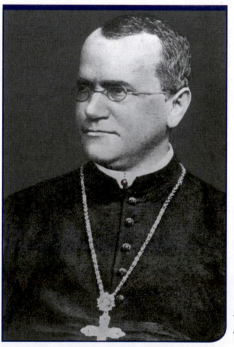

The theories of Charles Darwin (left) and discoveries of Gregor Mendel focused new attention on the inheritance of traits, both physical and behavioral, and provided the basis for both social Darwinism and eugenics.

about race, class, and the value of life. This new perspective focused on the inheritance of so-called genetic traits, which were believed to include everything from physical characteristics to moral behavior.

The school of thought known as **Social Darwinism** took the basic insights of the theory of evolution and applied them to social life, making the assumption that a society could determine between the "fit" and "unfit." Sociologist Herbert Spencer, who coined the phrase "survival of the fittest" in 1864, argued that the imagined laws of natural selection were justification for not intervening to help the poor.

These popular versions of evolutionary theory distorted the actual science of evolution in two important ways:

1. Evolution actually works extremely slowly, over millions of years, not over the course of a few generations as assumed by proponents of social Darwinism.

2. There is no way of knowing who is or is not "fit." According to the theory of evolution, "fitness" is determined by specific historical, environmental, and climatic contexts.

That is why diversity within a species is so important to its survival in a range of contexts that cannot be predicted in advance. The fittest species is the most diverse. A diverse species is capable of surviving and adapting to a changing environment.

The **eugenics** movement, which arose in the late 19th century, took the social Darwinist philosophy further, arguing that natural selection should be hastened through the implementation of policies that would encourage the "fit" Northern Europeans and upper classes to reproduce; in addition, the numbers of those defined as "unfit" should be reduced through sterilization. Francis Galton, a cousin of Charles Darwin, coined the term *eugenics*. The idea was relatively simple: If evolution works by preserving the fittest, why not aid that process by eliminating some of the unfit? At the very least, social Darwinists argued, society should not be helping the unfit to survive by providing them with forms of charity and welfare. Eugenicists' arguments appealed to those of all political stripes who sought answers to the economic crisis caused by the need to care for those in society who either could not care for themselves or were considered unfit to participate in society (Ekland-Olson and Beicken 2012; Lombardo 2008). In addition to eliminating the unfit, measures were suggested to encourage the "fittest" to marry each other and reproduce in order to increase the "fit" population. This all occurred within the broader context of a system of White supremacy, so that the White race was assumed to be the "fittest" race that could continue to be perfected.

Social Darwinism and eugenics gained a broad base of support among a number of groups, including progressive organizations fighting for women's suffrage, women's right to birth control, child welfare, temperance, and prison reform. If the poor and uneducated were not competent to make educated decisions if given the vote, then it followed that those groups were most in need of limiting the numbers of births in their families and most susceptible to alcoholism, violence, and crime.

Eugenics was legitimated and given the stamp of scientific truth when the AMA included among its published goals the application of a "scientific process of selection" to control the growth of the "unfortunate classes." Ways to do this included restrictions on immigration and who could marry, and compulsory sterilization for certain people (Lombardo 2008, 11).

Eliminating the "Unfit"

Many people believed that by removing from society those incapable of living up to high moral and physical standards, they could protect the purity and fitness of the White race. These efforts went so far as to attempt to protect the sensibilities of the fit by keeping "defectives" literally out of sight. The 1911 Chicago Ugly Law declared: "Any person who is diseased, maimed, mutilated or in any way deformed so as to be an unsightly or disgusting object, or an improper person to be allowed in or on the streets, highways, thoroughfares or public places in this city shall not therein or thereon expose himself or herself to public view" (quoted in Coco 2010, 23).

Eugenic ideology permeated immigration policy as well. Beginning with the Immigration Law of 1891, the federal government classified as "public charge" certain immigrants thought likely to depend on government assistance (Park 2011, 4) Any immigrant believed to suffer from a "loathsome or dangerous contagious disease" (which included pregnancy, poverty, and a lack of morals) was deported. Women were automatically assumed to be public charge if they were unmarried or widowed.

A plethora of new methods were devised to determine who was and was not "fit," ranging from the use of tools to measure the widths and angles of the face to the first IQ tests. Some of these intelligence measures were put to use at the immigration hub at New York's Ellis Island, where scores of women trained in methods of spotting the "feebleminded" were employed to identify misfits and administer IQ tests. Those immigrants defined as "morons" were swiftly deported. In 1913, Henry Goddard, psychologist, author, and leading eugenicist, claimed that this testing showed that about 80% of Jewish, Hungarian, Italian, and Russian immigrants were feebleminded. Deportations for the reason of feeblemindedness increased 350% that year and 570% the next, a situation that played a role in the setting of immigration quotas to limit the "inferior stock" of the "not quite White."

Charles Davenport, another prominent eugenicist, focused on the elimination of what he saw as undesirable inherited traits. He meticulously sought to identify every genetic trait, publishing his documentation in 1912 in his *Trait Book*. Public education about eugenics thus increased, and public health advocates sought methods for "race improvement through better marriage" (Lombardo 2008, 45). Fears of miscegenation were also fueled by eugenic sentiment.

During this period, 33 U.S. states adopted laws allowing eugenic sterilizations in order to decrease the reproduction of undesirable genetic traits (Ekland-Olson and Beicken 2012). The traits considered undesirable were found in people of many different heritages, and the grouping of such diverse people seems arbitrary to us now; however, people with the undesirable traits were united in the public mind as deviants, as a population of defectives who deviated from the norm of the healthy racial body required for a healthy nation.

The U.S. eugenics movement achieved its greatest success in the 1927 U.S. Supreme Court case of *Buck v. Bell*. In this case, the Court upheld Virginia's law requiring sterilization of those deemed "socially inadequate" and living on government support. Eugenicists argued that Carrie Buck, a resident at the Virginia Colony for Epileptics and Feebleminded who had given birth after being raped at age 16, could only produce socially inadequate offspring and was therefore a threat to both the White race and the nation (Lombardo 2008). Writing for the majority, Justice Oliver Wendell Holmes Jr. declared: "It is better for all the world, if instead of waiting to execute degenerate offspring for crime, or to let them starve for their imbecility, society can prevent those who are manifestly unfit from continuing their kind. . . . Three generations of imbeciles are enough" (quoted in Lombardo 2008, 287).

By the mid-1930s, most states had adopted laws similar to Virginia's, and more than 60,000 U.S. citizens were forcibly sterilized (Lombardo 2008). The United States was not alone in its efforts to "improve" its population; numerous other nations followed the example set by the United States and Britain, most notably Germany. Eugenic research, much of it conducted by U.S. scientists, was the foundation of Adolf Hitler's "final solution"—the elimination of the following identified categories of people: Jews, homosexuals, Romani (Gypsies), the disabled, Jehovah's Witnesses, political prisoners, habitual criminals, the asocial, and emigrants (United States Holocaust Memorial Museum, n.d.). All of these efforts revolved around the desire to "perfect" the Aryan race.

Bettmann / Bettmann / Getty Images

Stephen Jay Gould (1981, 166) sharply criticizes the early 20th-century American practice of subjecting newly arrived immigrants to intelligence screenings: "Consider a group of frightened men and women who speak no English and who have just endured an oceanic voyage in steerage. Most are poor and have never gone to school; many have never held a pen or pencil in their hand. They march off the boat; one of Goddard's intuitive women takes them aside. . . . Could their failure be a result of testing conditions, of weakness, fear, or confusion, rather than of innate stupidity?"

Despite widespread condemnation of Nazi practices of eugenics, in which many German doctors were complicit, the United States continued to carry out forced sterilizations in the period after World War II, with the goal of limiting the birth of "mental defectives." California led the way, sterilizing 20,000 people by 1963 (Cohen and Bonifield 2012). California's law required that anyone deemed a "ward of the state" could not be released from state custody without undergoing sterilization. Some of the victimized included teenagers who had been removed from their families because they had been neglected or abused. Between 1929 and 1974, North Carolina sterilized of more than 7,600 people, including young rape and incest victims (like Buck) who were blamed for being "promiscuous" (Snyderman 2012).

Eugenics was inherently about the construction of Whiteness, and it provides us with a clear example of the need to understand race intersectionally. Those White people who were seen as unhealthy and impure—the poor, the disabled, the homosexual, the not-quite-White Jew—were targeted for segregation or elimination. It was women's bodies, not men's, that were most often targeted for sterilization. The hierarchies of class, sexuality, ability, religion, and so on privileged the White race as the superior race.

Inventing the Homosexual

The eugenic search for hereditary "defects" or abnormalities led to efforts to locate homosexuality as something inherent in certain bodies. The invention of the homosexual—the idea that there is a homosexual body and a homosexual person (as opposed to simply sexual acts and desires)—arose in late 19th-century medical discourse. Havelock Ellis's *Studies in the Psychology of Sex* was published in 1897 and became one of the founding texts of sexology. Sexologists employed many of the same methods that race scientists used to measure or locate the bodily sources of such "defects" (Blumenfeld 2012; Somerville 2000). This resulted in members of the medical professions committing lesbians, gay males, bisexuals, and those who transgressed so-called normative gender identities and expressions (often against their will or under tremendous pressure) to hospitals, mental institutions, jails, and penitentiaries. Many were subjected to prefrontal lobotomies, electroshock, castration, and sterilization (Blumenfeld 2012).

The pathologizing of LGBT people of every race has continued since that time, with dire public health consequences. When the HIV/AIDS epidemic began in the early 1980s, gay men were among the first cases, and AIDS became known as a "gay men's disease." The false assumption that the disease was a result of individual lifestyle choices led heterosexuals to believe they were safe, and doctors to limit their study of the disease to men's symptoms only. It was more than a decade before symptoms unique to women, like cervical cancer, were recognized. By then, untold numbers of women had been misdiagnosed and denied appropriate treatment (Weber 2006, 28).

So-called **conversion therapy**, treatment programs meant to change the sexual orientations of gays and lesbians, remains largely legal. Although such programs are not medically oriented and are not run by doctors, in addition to being widely discredited and often harmful, they have proliferated in some states. The basis for conversion therapy is the idea that homosexuality is a mental disorder that can be cured. Some states now ban conversion therapy for minors (see Figure 5.1).

Figure 5.1 ■ Seven States Currently Ban the Practice of Conversion Therapy for Minors

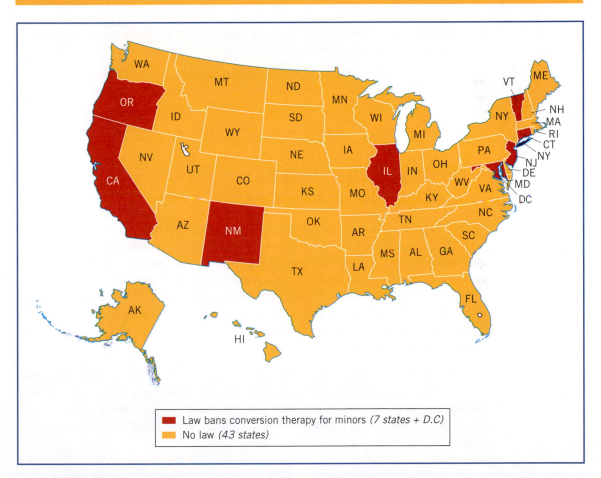

Law bans conversion therapy for minors *(7 states + D.C)*
No law *(43 states)*

Source: Movement Advancement Project, "Conversion Therapy Laws," http://www.lgbtmap.org/equality-maps/conversion_therapy#sthash .CPvnZdAr.dpuf.

Note: These laws prohibit licensed mental health practitioners from subjecting minors to harmful "conversion therapy" practices that attempt to change their sexual orientations or gender identities. This map reflects the states that prohibit conversion therapy. In 2015, Cincinnati, Ohio, passed the first city-level conversion therapy ban.

CRITICAL THINKING

1. Historically, how have the dynamics of gender, ability, and sexuality come into play in the service of White supremacy?

2. Can you think of specific innovations in contemporary medical technology that have the potential to bring the ideas of eugenics into public debate again? What safeguards might protect people from the misguided policies of the past?

3. Can you identify any characteristics you or any of your close friends or family members possess that were targeted for elimination by eugenicists?

4. Have you or anyone you know utilized traditional medicine or "alternative" medical practices? Why do you think some of these practices are more in vogue and acceptable today, after many years of being delegitimated in the United States?

■ THEORIZING INEQUALITY IN HEALTH AND HEALTH CARE

We have witnessed tremendous change in the American health care system in our lifetimes, especially within the past few years. Patients, practitioners, and government officials are still hotly debating what the system should look like, but in the meantime, the field of **medical sociology**, the sociological analysis of the field and practice of medicine and their social effects, has also changed. It is only in the past half century that medical sociology has come into its own as a significant field within the discipline of sociology, and sociology courses on health and illness have become more common.

Health and illness are not simply biological phenomena—they are also social phenomena. The sociology of health and health care challenges many of our basic assumptions about illness. In this section we will examine concealed and resistance stories that challenge the predominant stock stories about health and illness, such as these:

1. Race is a biological reality that can help explain disparities in health.

2. Health is a matter of individual and genetic factors.

3. Thanks to medical advances and the elimination or minimization of many infectious diseases, people today live longer than their predecessors in previous generations.

4. The field of medicine and health care employs objective science and operates independent of the social organization of society.

In our brief historical overview, we have seen the ubiquity of the first two stock stories, and the inequalities and White privilege they have justified. We now turn to the third and fourth stories above. These assumptions may seem like common sense on the surface, but many scientists and sociologists have been building a case against these arguments for quite some time.

Historical Advances in Health and Life Expectancy

People living in industrialized Western nations live much longer today than people in previous centuries. Over the course of the 19th and 20th centuries, average life expectancy has about doubled. Until about 100 years ago, most people died from infectious diseases, such as the flu and tuberculosis. Today the leading causes of death are chronic illnesses, such as cancer, heart disease, and diabetes. What accounts for this dramatic change? While advances in medicine played a significant role, social changes made the difference for many (Braveman and Gottlieb 2014; Conrad and Leiter 2012, McKeown 2014; Rasanathan and Sharkey 2016). Throughout the 1800s, advances in knowledge regarding hygiene and nutrition were much more important in the curtailing of infectious diseases than medical interventions such as immunizations (Aiello, Larson, and Sedlak 2008a, 2008b). Research on public health has documented the pivotal role of cleaner air and water, improved sewer and sanitation systems, and increased standards of living, including better nutrition and housing.

While overall life expectancy was increasing in the Western world, gains were not consistent across race and class groups, and disparities among groups have remained fairly steady. Education levels are one factor in these gaps. White men and women with a college education or higher have been found to have life expectancies at birth that are more than a decade longer than those for Black men and women with less than a high school

Fewer African Americans experience healthy aging and longevity than members of other groups.

degree. Between White and Black men with a college education or higher, the gap is approximately 5 years; when the Black men have fewer than 12 years of education, the gap is 16 years. Researchers are not hopeful about this gap narrowing in the coming years (Pollard and Scommegna 2013). German sociologist Friedrich Engels compared the life spans of the wealthy with the significantly shorter life spans of the working class, blaming social factors such as dangerous work environments and poor living conditions. In *The Philadelphia Negro,* first published in 1899, W. E. B. Du Bois examined African Americans' higher rates of disease and mortality compared with Whites. He also argued that social factors played a significant role in these disparities, blaming nonhygienic and poor living conditions and lack of protection from the elements (see Williams 2012, 283). Du Bois also identified racism itself as a variable:

> The most difficult social problem in the matter of Negro health . . . is the peculiar attitude of the nation toward the well-being of the race. There have . . . been few other cases in the history of civilized peoples where human suffering has been viewed with such peculiar indifference. (Du Bois 1899, 163, cited in Williams 2012, 287)

The Role of Objectivity in Medicine

Both conflict and functionalist schools of thought have contributed to the sociology of health and medicine. Conflict theorists argue that economic interests play the most significant role in determining health outcomes. Profit motives drive the definitions of disease, with pharmaceutical companies investing their research and development dollars in finding medications that will sell to large numbers of people, such as drugs for erectile dysfunction, rather than prioritizing their efforts based on public health needs. Economic interests also affect who is most likely to become ill, and the kind of health care they are likely to receive. Many researchers have argued that it is no coincidence that toxic waste dumps and other environmental hazards are most frequently located in or near poor communities, as we will examine later in this chapter. And because the U.S. health care system is driven by profits, the wealthy have better access to high-quality health care. Seen from this perspective, our medical system reinforces class inequality and serves as a form of social control.

Stock stories about health and health care ignore the role of institutional class and race inequity and unequal outcomes, and instead focus on the individual level and the biologized racial body. Sociologists have raised many critical questions about these assumptions and have highlighted the roles of a wide range of social factors.

CRITICAL THINKING

1. Other than those discussed above, what additional social and economic factors influence the U.S. health care system today? Compare and contrast our system with an alternative system in another developed nation.

2. What do you see as the most important institutional factors reproducing inequities and inequalities in medicine and health care today?

3. Select a social identity not examined in this chapter, such as disability, age, or gender identity, and research the health care inequalities that exist in relation to that identity. Identify at least three inequalities.

4. Sociologists shift our focus from the individual level to the social level. Which level do you see as more dominant among physicians today? Provide an example from your own experience.

■ APPLYING THE MATRIX TO HEALTH INEQUITY AND INEQUALITY

Health care as an institution is deeply enmeshed in other social institutions. For example, when a member of a family experiences health problems, other family members are affected, and specific social patterns can be observed. When you were a child and had to stay home from school because you were ill, who stayed home with you? For most children in the United States, the answer to that question would be the child's mother or another female family member (Lam 2014). Health and medicine are also intertwined with the world of work. If you have an aging relative who needs more care than the family can provide, that care is most likely provided by women of color. The low-paying jobs of nursing assistant, home health care worker, and hospice aide are some of those in which women of color are overrepresented (Glenn 2010). Just like all other social institutions, medicine and health care are imbued with hierarchies of race, gender, class, and other axes of inequality.

The matrix perspective, which draws upon the insights of earlier approaches, raises new questions and subjects for investigation:

1. *Race is inherently social.* We have explored some of the ways health and health care are actively involved in the social construction of race, as well as the social nature of health care and medicine as social institutions that reinforce inequities based on race, class, gender, sexuality, nationality, and ability.

2. *Race is a narrative.* Discourses of health and disease serve as important stories about bodies: what kinds of bodies exist, which bodies are defined as normal and which as defective, which bodies are valued and which are not. We examine the ways in which popular ideologies about bodies and health work to naturalize hierarchies of race, gender, class and sexuality, while at the same time constructing U.S. national identity.

3. *Racial identity is relational and intersectional.* We examine some of the many ways in which the construction of race is intertwined with the construction of gendered, classed, and sexualized bodies, and the provision of health care is shaped by the intersections of race, gender, class, sexuality, and ability.

4. *Race is institutional and structural.* This chapter emphasizes the importance of the institutions of health care and medicine as sources of racial constructs and the justification of racial inequality. Further, health and health care are key sites where racism is reproduced and experienced.

5. *We are active agents in the matrix.* We highlight racialized actors as active agents, not merely acted upon by social forces but also actively involved in resisting, challenging, and shaping those social forces themselves, within specific social, historical, economic, and geographical contexts.

An Intersectional Approach to Health and Health Care

Seeing our own health as a social issue may be difficult today, given our reality-show culture, which is filled with individual stories of success and failure. Television programs like *The Biggest Loser* and *The Dr. Oz Show* encourage us to think about a health problem such as obesity as an individual problem. The current discourse around obesity and fat frames the issue as simply one of individuals making poor choices. However, both class and race are correlated with weight. Sociologists argue that overall, social factors play a greater role in health outcomes than individual factors—something that is especially important to recognize when it comes to the issue of racial disparities in health. Seeing the causes of poor health as residing within the individual reinforces the notion that racial distinctions are real and have some genetic or biological reality, leading to disparate health outcomes (Daniels and Schulz 2006). In this manner, the institution of health care reproduces the stock narrative of race as biological and inequality as a product of poor choices.

Gender and Health Care

The provision of health care is an area in which we find many cases of both oppression and resistance that require an intersectional perspective. We have already seen evidence of this in our earlier examination of the rise of modern medicine. As a result of today's longer life spans, we now face the problem of providing care for an increasingly aging population, many members of which live with severe disabilities or chronic illness. In 2016, 44 million people in the United States were providing unpaid elder care, and just as child care has historically been defined as women's responsibility, the work of home health care has also fallen on the shoulders of women. This extended workload comes at a time when most women are employed outside the home. Women who can afford to do so often leave their jobs, cut back on their work hours, or move into less demanding jobs when they take on the task of providing care to elderly relatives, losing on average approximately $324,000 they would have made in the workplace (O'Donnell 2016). And it is more common for women of color, especially African American women, to manage jobs outside the home while simultaneously caring for disabled or aging family members. For many Asian American women, the strong ideology that commitment to family trumps individual choices, such as career, can lead to a sense of obligation to care for their elders, even if it means leaving their jobs and relocating to be near their families. Women in later generations of Asian immigrant families are much more likely to feel ambivalence about this, and to feel stuck between Eastern and Western ideologies (Glenn 2010; Weng and Robinson 2014).

Home health care workers, 87% of whom are women (Health Resources and Services Administration 2015), have been excluded from the protections and benefits guaranteed to other kinds of employees through legislation, such as a minimum wage and overtime pay. In 2015, the median wage among home health care workers was $11.00 per hour (U.S. Bureau of Labor Statistics 2017). Many have historically had no health insurance themselves, although that may have changed with the implementation of the Affordable Care Act, which made access to health care available to many previously without it (access that has now become uncertain under the Trump administration). The problems these women face will only grow, because they work in a field predicted to experience some of the fastest job growth in the coming decades.

Social inequities affect the provision of health care, and consequently have impacts on income as well. Shifting our attention to health itself, in the remaining subsections we examine a sampling of the many interconnected social factors and social identities, including ethnicity, age, gender, and immigration status, that influence group health patterns in the context of historical and structural inequities.

Class and Health

The most significant element in the relationship between groups and health outcomes is the linking factor of class. Those who live in poverty experience higher rates of illness, disease, and disability, but as individual wealth increases, health improves. People in the middle class may be thrust into poverty as a result of a chronic disease or disability because of tremendous health care expenses, inadequate health insurance, and/or inability to work. Further, growing up poor has lasting consequences. Despite an adult's current class status, growing up in poverty and facing the consequences of economic adversity early in life has negative impacts on health over the life span. For example, poor nutrition in childhood affects aspects of physical development, such as height, as well as cognitive development; childhood exposure to certain environmental dangers, such as high levels of lead, also affects cognitive development; and poverty in childhood has been associated with mental health disorders such as depression and anxiety, as well as decreased ability to control anger and general response inhibition (Capistrano, Bianco, and Kim 2016; Repka 2013; Strauss and Thomas 2007).

Specific health problems are highly correlated with class and income (Syme and Berkman 2009). Class-related variables such as education, occupation, income, and wealth have all been found to influence health. A lower class status not only leads to higher mortality rates but also produces higher morbidity rates, or incidence of illness. And these trends apply not just to identifiable illnesses; they are witnessed across the spectrum of health and wellness, including in rates of mental illness. Scholars have concluded that "those in the lower classes invariably have lower life expectancy and higher death rates from all causes of death, and that this higher rate has been observed since the 12th century when data on this question were first organized" (Syme and Berkman 2009, 24).

In nearly all the rest of the world's developed countries, socialized medicine and universal health care, often free, are the norm. Yet the United States spends far more on health care than any other nation, per person and as a share of gross domestic product (even since implementation of the Affordable Care Act), as illustrated in Figure 5.2.

The ACA (the future of which is in peril) was intended to improve health care access and cut costs while providing every U.S. citizen with health care coverage. Under the law, those whose incomes are below a certain level can receive subsidies to help pay their insurance premiums, and federal funding for Medicaid has been expanded to include the very poorest in the nation. The U.S. Supreme Court has ruled, however, that states can determine for themselves whether or not to expand Medicaid, and 26 states, many of them in the South, have declined to do so. These states are home to about half the country's population, "but about 68 percent of poor, uninsured blacks and single mothers. About 60 percent of the country's uninsured working poor are in those states" (Tavernise and Gebeloff 2013). While enabling access to high-quality care remains a priority, improving access does not fully eliminate health disparities (Syme and Berkman 2009).

Almost immediately after he took office, President Trump began prompting Congress to act on his campaign promise to repeal and replace the ACA. The proposed replacement, named the American Health Care Act when it was passed by the House of Representatives in May 2017, would allow states get waivers to set aside several provisions of the ACA, as long as the waivers would enable the states to (a) lower rates, (b) increase the number of insured, or (c) advance "the public interest of the state" (Amadeo 2017).

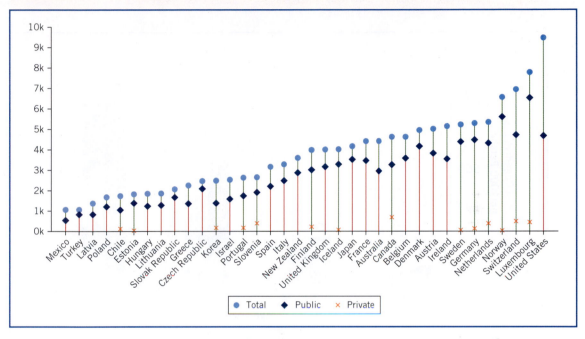

Source: Organisation for Economic Co-operation and Development, "OECD Data: Health Spending," https://data.oecd.org/healthres/health-spending.htm.

Race and Health

Because of the intersectional nature of social identities and relationships, where class dynamics are strong, we find that race is also part of the picture. The racial health gap actually increased in the 1980s as a consequence of the increasing racial income gap and widening racial inequality. While there is an overwhelming body of research documenting the impact of class on health and the interaction of class with race, the evidence also reveals that race itself is a significant factor, and sometimes a more significant factor, independent of class. For instance, depending on your race, you are more or less likely to have type 2 diabetes. Blacks, Hispanics, and Native Americans have a 50–100% higher risk than Whites of health problems and death caused by diabetes (Chow, Foster, Gonzalez, and McIver 2012). Whites experience the lowest levels of diabetes, while Native Americans face more than triple that rate. One out of three Native Americans is diabetic. Figures 5.3 and 5.4 provide a few examples of racial health disparities.

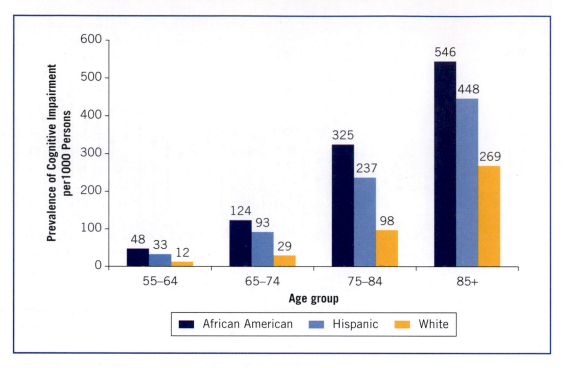

Source: Racial and Ethnic Disparities in Alzheimer's Disease: A Literature Review. February 2014. Office of the Assistant Secretary for Planning and Evaluation (ASPE), U.S. Department of Heath and Human Services.

Infants born prematurely are more likely to experience various health problems, ranging from mild to serious and chronic. Again, Whites are privileged to experience fewer preterm births, along with Asians and Pacific Islanders.

Overall, we find the greatest health inequities between Whites and African Americans and Native Americans. An "epidemiological paradox" explains the seemingly better health of Latino/as and Asian Americans. These two racialized groups are in fact heterogeneous, encompassing numerous diverse immigrant groups from different nations, with different resources, who immigrated at different points in history. When we collapse all Asians or all Latino/as into one large category, we lose sight of the differences within the group that influence health outcomes. For example, looking at infant mortality rates, Cuban Americans experience 4.7 deaths per 1,000

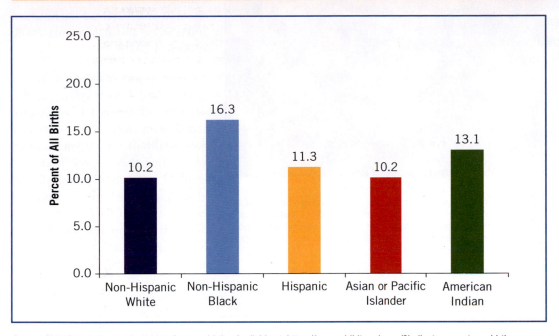

Source: Child Trends Databank. (2015). Preterm births. Available at: https://www.childtrends.org/?indicators=preterm-births

births, while the number for Puerto Ricans is 8.3. Combining these groups together under the label of Hispanics or Latino/as erases the inequities faced by specific ethnic subgroups (Zambrana and Dill 2006). Thus we see another of the problems inherent in relying on racial classifications.

Interestingly, the impact of immigration on health is different from what you might expect. All minority group immigrants experience significantly *better* health than their racial compatriots who are U.S.-born, including healthier birth weights, longer life expectancies, and lower rates of deadly diseases, including cancer and stroke (Ruiz, Hamann, Mehl, and O'Connor 2016; Waldstein 2010). Research has found, for example, that Mexican immigrants have much better health than U.S.-born Mexican Americans. One reason is that they experience stronger health in Mexico prior to coming to the United States. The longer they are in the United States, however, the more their health declines. Research comparing Caribbean Blacks with African Americans, and Asian immigrants with Asian Americans, has had similar findings, which also help us to understand why the health gap between Whites and others is smaller for racial groups with significant immigrant populations. These surprising findings force us to

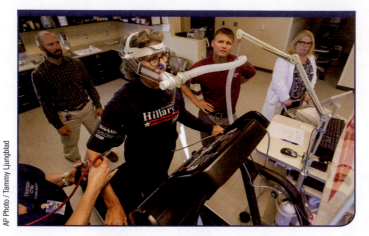

People of color are notably absent from clinical trials, in part because of this population's general mistrust of medical institutions. Other barriers to their participation in medical research include the language used in informational materials, which can be patronizing and incomplete, and the relative lack of researchers who are themselves people of color.

consider the role that simply living in the United States plays in undermining the health of people of color (De la Rosa 2002; Read and Emerson 2005; Stone and Balderrama 2008; Waldstein 2010).

Less access to and lower quality of health care can explain health inequities. Barriers to health care access are a factor in the relatively poor health of Native Americans, a group that has rarely been the focus of research on health disparities. A study examining rates of cancer among Native Americans found that, compared with Whites, Native Americans receive fewer health screenings, are diagnosed at later stages of a disease's progression, and have significantly higher cancer mortality rates. Despite the existence of early detection screening tests, Native Americans are 79% more likely than Whites to die from cervical cancer, 58% more likely to die from colorectal cancer, and 49% more likely to die from prostate cancer. Native Americans also report higher rates of dissatisfaction with the health care system (Guadagnolo et al. 2009).

African Americans face multiple barriers as well. Compared with Whites, they are less likely to have a regular location to seek health care, less likely to receive necessary medications, and more likely to experience delays in treatment. Factors like these, for example, mean that Blacks are 12% less likely than Whites to have their blood pressure under control, despite a 40% increased likelihood of having high blood pressure (National Institutes of Health 2015). Among the reasons for these kinds of outcomes are lack of access to health care, lower socioeconomic status, mistrust of providers and medical institutions, and limited health care literacy, as well as a lack of cultural competency and the continued prevalence of stereotypes among providers. Cumulatively, these factors lead to a shorter life span for African Americans compared to Whites.

Intersectional Complexity

Public health scholars Jackson and Williams (2006) have introduced the notion of an "intersectionality paradox" to describe seemingly contradictory research findings about the interactions of race, gender, and class. While very little research on health has utilized an intersectional approach, Warner and Brown (2011) have examined data showing that both African Americans and Hispanics generally suffer from higher levels of chronic disease and disability than do White people, and these researchers argue that gender also plays a role. They found that Black and Hispanic women have higher rates of chronic illness and disability than White women, and that there are greater disparities between men and women of color than between men and women who are White. In other words, the gender health gap is worse among people of color, and especially among African Americans.

Many studies also reveal that age is an interacting variable and that Black women experience the poorest health outcomes, which begin accelerating once they reach reproductive age. Warner and Brown (2011) have examined the ways in which race and gender intersect with age, looking at differences in ability/disability levels over the life course. They compared Whites, Blacks, and Mexican Americans and found that White men had the lowest disability levels, followed by White women and men of color, while Black and Hispanic women experienced the highest disability levels. They also found that these differing levels of disability increased at the same rate for each group, so the disparities remained constant over people's lifetimes. The only group for which this pattern did not hold was Black women, who experience a higher rate of disablement beginning in their reproductive years and continuing into their 60s.

Jackson and Williams (2006) also argue that to fully understand well-documented racial disparities, we must consider both class and gender. They examine the specific health inequities experienced by the Black middle class, including race-related stressors in the workplace, and find that Black middle-class men and Black middle-class women are both more vulnerable to specific sets of health problems. Recent research suggests that stress, which we examine next, is an important factor influencing health disparities.

Stress and Microaggressions

Émile Durkheim was the first sociologist to recognize the impact of stress on health (White 2009). Scholars now know that experiencing overt forms of discrimination has negative effects on both the mental and physical health of most minority group members (Sue 2010). Many studies have linked institutional racism and individual experiences of racism to poor health outcomes (Williams 2012; Sue 2010). Various studies of children and adolescents have found that youths of color report experiencing significant levels of racism, whether at school, engaged in online games and chat rooms, or elsewhere, that can be directly tied to negative mental health outcomes.

Racism and stress are key factors in explaining why some health inequities increase with age, producing a "cumulative disadvantage." Continued exposure to racism has negative impacts on the health of people of color, especially Blacks. Discrimination can lead to reduced access to desirable goods and services; **internalized racism,** or acceptance of society's negative characterization, can adversely affect health; racism can trigger increased exposure to traditional stressors (such as unemployment); and experiences of discrimination may constitute a neglected psychosocial stressor (Williams 2012, 284).

Similar research is being advanced in the field of psychology. First identified by Chester Pierce, founding president of the Black Psychiatrists of America, **micro-aggressions** "are brief verbal, non-verbal, and behavioral insults to a person or group, whether intentional or unintentional" (Hosokawa 2012, 21). They are a form of psychological stressor tied specifically to an individual's identity as a member of an oppressed group. The impact of microaggressions comes from their cumulative nature, and the way in which they evoke and serve as a reminder of a history of oppression. Imagine getting a paper cut. It stings for a moment and then you forget about it and move on. Now imagine getting a second paper cut, and then a third, and then a fourth—day after day, the paper cuts keep occurring. It is not long before you feel as if your whole body is cut and bleeding. That is how psychologists have described the experience of being exposed to repeated microaggressions. Those who experience a paper cut only occasionally may wonder why people of color make such a big deal of such little things, instead of brushing off a comedian's racist joke as "just kidding around," or dismissing someone's inadvertent racist comment by saying, "Hey, he made a mistake, what's the big deal?" As Sue (2010, 95) describes it: "Microaggressions are linked to a wider sociopolitical context of oppression and injustice (historical trauma) . . . [for] those who understand their own histories of discrimination and prejudice. Each small race-related slight, hurt, invalidation, insult, and indignity rubs salt into the wounds of marginalized groups in our society."

Phanie / Alamy Stock Photo

Constant exposure to microaggressions, for insance while working as a health aide in a nursing home, causes harm and creates health risks in every non-White group.

Research finds that every non-White racial group experiences harm and health risks as a result of microaggressions. As with the body's reaction to more overt stressors, the ongoing experience of microaggressions can lead to physiological responses that weaken the immune system, leaving people more vulnerable to illness and disease, including diabetes, high blood pressure, heart disease, and chronic respiratory problems (Sue 2010). The body's reaction to stress also facilitates the progression of such diseases. In a 2013 study, David H. Chae found that racial discrimination and anti-Black bias may accelerate the aging process in African American males (see Blake 2014). In addition to these physical consequences, exposure to microaggressions can threaten mental health functioning.

Those who are most affected by the stress of racism, sexism, and poverty are also least likely to have access to useful coping skills. Education, well-paying jobs, and access to health care and social services that help shore up our sense of worth and resilience are not evenly distributed in U.S. society (White 2009, 72). Women often bear the burden of supporting those who deal with stress (White 2009, 72) while at the same time taking over a greater share in caring for our aging population (Glenn 2010).

Researchers using complex statistical analyses have estimated the numbers of deaths each year due to specific social factors. They conclude that "245,000 deaths in the United States were attributable to low education, 176,000 to racial segregation, 162,000 to low social support, 133,000 to individual-level poverty, 119,000 to income inequality, and 39,000 to area-level poverty" (Galea, Tracy, Hoggatt, DiMaggio, and Karpati 2011, 1462). Yet no single factor explains all health inequities. Thinking about the visual image of how each individual is situated within the matrix, we have seen that within the institution of health care, a wide range of social identities and social factors, all of which are context specific (shaped by history and place), play important roles. But despite widespread understanding that social factors are some of the most significant influences on health, some scholars continue to seek answers in our biology.

A Legacy of Mistrust

One of the important concealed narratives that sociologists have identified is that medical theories determine the questions for study, framing them as scientific "problems" to be solved and guiding the possible answers, thus limiting what is even imaginable. This process has consequences. People defined as suffering from specific maladies can become subject to various medical, political, and legal forms of social control. Consider the case of **drapetomania**, a "mental illness" invented to explain why slaves tried to escape slavery.

Described by Samuel Cartwright in his book *Diseases and Peculiarities of the Negro Race* (1851), this disease could exist only in the context of a White supremacist society that sees slavery as the natural role for human beings defined as inferior. Slavery's stock story posited that slaves were happy to be slaves and were in their natural place according to God's plan. However, if they were happy and content as slaves, and slavery was God's will, what could explain the many cases of runaways? Drapetomania was the answer, and it also provided a cure—the amputation of the big toes. This remedy was successful because it physically prevented the slave from running away again. The case of drapetomania "was both a product of that society and helped to reinforce the power relations of that society" (White 2009, 43).

Mistrust of medicine is frequently a barrier for people of color. As one man put it, "I think that most of the people who are in control of research don't look like me, and I don't have confidence in how they perceive my value and my worth. I would be very reluctant to give anybody a blank check with respect to experimenting with my body and my life, my health" (quoted in Freimuth et al. 2001, 806). Given the history of medical experimentation, such mistrust is certainly understandable.

Perhaps the best-known medical experiment on a U.S. minority group is the Tuskegee Study of Untreated Syphilis in the Negro Male. This study, conducted from 1932 to 1972, is still the longest-running nontherapeutic medical study in U.S. history. Nearly 400 African American men with syphilis were recruited as subjects in Macon County, Alabama, by the U.S. Public Health Service, in collaboration with Tuskegee University, a historically Black institution. The men in the experimental group were never informed that they had syphilis, even as the study followed the natural progression of the disease and the study's doctors withheld treatment options such as penicillin, which became the standard of care for syphilis during the study period. It is estimated that between 28 and 100 of the 400 infected men died as a result of their untreated syphilis.

The narrative of this study (which was finally ended after a whistle-blower went to the press) helps explain why many Black people harbor fears and mistrust when it comes to the medical research establishment (Alsan and Wanamaker 2016; Boulware, Cooper, Ratner, LaVeist, and Powe 2003; Brenick, Romano, Kegler, and Eaton 2017; Thomas and Quinn 1991), Researchers argue that this history, combined with the cultural meanings of disease, has created a climate in which fears undermine public health efforts, such as those targeting AIDS in the African American community and many others (Thomas and Quinn 1991). Alsan and Wanamaker (2016) found that public news of the Tuskegee study in 1972 was directly correlated with a decline in Black men's trust of the medical establishment and visits to physicians, and with an increase in morbidity rates. Most significant, the researchers found a 1.4-year decrease in life expectancy among Black men over 45 years old.

The Role of Place and Environmental Racism

Where we live also affects our health, and segregated housing is a significant factor in health inequality. In 1899, W. E. B. Du Bois observed that poor people of color and poor Whites faced different living conditions that had impacts on their health. High levels of residential racial segregation persist in the United States, and people of color are more likely than Whites to be segregated in neighborhoods that are isolated from key social services and have poor living conditions, including environmental threats to health (Schulz et al. 2016). Poor Whites are more likely than poor people of color to live in economically diverse neighborhoods, with greater access to resources. As Williams (2012, 284) has reported, "In 100 of America's largest metropolitan areas, 75 percent of all African American children and 69 percent of all Latino children are growing up in more negative residential environments than are the worst-off white children." Neighborhood racial segregation also raises the risk of low birth weight beyond what would be expected from only economic differences (Debbink and Bader 2011; Gray, Edwards, Schultz, and Miranda 2014).

Environmental Risks

Race and class are both linked to exposure to environmental health risks. Hazardous waste dumps, landfills, incinerators, and other toxic sites are much more likely to be located in poor and minority neighborhoods than in wealthier, Whiter ones. People residing in neighborhoods that are primarily minority and lower-class are also exposed to higher levels of pollution, asbestos, and lead, and any playgrounds in these neighborhoods are usually older and unsafe (Massey 2004). A large body of research documents these realities and their impacts. For example, people of color and low-income Whites are significantly more likely to suffer from asthma, a difference that begins early in childhood. Research in California found that Whites are half as likely as people of color to live in areas where they face high cancer risks due to toxins in the air. Children of color face greater levels of pollution and lead poisoning at their schools, during a key period of development. Exposure to high levels of pollution contributes to lower academic performance, and lead poisoning produces permanent behavioral and neurological changes, including decreased IQ, as well as organ damage and even death (Agency for Toxic Substances and Disease Registry 2000).

Epidemiology

Social epidemiologists and sociologists are helping us to understand how race, class, and health are linked. Employing an "ecological perspective in health research" also adds to our understanding of these complex phenomena (McLaren and Hawe 2005). Public health specialists are currently showing a growing interest in this approach. *Ecological* is defined broadly here to include the entire context: all of the levels depicted in the matrix visual—history, place (both local and global), identity, the individual, and

Minority and poor neighborhoods are more likely to be near sources of exposure to toxins and environmental pollutants. Minority children are more likely to suffer from asthma and lead exposure as a result.

Chip Chipman/Bloomberg/Getty Images

so on (McLaren and Hawe 2005). These various theoretical perspectives acknowledge the importance of social structures and organizations, and culture and narratives of inequality, which all contribute to health disparities.

Epidemiology is the study of "the distribution of health issues (diseases or injuries) and health determinants in a population" (Conrad and Leiter 2012, 24). Epidemiologists focus on populations, rather than on individuals, to explain why some groups may be more likely to develop specific diseases; they look at factors such as the characteristics of the social groups themselves, the areas in which they live, and the environmental elements to which they are exposed.

The Human Genome Project

Today, research on race and genetics is progressing at a faster rate than ever before. In 1990, the internationally funded **Human Genome Project** (HGP) set out to map and sequence the entire spectrum of human genes. Recalling Davenport's attempt to create a comprehensive catalog of every human trait, sociologist Troy Duster (2003) refers to these contemporary efforts as a "backdoor to eugenics."

The HGP, which was completed in 2003, sparked renewed debate over the use of race in medicine and science. While geneticists acknowledge that race has no genetic basis, there is disagreement about the usefulness of race as a system of categories for sorting human differences. Some geneticists and biomedical researchers argue that our taken-for-granted racial classifications can be used as a means of dividing people into groups based on shared ancestry (Ossorio and Duster 2005, 117). However, scientists have discovered that approximately 85% of human genetic variation occurs *within* so-called races—far more than can be found between any racialized groups. People categorized as belonging to the same race may have very little in common genetically or biologically (Ossorio and Duster 2005, 117).

This view of genetic variation would seem to make racial categorizations useless. However, there are other interests at stake. One purpose of the HGP was to identify genetic markers for susceptibility to specific genetic disorders, so that gene therapies could be developed to prevent, treat, or cure them. According to the U.S. government's Human Genome Project website, "An important feature of the HGP project was the federal government's long-standing dedication to the transfer of technology to the private sector. By licensing technologies to private companies and awarding grants for innovative research, the project catalyzed the multibillion-dollar U.S. biotechnology industry and fostered the development of new medical applications." The website boasts that as a result of the HGP, many wide-ranging industries are booming, and "new entrepreneurs" are popping up to "offer an abundance of genomic services and applications" (Human Genome Project Information Archive 2013).

We have seen the growth of companies offering to provide us with information about our ancestors; the birth of the first racially targeted medicine, BiDil, a heart disease drug marketed to African Americans; and new methods of screening for birth "defects" and genetic diseases. While some of these advances may be welcome, they also carry unexamined assumptions from our eugenic past. For example, disability activists warn that screening for birth "defects" once again defines disabled bodies as "unfit" and as potential targets for elimination (Saxton 2010).

These developments also target individual consumers. The individualization of health and medicine directs our attention away from the larger issue of racial inequities in health and the factors that produce those inequities, supporting the stock story that locates inferiority in the bodies of people of color (Daniels and Schulz 2006; Hubbard and Wald 1999). Scholar Emily Martin (2006, 86) addresses the ethical dilemma raised by this approach in her critique of drugs tailored to specific racial groups. She asks, "Will making more and better medicines available to African Americans who suffer more stress due to poverty and racism provide something we want to call a solution, let alone a cure?"

Sociologists Ossorio and Duster (2005, 116) offer a way out of the trap of seeing race as either useful or not. They suggest an alternative perspective, informed by a sociological lens:

> Race and racial categories can best be understood as a set of social processes that can create biological consequences; race is a set of social processes with biological feedbacks that require empirical investigation. Researchers ought to be discussing when and how best to use race as a variable rather than arguing about the categorical exclusion or inclusion of race in science. Researchers ought to interrogate the meaning of observed racial differences. In doing so, they must recognize that race may be a consequence of differential treatment and experiences rather than an independent cause of differential outcomes.

One of the foundational arguments of a sociological perspective on health and medicine is that scientific knowledge is an inherently social enterprise (White 2009, 14). The scientific-medical eugenics discourse was the product of a specific social and historical context, and reflected the values of the dominant members of society. While some scholars refer to eugenics as pseudoscience, we have chosen not to do so, but to instead emphasize the fact that *all* scientific and medical knowledge is social. Eugenics is not a unique example of how medicine can be penetrated by social prejudices. Instead, medicine is always a social practice. It is carried out by social beings in specific social and cultural contexts.

■ RESISTING AND TRANSFORMING INEQUALITY IN HEALTH AND HEALTH CARE

The title of Sandra Morgen's 2002 book about the women's health movement, *Into Our Own Hands*, is an apt description of the steps taken by every community of color in the United States. In response to a long history of systemic racist violence, abuse, and neglect, we find remarkable numbers of individuals and communities facing these challenges head-on and working to meet their own health needs while simultaneously battling racist institutions and organizations. We have already seen one example in the history of the National Medical Association. Below we examine a few more.

Urban American Indian Health Care

Overall, people of color are more likely than their White counterparts to receive low-quality health care. Native Americans, however, face some unique circumstances. More than 560 tribes are currently recognized by the U.S. government and entitled to specific health care benefits. However, to receive those benefits, an individual must also be legally recognized, through a bureaucratic process, as a member of one of those tribes. Health care services provided by the Indian Health Service (IHS), a division of the U.S. Department of Health and Human Services established in 1955, are reserved for members of recognized tribes, generally provided on reservations, and concentrated in areas with the largest Indian populations. This means that some tribes benefit more than others (Fixico 2000). Where available, however, IHS-provided health care is free and likely to be culturally responsive and respectful of indigenous traditions. Despite some successes, however, the health disparities between Native Americans and Whites remain wide (Indian Health Service 2017).

About 70% of American Indians and Alaska Natives have moved away from reservations to urban areas, where obtaining health care is more difficult and expensive, and the care available is less culturally sensitive. According to the Urban Indian Health Commission (2007, 1), "Today's urban Indians are mostly the product of failed federal government policies that facilitated the urbanization of Indians, and the lack of sufficient aid to assure success with this transition has placed them at greater health risk." One example of this increased risk is the suicide rate among urban American Indian youth, which is 62% higher than the national average. In addition to the factors noted above, urban American Indians have few informal and formal community support networks to turn to for support, and they are unlikely to find traditional or even American Indian health care providers (Burrage, Gone, and Momper 2016; Filippi et al. 2016).

Comparatively little information is available on the specific health risks and needs facing American Indians and Alaska Natives, and even less is known about the health risks and needs of urban Native Americans. What research does exist provides evidence that Native Americans face disproportionate levels of depression and other mental health issues, type 2 diabetes, and poor cardiovascular health. Many also experience symptoms of, and are more likely to die from, these diseases at earlier ages. For example, compared to the U.S. population as a whole, Native Americans are more than three times as likely to die from diabetes-related strokes. The infant mortality rate for Native Americans is 33% higher than that for Whites, and their rate of deaths related to alcohol is 178% higher. Further, the majority of the non-elderly Native American population has been classified as either poor or near-poor, and while 25% qualify for Medicaid, only 17% report they are receiving benefits (Urban Indian Health Commission 2007).

In response to these circumstances, Native Americans have founded many urban health organizations to provide prevention and treatment services in culturally appropriate and respectful ways. These organizations have also been making efforts to improve data collection and research on this community, although limited funding has curtailed this work, which has yet to achieve its full potential. While these organizations can produce some measure of improvement at the individual and local levels, they argue that the Native American community faces issues that cannot be remedied without broader structural changes that address federal policy, including but not limited to the provision of health services, as well as socioeconomic factors. The history of extermination, segregation, broken promises, and recent patterns of government neglect will not be remedied by individual-level responses.

Race, Reproduction, and the Women's Health Movement

The first wave of the women's movement, besides fighting for suffrage in the early 20th century, also focused on access to birth control. At the time, any public discussion of contraception was against the law, which limited information access to well-off women who could consult with private doctors. Margaret Sanger, one of the leaders of the birth control movement, was arrested for promoting contraception through the U.S. mail. Again arrested and jailed for opening the first birth control clinic in 1916, she founded the American Birth Control League, which later became Planned Parenthood. Keenly aware of the barriers faced by immigrant women, Sanger used the racism and eugenics ideology of the time to argue that birth control would benefit White society by limiting the numbers of children born to immigrant families from Southern and Eastern Europe (DuBois and Dumenil 2012). Immigrant women would beg Sanger, who worked as a nurse, for information on how to prevent pregnancy, and she witnessed firsthand the poor health and needless deaths of many married women due to too many pregnancies.

Because of the racist inflection of the debate over birth control, and its connections with the eugenics movement, Black women sought to educate themselves about birth control and reproductive health, beginning with the women's clubs affiliated with the National Association of Colored Women. For Black women, as for many other marginalized women, the issue of reproductive rights included not only the right to use contraception but also the rights to choose to have children and to be free of nonconsensual sterilization.

Women's educational and occupational opportunities are limited if they have no control over their reproduction. Further, their economic dependence on men is reinforced and solidified when they have large numbers of children to care for. Growing directly out of the second wave of the women's rights movement, the women's health movement in the late 1960s and early 1970s particularly focused on increasing women's control over their reproductive and sexual health. Early on, women of color like Byllye Avery became "acutely aware of how little information existed about Black women's health and of how the movement [they were] part of defined issues, strategies, and services with little attention or awareness of the specific needs and perspectives of women of color" (Morgen 2002, 41). The mainstream women's movement's narrow focus on abortion and choice needed to be expanded to encompass the fuller range of women's reproductive needs and rights.

Avery, a board member of the National Women's Health Network, worked with others to form self-help groups for Black women, and initiated the NWHN's National Black Women's Health Project (NBWHP), which became its own organization in 1984. The NBWHP situated Black women's health within the larger context of not only sexism but also racism and class inequality, and broadened its focus from the "pro-choice" platform to one of **reproductive justice**, defined as "the right to have children, not have children, and to parent the children we have in safe and healthy environments. Reproductive justice addresses the social reality of inequality, specifically, the inequality of opportunities that we have to control our reproductive destiny" (SisterSong 2013). For example, when the NBWHP started the Center for Black Women's Wellness in Atlanta, alongside the many medical

RESISTANCE / STORY

Loretta Ross—Not Just Choice but Reproductive Justice

I was born in 1953 in Temple, Texas, the sixth of eight children in a churchgoing family. I was raped by a soldier at the age of 11 and then again by my mother's adult cousin. At age 16, I had an abortion. My mother would not consent to my obtaining birth control, although I was already a teen mother and attending my first year of college thousands of miles away from home. I was lucky—abortion had been legalized in Washington, D.C., in 1970, the year I desperately needed one, so I avoided the back alley. I had a safe and legal abortion, although my older sister had to forge my mother's signature on the consent form. I do not, in any way, regret my decision. What happened to me—rape, incest, parental blocking—should not happen to any other girl, and I'm proud to be a feminist fighting for all women's human rights. African American women have made consistent and critical activist contributions to the evolution of the reproductive rights movement in the United States, expanding the movement to highlight other aspects of our struggle to achieve reproductive freedom based on our experiences of pregnancy, infant mortality, sterilization abuse, welfare abuse, and sexuality in general.

I began my work as a reproductive justice activist in the early 1970s, focusing on sterilization abuse. I have witnessed the development of a strong reproductive freedom movement among Black women during this period. In doing research to support my activism, I discovered a long tradition of reproductive rights advocacy by Black women that was either undocumented or not widely understood. I became determined to reconnect the work of Black activists at the beginning of the 20th century to the work and ideology of those at the century's end.

I have spent 38 years launching and managing nonprofit feminist organizations, including SisterSong Women of Color Reproductive Justice Collective. The Collective was formed in 1997 to fulfill a need for a national movement by women of color to organize our voices to represent ourselves and our communities. SisterSong comprises 80 local, regional, and national grassroots organizations. SisterSong educates women of color on reproductive and sexual health and rights, and works toward improving access to health services, information, and resources that are culturally and linguistically appropriate through the integration of the disciplines of community organizing, self-help, and human rights education. The mission of SisterSong is to amplify and strengthen the collective voices of indigenous women and women of color to ensure reproductive justice through securing human rights.

Joining the women's movement not only transformed my life but also saved it. On my journey, I've learned about women's human rights, reproductive justice, White supremacy, and women of color organizing.

services the center provided, "vocational and educational training" were also offered (Morgen 2002, 49).

The conferences, workshops, and other activities of the NBWHP nurtured other new grassroots organizations in the 1980s, including the National Latina Health Organization, the Native American Women's Health Education Resource Center, and the National Asian Women's Health Organization. Each of these organizations maintains an emphasis on the diversity of women's needs within these communities, while at the same time addressing some of the specific challenges each constituent group faces.

Today, a vibrant movement is fighting for reproductive justice. Women with disabilities have embraced and advanced the reproductive justice framework based on their own history of sterilization, the treatment of people with disabilities as nonsexual beings, the risks posed by genetic testing that attempts to eliminate the disabled, and more. A reproductive justice approach moves disability rights activism from a focus on individual rights to a framework that examines access to services and support that can allow society to acknowledge the inherent value and worth of human beings with disabilities (Jesudason and Epstein 2011). While *Roe v. Wade* (1972) declared women's right to control their reproductive systems, restrictions limiting this right have proliferated. As of April 2016, 43 states had laws restricting access to abortion (https://www.guttmacher.org/). In 87% of U.S. counties, women have no access to an abortion provider.

The efforts of international nongovernmental organizations supporting women's health have also increased over the past few decades, while U.S. aid has declined. While reproductive health inequities reflect existing social and economic inequities, they also reinforce them. International family planning programs are one key component of improving women's lives around the world (Sedgh, Hussain, Bankole, and Singh 2007, 5). In developing nations, researchers have found that more than one in seven married women needs or wants contraception, but is not using any. The same is true for one in thirteen women ages 15 to 29 who have never married. The most common reason these women are not using contraception is a lack of access to "supplies and services," including counseling and education about contraceptive options (Sedgh et al. 2007, 5). Around the world, women are working together locally to improve women's health. In order to improve health and health care access among oppressed populations, those directly affected must be a part of the process of finding solutions.

A Path to the Future

One of the most important lessons we can learn from the many health care movements run by and for marginalized women is that strategies that narrowly target access and individual behavior are not enough. Health inequities are a social problem that requires much broader social change.

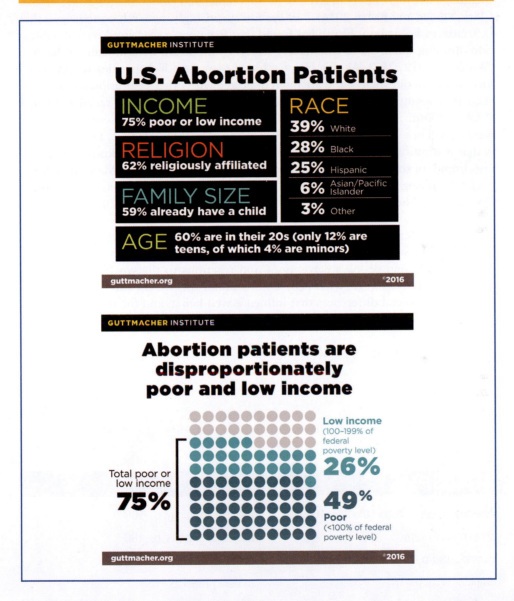

Sources: "U.S. Abortion Patients" May 9, 2016, Guttmacher Institute, https://www.guttmacher.org/infographic/2016/us-abortion-patients.

"Abortion patients are disproportionately poor and low income," May 9, 2016, Guttmacher Institute, https://www.guttmacher.org/infographic/2016/abortion-patients-are-disproportionately-poor-and-low-income.

Evidence suggests that policies targeting inequality at a broader level can reduce the health gap. For example, in the United States, states with higher levels of social spending have higher overall levels of health (Gallet and Doucouliagos 2017; Verma, Clark, Leider, and Bishai 2016). Perhaps not surprisingly, research on the views that U.S. citizens hold about health has found that few people see "employment, education, housing quality, and community safety as important determinants of health" (Williams 2012, 287). As this chapter has shown, health disparities reflect social inequalities in our society and are interconnected with other institutional structures, such as economy, education, the law, and a culture that reproduces racial inequality (Weber 2006). Simplistic individual-level responses, like telling someone to lose weight, will not solve the deep-rooted problems of health inequities. The good news is that institutions of medicine are taking a crucial first step in acknowledging the importance of social factors. In 2015, the Association of American Medical Colleges began requiring students taking the MCAT entrance exam to have background knowledge in the social sciences. As the association announced in 2012:

> A new section, "Psychological, Social, and Biological Foundations of Behavior," will test the ways in which these areas influence a variety of factors, including people's perceptions and reactions to the world; behavior and behavior change; what people think about themselves and others; cultural and social differences that influence well-being; and the relationships among socio-economic factors, access to resources, and well-being.

A truly interdisciplinary approach is essential to a real commitment to decreasing health inequities.

KEY TERMS

5

CHAPTER SUMMARY

LO 5.1   **Describe contemporary inequality in health and health care.**

Today's disparities among racial and ethnic groups in health and mortality are evidence of the historical and ongoing effects of structural racism. Racial disparities exist in health care access, disease prevention, identification of disease, treatment, care coordination, outcomes, patient satisfaction, and more. Today's health disparities have been significantly shaped by historical patterns of White privilege and White supremacy. Modern medicine displaced traditional methods of healing in many cultures, and played a central role in the construction of racial classifications and corresponding notions of difference. History is replete with examples of resistance to health inequities. African Americans developed their own health care systems in response to their exclusion from segregated institutions.

LO 5.2   **Examine various stock narratives of inequality in health and medicine.**

Our stock stories lead us to assume that medical advances are responsible for today's longer life spans; that the field of medicine and health care employs objective science; that race is a biological reality that can help explain disparities in health; and that health is strictly a matter of individual and genetic factors. Research, however, reveals the important roles of social factors such as hygiene and nutrition, as well as race and class.

LO 5.3   **Apply the matrix lens to the link between race and health care.**

The matrix perspective highlights various social factors contributing to racial health inequity and inequality, including stress, social relationships, socioeconomic factors, residential segregation, environmental factors, and mistrust, as well as the interactions of race, class, gender, age, and more. The field of social epidemiology highlights the relationships among race, class, and health, and explains the "epidemiological paradox" of better *overall* health among Asians and Latinos, racial groups with significant numbers of immigrants.

LO 5.4   **Explore alternatives to the current matrix of inequality in health and medicine.**

Disenfranchised groups have created many organizations to address and act as advocates for their health needs. Urban Indian health organizations and a wide array of health organizations founded by women of color place these groups' health needs within the broader context of social and institutional factors shaped by a history of racism. These organizations argue that health disparities cannot be remedied without broader structural changes. Organizations started and run by women of color and disabled women have fought for a more inclusive understanding of women's reproductive health needs.

EDUCATION

The Washington Post / The Washington Post / Getty Images

Despite the myth of education as the great equalizer, educational opportunities are not the same for all children across the United States.

CHAPTER OUTLINE

LEARNING OBJECTIVES

LO 6.1   Describe the current state of education in the United States and the key historical factors that have shaped it.

LO 6.2   Compare the major sociological theories of education.

LO 6.3   Analyze several matrix perspectives on education.

LO 6.4   Identify alternatives to the educational system that recognize intersectional realities.

The nation's only Catholic Black college, New Orleans's Xavier University, charges less than $20,000 a year for tuition and sends more Black students on to medical schools than any other educational institution in the United States. When Pierre Johnson arrived at Xavier several years ago to work toward fulfilling his lifelong ambition of becoming a doctor, he realized how inadequately he had been prepared at the all-Black Chicago high school he attended. Although he had been an outstanding student, his school had not even offered basic science courses like physics. As Johnson later told a *New York Times* reporter, "I wanted to be a doctor, but I did not even know what the periodic table was." With the intensive help and support of the faculty and his fellow Xavier students, Johnson earned admission to medical school at the University of Illinois, where he was the only Black student in his class. He is now a successful gynecologist in Illinois. Without Xavier, he says, "I wouldn't have made it" (quoted in Hannah-Jones 2015).

Johnson's shock at finding himself unprepared for college contradicts the primary stock story of the institution of education in the United States—that education serves as the great equalizer, that schooling can level the playing field for life opportunities and life chances, regardless of race, gender, or social and economic status. As Xavier's former president, Norman Francis, has stated, "Research shows if you are black and born poor, you are going to live in a poor neighborhood, going to go to a poor school, and by and large, you are going to stay that way. To come out of that system, you would have to rise much higher than other youngsters who had every resource" (quoted in Hannah-Jones 2015).

This story is part of a larger story—that educational opportunities are not the same for all. In this chapter, we examine how educational segregation is woven into the fabric of the United States, how different educations are creating different identities, and the important role of the matrix of race in this reality. The bottom line is this: Johnson was not "supposed" to be a doctor. Consider that in 1933, historian Carter G. Woodson argued that Black Americans were being indoctrinated and "taught their place" through the curricula in U.S. schools (Woodson [1933] 2016). In 1955, novelist and anthropologist Zora Neale Hurston criticized the Supreme Court's *Brown v. Board of Education* decision to desegregate schools, saying there were already adequate and important Black schools that more effectively served Black communities than any White school ever could (Hurston 1955).

Both claims are still debated, as the matrix of race still matters in the institution of education and vice versa. The institution of education in the United States has been shaped by decisions, definitions, and declarations about differences. In this chapter we will explore the history of U.S. public education and its expressed and concealed functions, and we will reflect on who gets an education and why. We begin with a look at who is getting an education today, and what "being educated" means.

■ THE SHAPING OF THE MATRIX OF U.S. EDUCATION

What does it mean to be educated? If you accept the arguments of C. Wright Mills (1956), you might conclude that education functions to maintain the social hierarchy by creating workers, who then sustain the wealth of the elite. A successful professional might tell you that education is a socialization process fundamentally about skills acquisition. The framers of U.S. democracy, such as Thomas Paine and Benjamin Franklin, believed that the purpose of education is to foster the critical thinking necessary for citizens in a free society. And middle-class parents paying a child's way through college might say that education is a way to move up the socio-economic ladder. Nathan Hare, who started the first Black studies program at San Francisco State University in 1969, sees the purpose of education as bringing about change, noting, "[If] education is not revolutionary in the current day [then it] is both irrelevant and useless" (quoted in Karenga 2002, 16–17). What does this mean? Who decides what is useful and relevant to learn? And for whom?

The institution of education is both vital and complex. While some see education as a solution for inequalities of all sorts, others see the education system as rife with inequalities—especially for those who are not White or affluent. The most recently available data (from the 2013–14 school year) show that nationally, 82% of all 9th-grade public school students graduated high school after 4 years, with Asian American (89%) and White (87%) students graduating at higher rates, and Latino (76%), Black (73%), and Native American (70%) students graduating at much lower rates (National Center for Education Statistics [NCES] 2016b). Graduation rates also vary widely from state to state. Clearly, education does not work equally for all.

Education Today

A study by researchers at Georgetown University found that while a college degree still provides a material boost to lifetime earnings, 10 years after graduation the alumni of elite institutions are outearning their peers from other colleges and universities, often by a significant amount, and male college graduates still earn much more per year than female graduates almost across the board (Carnevale, Rose, and Cheah 2011). Rising tuition costs and a weak job market have contributed to these inequalities, but as we will discuss in more detail below, they did not create them. The government plans to continue monitoring 10-year earnings data on its new College Scorecard website (Carey 2015).

Who Goes to School?

Many children in the United States begin their structured experience of education soon after birth, in institutionalized and organized child care. In 2010, there were about 20 million children under the age of 5 in the United States.

- Of these 20 million, 43.2% attended organized day-care or preschool facilities, and the remainder were under the care of parents, grandparents, siblings, or other relatives.

- Black and Latino children were a little less than half as likely as White and Asian children to attend preschool.

- Mothers with only high school educations were five times less likely to enroll their children in preschool than were mothers with college degrees (U.S. Census Bureau 2011).

In 2013–14 there were more than 104,000 elementary schools in the United States (some of which were combined elementary and secondary schools). Almost three-fourths (70.3%) of these were public schools, while the rest were private (including religious schools) (20.7%). Public elementary schools enroll slightly more than 35 million students, taught by some 2.2 million teachers. That makes the average student–teacher ratio 16.1 to 1 (NCES 2016b). Secondary schools (hosting different combinations of grades 7 through 12) number more than 41,000 in the United States. The vast majority of these are also public schools (73.1%). In public secondary schooling, 15 million students are taught by more than 1.2 million teachers—an average student–teacher ratio of 16.2 to 1 (NCES 2016b). From 2008 to 2013, public school enrollment increased by about 2%, while enrollment in private and religious schools declined over the same period. However, the public school enrollment of certain groups increased much more (Latinos, 18%; Asian Americans, 6%), while that of others decreased over this period (7% decrease for both Whites and Blacks; 11% decrease for Native Americans). By 2024, projections indicate a continued increase mirroring what was seen in the 2008–13 period, largely due to immigration from Asia (first) and Central and Latin America (second) (NCES 2016a) (see Figure 6.1).

Figure 6.1 ■ Racial and Ethnic Distributions of Public School Students Will Continue to Shift

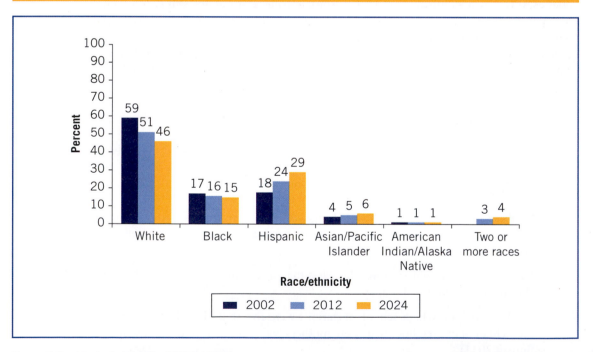

Source: National Center for Education Statistics (2016).

In the same school year (2013–14), 19.5 million students, ages 18 to 24, were enrolled in 7,253 Title IV institutions of postsecondary education (i.e., colleges and universities) (NCES 2016b). The majority of these students (59.3%) were White, while Blacks (14.7%), Latinos (15.8%), Asian Americans (6.4%), and Native Americans (0.8%) made up the rest. Compare this to a decade earlier, when Whites made up 69.1%, Blacks 12.7%, Latinos 10.5%, Asian Americans 6.6%, and Native Americans 1.1%. Hussar and Bailey (2016) have projected college enrollments a decade forward, to 2024, and they estimate that the proportion of Whites will decrease to 56%, that of Blacks will increase to 16.7%, and that of Latinos will increase to 17.5%, while the proportions of Asian Americans and Native Americans will remain largely the same. Indeed, a recent Pew study found that in 2012, Latinos' higher education enrollment rates surpassed those of Whites for the first time (49% of all 18- to 24-year-olds, compared to 47%) (Roach 2013).

We see that who enrolls and attends school has changed over time, and Figure 6.2 shows an even more interesting and disturbing pattern that requires explanation: The gains that Blacks and Latinos have made in graduating from high school as well as their immense gains in enrolling in and attending college have not resulted in proportionate attainment of the bachelor's degree. For instance, in the 2011–12 school year, Latinos made up 18% of all high school graduates, and they also made up 19% of the college enrollments, but by the time they were 25–29 years old they made up only 9% of those receiving bachelor's degrees. The challenges faced by

---

Figure 6.2 ■ There Are Racial Disparities in the Higher Education Pipeline

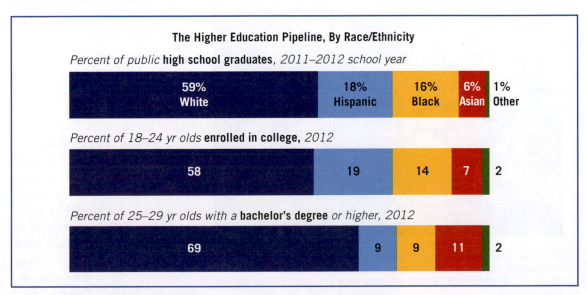

The Higher Education Pipeline, By Race/Ethnicity

Percent of public high school graduates, 2011–2012 school year

| 59% White | 18% Hispanic | 16% Black | 6% Asian | 1% Other |

Percent of 18–24 yr olds enrolled in college, 2012

| 58 | 19 | 14 | 7 | 2 |

Percent of 25–29 yr olds with a bachelor's degree or higher, 2012

| 69 | 9 | 9 | 11 | 2 |

Source: Chart: "The Higher Education Pipeline, By Race/Ethnicity." From "More Hispanics, blacks enrolling in college, but lag in bachelor's degrees," by Jans Manuel Krogstad and Richard Fry, Pew Research Center Fact Tank, April 24, 2014.

graduate students of color as they attempt to gain doctoral and professional degrees are even more pronounced (Brunsma, Embrick, and Shin 2017). Students of color face a pattern of poor access to the higher education pipeline, or the pathway to higher education, and the explanations for this pattern reside in the ways that the institution of education is woven by and within the matrix of race.

A Short History

Regardless of type or level of schooling, the institution of education in the United States has almost always been the site of conflict, debate, and confrontation over access, meanings of education, and what is taught, why, and to whom (as well as whose knowledge counts as knowledge worth having). This conflict is often between dominant (White, male, upper-class, heterosexual) groups and Blacks, Latinos, women, poor and working-class families, sexual minorities, and those with physical and mental disabilities. To understand current educational realities, we must first understand the formative moments in the shaping of the matrix of education.

The first public schools in the United States were established shortly after the American Revolution, and public education expanded rapidly in the 19th century, thanks to the efforts of such advocates as reformer Horace Mann and Tuskegee University founder Booker T. Washington. By 1910, nearly 72% of all children in the United States attended at least elementary school, and by 1930 most children received some form of compulsory education.

One of the key functions of Native American boarding schools run by Christian organizations and the federal government was to eradicate students' culture. The effects of this "soul wound" are still felt today, more than half a century after the program ended.

Native American Boarding Schools

Harvard University, founded by the Massachusetts legislature as Harvard College in 1636, was the first university built and chartered in the United States. The Harvard Indian College was established in 1655 to educate "the English & Indian Youth of this Country in knowledge: and godliness" (the school was closed in 1698) (McGrory 2011). Beginning in the early 1870s, the federal government set up boarding schools to educate Native American students in English, "civilization," Christianity, and the agricultural vocational trades. As one historian has observed, many Native Americans were, in this way, "stripped of their hair, their clothes, their beliefs, their language, and their culture, including, when possible, their prayers" (Owings 2011, xiv).

Until 1903, more than 460 boarding and day schools were built close to reservations; they were run by religious organizations using federal funds. Ultimately, more than 100,000 indigenous children were "educated" out of their cultures, languages, and ways of life. The effects linger, as recounted by Lakota woman Karen Artichoker:

> You see the impact of removing children from their homes, forcibly, putting them in a concentration camp type of setting, a POW type of setting, the boarding schools, and telling them anything Indian is not good, then sending them out into their community to do their work and to raise children they don't have a clue how to raise. We see our bonding with the oppressor still when we don't see each [other] competent as Indians. We don't see each other as being honest. We don't see ourselves as having a work ethic. If we didn't have that mainstream type of thinking about what's honorable and ethical, we're still sort of "savages." (quoted in Owings 2011, 155)

Consider the profound impacts that such cultural, spiritual, and psychological damage and erasure can have on a people—loss of language, community norms, parenting skills, tribal relationships, knowledge of one's own history, understanding of indigenous worldviews and identities, ability to develop skills useful to the life of the tribe, and more. The effects of such a collective experience linger, despite the fact that the last generation that went through the system was born in the 1950s; the long-term effects of the boarding school system have been described as a "soul wound" by some scholars (King 2008; Smith 2007). In a collective effort to move toward healing that wound, Native American activism arose in the 1960s and, along with several pieces of legislation concerning the Bureau of Indian Affairs, led to the closure of the vast majority of these schools and to the establishment of community schools and colleges run by the tribes themselves.

Early African American Education: "Separate but Equal"

After the emancipation of enslaved Africans in 1863 and the end of the Civil War in 1865, the period known as Reconstruction began. The nation faced four challenges in "reconstructing" the South after slavery and the Civil War:

1. To rebuild the crucial southern economy on free labor instead of slave labor

2. To change the South so that it could more effectively rejoin the United States

3. To integrate the freed Africans into U.S. society

4. To protect the freed Africans from harm

In the face of industrialization and capitalist development occurring in the northern United States, however, only the first challenge was achieved. The "education of the Negro" began in earnest as well, in schools that were separate from but supposedly equal to schools for Whites. The goal was to keep Blacks domesticated and subservient, with very limited skills exchangeable in the urban labor markets of the North and South. Not surprisingly, by 1870 the institutionalization of comprehensive and separate public school systems for Whites and Blacks was well under way.

Soon, however, educator and orator Booker T. Washington grew concerned about the increasing violence targeting the Black community and Black schools. In a now-famous speech he gave at the Atlanta Cotton States and International Exposition on September 18, 1895, Washington articulated the so-called **Atlanta Compromise.** Under this compromise, southern Blacks would agree to work, forgo their own political ambitions, and submit to White political rule. In exchange, southern Whites would guarantee basic education for Blacks, reduce intimidation toward them, and allow for due process in all legal matters involving Blacks. One year later, the U.S. Supreme Court, in the landmark *Plessy v. Ferguson* case, declared that racial segregation in public facilities was constitutional and fell under the doctrine of separate but equal. This decision heralded the Jim Crow era of legal segregation, which lasted nearly 100 years.

W. E. B. Du Bois and the Niagara Movement he founded inspired Blacks to reject the negative associations with their Blackness and laid the foundation for the modern civil rights movement.

Universal Images Group / Universal Images Group / Getty Images

School Desegregation

In 1900, W. E. B. Du Bois and the Black civil rights group he founded, the Niagara Movement, called for free education for all, *real* education, they cried, for "either the United States will destroy ignorance, or ignorance will destroy the United States" (Du Bois 1900). From Du Bois's criticism, the Harlem Renaissance was born, a period when Black scholars, scientists, and artists aimed to reject the negative characterizations of Blackness and assert the existence of the "New Negro." Thirty years later, Carter G. Woodson, as mentioned earlier, would lambast the educational system and decry the poverty it produced among

Blacks. These critiques and the social unrest they produced laid the foundation for what has been termed the modern civil rights movement. Several seminal court cases paved the way for this movement and significantly transformed the United States and its discourses regarding race, class, and gender. The launching event was the 1954 Supreme Court case of *Brown v. Board of Education of Topeka*.

Brown v. Board of Education effectively set aside the *Plessy v. Ferguson* decision and held that "separate" was by definition "unequal." Thurgood Marshall, who argued the case for the plaintiffs (and would later become the first Black American to sit on the U.S. Supreme Court), asserted that "separate but equal" was unfair and unconstitutional. He argued that the southern educational establishment should be forced to make all schools—both Black and White—equal. The South was trapped. For decades, Black schools had been significantly underfunded compared to White schools. According to testimony offered to the Court, the costs of equalizing the Black and White schools would essentially bankrupt the South. Evidence offered by child psychologist Kenneth Clark further demonstrated the damaging stigmas that were borne by Black children as a result of segregation. The psychological traumas inflicted by segregation further aggravated the already

Before the Supreme Court decision in *Brown v. Topeka Board of Education*, segregated schools for Blacks, like this one in rural Georgia, were considered equal to those available to whites.

Oliver Brown sued the Topeka Board of Education on behalf of his daughter, Linda, when she was denied admission to a white elementary school.

hostile situation faced by Blacks living in the South. Observing the paradox that produced "wholly unequal" educational systems for Black students, the

Court was forced to recognize that equality could not be provided under the current system, and that the only remedy was to set aside *Plessy*. *Brown v. Board of Education* followed a lesser-known but precedent-setting 1946 case, ***Mendez et al. v. Westminster School District of Orange County***, in which the Court declared unconstitutional the segregation of Mexican and Mexican American students into separate schools.

The history of education has affected our present and foreshadows our future. The institution of education in the United States has fundamentally involved decisions, definitions, and declarations about differences, including who is considered fully human, who is valued, whose histories are valued, who deserves what kind of education, and what kinds of futures can be envisioned for different classifications of peoples. All of these issues and more are related to interactions, opportunities, and outcomes within the institution of education.

When Sylvia Mendez was a child, whites and Mexicans attended separate schools, until her parents and several others in their California community, sued the schools and won. Mendez regularly speaks at schools about the importance of integration and in 2011 was awarded the Presidential Medal of Freedom by Barack Obama.

CRITICAL THINKING

1. What does it mean to be educated? What does it mean to "get" an education? What does it mean to "give" an education? These are core questions that any society must wrestle with. Be sure to start from the matrix of experience to begin discussing and answering these questions.

2. The institution of education was forged within the American crucible of race, class, and gender. How did these differential experiences in early American society aid in the formation of the institution of education? What do you see as some of the consequences and aftereffects of this early shaping of the matrix of education?

3. Is it important who controls the decisions that affect the institution of education? Give some historical and contemporary examples of the importance of such control. What happens when those who have been oppressed by the system control their own schools, curricula, and educations?

4. Can you describe any evidence of educational inequality in your schooling experiences up to this point?

■ THEORIES OF EDUCATION

How do we grapple with and begin to understand how education has functioned within the matrix of race in the United States? Sociology offers many potential theoretical perspectives, and these theories can help us understand the origins of our stock stories about education as an institution. In this section we discuss two of the primary theories of education—social-functional theory and human capital theory—and show how stock stories reflect each of these theories in the real world.

Social-Functional Theory: Education as a Socialization Process

One of the primary theoretical stock stories of education is the narrative of education as socialization. This rests on the idea that schools socialize students. Socialization is the process whereby members of a society are taught that society's dominant roles, norms, and values. Families once served the socialization function, but in postindustrial societies, other organizations have grown in socializing influence. The socialization function of education and school is to teach students to be competent members of society.

For French sociologist Émile Durkheim (1956, 1962, 1977), education's purpose was to instill a sense of "morality" and "cohesion" within individuals. By "morality," Durkheim meant that through education, children are subconsciously infused with the norms, rules, and values of their society (such as patriotism and the value of individual effort). This infusion of morality takes place through the structure of the classroom, the relationship between teacher and student, the structure of rules enforced throughout the school day, and other social and cultural structures in the school. The resulting conformity helps maintain the bonds between us that make us follow norms, thus producing social cohesion.

However, a theory that predicts social cohesion also implies that there are processes that might lead to breakdowns of that cohesion, inequalities within the system, and so on. The question, of course, is whose norms and values are being instilled? Whose cohesion is valued, and who has been excluded, marginalized, or devalued? If education socializes individuals into competent members of society, then who benefits from this process? These and other questions have motivated social scientists interested in critical studies of education for a very long time. The history laid out earlier in this chapter gives some indication.

Human Capital Theory: Education as Skills Acquisition

Many high schools, colleges, and universities aim to give their students the "skills they need to compete in the global economy" or for membership in the workforce in general. This theory invokes what we might call an **apprenticeship model of education**. In precapitalist societies, a master craftsman (usually a man) would take on one or more apprentices to train—whether in blacksmithing, baking, cobbling, or some other craft—passing on the skills the apprentices would need to eventually fill the master's role. In "dame schools" of the 17th, 18th, and 19th centuries, female teachers taught girls sewing, knitting, and embroidery (Forman-Brunell 2011), while during this same period boys from affluent families went to grammar schools to learn arithmetic, writing, Latin, and Greek (Zhboray 1993).

The skills acquisition function of education is echoed throughout many communities today in the common belief that education provides the skills we need to engage productively in society. In New York City, for instance, Mayor Bill de Blasio wants the city's public schools to offer computer science classes to all students by 2025, in a plan projected to cost $81 million and requiring the training of 5,000 teachers. With tech jobs increasing in the city, the director of the Office of Strategic Partnerships has stated, "I think there is acknowledgment that we need our students better prepared for these jobs and to address equity and diversity within the sector as well" (quoted in Taylor and Miller 2015, A22).

This provision of skills that are exchangeable within a social structure, or market, for other forms of capital has been described by economists, sociologists, and educational researchers alike as the development of **human capital** (Schultz 1961; Becker 1964; see also Coleman 1988). As Coleman (1988, S100) describes the concept: "Just as physical capital is created by changes in materials to form tools that facilitate production, human capital is created by changes in persons that bring about skills and capabilities that make them act in new ways."

Yet the knowledge we gain from the educational system often has little relevance to the specific skills we need in the workforce or on the job (Chang 2010; Rosenbaum 2001). In contemporary society, as in the apprentice model, most of the skills that people need to perform their jobs are learned *on* the job, through doing (practice), and not through knowing (theory). Despite this fact, the notion that education allows us to acquire job skills and/or makes us more desirable to potential employers remains one of the key legitimating narratives of education. The assumption that education leads to skills and skills lead to jobs has serious consequences for non-White and lower-class members of society, because it posits that (a) the playing field is level, (b) education delivers needed skills, and (c) race, class, and gender play no moderating role in the effects of these processes. Yet we know these things are not true.

CRITICAL THINKING

1. How do the stock theories of education—social-functional and human capital theories—help us understand the formative experiences that shaped the matrix of education, especially those of Native Americans and African Americans? Are these theories helpful for understanding these experiences?

2. Education, its socialization functions, and its human capital functions do not exist in a vacuum within our society. Education is linked to other institutions—work, family, and the mass media, for instance—in fundamental ways. How are any two of these institutions linked? How are the linkages the same or different for individuals from different locations within the matrix of race?

3. The institution of education is, according to the theories, central to both socialization and skills acquisition. It is also clearly important in the formation of identities. What lessons do these theories and/or the histories discussed above hold for our understanding of the relationship between education and identity for racial and ethnic minorities?

4. How were you socialized in high school? What norms and values were forged within your secondary education? Does attending the same high school as others mean that you experienced the same high school they did?

■ EXAMINING THE CONCEALED STORY OF RACE AND EDUCATION THROUGH THE MATRIX

The story of U.S. education is actually several parallel stories, as we can see if we use the matrix to view education as a social institution. What these parallel stories have in common is the recognition that we have created many different educational structures that serve different groups and purposes. Given all these different structures, some of which are based on race, gender, or ethnicity, it is not surprising that concealed stories are critical of the dominant educational narratives of the United States—that schools serve primarily as socializers and skill developers. These concealed stories speak to the stock stories we have examined in this chapter; sociologists themselves have told many of them. We will examine four concealed stories: education as a conversion tool, education as a site of class construction, education as a means of creating workers, and education as a citizen machine.

Education as a Conversion Tool

As societies spread across geographic and cultural space over time, whether through migration, conquest, colonialism, or imperialism, their members encounter others who are different from them in many ways. Often the institution of education becomes a tool that migrating settlers, conquering armies, or globalizing corporations use in the attempt to change the cognitions, the social arrangements, and even the meaning systems of their host societies. Like missionary work, education can be seen as an effort at a "conversion" of sorts. The story of education as a conversion tool is a critical take on the stock theory of education as socialization, and it goes something like this: "Your socialization is wrong; use ours. We will educate yours out of you, in order that you might become like us."

We can clearly see the role of education as conversion by looking at those who wrestled with their role as colonial subjects (or internal colonial subjects within the United States—some scholars consider Native Americans, African Americans, and Latinos, for instance, to constitute domestic, or internal, colonies *within* the United States, providing an exploitable workforce from which labor power can be extracted), and who continue to try to reclaim aspects of their social and cultural structures and identities. Frantz Fanon, in his classic books *Black Skin, White Masks* (1952) and *The Wretched of the Earth* (1961), writes caustically of the symbolic, cognitive, and cultural violence done to Algerians throughout French colonialism and the dominance of White supremacy. Introducing the concept of colonization of the mind, Fanon discusses the indelible mark of inferiority left on the psyches of colonized individuals and communities long after the colonizers have left. A deep and profound resocialization experience takes place in those who have been stripped of their dignity and self-determination.

In the United States, many education-as-conversion stories have been uncovered in the disciplines of Black studies, Chicano studies, women's studies, gender and sexuality studies, and indigenous studies. Many of these disciplines began as student movements aimed at changing dominant U.S. institutions—education, law, health, government—and they grew in earnest as a result of the civil rights movement. In the late 1960s, for example, the civil rights, freedom of speech, antiwar, and Black

San Francisco State University was the first college to offer a four-year Black Studies program, but it didn't come without a five-months-long student-led strike and many protests, including this occasion, when several members of the Black Student Union and the professor who would ultimately chair the new program, interrupted a speech by the university president.

Bettmann / Bettmann / Getty Images

Power movements converged on U.S. campuses, and Black students began demanding programs relevant to their lives and aspirations.

The first 4-year Black studies program was organized by Nathan Hare and Jimmy Garrett at San Francisco State in 1968. Between 1969 and 1973, approximately 300 to 600 programs sprang up across the United States at predominantly White colleges and universities, and today more than 200 schools maintain African American studies units, with 10 offering master's degrees (Patillo, cited in West 2012). While the discipline of Black studies provides a story of resistance, the fact that it is needed in the first place is evidence of the strength of the education-as-conversion reframing of the socialization stock story.

Education as a Site of Class Construction

Education has consistently perpetuated class inequality, going back as far as the earliest social structures of literacy. The notion that education provides a society and its members with the academic and cultural knowledge necessary to function is encouraged by the dominant classes in most contemporary societies. One interpretation of this belief is that if you do not receive an education, you are not a full-fledged member of society.

Scholars have been interested in this narrative primarily because of its obvious ties with class, control, and domination in virtually every known society (Apple 2013). Education has played a role not only in creating social classes but also in reproducing them generation after generation. One of the ways schools do this is by implicitly, structurally, and culturally embedding processes of distinction and the social construction of difference within their walls. Consider dress codes and even school uniforms. Dress codes are lists that schools create to specify what items of clothing *may not be worn* at school (e.g., bandanas, baggy pants), while uniform policies mandate what *must be worn* (e.g., specific khaki pants, specific colors)—many dress code and uniform policies have race, class, and gender overtones.

Cultural capital consists of the cultural resources—the meanings, codes, understandings, and practices—that individuals can accumulate and utilize to exchange for other goods in a social or economic market (Bourdieu and Passeron 1977; Bourdieu 1984; Lareau 1989, 2011). Cultural capital exists in three forms, according to Pierre Bourdieu (1986), an important 20th-century French sociologist:

- Embodied personal characteristics (such as the ability to see, feel, and think about the world in ways acceptable to the dominant class)
- Physical objects (like books, music, movies, and clothing recognized by the dominant class as worthy of attention)

- Institutionalized recognition (a college degree, for instance, which is an accepted credential that determines the graduate's worth in the job market)

Cultural capital is like a road map that helps us navigate social life because we have learned the "rules of the game."

At this point you might be saying, "Well, that sounds good, actually, because we want to be sure that schools imprint the rules of the game on their students so they can be competent members of society." However, the question is, *whose* rules and *whose* game? Lee, Park, and Wong (2016) studied second-generation Asian American students in the public education system and found that their identities were being shaped and also policed by the Whiteness of the structure of education. What's more, whose institution is education itself? For if Bourdieu is correct (and there is substantial evidence that he is), the dominant institutions of any given society serve the interests of the dominant classes. From this perspective, we can see a concealed story: that education reproduces the class structure by creating schools in society's image that expect students to know the rules of the game but do not actually teach them the rules. This has led to charges that schools are organized along male, White, middle-class, and heteronormative principles. Institutionalized cultural capital keeps this structure invisible to those who do not already have cultural capital—especially girls, non-Whites, and students from lower-class and disadvantaged families and communities. Thus, those without cultural capital have an increased probability of being unsuccessful from the institution's perspective.

Education as a Means of Creating Workers

While we generally assume, based on our stock stories about education, that we need an education in order to get a job, an alternative narrative focuses on the idea that schools exist to *create* (not educate) workers for the labor force. To consider this possibility further, think about the general rules we learn at school from a very early age, as listed in Table 6.1.

If we replace the school with the factory, the desk with the assembly line, the teacher with the boss, students with coworkers, and schoolwork with making products, we can see that the discipline of school literally mirrors the pulse of the factory, the rhythm of the workplace, the striving for output and profit for the corporate machine. Scholars have also argued that schools serve to create workers for the capitalist structure—not the *skills* needed, but the *identities* needed.

Karl Marx, in his analysis of capitalist development, argued that all institutions in capitalist societies are "epiphenomenal to social class." What he meant by this is that the dominant institutions in society—government, religious institutions, families, educational system, and so on—all exist in the forms they do, and operate in the

Table 6.1 ■ Dominant School Rules and Their Corresponding Roles at Work	
School Rule	Function for Occupational Structure
Arrive on time.	Punctuality
Keep your desk clean.	Image
Sit in your assigned seat.	Order
Ask the teacher for permission.	Hierarchy
Be silent and focus on your own work.	Individualism
Do what the teacher tells you to do.	Authority
Line up.	Rules
Eat when it is time for lunch.	Schedules
Do your best work.	Evaluation

ways they do, with the relationship structures they encourage, because they benefit the bourgeoisie (the owning class) and their interests.

In their classic 1976 book *Schooling in Capitalist America,* Bowles and Gintis echo this argument by comparing the structures of schools to the forms, relationships, and rules that operate within the world of work. Furthermore, they argue that schools (whether secondary or post-secondary) do not actually provide employers with workers who have the skills needed for particular jobs but instead provide employers with "suitably socialized workers," who come into the workforce trained not to question the system and to accept their socioeconomic fate. Scholars who follow this Marxist line of inquiry raise serious questions about the role education systems actually play in capitalist and other societies. In fact, as more people have attained higher levels of education, we would expect income inequality to be reduced, but it has actually worsened over time (Mayer 2010).

Scholars like Bowles and Gintis argue that school prepares children to be docile members of the workforce by teaching obedience, cooperation, and deference to authority.

Scholars who embrace the matrix perspective have also asked how the educational system fashions and constructs individuals' identities *as* women, *as* heterosexuals, *as* Blacks or Latinos, *as* (dis)abled, and *as* the myriad intersections across all these that fully inform their positions in the system. In his landmark work "The Afrocentric Idea in Education," Molefi Asante (1991, 171), speaks of his underlying premise about how education operates in society:

> These ideas represent . . . what education is capable of doing to and for an already politically and economically marginalized people—African Americans: (1) Education is fundamentally a social phenomenon whose ultimate purpose is to socialize the learner; to send a child to school is to prepare that child to become part of a social group. (2) Schools are reflective of the societies that develop them (i.e., a White supremacist–dominated society will develop a White supremacist educational system).

This narrative points to one of the most important lessons of sociology—the distinction between individual and group realities. On the one hand, it is clear that an individual who has more education will earn more income, on average, than someone with a lower level of education. On an individual level, the relationship between educational attainment and income is a strong one, supporting the stock stories about education as a skill provider and a path to social mobility.

However, on the group level, this has not been the case. Educational equity has *not* led to more income equality. In fact, the opposite has occurred—while more and more people have attained higher educational credentials over time, the income disparities between the rich and the poor have continued to widen. Thus, as a society, we have increased our human capital (e.g., skills, education) without increasing our socioeconomic equality. In fact, scholars recognize that the most efficient way to increase a nation's productivity is by increasing its mechanization and technological advancement (Chang 2010). Countries that do so, that actually "de-skill" their populaces through education institutions, make workers more replaceable and easier to control. The narrative that schools create workers for the bourgeoisie helps to partially account for this.

Education as a Citizen Machine

While we may like to imagine that education allows individuals to learn to question their reality, there is abundant evidence that it carefully constructs that reality for a specific purpose and with certain goals in mind. Through the curricula, social structures, and cultural meaning systems embedded in both, schools and the social institution of education socially construct age hierarchies, gendered identities, student roles, consumers, and ways to think, create, and question—including the creation of nationalistic sentiments, patriotic affiliations, and, ultimately, citizens. From the morning's recitation of the Pledge of Allegiance through a politically constructed curriculum, students in the United States (like students elsewhere) learn prescribed knowledge, from history and English to math and science. Education is continuously creating national citizens as well as citizens of a globally dominant, imperialist power.

Social scientists have been interested in this concealed narrative for education for some time. The primary research approach, often called **critical pedagogy,** stems from the work of Brazilian educator and philosopher Paulo Freire ([1970] 2000) and British sociologist of education Basil Bernstein (1971) and their students and colleagues. In his foreword to Freire's most important work, *Pedagogy of the Oppressed,* Richard Shaull ([1970] 2000, 34) explains Freire's view of education:

> Education either functions as an instrument that is used to facilitate the integration of the younger generation into the logic of the present system and bring about conformity to it, *or* it becomes "the practice of freedom," the means by which men and women deal critically and creatively with reality and discover how to participate in the transformation of their world.

Students of the institution of education must therefore pay very close attention to the old sociological adage that things are not what they seem. Education is a tool for both social control and liberation. The creation of citizens, the decision about who is and is not one, and the determination of what citizens should think, act, and do are mechanisms of social control for specific state purposes.

Throughout its history, education in the United States has been the subject of continuous efforts at reform by the federal government. In 1983, the National Commission on Excellence in Education published the report *A Nation at Risk: The Imperative for Educational Reform,* which prompted action from Ronald Reagan's administration. Since then, we have seen programs such as George H. W. Bush's Goals 2000, George W. Bush's No Child Left Behind, and Barack Obama's Race to the Top. With these national platforms, the federal government typically mandates reform but rarely funds it, and critics claim that such efforts also fundamentally fail to understand the structure and functioning of the institution of education. Nevertheless, all these reform efforts share one element: the goal of the development of the citizenry (especially imperial citizens, or citizens of the U.S. empire) and the furthering of the interests of multinational corporations.

At the time of this writing it is unclear what Donald Trump's educational platform will be; however, if his choice for secretary of education, Betsy DeVos, is any indication, one of the central components of the platform will be "school choice." The basic idea of school "choice" is this: While taxpayer dollars fund our public schools (and we will discuss below how this particularly American structure rigs the educational game), those who advocate school choice want taxpayer moneys to go to *all* schools (charter schools, private schools, religious schools, and so on), with parents then allowed to "choose" the schools they want their children to attend. This idea has its foundations in the White flight that occurred after the 1954 order to desegregate public schools. Indeed, as Singer (2017) observes, "before the federal government forced schools to desegregate, no one was all that interested in having an alternative to traditional public schools. But once whites got wind that the Supreme Court might make their kids go to school with black kids, lots of white parents started clamoring for 'choice.'" Time will tell what the Trump administration's plans for our schools will be and how these will create new citizens.

Education, Race, and Intersectional Realities

Each year since 1970 the U.S. Department of Education's National Center for Education Statistics has published a report titled *The Condition of Education,* a recent edition of which we have referenced and will continue to reference in this chapter (NCES 2016a), along with other sources that together represent the institution's official presentation on the developments and trends in education. Data do not speak for themselves, however; all of us use lenses to interpret data, as we will see next. Education is compulsory in the United States until the age of 16, but the ages at which children begin and end their education vary by state (NCES 2016a). And depending on their positions within the matrix of experience—their race, class, gender, sexuality, and abilities—the ways in which individuals experience the institution of education vary dramatically. Now that we have established a set of stories and lenses with which to understand the way education works (or does not work) for its constituents, we can map out its official structure, while recognizing that there are alternative structures, and that some children experience neither the official one nor any alternatives.

Social Class

We are born into the matrix and gendered, raced, and located in our positions in the socioeconomic structure. From Durkheim (1956) to Lareau (2011), sociologists of education have long identified social class as one of the most fundamental axes of inequality in all societies, determining who gets what and why in the educational system (for an overview of the field, see also Sadovnik 2011). Put another way, all educational processes and outcomes are grounded firmly in the student's class position and affected by the student's race, gender, and other locations.

The United States is the only nation that funds its public schools primarily on the basis of local and state, not federal, tax revenues (see Kozol 1991). What this means is that a given neighborhood or community can support the quality of its school system only to the extent that its local tax revenues, based on the income and wealth of its residents, can afford. This is the reason there are disadvantaged schools in disadvantaged neighborhoods and advantaged schools in advantaged neighborhoods. In addition, given the historical and contemporary linkages of class, race, immigration, poverty, and segregation, in the end, the school system is in a certain sense rigged. One disastrous consequence of such economic rigging is what some scholars have called the school-to-prison pipeline, in which race plays a fundamental part. The monetary and social disinvestment in and abandonment of many predominantly Black, Latino, and Native American schools and school districts disproportionately affects students of color, who achieve at lower rates, are not expected to achieve as much, are more likely to repeat a grade, are subject to increased surveillance and punishment, and, as we have seen, drop out at higher rates when compared to students from more affluent areas and more privileged positions within the matrix. So, we underfund certain schools, these students' opportunities are dismal, they drop out and commit crimes, and then they are put into prison (Redfield and Nance 2016). The United States currently spends much more on keeping an individual in prison than it would have cost to shepherd that same person through the education system as a child.

Given our narratives about the role of education in skills acquisition and social mobility, we should first ask whether the payoff is worth it. As Table 6.2 shows, the answer is yes, no, and, well, it depends. On average, those with more education earn more income. The median income for college graduates in 2015 was about $50,651 (National Association of Colleges and Employers 2015). However, there are significant gender and race differences. White men reap greater rewards at every educational level. And within every racial group there is a gender gap. White men with a high school diploma still earn significantly more money than White women with an associate of arts (AA) degree. This simple fact helps explain why more women today are seeking college degrees; men have greater income options without attending college.

Many students see a college degree as a requirement for landing a decent-paying job. However, college has grown increasingly expensive, and the past decade has shown that many graduates accumulate enormous debt in their pursuit of a degree. Overall, it is estimated that about 40 million U.S. adults have outstanding student debt and that the total owed is more than $1.2 trillion (Dynarski 2015). According to a recent study, more Black and Latino undergraduate students take out student loans than do Whites or Asians (Scott-Clayton and Li 2016) (see Figure 6.3). Additionally, Blacks and Latinos are more likely to shoulder a heavier debt burden than Whites or Asians while also having less income after graduation and coming from families with less wealth—the matrix of race allows us to see how entangled all these elements are.

Table 6.2 ■ Average Annual Earnings of U.S. Workers 18 Years Old and Older, by Educational Attainment, Race/Ethnicity, and Gender, 2010 (in U.S. dollars)

	White			African American		
	Total	Men	Women	Total	Men	Women
No high school diploma	22,497	26,774	16,147	19,317	20,182	15,280
High school graduate	31,286	36,823	24,062	26,100	30,500	22,145
AA degree	35,805	43,419	27,613	34,172	38,231	31,733
BA degree	55,630	66,716	42,678	44,867	50,658	42,228
	Hispanic			Asian American		
	Total	Men	Women	Total	Men	Women
No high school diploma	21,994	24,533	15,304	22,052	24,969	17,020
High school graduate	28,309	31,624	22,349	28,464	33,008	26,221
AA degree	35,820	42,331	29,545	37,071	43,020	30,121
BA degree	48,358	59,053	39,862	55,192	69,087	49,880

Source: American Council on Education, "Fact Sheet on Higher Education," http://www.acenet.edu/news-room/Documents/FactSheet-Average-Annual-Earnings-of-Workers-18-Years-Old-or-Older-by-Educational-Attainment-Race-and-Gender-2010.pdf.

Gender

Worldwide, according to UNESCO's most recent *World Atlas of Gender Equality in Education* (2012), only a handful of nations have achieved gender parity in education. They are most of the countries of the European Union, Indonesia, the Russian Federation, a few South American countries, Canada, and the United States. For the vast majority of these nations, this situation represents a significant gain since 1970. Despite advancements in school enrollment for girls around the world, however, women still make up the majority of illiterate adults—especially in South and West Asia, sub-Saharan Africa, and the Arab states.

In their Pulitzer Prize–winning book *Half the Sky: Turning Oppression into Opportunity for Women Worldwide,* Kristof and WuDunn (2009, 169–70) observe that "education is one of the most effective ways to fight poverty. . . . [It] is also a precondition for girls and women to stand up against injustice, and for women to be integrated into the economy." In 2011, Malala Yousafzai of Pakistan, 14 years old at the time,

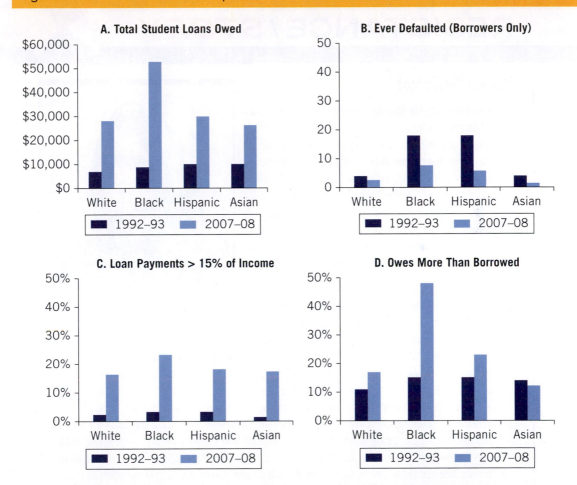

Figure 6.3 ■ There are Racial Disparities in Student Loan Debt Four Years After Graduation

A. Total Student Loans Owed

(bar chart with y-axis from $0 to $60,000; categories White, Black, Hispanic, Asian; legend 1992–93 and 2007–08)

B. Ever Defaulted (Borrowers Only)

(bar chart with y-axis from 0 to 50; categories White, Black, Hispanic, Asian; legend 1992–93 and 2007–08)

C. Loan Payments > 15% of Income

(bar chart with y-axis from 0% to 50%; categories White, Black, Hispanic, Asian; legend 1992–93 and 2007–08)

D. Owes More Than Borrowed

(bar chart with y-axis from 0% to 50%; categories White, Black, Hispanic, Asian; legend 1992–93 and 2007–08)

Source: Judith Scott-Clayton and Jing Li, "Black–White Disparity in Student Loan Debt More than Triples after Graduation," *Evidence Speaks Reports* 2, no. 3 (October 20, 2016), Brookings Institution, https://www.brookings.edu/research/black-white-disparity-in-student-loan-debt-more-than-triples-after-graduation.

was shot in the head and neck by a Taliban attacker because of her political blogging, organizing, and activism with girls and women in her community (and beyond) centered on the importance of education for all. Her experience reminds us that worldwide the education of girls and women fundamentally matters—but also that, while gains have been made, we still have far to go.

Malala Yousafzai

Some children receive stronger educations because the color of their skin is forever linked to opportunity; other children are not able to succeed in school because the curriculum is centered in experiences quite different from their own; still others are denied an education because they are female. This was the case with Malala Yousafzai. When she resisted, she almost paid for it with her life, but now she speaks for all of those children marginalized because of their racial, ethnic, gender, or other identities, emphasizing the importance of education. In 2013, she spoke at the United Nations:

Malala Yousafzai

Simon Davis / DFID

> I raise up my voice . . . so that those without a voice can be heard. Those who have fought for their rights: Their right to live in peace. Their right to be treated with dignity. Their right to equality of opportunity. Their right to be educated. . . . On the 9th of October, 2012, the Taliban shot me on the left side of my forehead. They shot my friends too. They thought that the bullets would silence us. But they failed. And then, out of that silence, came thousands of voices. . . . In many parts of the world, especially Pakistan and Afghanistan, terrorism, wars, and conflicts stop children to go to their schools. . . . Dear sisters and brothers, now it's time to speak up. . . . We call upon the world leaders that all the peace deals must protect women and children's rights. A deal that goes against the dignity of women and their rights is unacceptable. We call upon all governments to ensure free compulsory education for every child all over the world. . . . We call upon all communities to be tolerant—to reject prejudice based on caste, creed, sect, religion, or gender. To ensure freedom and equality for women so that they can flourish. We cannot all succeed when half of us are held back. . . . Let us empower ourselves with the weapon of knowledge and let us shield ourselves with unity and togetherness. . . . Education is the only solution. Education first.

Critical Thinking

- To what extent do cultural norms affect society's perception of the role and value of girls' education?
- To what extent should we honor those norms?

Source: Malala Yousafzai, speech to the United Nations Youth Takeover, July 12, 2013, https://secure.aworldatschool .org/page/content/the-text-of-malala-yousafzais-speech-at-the-united-nations.

Boys and girls experience schooling very differently. There are (at least) two useful general ways to examine this difference—by looking at what happens in schools and by looking at the cultural norms in society. Buchmann, DiPrete, and McDaniel (2008) reviewed the sociological literature on gender inequalities in education and found the following:

- Girls do less well on standardized tests than boys but get better grades (Duckworth and Seligman 2006).

- Girls' behavior in school, compared with that of boys, is more in line with institutional expectations of students (Downey and Vogt Yuan 2005).

- Girls show more interest in schooling than boys do (Rosenbaum 2001).

- In contrast to findings in earlier decades, high school boys and girls are now taking more similar classes (Hallinan and Sørensen 1987).

In general, girls engage much more fully than boys in many aspects of school. One of the reasons for this is society's very limited definition of masculinity. Teenage boys do not see engaging in schoolwork and getting good grades as a path to proving their masculinity. Instead, if they do these things, they may be bullied as geeks. When gender and race intersect, school success is even more problematic for boys. Among Black youth, getting good grades is often seen as "acting White."

In the wake of the founding of the Black Lives Matter movement, sparked by the 2014 shooting death of Michael Brown in Ferguson, Missouri, the African American Policy Institute released a report titled *Black Girls Matter: Pushed Out, Overpoliced, and Underprotected* (Crenshaw 2015). The report reviews research on Black girls' lives, particularly their lives and experiences in schools, details key findings, and offers suggestions. The following are some of the research findings described in the report:

- In New York and Boston, while both Black boys and Black girls are subject to larger achievement gaps and harsher forms of discipline than their White counterparts, for girls these consequences are often more stark.

In part because getting good grades is not seen as incompatible with femininity, as is often the case with masculinity, girls tend to be more engaged with many aspects of school.

The Washington Post / The Washington Post / Getty Images

- At-risk girls describe zero-tolerance schools as chaotic environments where discipline is prioritized over educational attainment; this leads them to disengage.

- Increased levels of law enforcement and other security measures within schools sometimes make girls feel less safe and less likely to attend school.

- Girls' attachment to and sense of belonging in school can be undermined if their achievements are overlooked or undervalued.

- Punitive rather than restorative responses to conflict contribute to girls' feelings of separation from school.

- The failure of schools to intervene in sexual harassment and bullying of girls contributes to girls' insecurity at school.

- Girls sometimes resort to "acting out" when their counseling needs are overlooked or disregarded.

- School-age Black girls experience a high incidence of interpersonal violence.

- Black and Latina girls are often burdened with familial obligations that undermine their capacity to achieve their schooling goals.

- Pregnancy and parenting make it difficult for girls to engage fully in school.

Clearly, the data show that race and gender together create the experience of schooling for Black girls. This report recommends the expansion of opportunities in schools to include Black girls, increase their feelings of safety, and ensure environments that are free of sexual harassment. So, while Malala rightly encourages us to work to ensure an education for all, especially girls, it is important to recognize that we must also keep a close eye on how education does and does not work for all girls, depending on their position within the matrix. Currently, with increasing Islamophobia in the United States and in American schools, girls like Malala are now daily undergoing a process of racialization the likes of which Muslim Americans have never seen—and it is deeply affecting their ability to succeed in American society (Selod 2015).

Sexual Minorities

In 1999, the Gay, Lesbian, and Straight Education Network (now known simply as GLSEN) began conducting the National School Climate Survey. This important survey, conducted every 2 years, seeks to measure students' experiences within their schools. In the most recent data collection, from the 2014–15 school year, a sample of 10,521 students across all 50 states and more than 3,000 school districts was canvassed (Kosciw, Greytak, Giga, Villenas, and Danischewski 2016). The results of the survey, since 1999, have consistently revealed a previously concealed story: LGBTQ students experience hostile school climates, absenteeism, lower educational aspirations and achievements, and poor psychological well-being. Respondents have reported verbal assaults on their sexuality, gender, and gender expression (while transgender is not about sexual orientation or sexuality, the data reported include these students along with LGB youth)(see Figures 6.4a and 6.4b). Physical assaults have been reported as well, and reports of intervention by fellow students have been rare. Such incidents are reported to school authorities only about 42% of the time, and to family members only about 43% of the time.

The report on the National School Climate Survey for the 2014–15 school year shows that while all LGBT students experience verbal and physical harassment in their schools, LGBT students of color experience such harassment in addition to the daily microaggressions that they receive when others make assumptions about their other statuses (such as race and class; Kosciw et al. 2016). The report, and LGBTQ students themselves, offer several solutions to these problems:

- Increased opportunities for gay–straight alliances been shown to have significant positive impacts on school cultures and climates.

- Curricula must be inclusive of the experiences of LGBTQ individuals, histories, and voices.

- Supportive teachers and administrators are essential.

- Comprehensive antibullying and antiharassment policies and laws should be in place.

CRITICAL THINKING

1. If the concealed story that education serves to create workers is correct, what other kinds of behavioral rules and normative expectations would employers in today's labor market find desirable? Do you think these differ for Blacks, Whites, and Latinos? For Black men and White women? How are such expectations manifested in schooling practices?

2. Now that you have been in college for a bit of time, can you explain the "rules of the game" (cultural capital) for college? Do these rules privilege certain locations in the matrix?

3. How has your education thus far encouraged you to question reality? What kinds of structures and relations have facilitated this? How has your education discouraged you from questioning reality?

4. Have you ever taken a Black studies/African American studies course? A women's studies or gender studies course? A sexualities course? If so, how did these classes function to decolonize (as Frantz Fanon would say) your mind? If not, how do you think such courses would help students to decolonize their minds? How would different students—Whites? Men? African Americans? Lesbians?—benefit differently from such courses?

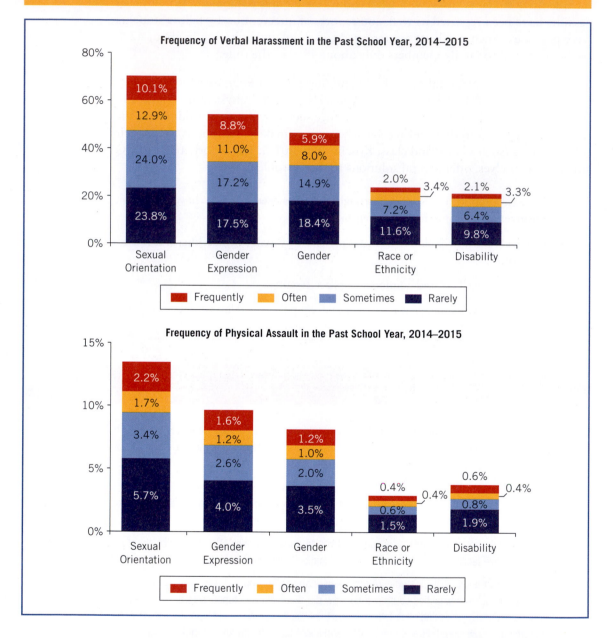

Frequency of Verbal Harassment in the Past School Year, 2014–2015

Sexual Orientation: Rarely 23.8%, Sometimes 24.0%, Often 12.9%, Frequently 10.1%
Gender Expression: Rarely 17.5%, Sometimes 17.2%, Often 11.0%, Frequently 8.8%
Gender: Rarely 18.4%, Sometimes 14.9%, Often 8.0%, Frequently 5.9%
Race or Ethnicity: Rarely 11.6%, Sometimes 7.2%, Often 3.4%, Frequently 2.0%
Disability: Rarely 9.8%, Sometimes 6.4%, Often 3.3%, Frequently 2.1%

Legend: Frequently, Often, Sometimes, Rarely

Frequency of Physical Assault in the Past School Year, 2014–2015

Sexual Orientation: Rarely 5.7%, Sometimes 3.4%, Often 1.7%, Frequently 2.2%
Gender Expression: Rarely 4.0%, Sometimes 2.6%, Often 1.2%, Frequently 1.6%
Gender: Rarely 3.5%, Sometimes 2.0%, Often 1.0%, Frequently 1.2%
Race or Ethnicity: Rarely 1.5%, Sometimes 0.6%, Often 0.4%, Frequently 0.4%
Disability: Rarely 1.9%, Sometimes 0.8%, Often 0.4%, Frequently 0.6%

Legend: Frequently, Often, Sometimes, Rarely

Source: Kosciw, J. G., Greytak, E. A., Giga, N. M., Villenas, C. & Danischewski, D. J. (2016). The 2015 National School Climate Survey: The experiences of lesbian, gay, bisexual, transgender, and queer youth in our nation's schools. New York: GLSEN.

■ ALTERNATIVE EDUCATIONAL MOVEMENTS AND THE FUTURE OF EDUCATION

In the late 1960s and early 1970s, Paulo Freire, an educator from Brazil, whom we met earlier, sought to reveal the oppressive foundations of capitalist educational systems, particularly in colonized countries, while simultaneously calling for the construction of a **pedagogy of liberation** whereby education can free people, not confine them. Freire was born into a middle-class family in Brazil but suffered from hunger in childhood as a result of the collapse of the Brazilian economy. He was inspired by this and by his later experiences in political exile to fight a colonial system that was built on and essentially maintained by the dehumanization and exploitation of the colonized such as himself. Believing that the capitalist system of education was instrumental in silencing the oppressed, he argued for a form of education through which the oppressed, in dialogue with one another and by drawing from personal experience, would come to critically question the oppressive system.

The Brazilian educator Paolo Freire believed that traditional education, as in this classroom near Rio de Janeiro, reinforces systems of oppression and inequality.

As Freire ([1970] 2000, 68) explains, "The struggle begins with men's recognition that they have been destroyed." The oppressed are then able to actively participate in their own liberation, and therefore in the transformation of society as a whole. Freire's transformational story about education motivated a broad movement around the world to create a liberatory model of education. Instead of walking through Freire's theoretical apparatus, in this section we will envision a new model using his insights. These insights are drawn heavily from the work of César Augusto Rossatto (2004).

Imagining New Educations

First, imagine a school where, in Freire's words, the "teacher-student" (because teachers are always students) begins with the notion that "student-teachers" (students are

Gender, racial, and class differences affect the labeling of students with disabilities as well as the level of services they receive. Students of color, especially black boys, are much more likely than white students to be labeled with intellectual disabilities and assigned to special education programs (USDOE 2016). Researchers Albanesi and Sauer (2013) have examined their own experience raising disabled children and engaging with the school structure, where they found their race and class privilege helped them be better advocates for school services that had to be fought for. They argue that "parents with privilege are encouraged and expected to pursue the individualized strategy (e.g., 'save my son') over collective strategies (e.g., 'how do we equitably address the needs of all children with disabilities?')," which reinforces the individualist approach.

seen as having experience and insight to offer their teachers) bring with them specific experiences based on their places within the matrix. A dialogue begins that includes respect for each other's knowledge and uncovers myths that hold us in oppression by identifying dominant and subordinate frames of reference. In this way the classroom constructs new languages of liberation. A key point of the model we are drawing here is that knowledge is constructed from daily life experiences as well as from reflections about the past and how it relates to and/or dominates the present and future. The goal is for student-teachers to explore their own connectedness to historical processes that may seem distant to them and act to bridge this distance. Building the curriculum becomes an ever-changing process that requires the participation of many stakeholders in the school community, including parents, students, teachers, and administrators. The dialogue grows outward from the school.

Second, the schools are transformed into local spaces for the reception, discussion, and distribution of the culture and knowledge of marginalized communities, in order to break down dominant ways of knowing and reconstruct a language of hope. The schools also become centers for participation and organization of the school communities in conjunction with other social movements. This reveals the political nature of schools and schooling that typically remains hidden, highlighting that the world is socially constructed and shaped by human action—or inaction. The world can be reconstructed, and student-teachers can be active participants in transforming the world, as opposed to passive recipients of secondhand knowledge of a world unchanged.

Third, based on this radical reimagining of education, schooling, curriculum, and the school, teacher-students and student-teachers learn to change their views of themselves and their relationship to the world. "Teacher education" becomes an opportunity for teacher-students to unlearn and rid themselves of old practices and beliefs that have served the system of oppression. In pursuit of new visions of the future, teacher-students and student-teachers participate in making a new history revitalized by democratic and critical pedagogy. A curriculum centered on *present* social, economic, and historical conditions, instead of being a continuation of the past, can begin a reconceptualization of society.

Fourth, education is socially contextualized and aware of power, as well as grounded in a commitment to an emancipatory world, a world where freedom, dignity, and self- and communal determination are central, as well as history-making, processes whereby we see ourselves as being the change we want to see in the world. Student-teachers understand that their perceptions and beliefs are based on worlds that they, as well as the larger society, have made. They engage in critical reflections on the sociopolitical nature of their school experience, asking whose interests it serves.

Fifth, student-teachers understand that they possess the right to speak, to disagree, to point out alterations, and to call for a renegotiation of the curriculum. In this way, they gain ownership of their education. Race, class, gender, and other differences are embraced as sites of creativity and critique in a multicultural society, allowing student-teachers the ability to see multiple perspectives and power relationships as well as to build a sense of communal identity. Education is committed to action. It challenges passivity by constructing meaning and initiating action. Drawing on feminist perspectives, it accepts that knowledge is based on emotion and affective capacity, not on reason alone. Personal and social transformations are based on new perceptions and conceptualizations, reached through dialogue.

Education as a Human Right

This brings us full circle. The Universal Declaration of Human Rights (UDHR) enshrines education as a human right. We need human rights principles not only to be taught in our classrooms but also to be structured into the social relationships that exist in our schools—and indeed wherever learning to be human takes place, which is everywhere. We need to move toward a liberation curriculum, one that recognizes that the world is socially constructed and shaped by human action and inaction, and that each person has a voice, experience, and knowledge, and therefore ideas and practices that we can use to alter the structure of the world for the betterment of all.

We need alternative models to civics, to political science, to social science, to history as taught in our schools and universities. Currently the structure trains and prepares citizens, not humans. The United Nations has been emphasizing the need for educating for human rights over the past several years. Unfortunately, in the United States, at all levels, progress in this area has been excruciatingly slow. People could demand courses about the UDHR in high schools and colleges; they could start discussions in their communities, at their workplaces, with their families, creating a grounded revolution of knowledge—but a new knowledge.

As part of the celebration of the 60th anniversary of the UDHR, the United Nations General Assembly declared 2009 the International Year of Human Rights Learning. Throughout the year, the General Assembly heavily promoted activities to strengthen and deepen human rights learning on the basis of the principles of universality, constructive international dialogue, and cooperation, with a view toward enhancing the promotion and protection of all human rights.

CRITICAL THINKING

1. Have you every studied abroad? Have you ever experienced education in another country? Have you had discussions with anyone else who has had these experiences? How would living in, studying in, or even studying/hearing about alternative educational experiences help us envision new educational realities that are more effective for all in the matrix?

2. Taking into account the ideas discussed above about imagining new educations and education as a human right, engage your peers in dialogue about ways in which we might forge new educational systems.

3. How might the institution of education and the process of schooling in the United States be different if African Americans had been centrally involved in the creation of the education system? If Latinos had been? If Asian American women had been? If the poor had been?

4. After reading this chapter, what actions can you take to improve the educational experience and outcomes for all students?

KEY TERMS

CHAPTER SUMMARY

LO 6.1   **Describe the current state of education in the United States and the key historical factors that have shaped it.**

Key factors that helped shape the contemporary educational system in the United States include the treatment of Native Americans, the development of the university system, the establishment of separate schools for Blacks and Whites, and the creation of training opportunities that differ by race, gender, ethnicity, and class. Experiences of schooling are fundamentally woven together with the threads of gender, class, and sexuality. These experiences are themselves critically about race. In order to understand the current realities and distributions of opportunities and outcomes for students, one needs to examine their locations in the matrix of race.

LO 6.2   **Compare the major sociological theories of education.**

Social-functional theory and human capital theory are two dominant explanations of education within the discipline of sociology. The former focuses on socialization, while the latter focuses on skills acquisition. These are similar stock theories, but they have different implications for our understanding of how education works in the matrix of race.

LO 6.3   **Analyze several matrix perspectives on education.**

From a critical matrix perspective, education can be seen as a site of conversion (to White American culture), a site of class construction (as a space for the dominant culture's ideas and interests), a site of creating workers (for the capitalist labor market), and a site where citizens are crafted (as Americans).

LO 6.4   **Identify alternatives to the educational system that recognize intersectional realities.**

Imagining new educations requires seeing our reality for what it is and allowing our vision to extend beyond that reality at the same time. Paulo Freire provides us with some inspiration in this regard, as does conceptualizing education as a human right.

CRIME, LAW, AND DEVIANCE

Nicholas Kamm / AFP / Getty Images

Blacks are more than twice as likely than Whites to be victims of police violence, a fact that has prompted numerous protests and confrontations between citizens and police.

LEARNING OBJECTIVES

LO 7.1 Examine the history of race, crime, and deviance.

LO 7.2 Analyze stock theories of race, crime, and deviance.

LO 7.3 Apply the matrix lens to the relationships among race, crime, and deviance.

LO 7.4 Formulate transformative narratives of crime and deviance.

In September 2016, concerned bystanders called police when Terence Crutcher, a 40-year-old Black man, abandoned his vehicle in the middle of the road in Tulsa, Oklahoma. When officers arrived, they found Crutcher, who was unarmed, approaching his vehicle with his hands in the air. He was shot dead by one of the responding police officers. Video taken from a police helicopter and by a police cruiser dashboard camera showed Crutcher standing next to the driver's side door of his car when he dropped to the ground, blood saturating his white shirt. The Tulsa police officer who fired the fatal shots, 5-year veteran Betty Shelby, claimed that Crutcher was acting erratically and that she suspected he was high on PCP. The officer stated that she feared for her life when she fired the shot that killed Crutcher. She was arrested and charged with first-degree manslaughter.

Blacks are more than twice as likely as Whites to be victims of police violence, and Hispanics are one-third more likely than Whites to be involved in violent incidents with police. Each day across the United States, an average of slightly more than two people are shot by police, and the victims are more likely to be persons of color than to be White (Guardian 2016).

If you turn on the television, go to the movies, or check out your social media feed, you might quickly conclude that the most significant stories of our time involve crime, law, and deviance. Are these issues deservedly prominent in our media, or are they socially constructed to reproduce the matrix of race? The way we frame deviance and label behavior and how these responses are shaped by the matrix of race are central questions in sociology.

Our stock stories teach us that laws protect us; they are created to preserve peace, promote tranquility, and allow us to pursue our collective best interests. The deviants who violate laws are committing crimes and must be punished accordingly. In the pursuit of justice, democracy is preserved and enhanced and freedoms are procured and embraced. Our stock stories assume that the law is color-blind—enforced the same way everywhere, for everyone, and without concern for race, class, or other differences. Using the matrix approach, we can reveal the concealed stories of crime and deviance in the United States, stories that have always been complicated by race, ethnicity, gender, and class. Historically, crime and punishment have been associated with attempts to preserve the racial order. In this chapter we will examine this and other narratives and observe how the matrix has influenced both our perceptions and the realities of crime, deviance, and the law.

■ A HISTORY OF RACE, CRIME, AND PUNISHMENT

What happens when being different defines criminal behavior and deviance? The historical record demonstrates that in the early days of the United States, high-status White males (e.g., ministers, merchants, landowners) were rarely the subjects of criminal proceedings. Punishments were most frequently meted out to Native Americans, African slaves, single women (particularly servants), poor White males, and unruly children (Patrick 2010). Deviance encompasses all actions or behaviors that defy social norms, from crimes to social expectations. Deviance can be as mild as wearing the wrong colors to a high school football game or as extreme as not wearing anything at all. When deviance takes forms that violate moral and ethical standards, like murder or theft, it may be covered under law and become a crime. Deviance in many ways defines a significant portion of our national identity. We will discover that as the social construction of "Whiteness" came into being, it also became the normative, or standard, structure by which our laws are constructed and deviance is defined.

Building a Foundation of Whiteness

Long before they ventured across the oceans to settle the Americas, Europeans were formulating the foundations of Whiteness. English colonists arrived in America with decidedly racist stereotypes about Africans, Native Americans, and others, assuming that members of these groups were savage, indolent, and sexually promiscuous (Jordan 1968). In fact, the Europeans who settled the Americas believed it was their destiny to extend Christian civilization and White supremacy around the globe.

Elite European males institutionalized, or established, Whiteness in an effort to control Blacks, Native Americans, women, and others. Women, across all socioeconomic statuses and racial groups, typically received harsher punishments than their male counterparts for violating sexual or marriage taboos. Gender-specific laws affecting all racial, ethnic, and class groups helped to sustain White privilege and White normative structures. **White privilege**, as we discussed briefly in Chapter 1, results from laws, practices, and behaviors that preserve and (re)create societal benefits for those people identified as White. **White normative structures** are those norms and institutions that obscure the racial intent of such laws, practices, and behaviors, creating the illusion that White privilege is natural and normal.

One of the first recorded instances within the English colonies in which judicial processes decreed differential judgments along both racial and gender lines occurred in 1630 in Jamestown, when colonist Hugh Davis was ordered to be "soundly whipt" for dishonoring God and shaming Christianity by sleeping with a Black woman (Bernasconi 2012, 215). Ten years later, also in Jamestown, another White man was ordered to do penance for impregnating an African female, while the African female was sentenced to whipping. So, even though the interracial relationship was condemned, the more extreme punishment was shifted to the Black female (Bernasconi 2012, 216).

Over the next few decades of the 17th century, the pattern of race, gender, and status inequities was replicated repeatedly. While all women experienced unique discrimination and bias, racial hierarchies were also gendered. White women, given authority over all other women through their connection to White males, were given authority over Blacks. White women could lose their status if they married or had intercourse with African, Native American, or Asian men. Colonial laws did not protect either Black or Native American women from rape. Laws also precluded them from defending themselves, either directly against their attackers or through the courts. Females of color were often cast as seducers (Browne-Marshall 2002).

Legislating White Privilege

Racial consciousness and fear have shaped our views of law and deviance since colonial times. **Racial consciousness** is the awareness of race shared by members of a racial group and the wider society. This consciousness perpetuates, legitimates, and normalizes racial hierarchies by making the notions of Whiteness, White privilege, and White supremacy real at the expense of people of color. The linking of White racial consciousness with notions of normalcy was first engraved into our national laws as early as 1790, with the passage of the U.S. Naturalization Law. This law limited citizenship to those immigrants who were "free white persons of good character." And when we look further into this law, we note that of children born abroad, only those whose fathers were U.S. residents were granted citizenship. The exclusion of children whose mothers might have been residents points to the gender bias of these early laws as well. We can only conclude that this process not only justified but also served to perpetuate White male privilege.

White privilege in the United States has its foundations in sets of rules created and preserved through a series of laws, mores, and beliefs that guaranteed White personal privilege over Blacks, Native Americans, Asians, Hispanics, and others. Privilege encouraged all Whites, including those of lower status, to identify with the ruling White elite, often at the expense of Black slaves. Whiteness and its privilege provided the illusion of elite status and control of the economic, political, and judicial systems, the ultimate arbiters of White privilege. More punishment could be meted out to Blacks than to Whites; Whites, not Blacks, could own and bear arms; Whites, not Blacks, had the right to self-defense. The lowliest of White servants could chastise, correct, and testify against Blacks (either free or enslaved). And the ultimate forms of degradations were reserved for Blacks, often at the hands of Whites. Only Blacks could be whipped naked; Black slave women could be raped, and any offspring that resulted would be slaves. Further, any White woman or free woman of color who, forgetful of her status, elected to have sex with or marry a Black male slave could be forced into slavery herself.

These laws were codified into what came to be called **slave codes** throughout the southern colonies. Under these laws White males were further empowered when they joined **slave patrols** (Durr 2015)—organized groups of White men with police powers who systematically enforced the slave codes. The first slave patrols began in 1757 in Georgia, where White landowners and residents were required to serve. A patrol, usually consisting of no more than seven men, would ride throughout the night, challenging any slaves they encountered and demanding proof that they were not engaging in unlawful activities (Cooper 2015). Slave patrols were active throughout the South until slavery's abolishment at the end of the Civil War.

With the end of the Civil War came a great many new laws aimed at controlling the now freed Blacks. These laws, known as **Jim Crow laws**, held sway across the United States from the 1880s onward, with some surviving into the 1960s.

Reservations and treaties served the same function for Native Americans. For many other racial and ethnic minority Americans, Whiteness and the laws were also effectively used for social control and the construction of deviance.

Defining Whiteness in the West

During the latter half of the 19th century, Whiteness was also being defined on the western frontier, this time at the expense of Native Americans. Formal U.S. policies and laws were explicitly formulated to aid White settlers and railroad

Slave rebellions demonstrate that deviance can be both deliberate and political. In the pre–Civil War United States, several rebellions and insurrections fanned the flames of White anxiety and fears, while legitimating the humanity of those considered slaves. During the 1831 rebellion led by Nat Turner, slaves went from plantation to plantation, freeing other slaves and killing Whites. A total of 55 to 65 Whites died. In retaliation, White militias and mobs killed more than 200 Blacks.

corporations in the forcible expulsion of Native Americans from their tribal lands. The U.S. Army supplied the force whereby thousands of acres of land were acquired. No new treaties were ratified, as "raid" replaced "trade" in White–Indian treaties (DiLorenzo 2010).

As the result of battles with the army, hundreds of Native Americans were held as prisoners and subjected to military "trials." Most of the adult male prisoners were quickly found guilty and sentenced to death. This presumption of guilt had nothing to do with whether or not they were actually warriors; rather, their mere presence at the scene of the fighting was enough. In the largest mass execution in U.S. history, 38 members of the Dakota tribe were hanged in 1862 in Mankato, Minnesota, on orders of the president of the United States, Abraham Lincoln. They were accused of killing 490 White settlers, including women and children, during the Santee Sioux uprising earlier in the year. The story that rarely gets told is that these Sioux were angered by repeated broken treaties and the failure of the United States to live up to its promises of food, supplies, and reparations. Enraged and starving, the Native Americans attempted to take back their lands by force. After the execution, the remaining Native Americans were resettled on "reservations" under a presidential executive order. From this period through the next few decades, Native Americans were consistently vilified as criminals, deviants, and savages, and their lands were systematically taken as Whites and Whiteness marched westward. Even a bloody civil war did not stop the U.S. attack on Native Americans. In 1867, General William Sherman, who was tasked with securing western lands and dealing with the Native Americans, wrote to Ulysses S. Grant, then commanding general of the U.S. Army, "We are not going to let a few thieving, ragged Indians check and stop our progress" (quoted in Goldfield 2011, 450). The consolidation of Native American lands, along with the end of the Civil War, marshaled a new period of Whiteness and social control.

The Effects of Immigration

During the California gold rush of 1848–52, Chinese immigrants began arriving in the United States to work as laborers on large construction projects. They helped construct the first transcontinental railroad, and they were quite successful at mining. As gold became scarce and the competition for good jobs increased, anti-Chinese bigotry intensified. Judicial decrees and legislative actions increasingly targeted not only Chinese but also other immigrants for increased police scrutiny and criminalization. As early as 1862 the state of California passed the Act to Protect Free White Labor against Competition with Chinese Coolie Labor, and to Discourage the Immigration of the Chinese into the State of California, or the Anti-Coolie Act. This law was a clear reaction to the fears of White laborers about competition for jobs. It imposed special taxes on Chinese miners and restrictions on immigration that ultimately led to the forced segregation of Chinese immigrants, resulting in the creation of what came to be known as Chinatowns. Chinese were stereotyped as criminals and prostitutes and thus were excluded from entry into the country. Other ethnic groups also deemed "undesirable" included Middle Easterners, Hindus, East Indians, and Japanese. Anti-Chinese laws, in various forms, held sway until 1943, when Chinese immigrants were finally made eligible for U.S. citizenship.

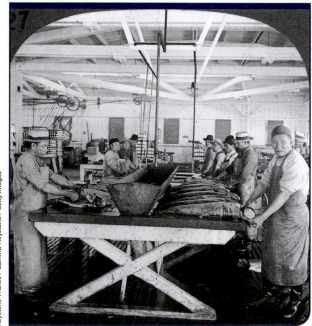

Keystone-France / Gamma-Keystone / Getty Images

Chinese immigration to the U.S. began in earnest around 1850, when "coolies" came to the country to work on major construction projects. Legislation aimed at preventing Chinese immigration, driven by fears of innate criminality, could not entirely stem the flow, and by the 1920s Chinese laborers had branched out into other industries, like salmon canning in Oregon.

At the beginning of the 20th century the United States experienced massive immigration of Southern Europeans, and a new set of White fears were launched. Southern Europeans, including the Irish, Italians, and Jews, now joined Blacks, Native Americans, and Asians as collectively perceived as the principal sources of criminality in the United States, particularly within urban communities. Associated with these concerns, the new science of sociology provided a scientific facade, assuaging White fears while explaining recently transplanted Europeans, Asians, Native Americans, and Blacks and their supposed criminality and deviance. Recently, we have developed a new terminology to use in the exploration of how laws, law enforcement, and courts racially profile various groups.

A Legacy of Racial Profiling

Crime, laws, and perceptions of deviance create, (re)produce, and reinforce status hierarchies based on race and ethnicity. At the intersections of these racial hierarchies are both gender and class. Consequently, as we look at how deviance is both constructed and enforced, we find that people of color, and males of color in particular, are most likely to be racially profiled by police, receive the stiffest sentences from the courts, are incarcerated at higher levels than Whites, and increasingly face the death penalty.

Imagine that one day a flyer appears in your mailbox. It declares that nowhere in North America is safe from "criminal Gypsies." According to the flyer, training is going to be provided that will help participants understand the "world of criminal Gypsies and Travelers," including their "fortune-telling frauds." The flyer mentions Polish Gypsies, Yugoslavian Gypsies, and other Romani groups. In fact, the Romani people have for decades been racially profiled across the United States. But they are not alone.

Racial profiling is the targeting of particular racial and ethnic groups by law enforcement and private security agencies, resulting in their subjection to ridicule, detention, interrogation, and search and seizure, often with no evidence of criminal activity. Racial profiling is based on the perception that certain racial, ethnic, religious, and national-origin groups are guilty until proven innocent. And while racial profiling violates the U.S. Constitution's guarantees of equal protection of the laws and freedom from unreasonable searches and seizures, it continues to be utilized.

Racial profiling has been a law enforcement tool in the United States since the establishment of slave patrols. From the beginning to the middle of the 19th century, it focused on the Irish, Italians, and other Southern European groups. Today, the most significant forms of racial profiling are aimed at Blacks, Hispanics, the Romani, Muslims, and Native Americans.

Slightly more than half of all adults in the United States believe that racial profiling is widespread. Some 53% believe that racial profiling plays a role in which motorists police pull over, and many believe that security personnel use racial profiling at airport security checkpoints (42%) and when deciding which shoppers to watch at stores and malls (49%). The majority of Blacks (67%) and Hispanics (63%), compared to only 50% of non-Hispanic Whites, feel that racial profiling is widespread (Bergner 2014).

The New York Police Department's so-called stop-and-frisk policy, once hailed as a marvel of modern policing, demonstrates the dangers of racial profiling. Since it was instituted in 2004, as many as 4 million citizens have been stopped and frisked by police. At least 83% of these have been Black and Latino, and 9 out of 10 have been completely innocent of any wrongdoing (Bergner 2014).

Law-abiding citizens have not been apathetic about being racially profiled. Governments, law enforcement officials, and corporations have been effectively sued for maintaining the practice. These suits have filled the media and highlight modern resistance stories. For example, a U.S. district court found that Joe Arpaio, then sheriff of Maricopa County in Arizona, had overseen a department that had systematically targeted Latinos during traffic operations. The suit alleged that the sheriff's office had violated constitutional guarantees of free speech, unlawful searches, and due process. Largely Hispanic neighborhoods were aggressively and regularly patrolled by Maricopa sheriff's deputies. A federal monitor was established to prevent continued misconduct and to safeguard the constitutional rights of the community (Osman 2015). Ironically, Joe Arpaio received the first Presidential pardon granted by President Trump in 2017.

Racial profiling is both caused and affected by the criminal justice system. So in addition to being targeted with more aggressive policing, people of color often find that the scales of justice are not always evenly balanced. When it comes to race, class, and gender, justice, as we will see in the next section, is anything but blind. Differential policing and law enforcement not only stigmatize marginalized people of color but also socially construct them as deviants. For example, the chief of police of Homer, Louisiana, once commented:

> If I see three or four young Black men walking down the street, I have to stop them and check their names. . . . I want them to be afraid every time they see the police that they might get arrested." (quoted in American Civil Liberties Union 2009, 52)

The urban poor have been systematically targeted by national and local law enforcement agencies since the founding of the United States. The urban unrest now rocking many U.S. cities reflects the increased stress fostered by a political climate that targets the poor and racial minorities.

1. How did Whiteness and deviance become the basis of criminalization, and what impact does this have on our perceptions of crime and deviance?

2. Racial profiling by police has consistently been demonstrated to lead to the increased surveillance and criminalization of both Blacks and Hispanics. How might similar types of racial profiling affect not only these groups but others within major institutions such as education, the military, and the economy? While we have concentrated on the negative aspects of racial profiling, could such profiling have positive aspects for Whites or females? Speculate on how these may manifest, not only in crime but also in other institutions.

3. Are there some individuals that we assume to be more violent, criminal, or deviant simply because of the groups to which they belong? What does this say about the social construction of deviance?

4. Consider your hometown or university. Does it include certain groups that are more likely to be associated with crime and deviance? Does this behavior surface in specific ways, at particular times, or in specific situations? Has this behavior been evidenced across several different periods?

■ SOCIOLOGICAL STOCK THEORIES OF CRIME AND DEVIANCE

The disciplines of sociology and criminology have, from their inception, been concerned with crime and deviance. These concerns have mirrored society's attempts to justify racial, gendered, and class hierarchies. Accordingly, the standard theories within sociology and criminology may be considered as stock stories. The theoretical orientations of these stock stories may be separated into two broad categories: biosocial theories of deviance and ecological perspectives on crime.

These standard stories have a common thread—they place the source of deviance at the micro, or personal, level. Therefore, either the individual or his or her community, culture, or environment is at odds with societal norms. And, by implication, if the individual or his or her community, culture, or environment could just be reformed, fixed, adjusted, or rehabilitated, then the deviance would be reduced or would cease to exist. Finally, as we shall see, these stock stories all fail to account adequately for the macro, or structural, factors that at best intervene in and at worst are the primary contributors to the social construction of deviance. As we will see later in the chapter, after a troubled start, sociologists armed with an intersectional or matrix perspective have been more adept at unraveling the discourse regarding race, class, gender, and crime and deviance. Let us now turn to these theories.

Biosocial Theories of Deviance

Classical sociological theories of crime and deviance represent a portion of our stock stories. The earliest and most systematic attempts to understand deviance linked it to biology. In the 19th century, Cesare Lombroso, viewed as the founder of modern criminology, ascribed crime and deviance to both ethnicity and race. He held that Africans, Asians, and American Indians were especially prone to crime and deviance (Greene and Gabbidon 2012, 96). Lombroso argued that so-called biological indicators such as a particular body type, a certain shape of face, high cheekbones, large ears, and small brain were all associated with a more primitive form of human being. These genetically determined characteristics were all external signs that marked individuals as potential criminals. According to Lombroso, all non-Europeans were more likely to be criminals because they were lower on the evolutionary scale. He argued that crime and deviance were biologically determined. This theory, based in **biological determinism**, holds that an individual's behavior is innately related to components of his or her physiology, such as body type and brain size. Lombroso's theory was later criticized for being too simplistic and highly ethnocentric. The samples he relied upon for his studies were unrepresentative of the population as a whole, because he focused primarily on Italian criminals who were convicted of crimes, comparing them with Italian soldiers. A whole range of structural, economic, and cultural factors were ignored or subsumed under these differences.

By the time Lombroso's research became known in the United States at the beginning of the 20th century, biological determinism was the dominant explanation for crime and deviance. Within the United States, the overrepresentation of African Americans and some immigrants in crime statistics caused many to link race and ethnicity to crime and deviance (Gould 1981). With time, the leading arguments regarding deviance and crime were linked to IQ and race.

While some recent scholars have revived the discourse linking crime and biology, they have stressed that a person's behavior is influenced by both biology and environment. Critiques of this approach have quickly pointed out the implicit race, gender, and class biases inherent in it, and that it fails to take into consideration social environment, a failure that can lead to the biological and social determinism of previous periods (Gould 1981).

If crime is related to environment, what does that say about the environment in which you live? If we were, for example, to do a measure of crime on many college campuses, we might conclude that offenders are likely to be White, male, and educated. This is primarily because most college campuses are predominantly White and presumably more educated than the general population. And it recognizes that males are most likely to be risk takers, hence more likely than females to be associated with deviance. Alternatively, within the United States, while Whites are more likely to use illegal drugs, including cocaine, marijuana, and LSD, Blacks are more likely to go to prison for drug offenses (Fellner 2009). Clearly, something more is happening.

Ecological Perspectives on Crime

From its inception, sociology in the United States was concerned with solving the myriad problems associated with industrialization, urbanization, slums, poverty, and crime that were rapidly transforming the nation at the beginning of the 20th century (Orcutt 1983). Sociologists attempted to explain the apparent links between crime and social location (including ethnicity, race, class, and gender). Some believed that members of minority communities received much more scrutiny from criminal justice professionals and thus were more likely to be prosecuted by the legal system (Tonry 1995). Others argued that Blacks and other minorities were simply more likely than Whites to commit serious crimes (Hindelang 1978).

For almost half of the 20th century, the ecological approach dominated the discourse on deviance within American sociology. This approach situates human behavior (norms, social control, deviance, and nondeviance) within the social structures external to the individual. The causes of crime, these theorists posited, are found in the community structures in which people live and interact. Community members interact to socially (re)create the conditions that account for criminal and noncriminal behavior. Several theoretical strands have been derived from the ecological approach to crime and deviance. The four most important of these are social disorganization, the culture of poverty, cultural conflict, and broken windows theory.

Social Disorganization

Social disorganization, one of the first derivatives of the ecological approach, links crime to neighborhood ecological patterns. Place matters, and the apparent ecological differences in levels of crime are explained by the structural and cultural factors that shape, distort, or encourage social order within communities. For example, high levels of immigration and migration often produce rapid community changes. These rapid changes may then lead to either the disruption or the breakdown of the structure of social relations and values, resulting in the loss of social controls over individual and group behavior. During the period of stress, social disorganization prevails, and crime, which is thus situational and not group specific, develops and persists.

Culture of Poverty

Rather than the community, some theorists began to conceive of culture as the nexus for deviance. It was argued that different levels of crime among various groups arose from differences in morality (Wirth 1931). Theorist Louis Wirth (1931, 485) wrote, "Where culture is homogeneous and class differences are negligible, societies without crime are possible." **Differential association theory** elaborates on this perspective, proposing that differences in criminal involvement among groups result from their different definitions of criminality. Those groups that normalize crime essentially develop a "culture of poverty," accounting not only for their lack of success but also for their continued leaning toward criminal lifestyles (Moynihan 1965; Lewis 1961, 1966a, 1966b). The **culture of poverty** approach views poverty as a set of choices made by unwed mothers that perpetuate crime, deviance, and other pathologies across generations. The process produces children who are both morally deficient and more apt to commit crime; in addition, they

Figure 7.1 ■ Children are More Likely to Be Born Into Poverty When Parents Lack Education

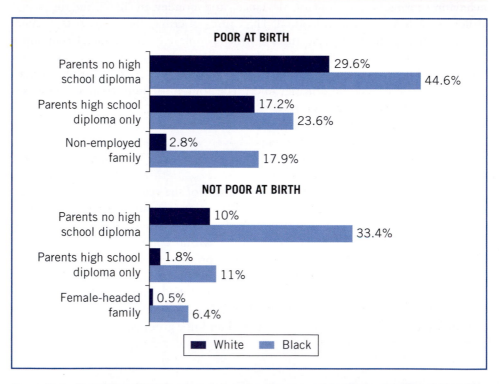

Source: Figure 3, p. 7 from "Child Poverty and Its Lasting Consequence" by Caroline Ratcliffe and Signe-Mary McKernan. Low-Income Working Families Paper 21, Urban Institute, September 2012. Retrieved from http://www.urban.org/UploadedPDF/412659-Child-Poverty-and-Its-Lasting-Consequence-Paper.pdf.

produce more unwed mothers with unwanted children. This self-perpetuating cycle of dependencies, it has been argued, is associated with poor families, and specifically with poor families of color. This perspective has been criticized as essentially blaming the victim—that is, holding the injured party entirely or partially responsible for the harm suffered. Such a perspective ignores the structural inequities that underlie poverty.

Recent research has documented that the most significant factor associated with growing up poor is low educational attainment (Figure 7.1). Other factors that are also important are single motherhood, family unemployment, young age of parents, and living in inner-city neighborhoods (Ratcliffe and McKernan 2012). So rather than a culture of poverty, there are definite structural conditions that lead to a cycle of poverty. We shall return to these structural conditions below.

Broken Windows Theory

Beginning in the early 1980s, criminologists began to speculate on the relationship between urban disorder and vandalism. Could cities fix their crime problems by simply fixing up the neighborhoods, picking up the litter, and, yes, fixing broken windows? **Broken windows theory** (Wilson and Kelling 1982) argues that stopping vandalism can lead to a significant decrease in serious crime. Police surveillance may be a means of controlling crime, but it does not eliminate or even curtail it. The presence of abandoned properties, vandalism, litter, and filth not only demoralizes community residents but also produces a form of nihilism (i.e., an extreme form of fatalism) that leaves people feeling overwhelmed, hopeless, and apt to give up. But while fixing broken windows and sprucing up neighborhoods may lead to increasing pride in a community, these actions do not sufficiently explain lower levels of crime and deviance. Combatting fear, making citizens feel empowered, and establishing partnership relations between community members and police are among the factors that lead to decreased crime levels (Xu, Fiedler, and Flaming 2015). Similar arguments have linked crime with the prevalence of lead in the environment.

The broken windows theory holds that addressing minor crimes like vandalism and jaywalking reinforces social norms around lawfulness and thus reduces crime.

pihpix / Alamy Stock Photo

CRITICAL THINKING

1. What does the acceptance of stock stories suggest regarding the natural, cultural, biological, or community basis of crime?

2. How might stock stories influence the way that crime is both perceived and prosecuted? How might such beliefs affect jury members in cases involving suspects who are members of racial minorities?

3. How do stock stories mirror our assumptions about racial and ethnic differences?

4. Have you experienced being categorized according to others' conceptualizations of how you should or should not act based on the group(s) with which you identify? If so, in what ways did this experience affect your choices? How did you ultimately deal with the characterizations of others? What does this suggest about your individual agency and stereotypical assumptions about you?

■ APPLYING THE MATRIX TO CRIME AND DEVIANCE

The matrix approach posits that powerful elites construct and enforce laws that protect their interests. Du Bois (1904) was the first to theorize and document the intersectional or matrix approach to crime and deviance. He began by dismissing the biological basis of crime and pointing out how social structures influence crime and deviance. Du Bois argued that crime and racial status are definitely linked, with the linkage most obvious among African Americans. He pointed out that in the United States, race, class, and gender are manipulated to maximize profits.

The matrix perspective helps us interrogate our assumptions about what is deviant and what is normal, or what is considered criminal and what is noncriminal. Even casual observation reveals that a given behavior might be rewarded in one context and penalized in another. Space often determines the appropriateness of specific acts. Consider war and contact sports: In both settings the use of certain forms of violence is considered legitimate, but that same behavior at a party or in a college classroom would not be appropriate. The matrix approach also reveals that certain persons occupying certain social spaces or identities, such as racial, class, and gender identities, may similarly find their actions differentially circumscribed and labeled deviant. When various physical spaces interact with social identities, different types and definitions of deviance can be identified.

The Spaces and Places of Crime and Deviance

Have you ever wondered when and where crime is most prevalent? The matrix approach focuses our attention on how individual behavior interacts with larger social structures. Issues of race and racism produce stress. One important theory helps us understand how this stress influences deviance.

General Strain Theory

One of the seminal Sociological approaches demonstrates the causal likes between levels of stress and deviance. **General strain theory** (Agnew 1992) proposes that racism produces stressful events and environments, which in turn lead to "negative emotions such as anger, fear, depression, and rage, and these emotional reactions lead to crime either directly or indirectly depending upon other contingencies such as coping mechanisms, peer and familial support, and self-esteem" (Piquero and Sealock 2010, 171). Thus it is suggested that people of color may view the United States from a particularly racialized perspective, where "race matters" because it significantly alters their chances for survival and success (Unnever and Gabbidon 2011). Systemic racism—that is, a system of inequality based on race, often within institutional settings, such as law enforcement and the criminal justice system—is often associated with differential outcomes in crime and deviance. Because of systemic racism, people of color are more likely than Whites to be victims of police abuse, racial profiling, and differential criminal sanctioning under get-tough policies associated with the war on crime and drugs. Systemic racism is at the root of the current mass incarceration of Blacks, who then experience a lifetime of legal and employment discrimination, housing segregation, and diminished opportunities (Alexander 2010).

Some criminologists argue that until we understand how race and racism create a hegemonic structure that has historically criminalized people of color, we will not be able to account for the apparent permanence of racial disparities in deviance and incarceration. Regardless of levels of crime or historical period, racial disparities in incarceration rates have been relatively constant (Hawkins 2011).

A Climate of Violence

Ethnographers such as Elijah Anderson flip the script by asking how racialization, gender, and disempowerment interact to produce increased surveillance, criminalization, and incarceration. Inner-city Black males find their lives more difficult as police assume they are the neighborhood problems that should be fixed, and detain, search, and often arrest them (Anderson 1990). The increased prevalence of men of color in the criminal justice system is more about this high level of surveillance than it is about these men's likelihood of criminality. Inner-city communities are surrounded by forces beyond their residents' control, and challenges to identity and manhood only intensify perceived problems and uncertainties. The only thing of value many young men can control is their reputation, or "rep." Losing it means losing credibility. The "code of the street"—the unwritten rules that enforce respect, justice, and rights—insulates community members from a profound sense of alienation from mainstream society, where many institutions seem punitive. Yet while the code helps to check wholesale violence, it actually perpetuates a climate of violence (Anderson 1994, 1999).

Incarceration rates are influenced by the disappearance of work as well as by differential labeling and negative stereotyping of young men of color by those who make and enforce the laws. Rios (2006) shows that these factors lead to increased surveillance by school officials in schools, by police within communities, and by families. At the intersection of race, class, gender, and age, poor young men of color face a "double bind." Thwarted in their efforts to be identified as "hardworking men," they choose "hypermasculinity" and deviance as a means of demonstrating their manhood (Rios 2006, 54). This hypermasculinity, with its aggravated aggressiveness and physicality, has been labeled "cool poise" (Anderson 1999). It has been both romanticized and glorified in hip-hop and "gangsta" rap music and linked to increasing levels of interpersonal conflicts, group violence and gang violence, and sexual exploitation of young women of color (Nettleton 2011, 140).

Unable to fulfill the role of "hardworking man," some turn to hypermasculinity and deviance to express their maleness.

Consequently, associating with violent peers, having a history of violent involvement, experiencing discrimination, and living in a neighborhood characterized by violence and disadvantage are all factors that have been found likely to reproduce violence among young men of color (Stewart and Simons 2009). Anderson (1999, 8) found that those who "internalized the code of the street and actually lived by it were more likely to be involved in later reported acts of violence."

The continual attention to acts of violence perpetrated by the urban poor is typically masked by the code words "getting tough on crime," a policy stance that accounts for the skyrocketing incarceration of persons of color (Alexander 2010). Similarly, the so-called war on drugs has been described as an undeclared war on women in general and Black women in particular (Bush-Baskette 1998). As we will see below, this undeclared war has resulted in an almost fourfold increase in the number of women imprisoned in recent years.

In summary, the matrix approach posits that race is a marker reflecting our social context (Burt, Simons, and Gibbons 2012, 3). Crime and deviance do not operate in a vacuum; they are part of the process by which the racial matrix is maintained and perpetuated. Of particular interest in this formulation is the prison–industrial complex.

The Structure and Context of Crime and Deviance

Over the past couple of decades, sociologists have pointed to **structural inequities** (i.e., society-wide conditions that result in unequal outcomes for particular groups in comparison with others), such as racism and social isolation, as the causal links to differential outcomes in crime and deviance (Massey and Sampson 2009). These new interpretations argue that racism, differential educational funding, and lack of opportunities may lead to a culture of poverty—not the other way around. All of these factors are structural; they affect the institutions of education, the job market, family formation, and community viability. These structural inequities produce poverty; poverty is not created by individuals, their cultures, or their communities (Cohen 2010). This aspect of the matrix highlights the interactions between micro-level behaviors and the structural systems and processes operating at the macro level.

The matrix informs us that crime and deviance are situational and contextually specific. This means that rather than culture or race, space and place provide the clues to understanding both. The implications that follow are that if we were to look at different situations and contexts, we would find different types of crime. Therefore, spaces and places like urban centers produce different types of deviance possibilities than do spaces and places such as corporations. We would also expect different types of deviance to be associated with different types of institutions. Similarly, the context of deviance is important.

Two Competing Perceptions of Reality

One media report argues that young Black men are 21 times more likely than their White counterparts to die at the hands of police. Another argues that more Whites are killed by police. They can't both be right, right? Wrong! They can. Consider the two reports. According to Gabrielson, Jones, and Sagara (2014), young Black males ages 15 to 19 were killed by police at a rate of 31.27 per million from 2010 through

Aerial Archives / Alamy Stock Photo

The U.S. inmate population has grown under the prison-industrial complex, necessitating the construction of enormous new facilities, like this one in Illinois.

2012, compared to a rate of just 1.47 per million for White males in the same age group. Alternatively, Bill O'Reilly (2014), then the popular host of his own program on Fox News, announced that his research concluded that in 2012 just 123 African Americans were shot by police, while 326 Whites were killed by police. When one considers that there are 43 million Blacks in the United States and 200.7 million Whites, the conclusion appears that Whites and Blacks have an almost equal chance of being shot by police.

So, how can both reports be right? The first set of numbers takes into consideration only those young men ages 15 to 19 and covers the period from 2010 to 2012. The second set of numbers does not specify an age range and deals with just one year. The other factor is where the numbers come from, and herein lies the real problem. No consistent data are recorded on police killings of civilians across the country. Gabrielson et al. cite data on fatal police shootings collected by the Federal Bureau of Investigation, but as extensive as their analysis is, it has flaws, in that the FBI relies on self-reported data from a small percentage of the nation's more than 17,000 law enforcement agencies. So, what we are left with are two competing perceptions of reality. These two perceptions have become increasingly evident as we have watched the unfolding of various grand jury deliberations regarding the deaths of Black males at the hands of police and the protests that have followed. In many ways, these constitute two different forms of concealed stories.

The Prison–Industrial Complex

In recent years, policies of aggressive policing targeting specific groups have greatly expanded the U.S. inmate population, helping to create what some have labeled the **prison–industrial complex** (Sudbury 2002). In this system, government and industry uses of surveillance, policing, and imprisonment have been merged in an effort to solve economic, social and political problems. Political support for mass-incarceration policies is influenced by private prison companies and by the businesses that supply goods and services to government prisons. The more recent politicization and racialization of crime and punishment has its roots in the 1968 presidential campaign of Richard Nixon. As jobs disappeared, unemployment skyrocketed, and urban unrest was observed, many began to call for more "law and order." This call was loudest from Nixon, who made being tough on crime the hallmark of his presidency.

The most significant increase in the adverse treatment of men of color occurred after the 1980 election of Ronald Reagan. The Reagan administration greatly publicized the drug war, highlighting the epidemic rise of crack cocaine in the inner cities. News stories, originating from White House staffers, began appearing, "publicizing inner-city crack babies, crack mothers, crack whores, and drug-related violence" (Alexander 2012). Racial inequities in

Richard Nixon, in his 1968 bid for the presidency, made "law and order" the linchpin of his southern strategy. In his first State of the Union address, he asserted that "we must declare and win the war against the criminal elements which increasingly threaten our cities, our homes and our lives." In this call for action, the "war on drugs" became the most visible outcome (Soss, Fording, and Schram 2011, 32–35).

criminalization intensified as voters and politicians decided to "get tough on crime." Clearly, the so-called war on crime has essentially been a war on race, as laws were passed to stiffen crime control, punishment, and sentencing. In the aftermath, racial disparities were not only worsened but also excused (Tonry 1994, 475–76).

The key force driving mass incarceration in the United States has been the war on drugs, which has led to policies that have resulted in a disproportionate increase in the criminalization of poor, non-White offenders (Alexander 2010; Mauer 2006; Provine 2007). Black and Latino males are disproportionately targeted by police in many major municipalities, including New York (New York Civil Liberties Union 2012), Los Angeles (Ayres 2008), and Chicago (Caputo 2014). In many states, laws concerning undocumented immigrants are in essence thinly disguised means of allowing law enforcement to engage in racial profiling; these states include Arizona, Alabama, Utah, South Carolina, Indiana, Georgia, Missouri, and Oklahoma (Rickerd and Lin 2012). Under the guise of race-neutral crime policies, racial hierarchies are preserved while the presumed criminality of racial minorities is made real. Consequently, while on the surface such laws seem to be nonracial, their effect is to perpetuate racial inequities (Alexander 2010; Tonry 1995).

After 1980, the federal prison population increased eightfold, at a cost to U.S. taxpayers of more than $6 billion a year. Since the mid-2000s, however, the numbers have dipped to 1999 levels; with 2013 admissions, the United States held an estimated 1,574,700 persons in both state and federal prisons (see Figure 7.2). Non-Hispanic

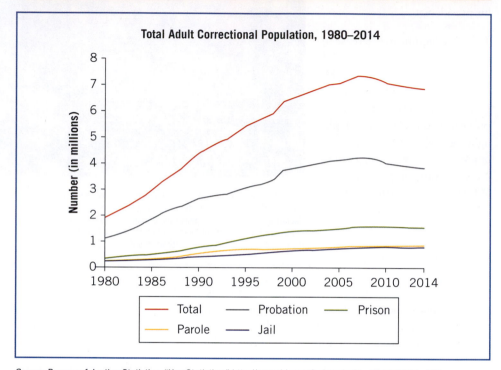

Figure 7.2 ■ The State and Federal Prison Population Has Increased Since 1980

Total Adult Correctional Population, 1980–2014

Legend: Total, Probation, Prison, Parole, Jail

Source: Bureau of Justice Statistics, "Key Statistics," http://www.bjs.gov/index.cfm?ty=kfdetail&iid=487.

Blacks (37%) made up the largest portion of male inmates, followed by non-Hispanic Whites (32%) and Hispanics (22%) (Carson 2014, 1–2).

In the same period, White women made up close to half (49%) of the female prison population, compared to Black women, who accounted for 22%. If, however, we look at rate of imprisonment, we see that Black women (at 113 per 100,000) are more than twice as likely as White females (51 per 100,000) to be incarcerated. Variations are also observed if we consider gender and age. Close to 3% of Black male U.S. residents, regardless of age, were imprisoned as of December 31, 2014 (2,805 inmates per 100,000), compared to 1% of Hispanic males (1,134 per 100,000) and slightly less than 0.5% of White males (466 per 100,000). Black males in the 18–19 age group had the highest imprisonment rates. These young men were more than nine times more likely than their White counterparts to be imprisoned (Carson 2014, 8).

The Poverty Link

Poverty lies at the heart of these trends. Poverty, aggravated by racial isolation and coupled with inadequate funding of schools, lack of employment, and aggressive policing, has both immediate and lasting effects. Gaps in income between different racial groups are reflected in some less-than-obvious ways. When we compare incarcerated with nonincarcerated people ages 27–42, stark differences are apparent (Figure 7.3). While the racial gaps remain, males see the greatest declines in average income. This reflects the fact that males, and White males in particular, start off with the highest earnings and so have more to lose. What is not so apparent, and provides further evidence of the effects of the matrix, is that Black women, who have significantly less to lose, are the second-biggest losers in terms of incarceration. Further, the smallest income losses are observed among Hispanic women, who have the lowest wages to start with (Figure 7.3).

Figure 7.3 ■ Incarcerated People Earn Less Prior to Incarceration Than Non-incarcerated People

	Incarcerated people (prior to incarceration)		Non-incarcerated people	
	Men	Women	Men	Women
All	$19,650	$13,890	$41,250	$23,745
Black	$17,625	$12,735	$31,245	$24,255
Hispanic	$19,740	$11,820	$30,000	$15,000
White	$21,975	$15,480	$47,505	$26,130

Figure 1. Median annual incomes for incarcerated people prior to incarceration and non-incarcerated people are ages 27–42, in 2014 dollars, by race/ethnicity and gender.

	Men	Women
All	52%	42%
Black	44%	47%
Hispanic	34%	21%
White	54%	41%

Figure 2. Percentage difference between the median annual incomes for incarcerated people prior to incarceration and non-incarcerated people ages 27–42, in 2014 dollars, by race/ethnicity and gender.

Source: Bernadette Rabuy and Daniel Kopf, "Prisons of Poverty: Uncovering the Pre-incarceration Incomes of the Imprisoned," Prison Policy Initiative, July 9, 2015, https://www.prisonpolicy.org/reports/income.html.

Among Black males without college educations, about 12% of those born after World War II are incarcerated, compared to 36% of those who reached their 30s in 2005. Even higher incarceration rates are observed among Black males born in the mid-1960s who dropped out of school. Of this group, between 60% and 70% are incarcerated. During this period, while the rate of incarceration for those without college more than tripled, it less than doubled among those with college. Consequently, a Black male dropping out of high school has an incarceration rate almost 50 times greater than the national average (Western 2006, 18). Ultimately, it is the community that bears the cost of so much imprisonment. As reported by Gonnerman (2004), this has produced "million-dollar blocks"—urban areas where $1 million or more has been spent to incarcerate the residents.

Different Sentencing Outcomes

Race, ethnicity, gender, and class disparities in sentencing outcomes have also been identified. Men are 15 times more likely than women to be convicted of crimes, and on average they receive sentences that are about 63% longer than those received by women. Women are also about twice as likely as men to avoid incarceration, even when convicted. Prosecutorial decisions regarding women might be influenced by such statistics, as well as by other elements. One of these might be that women simply commit less severe crimes and thus warrant less severe punishment. Another factor, labeled the "girlfriend theory," suggests that women are minor players caught up in the criminal actions of their boyfriends. Third, prosecutors might be lenient toward female defendants because of their family status—for instance, they may have young children, and incarceration would lead to family hardships. Fourth, women may be more likely to cooperate with prosecutors, and thus be granted plea deals (Starr 2012). Black women have been found to be three times more likely, and Hispanic women 69% more likely, than their White counterparts to be incarcerated (Sentencing Project 2005).

While inner-city drug use is highlighted on the front pages of tabloids across the country, drug use among middle-class youth is often ignored. Such drug abuse typically is more hidden and more likely to involve prescription medications, and thus is less likely to be criminalized. Middle- and upper-class young people are more likely to have access to both health insurance and prescription medications. Drugs such as oxycodone, hydrocodone, and codeine are now outpacing heroin and cocaine combined among substance abusers. Death rates from prescription drug overdoses nearly tripled between 1998 and 2006. White males ages 35–54 accounted for the highest proportion of deaths (Warner, Chen, and Makuc 2009).

Depending on the type of offense, most research finds that greater leniency is shown in sentencing when the victim is either Black or Hispanic. This is particularly true in sexual assault cases. When charged with crimes, Whites are more likely to receive

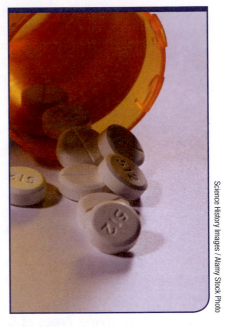

Abuse of prescription drugs, like oxycodone, is now outpacing that of street drugs like crack cocaine.

lower bail, thus suggesting a higher likelihood of prison time for Blacks and Hispanics. Hispanics, followed by Blacks, are also more likely to be denied release options. Regionally, Blacks charged with felonies in the South are least likely to have their cases dismissed. White males are also significantly more likely than either Hispanics or Blacks to have their charges reduced (Warner et al. 2009). Most research has found that Hispanic and Black males are more likely than their White counterparts to be singled out for severe punishment (Kutateladze, Lynn, and Liang 2012). And those with the least income and education are the most disadvantaged (Mustard 2001).

Capital Punishment

The United States is the only industrialized Western democracy that still allows capital punishment. Since 2009, Hispanics have constituted almost 20% of the new admissions to death rows across the United States (Snell 2010). Phillips (2008) has documented that Black defendants are 1.75 times more likely than White defendants to face the death penalty, and 1.5 times more likely than White defendants to actually be sentenced to death. Currently, 54% of prisoners on death rows in the United States are either Black or Latino, yet Blacks and Latinos make up only 27.9% of the total U.S. population (IndexMundi 2016).

The disparities in the application of the death penalty constitute an obvious indicator of more deeply ingrained inequalities across many institutional structures that maintain and perpetuate higher levels of violence in Black and Latino communities. When work disappears, there is an increase in ghetto-related behaviors, including the criminal activities associated with what some call an underground economy (Wilson 1996). Finally, what is the impact of structural inequality? For example, homicide rates over the past few decades point to obvious racial gaps. Black males are eight times more likely than their White counterparts to be homicide victims or offenders. They are also about five times more likely to be incarcerated for violent offenses. Comparatively, Hispanics also are more likely to be involved in violent crimes. Homicide continues to be the leading cause of death for Black males and the second leading cause of death for Latino males between the ages of 15 and 24 (Phillips 2002). These racial gaps can be explained only by structural inequalities. More specifically, almost the entire Hispanic–White gap and at least half of the Black–White gap could be eliminated by a reduction in residential mobility, improvements in education, and an increase in employment opportunities (Phillips 2002).

Identifying Types of Crime

Some types of crimes, victims, and criminals have become closely associated with particular races, classes, and genders. Dominant racial and ethnic groups, because they are better positioned than others, are more able to avoid criminal sanctions and being labeled deviant. The systemic linking of deviance with difference has much to do with both who is doing the linking and where the observations are being conducted. In most cases the assignment of deviance serves to legitimate both the status and the privileges of those in power. Deviance typically has been associated with young males who are members of racial and/or ethnic minorities. The fact that these youth also tend to be concentrated within urban areas, on reservations, or in rural enclaves has given rise to a long history of linking deviance to specific kinds of communities and groups. Crimes targeting women in all of these situations have tended to be either ignored or marginalized.

Differential Labeling

Differential labeling occurs when some individuals and groups are systematically singled out and declared deviant by virtue of their being in those particular groups. This labeling derives from the social construction of crime, law, and deviance by those who have power. Differential labeling underlies a persistently held belief within the United States that Blacks, Hispanics, and other disadvantaged groups are more prone to crime, violence, and disorder; more likely to receive support from welfare programs; and more likely to live in undesirable communities. Such stereotypes may also lead members of the stigmatized groups to respond in ways that confirm the beliefs. Women of all groups have also experienced differential labeling. Women of color in particular bear the historic scars of being labeled whores and gold diggers (Farrell and Swigert 1988, 3).

Differential labeling makes us more likely to associate racial minorities with crime. Deviance is in the eye of the observer. If we expect to see crime, then we will see it (Thomas and Thomas 1928, 571–72).

Differential labeling highlights the significance of the perceptions and social construction of deviance and crime. All too often, it can have devastating consequences. Over the past 7 years, the U.S. Department of Justice has been increasingly asked to evaluate incidents of the use of lethal force by local police. While it has identified 14 municipal law enforcement agencies suspected of engaging in a "pattern or practice" of violating civil rights through the use of excessive force, these findings have resulted in few lasting reforms (Weichselbaum 2015). Some have gone so far as to suggest that law enforcement has developed a warrior mindset rather than a guardian mindset (Stoughton 2015).

Hate Crimes

Crimes targeting individuals because of their group membership fall under the classification of hate crimes. The perpetrators of such crimes use violence and intimidation to further stigmatize and marginalize disenfranchised individuals and groups (Figure 7.4). These offenses are intended to protect and preserve hegemonic hierarchies associated with race, gender, sexuality, and class (Perry and Alvi 2011). The first federal legislation in the United States concerning hate crimes was the 1990 Hate Crime Statistics Act (Perry 2001, 2–3).

In 2014, the FBI reported that law enforcement agencies across the country reported a total of 5,850 hate crimes. Just over half were racially motivated crimes. Others targeted sexual orientation, religion, ethnicity, gender identity, disability, and gender. Almost two-thirds (65.1%) were crimes against persons; the rest were property crimes (FBI 2015). While Blacks remain the most

Mark Makela / Getty Images News / Getty Images

In early 2017, a string of hate crimes were recorded in which Jewish cemeteries were targeted. Roughly one-third of hate crimes target property.

targeted group, the number of incidents aimed at Blacks has steadily decreased, from about 6,000 per year in 1995 to 2,201 in 2015. Similarly, violence against lesbian, gay, bisexual, and transgender persons has been decreasing, but the number of crimes targeting LGBT people of color remains constant. LGBT people of color are more likely than their White counterparts to be the victims of hate crimes (Ahmed and Jindasurat 2014).

Most hate crime offenders are motivated either by a desire for excitement (66%) or by the belief that they are protecting their neighborhoods from perceived outsiders (25%). Few hate crime perpetrators commit these crimes in retaliation for being victimized (8%) or are motivated exclusively by bigotry (1%) (McDevitt, Levin, and Bennett 2002).

Figure 7.4 ■ Over Half of All Hate Crimes Reported in 2015 Were Racially Motivated

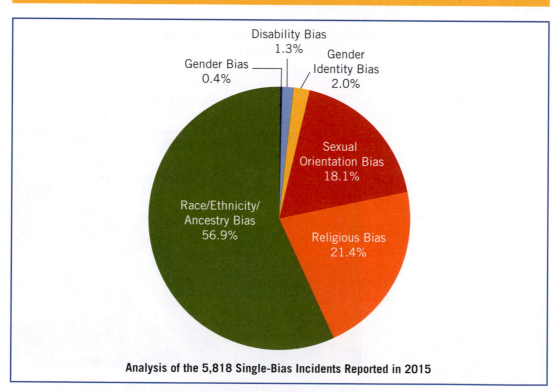

Analysis of the 5,818 Single-Bias Incidents Reported in 2015

Source: "Hate Crime in America, by the Numbers," Mike Brunker, Monica Alba, and Bill Dedman. NBC News, June 18, 2015.

Violence against Women

Throughout history, race, class, and gender have been elements in the selection of particular groups for victimization. Among women of color, sexual abuse has been used as a means of social control and to buttress a system that upholds both racial and masculine superiority. One in six women reports being the victim of attempted or completed rape. Of the 17.7 million women who fall into these categories, Native American and mixed-race women are by far the largest groups (34.1% and 24.4%, respectively). Since many rapes go unreported, these figures could be much higher. The leading causal factors associated with rape victims are high levels of poverty, unemployment, and hopelessness. Among all groups, persons in the poorest households experience violent victimizations at more than double the rate of persons in higher-income households (Harrell, Langton, Berzofsky, Couzens, and Smiley-McDonald 2014).

Across the United States, 1 in 5 women and 1 in 71 men will be raped at some point in their lives. Bisexual women report the highest rates of rape (74.9%), followed by lesbians (46.4%) and then heterosexual women (43%). The most common violent crime on U.S. college campuses is rape (Sampson 2002). By the time they graduate, at least a quarter of female college students have experienced sexual assault. Only 4% of these incidents are reported to law enforcement and 7% to any school official. A significant proportion of sexual assaults on college campuses involve LGBT students (9%) (National Sexual Violence Research Center 2015).

Many domestic workers and farmworkers, particularly those who are undocumented immigrants, may be hidden victims of sexual abuse. These victims, isolated physically, legally, or both, are least likely to report or to be able to prove charges of rape or abuse. An exhaustive 2006 study in New York found that 33% of domestic workers had experienced either verbal or physical abuse or were made to feel uncomfortable by their employers. Of these, one-third felt that their race/ethnicity or immigration status contributed to their employers' behavior (Domestic Workers United and DataCenter 2006). In fact, the rape of domestic workers is a worldwide problem. In 2012, the United Nations announced the ratification of a new treaty to protect domestic workers' rights. In many ways, crimes against immigrants and other so-called undocumented workers are forms of hate crimes.

Organized Crime

Gangs range in type from more or less informal groups whose members frequently commit crimes to more formal groups with clear hierarchies, histories, and cultures. These latter types of gangs participate in what can only be classified as **organized crime**.

Urban gangs associated with organized crime over the past decade have expanded their operations to include alien smuggling, human trafficking, and prostitution. These groups have also been highly integrated within specific communities. Urban gangs associated with the Irish, Italians, Jews, and Poles emerged in four major U.S. gang regions associated with European ethnic migration during the period 1880–1920. These almost exclusively consisted of street gangs operating in New York City and Chicago. During the 1960s and 1970s, the demographics of urban gangs shifted, reflecting changes in the U.S. population. Latino and Black gangs began to dominate in both of these cities. Significant differences in history can be identified between gangs in the western United States and those in the Northeast and the Midwest. Western gangs, for example, were never associated with White ethnics. Rather, for nearly half a century, Mexicans have dominated these gangs (Howell and Moore 2010).

The earliest gangs originating in New York and Chicago were dominated by adults engaged in criminal activity. Organized crime figures and political operatives created complex webs of criminal activity that controlled the streets in both cities. Gangs with younger members emerged and copied the styles of the earlier gangs, flourishing over time. These gangs tended to be associated with urban decay, unemployment, and overwhelmed social agencies (Howell and Moore 2010).

Today, four major gang regions can be identified in the United States. U.S.-based gangs operate behind prison walls (where they also recruit), in the military (where there are at least 53 separate gangs), and internationally, in Central America, Mexico, Africa, Europe, China, and the Middle East.

Contrary to popular stereotypes, three out of five gang members are adults (Howell and Moore 2010). Larger cities and suburban counties, with their longer histories of gang presence, are more likely to have older gang members. Most gang members are male, although nearly half of all gangs outside large cities report having some female members. Latinos and African Americans dominate gang membership (Figure 7.5). White gang members tend to be more prevalent in smaller, more rural areas (National Gang Center 2012). Gangs are associated primarily with poorer, urban communities. Their existence is seen as a response to both unemployment and the lack of other services (Egley, Howell, and Harris 2014). Gang membership may serve as a defensive response to perceived or real threats posed by social disorganization, economic disadvantage, and high levels of ethnic and racial conflict (Pyrooz, Fox, and Decker 2010). Racial and ethnic gangs serve a multitude of purposes for their members. They provide a sense of belonging, order, purpose, community, defense, and resources (status, drugs, and money) (Howell and Moore 2010).

White-Collar Crime

When most people think about crime, they might picture a male, typically a person of color, wearing a hoodie and sporting gold teeth, lurking on some dark street corner, just waiting to jump out and molest an innocent passerby. We all know those areas where it is "unsafe" to walk at night. Ironically, our perceptions of crime ignore some of the most significant criminal acts committed, those perpetrated by White professionals working in offices. This kind of crime—known as **white-collar crime**—is

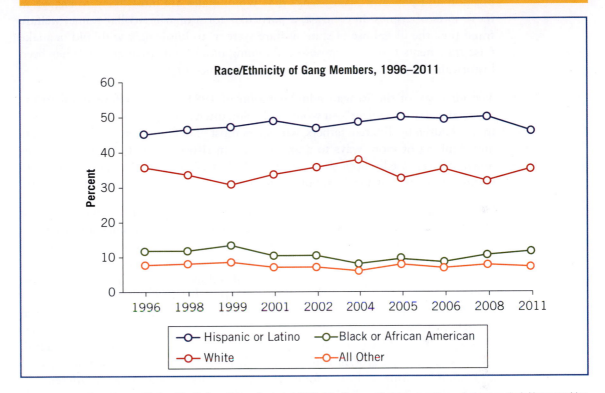

Race/Ethnicity of Gang Members, 1996–2011

Legend:
- Hispanic or Latino
- White
- Black or African American
- All Other

Source: National Gang Center, "National Youth Gang Survey Analysis," 2012, http://www.nationalgangcenter.gov/survey-analysis/demographics.

typically financially motivated and nonviolent, often committed by business or government professionals. It is estimated to cost U.S. citizens and corporations anywhere from $250 billion to $1 trillion each year (Friedrichs 2007)—and these criminals, in contrast with other types of offenders, are more likely to be male, White, highly educated, and employed (Wheeler, Weisburd, Waring, and Bode 1988).

White-collar crime has been defined as "crime committed by a person of respectability and high social status in the course of his [or her] occupation" (Sutherland 1949, 9). African Americans and other disadvantaged racial and ethnic groups are extremely unlikely to engage in corporate-level white-collar crimes like antitrust activities, although they are equally as likely as Whites to be charged with low-level white-collar crime such as embezzlement and fraud (Weisburd, Wheeler, Waring, and Bode 1991; Shover and Hochstetler 2006). Women, in general, are less likely to participate in white-collar crime (Weisburd et al. 1991). These differences manifest the clear structural opportunities that coincide with race, class, and gender. As Hagan (1994, 103) argues, since the opportunity to commit white-collar crime is linked to both class position and power, it makes sense that White males are most likely to engage in these sorts of crimes. In contrast, a particular form of white-collar crime, **welfare fraud** (i.e., the illegal use of state welfare systems to knowingly withhold or make false statements for the purposes of obtaining more funds than allowed) has been historically linked to poor women, especially women of color.

The ideology of the Reagan administration in 1981 linked welfare fraud to the "typical welfare recipient"—a woman of color, often African American, with five or more children by different fathers, who spent most of her days watching soap operas and thinking of more ways to scam the system (Rose 2000, 144). Although this image has repeatedly been shown to have little basis in reality, many people hold firmly to the myth, which is still promoted by right-wing media outlets (Rose 2000).

White-collar crimes are often cast as crimes of opportunity rather than crimes of deviousness. We tend to romanticize these criminals while demonizing other types of offenders. It is interesting to note that we rarely think of white-collar crime as being evidence of a culture of poverty or deviance. Therefore, we are less likely to link white-collar criminals to specific racial, ethnic, class, or gendered groups. Sutherland (1940), who originally coined the term *white-collar crime,* concluded that "the general public was, sadly, simply not aroused by white-collar crime." Even though as many as one in four U.S. households may be the victims of white-collar crimes, close to 90% of these crimes are not reported to law enforcement (Huff, Desilets, and Kane 2010). In 1968, the President's Commission on Law Enforcement and Administration of Justice found that U.S. adults tended to be "indifferent" to white-collar crime and in some cases actually sympathized with the perpetrators. More recently, federal judges have been found to be more likely to ignore federal sentencing guidelines and reduce the sentences for certain white-collar crimes, and more likely to follow sentencing guidelines in drug cases. Sentencing judges also tend to be more persuaded toward leniency by highly respectable and privately compensated counsel. In addition, sentencing judges are more likely to be swayed by high-profile defendants' histories of philanthropy and community service, the potential of long sentences for such defendants to disrupt economic or employment systems, and the defendants' loss of reputation (Shover and Hochstetler 2006, 98).

White-collar crime has been demonstrated to be as serious as street crime in the harm it produces (Piquero, Carmichael, and Piquero 2007). Among prominent white-collar offenders in recent years have been large corporations such as Halliburton, Lucent, Rite Aid, Cendant, Sunbeam, Waste Management, Enron, Global Crossing, Kmart, WorldCom, Adelphia, Xerox, and Tyco (Simon 2006).

Imagine the consequences when elected political leaders and major corporations conspire to illegally dump tons of garbage, construction waste, or other pollutants in your community. Such a scenario played out during the 1990s in Chicago, where local leaders and politicians were bribed to look the other way. The FBI, in a secret investigation dubbed Operation Silver Shovel, documented that construction and remodeling waste from mostly White neighborhoods on the city's North Side and from suburban communities was being dumped primarily into working-class and low-income African American and Latino communities on the West Side. In order to ensure the success of this operation, the perpetrators paid bribes of as much as $5,000 per month

Orjin F. Ellingvag / Corbis Historical / Getty Images

Investment adviser Bernie Madoff, utilizing a Ponzi scheme, bilked investors out of $64.8 billion. Madoff might well be the most famous, if not most successful, white-collar criminal in U.S. history, but he is not alone. Besides costing billions of dollars, corporate crime that exposes the public to environmental risks may endanger untold numbers of lives.

to Black and Latino aldermen beginning in the late 1980s. Black and Latino communities in Chicago account for close to 80% of the illicit trade in waste disposal (Pellow 2004).

CRITICAL THINKING

1. Examine a school or local newspaper. What types of stories are associated with deviance? Does the matrix help you better understand the types and forms of deviance? What types of deviance seem to be missing? What does this suggest about space and place?

2. Which of the following acts is most deviant: (a) cheating on a test, (b) cheating on your partner, (c) cheating on your taxes, or (d) cheating at cards? What accounts for your selection? Can you identify any situations in which that act would be considered appropriate or excusable?

3. What do you think would be the consequences of excessive policing and stiff punishment for those who engage in the acts listed in question 2? What does this suggest with reference to the interaction of race, class, and gender with different types of crime and deviance?

4. We all have at one time or another been involved with both crime and deviance. Thinking about one specific occurrence in your life, in what ways did this event demonstrate the interaction of race, class, and gender? How might such events affect your perceptions of those within particular groups and the causes of deviance?

■ TRANSFORMING THE NARRATIVE OF RACE, CRIME, AND DEVIANCE

The ways in which people, and youth in particular, perceive themselves are often framed by images in the news and entertainment media. These projections have significant impacts on how individuals see themselves as well as how the public, police, and courts respond to them. We do not often see positive news media portrayals of young people of color or their communities (Waymer 2009), and the effects of a steady stream of negative reporting on crime, poverty, and violence associated with inner-city areas are rarely considered. Without counterstories, the pictures these youths have of themselves, and the pictures others form, are negative, filled with deviance and violence. Thus we may be seeing self-fulfilling prophecies as life begins to imitate its representations. In this section we present some alternative stories, demonstrating that indeed there is hope for the future.

CONCEALED STORY: Keri

Hello, my name is Keri Blakinger. I was a senior at Cornell University when I was arrested for heroin possession. As an addict—a condition that began during a deep depression—I was muddling my way through classes and doing many things I would come to regret, including selling drugs to pay for my own habit. I even began dating a man with big-time drug connections that put me around large amounts of heroin. When police arrested me in 2010, I was carrying six ounces, an amount they valued at $50,000—enough to put me in prison for up to 10 years. Cornell suspended me indefinitely and banned me from campus. I had descended from a Dean's List student to a felon.

But instead of a decade behind bars and a life grasping for the puny opportunities America affords some ex-convicts, I got a second chance. In a plea deal, I received a sentence of 2½ years. After leaving prison, I soon got a job as a reporter at a local newspaper. Then Cornell allowed me to start taking classes again, and I graduated in 2014. What made my quick rebound possible?

I am white, female, and middle-class.

Source: Keri's story is used by permission of the author and the *Washington Post,* http://www.washingtonpost.com/posteverything/wp/2015/01/21/heroin-addiction-sent-me-to-prison-white-privilege-got-me-out-and-to-the-ivy-league.

Keri's story (see "Concealed Story" box) highlights the concealed reality of our justice system. Justice is not blind. Justice presumes that members of the community or society are equally represented in its decisions, judiciously represented by its laws, and treated equitably by its courts. Race riots, civil disobedience, protests, boycotts, and litigation are all forms of resistance that have been used effectively and continually to highlight racial injustice.

When Michael Brown, a young Black man, was shot and killed by police officer Darren Wilson in a St. Louis suburb in 2014, and the grand jury subsequently decided not to indict Wilson, several thousands of people protested. Police responded with tear gas, rubber bullets, armored vehicles, and helicopters. And even though more than 300 protesters were arrested, demonstrations continued to take place for months after the event. Similar stories have been repeated in dozens of cities across the nation, in such places as Cleveland, Ohio; Charlotte, North Carolina; Tulsa, Oklahoma; and San Diego, California. Other protests resulting from the police use of deadly force against Latinos have also occurred, in Bell and Los Angeles, California; Yuma, Arizona; and Reno, Nevada. Native Americans have also protested what they perceive as racial profiling by police. These events highlight how deviance as resistance can help not only to highlight the abuses of an inequitable system but also to push for the transformation of them. In 2016 alone, more than 24,000 inmates across 12 states and 29 prisons held hunger strikes, labor strikes, and other actions to protest what they perceived as unjust systems (Washington 2016). More than 2,000 military veterans joined Native Americans at Standing Rock Sioux Reservation in North Dakota in their protest against the construction of an oil pipeline, as demonstrators called attention to "assault and intimidation at the hands of the militarized police force" (Mele 2016).

TRANSFORMATIVE STORY:
Redefining Deviance

The matrix lens alerts us to the reality that groups and individuals throughout the American narrative have been quite effective at both resisting and surviving oppressive systems. Resistance consists of the conscious and unconscious attempts by individuals and groups to challenge the dominant values of society. Resistance serves to counter oppression by providing sites and spaces where stereotypes can be challenged and social and cultural hegemonies can be transformed, so while the normative structures define deviance as moral irregularities, resistance redefines it as resilience and moral alternatives (Scott 1985, 1992). Black, Latino, Native American, and other cultures developed in resistance to and negation of the dominant culture that not only racializes them but also serves to define them as deviant. These oppositional cultures reject the often demonized and ostracized racial identities inherent in racialized structures (Gardner 2004). When laws and structures are perceived as arbitrary and unjust, people feel anger, lack of self-control, and less committed to the community and each other. In such a situation deviance is likely (Colvin, Cullen, and Vander Ven 2002)—but deviance can also lead to forms of resistance.

Transformative stories are happening all around us. They are hidden within criminal proceedings and on the back pages of our newspapers, while the stock story is reported in the headlines. During a trial the victim is asked, "Do you see the person who attacked you?" And typically the confident victim points a finger at the handcuffed and nervous defendant. Nothing is more gripping; nothing is more definitive for jurors than that moment. But what happens when there is a case of mistaken identity, when the wrong person is accused, then convicted, then sentenced for a crime he or she did not commit?

Scientific Advances

This story begins in 1984 in Burlington, North Carolina. Jennifer Thompson, a 22-year-old college student, had gone to bed early in her off-campus apartment. As she slept, a man broke the light outside the apartment, cut the phone lines, and broke in. He then raped Thompson at knifepoint. She eventually tricked the rapist into letting her get up to fix him a drink, and she escaped out the back door. The rapist ran out as well, and 30 minutes later, he raped a second woman.

As Thompson recounted the events to the police later at the hospital, she provided all of the clues that she had observed regarding her rapist. Based on her recollections, the police were able to make a composite sketch. The sketch was aired on all the local news media and tips started coming in. One of those tips was about a man named Ronald Cotton, who worked at a restaurant near the scenes of both rapes. He also had a record, having pleaded guilty to breaking and entering, and, as a teenager, to sexual assault. Three days after the rape, police called Thompson to come in and view a photo lineup, out of which she identified Cotton as her attacker. Cotton was able to account for where he was, who he was with, and what he was doing during the time of the rape. The problem was that he confused his weekends, and the alibi that he provided was false. Based on this, he was arrested and arraigned, and ultimately he was convicted of rape. Ten years later, when technology had improved enough to make use of DNA evidence, Cotton asked his attorney to look into having the DNA in his case analyzed as a means of exonerating him. When a sample of sperm taken from one of the victims was tested, Cotton was excluded as a potential donor. Another man, ironically serving time in the same prison, was later proved by this same DNA evidence to be the perpetrator (Thompson 2013).

Since it was founded in 1992, the Innocence Project has been tracking possible cases of wrongful conviction. By 2016, through its efforts, a total of 344 convictions had been overturned by new DNA evidence. Among these cases, 20 of those convicted had been on death row. Of the 347 prisoners released, 215 were African Americans, 105 were Whites, 25 were Latinos, and 2 were Asian Americans. On average, they had served 14 years. If we were to compute the total years that would have been served by these wrongly convicted men if their innocence had not been established, we would arrive at a staggering 4,730 years. The average age of those exonerated at the time of their wrongful convictions was 26.5 (Innocence Project 2016).

Alternatives to Incarceration

Some state legislators, citing several decades of increasingly harsh laws, have begun proposing alternatives to incarceration, particularly for young offenders. In 2010, the U.S. Supreme Court ruled that sentencing juveniles to life without parole for homicide convictions violates the constitutional ban on cruel and unusual punishment. Judges are looking for creative ways to hold youth responsible for their crimes while at the same diverting them from prison. Community service has replaced incarceration for many youth. In these situations the focus is on repairing the harm the offenders have done, either to their victims or to their communities. This allows the youth to evaluate their behavior and gain a better understanding of how their actions affect others. It also offers a meaningful way to hold the juveniles accountable (Brown 2012).

Over the past few years, Congress and state governments have made significant progress in reducing the burgeoning U.S. prison population by passing legislation to shorten sentences for drug offenses and by offering clemency for certain nonviolent drug crimes. Unfortunately, these efforts may be derailed under the Trump administration, as federal prosecutors nationwide are now being encouraged to seek the strongest possible sanctions for those charged with serious offenses (Ford 2016).

Additional solutions require an investment in alternatives to detention and incarceration. Most criminal acts are related to drug abuse, and such crimes tend to be nonviolent and "victimless." Many states, such as Maryland, have begun to explore cost-effective approaches to sentencing for offenders in these kinds of cases that divert them from prison. Programs that provide offenders with community-based drug treatment, life skills training, literacy training, education, and job skills training have been highly successful. Many believe that investing in human capital in this way will produce a higher return to society than incarceration (McVay, Schiraldi, and Ziedenberg 2004).

Emphasizing Choice

Any remedy must take into consideration individual agency. People make choices, including the choice to commit crimes, although, as we have learned throughout this chapter, some choices are more constrained than others. Some people's criminal actions seem to be reactions to their being left out of the American Dream. When agency is denied or circumscribed by race, class, and gender, there is an increased likelihood that deviance will result. This deviance does not reflect a culture of crime or a culture of poverty; rather, it reflects a poverty of opportunities.

When we see that some upper-middle-class White males participate in fraudulent stock, banking, and mortgage schemes, or some poor Whites produce, distribute, and sell methamphetamine, or some Black and Hispanic individuals join gangs and precipitate violence, we must understand these acts as expressions of agency. Neither crime nor deviance is caused by race, ethnicity, gender, or class. People make choices, some good and some bad. These choices are circumscribed by environments, histories, and structural inequities. The prevalence of one specific type of crime or deviance is determined by the kinds of resources available within a particular community, institution, or situation and the kinds of choices people make.

The overwhelming majority of people in all racial and ethnic groups do not commit crimes—they make other choices. While society cannot force individuals to make different choices, it can both hold them accountable and provide effective alternatives to deviance. Even for those currently caught up in deviance, alternatives to detention have been demonstrated to deter further criminality. These alternatives include suspended sentences, probation, fines, restitution, community service, and deferred adjudication/pretrial diversion.

Adjusting the Narrative of Race and Deviance

Finally, we must shift away from an individualistic approach that defines specific individuals and communities as in need of "fixing." Using the matrix lens instead of the dominant cultural lens of White middle-class male privilege, we must understand that some differences in life outcomes are rooted in structural inequities. One size does not fit all, and racism, sexism, poverty, and homophobia influence identity, group formation, and community.

The matrix lens does not present people, communities, and groups as victims, though they might have been victimized. Rather, it projects them as agents, who see not only what is available but also what obstacles they must overcome to obtain it. By changing the lens we therefore ask a different set of questions: How do we empower, how do we incorporate, and how do we embrace the power of difference?

CRITICAL THINKING

1. How might prison riots, street protests, and legal actions transform our attitudes toward and the realities of crime and deviance?

2. Why is it difficult to transform our criminal justice system? What types of strategies have been devised? What other kinds of transformations seem likely?

3. What role does intersectionality play in crime and deviance? Identify and explain at least three ways in which this occurs. What does this suggest regarding our construction of crime and deviance?

4. In what ways does your status affect the likelihood that you will be charged with either a crime or being deviant? Are there types of crime or deviance that are strictly related to your being a student? Are there some behaviors that are considered deviant on a college campus that would be considered normal elsewhere?

KEY TERMS

biological determinism, p. 238	prison–industrial complex, p. 246
broken windows theory, p. 241	racial consciousness, p. 231
crime, p. 257	racial profiling, p. 235
culture of poverty, p. 240	slave patrols, p. 232
deviance, p. 230	social disorganization, p. 239
differential association theory, p. 240	structural inequities, p. 245
differential labeling, p. 252	welfare fraud, p. 258
general strain theory, p. 243	White normative structures, p. 231
Jim Crow laws, p. 232	White privilege, p. 231
organized crime, p. 255	white-collar crime, p. 256

CHAPTER SUMMARY

LO 7.1   Examine the history of race, crime, and deviance.

Race, gender, and class disparities are represented in who gets defined as either criminal or deviant. Historically these differentials can be traced to the slave codes, immigration policy, and the development of reservations for Native Americans. Taken together, these practices, policies, and laws account for the racially differentiated criminal justice system. Whiteness was created as a means of assuring that the racial state would be preserved. Laws were created to fortify this structure at the expense of people of color. Contemporary trends in scholarship on crime and deviance highlight the racial, gendered, and class differentials in how justice is administered across the United States. These disparities are observed throughout the justice system, in differential policing, racial profiling, and differential sentencing and incarceration rates.

LO 7.2   Analyze stock theories of race, crime, and deviance.

Classical sociological theories of crime and deviance represent a portion of our stock stories. As such, they reflect the dominant view that not only is our system just, but also those who violate the laws are appropriately sanctioned. Most of the theoretical orientations of these stock stories fall into four broad categories: biosocial theories of deviance, ecological perspectives, culture of poverty explanations, and broken windows theory. All of these have a common theme—they place the source of deviance at the micro level. Therefore, the individual or his or her community, culture, or environment is at odds with societal norms. And by implication, if the individual or his or her community, culture, or environment could just be reformed, fixed, adjusted, or rehabilitated, then the deviance would be reduced or nonexistent.

LO 7.3 **Apply the matrix lens to the relationships among race, crime, and deviance.**

The matrix of crime and deviance starts by recognizing that the assumptions about crime and deviance are intended to ensure that race, gender, and class differentials are preserved. The matrix informs us that certain socially defined people and groups (reflecting the interactions of race, class, and gender) situated in particular spaces and places are more apt to be labeled deviant than others. It also informs us that the nexus of various spaces interacts with social identities to produce different types and definitions of deviance. As we consider the various dimensions of the matrix lens, space and place help us to understand that crime and deviance are situationally and contextually specific. Therefore, urban areas produce different types of deviance possibilities than do corporate spaces. Hate crimes, which constitute a particular type of deviance, are utilized as means of social control. Among the outcomes of the linking of national and corporate policies around crime and deviance have been the militarization of the police and the creation of the prison–industrial complex. These policies have called for increased surveillance, criminalization, and incarceration of the members of designated racial and ethnic groups. Ultimately, this process also accounts for the fact that Blacks, Hispanics, and the poor are more likely to receive the death penalty.

LO 7.4 **Formulate transformative narratives of crime and deviance.**

Historically individuals and groups have not been complacent when faced with injustice. Rebellions and insurrections, riots, and protests have frequently been instrumental in movements calling for change. Over the past few years, many people have begun to question the racial, gender, and class disparities that dominate every phase of the American criminal justice system. Alternatives to detention and incarceration, particularly for nonviolent criminal acts, are showing promise in several states. And while we must continue to hold individuals responsible for their actions, we also need to recognize that some crimes and forms of deviance are the results of racism, sexism, poverty, and homophobia. The most effective way to reduce crime and deviance would be to decrease all forms of discrimination, increase opportunities, and enhance training and education.

POWER, POLITICS, AND IDENTITIES

Kyodo News / Kyodo News / Getty Images

Most of Donald Trump's supporters were White, non-Hispanic voters, as evidenced by the crowds that turned out to support him on the campaign trail.

LEARNING OBJECTIVES

LO 8.1   Explain contemporary political identities.

LO 8.2   Evaluate stock sociological theories regarding power, politics, and identity.

LO 8.3   Apply the matrix approach to U.S. political history.

LO 8.4   Formulate alternatives to the matrix of race and politics.

As the 45th president of the United States, Donald Trump looks a lot like the overwhelming majority of past presidents—male, rich, and White. Hailed by many as the ultimate outsider, he had never run for political office before his campaign for president. With Trump's upset victory, which saw him lose the popular vote but win the majority in the Electoral College, the 2016 election threw into sharp relief the already existing divides at the intersections of race, gender, and education. As we shall see, this election provided stark evidence that the U.S. electorate is extremely fragmented and polarized. Geographically speaking, Trump dominated rural and suburban areas, while his opponent, Hillary Clinton, was strongest in urban areas (Morin 2016). Voters were also divided by race, with most of Trump's support coming from non-Hispanic Whites, while most Blacks and Hispanics voted for Clinton (Tyson and Maniam 2016).

Every 4 years, the people of the United States elect a president, and candidates from each of the major political parties attempt to obtain the largest share of the votes. Success often is dependent on how well a candidate navigates the various political identities that define U.S. politics. What exactly are these political identities, and how do they define U.S. politics? In this chapter we will explore those questions, examine how various forms of political behavior have traditionally been accounted for, analyze political history and its lessons through the matrix, and discuss how new forms of political and social movements have affected political processes in the United States.

■ CONTEMPORARY POLITICAL IDENTITIES

Politics encompasses all of the processes, activities, and institutions having to do with governance. Like all other institutions, politics provides unique spaces and places in which various identities come into play. **Political identities** are the political positions, based on the interests and perspectives of social groups, with which people associate themselves. Across the United States, these political identities, representing race, gender, sexuality, language, region, and class, frequently intersect, interact, and intervene in multiple forms of political expression. Political identities have historically been a means by which nondominant groups can resist and transform political systems.

Understanding the Electorate

Traditionally, political analysis within the United States have stressed single group comparisons. The problem with comparing groups on a single indicator is that this method fails to capture the complex reality of voting behavior. As we saw above, it was not just White voters who supported Trump—it was White men and women living in both rural and suburban areas. As we examine the recent demographic shifts highlighted in Table 8.1, keep in mind that these shifts represent only a single dimension with regard to potential voters.

As the table shows, the 2016 electorate increased by about 5%. And although Whites still constituted slightly more than 70% of the projected eligible voters, the population of Whites grew more slowly than the populations of any other racial groups. More rapid growth was seen among both Hispanic (17%) and Asian (16%) eligible voters. Markedly smaller increases were associated with Blacks (6%) (Tyson and Maniam 2016).

Regional Differences

As we learned in our examination of colonial history in Chapter 2, the Spanish, French, and English frontier developments resulted in distinct regional differences that remained as the United States evolved as a nation. With time, population shifts

Table 8.1 ■ Growth of Eligible White Voters

Since 2012, whites have had the least growth in eligible voters

Projected change of the voting-eligible population by race/Hispanic origin
All figures in thousands

| | Nov.'12 eligible voters | Citizens reaching age 18 | COMPONENTS OF CHANGE, 2012–16 | | Deaths of citizens ages 18+ | Nov.'16 eligible voters | Change in eligible voters, 2012–16 |
			Naturalizations, ages 18+	Arrivals from Puerto Rico			
Total	215,081	+15,991	+3,201	+166	-8,662	225,778	■ 5%
White	152,862	+9,179	+644	+24	-6,625	156,084	▎2
Black	25,753	+2,303	+413	+9	-1,075	27,402	■ 6
Hispanic	23,329	+3,214	+1,167	+130	-537	27,302	■■■■ 17
Asian	8,032	+607	+930	+3	-286	9,286	■■■■ 16

Note: Eligible voters are U.S. citizens ages 18 and older. White, black and Asian includes only non-Hispanics. Hispanics are of any race. American Indians, Native Hawaiian/Pacific Islanders and muftirace Americans not shown.

Source: Jens Manuel Krogstad, "2016 Electorate Will Be the Most Diverse in U.S. History," Pew Research Center Fact Tank, February 3, 2016, http://www.pewresearch.org/fact-tank/2016/02/03/2016-electorate-will-be-the-most-diverse-in-u-s-history.

also occurred, influenced by economic trends and industrial and agricultural developments. The various U.S. geographical regions therefore reflect unique histories, cultures, wealth distributions, and political processes.

Political Identities by Place

Intersectionality informs us that political identities are more than just social groups—they intersect across multiple dimensions. Space is one dimension in which political identities vary significantly in the United States (see Figure 8.1). This is especially true for Blacks and Hispanics, who are more likely to identify according to racial identities. Among all groups, those living in the South and the Northeast are most likely to view reality through the lens of race. Whites, for the most part, are less likely to view themselves racially, and more likely to view class as the dominant feature of their identities. Across all groups, those living in the West are most likely to view class as central to their identities (McElwee 2016). Immediately, the questions of identity and intersectionality come into play. How, for example would living in a particular region affect people's different racial and class identities? More important for our purposes here, how might these differences play out politically?

Some recent research provides potential answers. Among predominantly White political districts, the relationship between income and political partisanship varies very

Figure 8.1 ■ Race and Place Help Shape Our Personal Identities

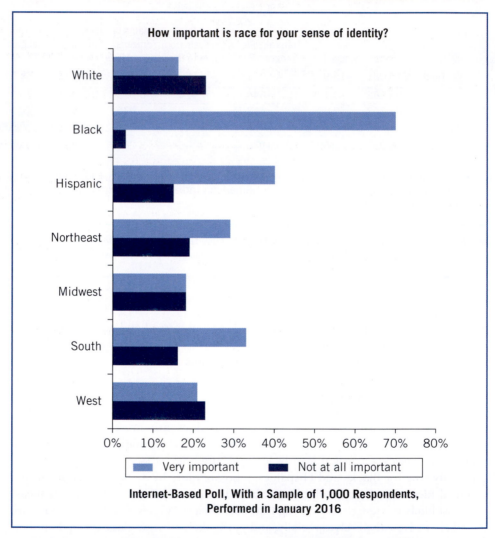

How important is race for your sense of identity?

Internet-Based Poll, With a Sample of 1,000 Respondents, Performed in January 2016

Source: Adapted from Sean McElwee, "Race versus Class in the Democratic Coalition," *The Nation,* March 7, 2016, https://www.thenation.com/article/race-versus-class-in-the-democratic-coalition.

little. Regional differences linking political partisanship and race are most likely to be associated with racially heterogeneous districts within states. So, in the Northeast, where large numbers of African Americans reside, there is an increased likelihood that the voters are Democrats. On the other hand, voters who live in affluent areas are only slightly more Republican than those in less affluent areas. In contrast, in specific rural areas with high concentrations of minority poverty (particularly the Black Belt, the Rio Grande Valley, and California's Central Valley), the links among White identity, income, and partisanship become more apparent. Alternatively, for racially diverse areas outside of the rural south, the link between party identification and income are very week (Hersh and Nall 2015).

Voter Disenfranchisement

Laws regulating voter **disenfranchisement**, or revocation of the right to vote, also differ regionally. Current laws in many states revoke the voting eligibility of anyone with a criminal conviction. The rate of disenfranchisement in the United States has kept pace with the growth in incarceration. Forty years ago, almost 1.2 million people were denied the right to vote due to criminal convictions. Twenty years later, that number had risen to 3.3 million. In 2010, a total of 5.9 million persons were disenfranchised (Uggen, Larson, and Shannon 2016). Of these disenfranchised voters, less than 23% are currently incarnated. This means that 77% of those who are disenfranchised have officially paid their debts to society and are free to do everything but vote. In the 2016 election, a record 6.1 million citizens were unable to vote because of laws restricting the voting rights for those convicted of felony-level crimes (Uggen et al. 2016).

States vary significantly in how they apply disenfranchisement laws. Seven states have revoked the right to vote for less than half of 1 percent of their populations, while in six southern states more than 7% of persons who would otherwise be eligible to vote have been disenfranchised. Among these, Hispanics and African Americans are more likely to be disenfranchised. In some states, such as Kentucky, Tennessee, and Virginia, the disenfranchisement among African Americans is more than 20% of the voting population. Many of these potential voters were caught in our nation's "get tough" policies on crime and the differential sentencing for those convicted of crimes involving crack cocaine (Uggen et al. 2016).

Some states have worked hard to reduce the growing numbers of disenfranchised among former inmates. In Virginia, Governor Terry McAuliffe restored voting rights to nearly 13,000 ex-felons in 2016. McAuliffe, calling it a voting rights issue, argued that most of those whose rights were restored had committed nonviolent crimes (Wines 2016).

The Role of Race, Class, and Gender

Other intersectional aspects of political identities are associated with how race and income interact. For example, slightly more than three-fourths of likely voters identify as White, compared to 9% identifying as Black and 6% Hispanic or Latino. Hispanics are almost four times as likely (23%) as Whites to be nonvoters, while those identifying as Black are 6% more likely to be nonvoters. An inverse relationship exists between nonvoting and both income and education (Pew Research Center 2015). The highest levels of nonvoting are associated with the lowest levels of education and income. And while higher income seems to be associated with a greater likelihood of voting, the same does not hold true for higher levels of education. The likelihood of voting is mixed across various levels of education (Pew Research Center 2015).

Being eligible or likely to vote and actually voting are two different things. Women across all racial groups are more likely to vote than men, and in the last two presidential election cycles, Black women have been the most likely to vote. Before that, White women had maintained this record. Women, including women of color, are increasingly being elected to political offices at all levels. As of 2017, of the 105 women serving in the U.S. Congress, 36.2% were women of color. Of the 21 women serving in the U.S. Senate, 4 were women of color. Of the 75 women serving in elective executive offices at the state level, 7 (9.3%) were women of color. This included one of the first two women of color to become a state governor, Susana Martinez, a Republican who took office as governor of New Mexico in 2011. Women of color made up just 2.2% of the total 312 statewide elective executives (Center for American Women and Politics 2017). Later in this chapter we will explore some of the historical reasons that women in general, and Black women in particular, might be more likely to vote than men.

Analyzing the 2016 Presidential Election

Democrats have traditionally relied on an alliance of identity groups (specifically Black voters and northern White voters). In 2008, this alliance accounted for the victory of Barack Obama, the first Black man to win the presidency of the United States. It resurfaced in 2012 to give President Obama a resounding victory in the so-called midwestern firewall states—Ohio, Michigan, and Wisconsin, all of which have large working-class populations (Gonyea 2012). In the 2012 election, voters under 25 years of age (millennials) accounted for about 9% of the electorate, and they favored Obama over his opponent, Republican Mitt Romney, by nearly 29 percentage points (Enten 2016). With the tremendous support of Black voters, Obama easily won a second term. But the same core identity groups failed to turn out for Democrats in 2016. Why?

Trump made significant gains among White working-class voters, not only in waning Democratic strongholds like western Pennsylvania, but also in historically Democratic Scranton, Pennsylvania, and eastern Iowa. White voters without a college education, a traditional Democratic voting bloc, also voted for Trump (see Figure 8.2). And for the first time in U.S. history, the Republican candidate garnered

Figure 8.2 ■ Fewer Northern White Voters Without a College Degree Voted Democrat in 2016

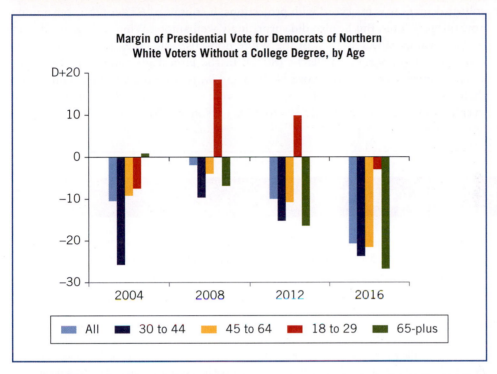

Margin of Presidential Vote for Democrats of Northern White Voters Without a College Degree, by Age

Legend: All | 30 to 44 | 45 to 64 | 18 to 29 | 65-plus

Source: Adapted from Nate Cohn, "How the Obama Coalition Crumbled, Leaving an Opening for Trump," *New York Times,* December 23, 2016, http://www.nytimes.com/2016/12/23/upshot/how-the-obama-coalition-crumbled-leaving-an-opening-for-trump.html.

more votes among low-income Whites than among affluent Whites. Trump also had the support of older White working-class voters.

When we examine the 2016 presidential election, we find that distinct intersectional realities associated with race, gender, and education are apparent. Historically, party affiliation—whether an individual is a registered Republican, Democrat, or independent—has been linked to stark differences by race, gender, age, and education. Research suggests that Democratic candidates currently hold significant advantages among voting Blacks, Asians, Hispanics, well-educated adults, and **millennials** (those in the generation born roughly from 1980 to 2000, currently ages 18 to 38). Republican candidates tend to be supported by Whites, particularly White men, those with lower education levels, evangelical Protestants, and the so-called **silent generation** (i.e., those born from 1925 to 1945, now ages 73 to 93) (Pew Research Center 2015).

In general, the presidential election of 2016 revealed that people with college degrees voted very differently than people without degrees. Clinton garnered 52% of the vote among voters with college degrees, while Trump scored similar support among those without a degree (52%). Trump's electoral support among Whites without college degrees was in accord with projections; he obtained 67% of the vote among noncollege Whites. But he also did surprisingly well among White college graduates (49%). Trump captured 58% of the White non-Hispanic vote, while Clinton garnered major support from Blacks (80%). In the largest gender voting gap since 1972, women were slightly more likely, at 54%, to support Clinton, while more than 53% of men supported Trump. Young voters ages 18 to 29 preferred Clinton over Trump by a wide margin: 53% to 45% (Tyson and Maniam 2016).

CRITICAL THINKING

1. Intersections of race, gender, and education affected the 2016 presidential election, but these were not the only factors. How might differences between geographical regions have influenced the election outcome?

2. An individual's education level may have an impact on how he or she votes. How might other factors, such as marital status, employment status, religion, and military service, affect a person's voting behavior?

3. Different levels of support for the candidates in the 2016 presidential race have been shown to be associated with particular areas of the country. How might these differences reflect the unique historical contexts of these areas? What do these suggest about how group identity and political identity are influenced by geography and/or historical sequences of events or processes?

4. In what ways do your own political beliefs reflect your identities (race, class, and/or gender), and in what ways do your identities shape your political beliefs?

■ CRITIQUING SOCIOLOGICAL THEORIES OF POWER, POLITICS, AND IDENTITY

Political sociology is the study of government, political behaviors, institutions, and processes that occur between the state and its society and citizens. More simply, political sociology is the study of power, politics, and identity. Our discussion of the stock sociological theories below is not intended to be an exhaustive look at the rich theoretical landscape; rather, our goal is to illustrate the major ways in which power, politics, and identity have been explained. These theories—pluralist approaches, the power elite model, and class approaches to power, politics, and identity—are central to the discipline and have long served to inform and guide political theorizing, research, and policy.

The Pluralist Approach

Pluralism posits that power within society is decentralized, widely shared, diffuse, and fragmented. Groups throughout society, reflecting business, labor, professions, religion, and culture, compete and often hold conflicting interests. Because no single group is dominant, **democratic equilibrium** (a dynamic working balance between and among various groups) is established. This means that democratic governance is conceived of as a system that regulates conflict between and among various interest groups. These interest groups include, but are not limited to, groups concerned with the economy (markets, industries, and finance), education, religion, and the military. Individuals join groups because groups have more power than individuals when it comes to achieving goals. The larger the group, the more influence it has. Political policies develop as a result of the continuous bargaining and compromises among various groups (Dahl 1961).

The essential democratic function of political institutions is to regulate the conflict among various groups. Multiple forms of conflict can surface along distinct interest group lines, so various political elites tend to be more or less engaged in the political process depending on which interests are prominent. For example, while Black political and civil rights elites were out front and actively involved with the recent water crisis in Flint, Michigan, few mainline political elites were so heavily involved. Alternatively, consider the Asian American electorate—a group that is virtually invisible in American politics. This reflects the fact that the "Asian" label gives the impression of a monolithic group, when in fact there is a significant degree of variation among Asian cultural groups (Wagner 2016). The democratic process is therefore dynamic, changing continually as different lines of conflict produce multiple and shifting power bases. Two types of groups are associated with the pluralist approach: **insider groups**, which hold the bulk of the power, and **outsider groups**, which are marginalized and have limited power (Dahl 1961).

Insider groups tend to be well recognized and established, holding positions of power and prestige within their communities. Their positions mean that they have considerable influence over elected officials at various levels of government. Members of these groups tend to have similar perspectives on a number of issues. The list of insider groups is virtually endless. It includes unions and professional organizations like the Teamsters Union and the American Medical Association; identity groups such as Protestants, Whites, and Blacks; gender groups; and corporations and marketing groups. Insider groups may use direct means such as voting, lobbying, and boycotts to influence political outcomes, political processes, and politicians.

Many of today's insider groups were outsider groups in the past. Blacks, Jews, and Catholics have become insider groups through effective political organizing,

The AARP is an insider group founded to promote the interests of retired people. The organization claims membership of more than 37 million people and has an annual budget of $1.6 billion (2016 AARP Annual Report), giving it considerable clout.

protests, and other forms of political activism. Outsider groups, which have significantly less power and prestige within their communities, tend to be marginalized in the political process and have less access to elected officials. Members of these groups may be recent immigrants (documented and undocumented, political refugees, and so on), people who belong to socially marginalized groups (including LGBT people), and people with special interests (such as animal rights or environmental justice).

The pluralist approach presumes that, at least among the various insider groups, power is dispersed equally. It also suggests that the system is fair, and that outsider groups get a chance at influencing the structures and one day achieving the status of insiders. The reality is that power tends to coalesce among a very few, well-placed insiders. For example, even as women and Blacks have become relative insiders over the past four decades, they do not share power equally with men and Whites. Also, their presence as insiders produces **binary constructs** (White/Black, male/female) that normalize and legitimate racial and gender hierarchies at the expense of other outsiders, such as other racial minorities and gender groups.

The pluralist approach has limited ability to actually deal with changing political climates and conditions. During these times of unrest, major upheavals are presented as interest group dynamics and conflicts that disrupt political processes. Since the terrorist attacks of September 11, 2001, many political candidates and elected officials have focused on Americans' fears of Islamic extremism. Muslims, regardless of political involvement or national origins, have become more likely to be targeted by political outcomes such as racial profiling laws and new immigration quotas and standards. The democratic equilibrium that pluralism assumes might actually be too simplistic and unrealistic (Domhoff 2005).

The Power Elite Model

The **power elite model** suggests that power is concentrated among a discrete group of elites who control the resources of significant social institutions. The power elite consists of members from three specific realms:

1. Holders of the highest political offices, such as the president of the United States, key cabinet members, and close advisers

2. Heads of major corporations and directors of corporate boards

3. High-ranking military personnel

While inherited wealth and position can help an individual attain the status of a power elite, individuals can also gain admittance to the highest circles by working hard and adopting elite values (Mills 1956). The power and authority derived from elite positions allow these members to influence governmental, financial, educational, social, civic, and cultural institutions. A relatively small group of elites, consequently, can have a significant impact on the majority of people across a nation. Over the past few decades, the power of the elites has been enhanced through the development of a military–industrial complex with strong governmental ties. Simultaneously, links between corporations and government elites have strengthened as the role of government has expanded into many aspects of our daily lives. In the United States, the Food and Drug Administration (FDA) must approve all foods and medicines intended for human consumption. But the FDA and Congress are frequently targeted by lobbying activity. In 2014, drug companies and their lobbying groups spent a total of $229 million to influence lawmakers, legislation, and politicians (Ludwig 2015).

The first major criticism of the power elite model is that it erroneously assumes equality among economic, political, and military elites. The link between political and military elites might be tenuous at best. For example, in 2014, just 20% of the members of the U.S. Congress were military veterans (Wellford 2014). Alternatively, veteran status might be a road to the White House. Slightly more than half (26 of 45) of U.S. presidents have served in the armed forces.

Another criticism of the power elite model is that it presents political and corporate elites as unified, while regional and economic interests interact to produce specific types of power structures. Consider the northern industrial and financial elites, who currently align with the Republican Party, and their common interests with southern Democrats and agricultural elites. Coming out of the Civil War, the Democratic Party surfaced in the South to thwart Reconstruction and the rising ambitions of the freed slaves (Ager 2013). The coalition of southern and northern elites remained constant for much of the 20th century, with only two deviations: one in 1935, when industrial union organizing dominated politics and elections in the North (forcing a split between northern and southern elites), and one in 1964, with the advent of the civil rights movement in the South (when again the northern and southern elites split). In the sections that follow, we will return to this example, as it demonstrates how White southern elites pursued a policy of segregation that not only harmed their long-term interests but also served to pit low-status Whites against low-status Blacks and Hispanics. The repercussions of these actions have lasted even to this day.

The Class Approach

The **class approach** to power, politics, and identity assumes that the type of economic system a society has determines the kind of political structures that evolve. Within the United States, those who control the economic production control the political processes. As implied by the saying "What is good for corporate America is good for America" (Nussbaum 2010), major corporations dominate our economy, and that translates to power across all major social institutions (Miliband 1977). We live in a society where major corporations and industries greatly influence political processes and outcomes. The social elites who control the markets control the government, and they in turn dominate other classes to perpetuate their power (Marx [1852] 1964). Two different intellectual traditions derive from this perspective:

1. **Instrumentalism** views the state as being dominated by an economic class that controls both political and economic spheres (Goldstein and Pevehouse 2009).

2. **Structuralism** posits that the state and all political institutions exist relatively independent of each other and are essentially by-products of conflict between and within class groups (Poulantzas 2008).

Critics of the class approach and its derivatives claim that that they tend to reduce all aspects of power to what happens in the market. These approaches do not account for those instances when members of the dominant class do not act in their own self-interest as they pursue either racial or gendered objectives. For example, from the 1920s to the 1940s, elite corporation owners were silent partners with the White labor force as labor unions denied membership to racial minorities and women. Elite employers first instigated racial strife by recruiting Black workers to take the place of White strikers, resulting in many riots across the country. Once settlements were reached, the newly hired Blacks were replaced by White immigrants, who were more acceptable to the unions (Restifo, Roscigno, and Qian 2013).

Further, class approaches tend to minimize racial, ethnic, and immigrant bases of power, such as the Congressional Black Caucus and the Congressional Hispanic Caucus, that serve as resistance and countervailing forces in our political structure. The biggest challenge for social change has to do with the gaps that exist among the various identity groups. Critical scholars point out that if coalitions could be forged across these various social locations (of race, class, gender, and age), a massive social movement could be fostered. Such a movement would be most effective in challenging the U.S. power structure. The civil rights movement of the 1960s could serve as a model for this kind of movement (Domhoff 2005).

CONCEALED STORY: Critical Race Theory

Critical race theory represents an attempt by scholars and activists to transform the relationships among race, racism, and power. Because critical race theorists tend to operate at the margins of the social sciences, their work is often dismissed by mainstream academia. In fact, the work of these theorists can be considered a type of concealed story that explains how the intersections of race, class, and gender inform a uniquely nuanced approach to power, politics, and identity.

One of the central themes of critical race scholars is their rejection of, significant challenges to, reinterpretations of, and/or new insights into the stock sociopolitical theories. Central among these critiques is the understanding that many of the stock theories have failed to adequately deal with race, gender, or ethnicity. Some critical race theorists have even gone so far as to argue that rather than revealing White male hegemony, stock theories have legitimated it (Fogg-Davis 2003).

A second theme of critical race scholars is that mainstream ideas, reflected disproportionately by White scholars, stress the importance of linking structural conditions, such as laws or the economy, to the self-interest of leaders, activists, or even regions to understand ethnic identity and the conflict that often occurs (Hochschild 2005). Alternatively, it is primarily scholars of color who have identified the racial underpinnings of politics as the principal source of ethnic identity and conflict (Hochschild 2005, 99). Historical examples of this include race riots, which always pit dominant racial groups against nondominant racial groups, who are often competing over perceived or actually scarce goods, such as labor, housing, and access to education. The fiercest ethnic conflicts appear to be at the lowest levels of White male–dominated industrial labor markets. These conflicts establish the importance of looking at power, politics, and identity through the intersections of race, class, and gender.

A third theme of critical race theorists is that the political realities that reaffirm racial hierarchies are normal. This means that the dominant political processes racialize different minority groups at different times, in response to shifting needs of the labor market (Delgado 2006). Black labor during the 1960s became more disposable and more easily displaceable by cheaper Mexican or Filipino agricultural workers. Politicians responded by passing lenient guest worker laws. Historically, White-dominated labor unions have been the first to challenge guest worker programs, but increasingly it appears that Black unskilled labor has been most harmed and displaced by such programs (Bronner 2013). As we will see, these realities, which pit one racial group against another, are frequent outcomes of racialized political processes.

Critical race theorist Kimberlé Williams Crenshaw (1991), who coined the term *intersectionality,* has argued that political processes are best understood through an intersectional lens. According to Crenshaw, the experiences that people face represent intersecting and interacting spheres that shape structural, political, and representational aspects of their being. The inequalities that result are therefore not the products of any single dimension, but the results of the intersection of two or more of them. On the other hand, intersectionality can also be a source of agency and advocacy. This agency is a form of **identity politics**, a political process or structure that relies on people of specific religions, racial and ethnic groups, or social backgrounds to form exclusive political alliances.

CRITICAL THINKING

1. What might account for the geographical voting patterns observed in the 2016 presidential election? How effective would the stock stories be in explaining the outcome?

2. We have seen how some institutions (such as the military and the economy) might influence political outcomes, and similarly how political institutions can affect the wider society. What other major institutions might have similar effects?

3. During different periods, different types of identities might be more prevalent or more visible than others. What does the 2016 presidential election suggest about how these identities interact with the political system? What does this suggest about the relevance of stock stories?

4. What are your political beliefs? To what extent do they reflect your family, education, gender, race, or geographical region? What intersections can you identify based on this?

■ APPLYING THE MATRIX OF RACE TO U.S. POLITICAL HISTORY

According to our nation's stock story, the original intent of our system of government was to diminish the conflict between "the haves" and "the have-nots." That is, since various interests divide people into different classes with radically different objectives and rationales, the principal purpose of government is to regulate these conflicts and ensure that fairness, or justice, is achieved. Our form of government, which is based on representation, is an attempt to ensure that we will not be governed by either the tyranny of the majority or the tyranny of the minority. The stock story of U.S. politics teaches us that our nation is a democracy in which every citizen, regardless of identifying characteristics, has a voice in the political process. The stock narrative also

Tom Williams / CQ-Roll Call Group / Getty Images

The Congressional Black Caucus is composed of most of the African-American members of the U.S. Congress and is an example of identity politics. The group is "committed to using the full Constitutional power, statutory authority, and financial resources of the federal government to ensure that African Americans and other marginalized communities in the United States have the opportunity to achieve the American Dream."

suggests that inequalities associated with race, class, gender, sexual orientation, and other forms of identity are aberrant and not part of the core values of our culture. This idea is part of the American Dream that draws thousands of immigrants and refugees to the United States each year. Accordingly, democracy fosters pluralism and welcomes diversity, as both are essential to the interests of freedom.

Using our stock story to guide us, we understand that conflicts arise in situations where resources are scarce (whether the scarcity is real or only perceived). Power, therefore, might be defined as the ability to acquire scarce resources. And if indeed the central role of political institutions is to diminish conflict, then they also serve the function of regulating power. It stands to reason that resource scarcity and the power associated with the acquisition of resources are both keyed to specific historical situations, institutional settings, and geographical locations. Further, individuals seeking to maximize their access to resources are likely to organize into groups to increase the efficiency of their resource acquisition. These assumptions align perfectly with the expectations of the matrix.

Certain resources associated with work and the economy, housing, and access to education are always scarcer than others. A person or group must first have access to these things, so citizenship or immigration status is of equal importance. We can also expect that both geographical and historical situations can have impacts on each of these potential sources of conflict. Our task in the next sections will be to explore how these conflicts have been resolved, and to what extent they reveal the importance of the intersections of race, class, and gender.

Building a Nation's Identity

Slavery

One of the most prized resources available in a democracy is freedom. In 1776, when the First Continental Congress met to create a government for our new nation, slaves made up approximately 20% of the entire population of the 13 colonies (Engerman, Sutch, and Wright 2004). While slavery existed in all of the colonies, political, social, and geographical conditions resulted in distinctly different attitudes toward slavery.

The southern colonies, consisting of Maryland, Virginia, the Carolinas, and Georgia, were staunch supporters of slavery. Their political economies rested on an agricultural base and almost year-round growing seasons. Elite landowners found that by using slave labor, their plantations could more profitably produce such crops as rice, cotton, and tobacco.

Slaves in the northern colonies (New Hampshire, Massachusetts, Rhode Island, and Connecticut) likely had more diversified skills than those in the heavily agricultural South (Melish 1998). The complex economies of the northern colonies allowed slaves to develop a wide variety of skills, from domestic to skilled trades. The tradition of northern slavery therefore allowed expansion from small-time farms to large agricultural production, the growth of local and regional markets, increased entrepreneurial activity, and the rise of industrialization. Some slave owners encouraged their slaves to work harder and more efficiently by offering them a share in the profits, which the slaves often used to buy their freedom. Ultimately, the northern elites determined that free labor was more productive than slave labor (Melish 1998). As the united colonies entered into the Revolutionary War, these different regional political economies and attitudes regarding slavery served to produce the nation's first set of political compromises.

The establishment of the U.S. Congress as a bicameral legislature, with Senate and House of Representatives, was a direct result of debates about whether and how to count slaves as part of the country's population. The southern states, with their relatively smaller populations, wanted the slaves to be counted equally to Whites to bolster their populations and thus their power in the government. The northern states, with their considerably larger populations and virtually no slaves, were in opposition. The **Great Compromise of 1787** was the result of this disagreement. According to the compromise, the Congress would be composed of two governing bodies, one in which population would determine the number of seats each state would hold (the House of Representatives), and one in which each state would have two members (the Senate). It was further decided that each slave would be counted as three-fifths of a person in population counts determining numbers of representatives as well as presidential electors, and for purposes of taxation.

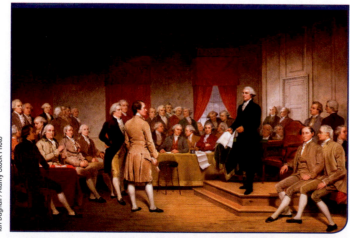

Ian Dagnall / Alamy Stock Photo

The Framers of the Constitution settled on the Great Compromise of 1787 to resolve a dispute between northern and southern states about how to fairly allot representation in Congress. The Compromise created the House of Representatives, where seats are distributed based on population, and the Senate, where each state is represented equally.

Citizenship

The next step in nation building that cemented the intersectional basis of our political institutions involved citizenship and immigration. One of the most significant aspects of power within any political system is to whom citizenship is granted. The status of **citizenship** reflects the legal processes that a country uses to regulate national identity, membership, and rights. Citizenship also establishes the political boundaries that define who is and is not included in the democratic franchise. The Naturalization Act of 1790 granted citizenship to "free white aliens" with 2 years' residence in the United States, but withheld it from slaves and women. The law further excluded all non-Whites, including Asians, enslaved Africans, and Native Americans, from citizenship. While citizenship was extended to all Whites after they had established residency, only property-owning men could exercise the right to vote or to hold political office (Tehranian 2000).

Sovereign Peoples

From the onset of the establishment of our nation, Native Americans were considered to be sovereign nationals. That is, the tribes were considered to be independent and held authority over their own citizens and lands. Since each tribe was an independent nation, the United States signed and ratified almost 390 treaties with various Native American tribes (Miller 2006). In all cases, the treaties were formal negotiations regarding the sale of land and property rights owned by the indigenous peoples but desired by the United States. Indigenous persons, as individuals, were expressly not considered citizens, and they paid no taxes. Even after the Civil War and the passage of the Fourteenth Amendment, which granted citizenship to "all persons born or naturalized in the United States," indigenous persons were excluded. Native Americans would not become U.S. citizens until 1924 (Miller 2006).

Immigration

From the outset, U.S. immigration policies were created expressly to preserve the racial character of the nation. Persons from Northern Europe and Western Europe, followed by Southern Europe, were favored over all other potential immigrants. The northern free states, with their concentration of both commercial businesses and manufacturing, were the clear choice of immigrants. In the 1840s, nearly half of immigrants to the United States were from Ireland alone. Of the approximately 4.5 million Irish immigrants who

From the nation's founding, Native Americans have been considered sovereign people. Their leadership, like the Lakota chiefs seen here in 1891, entered into many treaties with the U.S. government, many regarding land rights and ownership.

arrived between 1820 and 1930, most settled close to their points of arrival in cities along the East Coast (Omi and Winant 2015).

The mid-1800s gold rush attracted a significant number of Asian immigrants to the West Coast. By the early 1850s, lured by reports of available gold in California, some 25,000 Chinese had immigrated (Omi and Winant 2015). Almost 5 million German immigrants, also coming in large numbers during the 19th century, arrived in the Midwest, where they bought farms or settled near cities such as Milwaukee, St. Louis, and Cincinnati (Omi and Winant 2015).

Anglo-Saxon Protestants, nervous about the influx of so many newcomers, began voicing anti-immigrant sentiments. The anti-immigrant, anti-Catholic American Party (also known as the Know Nothings) lobbied for significant restrictions on immigration. The first group targeted was the Chinese in 1882, and immigrants from other Asian Pacific countries were targeted in 1917 (Jacobson 2006). In 1921 the Emergency Quota Act was adopted, limiting the numbers of immigrants to the United States by imposing quotas based on countries of birth, as determined by a **national origins formula.** The formula set quotas at 3% of the total number of foreign-born persons from a particular country, as recorded in the 1910 U.S. census. This meant that persons from Northern Europe had a higher likelihood of being admitted to the United States than persons from Eastern or Southern Europe and those from non-European countries. Latin American immigrants were excluded from these quotas until 1965, the same year that the discriminatory quotas based on race and national origins were limited. Actual numerical quotas limiting immigration from individual Latin American countries were imposed in 1976 (Ewing 2012). Use of the national origins formula continued until 1965, when it was replaced by rules laid out in the Immigration and Nationality Act of 1965.

Bettmann / Bettmann / Getty Images

Under the National Origins formula, immigration quotas were established that made it much more likely that a person from northern or western Europe would be admitted to the U.S. than those from elsewhere in the world.

The Black civil rights movement of the 1960s, which linked human rights and social justice, sheds light on American immigration policy. The 1965 Immigration and Nationality Act formally committed the United States, for the first time in its history, to accepting immigrants of all nationalities on roughly equal terms. The law eliminated quotas based on countries of origin, a system under which immigrants coming from Northern and Western Europe were given preferential treatment. The impact of this law was immediate and dramatic. For example, in 1960, seven out of every eight immigrants to the United States came from Europe; by 2010, nine out of ten came from other parts of the world. No other law passed in the

The 1965 Immigration and Nationality Act ended the preferential treatment enjoyed by immigrants from northern and western Europe, radically changing the demographic makeup of new arrivals to the country.

20th century has had such a significant demographic impact on our nation (Jelten 2015).

Civil War and Its Aftermath

Geography and history interact in particular ways. Over these unique spaces and places, two distinct patterns of racial political processes can be identified: **de jure political practices**, or processes that were enacted as formal laws, and **de facto political practices**, processes that, although not enshrined in law, were carried out by various entities. Collectively these political practices served to restrict or marginalize the political power, as well as the economic and social power, of specific racial and ethnic groups.

De Jure Political Practices

The Civil War, although centered on the issue of slavery, was equally about what political system should govern the country. In August 1862, in response to concerns about his resolve to free the slaves, President Abraham Lincoln wrote an open letter that appeared in the *New York Times*. Lincoln stated that the issue for him was not slavery but the preservation of the political union. He went further, declaring that he was prepared to abolish, uphold, or partially abolish slavery to uphold the union (Lincoln 1862). In the Emancipation Proclamation, issued one month later, Lincoln took the third choice, freeing some slaves while leaving others in slavery. Most historians agree that Lincoln's proclamation "freed" only those slaves under Confederate control, over which he had no power. The strategy worked in that it relied on either open rebellion or the fear of open rebellion among slaves. And this is what tipped the Civil War in the direction of the Union (Morris 2015).

In the aftermath of the Civil War, a half million Black men became voters in the South during the 1870s. Black women would have to wait until 1920, when all American women were granted the right to vote. Former slaves, now making up more than half of the voting population in many southern states, easily gave the Republican Party, the party of Lincoln, the political power. And for the first time, Blacks were elected to national, state, and local positions. But even with these majorities, Whites were still the majority of those elected at both the state and local levels. When federal troops left the old Confederacy, voting significantly declined among Blacks as White employers and groups like the Ku Klux Klan sought to preserve White political supremacy at all costs (Chancellor 2011).

Over the next few decades, many new laws were created that affected all aspects of life in the South. Most public spaces were segregated by race, and significant restrictions on voting were introduced, including **poll taxes**, taxes that individuals had to pay for 2 years in advance in order to register to vote; **literacy tests**, which required persons seeking to vote to read and interpret a section of the state constitution to the (always White) county court; and **grandfather clauses**, which gave the right to vote to anyone whose grandfather was qualified to vote prior to the Civil War. All of these laws benefited only White citizens. Prior to the enactment of these laws and during Reconstruction, 90% of Black males of voting age were eligible to vote. In 1892, after these laws were passed, less than 6% were eligible (Omi and Winant 2015). Blacks were not the only ones harmed by these devices. So-called old immigrants, mostly British, Irish, Germans, and Scandinavians, were strongly in favor of these restrictions. Those newly arrived from Italy, Russia, and other parts of Southern and Eastern Europe were not so fortunate, as they also found it difficult to pass the new voting tests (Omi and Winant 2015).

Poll tax receipts were issued to those who had paid the fees and were required as proof of payment before a person was permitted to register to vote.

With Blacks effectively removed from the electorate, Whites were in control of all federal and state legislative and executive offices, and so were able to pass a whole range of Jim Crow laws that enforced racial segregation throughout the South. These laws led not only to political disfranchisement but also to economic discrimination and social ostracism. In many ways, the laws specifically targeting African Americans were intended to deal with Native Americans and Chinese Americans as well (Upchurch 2004).

De Facto Political Practices

States in both the South and the North passed residential segregation laws. But in 1917, the U.S. Supreme Court held that such ordinances were unconstitutional. As a result, real estate agents and private developers began to write their own provisions into real estate contracts. These **restrictive covenants** barred the resale of houses to purchasers of a race different from that of the original homeowner. In 1948, the Supreme Court ruled that restrictive covenants were also unconstitutional. Unfortunately, the damage had already been done, as residential segregation had become entrenched. National housing policies from 1930 to 1950, under the Federal Housing Authority (FHA), also reinforced residential segregation. FHA rules required developers to include restrictive covenants and supported local housing policies that segregated public buildings owned by municipalities. In a practice known as **redlining,** areas worthy of mortgage lending were ranked and color coded, and those with the lowest rankings (typically outlined in red), so designated because they held "inharmonious" racial groups, were systematically denied good mortgage rates (Badger 2015).

Redlining was in use by the federal government until 1968, and it was also used by private banks as the country went through one of its most massive homeownership expansions in history. Income restrictions and income differences between Blacks and Whites helped create White suburbs and Black urban ghettos and Hispanic barrios (Tushnet 2003). In a 2015 suit against the largest bank in Wisconsin, the U.S. Department of Housing and Urban Development (HUD) argued that in the period 2008–9, Black and Hispanic borrowers in Wisconsin, Illinois, and Minnesota were wrongly excluded from getting loans. While the bank settled the dispute and denied any wrongdoing, HUD declared that it had gained a victory in "one of the largest redlining complaints" ever brought by the federal government against a lender (Badger 2015).

Redlining causes a domino effect, as lower-valued houses fall into disrepair, businesses and employment vacate the neighborhood, and only the poorest and most vulnerable are left behind. Schools decline, because their revenues are tied to local property and income taxes, and the level of education and the motivation to succeed dwindle, resulting in generations of youth that struggle to escape the cycle. The people who became involved in the 1960s civil rights movement found these circumstances ample reason to wage their war on racism.

CONCEALED RESISTANCE STORY: Claudette Colvin—Before Rosa, There Was Claudette

In 1955, Claudette Colvin, a 15-year-old Black woman, refused to give up her seat on a Montgomery, Alabama, bus to a White person. Someone knocked the books from her hands, beat her, and dragged her forcibly from the bus. When the police arrived, Colvin was arrested, charged with disorderly conduct for violating the segregation ordinance and with assault and battery. Her case immediately got the attention of local civil rights leaders, who debated whether it was worth contesting the charges. The civil rights leaders observed that Colvin's mother was a maid and her father mowed lawns. Although they were churchgoing people, they lived in the poorest section of Montgomery. As the local leaders continued to debate whether the Colvin case could be used to challenge segregation on Montgomery buses, it became known that Colvin was pregnant by a married man. While the leaders helped raise money for her defense, Colvin was deemed unacceptable to become the face of the Montgomery bus protest. Nine months later, another woman, Rosa Parks, would ride on the same bus and follow the same script originated by Colvin. The rest is history, as Rosa Parks became the face of the Montgomery bus boycott and the mother of the modern civil rights movement (Colvin 2016).

Dudley M. Brooks / The Washington Post / Getty Images

When she was 15, Claudette Colvin refused to give up her seat to a white passenger on a Montgomery, Alabama bus in 1955.

The Rise of Coalitional Politics and Social Movements

In many ways, identity politics paved the way for the massive political protests, resistance, and transformations associated with the civil rights movement of the 1950s and 1960s. This period is also distinguished by the rise to prominence of **coalitional politics**, in which political alliances are formed among various identity groups with the shared purpose of establishing specific political agendas.

Perhaps no single movement captured this new form of politics better than the **Black civil rights movement**, which began roughly in 1955 and continued through

1968. In this movement, southern Blacks—in partnership with their northern Black and White allies—challenged and effectively nullified the intimidation and segregation of the Old South. The movement was politically organized to effect change, resist oppression, and redefine the racial order through the courts, on the streets, through boycotts, and through the ballot box.

The Black civil rights movement utilized a series of well-orchestrated nonviolent protests and civil disobedience actions to force dialogues between activists and political institutions. Federal, state, and local governments, as well as businesses and communities, that discriminated against African Americans were targeted and highlighted. The protests included boycotts such as the Montgomery bus boycott of 1955–56; sit-ins targeting restaurants that refused to serve Blacks, such as in Greensboro, North Carolina, in 1960; and large-scale marches from Selma to Montgomery in 1965, protesting the inability of Blacks to vote.

Several major pieces of federal legislation resulted from these activities. One of the major victories of the movement came with passage of the Civil Rights Act of 1964. This act officially banned discrimination in employment practices based on race, color, religion, sex, or national origin. It also prohibited racial segregation in schools, workplaces, and public accommodations. This was followed the next year by the Voting Rights Act of 1965, which ended voting discrimination and extended federal protections to minorities. In that same year, the Immigration and Nationality Act removed racial and national barriers to immigration, which meant that Blacks from other nations could immigrate to the United States. In 1968, the Fair Housing Act banned discrimination in the sale and rental of housing.

During this same period, significant movements were also taking place among other identity groups. On September 8, 1965, a group of mostly male Filipino American grape workers, members of the Agricultural Workers Organizing Committee, walked out of the fields and began a strike against the Delano-Area Table and Wine Grape Growers Association. The workers were protesting decades of poor pay, substandard living conditions, and lack of benefits. They asked Cesar Chavez, leader of the mostly Latino National Farm Workers Association, to join their strike, along with his union's members. Chavez was a veteran union activist and understood how growers had historically pitted different low-skilled workers in disadvantaged racial groups (such as Blacks and Hispanics) against each other. Growers were able to keep wages low by continuously hiring the lowest bidders for services. When Chavez's union voted to join the Filipino workers by walking out on Mexican Independence Day, on September 16, 1965, a coalition was formed that bridged two different and often adversarial racialized labor groups. Soon the strike became a national boycott. As Latino and Filipino strikers banded together, their plight captured the attention of middle-class families in the big cities, who ultimately sided with the poor farmworkers and their families. Millions of families just stopped buying and eating grapes. By 1970, the table grape growers admitted defeat and agreed

By crossing racial lines and allying his National Farm Workers Association with Filipino groups, Cesar Chavez built a coalition that won major concessions from their employers.

to sign the first union contracts granting workers increased benefits and wages (United Farm Workers of America 2016).

In 2016, Standing Rock Indian Reservation in North Dakota became a household name when Native Americans defied large corporations and the government of the United States to protest the building of the Dakota Access Pipeline near the reservation. This was in the tradition of several other Native American protest movements aimed at preserving sacred sites, ensuring the protection of natural resources, and resisting corporate takeovers. The Standing Rock Sioux were not alone, as thousands of people from across the United States, from environmentalists to Black Lives Matter activists, traveled to the reservation to join hands and say no. Another Native American resistance movement took place in 2015, when the Rosebud Sioux tribe in South Dakota fought to keep the Keystone XL pipeline off its lands; also involved in those protests were environmentalists and other Native American tribes (Donnella 2016). These modern forms of resistance illustrate the viability and the reality of coalitional politics as an effective form of political activism.

■ BUILDING ALTERNATIVES TO THE MATRIX OF RACE AND POLITICS

The United States originated as a consequence of political activism, and the tradition of political activism has been central to every important phase of the nation's history, continuing to guide us in our quest to become "a more perfect union." On Monday, February 13, 2017, "A Day without Immigrants" was staged in major cities across the country as a response to President Trump's executive orders tightening immigration restrictions. Small businesses across the country were forced to close as immigrants stayed home to show just how important they are to the U.S. economy. In support of their efforts, employers and some other employees gave up wages and profits, also hoping to show the American consumer what an economy without immigrant labor would mean for goods and services (Lam 2017). These protests and others demonstrate that political activism makes a difference that can build alternatives to the matrix of race and politics.

1. Identities and political systems have changed over both times and places. Given the types of changes that we have seen, what may be the sources of change in the future? Alternatively, are there any political patterns linking identity to specific political parties or outcomes that may either endure into the future or be subject to change? What might account for these outcomes?

2. The labor and civil rights movements had significant impacts not only on identity but also on political coalitions. What other movements might have significantly influenced political institutions, identities, and outcomes? What does this suggest regarding the stability of political institutions?

3. Political identity is uniquely part of our political processes. What kinds of events might increase or decrease the likelihood that a particular political identity or collection of identities will remain viable or have the ability to transform political processes?

4. Identity politics is a very effective organizational tool, but identity movements can become mired in single issues. How might concentration on single issues and single identities serve not only to marginalize but also to limit the effectiveness of a social movement?

The Power of Political Activism

While much of our attention is drawn to political participation, other components of this terrain are just as important, including various forms of action where the primary goal is to promote, impede, or raise awareness of a particular issue or set of issues. **Political activism** normally involves various types of actions that go beyond voting. It may be as simple as posting opinions online or getting involved in a letter-writing campaign, or it may involve active participation in boycotts, protests, or demonstrations.

One of the major insights revealed by the intersectional approach is that while race, class, gender, sexuality, and other sites of identity interact to produce unique forms of inequality and discrimination, they can also become the basis of **agency**—that is, the ability to effect change, to act independently, and to exercise free choices. This agency, a vital component of identity politics, reflects the multiple ways and mechanisms by which individuals and groups challenge, resist, and cope with inequality and discrimination. The various forms of political activism, such as boycotts and harnessing social media, have been quite effective at producing social change. Identity politics also highlights the coalitions that form both within racial groups (as multiple ethnic groups coalesce into a panethnic or panracial identity) and across them. The various examples below highlight how identity politics significantly alters the political landscape.

Boycotts

Boycotting is one of the most significant forms of political activism. Boycotts are voluntary acts of protest in which individuals or groups seek to punish or coerce corporations, nations, or persons by refusing to purchase their products, invest in them, or otherwise interact with them. Boycotts are often used to raise awareness of issues while simultaneously pressuring the entities involved to change policies, practices, or structures. The earliest boycotts in the United States occurred during the American Revolution, when colonialists refused to purchase British goods. Other boycotts have served as means by which marginalized groups have challenged the political process:

- In 1905, the Chinese boycotted U.S. products in reaction to the extension of the Chinese Exclusion Act.

- From 1965 to 1970, the United Farm Workers of America led nationwide boycotts of grapes and lettuce in retail grocery stores to pressure growers to improve wages and working conditions.

- From 1954 to 1968, participants in the Black civil rights movement conducted a number of boycotts (including the Montgomery bus boycott) to protest unequal treatment of African Americans.

- From 1973 to 1995, LGBT groups led a boycott of Coors Brewing Company to protest its antigay hiring practices.

Harnessing Social Media

The day after Donald Trump became the 45th president of the United States, women across the United States and around the globe marched in protest. According to some estimates, as many as 2.5 million people—women as well as men who support women's rights—took to the streets. The demonstrations dominated the news and social media and elicited several tweets from the president. The movement to stage a Women's March began on Facebook the day after Hillary Clinton lost the November election, and the idea for the protest quickly went viral as many feared the consequences of a Trump presidency for reproductive, civil, and human rights (Przybyla and Schouten 2017). Although touted as an all-inclusive protest, drawing participants across all racial, ethnic, gender, and class groups, many criticized it as being a movement of primarily White, middle-class women (Bates 2017).

Other groups have also discovered the importance of social media as a tool for facilitating social activism. The story of the Black Lives Matter (BLM) movement

The National Women's March on January 21, 2017, drew millions of people workdwide.

demonstrates how political activism can be a form of resistance and transformation. BLM originated on social media in 2013 with the Twitter hashtag #BlackLivesMatter. It was a response to the acquittal of George Zimmerman for the shooting death of 17-year-old African American Trayvon Martin. The movement gained momentum and went national in 2014 after the police shooting deaths of two more African American males: Michael Brown in Ferguson, Missouri, and Eric Garner in New York City. This modern social movement is devoted to challenging police brutality and racial profiling. Since its inception, BLM has docu-

mented and protested the deaths of a number of African Americans who have been killed by police or died while in police custody. During the 2016 presidential campaign, representatives from BLM on several occasions entered into political discourse by attending candidate forums and pointing out how systemic racism is pervasive in the United States (Griffith 2016). While BLM has become an effective voice calling for both resistance and transformation, it has also produced some unanticipated consequences, including the revelation of underlying racial tensions affecting other minority groups.

Other interest groups have also found social media to be an effective tool for political activism. Black actors used the hashtag #OscarsSoWhite on several

In 2016, Chinese Americans, chanting "No scapegoat! No scapegoat!" carried signs and protested in support of Peter Liang, a former New York City police officer who was convicted in the fatal shooting of an unarmed Black man. Many of the protesters believed that Officer Liang was being used as a scapegoat due to his race. One of the protesters summed up their efforts by saying, "This movement, this community reaction, it won't be a Million Man March—it's not that. . . . It is representative of Asian Americans willing to take time away from their daily lives, to step up and say we don't like what's going on" (quoted in Rojas 2016).

social media platforms as part of their call for a boycott of the 2016 Academy Awards. Soon, more traditional news outlets, print and broadcast, began to cover the protest, which charged that the Oscars were too "pale, male and stale" (Pearson 2016). These kinds of comments made direct reference to the membership of the Academy of Motion Picture Arts and Sciences: At the time, roughly 87% of members were White, more than half (58%) were male, and close to two-thirds were 60 years old or older. Just 6% of Academy members were Black, 4% were Hispanic, and 2% were Asian. Women made up 42% of Academy members (Cieply and Barnes 2016). How effective was the boycott? Since that time, the Academy has expanded its membership somewhat and has appeared to make an effort to invite more women and people of color to join. Also, in 2017, 7 of the 20 actors nominated for Academy Awards were not White, compared to none the previous year (Robinson 2017).

Creating Change

If you are reading this text, then there is a good chance that you are a millennial, or that you regularly come into contact with millennials. Young people have historically voted in much lower numbers than other age groups across the United States, and the 2016 election was no different. In spite of the billions of dollars spent on the 2016 presidential campaigns, millennials were increasingly disengaged from the two-party-dominated election. Many of them gravitated to third-party or independent candidates. In some cases, third-party candidates held five-to-one margins among voters under 35 across all racial groups (Kilgore 2016).

The future looks to be even more variable, as millennials are soon to become the dominant force in the U.S. electorate. According to a recent portrait of millennials by the Pew Research Center (2014):

- Millennials are the most ethnically and racially diverse cohort in the nation's history. About 43% are non-White, the highest proportion of non-Whites in any generation. (About half of all newborns today in the United States are non-White, and the Census Bureau projects that by 2043 the U.S. population will be majority non-White; see Figure 8.3.)

- Millennials are possibly the most politically progressive age group in modern history.

- Millennials are the first generation for whom the Internet has been a constant. They grew up on social media and are a truly the digital generation.

The members of this generation are also more likely than those of other generations to be politically independent (50%), and close to a third are not affiliated with any religious group. It is noteworthy that these are the highest levels of political and religious disaffiliation recorded for any generation in the nearly quarter century that

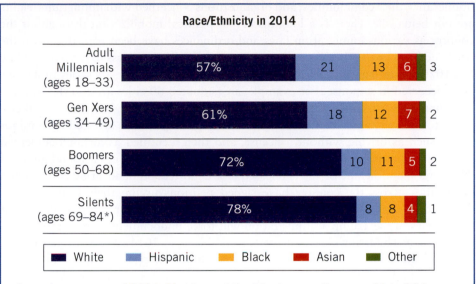

Figure 8.3 ■ Millennials are the Most Ethnically and Racially Diverse Cohort in Our Nation's History

Race/Ethnicity in 2014

	White	Hispanic	Black	Asian	Other
Adult Millennials (ages 18–33)	57%	21	13	6	3
Gen Xers (ages 34–49)	61%	18	12	7	2
Boomers (ages 50–68)	72%	10	11	5	2
Silents (ages 69–84*)	78%	8	8	4	1

Ages shown are as of 2014. Members of the Silent generation were 69 to 86 in 2014. Since the Current Population Survey aggregates those age 85 and older into one category, results for 69- to 84-year-olds are shown. Hispanics are of any race. Racial groups include only non-Hispanics. Figures may not add to 100% because of rounding. Shares less than 0.5% not shown.

Source: Chart: "Race/Ethnicity in 2014." From *Comparing Millennials to Other Generations*, Pew Research Center Social and Demographic Trends, March 19, 2015.

Pew has been conducting such research (Pew Research Center 2014). Less than a third (31%) of millennials believe that there is any real difference between the Republican and Democratic Parties. This generation, with the advent of the Internet, social media, and advancing globalization, is uniquely linked with the global universe. For millennials, political activity and organization are not limited by geography or by what is reported in or left out of the local press, radio, or television news coverage. With the world literally as close as a phone, tablet, or desktop, they can immediately and simultaneously communicate, agitate, transform, or just stay informed. They can show support for human rights or help build virtual communities across racial, gendered, political, class, national, educational, and geographic boundaries, or across any other boundaries imaginable (Pew Research Center 2014). And they can have a significant impact.

As we have seen, throughout U.S. history immigrants have frequently been targeted by both federal and state policies. Immigrants currently are undergoing similar sources of stress amid political rhetoric about building a wall along the U.S.–Mexico border, banning Muslim immigration, and deporting "undocumented" immigrants. Immigrants, their communities, and organizations concerned with immigrants' rights are not being idle. There is a long history of political mobilization throughout the country as various immigration laws and ordinances have been passed at both the state and local levels. These laws range from bans on Islamic dress to the Arizona law (SB 1070) requiring all immigrants to carry registration papers. A series of actions have occurred in response. For example, an estimated 60 cities around the country, including New York, Los Angeles, San Francisco, and Houston, have declared themselves to be "sanctuary cities." In a sanctuary city, if a person is arrested for a minor crime, such as driving without a license, and then identified as an undocumented immigrant, that person must serve the time or pay stipulated fines if found guilty of the charges, but then he or she is released, not deported. Students at 80 colleges and universities across the country have signed petitions urging their institutions to declare their campuses as sanctuaries. This movement reflects growing concerns that the policies of the Trump administration will force undocumented immigrants who came here as children to leave the country (CBS News 2016). For your generation, the question is not if you will bring about political change, but what forms that change will take. Will you be the change that you want to see in the world?

CRITICAL THINKING

1. In what ways might millennials effect transformative change? How might geography affect the likelihood of change?

2. How might political institutions better interact with other institutions (those dealing with the economy, family, education, or the military) to improve outcomes? What types of barriers or opportunities can you identify?

3. Our identities are shaped by and help shape the various institutions of which we are a part. In what ways might your identity become transformed given political actions that are now taking place? How might you, given your identity, be part of these changes?

4. The future belongs to all of us. Each generation, from oldest to youngest, has a stake in how well the political process operates. How might you, even at this point, become more involved in politics? What can you do within your institution or in the wider community?

KEY TERMS

agency, p. 293

binary constructs, p. 278

Black civil rights movement, p. 290

boycotts, p. 294

citizenship, p. 284

class approach, p. 280

coalitional politics, p. 290

critical race theory, p. 281

de facto political practices, p. 287

de jure political practices, p. 287

democratic equilibrium, p. 277

disenfranchisement, p. 273

grandfather clauses, p. 288

Great Compromise of 1787, p. 284

identity politics, p. 281

insider groups, p. 277

Instrumentalism, p. 280

literacy tests, p. 288

millennials, p. 275

national origins formula, p. 286

outsider groups, p. 277

pluralism, p. 277

political activism, p. 293

political identities, p. 270

political sociology, p. 276

politics, p. 270

poll taxes, p. 288

power, p. 283

power elite model, p. 278

redlining, p. 289

restrictive covenants, p. 289

silent generation, p. 275

structuralism, p. 280

CHAPTER SUMMARY

LO 8.1   Explain contemporary political identities.

The 2016 election of Donald Trump to the U.S. presidency highlights the relevance of political identities in our country. Trump, the 45th president, looks like the majority of those who have held the office—White, male, and rich. Alternatively, his election also demonstrates the importance of geographic space (he dominated in rural and suburban areas) and historical context (the Republican Party and conservative politics). The U.S. electorate is made up of various identity groups that reflect the matrix of race, class, gender, and region. These identities do not share equally in political outcomes, as witnessed by the significant number of Black and Hispanic felons who have been disenfranchised in recent years. Gender cannot be ignored, as we see how it interacts with race, education, and class, which helps to explain some recent political outcomes. One of these is that Black women, and women in general, are more likely to vote than their male counterparts but less likely to hold political office.

LO 8.2 Evaluate stock sociological theories regarding power, politics, and identity.

Political sociology has traditionally provided three central theories for understanding power, politics, and identity. These stock theories include pluralism, the power elite model, and the class approach. Pluralism argues that power is decentralized and widely shared among approximately equal groups. This perspective fails to provide sufficient insight into those systems in which power is not shared equally. The power elite model posits that power is concentrated among discrete groups of elites who control the resources of significant social institutions. Controlling these resources allows the elites also to control power and authority over governmental and political processes. Again, the model assumes both equality and consensus across the various elites. It fails to address what happens when power is in conflict across elites or how nonelite individuals and groups produce political change. The class approach argues essentially that those who control the economic system control the political processes. The class approach therefore tends to be reductionist, evaluating all politics from the vantage point of a person's position in the economic system. It fails to take into account how social movements radically outside the mainstream economic institutions have served to resist and transform the political process.

LO 8.3 Apply the matrix approach to U.S. political history.

Resource scarcity often underlies political struggles, and political systems come into being to regulate conflicts over these resources. In the process, differences associated with race, class, gender, and geography often become politicized. Our application of the matrix allows us to see how these political processes have played out over time, producing both de jure and de facto outcomes that have unique impacts. In the South, certain de jure forms of political structures came into being. These legal, more obvious forms of racialized politics had negative and differential impacts on Blacks, Chinese, and Native Americans and influenced how citizenship, freedom, and immigration were defined. In the North, less obvious de facto procedures were used in discriminatory federal housing policies that created White, middle-class suburbs and urban ghettos through redlining. Coalitional politics are associated with the convergence of identity politics in the form of massive political protests, resistance, and transformations during the civil rights movement of the 1950s and 1960s. This movement, driven by a coalition of southern Blacks and northern Whites and Blacks, effectively nullified the intimidation and segregation of the Old South. Such movements have not been exclusive to Blacks; among others, Filipino and Latino farmworkers and contemporary Native Americans have utilized similar social activism to influence political discourse.

LO 8.4 Formulate alternatives to the matrix of race and politics.

The members of the millennial generation are less likely than their counterparts in earlier generations to vote based on political party loyalty, but they might be more motivated by specific issues. Recent elections demonstrate that compared to other age cohorts, millennials are most likely to be politically independent. Millennials may change the very course of this country as they become the largest generation and as they become more economically viable and politically active. More diverse than any preceding generation, and with a strong understanding of the effective use of social media, millennials have a huge potential for bringing about political change. The question is not if they will create change, but when and what forms these changes will take.

SPORTS AND THE AMERICAN DREAM

Rezball is a favorite sport on Native American reservations. Requiring little more than a net and a ball, it has become an important communal experience for many.

LEARNING OBJECTIVES

LO 9.1   Explain the state of sport in the United States.

LO 9.2   Compare stock theories about U.S. sport.

LO 9.3   Apply the matrix approach to sport.

LO 9.4   Describe strategies for transforming the institution of sport.

Rezball, or reservation basketball, dominates the basketball courts on Native American reservations. The sport gained official certification from the National Collegiate Athletic Association (NCAA) in 2007. It differs from regular basketball in that it has fewer time-outs and no organized plays, and it serves to enhance identities at multiple levels by including both **communal experience,** or shared knowledge across group members occupying the same spaces, and **cultural values,** or are shared sets of beliefs and interpretations (Pember 2007). It is a game found both on reservations and in urban communities, played on dirt courts and in tribal gyms. Tournaments are played among families and friends, and during the games, Indian identity is shared and victory (regardless of who wins) is a community event (Manning 2016).

This fast-moving game has created its own stars and dreams. In these spaces we can find thousands of young players who make their mark in organized games, often playing for overflow crowds. Former rezball star Shoni Schimmel went on to play for two teams in the Women's National Basketball Association (WNBA), the Atlanta Dream and the New York Liberty, and in 2014 she was named Most Valuable Player in the WNBA All-Star Game. Off the court, Schimmel actively encourages Native American youth to pursue their dreams (Meyers 2016). The intricacies of rezball provide an example of how place and space, race, gender, class, and sports intersect. Sports are highly stratified, segregated, and reflective of these same intersections. This means that while some sports may appear to be more diverse than others, closer analysis of ownership, coaching, and fan bases reveals that an examination of sport, as an institution, can benefit from an intersectional approach. Let's first look at contemporary trends in sports and how they relate to the American Dream.

■ THE STATE OF SPORT TODAY

Sport encompasses a range of activities that involve physical exertion and skill. These activities are organized around sets of rules and can be played at either the individual or the team level. Today's athletes are remarkable, and some of the best set some dazzling new records at the 2016 Olympic Games in Rio de Janeiro. Team USA won a total of 121 medals, with the women capturing the most, garnering 61 individual medals, compared to 55 for the men, and another 5 in mixed events. They also won the majority of the gold medals (27 of 46). Among these stars were gymnast Simone Biles, who earned four golds and a bronze, a first for a U.S. gymnast in a single event, and swimmer Katie Ledecky, who set new world records in the 400- and 800-meter freestyle events (Myre 2016).

Across the country and in many of our colleges, high schools, and local communities, modern "gladiators" like these are writing new chapters in a long tradition of competition and victory, sometimes earning fame, high salaries, and lucrative endorsement deals. But all sports are not equal, as we will see in our exploration of the business of sports.

The Sports Industry

While the Olympics are spectacular, the most watched sport in the United States has traditionally been football, and the Super Bowl leads all other single sporting events. Games run by the National Football League (NFL) account for 34 of the 35 most-watched programs on TV (Thompson 2014).

Among the viewership numbers, some interesting demographics can be identified. The National Basketball Association (NBA) has the youngest audience (45% of its viewers are under 35) and the highest share of Black viewers (45%). Major League Baseball (MLB) and the National Basketball Association tie for the highest numbers of male viewers. The National Hockey League (NHL) has the richest audience (one-third of its viewers have annual incomes of more than $100,000), and Hispanics are more likely to view the games of Major League Soccer (MLS) teams. NASCAR's audience has the highest number of female viewers plus the most White viewers of either gender. The Professional Golfers' Association (PGA) has the oldest audience, with about 35% over the age of 55 (Thompson 2014). It should not come as any surprise that the sports we choose to watch reveal something about our values and interests, and that certain fan bases made up of distinct social groupings can have large impacts on the business of sport. The makeup of a sport's fan base not only affects television viewership but also links directly to both the salaries athletes can earn and the endorsement contracts they are offered.

Sport constitutes a significant portion of the U.S. economy, and the popularity of sports means that billions of dollars are generated each year. The business of sports today encompasses everything from food to memorabilia to stadium naming rights. In 2015, sports programming accounted for 35% of all broadcast TV advertiser spending. The largest television networks generated $8.47 billion in sports programming in 2014–15 (Crupi 2015). In one year, U.S. consumers spent a total of $498 billion on sports-related purchases (Plunkett Research 2012). Of this, $63.64 billion came from sales of sporting equipment and $21.4 billion was paid out in health club memberships (Peltz and Masunaga 2016). In 2016 the NFL, with income of $13 billion, led all other professional sports leagues in revenue (Kutz 2016). Also in 2016, among colleges and universities, 24 schools had revenues of at least $100 million annually for their athletic departments (Gaines 2016).

Sports Media

If we watch almost any sports media channel, we might conclude that sports in the United States are an equal opportunity employer. This is not correct. While women's participation in sports has increased at all levels since the 1970s, from high school through the professional level, serious media coverage of women's sports has been lacking (Cooky, Messner, and Hextrum 2013). In 2016, the Princeton women's NCAA basketball team won 30 games and lost none, setting an Ivy League season record that was previously held by a male team. This monumental accomplishment did not get nearly the amount of attention from the media as that paid to male teams. The Princeton women did not garner the same numbers of fans, TV rights, or marketing endorsements. This imbalance may be explained, at least in part, by the fact that sports reporters, writers, and editors are overwhelmingly White and male (Cooky et al. 2013).

The same rules apply for scholarships, positions, and endorsements. While female athletes make up more than half of the college student athlete population, they get only 43% of NCAA athletic opportunities. In 2014, women received 63,241 fewer NCAA athletic positions than their male counterparts (NCAA 2014). Men received about 55% of NCAA support for college athletes, while women received 45% (NCAA 2014).

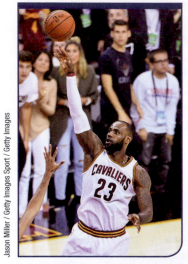

Jason Miller / Getty Images Sport / Getty Images

Christian Peterson / Getty Images Sport / Getty Images

Scott Barbour / Getty Images Sport / Getty Images

Hannah Foslien / Getty Images Sport / Getty Images

AP Photo / Andrew Patron

LeBron James, Phil Mickelson, Serena Williams, Robinson Cano, and Kei Nishikori are some of the highest paid athletes in the world.

In 2016, the top 10 female professional athletes made just 13.1% of the salaries of the top males. In that year, professional tennis player Serena Williams, who is the highest-paid female athlete in the world, made $28.9 million. But if she were a man, she would have been only the 40th highest-paid athlete (see Table 9.1). Maria Sharapova, a Russian-born U.S. tennis player who is ranked at 88th in income, is the only other woman in the top 100 highest-paid athletes (Forbes 2016). Four U.S. Black males—LeBron James, Kevin Durant, Kobe Bryant (all basketball players), and Cam Newton (football)—were among the 10 highest-paid athletes in 2016. The top-grossing world athletes in 2016 were both male international soccer players.

Table 9.1 ■ The World's Highest-Paid Athletes, 2016 (in millions of U.S. dollars)

Rank	Name	Total Pay	Salary/ Winnings	Endorsements	Sport
1	Cristiano Ronaldo	88	56	32	Soccer
2	Lionel Messi	81.4	53.4	28	Soccer
3	LeBron James	77.2	23.2	54	Basketball
4	Roger Federer	67.8	7.8	60	Tennis
5	Kevin Durant	56.2	20.2	36	Basketball
6	Novak Djokovic	55.8	21.8	34	Tennis
7	Cam Newton	53.1	41.1	12	Football
8	Phil Mickelson	52.9	2.9	50	Golf
9	Jordan Spieth	52.8	20.8	32	Golf
10	Kobe Bryant	50	25	25	Basketball
29	Kei Nishikori	33.5	3.5	30	Tennis
40	Serena Williams	28.9	8.9	20	Tennis
45	Robinson Cano	27	24	3	Baseball

Source: "The World's Highest-Paid Athletes," *Forbes,* 2016, https://www.forbes.com/athletes/list/#tab:overall.

Note: Among U.S. players, only two White males make it into the top 10, both golfers (Phil Mickelson and Jordan Spieth). U.S. White males, distributed broadly across most sports, are by far the most represented (accounting for 29). U.S. Black males, primarily within basketball and football, are the second most represented (accounting for 28). U.S. Hispanic males, almost exclusively found within baseball, are the third leading group of players (10). Only 3 Asians appear among the top 100 of the world's highest-paid athletes.

Players and Coaches

Both class and race are reflected in the biographies of successful athletes and coaches. An examination of the intersection of race, class, and family background structures demonstrates the unequal pathways into professional sports (Keating 2011). As we will see, these intersectional realities help us understand many of the variabilities associated with sports in this country.

Across the United States, we spend a lot of time thinking about and often constructing myths about our sports heroes. Athletes define and shape much of how we perceive ourselves as a people, and these perceptions, unfortunately, also become embedded within our various racial myths. These racial myths, often reflecting notions of innate superiority, can confuse and confound determination and motivation with community and culture. It is a widespread belief that many athletes rise to fame and fortune out of dismal poverty and family circumstances, but poor Blacks and Whites from broken families are not overrepresented in professional sports.

- Middle-class and more affluent Whites are 75% more likely than poor Whites to become NBA players.

- Blacks from two-parent families are 18% more likely than those from broken homes to become NBA athletes.

- White NBA players are 33% more likely to come from two-parent families than from single-parent families (Keating 2011).

Often when we speak of diversity, we are actually making reference to binary constructions of diversity—that is, we are accounting for only two major racial or ethnic groups. A more realistic measure of diversity would be one that accounts for the largest number of racial, ethnic, and gendered groups.

Most professional sports are at least somewhat segregated by race, ethnicity, and gender. With this caveat, if we were to consider the diversity of professional sports, only one sport can truly be called diverse (see Figure 9.1). Major League Soccer is the only professional sports league within the United States in which at least 50% of players are not of a single race or ethnicity. In contrast, three-quarters of NBA players, 70% of WNBA players, and 65% of NFL players are Black, and 60% of the players in Major League Baseball are White (Hoenig 2014). In 2016, although Latinos made up 17% of the U.S. population, they were underrepresented in all professional sports except Major League Baseball, where they made up 28.5% of the players. And diversity in sports pays off. The most diverse international soccer teams are also the most likely to win games (Maleskey and Saiegh 2014).

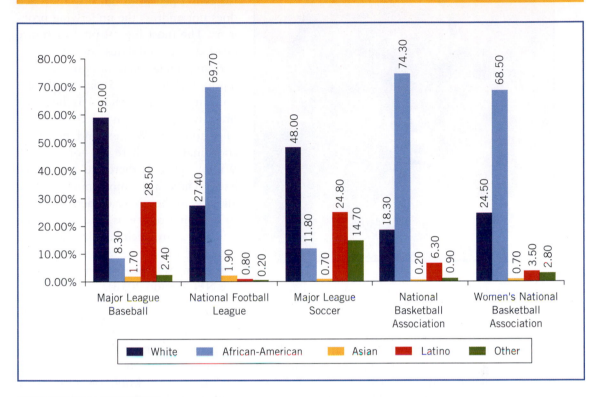

Source: Data from Lapchick (2017).

In the 2015–16 season, coaches across all leagues who identified as people of color represented just 33.3% of the head coaching positions (Lapchick 2016) The NBA, NFL, and MLS have made significant improvements in the development of coaches of color through more transparent hiring processes, increasingly diverse search committees, and the establishment of affirmative action policies. The National Football League, with the establishment of the Rooney Rule in 2003, mandated that the league develop a diverse pool of manager and general manager candidates. The rule specifically requires teams to interview minority candidates for head coaching and senior football operation jobs. A total of 22 head coaches were hired in the NFL from 2012 through 2016, and only one, Todd Bowles, hired as head coach for the New York Jets, was a person of color.

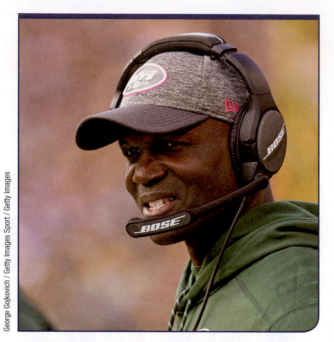

Todd Bowles, head coach with the New York Jets, was the only minority head coach hired in the NFL between 2012 and 2016, despite rules requiring teams to interview minority candidates for the positions.

Part of the issue is that while the Rooney Rule requires teams to interview at least one minority candidate for each open position, this approach does not address the underlying problems. The most logical pool of future head coach candidates consists of the current population of offensive coordinators (where only 5 out of 80 are minority), quarterback coaches and offensive quality control coaches (all of whom are White), and defensive coordinators (where 23 of 32 are White). This is therefore a pipeline issue. There are simply more Whites already on the career ladders that lead to coaching positions, and until more minorities are included in the lower coaching ranks, we will not see any real changes among head coaches in the NFL (Sando 2016).

In 1997, Bud Selig, then acting commissioner of baseball (he became commissioner in 1998), mandated that MLB create a diverse pool of managerial candidates in a manner similar to that later established in the NFL. In 2012, among managerial slots in the league, 32% of central staff were people of color, while women made up 39%. Two executive vice presidents and eight vice presidents were people of color, and women were also well represented among executives, with six senior vice presidents and five vice presidents (Lapchick 2012).

■ EXAMINING STOCK SOCIOLOGICAL THEORIES OF SPORT

The link between race and sport predates the actual sociology of sport, which has emerged as an academic field only in the past half century. Scholarly interest in the field may be linked to the increasingly significant amount of time devoted to sports on television, the development of professional sporting leagues, and the expansion of youth sports in local communities and educational institutions. There are four popular sociological theories about sport. Two pit biology and socialization against each other, with the biological viewpoint holding that certain groups are born with athletic abilities. The nurture perspective, in contrast, assumes that individuals are

1. Why might different U.S. regions, such as the South, the North, the Southwest, and the Midwest, produce different interactions among race, gender, and sport? How might both history and economic conditions affect these differences?

2. Sport is significantly influenced by other institutions, such as educational and community organizations. How might changes in these institutions (values, structure, or resources) lead to the increased or decreased participation of various groups in sport?

3. How have the interactions among race, gender, and sport changed across the United States? What might be some future trends in sport, based on current demographic and other potential shifts? For example, how might fan bases influence trends?

4. Are you into sport? If so, is your interest as an athlete, as a fan, or a little of both? What sports are you active in (either as a fan or as a participant)? What intersectional factors, such as your race, gender, class, and family background, might account for your support of particular sports?

socialized into becoming, or not becoming, athletes. Other scholars, assuming either nature or nurture, have been more interested in the functions served by sport in society and how sport serves to perpetuate certain myths about the United States. Finally, scholars who take a critical perspective argue that sport is a by-product of the U.S. economic system, where group differences in athleticism associated with race, gender, and class are manipulated to preserve power differentials. These dominant theories, reinforced and promoted by media and popular culture, are our sport stock stories.

The Nature Perspective

We live in a time when many of our behaviors have been linked to specific sets of genes. It's not surprising, then, that in our competitive culture companies have capitalized on this by claiming they can help parents identify, through genetic testing, which sports their kids are biologically programmed to succeed in and then recommend specific workouts based on the children's "innate" skills. One company claims that it can determine which youths are more susceptible to concussions, heart attacks, and other health problems. Critics point out that the advice being offered by these companies, based on questionable genetic testing, is not only likely to be inaccurate but also may pose potential ethical issues and health threats (Stein 2011). Let's take a look at the science.

The **nature perspective** posits that biological differences between genders and among racial, cultural, and national groups account for variations in athletic ability, performance, and success. On the surface, the link between biology and sport seems logical. Of course, some might argue, certain people and groups are just more athletic than others. These common stereotypes about race, gender, and sport are supported by the larger social narrative that defines differences as rooted in biology. Biological determinism argues that human behavior, intelligence, and athleticism are determined by genetics or by some other aspects of physiology (such as brain size or body type). Accordingly, it argues that Blacks run faster, run longer, and jump higher than Whites, but are genetically deficient in intelligence (Hall 2002, 114). No evidence, biological or otherwise, exists to support this linking of race, athleticism, and intelligence.

Current research has found more than 200 genetic variants associated with physical performance, and more than 20 genetic variants associated with elite athletic status. Genetic variants may also be associated with particular injury risks and outcomes. While these associations may exist, to date no genetic variations have been identified that provide predictability in terms of either athletic success or injury risk outcomes (Guth and Roth 2013). Further research has concluded that there is no association between genotypes and elite competitive status (Coelho et al. 2016). Other sports scholars and researchers theorize that rather than nature, nurture accounts for athletic success and related outcomes.

The Nurture Perspective

The **nurture perspective** views gender, racial, cultural, and national group differences in athleticism as products of socialization and environment. A whole range of behaviors are socialized, including those associated with notions of meritocracy, teamwork, rule conformance, gender norms, and sportsmanship. For example, sport is a space where the best athletes are rewarded, and in theory these rewards are not associated with race, gender, or class.

For years, gender norms have been reinforced by gender segregation within individual sports. Women rarely compete directly with men in a given sport, a practice that reinforces gender norms. Women athletes are, however consistently challenging these norms. Stock car racer Danica Patrick, winner of the 2008 Indy Japan 300 and third-place finisher in the 2009 Indianapolis 500, demonstrates that women can perform just as well as men in car racing. In 2003, professional golfer Annika Sörenstam decided to enter a PGA (men's) tournament. She faced a lot of backlash, but nevertheless, she competed.

The pushback that women encounter when they enter what are perceived to be male spaces in sport demonstrates how sport socialization tends to mirror the perceptions of sport within the wider community and nation. Major institutions, such as schools, media, teams, and local, state, and national government, use rewards and sanctions to reinforce this socialization (Sage and Eitzen 2015). Performing within a sport helps members learn how to obey rules, as they are rewarded when they accomplish acceptable tasks in acceptable ways and penalized when they violate these rules. Think for a moment about the following aspects of sport and how they reinforce rules:

- If a football player trips an opponent during a play, the player receives a foul for inappropriate or unfair behavior. The player has violated the rules—not only the rules of the game but also the rules of life.

- Sport teams and athletes are some of the most visible members of their schools and colleges, communities, and states.

- Team seasons, competitions, and rivalries structure our time in unique ways. There is March Madness, when college basketball teams vie for national honors, and bowl season, when college football dominates the airwaves and conversations. Baseball enthusiasts eagerly wait for spring training and the World Series. Then there are the Olympics, cheerleading competitions, fantasy bowls, and other competitions.

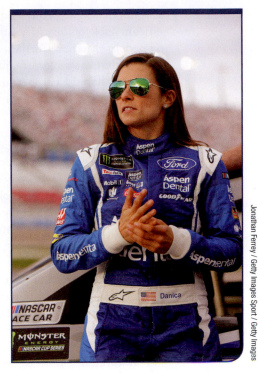

Indycar and NASCAR driver Danica Patrick has had success in these male-dominated sports, demonstrating that women can race at the highest level.

Jonathan Ferrey / Getty Images Sport / Getty Images

All of these aspects of sport provide opportunities for people to participate in a wide range of athletic activities. But participation is also to a great extent dictated by what is available within a community.

As we will examine in more depth, critical scholars have pointed out that sport socialization serves to preserve the dominant gender, racial, and class hierarchy. For example, fishing is typically cast as a male-dominated sport, and researchers have pointed out that women are rarely featured in fishing magazines. When they are depicted, usually in advertisements, they are often sexualized (their clothing and other "feminine" qualities are shown as obstacles to fishing for men) or they are presented as valued fishing companions for men (Carini and Weber 2015).

The links among race, nurture, and sport have also been demonstrated repeatedly. African American youth, compared to their White, Hispanic, and Asian counterparts, are more likely to receive encouragement to participate in sports from both family members and nonkin (Shakib and Veliz 2012). While there are more than

150 major league professional sports franchises in the United States, there is a significant lack of diversity among team ownership. The NBA's Charlotte Hornets, owned by Michael Jordan, is the only professional team among the six biggest leagues that has a Black majority owner. In the 2012, Pakistani-born American businessman Shahid Khan became the majority owner of the Jacksonville Jaguars in the NFL and thus became only the second person of color to gain this distinction (Hoenig 2014).

Critical theorists currently argue that **agency** (the capacity of individuals to make choices and to act independently given access, resources, and ability) interacts with sport in a process that links identities, nature, and nurture. This process recognizes that there are obvious biological differences among infants. These differences, related to motor skills and early childhood development, can have impacts later in life. Family and prenatal care can influence not only cognitive but also fine motor skills associated with sport. Lastly, if there is an environment, reflected in either culture or community, that values, encourages, and rewards athleticism, then we would expect these outcomes to be reflected in specific ways. For example, we tend to encourage gender differences in sport and athleticism, and this produces obvious gendered differences associated with specific types of sports (Hofstede, Dignum, Prada, Student, and Vanhée 2015). In high schools, girls have 1.3 million fewer opportunities than boys have to be involved in sports. This leads to an increased likelihood that female athletes have to look outside both high school and college to be involved in sports, and such alternative options typically do not exist, or if they do, they cost more money than school sports participation (Women's Sports Foundation 2017).

Class and space can also affect who has access to sport (Carrington 2013). Increasingly, shortfalls in public funds have forced school districts across the country to cut funding for their athletic programs. These cuts have had significant impacts particularly on lower-class families. In 2012, nearly 20% of lower-income parents were forced to restrict their children's participation in sports for monetary reasons. An estimated 61% of middle and high school children involved in sports were charged pay-to-play fees. Other expenses for the families of young athletes include the costs of equipment, uniforms, and team fees, which on average amount to an additional $381. Being a team member in an elite volleyball club can run as much as $3,500, with another $3,000 just for travel. Membership in a soccer club can exceed $4,000 a year, and that does not include tournaments and equipment (Killion 2013).

Research also has demonstrated that sport participation is linked to both race and gender. Black student-athletes tend to become concentrated and even overrepresented in sports like football, basketball, and boxing, and are nearly absent from all other sports (Coakley 2004). White athletes tend to have higher participation rates in swimming, soccer, baseball, and softball (Goldsmith 2003).

Some argue that sport serves as a means through which subordinate males and females can seek status, respect, empowerment, and upward mobility (Scraton and Flintoff 2013). The reality is quite the opposite. Being poor and from the inner city does not increase one's chances of becoming a sport star. Kids growing up in stable, more prosperous environments are more likely to develop the skills of persistence, self-regulation, and trust, all of which are basic to sport success (Stephens-Davidowitz 2013).

There are many more opportunities for boys to participate in school sports than for girls, and the increasing cost of participation can make it hard for lower income students to play.

The Functions of Sport

Functionalists believe that society is composed of a system of interrelated institutions that are structured according to the functions they perform (or the vital societal/community needs they fulfill). The **functionalist theory of sport** argues that sport fulfills a multitude of needs.

- *Shared values:* Sport both teaches and reinforces societal values. Parents encourage their children to play sports in the hopes that they will develop positive social values such as fair play, respect for others, and competition (Macri 2012).

- *Life skills:* Sport teaches and reinforces a set of core skills associated with moral development, social relationships, self-perception, motivation, and achievement. Ethics and good sportsmanship are considered vital, as they help individuals become good citizens who respect and abide by laws. Sport also teaches cooperation, respect for authority in the form of parents and coaches, and leadership (Weiss 2016).

- *Socioemotional function:* Sport helps individuals learn how to deal with conflict and anger management, encourages community bonding, and highlights the importance of rituals (Delaney 2015).

- *Social mobility:* Sport provides individuals and groups with opportunities to advance in socioeconomic status, both directly (through professional sport participation) and indirectly (through college scholarships) (Delaney 2015).

The principal critique of the functionalist theory of sport is that it tends to overemphasize the positive consequences of sport and assumes that all identity groups (race, class, and gender) benefit equally from sport. Proponents of this theory fail to grasp that sport is a social construction that preserves social hierarchies benefiting privileged individuals and groups while disadvantaging others.

Identity through Competition

Finally, the **symbolic interaction perspective on sport** posits that sports are created and maintained by shared meanings and social interaction. In other words, athletes' identities are formed as they participate in various sports and sport cultures. Sporting events are seen as ritual contests in which individuals seek to obtain heroic or iconic status. Competition provides order and control for these identities and various communities. For example, when the head coach of Auburn University's women's basketball team, Nell Fortner, walked onto the court for her first game in 2004, there were just 200 people in the stands. By 2012, when she left Auburn, her team was attracting crowds in excess of 12,000. Under Fortner, Auburn won the Southeastern Conference championship in 2009—the first time Auburn had won since 1989. Women's basketball is now the most popular team sport at Auburn. The fans come out in numbers because they want to see winners, and Auburn's success has helped to advance the profile of women's basketball nationally (Robinson 2017). A principal critique of the symbolic interaction perspective is that it provides limited ability to understand structural processes that create, maintain, and perpetuate inequalities among various identity groups (Giulianotti 2016).

We are left with the conclusion that while stock theories on sport do provide some insight, they leave much unanswered. For the rest of the picture, we turn to the matrix approach to sport.

■ APPLYING THE MATRIX TO SPORTS IN THE UNITED STATES

The matrix of race, class, and gender operates throughout the institution of sport. Geographic and social locations and identities across time influence how sport and athleticism develop, which groups and identities become involved, and the ways in which these might serve to facilitate change.

The stock story of U.S. sports has been central to our national narrative. However, our concealed stories reveal the historical, political, cultural, and social processes that have shaped the development of sport in the United States. What this history reveals is that for some, sport has provided access to the American Dream. Racial, ethnic, class, and gendered groups have frequently used sport as a means of social

CRITICAL THINKING

1. Clearly sport provides some useful functions within society. But in what ways do these functions reflect values specific to certain geographical areas? How might historical factors help explain the potential differences between these areas? More specifically, in what ways might history within specific areas, communities, or schools have impacts on who plays and what sports they might engage in?

2. Both the nature and nurture perspectives on sport seem to offer plausible arguments. But how might institutions such as family, school and community environment, and culture affect athleticism? What impact might sport have on the likelihood that an individual will be successful, marry, and have kids? What does this suggest about how sport may influence genetic outcomes? (For example, if society placed a value on tallness, would this lead to more tall people getting married and therefore propagating?)

3. Symbolic interactionism argues that how we interact with sport symbols and images can affect how sport is perceived, or valued. How does this symbolic interaction reflect cultural values? How might identities, as reflected in cultural, gendered, class, or school values, affect how sport is perceived? How might this account for the differences in athleticism associated with gender, race, and class?

4. In what ways do you believe your athleticism or lack thereof might be associated with nature or nurture?

mobility when other pathways were blocked. However, sport can be a source of both resistance and transformative change, as individuals and groups engaged in sport use their status to effect changes both within sport and in the wider society.

Analyzing Space and Place: Early American Sports Narratives

From the earliest point in U.S. history, sports blended the cultural and athletic traditions of Native Americans and European immigrants. Each new immigrant group arriving in North America brought along its own sporting traditions, which were absorbed and transformed to produce a unique American sport culture (Crawford 2013, 1–2). When Europeans settled the Americas, indigenous peoples, comprising as many as 500 separate nations, were actively engaged in a range of sport and game activities, including many that provided children with life experiences that would help them develop the competencies and experiences necessary for survival.

Sports and the Colonists

Several variations in sport and athleticism can be identified across U.S. regions and across historical times. Religious attitudes within the American colonies governed the recreational activities considered proper for men and women. In the North, elite

White women were encouraged to participate in ice skating, while southern women were expected to develop equestrian skills. Other recreational activities for women included dancing, quilting, and swimming. Women were also expected to be spectators at both horse and boat races (Borish 2014).

Puritans, believing that time was a sacred gift not to be wasted, condemned all sport (Daniels 1995). The Protestant Dutch in New York were more liberal, however, and allowed for bowling, golf, and boat and horse racing. The Quakers of Pennsylvania banned boxing but did allow those sports deemed useful and necessary for recreation, such as swimming, skating, hunting, and fishing.

The 19th-century southern planters modeled themselves on European nobility and attempted to duplicate their leisure activities. Within this culture, horse racing became a major sport. Fox and quail hunting and bloody sports such as bare-knuckle boxing and eye-gouging fights were also frequent events. All of these sport activities were associated with heavy gambling, where generations of wealth could be won or lost in a single match (Zirin 2000). Through gambling, southern elite gentlemen asserted their manliness while distinguishing themselves from poorer Whites and Black slaves (Carroll 2003). Sport not only helped reinforce the White gentry's values, but it also served to distinguish them from subordinate groups. Sporting venues quickly became the places where politics, economics, and culture were controlled. In many ways, sport became a proxy for power in the South (Crawford 2013).

Race, Gender, and Early American Sports

Slaves, both male and female, were often the featured attractions providing entertainment and profit to the southern plantation elite (Gems, Borish, and Pfister 2008). And while boxing and other sports provided Black slaves with entertainment and momentary escape from the harsh realities of slavery, for some they provided a more direct route to emancipation (Harris 2000).

Black women, regardless of their status, found that sport could be a means of rebellion. Many slave women excelled at swimming, which they often did in the nude, a practice that tended to go against religious and racial prohibitions for White women (Gems et al. 2008, 24). For northern White females, the bicycle became an instrument of rebellion. After the Civil War, women's colleges were a vanguard in this movement. Schools offered athletic options that included bicycle races. The bicycle became a symbol of women's liberation and resistance for suffragists such as Elizabeth Cady Stanton, Susan B. Anthony, and other feminists during the late 19th century (LaFrance 2014).

Latinos have also had an impact on sports within the United States. From 1519 to 1700, the Spanish imported cattle and horses and established ranches throughout the South and the Southwest. Cattle ranching became a dominant economic activity as early as the 1700s in Texas, Arizona, and New Mexico. The vaqueros (cowboys—the term is derived from *vaca*, the Spanish word for cow) on these ranches developed a range of skills using ropes made from braided rawhide, as well as skills in horsemanship, and they showed off these skills by competing with each other at rodeos, which were held to celebrate the annual cattle roundups. Rodeos became popular throughout the West and Southwest, and "Wild West"

Tom Molineux (1784–1818), born into slavery, was possibly the first heavyweight bare-knuckle boxing champion in the United States. Starting on the Virginia plantation of his birth, he often would fight fellow slaves while plantation owners placed wagers on the outcomes. After a particularly successful boxing match, for which his owner took in $100,000 in prize money (equivalent to about $1 million today), Molineux was granted his freedom and given $500 (equivalent to about $11,000 today).

shows featuring some of the most famous rodeo stars toured the country through much of the 1890s (Alamillo 2013).

Institutionalizing Sport: Industrialization, Immigration, and Team Sports

Theorists employing a matrix or intersectional approach have characterized sport as a mirror of capitalist society and have examined how sport has increasingly become globally commercialized. A matrix analysis of sport demonstrates that sporting events are more than media representations or cultural products. They become major institutional spaces where race, class, and gender intersections are manifested. The club movement served to preserve and magnify sport and race, class, and gender hierarchies.

The Club Movement

Industrialism encouraged increased immigration from Europe and spurred the **club movement** in the United States. The team sports that we know today developed out of this early movement, in which elite White ethnics formed exclusive clubs in urban industrial areas to promote group identity and enhance status. Typically, as these new ethnic groups entered the urban industrial centers, they were met with either acceptance or rejection. Immigrants from England, Scotland, and Wales tended to be more acceptable within the status communities of racialized White elites. These elite clubs tended to exclude Catholics, Jews, and women as part of an unwritten and often unspoken agreement among White Anglo-Saxon Protestant (WASP) men to preserve White male privilege and racial exclusion (Kendall 2008). Lower-status White ethnics, from other European countries such as Ireland, Italy, and Poland, responded by creating their own status clubs, which were closely linked to sports. Thus was born the sports club movement.

The sports club movement was a means by which lower-status White ethnics could gain elite status. The first sports clubs in the United States were formed by these groups. Cricket, racquet, and yacht clubs welcomed young men who shared an interest in various sports, and club membership became a principal means of status enhancement. Massive immigration and the perception that the United States was being swamped by the swarthy, unwashed masses led sports clubs to emphasize their aristocratic British cultural connections and lineage; thus they began introducing golf in the 1890s (Starn 2006). Golf courses and club facilities emulated aristocratic gardens and manor houses (Ceron-Anaya 2010).

Baseball and the American Dream

Baseball, considered by many to be the quintessential American game, has been far from a "field of dreams" for people of color. In the early 1850s, like its probable forerunner, cricket, the game was essentially a source of entertainment for middle-class White males. As industrialism and urbanization brought increasing numbers of immigrants to the United States, this rural pastime became part of the urban landscape and a form of escape. Baseball allowed many urban residents to imagine a more rural existence. Played in parklike settings with green fields and plenty of fresh air, it evoked images of a safe, secure haven from the harsh world. Baseball was from its inception a male-dominated sport with definite racial overtones (Kimmel 2005, 64). The historical view of baseball as a homogenized space where middle-class White males could be legitimated and glorified held sway up until the 1960s (Butterworth 2007).

The first baseball club originated in 1845 in Manhattan, when a group of young firefighters formed the Knickerbocker Baseball Club. Blue-collar workers were the mainstay viewers of the game until increased admission prices, lack of accessibility, and elimination of Sunday games transformed the audience to middle-class workers by the 1860s. The national leagues that developed continued to draw their players primarily from new immigrants and their audience from the White middle class until the late 1940s. This changed with the advent of World War II, when for the first time fans saw both Blacks and women on the field. Once these groups appeared on the national scene, it was too late to put them back in the bleachers or on the sidelines.

As many as 55 professional Black baseball teams existed from 1883 to 1898. Interestingly, about half of Black players in that period were part of these all-Black teams, while the remainder played on integrated teams. From the end of the Civil War until 1890, a number of Blacks played alongside Whites in both minor and major baseball league teams (Kleinknect 2017). When the National Association of Base Ball Players was formed in 1867, it formally banned all Black players. Despite this ban, as late as the 1870s several Black players were still active on mostly White minor league teams, and some persisted longer. In 1883, Moses "Fleetwood" Walker, from Oberlin College, signed with the Toledo, Ohio, team in the Northwestern League and became the first Black to play in a major league franchise. In the same year, another Black player, John W. "Bud" Fowler, a veteran of 10 years, signed with the Northwestern League. Even these slots were soon lost, however, when segregation became law and increased hostility toward Black, Hispanic, Asian, and other racial minority athletes became rampant. By the end of the 19th century, the ban on Black players in baseball was firmly established (Pennington 2006). Rather than admit defeat, Blacks and other athletes of color continued to play, but were often segregated into their own leagues. The first Black professional team, the Cuban Giants, was formed in 1885. Ironically, there were no Cubans or Hispanics on the team.

The story of baseball, with minor alterations, mirrors what was also happening in football, basketball, and other team sports. Therefore, as we move into the 20th century, segregated sports (by race, gender, and class) can be identified.

Identities and Resistance

Critical race theorists stress that confronting race and racism is central to any analysis of sport. This perspective argues that sport is a central social process that regularly legitimates, modifies, and re-creates racial hegemony. Critical race theory also aims to combat racial hegemony within sport, while at the same time recognizing that race is a social construction (Hylton 2010). Within sport, racism both dehumanizes and legitimates the racial "other." Thus, while the members of a given group might be the objects of racial derision, their participation in sport might also reconstruct or legitimate certain racial stereotypes.

The Legacy of Civil Rights

The civil rights movement of the mid-20th century had significant impact on sport in the United States. Through legislation, court actions, and organized efforts, the movement helped to abolish many of the formal mechanisms of racial discrimination. Almost every institutional sphere was affected, including sport.

As a registered conscientious objector, Black heavyweight boxing champion Cassius Clay repeatedly drew attention to racial injustices prevalent in the United States.

On December 3, 1943, singer/actor Paul Robeson headed a group of Blacks who met with baseball commissioner Kenesaw Mountain Landis and major league team owners at the Roosevelt Hotel in New York. After being introduced, Robeson remarked: "The time has come when you must change your attitude toward Negroes. . . . Because baseball is a national game, it is up to baseball to see that discrimination does not become an American pattern. And it should do this this year" (Robeson 1978, 152). Four years later, second baseman Jackie Robinson broke the major league color barrier. Other athletes, such as heavyweight boxing champion Muhammad Ali, would use their celebrity status as a form of resistance.

After converting to Islam, Cassius Clay changed his name to Muhammad Ali. One of his first announcements after his conversion concerned his objection to the Vietnam War: "I'm expected to go overseas to help free people in South Vietnam and at the same time my people here [African Americans] are being brutalized and mistreated, and this is really the same thing that's happening in Vietnam" (quoted in Hunt 2006, 285).

Critical scholars researching sport also became highly successful in bringing about change. Harry Edwards, political activist and scholar, was a key participant in a protest at the 1968 Olympic Games. Increasingly cynical, Edwards concluded that U.S. sport needed a wake-up call to address the long-standing racism that existed. He called for a Black athletic boycott of the 1968 Olympics and other sports activities to dramatize the racial inequities and obstacles confronting Blacks. But during a period of heightened racial awareness, Black athletes could not simply quit and be labeled as "failures."

Instead, during the medal awards ceremony for track and field, U.S. gold and bronze medalists John Carlos and Tommie Smith raised their fists as they stood on podium.

Women and the Impact of Title IX

It is only in the last two generations that young women in the United States have gained the ability to grow up actively engaged in sports. In 1972, President Richard M. Nixon signed into law the landmark U.S. Education Amendments, including **Title IX**, which declared that "no person in the United States shall, on the basis of sex, be excluded from participation in, be denied the benefits of, or be subjected to discrimination under any program or activity receiving federal financial assistance." The impact of Title IX was profound. In 1971, before it became law, fewer than 295 females participated in high school varsity athletics. This was just under 7% of all high school athletes. By 2001, a total of 2.8 million or 41.5% of all high school varsity athletes were females (see Table 9.1)

By 2012, the number of females in high school and college sports had grown to 3,373,000 (Dangerfield and Barra 2012; TitleIX.info, n.d.). Title IX did not solve gender inequities in sports, however. Today, roughly 28% of total money spent on high school and college athletes goes to women, and colleges spend 31% of recruiting dollars and 42% of athletic scholarship money on women (Title IX.info, n.d.).

The impacts of Title IX have not been universal across all women. In 2012, White females had a 51% participation rate in high school sports, but Black females were comparatively lower at 40%. Asian/ Pacific Islander and Hispanic female high school participation was even lower, at 34% and 32%, respectively. This differential access to sports by race and gender at the high school level carries forward to the intercollegiate level. For example, in Division I basketball, Black women represented 50.6% of the athletes in 2012, but they were significantly less likely to be on indoor and outdoor track and field teams (28.2% and 27.5%, respectively), and they were almost nonexistent in lacrosse (2.2%), swimming (2%), soccer (5.3%), and softball (8.22%). Finally, Title IX has not helped increase the proportion of women who are coaching women's teams at the intercollegiate level. In 1972, women filled 90% of coaching positions for women's teams. By 2012, only 44% of women's team's coaches were women (Rhoden 2012).

During the October 16, 1968, medal awards ceremony for track and field at the Mexico City Olympics, U.S. gold and bronze medalists John Carlos and Tommie Smith raised their fists in protest.

NCAA Photos / NCAA Photos / Getty Images

Table 9.2 ■ Five Most Frequently Played Women's Sports	
Sport	Percentage of U.S. High Schools with a Team
Basketball	98.8
Volleyball	95.7
Soccer	92.0
Cross-country	90.8
Softball	89.2

Source: Barbara Winslow, "The Impact of Title IX," History Now, 2012, https://www.gilderlehrman.org/history-by-era/seventies/essays/impact-title-ix.

A Female Founder's Fight

By Lynn Le, Founder of Society Nine

Fighting isn't always physical or contained within sport. Though my passion for mixed martial arts has led me to this place now—as the founder of a woman's combat sports brand—the truth is I had some life experiences along the way that instilled the fight in me.

I grew up in a very humble, hardworking Vietnamese immigrant household where we knew how to stretch dollars, always look presentable (because as my dad always said, you never knew what opportunities could be presented and you needed to look put together), and be fed. My parents were entrepreneurial with everything in their lives, from the household budget to what it was going to take to make the next professional move in order to improve the lives of their kids. We eventually made our way to a comfortable, middle-class lifestyle that was a result of my parents' devotion and conviction to provide. Their sacrifice and strength lit a fire in my belly. Honor and a duty to make my family proud were reasons to fight. To fight means to live with intent.

Tim Brown/Oxygen Media/NBCU Photo Bank via Getty Images

Lynn Le

Fighting and entrepreneurship have a lot of parallels. The most important thing it's taught me is that power is mine to define. Fighting helped me take ownership of what is inherently beautiful about my God-given body and mind. True femininity is pure resilience and unbridled strength—in and out of the gym. I will always be imperfect—we all are—but now, I'm proud to take ownership of my weaknesses and be vulnerable. It's helped me be a better entrepreneur, manager, daughter, sister, girlfriend, and friend.

What's thriving in my life right now is my start-up, Society Nine. The name was inspired by Title IX—and how far women have come since fighting for the right to play in college, to now professionally fighting among men on the mainstream stage. What is the future for female athletes? What are we capable of? This society represents the modern female fighter—she can do anything. I created Society Nine with the core athlete in mind—the athlete who does combat sports—but on a spiritual level, our heart belongs to the female fighter.

One of the most obvious boundaries maintained by sport is that of gender and gender identity. Not only does this boundary distinguish the types of athleticism appropriate for males and females, it also defines both masculinity and femininity. While today women can be found surfing, skateboarding, drag car racing, and skiing, many sports are still strongly male oriented, such as hockey, football, boxing, and wrestling. Sport reflects our cultural biases, but structural barriers also impede gender equity.

Women hold few positions of real power in the sports journalism industry (Nelson 2013). Research documents that gender subjectivity and stereotyping increase the likelihood that female athletes will be portrayed negatively in visual media (Brandt and Carstens 2011). This trend is evident in college newspapers across the United States. Female sports reporters are not only rare but also less likely to be involved in playing, watching, and writing about sports (Schmidt 2013).

CRITICAL THINKING

1. In what ways might either geography or history affect how sport is perceived and received? What does this suggest regarding our attitudes toward sport?

2. How does sport, or participating in sport, affect other institutions? How might other institutions affect sport?

3. How might sport affect an individual's identity? In what ways might this sport identity be influenced by other identities, such as race, class, and gender? How might differences in regional or community values influence these identities?

4. How has sport affected your life? What kinds of racial messages have been associated with your contacts with sport? What does this suggest about you, race, and sport?

■ CREATING A NEW PLAYING FIELD

Sport is an important institution within the United States. It not only provides needed exercise and opportunities but also helps stimulate change within both local communities and the wider society. How different athletes use their status in sport can enhance the visibility of often marginalized members within society.

The Role of Agency and Resistance

Much of our understanding of agency (i.e., sense of control, the ability to initiate, execute, and control one's actions, particularly to effect change) and resistance

Ezra Shaw / Getty Images Sport / Getty Images

Jesse Owens, by taking four gold medals at the Olympics in Berlin in 1936, destroyed Hitler's myth of Aryan supremacy. Tommie Smith and John Carlos, raising their black-gloved fists, asserted the importance of all humans as they received their Olympic medals in 1968. In 1988, the world was shocked as Jamaican bobsledders became internationally famous with their entry into the Olympics. And in Rio in 2016, Ibtihaj Muhammad (pictured) became the first U.S. athlete to compete in the Olympics wearing a hijab.

within sports is derived from personal narratives of athletes and coaches. Their stories have generated our knowledge of homophobia and sexism, racism, and ethnocentrism in sport. These narratives help us understand how we can bring about more tolerance within our communities, our institutions, and, ultimately, our society. They demonstrate how individuals have been able to transform not only how they perceive themselves but also how their identities are perceived and received within the wider community. These stories show that racial identities are not fixed and one-dimensional; rather, they are fluid and multifaceted (Iannotta and Kane 2002).

David Denson, first baseman for the Milwaukee Brewers' minor league affiliate in Helena, Montana, announced in August 2015 that he is gay. He became the first active player affiliated with a Major League Baseball organization to come out publicly (Hine 2016). A record 56 LGBT-identifying athletes competed in the Olympic Games in Rio de Janeiro in 2016. Clearly, these athletes represent a long list of athletes who have used their status as sport stars to engage in advocacy and resistance. These voices, collectively, have served to change not only sport but our country.

Closing the Athlete Graduation Gap

At the college level, the graduation gap between athletes of color and others is most significant within football and basketball, between Black and White players, and at the most sports-competitive schools, those in Division I of the NCAA. In 2016, about half of the Black male athletes in the top 65 basketball and football institutions graduated within 6 years. What makes these statistics even more troubling is that while Black males accounted for only 2.5% of undergraduates, they made up 56% of the football players and more than 60% of the men's basketball players (Harper 2016). But while Black male athletes' graduation rates appear to be declining, those of both White and Hispanic male athletes are on the rise (see Figure 9.2).

Figure 9.2 ■ In 2016, Graduation Rates for Male Athletes Varied by Race

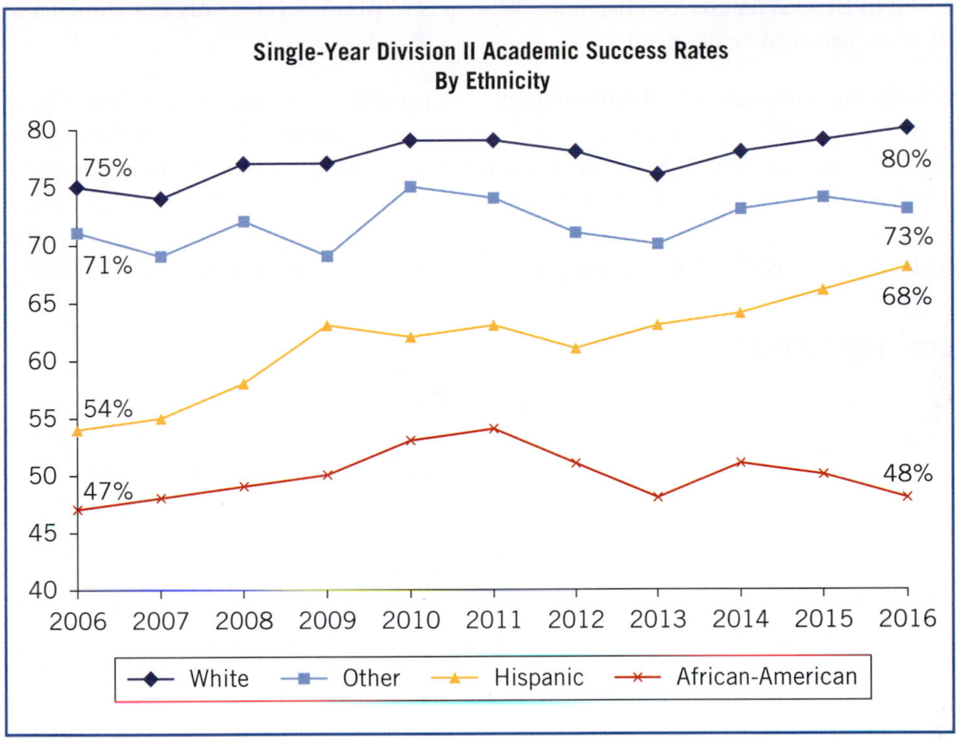

Single-Year Division II Academic Success Rates By Ethnicity

Source: NCAA Research Staff (2016).

What accounts for these differences? It might depend on the sport. Most Black college athletes are found within football (upward of 47% in NCAA Divisions I and II) and basketball (upward of 47% in NCAA Divisions I and II). Hispanic players rarely make up more than 3% of total players in these same sports. The highest sport participation for college Latino athletes is in baseball (6%) (Lapchick 2015).

Academic underperformance is particularly pronounced among male basketball, football, and hockey players in general, and Black men in particular (Shulman and Bowen 2001). Some observers have argued that the racial gap in college completion rates is less about sports and more about the resegregation of public education, with more subtle and less obvious forms of difference (Childress 2014).

In many states, private colleges and universities have tremendous advantages in recruiting top players, such as greater media exposure, better facilities, longer histories of victories, and scholarships. Already, many state championships in hockey, lacrosse, and soccer are dominated by private school teams. Trends are similar for both collegiate basketball and football (Cacabelos 2009). These teams also tend to be dominated by middle-class and more affluent White athletes, with few spots going to Blacks, Asians, or Hispanics. Who gets to play sports is only one dimension of what needs to be changed.

Scholarships also are not distributed equally, providing benefits for all. Just 7% of high school athletes who played varsity sports got college athletic scholarships in 2015–16 (Ecker 2017). Men are almost twice as likely as women to get athletic scholarships, and among minority youth, the largest proportion of these scholarships go to Black students (about 22.8%). Asian students receive the lowest proportion (0.1%). About 65% of all athletic scholarships go to White students (Westfall 2011).

Creating Change

Instead of waiting for change to happen, college athletes around the country have begun to organize themselves into unions. Currently more than 17,000 Division I college athletes belong to the National College Players Association (NCPA). This organization has testified in U.S. congressional hearings and briefings, appeared before state legislatures, and represented college athletes in the courts as they have sought improved athlete benefits, including a Student-Athletes' Bill of Rights. The NCPA has produced reports that document the value added to colleges and universities by football and men's basketball programs, which annually garner for their schools an average of $137,000 and $289,000, respectively (NCPA 2016). The nation's richest athletic departments made a record $6 billion in 2015, nearly $4 billion more than all the other schools combined (Lavigne 2016). The NCPA (2016) argues that some of these revenues should be used to minimize college athletes' brain trauma risks, raise scholarship amounts, pay more sports-related medical expenses, and improve graduation rates.

Many young athletes enter sports with the hope of one day playing professionally. Unfortunately, the likelihood of a high school or even a college athlete becoming a professional athlete is extremely low. Baseball players have the best chance, with 9.7% of NCAA players going on to enter MLB organizations; ice hockey players are next, with 6.6% later becoming professionals. For other sports, less than 2% of college players go on to play professionally (NCAA 2017).

The odds of an athlete graduating from college are much higher, with more than 70% in NCAA Division I, II, and III graduating within 6 years. But for some, even the dream of graduation is never realized. Just over half of Black athletes do not graduate within 6 years (Harper, Williams, and Blackman 2013). A number of proposals have been offered to remedy this situation. Some have argued that the best way to raise graduation rates is to make players ineligible to participate in both postseason play and championship contests if their team fails to graduate at least

40% of its players within a 6-year period. College presidents and university leaders must also do more to hold their sports programs accountable, including being transparent when it comes to data on graduation rates both by sport and within racial and ethnic groups. These data should be more specific in terms of grade point averages, classroom experiences, course enrollment, and major selection patterns (Harper et al. 2013).

Sport, as a collection of social institutions, reflects the values, customs, and histories of society. As an institution it also reflects the hierarchical relations between and among racial, gendered, and class groups within society. And these relations change as social dynamics, values, and attitudes change and as individuals and groups transcend the normal boundaries and challenge those very same norms. Despite the progress that individuals have made, however, it takes widespread institutional change to eliminate structural impediments to racial and gender equality in sport. Acknowledging the lack of sufficient mentors, sponsors, formal and informal networks, role models, leadership and coaching workshops, and opportunities would be a good start (Kamphoff and Gill 2013).

Further improvements in collegiate sport can come only if we reaffirm commitments to all students and remove lingering racial, gender, and class inequities. Given the interdependency and interrelatedness of institutions, systemic, society-wide change will be required to resolve these problems. Ultimately, we might just conclude that high-priced sports are not compatible with higher education.

CRITICAL THINKING

1. How does participation in sports affect racial identity? How does racial identity affect perceived competency in different sports? Some racial groups participating in sports appear to have different outcomes when it comes to college graduation. How might gender or class or even type of sport influence these outcomes?

2. Over time different racial groups appear to dominate particular sports. In what ways might this be a result of racial hierarchies operant within society, in different geographic areas, or in different historical periods? What does this suggest regarding the social construction of sport?

3. Sport provides many different types of opportunities and challenges for athletes. In what ways is racial identity reflected in these opportunities and challenges?

4. What might you do to effect changes in the institution of sport? As a student? As a consumer? As an athlete?

9

KEY TERMS

agency, p. 314

club movement, p. 319

communal experience, p. 303

cultural values, p. 303

functionalist theory of sport, p. 315

nature perspective, p. 312

nurture perspective, p. 312

sport, p. 304

symbolic interaction perspective on sport, p. 316

Title IX, p. 322

CHAPTER SUMMARY

LO 9.1   Explain the state of sport in the United States.

The institution of sport is an integral part of the nation. Millions of fans and players watch and actively participate in sports ranging from the high-powered, no-holds-barred rezball played on Native American reservations to the many individual and team sports represented at the Olympic Games. Football is the most popular American sport, capturing the largest TV audience. While the NFL is most popular among major sports leagues, however, Major League Soccer is the most diverse. Clear gender and racial hierarchies are reflected in what sports are played by whom, who is most rewarded (in terms of both income and endorsement deals), and who makes up the fan bases. Clearly the gendered segregation of sports has implications for both viewers and endorsement deals, accounting for the small number of women among the athletes who earn the highest salaries (just 2 of the top 100 earners are women). Also, the fact that males dominate in viewership explains to some extent their much higher levels of pay and their more lucrative endorsement contracts. Once we consider these, we are still left with the fact that only one professional sports league, Major League Soccer, is truly diverse; most national professional leagues have high concentrations of players in one or two racial groups.

LO 9.2   Compare stock theories about U.S. sport.

Four theoretical perspectives have traditionally been supported regarding U.S. sport: the nature perspective, the nurture perspective, the functionalist perspective, and the symbolic interactionist perspective. These represent stock stories, or the standard justifications that are used to explain the prevalence of sport and athleticism. The nature argument posits that biology and talent account for athleticism and sport development within specific groups and across the nation. The nurture perspective argues that environment, culture, and socialization explain how athletes and sport develop. Research indicates that both nature and nurture are significant but not sufficient to account for athletic ability and sport development. Functionalist theory explains the development of sport in terms of the vital or important needs accomplished by sport. These functions include shared values, life skills, socioemotional functions, and social mobility. The limitations of this theory include its overemphasis on the positive consequences of sport and its failure to account for unequal results for race, class, and gendered groups, and how sport serves to preserve inequalities. Symbolic interaction investigates the shared meanings that are created and maintained within sport, communities, and athletes. These shared meanings help produce sport cultures that replicate rituals, create sport heroes, and symbolically link sport to the community. Symbolic interaction provides limited insight into the structural processes that create, preserve, and distribute inequalities among various identity groups within sport. Collectively, while providing some insight into sport and athleticism, traditional stock theories offer a limited understanding regarding sport and athleticism.

LO 9.3 Apply the matrix approach to sport.

The matrix, with its focus on intersectional differences, helps fill the gaps in our understanding of how sport and athleticism create institutions that have differential impacts on racial, class, and gendered groups within U.S. society. The perspective anticipates that geographic and social locations, identities across time, and agency provide necessary insights into how this process operates. Institutional analysis demonstrates that sport and sporting events produce medial and cultural products. Through these processes race, class, and gender interactions are manifested. Space and place concerns within the matrix approach highlight the importance of geographical and historical spaces that affect social identities within sport. Identities are constantly affected by sports as they legitimate, modify, and re-create racial hegemonies. Finally, both agency and resistance have been demonstrated by multiple individuals and groups who have utilized their status within sport to transform both sport and the nation. An examination of U.S. sport through time reveals many concealed stories. Native Americans, long before European colonization, were active creators of sport and games. Most of these were directly associated with the needs of hunting and gathering communities. Consequently, stick games, racing, hunting, and archery were frequently vital parts of youth socialization. Industrialization served to transform the U.S. sport landscape as it drew an increasingly large number of immigrants and others into the urban centers. One of the significant outcomes of this transformation was the rise in team sports. From the early 19th century, elite sport clubs catering to White ethnics were established throughout the Northeast. Baseball and other team sports were soon to follow.

LO 9.4 Describe strategies for transforming the institution of sport.

Transformative stories are possible as athletes both individually and collectively push for change. Black male athletes at top-performing NCAA Division I institutions have the largest graduation gap among athletes. And this gap is widening. Some reasons for this may be increased pressure to perform athletically, lack of support (both financial and community), and limited number of mentors. But Black males are not the only college athletes with these problems—all male student-athletes, particularly in basketball, football, and hockey, underperform as students. These differences only highlight a series of other inequities that dominate collegiate sports and in many ways mirror those in the wider society. For example, male athletes are almost twice as likely as female athletes to receive collegiate athletic scholarships. And Black students receive significantly more athletic scholarships than either Asian or Hispanics students. Almost two-thirds of all athletic scholarships still go to White athletes. Student-athletes themselves are beginning to organize to challenge both institutions and governments, seeking better treatment, fairer processes, and increased support.

THE MILITARY, WAR, AND TERRORISM

Saul Loeb / AFP / Getty Images

Tammy Duckworth is a decorated veteran, the daughter of a veteran and an immigrant, and an exemplar of the unique mix of race, class, and gender that characterizes the United States.

LEARNING OBJECTIVES

LO 10.1 Examine the contemporary reality of race, class, and gender in the U.S. military.

LO 10.2 Explore the stock sociological theories regarding the U.S. military, war, and terrorism.

LO 10.3 Apply the matrix approach to U.S. military history, war, and terrorism.

LO 10.4 Evaluate the possibilities for a more inclusive future.

Politician, mother, wife, double amputee, disabled combat veteran, and hero—all of these describe U.S. Senator Tammy Duckworth of Illinois. Her story, like that of thousands of veterans throughout history, is entwined with society's collective narrative. Duckworth's father was a U.S. Marine Corps veteran who could trace his family's military roots back to the American Revolutionary War (Weinstein 2012). Her mother, a native of Thailand, is of Chinese ancestry. Duckworth joined the Army Reserve Officers' Training Corps as a graduate student and was soon commissioned a lieutenant in the U.S. Army Reserve. Since piloting was one of the few combat jobs open to women, she attended helicopter flight school. Upon graduation, she joined the Illinois National Guard. While she was earning her PhD in political science, her unit was deployed to Iraq. On November 12, 2004, her UH-60

Black Hawk helicopter was hit by a rocket-propelled grenade. She lost both of her legs and much of her right arm. Her valor earned her the Purple Heart, the Air Medal, and the Army Commendation Medal.

After leaving the military, Duckworth served as the director of the Illinois Department of Public Affairs from 2006 to 2009, after which she became assistant secretary of public and intergovernmental affairs at the U.S. Department of Veterans Affairs. Thousands were moved by her story when she spoke at the 2008 Democratic National Convention, and in 2011 she resigned her position at the Department of Veterans Affairs and announced her candidacy for the U.S. House of Representatives. She went on to win that election and represented Illinois's Eighth Congressional District from January 2013 to January 2017. In November 2016, she was elected to the U.S. Senate, where she now serves along with 20 other women and 79 men. Senator Duckworth has been a staunch supporter of American veterans and those who have disabilities, and her story uniquely reflects the matrix of race, class, and gender.

A single act of war or violence can define the life of a person, a community, and a nation. Consider the U.S. use of atomic bombs in Japan during World War II, or the terrorist acts carried out against the United States on September 11, 2001. Nothing seems so central to our collective experience, or as controversial, as war. Similarly, nothing seems so apt to bring us together or tear us apart, and nothing seems so central to the understanding of these moments as race, class, ethnicity, and gender.

■ CLASS, GENDER, AND RACE IN THE U.S. MILITARY

The five branches that make up the U.S. military—the Army, Navy, Air Force, Marine Corps, and Coast Guard—are authorized to use deadly force to support the national interests, specific entities, and citizens of the United States. The U.S. Department of Defense (DoD), an executive branch department of the federal government, is charged with coordinating all agencies and functions associated with national defense and U.S. armed forces. The DoD is the largest employer in the world, with an estimated 1.3 million service members on active duty and another 865,000 in reserve (Defense Manpower Data Center 2017); these numbers make it the third-largest military in the world, following China and India (Shaw 2016). The United States spends more on its military than any other country. In fact, U.S. military expenditures account for a third of all global defense spending (Taylor and Karklis 2016). The defense budget, representing 16% (or $602 billion) of the entire federal budget, is devoted primarily to costs related to the DoD. A smaller portion supports military operations in Afghanistan and other international security operations (Center on Budget and Policy Priorities 2016). Recruiting within the armed forces is closely tied to the economy and job prospects. The high unemployment rate among youth during the past decade has been associated with higher rates of enlistment. The demographic profile of the U.S. military tends to reflect these and other national trends (Alvarez 2009).

The military in the United States includes five branches: the U.S. Army, Navy, Air Force, Coast Guard, and Marine Corps.

While the military is predominantly male, White, and young, significant differences are seen across the various branches. For example, recruits going into the air force tend to be older, while about half of all Marine Corps recruits are 17–18 years old. Most army and navy recruits fall into the 19–20 age group (U.S. Department of Defense 2014).

Socioeconomics and Recruiting

Although a significant number of new soldiers come from large states such as California and Texas, close to 45% of all recruits hail from the southern region of the country. It might be tempting to assume that most recruits come from lower socio-economic groups, but the opposite is actually true. The largest proportion of armed forces recruits come from middle-class communities, from families with annual incomes in the range of $36,875 to $76,980. Tangentially, the majority of enlistees are married (52.3%), with the largest proportion of married recruits choosing the air force (57.3%), followed closely by the Coast Guard (54.8%). Fewer (42.6%) married enlisted recruits choose the Marine Corps (U.S. Department of Defense 2014).

The number of federal elected officials who are veterans was at an all-time low in 2013. Only 20% of them had served, and less than 1% of their children had enlisted (DeSilver 2013). This latter number matches the proportion of enlistees who come from Ivy League schools, where less than 1% decide to join the military (Roth-Douquet and Schaeffer 2006).

The U.S. military has, at least since World War II, been perceived as an avenue through which young people can see the world and gain highly marketable skills. The military, particularly the army, has offered a pathway out of poverty for many. The GI Bill, signed into law in 1944, provided opportunities for millions of World War II veterans to gain college degrees, buy homes, and receive preference in federal, state, and many corporate hiring pools. Recent research indicates that not all have benefited from military service, however, particularly children of immigrants (Homan and Pianin 2014).

Gender and Enlistment

In January 2016, the U.S. armed forces finally removed the last barriers preventing women from serving in all aspects of the military. Women can now drive tanks, fire mortars, lead infantry combat missions, and serve in elite military units such as the Green Berets, the Navy SEALs, and the Air Force Pararescue (Codinha 2017). However, women continue to be underrepresented in the military, making up only about 15% of the armed forces. Females are most likely to enlist in the air force, where they constitute 13.2% of enlisted personnel and 17.9% of commissioned officers (i.e., officers holding the rank of second lieutenant or above). The Marines have the smallest proportion of females, either as enlisted personnel (7.7%) or as commissioned officers (6.9%). In the Navy, Air Force, and Marine Corps, the proportion of female commissioned officers tends to mirror that of enlisted women. The greatest gap exists in the army, where just under 18% of officers and just over 13% of enlisted personnel are women (U.S. Department of Defense 2014).

Racial Minority Representation

In 2014, while racial minorities made up 23.4% of those ages 18 to 44 in the total U.S. population, they constituted 32.9% of enlisted personnel. Women of color are more likely to enlist in either the army or the navy. And within the army, the percentage of enlisted racial minority women is almost double that of racial minority men (see Figure 10.1).

Figure 10.1 ■ **Racial Groups Show Gender Differences across All Branches of Service**

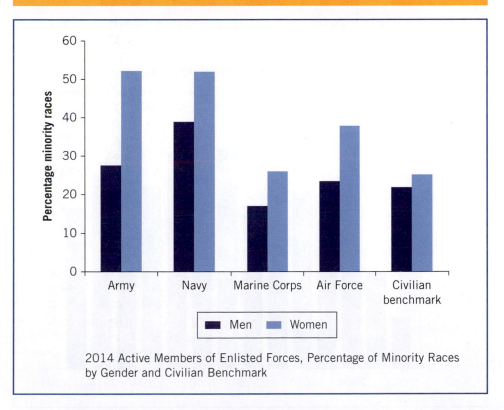

2014 Active Members of Enlisted Forces, Percentage of Minority Races by Gender and Civilian Benchmark

Source: U.S. Department of Defense, *Population Representation in the Military Services: Fiscal Year 2014 Summary Report* (Washington, DC: Office of the Under Secretary of Defense, Personnel and Readiness, 2014), http://www .people.mil/Portals/56/Documents/2014%20Summary.pdf?ver=2016-09-14-154051-563.

There has never been a U.S. war in which foreign-born persons have not participated on the side of the United States. From the Revolutionary War to the 1840s, nearly half of military recruits were foreign-born, and during the Civil War, nearly 20% of the Union army was made up of foreign-born troops. On average, 8,000 immigrants and noncitizen permanent residents enlist in the U.S. military annually (Powers 2016). Joining the armed forces is the fastest way to gain citizenship. It is estimated that more than two-thirds of non–U.S. citizen veterans ultimately become naturalized citizens (Batalova 2008). As Figure 10.2 shows, these trends have been generally increasing since 9/11, peaking at over 11,000 in 2011 and leveling off to slightly less than 8,000 annually by 2014 (Lawrence 2016).

Figure 10.2 ■ The Rate of Non–U.S. Citizen Veterans Becoming Naturalized Peaked in 2011

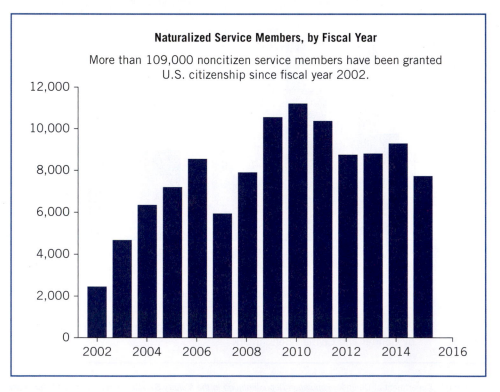

Source: Graph: "Naturalized Service Members, By Fiscal Year." Credit: Alyson Hurt/NPR. From "Service Members, Not Citizens: Meet the Veterans Who Have Been Deported," NPR Morning Edition, January 13, 2016.

A whole range of theories have been proposed, and a great deal of research has been conducted over the years in attempts to answer questions about the military, including who serves and under what conditions. Even a cursory examination of any news media reveals that the military, terrorism, and war are intricately interwoven into the American social landscape. And this landscape is reflective of our matrix and the intersection of race, class, and gender. An examination of the stock theories will shed some insight into why this is so.

CRITICAL THINKING

1. Does the fact that the United States has one of the world's largest military budgets improve the security of the United States or of the world?

2. How might other institutions, such as education, family, and health care, influence or be influenced by the current U.S. military? How might these same institutions influence the military?

3. What kinds of policies might increase diversity, including diversity in race, gender, and class, in the U.S. military?

4. In what ways are you affected by the military? Would you consider joining/serving? Why or why not?

■ MILITARY SOCIOLOGY STOCK THEORIES

Military sociology, the sociological analysis of armed forces and war, has been a central concern within the sociological discipline since at least World War I (Bottomore 1981). Three key sociological theories have controlled the field: functionalism, symbolic interactionism, and monopoly and materialist perspectives. Like all stock stories, these theories are both dominant within the discipline of sociology and traditionally relied upon as explanations. In many ways they also justify our use of the military, our involvement in wars, and our concerns regarding terrorism.

Functionalism

Functionalist theory assumes that institutions come into being to meet specific and basic societal needs. A **functionalist approach to the military** argues that the military, war, and terrorism serve specific and important tasks, or functions, within society. Some of these functions are socialization, integration, and reduction of conflict. **War**, defined as the use of organized force, represents a state of armed conflict between different nations, states, or groups within a nation or state. War functions to legitimate state claims, regulate conflict between states, minimize collateral damage among noncombatants, and extend the social, political, and economic values of the victor upon the vanquished (Park 1941). **Terrorism** is the unlawful use of force, particularly against civilians, in pursuit of political, economic, or social aims. Functionalism views terrorism as **dysfunctional**, as it disrupts social structures, increases stress, and violates norms and rules of engagement. An examination of how functionalist theorists view the military, war, and terrorism provides some key insights.

The Military Preserves Social Values

The military functions to preserve social values by encouraging patriotism, compliance with normative expectations, and order, both domestically and internationally. Accordingly, the stratification that occurs within the military, such as along racial and gender lines, reflects these functions. Those tasks considered most functionally important, such as those performed by officers and in combat roles, require higher levels of training and responsibility, and are therefore rewarded to a higher degree than other tasks and roles. For example, generals in the U.S. Army are graduates of the United States Military Academy at West Point; have advanced training in military tactics, troop deployment, leadership, and logistics; and have spent several years advancing through the ranks. On the other hand, an army private typically is qualified to serve after just 8 weeks of basic training. It is presumed that the inequality that results reflects the functional differentiation associated with the valuing of different tasks. Structural functionalists also stress the integrative functions served by the military (Cardoso 2001, 164). The military provides these functions at multiple levels. At the national level a strong military helps maintain social cohesion and relative calm, as it is perceived as a deterrent to hostile and wanton attacks. The military also serves at the individual level by socializing individuals and advancing such notions as patriotism, maturity, and solidarity.

War Is a Bonding Experience

War, viewed functionally, helps citizens develop a form of social bonding or solidarity. A nation and all of its citizens must come together to fight a common enemy. Recall the scene at the U.S. Capitol in the aftermath of the attacks on September 11, 2001, and similar scenes across the nation. Republicans and Democrats, Asians, Blacks, Whites, and Hispanics, urbanites and rural dwellers, gay, straight, and indifferent—all appeared to join hands in a collective show of solidarity. Wars produce cultural artifacts such as art, shared collective memories, and a sense of common purpose. And with the billions of dollars associated with modern wars, war also functions to stimulate the economy by providing jobs in the production of war/military goods and services. As we will see in our examination of the history of war, war has been a significant factor in the social mobility of women, people of color, immigrants, and the poor across the United States. Finally, wars have served to stimulate advances in technology, production processes, and sciences, leading to leaps forward in many areas, from airplanes and jets to space flight, medical innovations, mass transit, and the Internet (Lin 2010).

Terrorism Is Dysfunctional

Most sociologists ignored the topic of terrorism prior to the attacks on September 11, 2001. Since those pivotal events, a great deal of scholarly attention has been expended in efforts to understand them and prevent similar attacks. Terrorists, from a functionalist perspective, are viewed as deviants who violate basic norms of both civilization and war by targeting noncombatants. Unfortunately, the label of "terrorist" is applied depending on an individual's perspective. A person might be viewed as a terrorist by one group but seen as a revolutionary or even a patriot by another.

War, or violent attacks like those of September 11, 2001, can bring people together, like the more than 1,000 who gathered at this candlelight vigil in the wake of al-Qaeda's attack.

Race/Ethnicity Is the Missing Piece

Functionalist approaches to the military, war, and terrorism ignore how these institutions serve the interests of the powerful within society and fail to provide specific analysis of race and ethnicity. The emphasis on the idea that the military and war unify society obscures the fact that they can also be forces for disunity and oppression. As we have observed earlier, terrorism, while viewed as dysfunctional, may be functional and a form of resistance for those who feel that their freedoms are being denied. Specifically, who gets to label an individual or group as terrorist in many cases reflects the very power dynamics that the acts are intended to alter. The definition is critical and it is political, and often it also mirrors our concerns with race, class, and gender.

THE DESTRUCTION OF TEA AT BOSTON HARBOR.

Terrorism can be in the eye of the beholder. The United States originated from an act that may be seen as terrorism, when the Sons of Liberty boarded ships belonging to the East India Company in Boston Harbor and threw 342 chests of tea overboard to protest what they believed to be an unjust law.

Symbolic Interactionism

A **symbolic interactionist approach to the military** investigates how we attach meaning to things (flags and memorials), events (wars), and other representations (heroes and patriotism) in support of war, terrorism, and the military. Symbolic interactionists point out that military organizations have their own values, symbols, hierarchies, cultural rituals, and forms of socialization. The military socializes individuals to facilitate their entry into a specific community whose ultimate goal is to engage in war and conflict. In other words, the military creates symbolic meanings, representations, and recognitions that attempt to create a specific military personality that fosters group interaction, cohesion, and conformity.

Symbolic interactionism studies military life histories, the process of recruitment, and how civilians are transformed into soldiers. Establishing the legitimacy of the military and war is accomplished through the manipulation of symbols such as patriotism, heroes, enemies, and justice. The legitimacy of war, particularly, relies on the redefining of the killing of enemy soldiers, or combatants, as casualties of war. For example, using the term *collateral damage* instead of *victim* is one way this symbolism is extended to legitimate the "accidental" killing of innocents, or noncombatants (Cockerham 2003).

One of the critiques of symbolic interactionism is that it fails to account adequately for how social structures, identities, and military organizations interact (Giddens 1984). Symbolic interactionists have provided no insight, for example, into how racial, ethnic, and religious hostilities erupt into war, leading to events such as the 9/11 attacks (Cockerham 2003).

Monopoly and Materialist Perspectives

Finally, the **monopoly and materialist perspectives** posit that military organizations must maintain a legitimate monopoly on the use of force, and the use of this force is uniquely tied to the material instruments of war. In other words, the military argues that a central feature of the modern state is its monopoly over the legitimate use of coercive force (Weber 1978, 50–56). **Coercive force** is force in which intimidation is used to obtain compliance. The monopoly perspective suggests that the state and its agents have an exclusive right or privilege, granted by the citizens of the state, to use such force in order to gain compliance.

Contextualizing the Military

Clearly, the link between the military and its use of coercive force is important. Some scholars have argued that military institutions are a direct result of either the real or potential struggles of war and armed conflict (Kestnbaum 2009). They insist that if we are to understand the military, we must understand war. War highlights not only inequities but also the structural and organizational foundations of both conflict and coercion. National resources and their effective military mobilization determine the origins and likelihood of successful military campaigns. The basic questions that come from these lines of interest are concerned with how wars are waged and the consequences of wars for national existence (Kestnbaum 2009). Further, it is argued that the military force represents the essential quality of the modern state. By extension, both war and military violence are uniquely social events that create, maintain, and transform states as well as individuals and societies (Weber 1991).

Assuming Legitimacy

The major criticism of this approach is that it assumes that the military has a monopoly on the coercive use of force and, further, that such use is legitimate. This theory also assumes that **interstate forms of war** (conflicts involving national states, such as World Wars I and II) are somehow more legitimate than **intrastate forms of war** (conflicts that exist or occur within the boundaries of particular states). Third, this approach tends to overemphasize the material basis of war, dismissing or marginalizing other major sources of struggle, such as political, cultural, and other social dimensions and roots of both international and intranational forms of conflict (Kestnbaum 2009). Several implications follow from these criticisms. First, most of the wars fought by the United States prior to 9/11 were against nations, with clearly defined and universally recognized rules of war (as governed by the United Nations). The terrorist attacks of 9/11 signaled a shift in how wars are fought. Now, what are termed **nonstate actors** (individuals or organizations with economic, political, or social power that allows them to influence both national and international events, typically with violence) are most often the initiators of terrorist attacks, wars, and other conflicts. The reality is that most recent wars and other conflicts have involved nonstate actors. As we will see, nonstate actors such as ISIS (the so-called Islamic State), al-Qaeda, and Boko Haram are on the rise and pose a definite threat, not only to the United States but also to the world in general (Brady 2017).

Second, and more central to our concerns with the matrix, is that this approach ignores how the military, war, and terrorism tend to reflect, duplicate, and in some cases actually transform the race, class, and gender hierarchies present within society. Both state and nonstate actors utilize both organized and unorganized strategies to effect change. Wars and other conflicts are waged on multiple fronts and include actual combat as well as, and increasingly, campaigns of terror that may include lone terrorists and cells. Methods and strategies might range from simple tactics such as writing editorials and holding press conferences to hacking into secure networks and planting fictitious stories in formal news and social media outlets. As we will see when we apply the matrix to this institution, race, class, and gendered differences in the military's allocation of human resources duplicates the hierarchies within the host society. This means that military hierarchies, such as the hierarchy of the chain of command and the hierarchy of honors and other sanctions, tend to reflect status arrangements that are present within the wider society. Finally, this approach does not address the issues involved when a state uses the military to coerce compliance by domestic and/or indigenous groups, as when the U.S. military was used to control the Native American populations during westward expansion. The very presumption of the state's legitimacy hides the racial and gendered use of this force to preserve the racial hierarchy.

CONCEALED STORIES: Critical Race Theory and Military Sociology

Critical race theorists began to challenge the overly conservative and apologetic approach typically taken within military sociology. The earliest work by military sociologists found military organizations to be necessary features of modern democracies. At the core of such societies is a tension between violence and reason that war and the military serve to regulate and mediate (Foucault 1977). All of our moral values and intellectual definitions of right and wrong are derived from this viewpoint. Finally, the laws that we ultimately construct are a direct consequence of violence and war. Their intent, critical theorists insist, is to preserve peace and tranquility by establishing order, minimizing conflicts, and punishing violators. This means that power, inequalities, and social existence are anchored in relationships of force that are controlled through institutions, particularly those of the military (Foucault 2008). Therefore, the race, gender, and class inequities that exist are not only manifested but also in many ways preserved in military hierarchies. Obviously, as we will see, these inequalities actually preceded military hierarchies.

Finally, the military serves the interests of the corporate elite in their pursuit of profits and power. An informal alliance exists between the nation's military and the major industries that produce arms and other military materials, which seek to influence public policy. This alliance, termed the **military–industrial complex**, is dominated by major U.S. corporations and serves to preserve race, class, and gender hierarchies. By separating ownership from management, the corporations in the military–industrial complex have effectively emancipated themselves from stockholders. By reinvesting profits, they have eliminated the influence of both financiers and the capital market. And through effective lobbying, they have come to dominate and manipulate the state and governmental control (Galbraith 1967). The U.S. military–industrial complex is structured by violence and aimed at creating, preserving, and manipulating racial boundaries. This was clearly the case during the country's period of nation building and the Indian removal process (Perret 1989).

Contemporary research also highlights a stratified internal labor market within the military consisting of two spheres: one for enlisted personnel (working class) and one for officers (middle or managerial class). The different social locations or backgrounds of the people in each sphere reflect societal norms. For example, typically enlisted ranks require at least a high school degree, while officer grades require some college. These status distinctions, reflecting access to and quality of educational institutions, consequently tend to reflect the racial, gendered, and class hierarchies in the wider society. Hence, racial and ethnic minorities tend to be concentrated in the enlisted ranks, and women tend to be concentrated in the support, clerical, and medical fields (Booth and Segal 2005). Up until recently, women in the armed forces were also limited to noncombat positions, which further reduced their likelihood of promotion.

Lastly, as critical theorists have considered terrorism, again they have identified how race, class, and gender affect not only how particular acts are perceived but also who is most likely to be at risk of harm from terrorism. And, as to be expected, White, privileged males are less likely to perceive themselves at risk for various types of terrorism—typically, they view themselves as invulnerable. Women, across all groups, are more likely to be anxious about being the targets or victims of terrorist attacks (Finucane, Slovic, Mertz, Flynn, and Satterfield 2000). After 9/11, a national study found that women and racial/ethnic minorities were more likely than White males to have experienced sustained psychological distress and emotional as well as physical health problems (Chu, Seery, Ence, Holman, and Silver 2006).

CRITICAL THINKING

1. How might the stock stories of military sociology account for the terrorist attacks on 9/11?

2. In what ways do the stock stories reflect both the historical periods in which they were developed and the official perspective of the United States? Why are such stock stories appealing? What is the difficulty in automatically assuming their reliability?

3. How might the stock stories be utilized to minimize the concerns of racial, gender, and class groups or to marginalize such groups?

4. Almost all of us are affected in some way by the military, war, and acts of terrorism. How have these affected you or your family?

■ APPLYING THE MATRIX APPROACH TO U.S. MILITARY HISTORY, WAR, AND TERRORISM

Each war has shaped new traditions and created new social norms, heroes, and methods of military engagement. Exploring how various wars have also reflected our changing intersectional landscape of race, class, and gender will provide insight into the operation of the matrix within military organizations. One way to organize our discussion is to focus on those wars that have defined us as a people, and that have cost us the most in terms of human life. We begin with the Revolutionary War and then examine some of the U.S. government's hidden wars with Native Americans. With these as a backdrop and in the interests of brevity, we then explore the costliest wars (in terms of both people and capital) that the nation has waged: the Civil War, World War II, the Vietnam War, and our current wars on terrorism.

Revolutionary War

The Revolutionary War (1775–83) involved 217,000 colonial soldiers. Of those, 4,435 died in combat, and another 6,188 were wounded (U.S. Department of Veterans Affairs 2017). The U.S. military has always been a complex mix of race, class, gender, and sexual identities. Native Americans, Blacks, immigrants, Whites, women, the affluent class, the middle class, the working class, and the poor have all constituted significant portions of our military. This was also true of the first group of patriots to give their lives for this nation during the Boston Massacre on March 5, 1770. Crispus Attucks, a mulatto (African mixed race), a sailor by the name of Patrick Carr, an Irish immigrant, and two Englishmen—Samuel Maverick, a teenage apprentice, and a rope maker named Samuel Gray—all died from shots fired by the British soldiers that day. None were armed (Brooks 2011). These first to die in our country's history remarkably reflect the diversity of our nation and those willing to pay the ultimate sacrifice.

Boston silversmith Paul Revere called the nation to arms in 1775 and was answered by thousands of militiamen. On April 19, 1775, the first battle was waged in Concord, Massachusetts, where 89 men from Massachusetts died or were wounded. Within weeks of the first call, 6,000 men were mobilized. These were soon joined by 16,000 more from the other four New England colonies (Ferling 2010).

Black Soldiers

The British were the first to tap the support of Black slaves. Black militias were established in all of the English colonies. Virginia governor John Murray issued a proclamation on November 7, 1775, that granted full freedom to any and all Blacks willing to serve. The only caveat was that the offer applied only to slaves owned by the rebels, not to those owned by British Loyalists. The offer was aimed at punishing and threatening the rebels. North Carolinian Joseph Hews, one of the signers of the Declaration of Independence, accused the British of planning to "let loose Indians on our Frontiers" and to "raise the Negros against us" (quoted in Ashe 1908, 473).

Black men and women worked as British spies in New York. They created networks that helped others to escape, planned sabotage in rebellious cities, and otherwise aided in the British cause. More than 300 escaped slaves immediately joined the British within the first month of the war. Over the next few months more than

30,000 slaves would escape and fight for the British. This represented the single largest emancipation to take place within the United States until the Civil War. With the former slaves, the British established three full companies of colonial marines. These regiments took part in the sacking of Washington and fought in the Battle of Baltimore and along the coast (Lender 2016, 114).

George Washington was adamantly against the use of slaves in the military, but the ravages of the winter of 1777–78 and the devastation of the Continental army by both disease and desertion forced him to reconsider. He reluctantly granted Rhode Island permission to raise a regiment of free Blacks and slaves. A total of 5,000 free Blacks and slaves served in the Continental army, and the first integrated units of the U.S. military were created. Black and White men fought alongside each other almost on an equal footing, receiving the same pay, facing the same dangers, and providing the same levels of skill and courage (Lanning 2000, 73).

White Ethnic Soldiers

All forms of immigration were halted when the Revolutionary War began, but a large percentage of White immigrants and their descendants served in the Revolutionary War. For example, Irish and German immigrants fought on both sides of this war, but those living in the Mid-Atlantic states comprised the largest proportion of recruits in the Continental army. Roughly one out of every four Continental soldiers was of Irish descent, and both groups fought in all-Irish and all-German battalions. When the Revolutionary War broke out, many European nations provided soldiers to both sides. Of these, several German states actually provided mercenaries to the British army (Lutz 2008).

The Role of Women

The Revolutionary War afforded women on both sides of the conflict a variety of roles, including combat. One of the little-known achievements of women during the Revolutionary War was a successful boycott of British goods starting in the 1760s and continuing through the 1770s. Many women avoided purchasing British goods by making their own products at home, particularly clothing, and therefore effectively changed the consumption patterns of households. Acts of sabotage were also frequently carried out by women; for example, Catherine Van Rensselaer Schuyler, wife of General Philip Schuyler, burned the wheat fields around Albany, New York, thus denying the harvest to British forces (Best 2012, 23). Both the British and colonial forces utilized women in their traditional roles as homemakers and domestic servants to carry out espionage. As cooks and maids, who were routinely ignored, women were able to gain unrestricted access to military operations and move easily to gather information about troop movements, leadership changes, and equipment shortages. Some reported directly to General Washington and became highly accomplished spies. Of special note is Ann Simpson Davis, whom Washington personally selected to carry messages to his generals in Pennsylvania. Slipping through British-occupied areas unnoticed, she would often carry secret messages in sacks of grain or in her clothing. She received a letter of commendation for her services from Washington (Rhoades-Piotti 2017, 251). Women also served in more conventional roles as nurses and medics (Figley, Pitts, Chapman, and Elnitsky 2015).

Wars and Native Americans

Some of the most violent and cruel wars in U.S. history took place on our own soil, against Native American populations. American military forces fought 29 major wars against Native Americans, stretching from precolonial times to well into the 20th century. These wars cost thousands of lives, and Native Americans lost thousands of acres of land, from Georgia to Ohio, from Illinois to Alabama, and from Florida to Texas. The only other war on our soil to match this dreadful toll in both destruction and lives lost was the Civil War (Stout 2009).

Native Americans and the Revolutionary War

General George Washington, fearful of the Native Americans' potential strategic advantage, attempted to neutralize their ability to act at the start of the Revolutionary War. With few exceptions, the Native Americans sided with the British. Four of the six Iroquois nations joined forces with the British, and Loyalist forces devastated the Continental forces in western New York and Pennsylvania in 1778 and 1779. In spite of significant Native American support, not a single Native American representative was invited to the European treaty negotiations that concluded the war in 1783. As a result, the British ceded much of lands occupied by Native Americans between the Appalachian Mountains and the Mississippi River (Callaway 1995).

During the Revolutionary War, the Seminoles and a large contingent of African ex-slaves also allied with the British. This alliance was not without its difficulty, as the Seminoles also held slaves. Slavery among the Native Americans was radically different from that found among the Europeans. Among the Seminoles, slaves gradually became part of the group through marriage. After the Revolutionary War, southern slaveholders became increasingly alarmed at the armed Black and Native American communities throughout Florida. The territory, formally under Spanish rule, was a safe haven for escaped slaves. The first effort to deal with the escaped slaves was in the Treaty of New York (1790), which attempted to force Seminoles to honor new boundary lines and return African slaves to their masters. The Seminoles and other Native Americans refused to honor the treaty and return the Black fugitive slaves. From these humble beginnings the Black Seminoles came into being. Black Seminole culture, a blend of African, Native American, Spanish, and slave traditions, solidified during the 1800s (Ray 2007, 100).

War of 1812

A total of 286,730 soldiers fought in the **War of 1812** (1812–15). Of these, 2,260 died in combat, and another 4,505 were wounded (U.S. Department of Veterans Affairs 2017). Land, specifically Native American land, was the principal source of the tensions that gave rise to this conflict between the United States and Great Britain over British violations of U.S. maritime and trading rights with Europe. It quickly became a war that pitted the United States against the Native Americans, who were allied with Britain and France. All of the major players wanted to consolidate or actuate their claims on Native American homelands throughout the interior of the continent. Tribal nations immediately understood the risk to their lands, and a diverse group of Native American military leaders banded together. A faction of the Seneca joined with the Americans in the Battles of Fort George and Chippewa. Most other Native Americans sided with the British against the United States, believing that a British victory would lead to a cessation of land expansions. About a dozen Native American nations participated in the war (Fixico 2008).

One of the most diverse groups of soldiers participating in this war consisted of Choctaw Indians, free Blacks, Creoles, slaves, pirates, and Filipino sailors. Operating out of a swamp, this motley crew fought the decisive **Battle of New Orleans** in January 1815. In this battle, considered the final major battle of the war, the invading British army was defeated; the British had been intent on seizing New Orleans and subsequently all of the lands associated with the Louisiana Purchase. Although the British were defeated, the increasingly bitter relationship between the United States and the Seminoles continued. The War of 1812 was also the harbinger of the various Seminole Wars (Warshauer 2007).

The U.S. victory in the War of 1812 marked the acceleration of westward expansion and the destruction of much of what had been Native American lands. Andrew Jackson wasted no time in pushing for passage of the Indian Removal Act; this 1830 law banished all Native Americans to lands west of the Mississippi River. The Indian Removal Act is most directly associated with what became known as the **Trail of Tears** (1838–39), the name given by Native Americans to the devastating relocation process, which resulted in thousands of deaths from disease and exposure as tribes were forced to leave their lands (Warshauer 2007).

Seminole Wars

During the War of 1812, both African escaped slaves, known as maroons, and Black Seminoles waged war against the United States. Their combined strength made them targets of General Andrew Jackson. After the War of 1812 was concluded, Jackson led army forces in an attack on Fort Gadsden (also known as the Negro Fort) in an attempt to disrupt Florida's maroon communities. Thus the first of the **Seminole Wars** (1817–18) began. The Seminole Wars were three conflicts in Florida between the United States and the Seminoles. Often these conflicts were instigated by the British against U.S. settlers migrating south into Seminole territory. The fact that the Seminoles provided sanctuary to escaping Black slaves also precipitated these conflicts. The three Seminole Wars were never officially declared "wars" by the U.S. government. They were essentially the continuation of the U.S. policy aimed at stripping Native Americans of their lands and forcing them west of the Mississippi. Collectively, the Seminole Wars resulted in the removal of almost 4,000 Seminoles to Oklahoma. In later years, some Black Seminoles went on to become members of the famed Buffalo Soldiers (Calvin 2015).

By 1837, John Horse was an ex-slave and a formidable military leader and member of the Seminole tribe. He launched several successful campaigns throughout the Florida Everglades. At the age of 36, he was elevated from subchief to war chief. He commanded both fellow ex-slaves and Black Seminoles. Black Seminoles had been instrumental in the liberation of slaves from plantations throughout Florida and Georgia, and were frequent instigators of Native American rebellions against the U.S. government's policy of forced removal to present-day Oklahoma. Captured by Union troops in November 1837, John Horse met and became allies with another Seminole war leader—Wild Cat. After their escape, they inspired hope and resistance among both Black and Seminole people. The ultimate battle would come on Christmas Day in 1837, as a sizable U.S. force pursued the Seminoles into the Everglades of southern Florida. With fewer than 380 defenders, the Seminoles faced Union soldiers totaling more than 1,000. Thus began the Battle of Lake Okeechobee, the bloodiest contest of the Seminole Wars. His forces decimated, John Horse and his followers fled south with the Seminoles toward the last safe zone in Florida. Fearing for the survival of his own wife and children, John Horse surrendered during the spring of 1838. By the end of the summer of 1838, he and his family had joined other Native Americans in Indian Territory in present-day Oklahoma (Bird 2008; Tucker 1992).

Mexican–American War

From 1846 to 1848, the United States was at war with Mexico. A total of 78,718 soldiers were engaged in the **Mexican–American War**. Among those who served, a total of 1,733 died, while 4,125 suffered nonmortal wounds (U.S. Department of Veterans Affairs 2017). The Mexican–American War was primarily an outcome of the U.S. government's desire to annex Texas, California, and other Mexican territories. U.S. forces launched a three-pronged offensive: from the north through Texas, from the east through the Port of Veracruz, and from the west through present-day California and New Mexico. The Mexican–American

War was concluded in 1848 with the signing of the Treaty of Guadalupe Hidalgo. In this treaty, Mexico ceded all lands now considered the American Southwest. In return, all Mexicans living on that land were to be granted full U.S. citizenship. Actions taken by both the U.S. Congress and the Supreme Court denied American citizenship to both Black Mexicans and Pueblo Indians, even though both groups had previously been Mexican citizens. Black Mexicans in Texas were given the choice of staying in Texas and becoming slaves or being deported to Mexico, where slavery was outlawed. Pueblo Indians would not gain the right to vote until 1924. Finally, many other Mexican Americans lost their lands to White American settlers. The Mexican–American War highlighted not only the differences between regions but also the influence of slavery. The nation was on a collision course that could only lead to civil war.

After the Mexican-American War, Mexico ceded a huge swath of land to the U.S. with the condition that all the Mexican citizens residing there be granted American citizenship. Despite these terms, the U.S. denied citizenship to many black Mexicans and Pueblo Indians in the region.

Civil War

If the Revolutionary War defined the United States as a republic, then the Civil War defined it as a nation. The Civil War was a struggle over who would be covered under "we the people" and who would not. Consequently, this conflict also helped define the meaning of U.S. citizenship. The war affected not only native-born Whites and African Americans but also foreign-born residents and Native Americans. A total of 2,213,363 soldiers served in the Union army, and 1,050,000 served in the Confederate army. A total of 140,414 Union soldiers died in battle, as did 74,524 Confederate soldiers. Among Union soldiers, 281,881 suffered nonmortal wounds; it is unknown how many Confederate soldiers were wounded (U.S. Department of Veterans Affairs 2017).

The Union, the Confederacy, and Ethnicity

On the eve of the Civil War, the United States was truly becoming a nation of immigrants. For the first time the **old immigrants** (people who came in the earliest waves of immigration, from England, Scotland, and Wales) were being supplanted by **new immigrants** (people from Ireland, Switzerland, Poland, Germany, and other Southern European countries). In 1860, about 13% of the U.S. population was foreign-born. This group overwhelmingly not only supported the Union cause but also volunteered for the army in numbers that far exceeded their proportion in the U.S. population. A quarter of the Union armed forces were foreign-born (i.e., 543,000 out of the more than 2 million Union soldiers). Collectively, immigrants and the sons of immigrants accounted for about 43% of the Union army. Many of these were segregated into ethnic regiments (Doyle 2015). In contrast, the Confederate army was 91% native-born, primarily the descendants of old immigrants.

Race and Gender in the Civil War

The Union army, despite intense prejudices, actively recruited Native Americans under the condition that they would fight only in Indian Territory. Two regiments— the First and Second Indian Home Guards—were established. Initially serving under White officers, Native Americans eventually assumed leadership of these regiments.

The start of hostilities put a strain on the Union army and forced it to abandon many of its forts in Indian Territory. This provided a unique opportunity for the Confederates to open up an alliance with the Creek, Cherokee, Choctaw, Chickasaw, and Seminole. Their geographic location also ensured that they were culturally tied to the Confederacy. Native American tribes siding with the Confederates were part of the Texas regiments and fought against Union troops (National Park Service 2010).

Although it is difficult to document the contributions of women during the Civil War, we do know of distinguished service by some women. At least 250 women, dressed as men, are known to have fought on both sides of the war (Blanton and Cook 2002). Harriet Tubman, who was born a slave, served as a spy, scout, and hospital nurse during the war. Because of Tubman's knowledge of escape routes from the South, Union officers recruited her to organize an intelligence service to provide troop deployment and other tactical information on Confederate military operations (Moore 1991).

Rape is one of those peculiar atrocities of war visited upon women, and it remains a widespread weapon of war today. The Civil War was no exception. Even though President Lincoln—in General Order No. 100, known as the Lieber Code of 1863— established strict guidelines prohibiting wartime atrocities, particularly rape, such atrocities nevertheless occurred. What is important about the Lieber Code is that it represents the first time Black women were afforded protections against rape by White men. As many as 450 cases involving sexual crimes were tried by Union military courts (Feimster 2013), and at least 20 of these cases were prosecuted on behalf of "colored" women (Stutzman 2009).

Cathay Williams

Cathay Williams (1844–92) was the first documented woman ever to enlist and serve in the U.S. Army while posing as a man. Williams was born a slave on the Johnson plantation on the outskirts of Jefferson City, Missouri. In 1861, as Union forces occupied Jefferson City during the early period of the Civil War, the slaves were declared contraband, and many were forced into military service in support roles such as cooks, laundresses, and nurses. Williams, then 17 years old, was pressed into service in the Eighth Indiana Volunteer Infantry Regiment, under the command of Colonial William Plummer Benton. Over the next few years, as a soldier in the Eighth Indiana, Williams participated in campaigns in Arkansas, Louisiana, and Georgia. She participated in the Battle of Pea Ridge and the Red River Campaign. Later, Williams was transferred to Washington, D.C., where she served with General Phillip Sheridan's battalion. As the war drew to a close, she worked at Jefferson Barracks. After the war, Williams enlisted for a 3-year term in the U.S. Regular Army on November 15, 1866, in St. Louis, Missouri. During this term she served with the famed Buffalo Soldiers. When she suffered a bout of smallpox, a medical examiner discovered that she was a woman. As a result, she was discharged from the army on October 14, 1868.

Courtesy of the National Archives and Records Administration

Cathay Williams, who later altered her name to William Cathay, hid her gender as the nation's only female Buffalo Soldier, as a private from 1866 to 1868. A bronze bust memorial was dedicated to her on July 22, 2016, at the Richard Allen Cultural Center and Museum in Leavenworth, Kansas.

After the Civil War, the army disbanded all of the volunteer "colored" regiments and established six segregated Black regiments under White officers. In 1869, the infantry regiments were reconstituted into the 24th and the 25th Infantries. Two cavalry regiments, the 9th and the 10th, remained intact. These regiments saw combat in both the Southwest and the West in the so-called Indian War, and during the Spanish–American War.

World War II

World War II (U.S. involvement 1941–45) was, among other things, a scramble for raw resources such as oil, gold, and diamonds that spanned Europe, Africa, Asia, and the Middle East. A total of 16,112,566 Americans served in World War II. Of those, 53,402 died in battle and 670, 846 were wounded. In 2017, 1,711,000 World War II veterans were still living (U.S. Department of Veterans Affairs 2017).

Unrest at Home and Abroad

From its beginning in 1939, World War II was cast as a race war as Adolf Hitler and Nazi Germany stormed through Poland and the Soviet Union, killing Jews (some 6 million over the course of the war) and declaring Slavs (mainly ethnic Poles, Serbs, and Russians) to be subhuman (Timm 2010). The Japanese, allied with Germany in this effort, believed that they were the superior race and attempted to overpower China and other Asian countries. The Japanese held the United States in equal contempt, describing Americans as a decadent and mongrel people (Baofu 2014).

Meanwhile, here in the United States, after the bombing of Pearl Harbor by the Japanese in December 1941, 120,000 citizens of Japanese ancestry were ordered into concentration camps. As our nation castigated both Germany and Japan for their racist imperialism, Jim Crow laws ruled the South and the military. American cities were repeatedly rocked by race riots. Whites attacked Blacks in shipyards in Mobile, Alabama; Whites targeted both Blacks and immigrants in Detroit; White workers rioted in Beaumont, Texas; and White servicemen beat Mexican Americans in Los Angeles during the so-called Zoot Suit Riots. In 1943 alone, 242 separate violent attacks targeting African Americans occurred in 47 U.S. cities as southern White migrants clashed with Black residents over access to public spaces, jobs, and housing (Honey 2007).

African Americans: Upward Mobility and Continued Discrimination

During the war, some 400,000 women served in the American military, primarily in the Women's Army Corps and the Army and Navy Nurse Corps. Black women constituted the largest group of women of color within the Women's Army Corps, accounting for 10.6% of the total (Honey 2007). Black women in particular made significant gains in the labor force during the war, although these advances were significantly curtailed by legally sanctioned racial and gendered segregation across the entire country.

While President Franklin Roosevelt's 1941 Executive Order 8802 prohibited racial discrimination in the defense industries and civil service jobs, this rule was rarely enforced. Most employers turned to non-Whites only when they had exhausted the White labor supply. Even then, non-Whites were relegated to the most menial and dangerous positions, frequently on night shifts and in janitorial slots. Unions further hindered Black women's ability to gain employment in unionized blue-collar jobs. When Black people were hired, they were forced to use separate restrooms and were often paid the lowest salaries for the most difficult work. **Hate strikes**, a series of White supremacist wildcat strikes, were triggered throughout the war, such as in 1943 when White women working at the Baltimore Western Electric plant demanded toilet facilities separate from those used by the Black women working at the plant. Ultimately, the racial restrictions in the military–industrial complex forced Black women to remain in the private sector, serving as maids (Honey 2007).

Fully qualified African American nurses often found that racial segregation and discrimination hampered their entry into military service during World War II. And even those who made it in found Jim Crow discrimination waiting for them at the door. In 1945, thanks to pressure applied by First Lady Eleanor Roosevelt, 60 Black women were sent to Lovell Hospital at Fort Devens (outside Boston) to be trained as medical technicians. The commanding officer objected to Black medical technicians placing thermometers in the mouths of White servicemen, and he ordered these women to be reclassified from medical technicians to orderlies. A group of African American servicewomen met with the commanding officer, only to be insulted and dismissed. They walked out of the meeting and refused to report to work the next morning. After being threatened with charges of mutiny, most returned to work. Six did not. When these six were threatened with execution, still four stayed away. They were eventually court-martialed for refusing to obey orders, found guilty, and sentenced to a year of hard labor. The also received dishonorable discharges. A national protest led by the NAACP, the ACLU, and Mary McLeod Bethune's National Council of Negro Women forced a reversal of the decision (Bray 2016), but resistance to African American women serving across all of the armed forces persisted throughout the war (Wynn 2010).

For many Black men, the military offered decent wages and the potential for upward mobility after the war. But the military life, they discovered, was a continuation of the discrimination and segregation prevalent in the wider society. Often both the military and government officials looked upon Black soldiers as inferior. They rejected Blacks as leaders, assuming that Blacks would serve best under White officers. While the U.S. Army maintained separate Black regiments, the navy restricted Blacks to positions as cooks, janitors, and waiters. The Marine Corps refused to allow Blacks to join altogether. But possibly the worst treatment occurred among those Blacks serving in the South. Here even Nazi prisoners of war were accorded better treatment than Black soldiers. Prisoners of war could dine with Whites, often ride on the trains, and even go into town to view movies. Black soldiers and civilians were denied all of these (Wynn 2010).

In 1940 just 4,000 African Americans served in the U.S. Navy, most of them as cooks or dishwashers or in the engine rooms. Another 12,500 served in naval construction units such as the Seabees and another thousand in the Coast Guard. It was not until 1943 that African Americans were admitted into all naval branches on a proportional basis, and the first Black naval officers were appointed in February 1944. Segregation still prevailed, and the only way Blacks could crew a ship was if it was entirely Black. In 1944 the USS *Mason* and the submarine chaser *PC-1264*, both with all-Black crews, were commissioned to escort destroyers. That same year the first integrated crews were introduced on 25 auxiliary vessels. By the end of the war, 165 African Americans were serving in the navy and 5,000 in the Coast Guard. The overwhelming majority of these, 95%, still served in mess halls. Only 54 Black naval officers and 700 Coast Guard officers were serving at the close of hostilities, in 1945 (Wynn 2010).

Labor Shortages and the Bracero Program

Latino men and women also benefited from the labor needs of the military–industrial complex during World War II. In 1942, labor shortages on railroads, in mining operations, at shipyards, and in agriculture forced the U.S. government to establish the **Bracero Program**, which allowed 50,000 agricultural workers and 765 railroad workers from Mexico to enter the United States as contract guest workers (*bracero* is the Spanish word for manual laborer). These workers were critical to the nation's wartime economy. The program established basic workers' rights (sanitation, adequate shelter and food) and a minimum wage of 30 cents an hour. Through various extensions of the program, 4.6 million contracts were signed from 1942 to 1964, with many workers coming back year after year. From its inception, however, the Bracero Program was fraught with problems, as desperate Mexican workers were often relegated to the most difficult, least desirable, and lowest-paying jobs in agriculture. In theory the workers were protected, with guaranteed sanitary housing, decent meals at reasonable prices, occupational insurance at the farm owners' expense, and free transportation back to Mexico at the ends of their contracts. In reality, these rules were often and flagrantly broken as farm wages dropped and abuses ran rampant (Gonzalez 2013).

Asian Americans in the Enlisted Ranks

One particular group that faced systematic discrimination during the war consisted of about 500 Nisei (second-generation Japanese—i.e., children of immigrants) women who served in the U.S. forces in the enlisted ranks and worked as office personnel, translators, and medical professionals. They had to contend not only with the reality that their families were being held in internment camps but also with the Japanese cultural expectation that women should be docile and subservient to men. For many of these women, their wartime experience was a turning point in their lives as they navigated racial, gender, and national identities. The military experience for Japanese American (as well as for Korean and

Chinese American) women was different from that of African American women in that they did not serve in segregated units (Moore 2003).

Correcting the Record

The **Medal of Honor**, often called the Congressional Medal of Honor because it is awarded in the name of Congress, is the highest military honor that an individual can receive for combat heroism. Racial discrimination was so extreme during World War II that not a single African American received a Medal of Honor during the war or immediately after. This injustice began to be remedied somewhat only after researchers at

The 100th Infantry Battalion, or the 42nd Regimental Combat Team, composed exclusively of Japanese Americans, was one of the most highly decorated units in the U.S. military, yet the battalion's members were denied the nation's highest combat award. Among the unit's citations were an accumulated 18,000 individual decorations, but only one wartime Medal of Honor, 53 Distinguished Service Crosses, 9,486 Purple Hearts, and 7 Presidential Unit Citations. Anti-Japanese sentiment would deny many the nation's highest honor. It would take another 57 years before 21 more would receive the Medal of Honor (Williams 2000).

Shaw University conducted a study in the mid-1990s and found that systematic racial discrimination had prevented Blacks from being considered (Converse, Gibran, Cash, Griffith, and Kohn 1997).

Of the 3,488 Medals of Honor awarded as of June 2016, 263 have gone to Irish Americans, 87 to African Americans, 42 to Hispanic Americans, 47 to Asian Americans, 22 to Native Americans, 25 to Italian Americans, and at least 28 to Jewish Americans. Only one Medal of Honor has been awarded to a woman. The numbers of Medal of Honor recipients of various races and ethnicities are even more telling when we look behind the scenes. Most of the Jewish, Hispanic, Asian, and African American recipients have been recognized only after decades of anonymity and historical amnesia. Over the past three decades, each U.S. president has held special ceremonies to honor these heroes for their service and sacrifices. These delayed recipients of the nation's highest recognition of valor have been identified through a congressionally mandated review.

On January 13, 1997, President Bill Clinton awarded the Medal of Honor to seven African American World War II veterans. Only one recipient, Vernon Baker, was still alive to receive it. On June 21, 2000, after more than 50 years, the government recognized and awarded 22 Asian American soldiers for their valor during World II. In awarding these medals, President Clinton stated, "It's long past time to break the silence about their courage . . . rarely has a nation been so well-served by a people it has so ill-treated" (quoted in Williams 2000). Most recently, President Barack Obama awarded the Medal of Honor to 24 overlooked Black, Hispanic, and Jewish heroes. In all of these cases, a military tribunal declared that all were "denied Medal(s) of Honor years ago because of bias" (Straw 2014).

CONCEALED STORY: Marcario García

Marcario García answered his nation's call to go to war. García, a native of Mexico, grew up in the Fort Bend area in Texas. In November 1942 he was drafted and was soon bound for the European theater. There, during the Normandy attack in November 1944, he was wounded. When VE Day ended the war in Europe on May 8, 1945, he returned to the United States and his hometown. VJ Day, announcing the Japanese surrender and the end of World War II, occurred on August 14, 1945. Less than two weeks later, on August 23, 1945, Harry Truman awarded García the Medal of Honor in a White House ceremony. García was a hometown hero.

Courtesy of the National Archives and Records Administration

Marcario Garcia

A fabulous party was held to celebrate the local hero. A story in the *Houston Post* on September 7, 1945, was headlined "Sugar Land War Hero." But just a day after this public welcome, Staff Sergeant García was refused service at the Oasis Café in the nearby city of Richmond. He was then beaten with a bat, resulting in his hospitalization; he was subsequently charged with drunkenness and disorderly conduct. The charges were ultimately dropped, but this incident illustrates the racial climate in America at the time—a climate in which individuals could honorably serve, putting their lives on the line on foreign battlefields, and still come home to a place where their basic freedoms were circumscribed by race, class, and gender.

Source: Michael A. Olivas, "The 'Trial of the Century' That Never Was: Staff Sgt. Marcario García, the Congressional Medal of Honor, and the Oasis Café," *Indiana Law Journal* 83, no. 4 (2008): 1391–1403.

Although five Native Americans who served in World War II were Medal of Honor recipients, few have acknowledged the clandestine and important mission served by the group known as code talkers. Their story is both unique and important. The Japanese military had become very adept at breaking the sophisticated codes utilized by the U.S. forces. In the search for a solution, it was suggested that the language of the Navajo might be effective in thwarting the Japanese code breakers. This language, without an alphabet or symbols, was in use only in remote areas of the American Southwest. At the onset of World War II no more than 30 non-Navajo could understand the language. Therefore its potential as code was immediately recognized. During one of the most hard-fought battles in the Pacific theater, at Iwo Jima, a strange language was intercepted coming from American radios. The secret messages were derived from the Navajo language and transmitted by Native American soldiers. A total of 400 Navajo served in the Marines Corps as code talkers. While the value of what they contributed was significant, it was not until September 17, 1992, that they were honored in a ceremony at the Pentagon (Asturias 2008).

Vietnam War

The Vietnam War (1954–75), one of the most contentious conflicts this nation has seen, continues to define U.S. politics, military wisdom, and national policy. President George H. W. Bush euphemistically declared that the 1991 Persian Gulf War would "not be another Vietnam," and all succeeding presidents have found themselves arguing with the war's ghost—Bill Clinton in the Balkans, George W. Bush in Iraq, and Barack Obama in Afghanistan. The Vietnam War resulted in an estimated 1.1 million Vietnamese army and Viet Cong military deaths and another 533,000 civilian deaths. Of the 2.1 million U.S. men and women who served, 90,220 died and 153,303 were wounded. Today, an estimated 7,391,000 Vietnam veterans are living (U.S. Department of Veterans Affairs 2017). The Vietnam War coincided with various civil rights movements—the Black civil rights movement, the women's liberation movement, the Native American movement—and a whole slew of countercultural movements, and, of course, it was the entire reason for the antiwar movement. But this does not totally explain why this was the most unpopular, most debated, most contentious war in U.S. history.

The Vietnam War challenged Americans and their leaders to reconsider how wars should be fought and, more important, by whom. As images of body bags and military misconduct in combat filled the airwaves, talk about a new military emerged among both military leaders and politicians. The draft was one casualty of the Vietnam War. While draftees made up only 25% of the U.S. military at that time, they were more than half of the army's battle casualties. More than half of the young men of draft-eligible age between 1964 and 1973 never served. Richard Nixon promised to end the draft when he was campaigning for the presidency in

Blacks were overrepresented in the military during the Vietnam War and made up a yet larger proportion of casualties.

1968. In February 1970, a presidential commission recommended the creation of an all-volunteer force (Eikenberry 2013). The Vietnam War forced the nation to reconsider how race and duty intersect.

More Blacks served in Vietnam than in any war before or since. During the height of the war (1965–69), Blacks accounted for 11% of the American population but made up 12.6% of the soldiers in Vietnam. They also made up 14.1% of the war dead (National Archives 2016). Military recruitment advertisements were carefully crafted to feature African American men and women but avoided overrepresenting them. The advertising agencies charged with crafting these ads took into consideration both the arguments of civil rights activists that Blacks were overrepresented among war casualties and the fears that an all-volunteer military would become disproportionately populated by lower-income minorities. The ads they developed attempted to strike a balance, featuring Blacks and Whites, and males and females, in identical environments (Bailey 2009).

As noted above, the Vietnam War took place during the height of several civil rights movements. Most significantly, Black civil rights activists began to point out the multiple forms of racism associated with the military. Under pressure from civil rights groups, President John F. Kennedy in 1962 reactivated the Committee on Equal Opportunity in the Armed Forces. The committee released a report in 1964 that identified several racial problems. It noted that while African Americans made up close to 13% of the U.S. population, they constituted only 9% of the various branches of the armed forces. Throughout the military, Black troops were unevenly promoted, and their opportunities were restricted within both the National Guard and the Army Reserve. Most still served in segregated units, and they faced high levels of discrimination both on military bases and in the surrounding communities (Coffey 1998).

As U.S. involvement in Vietnam increased, so did the numbers of African American recruits. These increases were associated with a discriminatory draft and other governmental policies. For example, the draft deferments for both college and employment favored middle-class White youth. A majority of those drafted were poor, undereducated, and urban. Blue-collar workers and the unemployed faced an increased likelihood of being drafted. Finally, less than 1% of those serving on Selective Service draft boards (boards made up of citizen volunteers charged with determining who within their communities would serve or receive deferments, postponements, or exemptions) were Black, and the draft boards in seven states had no Blacks at all (Coffey 1998).

Most of the deaths of Black soldiers in Vietnam occurred during the war's first phase. Blacks were overrepresented in the infantry at that time and consequently had significantly higher casualties. Interestingly, as the military shifted to a withdrawal phase, deaths among Black servicemen declined, while a disproportionate number of Hispanics died in combat. Some speculate that this shift reflects the effectiveness of civil rights activism, which applied pressure to decision makers to replace African Americans with members of less politically mobilized ethnic groups, such as Hispanics, during the withdrawal phase of the war (Talbot and Oplinger 2014).

Obviously absent from the binary construct of military advertisements was the possibility of recruiting either Latino or Asian Americans. Part of this might have been deliberate avoidance, particularly of Hispanics, as Chicano antiwar leaders were extremely vocal about their opposition to any form of military service (Oropeza 2005).

Vietnam veterans constitute nearly half of all homeless veterans today. Of these, close to 45% are African American or Hispanic, despite the fact that these groups make up only 10.4% and 3.4%, respectively, of the U.S. veteran population (National Coalition for Homeless Veterans 2017).

Wars on Terrorism

Terrorists function to disrupt social, political, and economic processes, with the aim of accomplishing specific ends. There are three forms of terrorism: individual, group, and state sponsored. Many observers today believe that state-sponsored terrorism is the biggest challenge to world peace.

The **war on terrorism**, also often called the global war on terrorism or the war on terror, consists of a series of military and legislative campaigns that began after the September 11, 2001, attacks on the United States. These have involved both covert and overt military operations, new legislation aimed at increasing national security, and efforts to block the flow of money going to terrorists. Those critical of such efforts argue that they stem primarily from an ideology of fear and repression that targets specific groups, and that they actually promote violence, thus strengthening terrorist recruitment efforts (Hafetz 2011).

The phrase "war against terrorism" first appeared in 1984 in reaction to the 1983 Beirut barracks bombings, a set of terrorist attacks that occurred during Lebanon's Civil War. In the attacks, two truck bombs were used to target separate buildings that housed peacekeeping forces, specifically U.S. and French soldiers. In the suicide attacks, 241 American and 58 French soldiers, 6 civilians, and 2 attackers were killed. The Reagan administration used these provocations to seek enhanced powers to freeze the assets of terrorist groups and respond quickly to perceived threats with military action. The U.S. strike on Libya in April 1986 was the first strategic use of this policy. In this attack, code-named Operation El Dorado Canyon, the U.S. military conducted air strikes in retaliation for Libyan sponsorship of terrorism against Americans. During the same period, the Reagan administration was also covertly involved in trying to topple several governments. One example is the Iran-Contra affair, in which senior administration officials violated the law by facilitating the acquisition of military arms for both Iran and the Contras in Nicaragua, as part of an attempt to destabilize autonomous governments. A total of $212 million in covert U.S. military aid flowed into Central American states in 1986 alone. By 1992, when a United Nations–brokered peace was established, more than 80,000 Salvadorans had been killed, 8,000 more had disappeared, and more than a million of El Salvador's 5 million citizens had been displaced (Sandford 2003, 70). Often indigenous peasants were targeted, as was the case in Guatemala, where more than 200,000 people died (Sullivan and Jordan 2004). These covert operations included disseminating propaganda and arming and training Indian leaders willing to fight (Krauss 1986, 569).

The current war on terrorism is associated with the events that occurred on September 11, 2001. Since that time, Arab and Muslim Americans have been systematically targeted, racialized, and often ostracized for acts they did not commit, accused of things they did not do, and presumed guilty despite their firm assertion of their commitment to the United States as citizens (Aziz 2012). Pervasive levels of **Islamophobia**, or intense fear and paranoia regarding Muslims and Arabs (both those living in the United States and those abroad), have consistently and increasingly been identified among U.S. citizens, and hate crimes against people assumed to be Muslim have spiked dramatically (Ogan, Wilnat, Pennington, and Bashir 2013). These anxieties suggest simmering resentment and condemnation of Arab and Muslim Americans. Islamophobia ultimately asserts that a fundamental incompatibility exists between Islam and Western values associated with democracy, tolerance, and civility (Panagopoulos 2009).

Anti-Muslim crimes have increased fivefold since the 2001 attacks on the United States (see Figure 10.3). In the year prior to 9/11, hate crimes targeting Muslims averaged between 20 and 30 per year. In 2001 that number jumped to 500. Since then, hate crimes against Muslims have averaged 100–150 annually (Ingraham 2015).

Figure 10.3 ■ 9/11 Changed Things for American Muslims

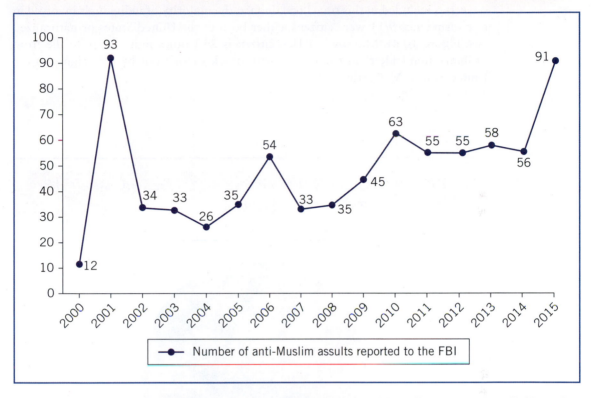

Source: "Anti-Muslim hate crimes are still five times more common today than before 9/11," by Christopher Ingraham. *Washington Post*, February 11, 2015.

To a great extent, how we ultimately view terrorism is structured by the intersectional lens that we have constructed. We rarely think of terrorists as being rich, wealthy, White, and female (Cole 2011). The reality is that women, particularly affluent White women, are being effectively recruited by various terrorist organizations. These women are attracted to such organizations because they perceive that by joining they can be empowered and add meaning to their lives. These groups use Twitter, Facebook, and other social media sites as primary arenas for recruitment of both women and men (Ferran and Kreider 2015).

Early in his administration, President Donald Trump vowed that he would protect the American people from terrorists. He signed an executive order banning entry into the United States for 90 days by all persons from seven Muslim-majority countries: Iran, Iraq, Libya, Somalia, Sudan, Syria, and Yemen. None of the terrorists responsible for any attacks within the United States has come from any of the countries included in this travel ban. In fact, the majority of individuals involved in terrorism since 9/11 were citizens, either born in the United States or naturalized (see Figure 10.4). Moreover, a U.S. citizen is 253 times more likely to die from ordinary homicide than from a terrorist attack carried out by a foreigner in the United States (McCarthy 2017).

Figure 10.4 ■ The Majority of America's Post 9/11 Era Terrorists Are U.S. Born or Naturalized Citizens

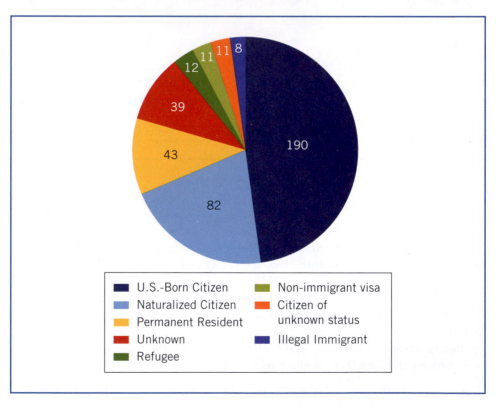

Source: Adapted from "Most Terrorists in the U.S. Since 9/11 Have Been American Citizens or Legal Residents," by Niall McCarthy. *Forbes,* January 31, 2017.

CRITICAL THINKING

1. In what ways have the wars in which the United States has been involved changed over both times and places? What does this suggest about us as a nation? What are the implications for our future?

2. The U.S. military, as an institution, has been transformed by wars and terrorism. What changes have occurred in how the United States conducts wars?

3. What does the belated awarding of Medals of Honor suggest about the operation of the racial matrix (both historically and in contemporary times)? What may account for these shifts?

4. How have you been affected by the war on terrorism? How have your family and friends been affected? What does this suggest about race, gender, and class?

■ A MORE INCLUSIVE FUTURE

In 2001, when the United States started the current war on terrorism, the cost of that war was estimated at $31 billion. By 2003 that figure was up to $111.9 billion, and 65,000 troops from 42 nations had become involved. And in 2017, the figure was $97.9 billion. To date, the United States has spent some $2.02 trillion on the war on terrorism. And there is no end in sight (Amadeo 2017).

It is almost inconceivable to think of a time when we might be free of conflict. However, we can develop more sane, reasonable, and just ways of resolving conflict that avoid the destructive and vastly inequitable structures, processes, and practices that all too frequently reflect race, class, and gender. Engaged citizens are the most significant deterrent to domestic terrorism. Engaged citizens are also the most effective safeguards when national policies are misdirected.

Strength through Diversity

Our best chance of averting wars lies in efforts to increase world security by working toward sustainable jobs and economies. Asserting the basic dignity of all, regardless of race, class, ethnicity, religion, age, or gender, is a good starting place. We cannot fight wars, protect our shores, or fight terrorism abroad or at home through racism, sexism, ethnocentrism, or Islamophobia. Measures such as random bag checks, airport strip searches, and racial profiling have done little to make us any safer, but they have increased the threats to our basic freedoms. Homeland security begins with a basic level of trust between us as citizens of the United States and of the world. At the core of the American judicial system is the presumption of innocence, yet we have targeted our citizens for internment, hostility, and even death, with no basis for our accusations other than our fear. Fear is a poor substitute for trust, and it erodes the very democratic principles that we cherish.

Our military institutions, the most diverse institutions in the nation, hold the key to the effective and efficient use of all our human resources. Encouraging all citizens to serve in, participate with, and provide oversight of our military institutions can be the greatest deterrent to abuses, the greatest safeguard to peace, and the most effective weapon against terrorism.

In May 2016, a group of fourth-year female cadets at the U.S. Military Academy at West Point posed for a picture in their dress gray uniforms with crossed sabers, reflecting a long tradition of academy graduates. The difference was that all 16 of these women were Black. The photo was disseminated across social media channels, and many interpreted it as part of the Black Lives Matter movement. It is also important to note that these Black women were raising their fists, a gesture that historically has been taken as a political statement. An investigation by the army found that this was not a political protest, but the academy superintendent publicly chastised the cadets just the same, noting that "a symbol or gesture that one group of people may find harmless may offend others. As Army officers, we are not afforded the luxury of a lack of awareness" (quoted in Sicard 2016).

If we are going to diversify the military, the change needs to start from the top (Sicard 2016)—something on which 25 four-star generals, admirals, and other military leaders agree (Duster 2013). While race and gender are factors in the appointment process, those admitted to our military academies continue to be among the best that our nation has to offer. In the West Point class of 2016, 1,150 cadets graduated. Among these were 322 minorities, 15 international cadets, and 35 combat veterans. The 2019 graduating class is the most diverse in the academy's 214-year history (Sicard 2016). These same patterns need to be replicated across all military academies if the armed forces are going to become truly diverse.

World Security through Sustainable Economies

The one clear enemy of democracy is tyranny. And the principal allies of tyranny are poverty, hopelessness, and inequity. If we are going to stop terrorism, then we must first prevent it by supporting equal access to education; alleviating poverty, hunger, and misery; and promoting civil liberties and freedom (Martin 2015).

Wars are more likely to occur where lawlessness, hopelessness, and helplessness prevail. The most likely to suffer are those most vulnerable, regardless of whether they are in the United States or abroad. In such situations it is difficult to determine who is right or wrong, evil or good. In reality, none of these terms make any sense in the face of devastated lives, pain, and suffering. We should realize that during our own Revolutionary War, we were the extremists, the terrorists, and the discontents.

As a nation among other nations, the United States needs to join with the United Nations to help sustain the rule of law around the world. All parties need to be brought to the table, and all need to be held to the same standard. The International Criminal Court offers a place where the world can hold accountable those who commit crimes against humanity, whether they are state agents or nonstate actors (Rothkopf and Lord 2013).

Within our own country, we need to encourage service by all as part of what it means to be a citizen. The idea that military service and other forms of public service should be shared equally by all, regardless of race, class, or gender, reflects the fact that we all have a stake in this democracy. The most secure democracy is one in which all citizens participate.

CRITICAL THINKING

1. How do the societal values of diversity and inclusion become manifested in the military? How might our values effect changes in the military?

2. How could the establishment of more global institutions lead to decreasing numbers of terrorist acts? What role should the United States play in such institutions? What role should the United Nations and the International Criminal Court play?

3. Over time, who might be considered a terrorist or a patriot changes. How might such shifting definitions be applied within our country? How might our attitudes toward non–U.S. identities and marginalized U.S. identities affect our struggles toward democracy?

4. What kinds of information, messages, or images prevail regarding people who are not like you, not of your same culture or nationality? Are these barriers or bridges to interactions?

KEY TERMS

Battle of New Orleans, p. 349

Bracero Program, p. 356

coercive force, p. 342

dysfunctional, p. 340

functionalist approach to the military, p. 339

hate strikes, p. 355

interstate forms of war, p. 343

intrastate forms of war, p. 343

Islamophobia, p. 362

Medal of Honor, p. 357

CHAPTER SUMMARY

LO 10.1 Examine the contemporary reality of race, class, and gender in the U.S. military.

The contemporary U.S. military accounts for 16% of the total U.S. budget, which represents a third of all moneys spent globally on defense. Although it is predominantly male, White, and young, the U.S. military is one of the most diverse institutions in the nation. Race, gender, and age differences occur across all the branches. Younger recruits tend to join the Marine Corps, while the air force attracts older recruits. Women are underrepresented in all branches, but they are most likely to enlist in the air force. Close to a third of all enlisted personnel are members of racial minority groups. While racial minorities constitute 23.4% of those eligible to enlist, they make up 32.9% of enlisted ranks. Middle- and upper-class individuals are least likely to be found among enlisted personnel. Clear gender differences are evident across the various services. Women of color are more likely to serve in either the army or the navy than in other military branches. Immigrants continue to join the military as a means of becoming naturalized citizens.

LO 10.2 Explore the stock sociological theories regarding the U.S. military, war, and terrorism.

Three central sociological theories dominate the field of military sociology and represent stock stories. The functionalist approach holds that the military, war, and terrorism serve specific and important tasks within society. Symbolic interactionism investigates how we attach meaning to such things as war and remembrance, flags and memorials, and other representations that support wars, terrorism, and the military. Monopoly and materialist perspectives posit that military organizations maintain a legitimate monopoly on the use of coercive force that is uniquely tied to the material instruments of war. Stock theories tend to oversimplify the military, war, and terrorism while underemphasizing the impacts of race, class, and gender. Functionalism, specifically, fails to anticipate change and tends to ignore powerful interests within society. Symbolic interactionism, with its emphasis on micro-level analysis, fails to account adequately for social structure, identity, and military organizations. And monopoly and materialist perspectives, by linking all manifestations of the military, war, and terrorism to the state, fails to anticipate how nonstate entities, civil war, and ethnic/racial conflict can be the sources of war and military conflict. Critical sociologists have stressed the intersections of race, class, and gender as being central in any theories, scholarship, and research interrogating the military, war, and terrorism. Critical race theory also examines how military hierarchies represent internally stratified labor markets that reflect hierarchies in wider society. Terrorism often highlights the vulnerability of specific racial groups

LO 10.3 Apply the matrix approach to U.S. military history, war, and terrorism.

Every generation of U.S. citizens since the birth of the nation has witnessed wars. These wars have served to define our national character, norms, and identity. Each war has served to shape new traditions, new heroes, and new ways of deploying military technology. Concentrating on the most significant wars throughout our history provides a central set of events by which and through which the matrix lens can be utilized. The Revolutionary War highlights that the military of the United States has never been homogeneous, as Native Americans, Blacks, immigrants, Whites, women, and various class groups have participated. Our national identity was initially forged in this war. Across our history, the U.S. military engaged in 29 major wars with Native American populations. These wars were responsible for the loss of thousands of lives as well as Native Americans' loss of tribal lands. The Civil War highlights the importance of race, class, and gender. At least 250 women, often dressed as men, fought on both sides. Rape, a particular atrocity of war, targeted women, especially Black women. World War II highlighted the nation's bifurcated stance with regard to race. On the one hand, the United States was waging a war against fascism and racial imperialism, while on the other it was upholding Jim Crow laws in both the South and the military. The Vietnam War, our most contentious war, revealed the ugly scars of racism as both Blacks and Hispanics were significantly overrepresented among U.S. casualties. Agitation over these deaths and the morality of the war challenged our country and its leaders to reconsider how wars should be fought. Amid these controversies an all-volunteer force was created. Wars against terrorism, involving both covert and overt military operations, security legislation, and new regulations, derive from the September 11, 2001, attacks on U.S. soil. The current war on terrorism has tended to target both Muslims and Arabs, principally from the Middle East. Such concerns seem to be misplaced, as the average U.S. citizen is more than 253 times more likely to die from a homicide than from a terrorist attack carried out by a foreigner in the United States.

LO 10.4 Evaluate the possibilities for a more inclusive future.

Our military institutions, the most diverse institutions in the nation, hold the key to the effective and efficient use of all our human resources. Encouraging all citizens to serve in, participate with, and provide oversight of our military institutions can be the greatest deterrent to abuses, the greatest safeguard to peace, and the most effective weapon against terrorism. Wars are more likely to occur where lawlessness, hopelessness, and helplessness prevail. The most likely to suffer are those most vulnerable, regardless of whether they are in the United States or abroad. In such situations it is difficult to determine who is right or wrong, evil or good. In reality, none of these terms make any sense in the face of devastated lives, pain, and suffering. We should realize that during our own Revolutionary War, we were the extremists, the terrorists, and the discontents.

CONCLUSION

We have provided you with the tools and knowledge to examine the social construction of identities and the systems and experiences of oppression and privilege that pervade social institutions. While our text concludes here, your work is only beginning!

You now have the ability to center other social identities in the Matrix. Identify an important identity in your own life, whether gender, class, ability, or some other constructed identity shaped by inequality. As you pay more attention to racial dynamics in the institutions you exist in, start to think about one of these other identities in detail at the same time. Alternatively, start to pay close attention to how racial dynamics intersect with other specific identities, on a micro level, as well as in the way people are treated, the general culture, the policies and informal practices, and more. For people with privilege, it takes training and practice to actually see the privileges you benefit from. Yet when we take up an intersectional lens, we can see that we each benefit from some form of privilege, so we are each implicated in the vast inequality that pervades our nation and the globe.

We also encourage you to examine other institutions not included in this text. Perhaps the easiest one to start with is the media. What are the stock stories we learn from the media about race, racism, and specific racial groups? How have they changed over time? Find examples of concealed and resistance stories. Think creatively about some of the ways media can be transformed to advance equality rather than to reinforce the status quo.

While this text has primarily examined our domestic context, scholars are exploring race on a global scale. Of course we know that constructions of race vary geographically. Examine the ways that racial constructs vary across nations and cultures. In some nations it is not race, but ethnicity or religion that is the primary source of oppression and privilege. We also need to ask how the dominance of whiteness on a global scale has historically been imposed, maintained, and is advancing.

The issues we have examined throughout this text are serious, impacting people's quality of life and life itself. They can seem overwhelming, and they are. But that should not be an excuse for doing nothing. Knowing what you now know, is doing nothing an option for you anymore? There are many, many different ways to do something, no matter where you live, your career field, or any other details of your life. You do not have to drop everything and become a full-time activist, but you can support activists and activist organizations.

Other small changes that can take place on a daily basis: Interrupt racist jokes, statements of prejudice, etc. Try to explain why you find them offensive. You are always educating others with what you say and do. It may be hard to find the courage, but it gets easier with practice, and there are many books and online tools designed to help you. Question policies, practices, and the curricular offerings in your school and workplace. Students have more power than they realize. Look at the racial demographics of students and faculty on your campus. Question any inequality you may find. Write to members of congress. Educate others. Speak up.

When we do nothing, we are complicit in reproducing racism, oppression, and privilege. Continue to educate yourself about oppression and privilege. They are everywhere. Study history. There have been many white people who have devoted their lives (and lost them) in fighting racism. There are many men who have fought historically for women's rights. Seeing these role models is important. It is just as important to find a support network of others you can continue to examine oppression and privilege with. Develop real relationships with people who vary from you racially, and carefully listen to their stories, but do not expect them to educate you. Learn from the oppressed and follow their lead.

Acknowledge that you will make mistakes and accept that. That is how we learn. This is a lifelong journey, and humility is important. Much has been written about how to do ally work. These are easy to find online. You can also find many "action continuums" to consider where you stand. Do your behaviors and words draw upon common derogatory stereotypes? Do you tacitly support the reproduction of racism, sexism, heterosexism, and other systems of oppression through your silence? Do you work to educate yourself and others? Do you work toward creating change on campus, in your family, on the job, etc?

Remember, institutions constrain our roles and behaviors, but they are also reproduced on a daily basis by the people within them. Everything we do, we do within an institution. It is individual people, working together, who get campus policies changed. In fact, Ethnic Studies programs are largely the result of student demand. People implement and can challenge law, policies, and practices. As we have seen throughout this text, many of the answers we need already exist; what is missing is enough people with the will to make change happen. What role will you play?

affirmative action: Programs, begun under the administration of President Richard Nixon, requiring employers receiving federal funding to take affirmative steps to eliminate discrimination based on race, ethnicity, national origin, or gender in the hiring and treatment of employees.

agency: The ability to effect change, to act independently, and to exercise free choices.

American Medical Association: A formal organization established by physicians as a way of defining themselves as the only authentic and legitimate practitioners of medicine.

ancestry: An individual's point of origin, lineage, or descent.

apprenticeship model of education: A form of education in which skills are transferred from a master/teacher to an apprentice/student and the skills needed to perform a job are learned on the job.

assimilation: The process through which people gradually accept and adapt to the dominant culture after immigrating to a new society. The stages of assimilation generally begin with adoption of the dominant language and cultural patterns and then advance to increased interaction between newcomers and dominant group members, reduced levels of prejudice and discrimination, intermarriage, and eventually full integration and acceptance.

Atlanta Compromise: An agreement articulated by Booker T. Washington in 1895 to pacify White business owners; it suggested that Blacks and Whites could work together to play their economic roles while remaining socially separate.

Bacon's Rebellion of 1676: A revolt in which Black, Irish, Scottish, and English bond servants fought against the planter elite in Virginia.

Battle of New Orleans: The final major battle of the War of 1812, in which the British army was defeated and prevented from seizing New Orleans and subsequently all the lands associated with the Louisiana Purchase.

binary constructs: In relation to identity groups, the representation of two groups in opposition (such as White/Black, male/female); such constructs normalize and legitimate racial and gender hierarchies at the expense of other outsiders, such as other racial minorities (Jews, Hispanics, Italians) and gender groups (LGBT).

biological determinism: The concept that an individual's behavior is innately related to components of his or her physiology, such as body type and brain size.

Black civil rights movement: A movement orchestrated by southern Blacks—in partnership with northern allies, both White and Black—in the period 1955–68 that not only challenged but also effectively nullified the intimidation and segregation of the Old South.

Black Code: France's Colonial Ordinance of 1685, which legislated the life, death, purchase, marriage, and religion of slaves, as well as the treatment of slaves by their masters.

boycotts: Voluntary acts of protest in which individuals or groups seek to punish or coerce corporations, nations, or persons by refusing to purchase their products, invest in them, or otherwise interact with them.

Bracero Program: Guest worker program established in 1942 because of labor shortages caused by World War II; allowed Mexican contract laborers to enter the United States to work in agriculture and on railroads.

broken windows theory: A theory of crime that asserts that a relationship exists between urban disorder and vandalism, such that if vandalism can be stopped, serious crime will decrease.

Brown v. Board of Education of Topeka: The landmark 1954 U.S. Supreme Court case that struck down the 1896 decision in *Plessy v. Ferguson,* making the racial segregation of public accommodations, including public schools, illegal.

capitalism: A type of economy in which the means of production are held and controlled by private owners, not the government, and in which prices are set by the forces of supply and demand with minimal government interference.

chattel slavery: Slavery in which the enslaved persons are considered personal property, owned by their masters for life, and their children are the owners' property as well.

citizenship: A status reflecting the legal process countries use to regulate national identity, membership, and rights.

class: A person's location in the social stratification, which encompasses particular levels of access to and control over resources for survival.

class approach: An approach to issues of power, politics, and identity that assumes that power is derived from having control over specific economic structures within society.

club movement: A late 19th-century movement in the United States through which lower-status White ethnics sought to gain elite status through the establishment of exclusive sport groups.

coalitional politics: Politics characterized by alliances of various identity groups whose shared purpose is to establish a specific political agenda.

coercive force: Force that involves the use of intimidation to obtain compliance.

colonialism: A set of hierarchical relationships in which groups are defined culturally, ethnically, and/or racially and in which these relationships serve to guarantee the political, social, and economic interests of the dominant group.

colonization of the mind: From the work of Frantz Fanon, the concept that our cognitions, our ideologies, and our worldviews are often those of those in power.

color blindness: The view (or assertion) that one does not see race or ethnicity, only humans.

color-blind racism: An ideology with four components: *abstract liberalism,* which encompasses abstract concepts of equal opportunity, rationality, free choice, and individualism and is used to argue that discrimination is no longer a problem, and any individual who works hard can succeed; *naturalization,* in which ongoing inequality is reframed as the result of natural processes rather than social relations; *cultural racism,* in which inherent cultural differences are used to separate racialized groups; and *minimization of racism,* or the argument that we now have a fairly level playing field, everyone has equal opportunities to succeed, and racism is no longer a real problem.

communal experience: Shared knowledge across group members occupying the same spaces.

concealed stories: Narratives consisting of the data and voices that stock stories ignore; these stories often convey a very different understanding of identity and inequity.

conversion therapy: Treatment programs that purport to change the sexual orientations of gays and lesbians.

crime: A form of deviance that violates moral and ethical standards and is generally defined as such by law.

critical pedagogy: Strategies of education that seek to create structures of liberation rather than reproduce the status quo.

critical race theory: A theoretical approach that represents an attempt by scholars and activists to transform the relationships among race, racism, and power.

cultural capital: The resources that individuals have, from their social networks, that enable them to interact in certain social situations and move up the socioeconomic ladder through the adoption of particular styles, tastes, and dispositions.

cultural values: Sets of beliefs and interpretations that are shared across group members.

culture of poverty: An approach to crime and deviance that associates self-perpetuating cycles of dependency with poor families, specifically poor families of color.

curandero/as: Traditional or native healers in Latino/a cultures.

Dawes Act: Law passed by the U.S. Congress in 1887 that required Native American nations to divide their communal reservations into individual plots of 160 acres, with each assigned to a family head. The remaining land was given to White homesteaders and various corporations, such as railroads and ranching companies.

de facto political practices: Extralegal processes and methods that restrict political and other rights.

de jure political practices: Legal enactments and processes that restrict political and other rights.

democratic equilibrium: A dynamic working balance between and among various groups.

deviance: Actions and behaviors that defy social norms, from crimes to failures to meet social expectations.

differential association theory: A theory that proposes that differences in criminal involvement among groups result from the groups' different definitions of criminality.

differential labeling: The systematic singling out of individuals for labeling as deviant by virtue of their membership in particular groups.

discrimination: The differential allocation of goods, resources, and services, and the limitation of access to full participation in society, based on an individual's membership in a particular social category.

disenfranchisement: Revocation of the right to vote.

drapetomania: A "mental illness" invented to explain why slaves tried to escape slavery.

dysfunctional: Disruptive to social structures, increasing stress and violating norms and rules of engagement.

economic restructuring: The shift from a manufacturing- to a service-based economy in urban areas.

epidemiology: The study of the causes and distribution of diseases and injuries in a population.

ethnicity: Identity that encompasses cultural aspects of an individual's life, including religion, tradition, language, ancestry, nation, geography, history, belief, and practice.

eugenics: A science concerned with improving genetic quality or desired characteristics of a population through practices of breeding and/or extermination.

Fair Deal: A series of federal programs initiated in the late 1940s and early 1950s by President Harry Truman to protect workers from unfair employment practices, raise the minimum wage, and provide housing assistance, among other goals.

formal or overt racism: Discriminatory practices and behaviors that are sanctioned by official rules, codes, or laws of an organization, institution, or society.

frontiers: Contested spaces or borders, such as those between the Spanish, French, and English colonies in the Americas.

functionalist approach to the military: The theory that the military, war, and terrorism serve specific and important tasks, or functions, within society, including socialization, integration, and reduction of conflict.

functionalist theory of sport: A theory that argues that sport fulfills a multitude of societal needs, such as shared values, acquisition of life skills, conflict management, and social mobility.

general strain theory: A theory that proposes that racism produces stressful events and environments, which in turn lead to emotional reactions (such as anger, fear, depression, and rage) that indirectly or directly lead to acts of crime.

genocide: The large-scale, systematic destruction of a people or nation.

gestational surrogacy: The practice of a woman carrying an implanted embryo, not her own, to full term for the biological parent(s).

GI Bill of Rights: The Servicemen's Readjustment Act, passed in 1944 to support veterans. The law included provisions for low-cost guaranteed loans for college degrees, new homes, and businesses; job training; and unemployment benefits.

grandfather clauses: Legal provisions used in the South to restrict voting rights; such clauses granted the right to vote to anyone whose grandfather qualified to vote prior to the Civil War.

Great Compromise of 1787: Compromise reached during the Constitutional Convention, under which the Congress would be composed of two governing bodies, one in which population would determine the number of seats each state would hold (the House of Representatives), and one in which each state would have two members (the Senate). It was further decided that each slave would be counted as three-fifths of a person in population counts determining numbers of representatives as well as presidential electors, and for purposes of taxation.

Great Migration: The movement, from 1916 to 1970, of more than 6 million African Americans out of the rural South to the urban areas of the North, Midwest, and West, in search of greater safety and higher-paying, industrial jobs.

hate strikes: A series of White supremacist wildcat strikes that took place throughout World War II, targeting Black workers competing with White labor.

human capital: The resources that individuals have from their education and training that can be traded for status in an occupational market.

Human Genome Project: An international research collaboration (begun in 1990, completed in 2003) that mapped all human genes.

identity politics: A political process/structure that relies on people of specific religions, racial and ethnic groups, or social backgrounds to form exclusive political alliances.

ideology of domesticity: An ideology in which the home and family became defined as women's realm, and women were not expected to work for pay outside the home. This ideal was generally attainable only by well-off White families.

income: The sum of earnings from work, profit from items sold, and returns on investments.

indentured servants: Persons who are legally bound to work for their masters for a set number of years.

informal or covert racism: Discriminatory practices and behaviors that are not formally sanctioned but rather are often assumed to be the natural, legitimate, and normal workings of society and its institutions.

insider groups: Those groups that hold the bulk of the power in society.

instrumentalism: Derived from the class approach to issues of power, politics, and identity, assumes that the state is dominated by an elite class that controls both the political and economic spheres.

internalized racism: The acceptance by members of minority groups of White society's negative beliefs about, actions toward, and characterizations of them.

intersectional theories: Theories that argue that race and gender (as well as other salient social identities) are intertwined and inseparable, and no individual social identity can be fully comprehended on its own.

interstate forms of war: Conflicts involving national states, such as World Wars I or II; considered to be legitimate wars.

intrastate forms of war: Conflicts that exist or occur within the boundaries of particular states; considered to be less legitimate than interstate wars.

Islamophobia: Intense fear and paranoia regarding Muslims and Arabs, both those living in the United States and those abroad.

Jim Crow laws: Laws designed to preserve Whiteness by criminalizing and sanctioning Blacks, Native Americans, and other racial and ethnic minorities; such laws were widespread across the United States from the 1880s to the 1960s.

Jim Crow racism: Racism supported by the laws and practices that originated in the American South to enforce racial segregation.

left-handed marriages: Temporary alliances between men and women equivalent to common-law marriages, particularly common in the French colonies in the Americas. These unions often resulted in children who served as interpreters and mediators.

legacy of slavery thesis: A theoretical approach that argues that Black family structures are the result of the long history of structural inequality faced by Blacks since slavery.

literacy tests: De jure enactments employed in the South to disadvantage Blacks by restricting the access to vote to those who could read and interpret sections of the state constitution.

marriage promotion programs: State and federal programs that teach relationship and communication skills to women in poverty, with the aim of increasing their chances of marriage, as marriage is assumed to be a solution to poverty for single mothers. No research evidence exists to support the ideas on which such programs are based.

marriage squeeze: A change in demographic patterns leading to fewer marriages and fewer suitable partners for Black women.

Marxist theories: Social theories concerning the impacts of economic change on class relations and conditions, as examined in the work of Karl Marx.

matrix: The surrounding environment in which something (e.g., values, cells, humans) originates, develops, and grows. The concept of a matrix captures the basic sociological understanding that contexts— social, cultural, economic, historical, and otherwise—matter.

Medal of Honor: The highest military honor awarded in the United States for combat heroism; often called the Congressional Medal of Honor because it is awarded in the name of Congress.

medical sociology: The sociological study of the field and practice of medicine and their social effects.

Mendez et al. v. Westminster School District of Orange County: The 1946 U.S. Supreme Court case in which the segregation of Mexicans and non-Mexicans in public schools was found to be unconstitutional.

Mexican–American War: Conflict (1846–48) primarily associated with the U.S. government's desire to annex Texas, California, and other Mexican territories.

microaggressions: Intentional or unintentional brief insults to a person or group; these may be verbal, nonverbal, or behavioral.

military–industrial complex: The informal alliance between the U.S. military and major industries that produce arms and other military materials and seek to influence public policy.

military sociology: The sociological study of armed forces and war.

millennials: People in the generation born roughly from 1980 to 2000.

miscegenation: The mixing of different racial groups.

monopoly and materialist perspectives: Perspectives on the military that posit that military organizations must maintain a legitimate monopoly on the use of force, and the use of this force is uniquely tied to the material instruments of war.

morbidity rates: Rates of disease.

mortality rates: Rates of death.

national origins formula: A formula instituted under the 1921 Emergency Quota Act to set annual limits on the numbers of immigrants admitted to the United States from individual countries; quotas were calculated at 3% of the total number of foreign-born persons from particular countries as recorded in the 1910 U.S. census.

nature perspective: A view of sport that posits that biological differences between genders and among racial, cultural, and national groups account for variations in athletic ability, performance, and success.

neoliberal theory: A social theory that embraces individualism, free markets, free trade, and limited government intervention or regulation. Also known as *market fundamentalism*.

New Deal: A series of programs initiated in the mid-1930s by President Franklin Roosevelt in response to the Great Depression, with the aim of providing economic relief and instituting banking reform.

new immigrants: Immigrants to the United States from Ireland, Switzerland, Poland, Germany, and other Southern European countries between 1886 and 1920.

nonstate actors: Individuals and organizations with economic, political, or social power that allows them to influence both national and international events, typically with violence.

nuclear family: A family consisting of a mother, a father, and their children (biological or adopted), living together. The idea of the "ideal" and "traditional" nuclear family usually assumes a working father and stay-at-home mother.

nurture perspective: A view of sport that sees gender, racial, cultural, and national group differences in athleticism as products of socialization and environment.

old immigrants: Immigrants to the United States from England, Scotland, and Wales.

one-drop rule: The rule, based on a definition in the 1924 Racial Integrity Act, that a person was to be considered Black if he or she had any Black or Native American ancestry at all (i.e., "one drop" of Black blood).

oppression: The systematic devaluing, undermining, marginalizing, and disadvantaging of certain social identity groups in contrast to a privileged norm.

organized crime: Crime involving groups of people participating in highly centralized criminal enterprises.

outsider groups: Those groups within a society that are marginalized and have limited power.

panethnicity: The placing of various regional groups into one large ethnic category.

pedagogy of liberation: From the work of Paulo Freire, an empowering approach to education in which the pedagogical process goes both ways—teachers becoming students, students becoming teachers—leading to altered social structures of liberation and equality.

phenotypical traits: Physical traits such as skin color, hair texture, and facial features typically used to characterize people into racial groups.

pigmentocracies: Governments and other social structures that grant political power based on a hierarchy defined by skin tone, regardless of race or social status.

plaçage: The name given to the social arrangement of left-handed marriages by free people of color in the colonial era. A woman involved in such an arrangement had a status lower than that of a wife but higher than that of a concubine.

Plessy v. Ferguson: The landmark 1896 case in which the U.S. Supreme Court declared the doctrine of separate but equal to be constitutional and the law of the land, leading to Jim Crow segregation in all public facilities.

pluralism: An approach to the issue of power within society that posits that power is decentralized, widely shared, diffuse, and fragmented.

political activism: Actions of political involvement that go beyond voting; includes posting opinions online and participating in letter-writing campaigns, boycotts, protests, and demonstrations.

political identities: Political positions based on the interests and perspectives of social groups with which people identify.

political sociology: The study of government, political behaviors, institutions, and processes that occur between the state and its society and citizens.

politics: All of the processes, activities, and institutions having to do with governance.

poll taxes: Taxes a person must pay to qualify to vote; before the practice of levying such taxes was prohibited, southern states enacted poll tax laws as a way of restricting voting by Blacks.

power: The ability to acquire scarce resources.

power elite model: A model of the distribution of power in society that posits that power is concentrated among discrete elites of relatively equal power; these elites control the resources of significant social institutions.

prejudice: A judgment of an individual or group, often based on race, ethnicity, religion, gender, class, and other social identities.

prison–industrial complex: The system resulting from policies of aggressive policing targeting specific groups, which have greatly expanded the U.S. inmate population. In this system, government and industry uses of surveillance, policing, and imprisonment have been merged in an effort to solve economic, social, and political problems.

privilege: The systemic favoring, valuing, validating, and including of certain social identities over others.

quadroon: A person who is one-fourth Black by descent.

quinceañera: The custom in many Latino cultures of celebrating a girl's transformation from a child to an adult at age 15.

race: A social and cultural system by which people are categorized based on presumed biological differences.

racial caste system: A hierarchical social system based on race that is considered to be permanent.

racial categorizations: Categorizations of people according to race that employ reputed differences in behaviors, skill sets, and inherent intelligence; such categorizations are uniquely social creations that have been purposefully constructed.

racial consciousness: The awareness of race shared by members of a racial group and the wider society.

racial frames: The ideological justifications, processes, procedures, and institutions that define and structure society.

racial profiling: The targeting of particular racial and ethnic groups by law enforcement and private security agencies.

racial violence: Violence in which one racial group is pitted against another.

racism: A system of oppression by which those groups with relatively more social power subordinate members of targeted racial groups who have relatively little social power.

redlining: A practice of evaluating mortgage lending potential for designated areas that typically discriminated against racial and ethnic minorities.

relational aspects of race: A concept that encompasses the defining of categories of race in opposition to each other (e.g., to be White means one is not Black, Asian, Hispanic, or Native American) and according to where they fall along the continuum of hierarchy.

reproductive justice: A concept involving the right to have or not have children, and to parent children in safe and healthy environments.

resistance stories: Narratives that directly challenge stock stories by speaking of defying domination and actively struggling for racial justice and social change.

resocialization: A process whereby an individual is taught new norms and is expected to act accordingly in order to fulfill institutional and social obligations.

restrictive covenants: Rules inserted into real estate contracts that specify which racial groups may purchase the land.

revisionist thesis: A theoretical approach, developed in direct response to stereotypes and the legacy of slavery thesis, involving research that redirects attention to the strength and resilience of Black families.

Seminole Wars: Three conflicts (circa 1817–98) that took place in Florida between the U.S. military and the Seminole, who allied with African escaped slaves and Black Seminoles.

separate spheres: The concept that men's area of influence, or sphere, is the world outside the home, and women's sphere is the home and domesticity. The ideology of separate spheres for men and women developed along with industrialization and created a public/private dichotomy.

settler colonies: Colonies created by external, imperialist nations in which those nations control political, economic, social, and cultural mechanisms through a colonial elite.

silent generation: People born from 1925–45.

slave patrols: Organized groups of White men with police powers who systematically enforced the slave codes in the pre–Civil War South.

social cohesion: A sense of togetherness in a social structure.

social construction of race: The concept that the outcomes of the systematic distribution of rewards, privileges, and sanctions across populations through time have produced and reproduced social hierarchies that reflect society's racial categorizations.

social Darwinism: An ideology that attempts to apply Charles Darwin's theory of natural selection to people at the individual or group level over a few generations, based on

a misguided and incorrect interpretation of Darwin's work.

social disorganization: A theory that links crime to neighborhood ecological patterns.

social institutions: Patterned and structured sets of roles and behaviors centered on the performance of important social tasks within any given society.

socialization: The process through which individuals are taught the norms and expectations of their societies.

split labor market: A labor market in which higher-paid workers, largely White, try to protect their jobs and wages (often through unions) by excluding new groups (often minorities) entering the labor market from the higher-paying jobs.

sport: A range of activities that involve physical exertion and skill. These activities are organized around sets of rules and can be played at either the individual or the team level.

stereotypes: Assumptions or generalizations applied to an entire group.

stock stories: The narratives of the dominant group, often embraced by those whose oppression these stories reinforce. Such stories are shaped by the White racial frame, and they inform and organize the practices of social institutions and are encoded in law, public policy, public space, history, and culture.

structural inequities: Institutional processes that deferentially distribute rewards such as status, privilege, compensation and access according to membership in specific categories or group membership.

structuralism: Derived from the class approach to issues of power, politics, and identity, assumes that the state and all political institutions exist relatively independent of each other and are essentially by-products of conflict between and within class groups.

symbolic interaction perspective on sport: An approach that posits that sports are created and maintained by shared meanings and social interaction.

symbolic interactionist approach to the military: A theoretical approach concerned with how people attach meaning to things (flags and memorials), events (wars), and other representations (heroes and patriotism) in support of war, terrorism, and the military.

systemic nature of racial oppression: The manifestation of core racist realities, values, and ideologies in all of the major institutions within society.

terrorism: The unlawful use of force, particularly against civilians, in pursuit of political, economic, or social aims.

Title IX: Legislation enacted in 1972 that declared that "no person in the United States shall, on the basis of sex, be excluded from participation in, be denied the benefits of, or be subjected to discrimination under any program or activity receiving federal financial assistance."

traditional medicine: Physical, mental, and spiritual healing that makes use of indigenous knowledge, skills, and practices that have been passed down over generations.

Trail of Tears: Name given by Native Americans to the forced relocation, 1838–39, of tribal groups from their traditional lands to Indian Territory, west of the Mississippi River; during this relocation, thousands died of exposure and disease.

transforming stories: Narratives that demonstrate how change and social justice come about.

transmigrants: People who live their lives crossing national borders, for whom participating in more than one nation is central to their lives.

triple glass ceiling: Limits placed on women because of threefold discrimination based on race, gender, and class.

Turner thesis: The theory, developed by historian Frederick J. Turner in the late 19th century, that the American identity—including democratic governance, rugged individualism, innovative thinking, and egalitarian viewpoints—was forged in the nation's frontier experience.

war: The use of organized force; a state of armed conflict between nations, states, or groups within a nation or state.

War of 1812: A military conflict between the United States and Great Britain that began because of British violations of U.S. maritime and trading rights with Europe and quickly became a war pitting the United States against Native Americans, who forged alliances with Britain and France.

war on terrorism: A series of military and legislative campaigns that began after the September 11, 2001, attacks on the United States.

wealth: The market value of all assets owned (such as homes, cars, artwork, jewelry, businesses, and savings and retirement accounts) minus any debts owed (such as credit card debts, mortgages, and college loans).

welfare: Policies and programs designed to support people in great financial need. Examples of forms of welfare are food stamps, Social Security benefits, Medicare, and Medicaid.

welfare fraud: The illegal use of deception to collect more funds than allowed from state welfare systems.

White flight: The movement of Whites from urban areas to suburbs in response to Black civil rights activism.

White normative structures: Norms and institutions that obscure the racial intent of laws, practices, and behaviors that preserve and (re)create societal benefits for White people, creating the illusion that White privilege is natural and normal.

White privilege: The advantage that White people have (over Blacks, Native Americans, Asians, Hispanics, and others) as the result of laws, practices, and behaviors that preserve and (re)create societal benefits for them.

white-collar crime: Crime, typically nonviolent, committed by business or government professionals; the motivation for such crime is often financial.

Whiteness studies: An interdisciplinary subfield of scholarship examining Whiteness and White privilege that includes contributions by literary theorists, legal scholars, anthropologists, historians, psychologists, and sociologists.

World War II: A major worldwide conflict (U.S. involvement 1941–45) that spanned Europe, Africa, Asia, and the Middle East.

■ ■ REFERENCES

■ CHAPTER 1

Adams, Maurianne, Lee Anne Bell, and Pat Griffin, eds. 1997. *Teaching for Diversity and Social Justice: A Sourcebook.* New York: Routledge.

African American Policy Forum. 2009. "A Primer on Intersectionality." Accessed April 7, 2017. http://static .squarespace.com/static/53f2 0d90e4b0b80451158d8c/53 f399a5e4b029c2ffbe26c c/53f399c8e4b029c2ffbe 2b28/1408473544947/598 19079-Intersectionality-Primer .pdf?format=original.

Almeida, Rhea, Pilar Hernández-Wolfe, and Carolyn Tubbs. 2011. "Cultural Equity: Bridging the Complexity of Social Identities with Therapeutic Practices." *International Journal of Narrative Therapy and Community Work* 3: 43–56.

Anderson, Monica. 2017. "African Immigrant Population in U.S. Steadily Climbs." Fact Tank, Pew Research Center, February 14. Accessed April 7, 2017. http://www .pewresearch.org/fact-tank/2017/02/14/african-immigrant-population-in-u-s-steadily-climbs.

Anzaldúa, Gloria. 2007. *Borderlands/La Frontera: The New Mestiza.* 3rd ed. San Francisco: Aunt Lute Books.

Barnett, Bernice McNair. 1995. "Black Women's Collectivist Movement Organizations: Their Struggles during the 'Doldrums.'" In *Feminist Organizations: Harvest of the New Women's Movement,* edited by Myra Marx Ferree and Patricia Yancey Martin. Philadelphia: Temple University Press.

Barzun, Jacques. (1937) 1965. *Race: A Study in Superstition.* New York: Harper.

Battiste, Marie. 2002. "Indigenous Knowledge and Pedagogy in First Nations Education: A Literature Review with Recommendations." Paper prepared for the National Working Group on Education and the Minister of Indian Affairs, Indian and Northern Affairs Canada. Accessed July 19, 2011. http:// www.afn.ca/uploads/files/ education/24._2002_oct_ marie_battiste_ indigenousknowledge andpedagogy_lit_review_for_ min_working_group.pdf

Baunach, Dawn Michelle. 2012. "Changing Same-Sex Marriage Attitudes in America from 1988 through 2010." *Public Opinion Quarterly* 76, no. 2: 364–78.

Bell, Lee Anne. 2010. *Storytelling for Social Justice: Connecting Narrative and the Arts in Antiracist Teaching.* New York: Routledge.

Bonilla-Silva, Eduardo. 2003. "'New Racism,' Color-Blind Racism, and the Future of Whiteness in America." In *White Out: The Continuing Significance of Race,* edited by Ashley W. Doane and Eduardo Bonilla-Silva. New York: Routledge.

———. 2010. *Racism without Racists: Color-Blind Racism and the Persistence of Racial Inequality in the United States.*

3rd ed. Lanham, MD: Rowman & Littlefield.

Brandt-Rauf, P. W., and S. I. Brandt-Rauf. 1987. "History of Occupational Medicine: Relevance of Imhotep and the Edwin Smith Papyrus." *British Journal of Industrial Medicine* 44: 68–70.

Brodkin, Karen. 1998. *How Jews Became White Folks and What That Says about Race in America.* New Brunswick, NJ: Rutgers University Press.

Brown, Catrina, and Tod Augusta-Scott, eds. 2007. *Narrative Therapy: Making Meaning, Making Lives.* Thousand Oaks, CA: Sage.

Bush, Melanie E. L. 2011. *Everyday Forms of Whiteness: Understanding Race in a "Post-racial" World.* 2nd ed. Lanham, MD: Rowman & Littlefield.

Case, Kim, ed. 2013. *Deconstructing Privilege: Teaching and Learning as Allies in the Classroom.* New York: Routledge.

Clandinin, D. Jean, and Heather Raymond. 2006. "Note on Narrating Disability." *Equity & Excellence in Education* 39, no. 2: 101–4.

Coates, Rodney D. 2011. "Covert Racism: An Introduction." In *Covert Racism: Theories, Institutions, and Experiences,* edited by Rodney D. Coates. Leiden, Netherlands: Brill.

Collins, Patricia Hill. 2000. *Black Feminist Thought: Knowledge, Consciousness, and the Politics of Empowerment.* 2nd ed. New York: Routledge.

———. 2004. *Black Sexual Politics: African Americans, Gender, and the New Racism.* New York: Routledge.

Connor, David J. 2006. "Michael's Story: 'I Get into Such Trouble Just by Walking': Narrative Knowing and Life at the Intersections of Learning Disability, Race, and Class." *Equity & Excellence in Education* 39, no. 2: 154–65.

Crenshaw, Kimberlé. 1991. "Mapping the Margins: Intersectionality, Identity Politics, and Violence against Women of Color." *Stanford Law Review* 43, no. 6: 1241–99.

Cunnigen, Donald, and Marino A. Bruce, eds. 2010. *Race in the Age of Obama.* Bingley, England: Emerald Books.

Dasien, Andrew. 2008. "Hutu and Tutsi before Colonialism." All Quiet on the Quaker Front: A U.S. Quaker in Burundi, June 12. Accessed August 3, 2015. http://www .quakerfront.com/2008/ 06/12/hutu-tutsi-before- colonialism.

Davis, Angela Y. 1983. *Women, Race and Class.* New York: Vintage Books.

———. 1990. *Women, Culture and Politics.* New York: Vintage Books.

Desmond, Matthew, and Mustafa Emirbayer. 2010. *Racial Domination, Racial Progress: The Sociology of Race in America.* New York: McGraw-Hill.

Espiritu, Yen Le. 1994. *Asian American Panethnicity: Bridging Institutions and Identities.* Philadelphia: Temple University Press.

Feagin, Joe R. 2000. *Racist America: Roots, Current Realities, and Future Reparations.* New York: Routledge.

———. 2010. *The White Racial Frame: Centuries of Racial Framing and Counter-framing.* New York: Routledge.

Feagin, Joe R., and José A. Cobas. 2013. *Latinos Facing Racism: Discrimination, Resistance, and Endurance.* Boulder, CO: Paradigm.

Fearon, James D. 2002. "Ethnic Structure and Cultural Diversity around the World: A Cross-National Data Set on Ethnic Groups." Paper presented at the annual meeting of the American Political Science Association, Boston, August 28.

Ferber, Abby L. 2012. "The Culture of Privilege: Color- Blindness, Postfeminism, and Christonormativity." *Journal of Social Issues* 68, no. 1: 63–77.

Ferber, Abby L., Christina M. Jiménez, Andrea O'Reilly Herrera, and Dena R. Samuels, eds. 2009. *The Matrix Reader: Examining the Dynamics of Oppression and Privilege.* Boston: McGraw Hill.

Ferber, Abby L., and Dena R. Samuels. 2010. "Oppression without Bigots." SWS Factsheet, Sociologists for Women in Society. Accessed April 4, 2017. https://www .socwomen.org/wp-content/ uploads/2010/05/fact_3- 2010-oppression.pdf.

Ferrante, Joan, and Prince Brown Jr. 2001. *The Social Construction of Race and Ethnicity in the United States.* 2nd ed. Upper Saddle River, NJ: Prentice Hall.

Fields, Karen E., and Barbara J. Fields. 2012. *Racecraft: The Soul of Inequality in American Life.* London: Verso Books.

Fish, Jefferson M. 2011. "What Does the Brazilian Census Tell Us about Race?" Looking in the Cultural Mirror (blog), *Psychology Today,* December 6. Accessed April 4, 2017. https://www .psychologytoday.com/ blog/looking-in-the-cultural- mirror/201112/what-does- the-brazilian-census-tell-us- about-race.

Freedman, Estelle B. 2002. *No Turning Back: The History of Feminism and the Future of Women.* New York: Ballantine Books.

Frye, Marilyn. 2007. *The Politics of Reality*: Essays in Feminist Theory. Berkeley, CA: Crossing Press.

Gallagher, Charles. 2009. "Color- Blinded America or How the Media and Politics Have Made Racism and Racial Inequality Yesterday's Social Problem." In *The Matrix Reader: Examining the Dynamics of Oppression and Privilege,* edited by Abby L. Ferber, Christina M. Jiménez, Andrea O'Reilly Herrera, and Dena R. Samuels, 548–51. Boston: McGraw-Hill.

Gans, Herbert J. 1971. "The Uses of Poverty: The Poor Pay All." *Social Policy* 2, no. 2 (July/August): 14–21.

Garcia, Alma M. 1997. *Chicana Feminist Thought: The Basic Historical Writings.* New York: Routledge.

Gould, Stephen Jay. 1981. *The Mismeasure of Man.* New York: W. W. Norton.

Graham, David. 2016. "The Stubborn Persistence of Confederate Monuments." *Atlantic,* April. Accessed April 30, 2017. https://www .theatlantic.com/politics/ archive/2016/04/the-stubborn- persistence-of-confederate- monuments/479751.

Grosfoguel, Ramán. 2004. "Race and Ethnicity or Racialized

Ethnicities? Identities within Global Coloniality." *Ethnicities* 4: 315–36.

Haney López, Ian. 2006. *White by Law: The Legal Construction of Race.* Rev. ed. New York: New York University Press.

Hannah-Jones, Nikole. 2016. "The End of the Postracial Myth." *New York Times Magazine,* November 15. Accessed March 5, 2017. https://www.nytimes.com/interactive/2016/11/20/magazine/donald-trumps-america-iowa-race.html.

Harding, Sandra, ed. 1993. *The "Racial" Economy of Science: Toward a Democratic Future.* Bloomington: Indiana University Press.

Hartigan, John, Jr. 2010. *Race in the 21st Century: Ethnographic Approaches.* New York: Oxford University Press.

Hillinbrand, Carole. 2000. *The Crusades: Islamic Perspectives.* New York: Routledge.

hooks, bell. 2000. *Feminist Theory from Margin to Center.* 2nd ed. Cambridge, MA: South End Press.

Hull, Gloria T., Patricia Bell Scott, and Barbara Smith. 2015. *All the Women Are White, All the Blacks Are Men, but Some of Us Are Brave: Black Women's Studies.* 2nd ed. New York: Feminist Press.

Irons, Jenny. 2010. *Reconstituting Whiteness: The Mississippi State Sovereignty Commission.* Nashville: Vanderbilt University Press.

Jacobson, Matthew Frye. 1998. *Whiteness of a Different Color: European Immigrants and the Alchemy of Race.* Cambridge, MA: Harvard University Press.

Johnson, Allan G. 2006. *Privilege, Power, and Difference.* 2nd ed. Boston: McGraw-Hill.

Ken, Ivy. 2008. "Beyond the Intersection: A New Culinary Metaphor for Race-Class-Gender Studies." *Sociological Theory* 26, no. 2: 152–72.

Khan, M. A. 2009. *Islamic Jihad: A Legacy of Forced Conversion, Imperialism, and Slavery.* Bloomington, IN: iUniverse.

Landrieu, Mitch. 2017. "We Can't Walk Away from This Truth." *Atlantic,* May. Accessed April 30, 2017. https://www.theatlantic.com/politics/archive/2017/05/we-cant-walk-away-from-this-truth/527721.

Linshi, Jack. 2014. "10 Million Americans Switched Their Race or Ethnicity for the Census." *Time,* August 7. Accessed April 7, 2017. http://time.com/3087649/census-race-ethnicity-report.

Lorde, Audre. (1984) 2007. *Sister Outsider: Essays and Poems.* Berkeley, CA: Crossing Press.

Markus, Hazel Rose, and Paula M. L. Moya. 2010. *Doing Race: 21 Essays for the 21st Century.* New York: W. W. Norton.

McIntosh, Peggy. 1988. "White Privilege and Male Privilege: A Personal Account of Coming to See Correspondences through Work in Women's Studies." Working Paper 189, Wellesley College Center for Research on Women.

McNamee, Stephen, and Robert K. Miller Jr. 2014. *The Meritocracy Myth.* 3rd ed. Lanham, MD: Rowman & Littlefield.

Moore, Eddie, Jr., Marguerite W. Penick-Parks, and Ali Michael, eds. 2015. *Everyday White People Confront Racial and Social Injustice: 15 Stories.* Sterling, VA: Stylus.

Morrison, Toni. 1992. *Playing in the Dark: Whiteness and the Literary Imagination.* New York: Vintage Books.

Mills, Charles. 1997. *The Racial Contract.* Ithaca, NY: Cornell University Press.

National Education Association. 2015. "Ensuring Safe Schools for All Students." Accessed August 3, 2015. http://www.nea.org/tools/30437.htm.

Omi, Michael, and Howard Winant. 1994. *Racial Formation in the United States: From the 1960s to the 1990s.* 2nd ed. New York: Routledge.

Ortiz, Vilma, and Edward Telles. 2012. "Racial Identity and Racial Treatment of Mexican Americans." *Race and Social Problems* 4, no. 1 (April): 41–56.

Painter, Nell Irvin. 2015. "What Is Whiteness?" *New York Times Sunday Review,* June 6. Accessed August 4, 2015. http://www.nytimes.com/2015/06/21/opinion/sunday/what-is-whiteness.html?_r=0.

Park, Madison. 2017. "Removal of Confederate Monuments Stirs Backlash in Statehouses." CNN, May 12. Accessed June 10, 2017. http://www.cnn.com/2017/05/12/us/confederate-monument-state-bills/index.html.

Perez, Chris. 2015. "Meet the Biracial Twins No One Believes Are Sisters." *New York Post,* March 2. Accessed June 7, 2017. http://nypost.com/2015/03/02/meet-the-bi-racial-twins-no-one-believes-are-sisters.

Plaut, Victoria C. 2010. "Diversity Science: Why and How Difference Makes a Difference." *Psychological*

Inquiry 21, no. 2: 77–99. doi:10.1080/10478401003 676501.

Portis, Larry. 2007. "'Arabs' and 'Jews' as Significant Others: Zionism and the Ambivalence of 'Orientalism' in the United-Statesian Imagination." *Middle Ground: Journal of Literary and Cultural Encounters* 1: 75–96.

Radford, Tim. 2015. "Irish DNA Originated in Middle East and Eastern Europe." *Guardian,* December 28. Accessed April 5, 2017. https://www.theguardian .com/science/2015/dec/28/ origins-of-the-irish-down-to- mass-migration-ancient-dna- confirms.

Ritvo, Harriet. 1997. *The Platypus and the Mermaid, and Other Figments of the Classifying Imagination.* Cambridge, MA: Harvard University Press.

Robnett, Belinda. 1999. *How Long? How Long? African- American Women in the Struggle for Civil Rights.* Oxford: Oxford University Press.

Ruiz, Vicki L. 1999. *From Out of the Shadows: Mexican Women in Twentieth-Century America.* Oxford: Oxford University Press.

Rumbaut, Ruben. 2011. "Pigments of Our Imagination: The Racialization of the Hispanic-Latino Category." Immigration Policy Institute, April 27. Accessed September 13, 2016. http:// www.migrationpolicy .org/article/pigments-our- imagination-racialization- hispanic-latino-category.

Russell, Joseph, and Jeanne Batalova. 2012. "European Immigrants in the United States." Migration Policy Institute, July 26. Accessed

August 18, 2016. http://www .migrationpolicy.org/article/ european-immigrants-united- states-1.

Segal, Ronald. 2001. *Islam's Black Slaves: The Other Black Diaspora.* New York: Farrar, Straus and Giroux.

Smaje, Chris. 2000. *Natural Hierarchies: The Historical Sociology of Race and Caste.* Oxford: Blackwell.

Smedley, Audrey. 2007. *Race in North America: Origin and Evolution of a Worldview.* 3rd ed. Boulder, CO: Westview Press.

Snively, Gloria, and John Corsiglia. 2001. "Discovering Indigenous Science: Implications for Science Education." *Science Education* 85, no. 1: 6–34.

Sollors, Werner, ed. 1989. *The Invention of Ethnicity.* New York: Oxford University Press.

Spade, Joan Z., and Jeanne H. Ballantine, eds. 2011. *Schools and Society: A Sociological Approach to Education.* Thousand Oaks, CA: Sage.

Spelman, Elizabeth V. 1988. *Inessential Woman: Problems of Exclusion in Feminist Thought.* Boston: Beacon Press.

Sue, Derald Wing. 2010. *Microaggressions in Everyday Life: Race, Gender, and Sexual Orientation.* Hoboken, NJ: John Wiley.

Takei, Isao, and Arthur Sakamoto. 2011. "Poverty among Asian Americans in the 21st Century." *Sociological Perspectives* 54, no. 2: 251–76.

Telles, Edward, and the Project on Ethnicity and Race in Latin America. 2014. *Pigmentocracies: Ethnicity, Race, and Color in Latin America.* Chapel Hill:

University of North Carolina Press.

Tochluk, Shelly. 2008. *Witnessing Whiteness: First Steps toward an Antiracist Practice and Culture.* Lanham, MD: Rowman & Littlefield.

U.S. Bureau of Labor Statistics. 2010. *Highlights of Women's Earnings in 2009.* Report 1025, June. Washington, DC: U.S. Department of Labor. Accessed April 1, 2017. https://www .bls.gov/opub/reports/ womens-earnings/archive/ womensearnings_2009.pdf

U.S. Census Bureau. 2012. "2010 Census Shows Nearly Half of American Indians and Alaska Natives Report Multiple Races." Press release, January 25. Accessed April 1, 2017. https://www.census .gov/newsroom/releases/ archives/2010_census/cb12- cn06.html.

———. 2015. "Annual Estimates of the Resident Population by Sex, Race Alone or in Combination, and Hispanic Origin for the United States, States, and Counties: April 1, 2010 to July 1, 2014." American FactFinder. Accessed June 12, 2017. https://factfinder.census .gov/faces/tableservices/ jsf/pages/productview .xhtml?src=bkmk.

Van Ausdale, Debra, and Joe R. Feagin. 2001. *The First R: How Children Learn Race and Racism.* Lanham, MD: Rowman & Littlefield.

Villalon, Roberta. 2010. *Violence against Latina Immigrants: Citizenship, Inequality, and Community.* New York: New York University Press.

Wade, Lizzie. 2014. "Genetic Study Reveals Surprising Ancestry of Many Americans." *Science,*

December 18. Accessed April 2, 2017. http://www.sciencemag.org/news/2014/12/genetic-study-reveals-surprising-ancestry-many-americans.

Walters, Alicia. 2015. "I Became a Black Woman in Spokane. But, Rachel Dolezal, I Was a Black Girl First." *Guardian,* June 14. Accessed August 3, 2015. http://www.theguardian.com/commentisfree/2015/jun/14/became-a-black-woman-spokane-rachel-dolezal-black-girl.

Ware, Kallistos. 1980. *The Orthodox Church.* New York: Penguin.

Warren, Carroll. 1993. *The Glory of Christendom.* Front Royal, VA: Christendom Press.

Wootson, Cleve R., Jr. 2017. "New Orleans Protesters Launch Last-Ditch Effort to Protect Confederate Monuments." *Chicago Tribune,* April 30. Accessed April 30, 2017. http://www.chicagotribune.com/news/nationworld/ct-new-orleans-confederate-monuments-20170430-story.html.

Wright, Louis B. 1970. *Gold, Glory and the Gospel.* New York: Atheneum Press.

Yoshino, Kenji. 2007. *Covering: The Hidden Assault on Our Civil Liberties.* New York: Random House.

Yudell, Michael, Dorothy Roberts, Rob DeSalle, Rob, and Sarah Tishkoff. 2016. "Taking Race Out of Human Genetics." *Science* 351, no. 6273: 564–65.

Zong, Jie, and Jeanne Batalova. 2016. "Asian Immigrants in the United States." Migration Policy Institute, January 6. Accessed April 4, 2017. http://www.migrationpolicy.org/article/asian-immigrants-united-states.

Zuberi, Tukufu. 2001. *Thicker than Blood: How Racial Statistics Lie.* Minneapolis: University of Minnesota Press.

■ CHAPTER 2

Adelman, Jeremy, and Stephen Aron. 1999. "From Borderlands to Borders: Empires, Nation-States, and the Peoples in between in North American History." *American Historical Review* 104, no. 3 (June): 814–41.

Alegria, Ricardo. 1990. *Juan Garrido, el Conquistador Negro en Antillas, Florida, Mexico y California c. 1503–1540.* San Juan, Puerto Rico: Centro de Estudios Avanzados de Puerto y el Caribe.

Allen, Theodore W. 1997. *The Invention of the White Race: The Origin of Racial Oppression in Anglo-America.* New York: Verso Books.

——. 2012. *The Invention of the White Race: The Origin of Racial Oppression in Anglo-America.* Vol. 2. New York: Verso Books.

Aptheker, Herbert. 1993. *African Negro Slave Revolts.* 6th ed. New York: International Publishers.

Arends, Jacques. 1995. "Demographic Factors in the Formation of Sranan." In *The Early Stages of Creolization,* edited by Jacques Arends, 233–86. Amsterdam: John Benjamins.

Arnaiz-Villena, C. Parga-Lorazano, E. Moreno, C. Areces, D. Rey, and P. Gomez-Prieto. 2010. "The Origin of Amerindians and the Peopling of the Americas According to HLA Genes: Admixture with Asian and Pacific People." *Current Genomics* 11, no. 2 (April): 103–14.

Asbury, Herbert. (1936) 2003. *The French Quarter: An Informal History of the New Orleans Underworld.* New York: Alfred A. Knopf.

Barrera, Mario. 1976. "Colonial Labor and Theories of Inequality: The Case of International Harvester." *Review of Radical Political Economics* 8, no. 2: 1–18.

Beal, Timothy K. 2008. *Religion in America: A Short History.* London: Oxford University Press.

Beckles, Hilary McD. 1990. "A 'Riotous and Unruly Lot': Irish Indentured Servants and Freemen in the English West Indies, 1644–1713." *William and Mary Quarterly* 47, no. 4 (October): 503–22.

Belchior, Elias. 2007. "White Rights, Black Rights, Human Rights." In *Human Rights in Brazil 2007,* edited by Evanize Sydow e Maria Luisa Mendonça. São Paulo: Social Network for Justice and Human Rights.

Belmessous, Saliha. 2005. "Assimilation and Racialism in Seventeenth and Eighteenth-Century French Colonial Policy." *American Historical Review* 110, no. 2 (April): 322–49.

Beltran, Erika. 2010. Review of *New England Frontier: Puritans and Indians 1620–1675,* by Alden T. Vaughan. Race, Class and Ethnicity in American History (blog), October 17. Accessed May 30, 2017. http://todiefree .blogspot.com/2010/10/new- england-frontier-puritans-and- .html.

Berlin, Ira. 1998. *Many Thousands Gone: The First Two Centuries of Slavery in North America.* Boston: Harvard University Press.

———. 2003. *Generations of Captivity: A History of African-American Slaves.* Cambridge, MA: Harvard University Press.

Bernhard, Virginia. 1999. *Slaves and Slaveholders in Bermuda, 1616–1782.* Columbia: University of Missouri Press.

Biancardi, Paul. 2015. "ESPN 100: Where Would We Have Ranked Thon Maker?" ESPN, August 26. Accessed June 13, 2017. http:// www.espn.com/blog/ ncbrecruiting/on-the-trail/ insider/post?id=14409.

Blackman, Robin. 1997. *The Making of New World Slavery: From the Baroque to the Modern, 1492–1800.* New York: Verso Books.

Blauner, Robert. 1972. *Racial Oppression in America.* New York: Harper and Brothers.

Bonilla-Silva, Eduardo. 2008. "'Look, a Negro': Reflections on the Human Rights Approach to Racial Inequality." In *Globalization and America: Race, Human Rights, and Inequality,* edited by Angela J. Hattery, David G. Embrick, and Earl Smith, 9–22. Lanham, MD: Rowman & Littlefield.

Bowles, Samuel, and Herbert Gintis. 2011. *Schooling in Capitalist America: Educational Reform and the Contradictions of Economic Life.* New York: Haymarket Books.

Boxer, C. R. 1975. *Women in Iberian Expansion Overseas, 1415–1815.* New York: Oxford University Press.

Bradford, William. 1901. *Of Plymouth Plantation.* Boston: Wright and Potter.

Breen, T. H. 1973. "A Changing Labor Force and Race Relations in Virginia 1660–1710." *Journal of Social History* 7, no. 1 (Autumn): 3–25.

Brown, Kathleen. 1996. *Good Wives, Nasty Wenches, and Anxious Patriarchs: Gender, Race, and Power in Colonial Virginia.* Chapel Hill: University of North Carolina Press.

Buchanan, Kelly. 2011. "Slavery in the French Colonies: Le Code Noir (the Black Code) of 1685." In Custodia Legis (blog), Law Library of Congress, January 13. Accessed May 5, 2016. https://blogs.loc.gov/ law/2011/01/slavery-in-the- french-colonies.

Caspari, Rachel 2003. "From Types to Populations: A Century of Race, Physical Anthropology, and the Anthropological Association." *American Anthropology* 105, no. 1: 65–76.

Chambliss, William J. 1989. "State-Organized Crime— The American Society of Criminology, 1988 Presidential Address." *Criminology* 27, no. 2: 183–208.

Childress, Sarah. 2014. "School Segregation Is Back, 60 Years after 'Brown.'" *Frontline,* PBS, May 15. Accessed April 9, 2017. http://www.pbs.org/wgbh/ frontline/article/report- school-segregation-is-back- 60-years-after-brown.

Clayton, Lawrence. 2009. "Bartolomé de las Casas

and the African Slave Trade." *History Compass* 7, no. 6 (November): 1526–41.

Clough, Patricia Ticineto. 2003. "Affect and Control: Rethinking the Body 'beyond Sex and Gender.'" *Feminist Theory* 4, no. 3: 359–64.

Cohn, D'Vera, and Andrea Caumont. 2016. "10 Demographic Trends That Are Shaping the U.S. and the World." Fact Tank, Pew Research Center, March 31. Accessed June 20, 2017. http://www.pewresearch.org/ fact-tank/2016/03/31/10- demographic-trends-that- are-shaping-the-u-s-and- the-world.

Colburn, David R., and Jane L. Landers, eds. 1995. *The African American Heritage of Florida.* Gainesville: University Press of Florida.

Conley, Dalton. 2011. *You May Ask Yourself. A Guide to Thinking Like a Sociologist.* 2nd ed. New York: W. W. Norton.

Cook, Sherburne F. 1976. *The Population of the California Indians, 1769–1970.* Berkeley: University of California Press.

Corris, Peter. 1973. *Passage, Port and Plantation: A History of Solomon Islands Migration, 1870–1940.* Melbourne: Melbourne University Press.

Deagan, Kathleen. 1983. "Spanish-Indian Interaction in Sixteenth-Century Florida and Hispaniola." In *Cultures in Contact,* edited by William Fitzhugh, 281–318. Washington, DC: Smithsonian Institution Press.

———. 1985. *Spanish St. Augustine: The Archaeology of a Colonial Creole Community.* New York: Academic Press.

——. 1996. "Colonial Transformations: Euro-American Cultural Genesis in the Early Spanish American Colonies." *Journal of Anthropological Research* 52, no. 2 (Summer): 135–60.

——. 2004. "Reconsidering Taíno Social Dynamics after Spanish Conquest: Gender and Class in Culture Contact Studies." *American Antiquity* 69: 597–626.

Deagan, Kathleen, and José María Cruxent. 1993. "From Contact to *Criollos*: The Archaeology of Spanish Colonization in Hispaniola." *Proceedings of the British Academy* 81: 67–104.

——. 2002. *Columbus's Outpost among the Taínos: Spain and America at La Isabela, 1493–1498.* New Haven, CT: Yale University Press.

Deloria, Vine, Jr. 1988. *Custer Died for Your Sins: An Indian Manifesto.* Oklahoma City: University of Oklahoma Press.

Diamond, Jared. 1999. *Guns, Germs, and Steel: The Fates of Human Societies.* New York: W. W. Norton.

Diggs, Irene. 1953. "Color in Colonial Spanish America." *Journal of Negro History* 38, no. 4 (October): 403–27.

Fanon, Frantz. 1965. *The Wretched of the Earth.* New York: Grove Press.

Foner, Eric. 2006. *Give Me Liberty! An American History.* Vol. 1. New York: W. W. Norton.

Frank, Andre Gunder. 1976. *On Capitalist Underdevelopment.* New York: Oxford University Press.

Frazier, E. Franklin. 1949. *The Negro in the United States.* New York: Macmillan.

Fry, Richard. 2011. "Hispanic College Enrollment Spikes, Narrowing Gaps with Other Groups." Pew Research Center, August 25. Accessed June 13, 2017. http://www.pewhispanic.org/2011/08/25/hispanic-college-enrollment-spikes-narrowing-gaps-with-other-groups.

Galenson, David W. 1984. "The Rise and Fall of Indentured Servitude in the Americas: An Economic Analysis." *Journal of Economic History* 44, no. 1 (March): 1–26.

Gallay, Alan. 2002. *The Indian Slave Trade: The Rise of the English Empire in the American South, 1670–1717.* New Haven, CT: Yale University Press.

Gardner, Charles F. 2017. "Bucks Rookie Thon Maker Could Be All-Star in the Making." *Milwaukee Journal Sentinel,* February 19. Accessed April 5, 2017. http://www.jsonline.com/story/sports/nba/bucks/2017/02/19/bucks-rookie-thon-maker-could-all-star-making/98043082.

Garrigus, John D. 2007. "Opportunist or Patriot? Julien Raimond (1744–1801) and the Haitian Revolution." *Slavery and Abolition* 28, no. 1 (April): 1–21.

Gill, Harold B. 2003. "Colonial Germ Warfare." *Colonial Williamsburg Journal* 4 (Spring). Accessed May 30, 2017. http://www.history.org/foundation/journal/spring04/warfare.cfm.

Gould, Stephen Jay. 1981. *The Mismeasure of Man.* New York: W. W. Norton.

Goyette, Braden, and Alissa Scheller. 2016. "15 Charts That Prove That We're Far from Post-racial." Huffington Post, March 3. Accessed June 13, 2017. http://www.huffingtonpost.com/2014/07/02/civil-rights-act-anniversary-racism-charts_n_5521104.html.

Greene, Lorenzo Johnston. 1942. *The Negro in Colonial New England, 1620–1776.* New York: Columbia University Press.

Greer, Allan. 1997. *The People of New France.* Toronto: University of Toronto Press.

Gutiérrez, Gustavo. 1974. *A Theology of Liberation.* Maryknoll, NY: Orbis Books.

Gutiérrez, José Angel, Michelle Meléndez, and Sonia Adriana Noyola. 2007. *Chicanas in Charge: Texas Women in the Public Arena.* Lanham, MD: AltaMira Press.

Haan, Richard L. 1973. "Another Example of Stereotypes on the Early American Frontier: The Imperialistic Historians and the American Indian." *Ethnohistory* 20, no. 2 (Spring): 143–52.

Hall, Gwendolyn Midlo. 1992. *Africans in Colonial Louisiana.* Baton Rouge: Louisiana State University Press.

Harper, Douglas. 2003. "Colonial Slavery: Northern Profits from Slavery." Varsity Tutors, Archiving Early America. Accessed May 30, 2017. http://www.earlyamerica.com/review/2004_summer_fall/northern_profits.htm.

Hening, William Waller. 1819. *The Statutes at Large, Being the Collection of All the Laws of Virginia from the Third Session of the Legislature in the Year 1619.* 13 vols. Richmond, VA: W. Gray Printers.

Holmes, Jack D. L. 1970. "The Abortive Slave Revolt at Pointe Coupee, Louisiana, 1795." *Louisiana History* 11, no. 4: 341–62.

Hugh, Thomas. 1997. *The Slave Trade.* New York: Simon & Schuster.

Jackson, Robert. 2006. "República de Indios." In *Iberia and the Americas: Culture, Politics, and History—A Multidisciplinary Encyclopedia,* edited by J. Michael Francis, 901–3. Santa Barbara, CA: ABC-CLIO.

Janiewski, Dolores. 1995. "Gendering, Racializing and Classifying: Settler Colonization in the United States, 1950–1990." In *Unsettling Settler Societies: Articulations of Gender, Race, Ethnicity and Class,* edited by Daiva K. Stasiulis and Nira Yuval-Davis. London: Sage.

Jennings, Francis. 1975. *The Invasion of America: Indians, Colonialism, and the Cant of Conquest.* New York: W. W. Norton.

Karenga, Maulana. 2002. *Introduction to Black Studies.* 3rd ed. Los Angeles: University of Sankore Press.

Keen, Benjamin, and Keith Haynes. 2009. *A History of Latin America.* Boston: Houghton Mifflin Harcourt.

Kit-Powell, Rodney. 2013. "Seminole Wars Shaped Florida's History." *Tampa Tribune,* July 14. Accessed September 9, 2013. http:// tbo.com/events/seminole-wars-shaped-floridas-history-20130714.

Kotkin, Joel. 2010. "The Changing Demographics of America." *Smithsonian Magazine,* August. Accessed September 9, 2013. http:// www.smithsonianmag .com/travel/the-changing-demographics-of-america-538284.

Kramsch, Olivier Thomas, and Sabine Motzenbacker. 2004. "On the 'Pirate Frontier': Re-conceptualizing the Space of Ocean Governance in Light of the *Prestige* Disaster." Research Team Governance and Place Working Paper Series 2004/1, University of Nijmegen. Accessed September 9, 2013. http://www.ru.nl/publish/ pages/515103/2004-1.pdf.

Krogstad, Jens Manuel. 2015. "Reflecting a Racial Shift, 78 Counties Turned Majority-Minority since 2000." Fact Tank, Pew Research Center, April 8. Accessed May 8, 2017. http://www.pewresearch .org/fact-tank/2015/04/08/ reflecting-a-racial-shift-78-counties-turned-majority-minority-since-2000.

Kromm, Chris, and Sue Sturgis. 2008. *Hurricane Katrina and the Guiding Principles on Internal Displacement: A Global Human Rights Perspective on a National Disaster.* Durham, NC: Institute for Southern Studies. Accessed June 13, 2017. https://www .brookings.edu/wp-content/ uploads/2012/04/0114_ ISSKatrina.pdf.

Landers, Jane L. 1984. "Spanish Sanctuary: Fugitives in Florida, 1687–1790." *Florida Historical Quarterly* 62 (January): 296–313.

———. 1997. "Africans in Spanish Colonies." *Historical Archaeology* 31, no. 1: 84–103.

Lange, Matthew, James Mahoney, and Mathias vom Hau. 2006. "Colonialism and Development: A Comparative Analysis of Spanish and British Colonies." *American Journal of Sociology* 111, no. 5 (March): 1412–62.

Lewis, Kevin, Marco Gonzalez, and Jason Kaufman. 2011. "Social Selection and Peer Influence in an Online Social Network." *Proceedings of the National Academy of Sciences* 109, no. 1: 68–72.

Li, Stephanie. 2007. "Resistance, Silence, and Placées: Charles Bon's Octoroon Mistress and Louisa Picquet." *American Literature* 79, no. 1 (March): 85–112.

Linnaeus, Carolus. 1758. *Systemae Naturae.* 10th ed. Stockholm: Laurentii Salvii.

Lord, Lewis, and Sarah Burke. 1991. "America Before Columbus." *U.S. News & World Report,* July 8, 22–27. Accessed June 1, 2017. http://web.archive.org/ web/20020827104452/ http://www.millersville .edu/~columbus/data/art/ LORD-01.ART.

Maciag, Mike. 2015. "A State-by-State Look at Growing Minority Populations." *Governing,* June 25. Accessed April 4, 2017. http://www.governing.com/ topics/urban/gov-majority-minority-populations-in-states.html.

Mann, Charles. 2005. *1491: New Revelations of the Americas before Columbus.* New York: Borzoi Books.

Martinez, Maria Elena. 2004. "Limpieza de Sangre, Racial Violence, and Gendered Power in Early Colonial Mexico." *William and Mary Quarterly,* 3rd ser., 61, no. 3 (July): 479–520.

———. 2008. *Limpieza de Sangre, Religion, and Gender in Colonial Mexico.* Stanford, CA: Stanford University Press.

Martinez-Alier, Veren. (1974) 1989. *Marriage, Class and Color in Nineteenth-Century Cuba:*

A Study of Racial Attitudes and Sexual Values in a Slave Society. Ann Arbor: Michigan University Press.

McEwan, Bonnie G. 1991. "The Archaeology of Women in the Spanish New World." *Historical Archaeology* 25, no. 4: 33–41.

Mendoza, Ruben. 1997. "Metallurgy in Meso and Native America." In *Encyclopaedia of the History of Science, Technology, and Medicine in Non-Western Cultures,* edited by H. Selin, 702–6. Dordrecht: Kluwer Academic.

Mills, Charles. 1997. *The Racial Contract.* Ithaca, NY: Cornell University Press.

Moitt, Bernard. 2001. *Women and Slavery in the French Antilles, 1635–1848.* Bloomington: Indiana University Press.

Moje, Elizabeth Birr, Josephine Peyton Young, John E. Readence, and David W. Moore. 2000. "Reinventing Adolescent Literacy for New Times: Perennial and Millennial Issues." *Journal of Adolescent & Adult Literacy* 43, no. 5: 400–410.

National Archives. 2000. "Educator Resources: The *Amistad* Case." Accessed April 23, 2013. http://www.archives.gov/education/lessons/amistad.

Novack, George E. 1939. "Negro Slavery in North America." *New International* 5, no. 10 (October): 305–8. Accessed April 23, 2013. https://www.marxists.org/archive/novack/1939/10/x01.htm.

Orfield, Gary. 2009. *Reviving the Goal of an Integrated Society: A 21st Century Challenge.* Los Angeles: UCLA Civil Rights Project.

Palmer, Vernon V. 1995. "The Origins and Authors of the Code Noir." *Louisiana Law Review* 56, no. 363: 363–408.

Parise, Agustin. 2008. "Slave Laws and Labor Activities During the Spanish Colonial Period: A Study of the South American Region of Río de la Plata." *Rutgers Law Record* 32, no. 1: 1–39.

Parker, Martin. 2009. "Pirates, Merchants and Anarchists: Representations of International Business." *Management and Organizational History* 4, no. 2: 167–85.

Pateman, Carole. 1988. *The Sexual Contract.* Stanford, CA: Stanford University Press.

PBS. 2000. "Africans in America: America's Journey through Slavery." Accessed April 22, 2013. http://www.pbs.org/wgbh/aia/part1/1p285.html.

Perrin, Andrew. 2015. "Social Media Usage: 2005–2015." Pew Research Center, October 8. Accessed June 13, 2017. http://www.pewinternet.org/2015/10/08/social-networking-usage-2005-2015.

Phillips, William D. 1985. *Slavery from Roman Times to the Early Transatlantic Trade.* Minneapolis: University of Minnesota Press.

Pitts, Leonard. 2012. "A Whiter Shade of Privilege." *Columbia Daily Tribune,* March 28. Accessed April 22, 2013. http://m.columbiatribune.com/news/2012/mar/28/a-whiter-shade-of-privilege/?commentary.

Postma, Johannes. 1990. *The Dutch in the Atlantic Slave Trade, 1600–1815.* Cambridge: Cambridge University Press.

Rasmussen, Daniel. 2011. *"American Rising": When Slaves Attacked New Orleans.* New York: HarperCollins.

Rediker, Marcus Buford. 2004. *Villains of All Nations: Atlantic Pirates in the Golden Age.* London: Bath Press.

Reynolds, David S. 2005. *John Brown, Abolitionist: The Man Who Killed Slavery, Sparked the Civil War, and Seeded Civil Rights.* New York: Vintage Press.

Riding, Alan. 1992. "6 Ships, 2 Queens, Many Headaches." *New York Times,* March 15. Accessed June 1, 2017. http://www.nytimes.com/1992/03/15/movies/film-6-ships-2-queens-many-headaches.html?ref=alanriding.

Robenstine, Clark. 1992. "French Colonial Policy and the Education of Women and Minorities: Louisiana in the Early Eighteenth Century." *History of Education Quarterly* 32, no. 2 (Summer): 193–211.

Roediger, David R. 2007. *The Wages of Whiteness: Race and the Making of the American Working Class.* Chicago: Haymarket Press.

Rupp, Leila J. 2001. "Toward a Global History of Same-Sex Sexuality." *Journal of the History of Sexuality* 10, no. 2 (April): 287–302.

Rushforth, Brett. 2003. "'A Little Flesh We Offer You': The Origins of Indian Slavery in New France." *William and Mary Quarterly,* 3rd ser., 60, no. 4 (October): 777–808.

Sassaman, Kenneth E. 2005. "Poverty Point as Structure, Event, Process." *Journal of Archaeological Method and Theory* 12, no. 4 (December): 335–64.

Schafer, Daniel L. 1993. "'A Class of People Neither Freemen nor Slave': From Spanish Race Relations in Florida, 1821–1861." *Journal of Social History* 26, no. 3 (Spring): 587–609.

Shin, Hyon B., and Robert A. Kominski. 2010. *Language Use in the United States: 2007.* Washington, DC: U.S. Census Bureau.

Shippen, Peggy. 2004. "Sex Ratios." In *Women in Early America: Struggle, Survival, and Freedom,* edited by Dorothy A. Mays, 356–58. Santa Barbara, CA: ABC-CLIO.

Simms, Ellen Yvonne. 2009. "Miscegenation and Racism: Afro-Mexicans in Colonial New Spain." *Journal of Pan African Studies* 2, no. 3 (March): 228–54.

Singler, John Victor. 1995. "The Demographics of Creole Genesis in the Caribbean: A Comparison of Martinique and Haiti." In *The Early Stages of Creolization,* edited by Jacques Arends, 203–32. Amsterdam: John Benjamins.

Smedley, Audrey. 2007. *Race in North America: Origin and Evolution of a Worldview.* 3rd ed. Boulder, CO: Westview Press.

Smith, Charles E. 1966. "Negro-White Intermarriage: Forbidden Sexual Union." *Journal of Sex Research* 2, no. 3 (November): 169–77.

Soyinka, Wole. 1990. *Myth, Literature and the African World.* New York: Cambridge University Press.

Spade, Joan Z., and Jeanne H. Ballantine, eds. 2011. *Schools and Society: A Sociological Approach to Education.* Thousand Oaks, CA: Sage.

Spear, Jennifer M. 2003. "Colonial Intimacies: Legislating Sex in French Louisiana." *William and Mary Quarterly,* 3rd ser., 60, no. 1 (January): 75–98.

Stanish, Charles. 2000. "Negotiating Rank in an Imperial State: Lake Titicaca Basin Elite under Inca and Spanish Control." In *Hierarchies in Action: Cui Bono?,* edited by Michael W. Diel. Carbondale: Southern Illinois University.

Stasiulis, Daiva K., and Radha Jhappan. 1995. "The Fractious Politics of a Settler Society: Canada." In *Unsettling Settler Societies: Articulations of Gender, Race, Ethnicity and Class,* edited by Daiva K. Stasiulis and Nira Yuval-Davis. London: Sage.

Stasiulis, Daiva K., and Nira Yuval-Davis. 1995. "Beyond Dichotomies: Gender, Race, Ethnicity and Class in Settler Societies." In *Unsettling Settler Societies: Articulations of Gender, Race, Ethnicity and Class,* edited by Daiva K. Stasiulis and Nira Yuval-Davis. London: Sage.

Stern, Steve J. 1982. *Peru's Indian Peoples and the Challenge of Spanish Conquest: Huamanga to 1640.* Madison: University of Wisconsin Press.

Stinchcombe, Arthur L. 1994. "Freedom and Oppression of Slaves in the Eighteenth-Century Caribbean." *American Sociological Review* 59, no. 6 (December): 911–29.

Stolcke, Verena. 2004. "New World Engendered: The Making of the Iberian Transatlantic Empires." In *A Companion to Gender History,* edited by Teresa A. Meade and Merry E. Wiesner-Hanks. Oxford: Blackwell.

Stoler, Ann L. 1989. "Making Empire Respectable: The Politics of Race and Sexual Morality in 20th-Century Colonial Cultures." *American Ethnologists* 16, no. 4 (November): 634–60.

Strommen, Linda Teran, and Barbara Fowles Mates. 2004. "Learning to Love Reading: Interviews with Older Children and Teens." *Journal of Adolescent & Adult Literacy* 48, no. 3: 188–2000.

Taylor, Paul, and Scott Keeter, eds. 2010. *Millennials: A Portrait of Generation Next.* Washington, DC: Pew Research Center. Accessed June 13, 2017. http://www.pewsocialtrends.org/files/2010/10/millennials-confident-connected-open-to-change.pdf.

Telles, Edward, and the Project on Ethnicity and Race in Latin America. 2014. *Pigmentocracies: Ethnicity, Race, and Color in Latin America.* Chapel Hill: University of North Carolina Press.

Thomas, G. E. 1975. "Puritans, Indians, and the Concept of Race." *New England Quarterly* 48, no. 1 (March): 3–27.

Towle, Evan B., and Lynn Marie Morgan. 2002. "Romancing the Transgender Native: Rethinking the Use of the 'Third Gender' Concept." *GLQ: A Journal of Lesbian and Gay Studies* 8, no. 4: 469–97.

Trocolli, R. 1992. "Colonization and Women's Production: The Timucua of Florida." In *Exploring Gender through Archaeology: Selected*

Papers from the 1991 Boone Conference, edited by C. Claassen and M. C. Beaudry, 95–102. Madison, WI: Prehistory Press.

Turner, Frederick J. 1920. *The Frontier in American History.* New York: Holt.

Tyson, Alec, and Shiva Maniam. 2016. "Behind Trump's Victory: Divisions by Race, Gender, Education." Fact Tank, Pew Research Center, November 9. Accessed June 17, 2017. http://www.pewresearch.org/fact-tank/2016/11/09/behind-trumps-victory-divisions-by-race-gender-education.

Usner, Daniel H. Jr. 1979. "From African Captivity to African Slavery: The Introduction of Black Laborers to Colonial Louisiana." *Louisiana History* 20, no. 1: 25–48.

Voss, Barbara. 2008. "Gender, Race, and Labor in the Archaeology of the Spanish Colonial Americas." *Current Anthropology* 49, no. 5 (October): 861–93.

Weatherford, Jack. 1989. "Examining the Reputation

of Christopher Columbus." *Baltimore Evening Sun,* October 6. Reprinted by Clergy and Laity Concerned. Accessed June 1, 2017. http://www.hartford-hwp.com/Taino/docs/columbus.html.

Weber, David J. 2000. "The Spanish Borderlands of North America: A Historiography." *OAH Magazine of History* 14, no. 4 (Summer): 5–11.

Williams, Joseph P. 2014. "College of Tomorrow: The Changing Demographics of the Student Body." *U.S. News & World Report,* September 22. Accessed April 4, 2017. https://www.usnews.com/news/college-of-tomorrow/articles/2014/09/22/college-of-tomorrow-the-changing-demographics-of-the-student-body.

Wilson, Natalie. 2011. *Seduced by "Twilight": The Allure and Contradictory Messages of the Popular Saga.* Jefferson, NC: McFarland.

Wolfe, Patrick. 2006. "Settler Colonialism and the

Elimination of the Native." *Journal of Genocide Research* 8, no. 4 (December): 387–409.

Young, R. J. C. 2001. *Postcolonialism: An Historical Introduction.* London: Blackwell.

Zarya, Valentina. 2016. "The Percentage of Female CEOS in the Fortune 500 Drops to 4%." *Fortune,* June 6. Accessed April 9, 2017. http://fortune.com/2016/06/06/women-ceos-fortune-500-2016.

Zerubavel, Eviatar. 1993. *Time Maps: Collective Memory and the Social Shape of the Past.* Chicago: University of Chicago Press.

Zinn, Howard. 1980. *A People's History of the United States.* New York: Harper & Row.

Zion, James W., and Robert Yazzie. 1997. "Indigenous Law in North America in the Wake of Conquest." *Boston College International and Comparative Law Review* 20: 55–84.

■ CHAPTER 3

American Psychological Association. n.d. "Undocumented Americans." Accessed December 23, 2016. http://www.apa.org/topics/immigration/undocumented-video.aspx.

Amott, Teresa, and Julie Matthaei. 1996. *Race, Gender, and Work: A Multicultural Economic History of Women in the United States.* Boston: South End Press.

Avishai, Orit, Melanie Heath, and Jennifer Randles. 2012.

"Marriage Goes to School." *Contexts* 11, no. 3: 34–38

Baca Zinn, Maxine. 2012. "Patricia Hill Collins: Past and Future Innovations." *Gender & Society* 26, no. 1: 28–32.

Baca Zinn, Maxine, and Barbara Wells. 2000. "Diversity within Latino Families: New Lessons for Family Social Science." In *Handbook of Family Diversity,* edited by David H. Demo, Katherine R. Allen, and Mark A. Fine, 252–73. New York: Oxford University Press.

Baker, Peter. 2012. "Same-Sex Marriage Support Shows Pace of Social Change Accelerating." *New York Times,* May 11. Accessed August 24, 2013. http://www.nytimes.com/2012/05/11/us/same-sex-marriage-support-shows-pace-of-social-change-accelerating.html?_r=0.

Baldwin, James. 1963. *The Fire Next Time.* New York: Vintage.

Barber, Clifton E., and L. Diego Vega. 2011. "Conflict, Cultural Marginalization, and Personal Costs of Filial

Caregiving." *Journal of Cultural Diversity* 18, no. 1: 20–28.

Beoku-Betts, Josephine A. 2000. "We Got Our Way of Cooking Things: Women, Food, and Preservation of Cultural Identity among the Gullah." In *How Sweet the Sound: The Spirit of African American Family,* edited by Nancy-Elizabeth Fitch, 414–32. Orlando, FL: Harcourt Brace.

Berkin, Carol. 1996. *First Generations: Women in Colonial America.* New York: Hill and Wang.

Blassingame, John W. 1976. *The Slave Community: Plantation Life in the Antebellum South.* New York: Oxford University Press.

Bradfield, Stuart. 2011. "American Indian Heritage Month: Commemoration vs. Exploitation." ABC-CLIO. Accessed October 29, 2013. http://www .historyandtheheadlines. abc-clio.com/ContentPages/ ContentPage.aspx?entryId= 1171791&currentSection=11 61468&productid=5.

Bronson, Po, and Ashley Merryman. 2009. "Even Babies Discriminate." *Newsweek,* September 4. Accessed September 12, 2013. http://www .newsweek.com/even- babies-discriminate- nurtureshock-excerpt-79233.

Buckley, Cara. 2013. "Gay Couples, Choosing to Say 'I Don't.'" *New York Times,* October 25. Accessed October 27, 2013. http://www.nytimes .com/2013/10/27/ style/gay-couples- choosing-to-say-i-dont. html?pagewanted=1&_ r=3&smid=fb-share.

Buss, Fran Leeper. 1985. *Dignity: Lower-Income Women Tell of Their Lives and Struggles.* Ann Arbor: University of Michigan Press.

Butler, Edgar W., and Celia Mancillas Bazan. 2011. "Beyond National Borders: Family Frontiers and Expulsion from the US." *Journal of Borderlands Studies* 26, no. 1: 53–63.

Calderon, Jose Zapata. 2005. "Inclusion or Exclusion: One Immigrant's Experience of Cultural and Structural Barriers to Power Sharing and Unity." In *Minority Voices: Linking Personal Ethnic History and the Sociological Imagination,* edited by John P. Myers, 106–20. Boston: Pearson.

Carby, Hazel. 1986. "'On the Threshold of Woman's Era': Lynching, Empire, and Sexuality in Black Feminist Theory." In *"Race," Writing, and Difference,* edited by Henry Louis Gates Jr. Chicago: University of Chicago Press.

Chase, Susan E., and Mary F. Rogers. 2001. *Mothers and Children: Feminist Analyses and Personal Narratives.* New Brunswick, NJ: Rutgers University Press.

Coles, Roberta L. 2009. *The Best Kept Secret: Single Black Fathers.* Lanham, MD: Rowman & Littlefield.

Collins, Patricia Hill. 1998. "It's All in the Family: Intersections of Gender, Race, and Nation." *Hypatia* 13, no. 3: 62–82.

Coontz, Stephanie. 2010a. "The Evolution of American Families." In *Families as They Really Are,* edited by Barbara J. Risman, 30–47. New York: W. W. Norton.

———. 2010b. "Not Much in Those Census Stories." In *Families as They Really Are,* edited by Barbara J. Risman. New York: W. W. Norton.

Coontz, Stephanie, and Nancy Folbre. 2010. "Briefing Paper: Marriage, Poverty, and Public Policy." In *Families as They Really Are,* edited by Barbara J. Risman, 185–93. New York: W. W. Norton.

Cott, Nancy F. 2000. *Public Vows: A History of Marriage and the Nation.* Cambridge, MA: Harvard University Press.

Cunnigen, Donald. 2005. "Race, Class, Civil Rights, and Jim Crow America: Silences and Smiles." In *Minority Voices: Linking Personal Ethnic History and the Sociological Imagination,* edited by John P. Myers, 75–105. Boston: Pearson.

Davis, Kingsley. 1984. "Wives and Work: The Sex Role Revolution and Its Consequences." *Population and Development Review* 10, no. 3: 397–417.

Devries, K. M., J. Y. T. Mak, C. García-Moreno, M. Petzold, J. C. Child, G. Falder, S. Lim, L. J. Bacchus, R. E. Engell, L. Rosenfeld, C. Pallitto, T. Vos, N. Abrahams, and C. H. Watts. 2013. "The Global Prevalence of Intimate Partner Violence against Women." *Science* 340, no. 6140: 1527–28.

Dodson, Jualynne Elizabeth. 2007. "Conceptualizations and Research of African American Family Life in the United States: Some Thoughts." In *Black Families,* 4th ed., edited by Harriette Pipes McAdoo, 51–68. Thousand Oaks, CA: Sage.

Dornbusch, Sanford, and Myra H. Strober, eds. 1988. *Feminism, Children, and the New Families.* New York: Guilford Press.

Dreby, Joanna. 2010. *Divided by Borders: Mexican Migrants and Their Children.* Berkeley: University of California Press.

Du Bois, W. E. B. 1899. *The Philadelphia Negro: A Social Study.* Philadelphia: University of Pennsylvania Press.

Edelman, Marian Wright. 2007. "A Portrait of Inequality." In *Black Families,* 4th ed., edited by Harriette Pipes McAdoo, 319–27. Thousand Oaks, CA: Sage.

Edin, Kathryn, Laura Tach, and Ronald Mincy. 2009. "Claiming Fatherhood: Race and the Dynamics of Paternal Involvement among Unmarried Men." *Annals of the American Academy of Political and Social Science* 621: 149–77.

Feagin, Joe R. 2000. *Racist America: Roots, Current Realities, and Future Reparations.* New York: Routledge.

Fenelon, James V. 2005. "Dakota Woman, Mixed-Blood Man: American Indians from the Northern Plains." In *Minority Voices: Linking Personal Ethnic History and the Sociological Imagination,* edited by John P. Myers, 27–50. Boston: Pearson.

Ferber, Abby L. 1998. *White Man Falling: Race, Gender, and White Supremacy.* Lanham, MD: Rowman & Littlefield.

Flavin, Jeanne. 2009. *Our Bodies, Our Crimes: The Policing of Women's Reproduction in America.* New York: New York University Press.

Franklin, Donna. 2010. "African Americans and the Birth of Modern Marriage." In *Families as They Really Are,* edited by Barbara J. Risman, 63–74. New York: W. W. Norton.

Franklin, John Hope. 1947. *From Slavery to Freedom: A History of American Negroes.* New York: Alfred A. Knopf.

Franzen, Trisha. 1996. *Spinsters and Lesbians: Independent Womanhood in the United States.* New York: New York University Press.

Frazier, E. Franklin. 1948. *The Negro Family in the United States.* New York: Citadel Press.

Gates, Gary J. 2012. "Same-Sex Couples in Census 2010: Race and Ethnicity." Williams Institute, April. Accessed June 16, 2017. https://williamsinstitute.law.ucla.edu/wp-content/uploads/Gates-CouplesRaceEthnicity-April-2012.pdf.

Genetin-Pilawa, C. Joseph. 2008. "'All Intent on Seeing the White Woman Married to the Red Man': The Parker/Sackett Affair and the Public Spectacle of Intermarriage." *Journal of Women's History* 20, no. 2: 57–85.

Genovese, Eugene D. 1974. *Roll, Jordan, Roll: The World the Slaves Made.* New York: Random House.

Gharib, Malaka. 2016 "A Quinceañera Got a Million RSVPs: The Story behind the Ritual." Goats and Soda (blog), Southern California Public Radio, December 13. Accessed April 15, 2017. http://www.npr.org/sections/goatsandsoda/2016/12/13/505298710/a-quincea-era-got-a-million-rsvps-the-story-behind-the-ritual.

Giddings, Paula. 1984. *When and Where I Enter: The Impact of Black Women on Race and Sex in America.* New York: William Morrow.

Glick-Schiller, Nina. 2003. "The Centrality of Ethnography in the Study of Transnational Migration: Seeing the Wetlands instead of the Swamp." In *American Arrivals,* edited by Nancy Foner, 99–128. Santa Fe, NM: School of American Research Press.

Goings, Kenneth W. 1994. *Mammy and Uncle Mose: Black Collectibles and American Stereotyping.* Bloomington: Indiana University Press.

Hamm, Deborah. 2013. "Autonomy, Justice, and Injustice with Indian Gestational Surrogacy." *Voices in Bioethics* (Fall). Accessed June 12, 2017. http://www.voicesinbioethics.net/opeds/2013/10/15/indian-gestational-surrogacy?rq=indian%20gestational%20surrogacy.

Harding, Vincent. 2000. "From the Shores of Africa." In *How Sweet the Sound: The Spirit of African American Family,* edited by Nancy-Elizabeth Fitch, 40–59. Orlando, FL: Harcourt Brace.

Hattery, Angela J., and Earl Smith. 2007. *African American Families.* Thousand Oaks, CA: Sage.

———. 2016. *The Social Dynamics of Family Violence.* Boulder, CO: Westview Press.

Heath, Melanie. 2013. "State of Our Unions: Marriage Promotion and the Contested Power of Heterosexuality." In *Sex, Gender, and Sexuality: The New Basics,* edited by Abby L. Ferber, Kimberly

Holcomb, and Tre Wentling, 292–99. New York: Oxford University Press.

Heath, Melanie, Jennifer Randles, and Orit Avishai. 2016. "Marriage Movement." In *The Wiley Blackwell Encyclopedia of Family Studies,* edited by Constance L. Shehan. Malden, MA: John Wiley.

Herdt, Gilbert H., ed. 1996. *Third Sex, Third Gender: Beyond Sexual Dimorphism in Culture and History.* New York: Zone.

Hill, Shirley A. 2005. *Black Intimacies: A Gender Perspective on Families and Relationships.* Walnut Creek, CA: AltaMira Press.

Hirata, Lucie Cheng. 1979. "Free, Indentured, Enslaved: Chinese Prostitutes in Nineteenth-Century America." *Signs* 5, no. 1: 3–29.

Hurtado, Aida. 2003. *Voicing Chicana Feminisms: Young Women Speak Out on Sexuality and Identity.* New York: New York University Press.

Hymowitz, Carole, and Michaele Weissman. 1978. *A History of Women in America.* New York: Bantam Books.

Ichioka, Yuji. 1977. "Ameyuki-san: Japanese Prostitutes in Nineteenth-Century America." *Amerasia* 4, no. 1: 1–21.

———. 1980. "*Amerika Nadeshiko*: Japanese Immigrant Women in the United States, 1900–1924." *Pacific Historical Review* 49, no. 2: 339–57.

Ingraham, Chrys. 2013. "Heterosexuality: It's Just Not Natural." In *Sex, Gender, and Sexuality: The New Basics,* edited by Abby L. Ferber, Kimberly Holcomb, and Tre Wentling, 99–106.

New York: Oxford University Press.

James, Susan Donaldson. 2013. "Infertile Americans Go to India for Gestational Surrogates." ABC News, November 7. Accessed May 16, 2015. http://abcnews.go.com/Health/infertile-americans-india-gestational-surrogates/story?id=20808125.

Jones, Jeffrey M. 2016. "Same-Sex Marriages Up One Year after Supreme Court Verdict." Gallup, Social Issues, June 22. Accessed December 27, 2016. http://www.gallup.com/poll/193055/sex-marriages-one-year-supreme-court-verdict.aspx?g_source=Social%20Issues&g_medium=newsfeed&g_campaign=tiles

Jones, Rachel K., and Jenna Jerman. 2017. "Abortion Incidence and Service Availability in the United States, 2011." *Perspectives on Sexual and Reproductive Health* 46, no. 1: 3–14.

Joyner, Charles. 2000. "Gullah: A Creole Language." In *How Sweet the Sound: The Spirit of African American Family,* edited by Nancy-Elizabeth Fitch, 461–86. Orlando, FL: Harcourt Brace.

Kohler-Hausmann, Julilly. 2007. "The Crime of Survival: Fraud Prosecutions, Community Surveillance, and the Original Welfare Queen." *Journal of Social History* 41, no. 2: 329–54.

Lefkovitz, Alison. 2011. "Men in the House: Race, Welfare, and the Regulation of Men's Sexuality in the United States, 1961–1972." *Journal of the History of Sexuality* 20, no. 3: 594–614.

Lew, William W. 2005. *Minidoka Revisited: The Paintings of Roger Shimomura.* Clemson, SC: Clemson University, distributed by University of Washington Press.

Lopez, Iris. 1987. "Sterilization among Puerto Rican Women in New York City: Public Policy and Social Constraints." In *Cities of the United States: Studies in Urban Anthropology,* edited by Leith Mullings, 269–91. New York: Columbia University Press.

Luibhéid, Eithne. 2002. *Entry Denied: Controlling Sexuality at the Border.* Minneapolis: University of Minnesota Press.

MacLean, Maggie. 2014. "19th Century Midwives." History of American Women (blog). Accessed December 27, 2016. http://www.womenhistoryblog.com/2014/06/19th-century-midwives.html.

Madison, D. Soyini, ed. 1994. *The Woman That I Am: The Literature and Culture of Contemporary Women of Color.* New York: St. Martin's Press.

Marks, Stephen R. 2000. "Teasing Out the Lessons of the 1960s: Family Diversity and Family Privilege." *Journal of Marriage and the Family* 62, no. 3 (August): 609–22.

Martin, Steven. 2008. "Recent Changes in Fertility Rates in the United States: What Do They Tell Us about Americans' Changing Families?" Council on Contemporary Families, February 11. Accessed February 11, 2013. https://contemporaryfamilies.org/wp-content/uploads/2013/10/2008_Briefing_Martin_Fertility-rates-Americans.pdf.

McAdoo, Harriette Pipes, ed. 2007. *Black Families.* 4th ed. Thousand Oaks, CA: Sage.

McLanahan, Sara S., and Marcia J. Carlson. 2002. "Welfare Reform, Fertility, and Father Involvement." *Future of Children* 12, no. 1: 147–65.

Meacham, Mike. 1983. "The Myth of the Black Matriarchy Under Slavery." *Mid-American Review of Sociology* 8, no. 2 (Winter): 23–41.

Moore, Mignon R. 2011. *Invisible Families: Gay Identities, Relationships, and Motherhood among Black Women.* Berkeley: University of California Press.

Moses, Lucia. 2012. "Data Points: Modern Families: Nontraditional Families Are Open to Advertising but Turned Off by Most Messaging." *Adweek,* August 22. Accessed March 23, 2013. http://www.adweek.com/news/advertising-branding/data-points-modern-families-142950.

Movement Advancement Project. 2017. "Marriage and Relationship Recognition Laws." Accessed April 16, 2017. http://www.lgbtmap.org/equality-maps/marriage_relationship_laws.

MSN News. 2012. "Racism 'Harms Children's Learning.'" March 9. Accessed October 21, 2013. http://news.uk.msn.com/racism-harms-childrens-learning.

Myers, John P., ed. 2005. *Minority Voices: Linking Personal Ethnic History and the Sociological Imagination.* Boston: Pearson.

Mathews, Shailer. 1896. "Christian Sociology, III: The Family." *American Journal of Sociology* 1, no. 4: 457–72.

National Coalition Against Domestic Violence. 2015. "Domestic Violence National Statistics." Accessed June 2, 2017. http://ncadv.org/files/National%20Statistics%20Domestic%20Violence%20NCADV.pdf.

Otsuka, Julie. 2011. *The Buddha in the Attic.* New York: Vintage.

Pan American Health Organization. n.d. "Domestic Violence during Pregnancy." Fact sheet, Women, Health & Development Program. Accessed October 29, 2012. http://www.paho.org/english/ad/ge/vawpregnancy.pdf.

Parker, Kim, and Wendy Wang. 2013. "Modern Parenthood: Roles of Moms and Dads Converge as They Balance Work and Family." Pew Research Center, March 14. Accessed June 13, 2013. http://www.pewsocialtrends.org/2013/03/14/modern-parenthood-roles-of-moms-and-dads-converge-as-they-balance-work-and-family.

Pew Research Center. 2010. "The Decline of Marriage and Rise of New Families." November 18. Accessed November 3, 2013. http://www.pewsocialtrends.org/2010/11/18/the-decline-of-marriage-and-rise-of-new-families.

———. 2012. "The Rise of Intermarriage." February 16. Accessed November 3, 2013. http://www.pewsocialtrends.org/2012/02/16/the-rise-of-intermarriage/2.

———. 2013a. "The Rise of Asian Americans." Accessed November 8, 2013. http://www.pewsocialtrends.org/asianamericans-graphics.

———. 2013b. "A Survey of LGBT Americans." June 13. Accessed December 27, 2016.

http://www.pewsocialtrends.org/2013/06/13/a-survey-of-lgbt-americans.

———. 2015. "Multiracial in America: Proud, Diverse and Growing in Numbers." June 11. Accessed December 23, 2016. http://www.pewsocialtrends.org/2015/06/11/multiracial-in-america.

———. n.d. "Parental Time Use." Accessed January 23, 2017. http://www.pewresearch.org/data-trend/society-and-demographics/parental-time-use.

Pinder, Sherrow O. 2013. *American Multicultural Studies: Diversity of Race, Ethnicity, Gender and Sexuality.* Thousand Oaks, CA: Sage.

Prell, Riv-Ellen. 1999. *Fighting to Become Americans: Jews, Gender, and the Anxiety of Assimilation.* Boston: Beacon Press.

Proctor, Bernadette D., Jessica L. Semega, and Melissa A. Kollar. 2016. *Income and Poverty in the United States: 2015.* U.S. Census Bureau, Current Population Reports, P60-256(RV). Washington, DC: Government Printing Office. https://www.census.gov/content/dam/Census/library/publications/2016/demo/p60-256.pdf.

Rauch, Jonathan. 2004. *Gay Marriage: Why It Is Good for Gays, Good for Straights, and Good for America.* New York: Henry Holt.

Reeve, Elspeth, and Philip Bump. 2013. "A Map Showing the Country's Sudden Move towards Marriage Equality." *Atlantic Wire,* April 11. Accessed June 2, 2017. http://www.theatlanticwire.com/politics/2013/04/gay-rights-marriage-map-gif/64148.

Reich, Jennifer. 2003. *Fixing Families: Parents, Power, and the Child Welfare System.* New York: Routledge.

Risman, Barbara J., ed. 2010. *Families as They Really Are.* New York: W. W. Norton.

Rockquemore, Kerry Ann, and Loren Henderson. 2010. "Interracial Families in Post–Civil Rights America." In *Families as They Really Are,* edited by Barbara J. Risman, 90–114. New York: W. W. Norton.

Roscoe, Will. 1998. *Changing Ones: Third and Fourth Genders in Native North America.* New York: St. Martin's Press.

Sieglera, Ilene C., Beverly H. Brummetta, Redford B. Williams, Thomas L. Haney, and Peggy Dilworth-Anderson. 2010. "Caregiving, Residence, Race, and Depressive Symptoms." *Aging & Mental Health* 14, no. 7 (September 2010): 771–78.

Skinner, Allison L., and Caitlin M. Hudac. 2017. "'Yuck, You Disgust Me!': Affective Bias against Interracial Couples." *Journal of Experimental Social Psychology* 68 (January): 68–77.

Smith, Mychal Denzel. 2017. "The Dangerous Myth of the 'Missing Black Father.'" *Washington Post,* January 10. Accessed February 6, 2017. https://www .washingtonpost .com/posteverything/ wp/2017/01/10/the-dangerous-myth-of-the-missing-black-father/?utm_ term=.6d76a1b06661.

Soehl, Thomas, and Roger Waldinger. 2010. "Making the Connections: Latino Immigrants and Their Cross-Border Ties." *Ethnic and Racial Studies* 33, no. 9: 1489–1510.

Solinger, Rickie. 2001. *Beggars and Choosers: How the Politics of Choice Shapes Adoption, Abortion, and Welfare in the United States.* New York: Hill and Wang.

———. 2007. *Pregnancy and Power: A Short History of Reproductive Politics in America.* New York: New York University Press.

———. 2010. "The First Welfare Case: Money, Sex, Marriage, and White Supremacy in Selma, 1966—A Reproductive Justice Analysis." *Journal of Women's History* 22, no. 3: 13–38.

———. 2013. *Wake Up Little Susie: Single Pregnancy and Race before* Roe v. Wade. New York: Routledge.

Southern Poverty Law Center. 2012. "Court Rules in SPLC Suit That Florida Tuition Policy Discriminates against Children of Undocumented Immigrants." September 4. Accessed June 2, 2017. http://www.splcenter .org/get-informed/news/ court-rules-in-splc-suit-that-florida-tuition-policy-discriminates-against-childre.

Spar, Deborah. 2012. "American Women Have It Wrong." *Newsweek,* October 1–8, 38–48.

Strah, David, with Susanna Margolis. 2003. *Gay Dads.* New York: Penguin.

Tehranian, John. 2009. *White Washed: America's Invisible Middle Eastern Minority.* New York: New York University Press.

Thorpe, Helen. 2011. *Just Like Us: The True Story of Four Mexican Girls Coming of Age in America.* New York: Scribner.

Towle, Evan B., and Lynn Marie Morgan. 2002. "Romancing the Transgender Native: Rethinking the Use of the 'Third Gender' Concept." *GLQ: A Journal of Lesbian and Gay Studies* 8, no. 4: 469–97.

Twine, France Winddance. 2011. *Outsourcing the Womb: Race, Class, and Gestational Surrogacy in a Global Market.* New York: Routledge.

U.S. Census Bureau. 2015. "Families and Living Arrangements: Current Population Survey." Accessed January 23, 2017. https://www .census.gov/hhes/ families/data/cps2015C .html.

———. 2016. "Families and Living Arrangements: Historical Time Series." Accessed January 19, 2017. https:// www.census.gov/hhes/ families/data/historical.html.

Valenti, Jessica. 2012. "Smart Women Not Having Kids, or Getting Support." WeNews, September 15. Accessed June 2, 2017. http://womensenews.org/ story/books/120915/smart-women-not-having-kids-or-getting-support# .UFz1tceUtHM.email.

Villalon, Roberta. 2010. *Violence against Latina Immigrants: Citizenship, Inequality, and Community.* New York: New York University Press.

Vizenor, Gerald. 1995. *Native American Literature.* New York: HarperCollins.

Wang, Wendy. 2012. "The Rise of Intermarriage: Rates, Characteristics Vary by Race and

Gender." Pew Research Center, February 16. http://www .pewsocialtrends. org/2012/02/16/the-rise-of-intermarriage.

———. 2015. "Interracial Marriage: Who Is 'Marrying Out'?" Fact Tank, Pew Research Center, June 12. Accessed December 23, 2016. http:// www.pewresearch.org/fact-tank/2015/06/12/interracial-marriage-who-is-marrying-out.

Ward, Lester F. 1899. *Outlines of Sociology.* London: Macmillan.

Wong, Nellie. 1983. "When I Was Growing Up." In *This Bridge Called My Back: Writing by Radical Women of Color,* edited by Cherrie Moraga and Gloria Anzaldúa. Latham, NY: Kitchen Table/Women of Color Press.

Wu, Judy Tzu-Chun. 2001. "Was Mom Chung a 'Sister Lesbian'? Asian American Gender Experimentation and Interracial Homoeroticism." *Journal of Women's History* 13, no. 1 (Spring): 58–82. doi:10.1353/ jowh.2001.0028.

Yang, Philip Q. 2011. *Asian Immigration to the United States.* Cambridge: Polity Press.

Zaher, Claudia. 2002. "When a Woman's Marital Status Determined Her Legal Status: A Research Guide on the Common Law Doctrine of Coverture." *Law Library Journal* 94, no. 3.

Zambrana, Ruth Enid. 2011. *Latinos in American Society: Families and Communities in Transition.* Ithaca, NY: Cornell University Press.

■ CHAPTER 4

Acker, Joan. 1989. *Doing Comparable Worth.* Philadelphia: Temple University Press.

———. 2006. "Inequality Regimes: Gender, Class, and Race in Organizations." *Gender & Society* 20: 441–64.

Alderson, Arthur S. 2015. "Globalization and Deindustrialization: Direct Investment and the Decline of Manufacturing Employment in 17 OECD Nations." *Journal of World-Systems Research* 3, no. 1: 1–34.

American Association of University Women. 2014. "The Simple Truth about the Gender Pay Gap." Accessed April 8, 2016. http://www .aauw.org/files/2014/03/ The-Simple-Truth.pdf.

American Immigration Council. 2016. "How the United States Immigration System Works." Fact sheet, August 12. Accessed April 10, 2017. http://www.immigrationpolicy .org/just-facts/how-united-states-immigration-system-works-fact-sheet.

Amott, Teresa, and Julie Matthaei. 1996. *Race, Gender, and Work: A Multicultural Economic History of Women in the United States.* Boston: South End Press.

Andersen, Margaret L. 2001. "Restructuring for Whom? Race, Class, Gender, and the Ideology of Invisibility." *Sociological Forum* 16, no. 2 (June): 181–201.

Badger, Emily. 2015. "When Work Isn't Enough to Keep You off Welfare and Food Stamps." Wonkblog (blog), *Washington Post,* April 14. Accessed April 7, 2016. https://www .washingtonpost.com/news/ wonk/wp/2015/04/14/when-work-isnt-enough-to-keep-you-off-welfare-and-food-stamps.

Barlett, Donald L., and James B. Steele. 1998. "Corporate Welfare." *Time,* November 9. Accessed January 25, 2013. http://content .time.com/time/magazine/ article/0,9171,989508,00.html.

Barnes, Mario L., Erwin Chemerinsky, and Angela

Onwuachi-Willig. 2015. "Judging Opportunity Lost: Assessing the Viability of Race-Based Affirmative Action after *Fisher v. University of Texas.*" *UCLA Law Review* 62: 272–305.

Bauer, Mary, and Meredith Stewart. 2013. "Close to Slavery: Guestworker Programs in the United States." Southern Poverty Law Center, February 18. Accessed March 1, 2015. http://www.splcenter.org/ get-informed/publications/ close-to-slavery-guestworker-programs-in-the-united-states.

BBC News. 2011. "Q&A: What Is GDP?" Business, April 26. Accessed April 7, 2016. http://www.bbc.com/news/ business-13200758.

Benner, Chris, and Kyle Neering. 2016. "Silicon Valley Technology Industries: Contract Workforce Assessment." Everett Program, University of California, Santa Cruz, March 29. Accessed April 8, 2016. http://www.everettprogram

.org/main/wp-content/uploads/Contract-Workforce-Assessment.pdf.

Bernard, Tara Siegel. 2013. "Fired for Being Gay? Protections Are Piecemeal." *New York Times,* May 31. Accessed February 11, 2014. http://www.nytimes.com/2013/06/01/your-money/protections-for-gays-in-workplace-are-piecemeal.html.

Berry, Brent, and Eduardo Bonilla-Silva. 2007. "'They Should Hire the One with the Best Score': White Sensitivity to Qualification Differences in Affirmative Action Hiring Decisions." *Ethnic and Racial Studies* 31, no. 2: 215–42. doi:10.1080/01419870701337619.

Bertrand, Marianne, and Sendhil Mullainathan. 2003. "Are Emily and Greg More Employable than Lakisha and Jamal? A Field Experiment on Labor Market Discrimination." Working Paper 9873, National Bureau of Economic Research. http://www.nber.org/papers/w9873.pdf.

Bonacich, Edna. 1972. "A Theory of Ethnic Antagonism: The Split Labor Market." *American Sociological Review* 37, no. 5: 547–59.

Bricker, Jesse, Alice Henriques, Jacob Krimmel, and John Sabelhaus. 2015. "Measuring Income and Wealth at the Top Using Administrative and Survey Data." Finance and Economics Discussion Series 2015-030, Board of Governors of the Federal Reserve System. Accessed June 1, 2017. http://dx.doi.org/10.17016/FEDS.2015.030.

Brodkin, Karen. 1998. *How Jews Became White Folks and What That Says about Race in America.* New Brunswick,

NJ: Rutgers University Press.

Brunori, David. 2014. "Where Is the Outrage over Corporate Welfare?" *Forbes,* March 14. Accessed April 2, 2016. http://www.forbes.com/sites/taxanalysts/2014/03/14/where-is-the-outrage-over-corporate-welfare/#7540e9126881.

Business Dictionary. n.d. "Gross Domestic Product." Accessed April 7, 2016. http://www.businessdictionary.com/definition/gross-domestic-product-GDP.html.

Caiazza, Amy, April Shaw, and Misha Werschkul. 2004. "Women's Economic Status in the States: Wide Disparities by Race, Ethnicity, and Region." Institute for Women's Policy Research, October 31. Accessed June 2, 2017. https://iwpr.org/publications/womens-economic-status-in-the-states-wide-disparities-by-race-ethnicity-and-region.

Chomsky, Aviva. 2007. *"They Take Our Jobs!" and 20 Other Myths about Immigration.* Boston: Beacon Press.

Chua, Amy, and Jed Rubenfeld. 2014. *The Triple Package: How Three Unlikely Traits Explain the Rise and Fall of Cultural Groups in America.* New York: Penguin.

CNN. 2012. "U.S. Finalizes $3.4 Billion Settlement with American Indians." November 27. Accessed June 16, 2017. http://www.cnn.com/2012/11/26/politics/american-indian-settlment.

Coalition of Immokalee Workers. 2012. "Consciousness + Commitment = Change: How and Why We Are Organizing." Accessed February 22,

2013. http://ciw-online.org/about/#facts.

Coates, Rodney D. 2004. "If a Tree Falls in the Wilderness: Reparations, Academic Silences, and Social Justice." *Social Forces* 83, no. 2: 841–64.

Coates, Ta-Nehisi. 2014. "The Case for Reparations." *Atlantic,* June. Accessed February 27, 2015. http://www.theatlantic.com/features/archive/2014/05/the-case-for-reparations/361631.

Cohen, Phillip. 2014. "Was the War on Poverty a Failure? Or Are Anti-poverty Efforts Simply Swimming against a Stronger Tide?" Council on Contemporary Families, January 6. Accessed February 20, 2014. http://www.contemporaryfamilies.org/was-war-on-poverty-a-failure-report.

Coleman, Rhonda Janney. 2001. "Coal Miners and Their Communities in Southern Appalachia, 1925–1941." *West Virginia Historical Society Quarterly* 15, no. 2 (April). Accessed February 20, 2014. http://www.wvculture.org/history/wvhs1502.html.

Collins, Jane L., and Victoria Mayer. 2010. *Both Hands Tied: Welfare Reform and the Race to the Bottom of the Low-Wage Labor Market.* Chicago: University of Chicago Press.

Columbia Center for New Media Teaching and Learning. 2014. "Mapping the African American Past." Accessed March 1, 2014. http://maap.columbia.edu/place/22.html.

Conley, Dalton. 2009. *Being Black, Living in the Red: Race, Wealth, and Social Policy in*

America. Berkeley: University of California Press.

Conrad, David E. 1982. "Tenant Farming and Sharecropping." Oklahoma Historical Society, Encyclopedia of Oklahoma History and Culture. Accessed April 2, 2013. http://digital.library.okstate .edu/encyclopedia/entries/T/ TE009.html.

Corporation for Enterprise Development. 2014. "Assets and Opportunity Scorecard." Accessed February 24, 2014. http://assetsandopportunity .org/scorecard.

Couch, Kenneth A., and Robert Fairlie. 2010. "Last Hired, First Fired? Black–White Unemployment and the Business Cycle." *Demography* 47, no. 1: 227–47.

Council of Economic Advisers. 2015. "Gender Pay Gap: Recent Trends and Explanations." Issue Brief, April. Accessed April 8, 2016. https://www.whitehouse.gov/ sites/default/files/docs/equal_ pay_issue_brief_final.pdf.

Darity, William A., Jr., and Samuel L. Myers Jr. 1998. *Persistent Disparity: Race and Economic Inequality in the United States since 1945.* Cheltenham, England: Edward Elgar.

DeSilver, Drew. 2013. "U.S. Income Inequality, on Rise for Decades, Is Now Highest since 1928." Fact Tank, Pew Research Center, December 5. Accessed June 16, 2017. http://www.pewresearch.org/ fact-tank/2013/12/05/u-s-income-inequality-on-rise-for-decades-is-now-highest-since-1928.

Dickler, 2009. "The Hidden Job Market." CNN Money, June 10. Accessed June 24, 2014. http://money.cnn .com/2009/06/09/

news/economy/hidden_ jobs.

Dollars and Sense for a Fair Economy, ed. 2004. *The Wealth Economy Reader,* Boston: United for a Fair Economy.

Doob, Christopher Bates. 2005. *Race, Ethnicity, and the American Urban Mainstream.* Boston: Pearson.

Du Bois, W. E. B. 1918. "The Black Man and the Unions." TeachingAmerican History.org, Ashbrook Center, Ashland University. Accessed February 22, 2013. http:// teachingamerican history.org/library/document/ the-black-man-and-the-unions.

Dunn, John H., Jr. 2012. "The Decline of Manufacturing in the United States and Its Impact on Income Inequality." *Journal of Applied Business Research* 28, no. 5: 995–1000.

Edin, Kathryn J., and H. Luke Shaefer. 2015. *$2.00 a Day: Living on Almost Nothing in America.* Boston: Houghton Mifflin Harcourt.

Eitzen, D. Stanley, and Maxine Baca Zinn. 2000. "The Missing Safety Net and Families: A Progressive Critique of the New Welfare Legislation." *Journal of Sociology & Social Welfare* 27, no. 1: 53–72.

Engemann, Kristie M., and Howard J. Wall. 2009. "The Effects of Recessions across Demographic Groups." Working Paper 2009-052A, Federal Reserve Bank of St. Louis. Accessed June 4, 2017. http:// research.stlouisfed.org/ wp/2009/2009-052.pdf.

Equal Employment Opportunity Commission. 2010. "Pre-1965: Events Leading to the Creation of EEOC." Accessed February

22, 2014. http://www.eeoc .gov/eeoc/history/35th/ pre1965/index.html.

Eriksson, Stefan, Per Johansson, and Sophie Langenskiöld. 2012. "What Is the Right Profile for Getting a Job? A Stated Choice Experiment of the Recruitment Process." Discussion Paper 6691, IZA Institute for the Study of Labor, June. http://ftp.iza .org/dp6691.pdf.

Farber, Henry S. 2011. "Job Loss in the Great Recession: Historical Perspective from the Displaced Workers Survey, 1984–2010." Working Paper 17040, National Bureau of Economic Research. http://www.nber .org/papers/w17040.pdf.

Feagin, Joe R. 2000. *Racist America: Roots, Current Realities, and Future Reparations.* New York: Routledge.

Ferber, Abby L. 2014. "We Aren't Just Color-Blind, We Are Oppression-Blind!" In *Privilege: A Reader,* 3rd ed., edited by Michael S. Kimmel and Abby L. Ferber, 226–39. Boulder, CO: Westview Press.

Fishback, Price. 1984. "Segregation in Job Hierarchies: West Virginia Coal Mining, 1906–1932." *Journal of Economic History* 44, no. 3 (September): 755–74.

Flippen, Chenoa A., and Emilio A. Parrado. 2015. "Perceived Discrimination among Latino Immigrants in New Destinations: The Case of Durham, North Carolina." *Sociological Perspectives* 58, no. 4: 666–85.

Foged, Mette, and Giovanni Peri. 2016. "Immigrants' Effect on Native Workers: New Analysis on Longitudinal Data." *American Economic*

Journal: Applied Economics 8, no. 2: 1–34.

Forbes, Kristin. 2004. "U.S. Manufacturing: Challenges and Recommendations." *Business Economics* 39, no. 3: 30–37.

Foster, Carly Hayden. 2008. "The Welfare Queen: Race, Gender, Class, and Public Opinion." *Race, Gender, Class* 15, nos. 3–4: 162–79.

Foster, Thomas B., and Rachel Garshick Kleit. 2015. "The Changing Relationship between Housing and Inequality, 1980–2010." *Housing Policy Debate* 25, no. 1: 16–40.

Freeman, Jo. 1991. "How 'Sex' Got into Title VII: Persistent Opportunism as a Maker of Public Policy." *Law and Inequality* 9, no. 2: 163–84.

Freiberg, Fred, and Gregory D. Squires. 2015. "Changing Contexts and New Directions for the Use of Testing." *Cityscape* 17, no. 3.

Fry, Richard, and Paul Taylor. 2013. "A Rise in Wealth for the Wealthy; Declines for Lower 93%." Pew Research Center, April 23. Accessed February 22, 2013. http:// www.pewsocialtrends .org/2013/04/23/a-rise-in-wealth-for-the-wealthydeclines-for-the-lower-93/2/#chapter-1-the-uneven-wealth-recovery-among-the-nations-households.

Garfinkel, Irwin, David Harris, Jane Waldfogel, and Christopher Wimer. 2016. "Doing More for Our Children: Modeling a Universal Child Allowance or More Generous Child Tax Credit." Century Foundation, March 16. Accessed April 7, 2016. https://tcf.org/content/report/doing-more-for-our-children.

Gleckman, Howard. 2015. "How Many Americans Get Government Assistance? All of Us." *Forbes,* June 4. Accessed March 1, 2017. http://www.forbes.com/ sites/beltway/2015/06/04/ how-many-americans-get-government-assistance-all-of-us/#7790a3e120eb.

Grabell, Michael. 2013. "The 4 A.M. Army." *Time,* June 27. Accessed March 2, 2014. http://nation.time .com/2013/06/27/the-4-am-army/#ixzz2YryHi4Le.

Greenberg, Allen. 2013. "Muslim Job Candidates May Face Greater Discrimination." BenefitsPRO, December 2. Accessed April 10, 2016. http://www.benefitspro .com/2013/12/02/muslim-job-candidates-may-face-greater-discriminat.

Greenhouse, Stephen. 2010. "Muslims Report Rising Discrimination at Work." *New York Times,* September 23. Accessed June 24, 2014. http://www.nytimes .com/2010/09/24/ business/24muslim. html?pagewanted=all&_r=0.

Gurrieri, Vin. 2016. "Provisions to Cut EEOC Bias Case Backlog Advance in Senate." Law360, April 25. Accessed June 16, 2017. https://www.law360.com/ articles/788478/provisions-to-cut-eeoc-bias-case-backlog-advance-in-senate.

Higginbotham, Elizabeth. 2001. *Too Much to Ask: Black Women in the Era of Integration.* Chapel Hill: University of North Carolina Press.

Hill, Herbert. 1985. *Black Labor and the American Legal System: Race, Work, and the Law.* Madison: University of Wisconsin Press.

Hill, Linda. 2013. "Equal Pay for Equal Value: The Case for Care Workers." *Women's Studies Journal* 27, no. 2: 14–31.

Hosoda, Megumi, Lam T. Nguyen, and Eugene Stone-Romero. 2012. "The Effects of Hispanic Accents on Employment Decisions." *Journal of Managerial Psychology* 27, no. 4: 347–64.

Hoynes, Hilary W., Douglas L. Miller, and Jessamyn Schaller. 2012. "Who Suffers During Recessions?" Working Paper 17951, National Bureau of Economic Research. Accessed June 4, 2017. http://www.nber.org/ papers/w17951.pdf.

Ignatiev, Noel. 2008. *How the Irish Became White.* New York: Routledge.

Immigration Policy Center. 2013. "The Economic Blame Game: Immigration and Unemployment." Fact Sheet, June. Accessed April 10, 2016. http://www .immigrationpolicy.org/ just-facts/economic-blame-game-immigration-and-unemployment.

Ingraham, Christopher. 2015. "If You Thought Income Inequality Was Bad, Get a Load of Wealth Inequality." *Washington Post,* May 21. Accessed June 16, 2017. https://www .washingtonpost.com/news/ wonk/wp/2015/05/21/the-top-10-of-americans-own-76-of-the-stuff-and-its-dragging-our-economy-down.

Investopedia. n.d. "Gross Domestic Product—GDP." Accessed April 7, 2016. http://www.investopedia .com/terms/g/gdp.asp.

Iversen, Roberta Rehner, and Annie Laurie Armstrong. 2006. *Jobs Aren't Enough: Toward a New Economic Mobility for Low-Income Families.* Philadelphia: Temple University Press.

Kang, Miliann. 2010. *The Managed Hand: Race, Gender, and the Body in Beauty Service Work.* Berkeley: University of California Press.

Kantor, Jodi, Thomas Fuller, and Noam Scheiber. 2016. "Why Parental Leave Policies Are Changing." *New York Times,* April 6. Accessed April 8, 2016. http://www.nytimes.com/2016/04/07/us/why-parental-leave-policies-are-changing.html?emc=eta1&_r=0.

Kaplan, Jonathan, and Andrew Valls. 2007. "Housing Discrimination as a Basis for Black Reparations." *Public Affairs Quarterly* 21, no. 3: 255–73.

Katznelson, Ira. 2005. *When Affirmative Action Was White: An Untold History of Racial Inequality in Twentieth-Century America.* New York: W. W. Norton.

Kaufman, Wendy. 2011. "A Successful Job Search: It's All about Networking." *All Things Considered,* NPR, February 3. Accessed June 25, 2014. http://www.npr.org/2011/02/08/133474431/a-successful-job-search-its-all-about-networking.

Kennedy, John F. 1961. Executive order 10925. March 6. Accessed March 5, 2017. https://www.eeoc.gov/eeoc/history/35th/thelaw/eo-10925.html.

King, Eden B., and Afra Ahmad. 2010. "An Experimental Field Study of Interpersonal Discrimination toward Muslim Job Applicants." *Personnel Psychology* 63, no. 4: 881–906.

Kirschenman, Joleen, and Kathryn M. Neckerman. 1991. "'We'd Love to Hire Them but . . .': The Meaning of Race for Employers." In *The Urban Underclass,* edited by Christopher Jencks and Paul E. Peterson. Washington, DC: Brookings Institution Press.

Kneebone, Elizabeth, and Natalie Holmes. 2015. "New Census Data Finds Scant Progress against Poverty." Brookings Institution, September 18. Accessed April 3, 2016. http://www.brookings.edu/blogs/the-avenue/posts/2015/09/17-acs-poverty-data-kneebone-holmes.

Kochhar, Rakesh. 2011. "Two Years of Economic Recovery: Women Lose Jobs, Men Find Them." Pew Research Center, July 6. Accessed June 2, 2017. http://www.pewsocialtrends.org/2011/07/06/two-years-of-economic-recovery-women-lose-jobs-men-find-them.

Kochhar, Rakesh, Richard Fry, and Paul Taylor. 2011. "Wealth Gaps Rise to Record Highs Between Whites, Blacks, Hispanics." Pew Research Center, July 26. Accessed March 22, 2013. http://www.pewsocialtrends.org/2011/07/26/wealth-gaps-rise-to-record-highs-between-whites-blacks-hispanics.

Kolchin, Peter. 2002. "Whiteness Studies: The New History of Race in America." *Journal of American History* 89, no. 1 (June): 154–73.

Kusisto, Laura. 2015. "Many Who Lost Homes to Foreclosure in Last Decade Won't Return." *Wall Street Journal,* April 20. Accessed March 2, 2017. https://www.wsj.com/articles/many-who-lost-homes-to-foreclosure-in-last-decade-wont-return-nar-1429548640.

Lareau, Annette. 2011. *Unequal Childhoods: Class, Race, and Family Life.* 2nd ed. Berkeley: University of California Press.

Llewellyn Consulting. 2016. "Which Countries in Europe Offer the Fairest Paid Leave and Unemployment Benefits?" Glassdoor, February. Accessed April 7, 2016. https://research-content.glassdoor.com/app/uploads/sites/2/2016/02/GD_FairestPaidLeave_Final.pdf.

Lucas, Kintto. 2007. "Latin America: Indigenous, Black Women Face 'Triple Glass Ceiling.'" Inter Press Service, August 9. Accessed April 10, 2016. http://www.ipsnews.net/2007/08/latin-america-indigenous-black-women-face-lsquotriple-glass-ceilingrsquo.

Lui, Meizhu, Barbara Robles, Betsy Leondar-Wright, Rose Brewer, and Rebecca Adamson, with United for a Fair Economy. 2006. *The Color of Wealth: The Story behind the U.S. Racial Wealth Divide.* New York: New Press.

Madrick, Jeff. 2016. "Handouts Are Often Better Than a Hand Up." *New York Times,* April 7. Accessed April 7, 2016. http://www.nytimes.com/2016/04/07/opinion/handouts-are-often-better-than-a-hand-up.html?emc=eta1&_r=0.

Making Change at Walmart. 2014. "Walmart and Workers." Accessed June 24, 2014. http://changewalmart.org/issues/workers.

Marx, Karl. (1848) 2001. "Classes in Capitalism and Precapitalism." In *Social Stratification in Sociological Perspective,* 2nd ed., edited by David Grusky, 91–101.

McCarthy, Thomas. 2004. "Coming to Terms with Our Past, Part II: On the Morality and Politics of Reparations for Slavery." *Political Theory* 32, no. 6: 750–72.

McDonald, Stephen. 2015. "Protecting Hiring Managers from Themselves: Organizational Dynamics and Discriminatory Online Candidate Screening." Paper presented at the Conference of the Society for the Advancement of Socio-Economics, London, July 2–4.

McGee, Robert W. 2003. "Trade Policy as Corporate Welfare: The Case of the U.S. Steel Industry." Paper presented at the fifteenth annual conference of the International Academy of Business Disciplines, Orlando, FL, April 3–6. https://www.researchgate.net/profile/Robert_Mcgee2/publication/228238238_Trade_Policy_as_Corporate_Welfare_The_Case_of_the_U.S._Steel_Industry/links/00b7d5252c1f540d4c000000.pdf.

McKernan, Signe-Mary, Caroline Ratcliffe, Eugene Steuerle, and Sisi Zhang. 2013. "Less than Equal: Racial Disparities in Wealth Accumulation." Urban Institute, April. Accessed June 2, 2017. http://www.urban.org/sites/default/files/publication/23536/412802-less-than-equal-racial-disparities-in-wealth-accumulation.pdf.

Mine Safety and Health Administration. 2012. "Injury Trends in Mining." U.S. Department of Labor. Accessed April 1, 2013. http://www.msha.gov/MSHAINFO/FactSheets/MSHAFCT2.HTM#.UxTGv_ldV8E.

Mong, Sherry N., and Vincent J. Roscigno. 2010. "African American Men and the Experience of Employment Discrimination." *Qualitative Sociology* 33, no. 1: 1–21.

Monaghan, Angela. 2014. "US Wealth Inequality—Top 0.1% Worth as Much as the Bottom 90%." *Guardian,* November 13. Accessed June 16, 2017. https://www.theguardian.com/business/2014/nov/13/us-wealth-inequality-top-01-worth-as-much-as-the-bottom-90.

Moore, Marjorie, and Jo Jones. 2001. "Cracking the Concrete Ceiling: Inquiry into the Aspirations, Values, Motives, and Actions of African American Female 1890 Cooperative Extension Administrators." *Journal of Extension* 39, no. 6 (December).

Moore, Natalie. 2016. *The South Side: A Portrait of American Segregation.* New York: St. Martin's Press.

Morin, Rich, Paul Taylor, and Eileen Patten. 2012. "A Bipartisan Nation of Beneficiaries." Pew Research Center, December 18. Accessed April 7, 2016. http://www.pewsocialtrends.org/2012/12/18/a-bipartisan-nation-of-beneficiaries.

Movement for Black Lives. n.d. "Reparations." Accessed June 13, 2017. https://policy.m4bl.org/reparations.

National Academies of Sciences, Engineering, and Medicine. 2016. *The Economic and Fiscal Consequences of Immigration.* Washington, DC: National Academies Press. Accessed March 5, 2017. http://sites.nationalacademies.org/dbasse/cnstat/economic-and-fiscal-consequences-of-immigration.

Neckerman, Kathryn M., and Joleen Kirschenman. 1991. "Hiring Strategies, Racial Bias, and Inner-City Workers." *Social Problems* 38, no. 4: 433–47.

Neubeck, Kenneth J. 2006. *When Welfare Disappears: The Case for Economic Human Rights.* New York: Routledge.

Neubeck, Kenneth J., and Noel A. Cazenave. 2001. *Welfare Racism: Playing the Race Card against America's Poor.* New York: Routledge.

O'Connor, Clare. 2014. "Walmart Workers Cost Taxpayers $6.2 Billion in Public Assistance." *Forbes,* April 15. Accessed April 2, 2016. http://www.forbes.com/sites/clareoconnor/2014/04/15/report-walmart-workers-cost-taxpayers-6-2-billion-in-public-assistance/#55aa04657cd8.

Oliver, Melvin L., and Thomas M. Shapiro. 2006. *Black Wealth/White Wealth.* 2nd ed. New York: Routledge.

Oliveri, Rigel Christine. 2009. "Between a Rock and a Hard Place: Landlords, Latinos, Anti-illegal Immigrant Ordinances, and Housing Discrimination." *Vanderbilt Law Review* 62, no. 1: 55–124.

Organisation for Economic Co-operation and Development. 2015. *In It Together: Why Less Inequality Benefits All.* Paris: OECD Publishing. Accessed January 16, 2017. http://www.oecd.org/social/in-it-together-why-less-inequality-benefits-all-9789264235120-en.htm.

Ortega, Ramona, Gregory K. Plagens, Peggy Stephens, and RaJade M. Berry-James. 2012. "Mexican American Public Sector Professionals: Perceptions of Affirmative Action Policies and

Workplace Discrimination." *Review of Public Personnel Administration* 32, no. 1: 24–44. doi:10.1177/07343 71X11408705.

Ortiz, Susan Y., and Vincent J. Roscigno. 2009. "Discrimination, Women, and Work: Processes and Variations by Race and Class." *Sociological Quarterly* 50, no. 2: 336–59.

Pager, Devah. 2003. "The Mark of a Criminal Record." *American Journal of Sociology* 108, no. 5: 937–75.

———. 2007. "The Use of Field Experiments for Studies of Employment Discrimination: Contributions, Critiques, and Directions for the Future." *Annals of the American Academy of Political and Social Science* 609: 104–33.

———. 2008. *Marked: Race, Crime, and Finding Work in an Era of Mass Incarceration.* Chicago: University of Chicago Press.

Pager, Devah, and Hana Shepherd. 2008. "The Sociology of Discrimination: Racial Discrimination in Employment, Housing, Credit, and Consumer Markets." *Annual Review of Sociology* 34: 181–209.

Pager, Devah, and Bruce Western, 2012. "Identifying Discrimination at Work: The Use of Field Experiments." *Journal of Social Issues* 68, no. 2: 221–37.

Pager, Devah, Bruce Western, and Bart Bonikowski. 2009. "Discrimination in a Low-Wage Labor Market: A Field Experiment." *American Sociological Review* 74, no. 5: 777–99.

Pearce, Diana, with Jennifer Brooks. 2004. "The Self-Sufficiency Standard for Colorado 2004: A Family Needs Budget." Report prepared for the Colorado Fiscal Policy Institute. Accessed February 21, 2013. June http://www.larimer.org/compass/fnb_report2.pdf.

Pew Research Center. 2012. "The Rise of Asian Americans." June 19. Accessed February 21, 2013. http://www.pewsocialtrends.org/2012/06/19/the-rise-of-asian-americans.

Picchi, Aimee. 2015. "How Low-Wage Employers Cost Taxpayers $153B a Year." CBS Moneywatch, April 13. Accessed June 4, 2017. http://www.cbsnews.com/news/how-low-wage-employers-cost-taxpayers-153-billion-a-year.

Piketty, Thomas. 2014. *Capital in the Twenty-First Century.* Translated by Arthur Goldhammer. Cambridge, MA: Harvard University Press.

Piketty, Thomas, and Emmanuel Saez. 2014. "Inequality in the Long Run." *Science* 344, no. 6186: 838–43, and supplementary text online, 1–8. Accessed April 7, 2016. http://eml.berkeley.edu/~saez/piketty-saezScience14.pdf.

Piven, Frances Fox. 2002. "Welfare Policy and American Politics." In *Work, Welfare and Politics: Confronting Poverty in the Wake of Welfare Reform,* edited by Frances Fox Piven, Joan Acker, Margaret Hallock, and Sandra Morgen. Eugene: University of Oregon Press.

Qian, Zhenchao. 2012. "During the Great Recession, More Young Adults Lived with Parents." Census Brief prepared for Project US2010. Accessed April 8, 2016. https://www.s4.brown.edu/us2010.

Rahill, Guitele J. 2015. "A World More Concrete: Real Estate and the Remaking of Jim Crow South Florida." *Ethnic and Racial Studies* 38, no. 13: 2462–64.

Ray, Rebecca, and John Schmitt. 2007. "No-Vacation Nation USA: A Comparison of Leave and Holiday in OEC Countries." European Economic and Employment Policy Brief 3, ETUI-REHS. Accessed June 2, 2017. http://www.law.harvard.edu/programs/lwp/papers/No_Holidays.pdf.

Roediger, David R. 2007. *The Wages of Whiteness: Race and the Making of the American Working Class.* Chicago: Haymarket Press.

Rooth, Dan-Olof. 2010. "Automatic Associations and Discrimination in Hiring: Real World Evidence." *Labour Economics* 17, no. 3: 523–34.

Roscigno, Vincent J. 2007. *The Face of Discrimination: How Race and Gender Impact Work and Home Lives.* Lanham, MD: Rowman & Littlefield.

Roscigno, Vincent J., Lisa M. Williams, and Reginald A. Byron. 2012. "Workplace Racial Discrimination and Middle-Class Vulnerability." *American Behavioral Scientist* 56, no. 5: 696–710.

Rugh, Jacob S., and Douglas S. Massey. 2010. "Racial Segregation and the American Foreclosure Crisis." *American Sociological Review* 75, no. 5: 629–51.

Saez, Emmanuel, and Gabriel Zucman. 2016. "Wealth

Inequality in the United States since 1913: Evidence from Capitalized Income Tax Data." *Quarterly Journal of Economics,* published online February 16. doi:10.1093/qje/qjw004.

Schow, Ashe. 2013. "Recovery Woes: America's Second Largest Employer Is a Temp Agency." *Washington Examiner,* July 8. Accessed January 16, 2017. http://washingtonexaminer.com/recovery-woes-americas-second-largest-employer-is-a-temp-agency/article/2532778.

Shapiro, Thomas M. 2004. *The Hidden Cost of Being African American: How Wealth Perpetuates Inequality.* Oxford: Oxford University Press.

Sherman, Erik. 2015. "America Is the Richest, and Most Unequal, Country." *Fortune,* September 30. Accessed January 16, 2017. http://fortune.com/2015/09/30/america-wealth-inequality.

Sierminska, Eva, and Yelena Takhtamanova. 2011. "Job Flows, Demographics, and the Great Recession." In *Who Loses in the Downturn? Economic Crisis, Employment, and Income Distribution,* edited by Herwig Immervoll, Andreas Peichl, and Konstantinos Tatsiramos, 115–54. Bingley, England: Emerald Books.

Silicon Valley Rising. 2016. "Tech's Invisible Workforce." Accessed April 7, 2016. http://www.siliconvalleyrising.org/TechsInvisibleWorkforce.pdf.

Slivinski, Stephen. 2007. "The Corporate Welfare State: How the Federal Government Subsidizes U.S. Business." *Policy Analysis,* no. 592 (May 14). Accessed April 2, 2016. http://www.occupybanksters.com/images/graphs/corporate-welfare/corporate-welfare_003_pa592.pdf.

Strauss, Jack. 2013. "Allies, Not Enemies: How Latino Immigration Boosts African American Employment and Wages." American Immigration Council, June 12. Accessed June 2, 2017. https://www.americanimmigrationcouncil.org/research/allies-not-enemies-how-latino-immigration-boosts-african-american-employment-and-wages.

Swaine, Jon. 2014. "Jamaicans Lead Caribbean Calls for Britain to Pay Slavery Reparations." *Telegraph,* February 15. Accessed February 20, 2014. http://www.telegraph.co.uk/news/worldnews/centralamericaandthecaribbean/jamaica/10640560/Jamaicans-lead-Caribbean-calls-for-Britain-to-pay-slavery-reparations.html.

Tasch, Barbara. 2015. "The 23 Richest Countries in the World." Business Insider, July 23. Accessed January 16, 2017. http://www.businessinsider.com/the-23-richest-countries-in-the-world-2015-7.

———. 2016. "The 25 Poorest Countries in the World." Business Insider, April 3. Accessed January 16, 2017. http://www.businessinsider.com/the-25-poorest-countries-in-the-world-2016-4.

Thomas, Alexandar R. 1998. "Ronald Reagan and the Commitment of the Mentally Ill: Capital, Interest Groups, and the Eclipse of Social Policy." *Electronic Journal of Sociology* 3, no. 4. Accessed April 2, 2016. https://www.sociology.org/content/vol003.004/thomas.html.

Tilbury, Farida, and Val Colic-Peisker. 2006. "Deflecting Responsibility in Employer Talk about Race Discrimination." *Discourse and Society* 17: 651–76.

Tilcsik, András. 2011. "Pride and Prejudice: Employment Discrimination against Openly Gay Men in the United States." *American Journal of Sociology* 117, no. 2 (September): 586–626.

U.S. Bureau of Labor Statistics. 2015. "Data Tables for the Overview of May 2015 Occupational Employment and Wages." Accessed June 2, 2017. http://www.bls.gov/oes/2015/may/featured_data.htm#largest2.

———. 2016. "Labor Force Statistics from the Current Population Survey." Accessed June 2, 2017. http://www.bls.gov/cps/cpsaat11.htm.

U.S. Department of Justice, Civil Rights Division. 2010. "Information and Technical Assistance on the Americans with Disabilities Act." Accessed February 22, 2013. http://www.ada.gov/2010_regs.htm.

U.S. Department of Labor. 2001. "Facts on Executive Order 11246—Affirmative Action." Accessed March 12, 2013. http://www.dol.gov/ofccp/regs/compliance/aa.htm.

———. 2011. "The Asian-American Labor Force in the Recovery." July 22. Accessed April 7, 2016. http://www.dol.gov/_sec/media/reports/asianlaborforce.

———. 2014. "The Economic Status of Asian Americans and Pacific Islanders in the Wake of the Great Recession." Accessed March 5, 2017. https://www.dol.gov/_sec/media/reports/20140828-aapi.pdf.

West, Cassandra. 1999. "A 'Concrete Ceiling' Lingers over Women of Color." *Chicago Tribune,* August 4. Accessed April 10, 2016. http://articles.chicagotribune.com/1999-08-04/features/9908040296_1_glass-ceiling-minority-women-sheila-wellington.

Western, Bruce, and Jake Rosenfeld. 2011. "Unions, Norms, and the Rise in U.S. Wage Inequality." *American Sociological Review* 76, no. 4: 513–37.

Wilkerson, Isabel. 2010. *The Warmth of Other Suns: The Epic Story of America's Great Migration.* New York: Random House.

Williams, Jimmy. 2013. "Welfare Queens? Welfare Kings Rule the Land." *U.S. News & World Report,* December 20. Accessed April 2, 2016. http://www.usnews.com/opinion/blogs/jimmy-williams/2013/12/20/dont-forget-the-corporate-welfare-kings-and-their-tax-code-subsidies.

Wilson, George, and Debra Branch McBrier. 2005. "Race and Loss of Privilege: African American/White Differences in the Determinants of Job Layoffs from Upper-Tier Occupations*." Sociological Forum* 20: 301–21.

Wilson, George, and Vincent J. Roscigno. 2010. "Race and Downward Occupational Mobility from Privileged Occupations: African American/White Dynamics across the Early Work-Career." *Social Science Research* 39: 67–77.

Wilson, William Julius. 1991–92. "Another Look at *The Truly Disadvantaged.*" *Political Science Quarterly* 106, no. 4: 639–56.

———. 1996. "When Work Disappears." *Political Science Quarterly* 111, no. 4: 567–95.

Wingfield, Adia Harvey. 2012. *No More Invisible Man: Race and Gender in Men's Work.* Philadelphia: Temple University Press

Wolfers, Justin. 2015. "The Gains from the Economic Recovery Are Still Limited to the Top One Percent." *New York Times,* January 27. Accessed June 4, 2017. http://www.nytimes.com/2015/01/28/upshot/gains-from-economic-recovery-still-limited-to-top-one-percent.html.

Worldatlas. 2017. "The Richest Countries in the World." Accessed January 16, 2017. http://www.worldatlas.com/articles/the-richest-countries-in-the-world.html.

Zack, Naomi. 2003. "Reparations and the Rectification of Race." *Journal of Ethics* 7, no. 1: 139–51.

Zong, Jie, and Jeanne Batalova. 2015. "Indian Immigrants in the United States." Migration Policy Institute, May 6. Accessed March 5, 2017. http://www.migrationpolicy.org/article/indian-immigrants-united-states.

■ CHAPTER 5

Agency for Healthcare Research and Quality. 2016. *2015 National Healthcare Quality and Disparities Report and 5th Anniversary Update on the National Quality Strategy.* AHRQ Pub. No. 16-0015. Washington, DC: AHRQ, U.S. Department of Health and Human Services. Accessed June 3, 2017. https://www.ahrq.gov/sites/default/files/wysiwyg/research/findings/nhqrdr/nhqdr15/2015nhqdr.pdf.

Agency for Toxic Substances and Disease Registry. 2000. *Lead Toxicity.* Publication No. ATSDR-HE-CS-2001-0001. Washington, DC: U.S. Department of Health and Human Services.

Aiello, Allison E., Elaine L. Larson, and Richard Sedlak. 2008a. "Foreword." *American Journal of Infection Control* 36, no. 10 (suppl.): S109.

———. 2008b. "Hidden Heroes of the Health Revolution: Sanitation and Personal Hygiene." *American Journal of Infection Control* 36, no.10 (suppl.): S128–51.

Alsan, Marcella, and Marianne Wanamaker. "Tuskegee and the Health of Black Men." Working Paper 22323, National Bureau of Economic Research. Accessed June 27, 2017. http://www.nber.org/papers/w22323.pdf.

Amadeo, Kimberly. 2017. "Donald Trump on Health Care." The Balance, June 26. Accessed June 27, 2017. https://www.thebalance.com/how-could-trump-change-health-care-in-america-4111422.

Association of American Medical Colleges. 2012. "New Medical College Admission Test Approved: Changes Add Emphasis on Behavioral and Social Sciences." Press release, February 16. Accessed March 31, 2015. https://www.aamc.org/newsroom/newsreleases/273712/120216.html.

———. 2014. "Diversity in the Physician Workforce: Facts and Figures 2014." Accessed March 31, 2015. http://aamcdiversityfactsandfigures.org.

Barnes, Colin. 2010. "A Brief History of Discrimination and Disabled People." In *The Disability Studies Reader,* 3rd ed., edited by Lennard J. Davis, 20–32. New York: Routledge.

Blake, Kelly. 2014. "Racism May Accelerate Aging in African American Men." UMD Right Now, January 7. Accessed June 2, 2017. http://www.umdrightnow.umd.edu/news/racism-may-accelerate-aging-african-american-men.

Blumenfeld, Warren J. 2012. "One Year Sick and Then Not: On the Social Construction of Homosexuality as Disease.'" Warren Blumenfeld's Blog, December 27. Accessed December 12, 2013. http://www.warrenblumenfeld.com/?s=homosexuality+disease.

Boulware, L. Ebony, Lisa A. Cooper, Lloyd E. Ratner, Thomas A. LaVeist, and Neil R. Powe. 2003. "Race and Trust in the Health Care System." *Public Health Reports* 118, no. 4: 358–65.

Braveman, Paula. 2012. "Health Inequalities by Class and Race in the US: What Can We Learn from the Patterns?" *Social Science & Medicine* 74: 665–67.

Braveman, Paula, and Laura Gottlieb. 2014. "The Social Determinants of Health: It's Time to Consider the Causes of the Causes." *Public Health Reports* 129, no. 1 (suppl. 2): 19–31.

Brenick, Alaina, Kelly Romano, Christopher Kegler, and Lisa A. Eaton. 2017. "Understanding the Influence of Stigma and Medical Mistrust on Engagement in Routine Healthcare among Black Women Who Have Sex with Women." *LGBT Health* 4, no. 1: 4–10.

Brown, Roscoe C. 1937. "The National Negro Health Week Movement." *Journal of Negro Education* 6, no. 3 (July): 553–64.

Burrage, Rachel L., Joseph P. Gone, and Sandra L. Momper. 2016. "Urban American Indian Community Perspectives on Resources and Challenges for Youth Suicide Prevention." *American Journal of Community Psychology* 58, nos. 1–2: 136–49.

Capistrano, Christian G., Hannah Bianco, and Pilyoung Kim. 2016. "Poverty and Internalizing Symptoms: The Indirect Effect of Middle Childhood Poverty on Internalizing Symptoms via an Emotional Response Inhibition Pathway." *Frontiers in Psychology* 7. doi:10.3389/fpsyg.2016.01242.

Castillo, Michelle. 2013. "U.S. Life Expectancy Lowest among Wealthy Nations Due to Disease, Violence." CBS News, January 10. Accessed April 2, 2015. http://www.cbsnews.com/news/report-us-life-expectancy-lowest-among-wealthy-nations-due-to-disease-violence.

Centers for Disease Control and Prevention. 2017. "Stroke Facts." Accessed June 19, 2017. https://www.cdc.gov/stroke/facts.htm.

Charatz-Litt, C. 1992. "A Chronicle of Racism: The Effects of the White Medical Community on Black Health." *Journal of the National Medical Association* 84, no. 8 (August): 717–25.

Chow, Edward A., Henry Foster, Victor Gonzalez, and LaShawn McIver. 2012. "The Disparate Impact of Diabetes on Racial/Ethnic Minority Populations." *Clinical Diabetes* 30, no. 3: 130–33.

Coco, Adrienne Phelps. 2010. "Diseased, Maimed, Mutilated: Categorizations of Disability and an Ugly Law in Late Nineteenth-Century Chicago." *Journal of Social History* 44, no. 1: 23–37.

Cohen, Elizabeth, and John Bonifield. 2012. "California's Dark Legacy of Forced Sterilizations." CNN, March 15. Accessed December 11, 2012. http://www.cnn.com/2012/03/15/health/california-forced-sterilizations.

Conrad, Peter, and Valerie Leiter, eds. 2012. *The Sociology of Health and Illness: Critical Perspectives.* 9th ed. New York: Worth.

Cornwell, John. 2003. *Hitler's Scientists: Science, War, and the Devil's Pact.* New York: Penguin.

Daniels, Jessie, and Amy J. Schulz. 2006. "Constructing Whiteness in Health Disparities Research." In *Gender, Race, Class, and Health: Intersectional Approaches,* edited by Amy J. Schulz and Leith Mullings, 89–127. San Francisco: Jossey-Bass.

Davis, Lennard J. 2010. "Constructing Normalcy." In *The Disability Studies Reader,* 3rd ed., edited by Lennard J. Davis, 3–19. New York: Routledge.

Debbink, Michelle Precourt, and Michael D. M. Bader. 2011. "Racial Residential Segregation and Low Birth Weight in Michigan's Metropolitan Areas." *American Journal of Public Health* 101, no. 9: 1714–20.

De la Rosa, Iván A. 2002. "Perinatal Outcomes among Mexican Americans: A Review of an Epidemiological Paradox." *Ethnicity & Disease* 12 (Autumn): 480–87.

DuBois, Ellen Carol, and Lynn Dumenil. 2012. *Through Women's Eyes: An American History.* 3rd ed. Boston: Bedford/St. Martin's.

Du Bois, W. E. B. 1899. *The Philadelphia Negro: A Social Study.* Philadelphia: University of Pennsylvania Press.

Duster, Troy. 2003. *Backdoor to Eugenics.* 2nd ed. New York: Routledge.

Ekland-Olson, Sheldon, and Julie Beicken. 2012. *How Ethical Systems Change: Eugenics, the Final Solution, Bioethics.* New York: Routledge.

Feagin, Joe R., and Karyn D. McKinney. 2003. *The Many Costs of Racism.* Lanham, MD: Rowman & Littlefield.

Ferber, Abby L. 1998. *White Man Falling: Race, Gender, and White Supremacy*. Lanham, MD: Rowman & Littlefield.

Filippi, Melissa K., David G. Perdue, Christina Hester, Angelia Cully, Lance Cully, K. Allen Greiner, and Christine M. Daley. 2016. "Colorectal Cancer Screening Practices among Three American Indian Communities in Minnesota." *Journal of Cultural Diversity* 23, no. 1: 21–27.

Fixico, Donald L. 2000. *The Urban Indian Experience.* Albuquerque: University of New Mexico Press.

Freimuth, Vicki S., Sandra Crouse Quinn, Stephen B. Thomas, Galen Cole, Eric Zook, and Ted Duncan. 2001. "African Americans' Views on Research and the Tuskegee Syphilis Study." *Social Science & Medicine* 52: 797–808.

Galea, Sandro, Melissa Tracy, Katherine J. Hoggatt, Charles DiMaggio, and Adam Karpati. 2011. "Estimated Deaths Attributable to Social Factors in the United States." *American Journal of Public Health* 101, no. 8: 1456–65.

Gallet, Craig A., and Hristos Doucouliagos. 2017. "The Impact of Healthcare Spending on Health Outcomes: A Meta-regression Analysis." *Social Science & Medicine* 179: 9–17.

Glenn, Evelyn Nakano. 2010. *Forced to Care: Coercion and Caregiving in America.* Cambridge, MA: Harvard University Press.

Gorman, Bridget K., and Jen'nan Ghazal Read. 2006. "Gender Disparities in Adult Health: An Examination of Three Measures of Morbidity." *Journal of Health and Social Behavior* 47 (June): 95–110

Gould, Stephen Jay. 1981. *The Mismeasure of Man*. New York: W. W. Norton.

Gray, Simone C., Sharon E. Edwards, Bradley D. Schultz, and Marie Lynn Miranda. 2014. "Assessing the Impact of Race, Social Factors and Air Pollution on Birth Outcomes: A Population-Based Study." *Environmental Health* 13, no. 4. doi:10.1186/1476-069X-13-4.

Green, Tiffany L., and William A. Darity Jr. 2010. "Under the Skin: Using Theories from Biology and the Social Sciences to Explore the Mechanisms behind the Black–White Health Gap." *American Journal of Public Health* 100 (suppl. 1): 36–38.

Guadagnolo, B. Ashleigh, Kristen Cina, Petra Helbig, Kevin Molloy, Mary Reiner, E. Francis Cook, and Daniel Petereit. 2009. "Medical Mistrust and Less Satisfaction with Health Care among Native Americans Presenting for Cancer Treatment." *Journal of Health Care for the Poor and Underserved* 20, no. 1 (February): 210–26.

Health Resources and Services Administration. 2015. "Sex, Race, and Ethnic Diversity of U.S. Health Occupations (2010–2012)." U.S. Department of Health and Human Services. Accessed Jun 2, 2017. https://bhw.hrsa.gov/sites/default/files/bhw/nchwa/diversityushealthoccupations.pdf.

Hertzman, Clyde. 2012. "Putting the Concept of Biological Embedding in Historical Perspective." *Proceedings of the National Academy of Sciences* 109 (suppl. 2): 17160–67.

Hosokawa, Michael C. 2012. "Please Don't." *Annals of Behavioral Science and Medical Education* 18, no. 1: 21–22.

Hubbard, Ruth, and Elijah Wald. 1999. *Exploding the Gene Myth*. Boston: Beacon Press.

Human Genome Project Information Archive.

2013. "About the Human Genome Project." Accessed December 30, 2013. http://web.ornl.gov/sci/techresources/Human_Genome/project/index.shtml.

Indian Health Service. 2017. "Disparities." Fact sheet, April. Accessed May 14, 2017. https://www.ihs.gov/newsroom/factsheets/disparities.

International Society for Ethnopharmacology. 2012. "Vision." Accessed December 25, 2013. http://www.ethnopharmacology.org/ISE_about_us.htm.

Jackson, Pamela Braboy, and David R. Williams. 2006. "The Intersections of Race, Gender, and SES: Health Paradoxes." In *Gender, Race, Class, and Health: Intersectional Approaches,* edited by Amy J. Schulz and Leith Mullings, 131–62. San Francisco: Jossey-Bass.

Jesudason, Sujatha, and Julia Epstein. 2011. "The Paradox of Disability in Abortion Debates: Bringing the Pro-choice and Disability Rights Communities Together." *Contraception* 84, no. 6: 541–43.

Korosec, Kirsten. 2017. "2016 Was the Deadliest Year on American Roads in Nearly a Decade." *Fortune,* February 15. Accessed June 19, 2017. http://fortune.com/2017/02/15/traffic-deadliest-year.

Lam, Bourree. 2014. "Who Stays Home When the Kids Are Sick?" *Atlantic,* October. Accessed May 14, 2017. https://www.theatlantic.com/business/archive/2014/10/who-stays-home-when-the-kids-are-sick/382011.

Lombardo, Paul A. 2008. *Three Generations and No Imbeciles: Eugenics, the Supreme Court, and* Buck v. Bell. Baltimore: Johns Hopkins University Press.

Martin, Emily. 2006. "Moods and Representations of Social Inequality." In *Gender, Race, Class, and Health: Intersectional Approaches,* edited by Amy J. Schulz and Leith Mullings, 60–88. San Francisco: Jossey-Bass.

Massey, Rachel. 2004. "Environmental Justice: Income, Race, and Health." Global Development and Environment Institute, Tufts University. Accessed June 2, 2017. http://www.ase.tufts.edu/gdae/education_materials/modules/Environmental_Justice.pdf.

McKeown, Thomas. 2014. *The Role of Medicine: Dream, Mirage, or Nemesis?* 2nd ed. Princeton, NJ: Princeton University Press.

McLaren, Lindsay, and Penelope Hawe. 2005. "Ecological Perspectives in Health Research." *Journal of Epidemiology & Community Health* 59, no. 1: 6–14.

Mora, Pat. 1984. *Chants.* Houston, TX: Arte Público Press.

———. 1993. *Nepantla: Essays from the Land in the Middle*. Albuquerque: University of New Mexico Press.

Morgen, Sandra. 2002. *Into Our Own Hands: The Women's Health Movement in the United States, 1969–1990.* New Brunswick, NJ: Rutgers University Press.

National Institutes of Health. 2015. "Risk Factors for High Blood Pressure." September 10. Accessed May 14, 2017. https://www.nhlbi.nih.gov/health/health-topics/topics/hbp/atrisk.

National Medical Association. n.d. "History." Accessed June 2, 2017. http://www.nmanet.org/page/History.

O'Donnell, Liz. 2016. "The Crisis Facing America's Working Daughters." *Atlantic,* February 9. Accessed June 15, 2017. https://www.theatlantic.com/business/archive/2016/02/working-daughters-eldercare/459249.

Olakanmi, Ololade. n.d. "The AMA, NMA, and the Flexner Report of 1910." Paper prepared for the Writing Group on the History of African Americans and the Medical Profession, American Medical Association. Accessed June 2, 2017. http://www.ama-assn.org/resources/doc/ethics/flexner.pdf.

Olshansky, S. Jay, Toni Antonucci, Lisa Berkman, Robert H. Binstock, Axel Boersch-Supan, John T. Cacioppo, Bruce A. Carnes, Laura L. Carstensen, Linda P. Fried, Dana P. Goldman, James Jackson, Martin Kohli, John Rother, Yuhui Zheng, and John Rowe. 2012. "Differences in Life Expectancy Due to Race and Educational Differences Are Widening, and Many May Not Catch Up." *Health Affairs* 31, no. 8 (August): 1803–13.

Ossorio, Pilar, and Troy Duster. 2005. "Race and Genetics: Controversies in Biomedical, Behavioral, and Forensic Sciences." *American Psychologist,* 60, no. 1 (January): 115–28.

Park, Lisa Sun-Hee. 2011. *Entitled to Nothing: The Struggle for Immigrant Health Care in the Age of Welfare Reform.* New York: New York University Press.

Parker-Pope, Tara. 2013. "Tackling a Racial Gap in Breast Cancer Survival."

New York Times, December 20. Accessed June 2, 2017. http://www.nytimes .com/2013/12/20/health/ tackling-a-racial-gap-in-breast-cancer-survival. html?_r=0.

Pollard, Kelvin, and Paola Scommegna. 2013. "The Health and Life Expectancy of Older Blacks and Hispanics in the U.S." Population Reference Bureau, *Today's Research on Aging,* no. 28 (June). Accessed June 19, 2017. http://www.prb.org/pdf13/ TodaysResearchAging28 .pdf.

Pollitt, Phoebe Ann 1996. "From National Negro Health Week to National Public Health Week." *Journal of Community Health* 21, no. 6: 401–7.

Randall, Alice. 2012. "Black Women and Fat." *New York Times,* May 6. Accessed June 2, 2017. http://www .nytimes.com/2012/05/06/ opinion/sunday/why-black-women-are-fat.html?_r=0.

Rasanathan, Kumanan, and Alyssa Sharkey. 2016. "Global Health Promotion and the Social Determinants of Health." In *Introduction to Global Health Promotion,* edited by Rick S. Zimmerman, Ralph J. DiClemente, Jon K. Andrus, and Everold N. Hosein, 49–64. San Francisco: Jossey-Bass.

Read, Jen'nan Ghazal, and Michael O. Emerson. 2005. "Racial Context, Black Immigration and the U.S. Black/White Health Disparity." *Social Forces* 84, no. 1: 181–99.

Repka, Matt. 2013. "Enduring Damage: The Effects of Childhood Poverty on Adult Health." *Chicago Policy Review,* November 27.

Robert Wood Johnson Foundation. 2011. "Race, Socioeconomic Factors and Health." Exploring the Social Determinants of Health, Issue Brief 6, April. Accessed June 4, 2017. http://www .rwjf.org/content/dam/farm/ reports/issue_briefs/2011/ rwjf70446.

Ruiz, John M., Heidi A. Hamann, Matthias R. Mehl, and Mary-Frances O'Connor. 2016. "The Hispanic Health Paradox: From Epidemiological Phenomenon to Contribution Opportunities for Psychological Science." *Group Processes & Intergroup Relations* 19, no. 4: 462–76.

Savitt, Todd L. 1982. "The Use of Blacks for Medical Experimentation and Demonstration in the Old South." *Journal of Southern History* 48, no. 3 (August): 331–48.

Saxton, Marsha. 2010. "Disability Rights and Selective Abortion." In *The Disability Studies Reader,* 3rd ed., edited by Lennard J. Davis, 120–32. New York: Routledge.

Schulz, Amy J., Graciela B. Mentz, Natalie Sampson, Melanie Ward, Rhonda Anderson, Ricardo de Majo, Barbara A. Israel, Toby C. Lewis, and Donele Wilkins. 2016. "Race and the Distribution of Social and Physical Environmental Risk." *Du Bois Review* 13, no. 2: 285–304.

Sedgh, Gilda, Rubina Hussain, Akinrinola Bankole, and Susheela Singh. 2007. "Women with an Unmet Need for Contraception in Developing Countries and Their Reasons for Not Using a Method." Occasional Report 37, Guttmacher Institute, June. Accessed February 13, 2015. http://www.guttmacher .org/pubs/2007/07/09/ or37.pdf.

SisterSong. 2013. "What Is Reproductive Justice?" Accessed February 13, 2015. http://sistersong.net/ index.php?option=com_ content&view =article&id=141.

Smedley, Brian, Michael Jeffries, Larry Adelman, and Jean Cheng. 2008. "Race, Racial Inequality and Health Inequities: Separating Myth from Fact." Briefing Paper, Opportunity Agenda and California Newsreel. Accessed June 2, 2017. http://www.unnaturalcauses .org/assets/uploads/file/ Race_Racial_Inequality_ Health.pdf.

Snyderman, Nancy. 2012. "North Carolina Budget Drops Payment to Forced Sterilization Victims." NBC News, June 20. Accessed December 30, 2013. http:// usnews.nbcnews.com/_ news/2012/06/20/12321330-north-carolina-budget-drops-payment-to-forced-sterilization-victims?lite.

Somerville, Siobhan B. 2000. *Queering the Color Line: Race and the Invention of Homosexuality in American Culture.* Durham, NC: Duke University Press.

Spanakis, Elias K., and Sherita Hill Golden. 2013. "Race/ Ethnic Difference in Diabetes and Diabetic Complications." *Current Diabetes Reports* 13, no. 6: 814–23.

Stone, Lisa Cacari, and C. H. Hank Balderrama. 2008.

"Health Inequalities among Latinos: What Do We Know and What Can We Do?" *Health and Social Work* 33, no. 1: 3–7.

Strauss, John, and Duncan Thomas. 2007. "Health over the Life Course." California Center for Population Research, November. Accessed May 8, 2017. http://papers.ccpr.ucla.edu/papers/PWP-CCPR-2007-011/PWP-CCPR-2007-011.pdf.

Striegel-Moore, Faith-Anne Dohm, Kathleen M. Pike, Denise E. Wifley, and Christopher G. Fairburn. 2002. "Abuse, Bullying, and Discrimination as Risk Factors for Binge Eating Disorders." *American Journal of Psychiatry* 159, no. 11: 1902–7.

Sue, Derald Wing. 2010. *Microaggressions in Everyday Life: Race, Gender, and Sexual Orientation.* Hoboken, NJ: John Wiley.

Sullivan, Louis W., and Ilana Suez Mittman. 2010. "The State of Diversity in the Health Professions a Century after Flexner." *Academic Medicine* 85, no. 2: 246–53.

Syme, S. Leonard, and Lisa F. Berkman. 2009. "Sociology, Susceptibility, and Sickness." In *The Sociology of Health and Illness: Critical Perspectives,* 8th ed., edited by Peter Conrad, 24–30. New York: Worth.

Tavernise, Sabrina, and Robert Gebeloff. 2013. "Millions of Poor Are Left Uncovered by Health Law." *New York Times,* October 2. Accessed June 1, 2017. http://www.nytimes.com/2013/10/03/health/millions-of-poor-are-left-uncovered-by-health-law.html?pagewanted=all&mcubz=1.

Thomas, Stephen B., and Sandra Crouse Quinn. 1991. "Public Health Then and Now: The Tuskegee Syphilis Study, 1932 to 1972: Implications for HIV Education and AIDS Risk Education Programs in the Black Community." *American Journal of Public Health* 81, no. 11: 1498–505.

United States Holocaust Memorial Museum. n.d. "The Murder of the Handicapped." The Holocaust: A Learning Site for Students. Accessed December 28, 2013. http://www.ushmm.org/outreach/en/article.php?ModuleId=10007683.

Urban Indian Health Commission. 2007. *Invisible Tribes: Urban Indians and Their Health in a Changing World.* Seattle: Urban Indian Health Commission. Accessed May 14, 2017. https://www2.census.gov/cac/nac/meetings/2015-10-13/invisible-tribes.pdf.

U.S. Bureau of Labor Statistics. 2017. "Occupational Employment and Wages, May 2016." Accessed June 1, 2017. http://www.bls.gov/oes/current/oes311011.htm.

U.S. Department of Health and Human Services, Office of Minority Health. 2011. "Pathways to Integrated Health Care: Strategies for African American Communities and Organizations." Accessed June 4, 2017. http://minorityhealth.hhs.gov/Assets/pdf/Checked/1/PathwaystoIntegratedHealthCareStrategiesforAfricanAmericans.pdf.

Verma, Reetu, Samantha Clark, Jonathon P. Leider, and David Bishai. "Impact of State Public Health Spending on Disease Incidence in the United States from 1980 to 2009." *Health Services Research* 52, no. 1. doi:10.1111/1475-6773.12480.

Waldstein, Anna. 2010. "Popular Medicine and Self-Care in a Mexican Migrant Community: Toward an Explanation of an Epidemiological Paradox." *Medical Anthropology* 29, no. 1: 71–107.

Warner, David F., and Tyson Brown. 2011. "Understanding How Race/Ethnicity and Gender Define Age-Trajectories of Disability: An Intersectionality Approach." *Social Science & Medicine* 72: 1236–48.

Washington, Harriett A. 2008. *Medical Apartheid: The Dark History of Medical Experimentation on Black Americans from Colonial Times to the Present.* New York: Anchor Books.

Weber, Lynn. 2006. "Reconstructing the Landscape of Health Disparities Research: Promoting Dialogue and Collaboration between Feminist Intersectional and Biomedical Paradigms." In *Gender, Race, Class, and Health: Intersectional Approaches,* edited by Amy J. Schulz and Leith Mullings, 21–59. San Francisco: Jossey-Bass.

Weng, Suzie S., and Jacqueline Robinson. 2014. "Intergenerational Dynamics Related to Aging and Eldercare in Asian American Families: Promoting Access to Services." In *The Collective Spirit of Aging across Cultures,* edited by Halaevalu F. Ofahengaue Vakalahi, Gaynell M. Simpson, and Nancy Giunta, 157–71. Dordrecht: Springer.

White, Kevin. 2009. *An Introduction to the Sociology*

of Health and Illness. Thousand Oaks, CA: Sage.

Williams, David R. 2012. "Miles to Go before We Sleep: Racial Inequities in Health." *Journal of Health and Social Behavior* 53, no. 3: 279–95.

World Health Organization 1996. "Traditional Medicine." Accessed December 25, 2013. http://www.who.int/inf-fs/en/fact134.html.

Zambrana, Ruth E., and Bonnie Thornton Dill. 2006.

"Disparities in Latina Health: An Intersectional Analysis." In *Gender, Race, Class, and Health: Intersectional Approaches,* edited by Amy J. Schulz and Leith Mullings, 192–227. San Francisco: Jossey-Bass.

■ CHAPTER 6

Apple, Michael. 2013. *Knowledge, Power, and Education: The Selected Works of Michael Apple.* London: Routledge.

Asante, Molefi Kete. 1991. "The Afroectric Idea in Education." *Journal of Negro Education* 60, no. 2: 170–80.

Becker, Gary. 1964. *Human Capital.* New York: National Bureau of Economic Research.

Bernstein, Basil. 1971. *Class, Codes and Control,* Vol. 1, *Theoretical Studies towards a Sociology of Language.* Oxford: Routledge.

Bourdieu, Pierre. 1984. *Distinction: A Social Critique of the Judgment of Taste.* Cambridge, MA: Harvard University Press.

——. 1986. "The Forms of Capital." In *Handbook of Theory and Research for the Sociology of Education,* edited by John G. Richardson, 241–58. Westport, CT: Greenwood Press.

Bourdieu, Pierre, and Jean-Claude Passeron. 1977. *Reproduction in Education and Society.* London: Sage.

Bowles, Samuel, and Herbert Gintis. 1976. *Schooling in Capitalist America.* New York: Basic Books.

Brunsma, David L., David G. Embrick, and Jean H. Shin. 2017. "Graduate Students of Color: Race, Racism, and Mentoring in the White Waters of Academia." *Sociology of Race and Ethnicity* 31. doi:10.1177/2332649 216681565.

Buchmann, Claudia, Thomas A. DiPrete, and Anne McDaniel. 2008. "Gender Inequalities in Education." *Annual Review of Sociology* 34: 319–37.

Carey, Kevin. 2015. "How One's Choice of College Affects Future Earnings." *New York Times,* September 15, A3.

Carnevale, Anthony P., Stephen J. Rose, and Ban Cheah. 2011. "The College Payoff: Education, Occupations, Lifetime Earnings." Center on Education and the Workforce, Georgetown University. Accessed March 11, 2017. https://www2.ed.gov/policy/highered/reg/hearulemaking/2011/collegepayoff.pdf.

Chang, Ha-Joon. 2010. *23 Things They Don't Tell You about Capitalism.* New York: Bloomsbury.

Coleman, James S. 1988. "Social Capital in the Creation of Human Capital." *American Journal of Sociology* 94 (suppl. 1): S95–S120.

Crenshaw, Kimberlé Williams. 2015. *Black Girls Matter: Pushed Out, Overpoliced, and Underprotected.* New York: African American Policy Forum. Accessed June 2, 2017. http://www.aapf.org/recent/2014/12/coming-soon-blackgirlsmatter-pushed-out-overpoliced-and-underprotected.

Diaz, Elizabeth M., and Joseph G. Kosciw. 2009. *Shared Differences: The Experiences of Lesbian, Gay, Bisexual, and Transgender Students of Color in Our Nation's Schools.* New York: Gay, Lesbian and Straight Education Network. Accessed June 5, 2017. https://www.glsen.org/sites/default/files/Shared%20Differences.pdf.

Downey, Douglas, and Anastasia S. Vogt Yuan. 2005. "Sex Differences in School Performance during High School: Puzzling Patterns and Possible Explanations." *Sociological Quarterly* 46, no. 2: 299–321.

Du Bois, W. E. B. 1900. "Address to the Nation." Accessed December 3, 2012. http://users.wfu.edu/zulick/341/niagara.html.

Duckworth, Angela, and Martin Seligman. 2006. "Self-Discipline Gives Girls the Edge: Gender in Self-Discipline, Grades, and Achievement Test Scores." *Journal of Educational Psychology* 98, no. 1: 198–208.

Durkheim, Émile. 1956. *Education and Sociology.* New York: Free Press.

———. 1962. *Moral Education.* New York: Free Press.

———. 1977. *The Evolution of Educational Thought.* London: Routledge & Kegan Paul.

Dynarski, Susan. 2015. "New Data Give Clearer Picture of Student Debt." *New York Times,* September 10.

Fanon, Frantz. 1952. *Black Skin, White Masks.* New York: Grove Press.

———. 1961. *The Wretched of the Earth.* New York: Grove Press.

Forman-Brunell, Miriam. 2011. *Babysitter: An American History.* New York: New York University Press.

Freire, Paulo. (1970) 2000. *Pedagogy of the Oppressed.* 30th anniversary ed. New York: Bloomsbury.

Hallinan, Maureen T., and Aage B. Sørensen. 1987. "Ability Grouping and Sex Differences in Mathematics Achievement." *Sociology of Education* 60, no. 2: 63–72.

Hannah-Jones, Nikole. 2015. "A Prescription for More Black Doctors." *New York Times Magazine,* September 9. Accessed June 5, 2017. https://www .nytimes.com/2015/09/13/ magazine/a-prescription- for-more-black-doctors .html?mcubz=1&_r=0.

Hurston, Zora Neale. 1955. "Court Order Can't Make the Races Mix." *Orlando Sentinel,* August. Accessed March 11, 2017. https://www.lewrockwell .com/1970/01/zora-neale- hurston/court-order-cant- make-the-racesmix.

Hussar, William J., and Tabitha M. Bailey. 2016. *Projections of Education Statistics to 2024.* NCES 2013-008. Washington, DC: U.S. Department of Education, National Center for Education Statistics.

Karenga, Maulana. 2002. *Introduction to Black Studies.* 3rd ed. Los Angeles: University of Sankore Press.

King, Marsha. 2008. "Tribes Confront Painful Legacy of Indian Boarding Schools." *Seattle Times,* February 3. Accessed March 11, 2017. http://www.seattletimes .com/seattle-news/tribes- confront-painful-legacy-of- indian-boarding-schools.

Kosciw, Joseph G., Emily A. Greytak, Noreen M. Giga, Christian Villenas, and David J. Danischewski. 2016. *The 2015 National School Climate Survey: The Experiences of Lesbian, Gay, Bisexual, Transgender, and Queer Youth in Our Nation's Schools.* Washington, DC: Gay, Lesbian and Straight Education Network. Accessed June 5, 2017. https://www .glsen.org/sites/default/ files/2015%20National%20 GLSEN%202015%20 National%20School%20 Climate%20Survey%20 %28NSCS%29%20-%20 Full%20Report_0.pdf.

Kozol, Jonathan. 1991. *Savage Inequalities: Children in America's Schools.* New York: Crown.

Kristof, Nicholas D., and Sheryl WuDunn. 2009. *Half the Sky: Turning Oppression into Opportunity for Women Worldwide.* New York: Alfred A. Knopf.

Krogstad, Jens Manuel, and Richard Fry. 2014. "More Hispanics, Blacks Enrolling in College but Lag behind in Bachelor's Degrees." Fact Tank, Pew Research Center, April 24. Accessed March 11, 2017. http:// www.pewresearch.org/ fact-tank/2014/04/24/ more-hispanics-blacks- enrolling-in-college-but-lag- in-bachelors-degrees.

Lareau, Annette. 1989. *Home Advantage: Social Class and Parental Involvement in Elementary Education.* Lanham, MD: Rowman & Littlefield.

———. 2011. *Unequal Childhoods: Class, Race, and Family Life.* 2nd ed. Berkeley: University of California Press.

Lee, Stacey, Eujin Park, and Jia-Hui Stefanie Wong. 2016. "Racialization, Schooling, and Becoming American: Asian American Experiences." *Educational Studies,* published online December 14. doi:10.1080/0 0131946.2016.1258360.

Mayer, Susan. 2010. "The Relationship between Income Inequality and Inequality in Schooling." *Theory and Research in Education* 8, no. 1: 5–20.

McGrory, Brian. 2011. "Centuries of Interruption and a History Rejoined: Wampanoag Grad to Be Harvard's First since 1665." *Boston Globe,* May 11. Accessed June 5, 2017. http://www.boston.com/ news/local/massachusetts/ articles/2011/05/11/ wampanoag_grad_ to_be_harvards_first_ since_1665/?page=2.

Mills, C. Wright. 1956. *The Power Elite.* New York: Oxford University Press.

Mulhere, Kaitlin. 2015. "Students Are Totally Clueless about Financial Aid and It's Costing

Them a Lot of Money." *Money,* August 3. Accessed June 5, 2017. http://time.com/money/3982343/financial-aid-new-america-report.

National Association of Colleges and Employers. 2015. "Average Starting Salary for Class of 2015 Climbs 5.2%." Accessed March 11, 2017. http://www.naceweb.org/s11182015/starting-salary-class-2015.aspx.

National Center for Education Statistics. 2016a. *The Condition of Education: 2016.* Washington, DC: National Center for Education Statistics. Accessed March 11, 2017. https://nces.ed.gov/pubs2016/2016144.pdf.

——. 2016b. *Digest of Education Statistics: 2015*. Washington, DC: National Center for Education Statistics. Accessed June 2, 2017. https://nces.ed.gov/pubs2016/2016014.pdf.

——. 2016c. "Public High School Graduation Rates." Accessed March 11, 2017. https://nces.ed.gov/programs/coe/indicator_coi.asp.

National Commission on Excellence in Education. 1983. *A Nation at Risk: The Imperative for Educational Reform.* Washington, DC: Government Printing Office.

Owings, Allison. 2011. *Indian Voices: Listening to Native Americans.* New Brunswick, NJ: Rutgers University Press.

Redfield, Sarah E., and Jason P. Nance. 2016. *School to Prison Pipeline: Preliminary Report.* Washington, DC: American Bar Association. Accessed June 27, 2017. https://www.americanbar.org/content/dam/aba/administrative/

diversity_pipeline/stp_preliminary_report_final.authcheckdam.pdf.

Roach, Ronald. 2013. "Analysis: 2012 Higher Education Enrollment Rate of Latino High School Graduates Surpassed That of Whites." Diverse Issues in Higher Education, September 10. Accessed October 10, 2013. http://diverseeducation.com/article/55874/?utm_campaign=Diverse%20Newsletter%203&utm_medium=email&utm_source=Eloqua&elq=6033d094985546ac87fb2972f4c4139e&elqCampaignId=62#.

Rosenbaum, James E. 2001. *Beyond College for All: Career Paths for the Forgotten Half.* New York: Russell Sage Foundation.

Rossatto, César Augusto. 2004. "Social Justice in Times of McCarthyism Renaissance: Surveillance, Ethics, and Neoliberalism. In *Social Justice in These Times,* edited by James O'Donnell, Marc Pruyn, and Rudolfo Chávez Chávez, 215–34. Greenwich, CT: Information Age.

Sadovnik, Alan R., ed. 2011. *Sociology of Education: A Critical Reader.* 2nd ed. New York: Routledge.

Schultz, Theodore. 1961. "Investment in Human Capital." *American Economic Review* 51: 1–17.

Scott-Clayton, Judith, and Jing Li. 2016. "Black–White Disparity in Student Loan Debt More than Triples after Graduation." *Evidence Speaks Reports* 2, no. 3 (October 20), Brookings Institution. Accessed March 14, 2017. https://www.brookings.edu/research/

black-white-disparity-in-student-loan-debt-more-than-triples-after-graduation.

Selod, Saher. 2015. "Citizenship Denied: Racialization of Muslim American Men and Women Post 9/11." *Critical Sociology* 41: 77–95.

Shaull, Richard. (1970) 2000. Foreword to *Pedagogy of the Oppressed,* by Paulo Freire. 30th anniversary ed. New York: Bloomsbury.

Singer, Steven M. 2017. "The Racist Roots and Racist Indoctrination of School Choice." Gadfly on the Wall (blog), January 15. Accessed March 11, 2017. https://gadflyonthewallblog.wordpress.com/2017/01/15/the-racists-roots-and-racist-indoctrination-of-school-choice.

Smith, Andrea. 2007. "Soul Wound: The Legacy of Native American Schools." *Amnesty International Magazine,* March 26. Accessed March 11, 2017. http://www.amnestyusa.org/node/87342.

Taylor, Kate, and Claire Cain Miller. 2015. "Mayor to Put Schools' Focus on the Science of Computers." *New York Times,* September 16, A22, A25.

UNESCO. 2012. *World Atlas of Gender Equality in Education.* Paris: UNESCO. Accessed March 28, 2013. http://www.unesco.org/new/en/education/themes/leading-the-international-agenda/gender-and-education/resources/the-world-atlas-of-gender%20equality-in-education.

U.S. Census Bureau. 2011. "Who's Minding the Kids? Child Care Arrangements: Spring 2010, Detailed Tables." Accessed July 12,

2013. http://www.census
.gov/hhes/childcare/data/
sipp/2010/tables.html.

U.S. Department of Education.
2016. *Racial and Ethnic
Disparities in Special
Education: A Multi-year
Disproportionality Analysis by
State, Analysis Category, and
Race/Ethnicity.* Washington,
DC: U.S. Department
of Education. Accessed
March 11, 2017. https://
www2.ed.gov/programs/

osepidea/618-data/LEA-racial-
ethnic-disparities-tables/
disproportionality-analysis-by-
state-analysis-category.pdf.

West, Cassandra. 2012. "Black
Studies Programs Now
Flourishing despite Early
Struggles." *Diverse Issues in
Higher Education* 29,
no. 11. Accessed
June 26, 2017. https://
www.questia.com/
magazine/1G1-296952044/
black-studies-programs-

now-flourishing-despite-
early.

Woodson, Carter Godwin. (1933)
2016. *The Mis-education of
the Negro.* Baltimore: Black
Classic Press.

Zhboray, Ronald. 1993. *Fictive
People: Antebellum
Economic Development
and the American Reading
Public.* New York: Oxford
University Press.

■ CHAPTER 7

Agnew, Robert. 1992. "Foundation
for a General Strain Theory
of Crime and Delinquency."
Criminology 30, no. 1: 47–87.

Ahmed, Osman, and Chai
Jindasurat. 2014. *Lesbian,
Gay, Bisexual, Transgender,
Queer, and HIV-Affected
Hate Violence in 2013.*
New York: National
Coalition of Anti-Violence
Programs. Accessed
June 17, 2014. http://
www.cuav.org/wp-content/
uploads/2016/12/
2013_ncavp_hvreport_
final.pdf.

Alexander, Michelle. 2010. *The
New Jim Crow: Mass
Incarceration in the Age of
Colorblindness.* New York:
New Press.

———. 2012. "The New Jim Crow:
How the War on Drugs
Gave Birth to a Permanent
American Undercaste."
Common Dreams, March 27.
Accessed June 13,
2014. https://www
.commondreams.org/
view/2012/03/27.

American Civil Liberties Union.
2009. *The Persistence of
Racial and Ethnic Profiling
in the United States.* New

York: ACLU. Accessed June
5, 2017. https://www.aclu.
org/files/pdfs/humanrights/
cerd_finalreport.pdf.

American Psychological
Association Zero Tolerance
Task Force. 2008. "Are
Zero Tolerance Policies
Effective in the Schools?
An Evidentiary Review
and Recommendations."
American Psychologist 63:
852–62.

Amnesty International. 2007. *Maze
of Injustice: The Failure to
Protect Indigenous Women
from Sexual Violence in the
USA.* London: Amnesty
International.

Anderson, Craig A., and Brad
J. Bushman. 2002. "The
Effects of Media Violence
on Society." *Science* 29, no.
5564 (March): 2377–79.

Anderson, Elijah. 1990. "The
Police and the Black Male."
In *Constructions of Deviance:
Social Power, Context, and
Interaction,* edited by
Patricia A. Adler and
Peter Adler. Belmont,
CA: Wadsworth.

———. 1994. "The Code of the
Streets." *Atlantic Monthly,*
May, 80–94.

———. 1999. *Code of the Street:
Decency, Violence, and the
Moral Life of the Inner City.*
New York: W. W. Norton.

Andreescu, Viviana, John Eagle
Shutt, and Gennaro F. Vito.
2011. "The Violent South:
Culture of Honor, Social
Disorganization, and Murder in
Appalachia." *Criminal Justice
Review* 36, no. 1: 76–103.

Ayres, Ian. 2008. "Racial Profiling
in L.A.: The Numbers Don't
Lie." *Los Angeles Times,*
October 23. Accessed June
5, 2017. http://articles
.latimes.com/2008/oct/23/
opinion/oe-ayres23.

Bachman, Ronet. 1992. *Death and
Violence on the Reservation:
Homicide, Family Violence,
and Suicide in American
Indian Populations.* New
York: Auburn House.

Baldus, David C., George G.
Woodworth, and Charles
A. Pulaski Jr. 1990. *Equal
Justice and the Death
Penalty: A Legal and
Empirical Analysis.* Boston:
Northeastern University
Press.

Balfanz, Robert, Kurt Spiridakis,
Ruth Curran Neild, and Nettie
Legters. 2003. "High-Poverty

Secondary Schools and the Juvenile Justice System: How Neither Helps the Other and How That Could Change." In "Deconstructing the School-to-Prison Pipeline," edited by Johanna Wald and Daniel J. Losen, special issue, *New Directions for Youth Development* 99 (Fall): 71–89.

Baptist, Edward E. 2001. "Cuffy, Fancy Maids, and One-Eyed Men: Rape, Commodification, and the Domestic Slave Trade in the United States." *American Historical Review* 106, no. 5: 1619–50.

Beckett, Katherine, and Naomi Murakawa. 2016. "Mapping the Shadow Carceral State: Toward an Institutionally Capacious Approach to Punishment." *Theoretical Criminology* 16, no. 1: 221–44.

Behrens, Angela, Christopher Uggen, and Jeff Manza. 2003. "Ballot Manipulation and the 'Menace of Negro Domination': Racial Threat and Felon Disenfranchisement in the United States, 1850–2002." *American Journal of Sociology* 109, no. 3 (November): 559–605.

Bell, Derrick, Jr. 1988. "White Superiority in America: Its Legal Legacy, Its Economic Costs." *Villanova Law Review* 33, no. 5: 767–79.

Bell, Jamaal. 2010. "Race and Human Trafficking in the U.S.: Unclear but Undeniable." Huffington Post, May 10. Accessed January 10, 2014. http://www.huffingtonpost.com/jamaal-bell/race-and-human-traffickin_b_569795.html.

Bergner, Daniel. 2014. "Is Stop-and-Frisk Worth It?" *Atlantic,* April. Accessed November 17, 2016. http://www.theatlantic.com/magazine/archive/2014/04/is-stop-and-frisk-worth-it/358644.

Bernasconi, Robert. 2012. "Crossed Lines in the Racialization Process: Race as a Border Concept." *Research in Phenomenology* 42, no. 2: 206–28.

Bevilacqua, Laura, Stéphane Doly, Jaakko Kaprio, Qiaoping Yuan, Roope Tikkanen, Tiina Paunio, Zhifeng Zhou, Juho Wedenoja, Luc Maroteaux, Silvina Diaz, Arnaud Belmer, Colin A. Hodgkinson, Liliana Dell'Osso, Jaana Suvisaari, Emil Coccaro, Richard J. Rose, Leena Peltonen, Matti Virkkunen, and David Goldman. 2010. "A Population-Specific HTR2B Stop Codon Predisposes to Severe Impulsivity." *Nature* 468, no. 7327: 1061–66. doi:10.1038/nature09629.

Biko, Agonizo. 2004. "Imperialism, Crime and Criminology: Towards the Decolonisation of Criminology." *Crime, Law and Social Change* 41: 343–58.

Black, Donald. 1993. *The Social Structure of Right and Wrong.* New York: Cambridge University Press.

Blankley, Bethany. 2014. "As Christianity Exits Europe, 'Criminal Muslims' Fill Void with Rabid Violence." *Washington Times,* December 29. Accessed January 9, 2015. http://www.washingtontimes.com/news/2014/dec/29/bethany-blankley-christianity-exits-europe-crimina/?page=all.

Blau, Judith R., and Peter M. Blau. 1982. "The Cost of Inequality: Metropolitan Structure and Violent Crime." *American Sociological Review* 47: 114–29.

Blau, Peter M., and Joseph E. Schwartz. 1984. *Crosscutting Social Circles: Testing a Macrostructural Theory of Intergroup Relations.* New York: Academic Press.

Blauner, Robert. 1972. *Racial Oppression in America.* New York: Harper & Row.

Bogle, Donald. 2001. *Toms, Coons, Mulattoes, Mammies, and Bucks: An Interpretive History of Blacks in American Films.* London: Continuum.

Brame, Robert, Shawn D. Bushway, Ray Paternoster, and Michael G. Turner. 2014. "Demographic Patterns of Cumulative Arrest Prevalence by Ages 18 and 23." *Crime & Delinquency* 60, no. 3: 471–86.

Braveheart-Jordan, Maria, and Lemyra DeBruyn. 1995. "So She May Walk in Balance: Integrating the Impact of Historical Trauma in the Treatment of Native American Indian Women." In *Racism in the Lives of Women: Testimony, Theory, and Guides to Antiracist Practice,* edited by Jeanne Adleman and Gloria M. Enguidanos, 345–68. Binghamton, NY: Haworth.

Brown, Sarah Alice. 2012. "Trends in Juvenile Justice State Legislation: 2001–2011." National Conference of State Legislatures, June. Accessed April 12, 2014. http://jdaihelpdesk.org/miscellaneous/Trends%20in%20Juvenile%20Justice%20State%20Legislation%202001-2011%20(8-7-2012).pdf.

Browne-Marshall, Gloria J. 2002. "The Realities of Enslaved Female Africans in America." Excerpted from Gloria J. Brown-Marshall, "Failing Our

Black Children: Statutory Rape Laws, Moral Reform and the Hypocrisy of Denial." Accessed October 17, 2011. http://academic.udayton.edu/race/05intersection/gender/rape.htm.

Buenker, J. 1999. "Overview of Violence Theories: History." In *The Encyclopedia of Violence in America,* Vol. 3, edited by R. Gottesman, 314–15. New York: Scribner.

Burt, Callie Harbin, Ronald L. Simons, and Frederick X. Gibbons. 2012. "Racial Discrimination, Ethnic-Racial Socialization, and Crime: A Micro-sociological Model of Risk and Resilience." *American Sociological Review* 20, no. 10: 1–30.

Bush-Baskette, Stephanie R. 1998. "The War on Drugs as a War against Black Women." In *Crime Control and Women: Feminist Implications of Criminal Justice Policy,* edited by Susan L. Miller. Thousand Oaks, CA: Sage.

Caputo, Angela. 2014. "Data: Black Chicagoans at Higher Risk of Being Shot by Police." *Chicago Reporter,* January 23. Accessed June 13, 2014. http://chicagoreporter.com/data-black-chicagoans-higher-risk-being-shot-police#.U5sFqPldXmc.

Carson, E. Ann. 2014. "Prisoners in 2013." Bulletin, NCJ 247282, U.S. Department of Justice, Bureau of Justice Statistics, September. Accessed September 27, 2016. http://www.bjs.gov/content/pub/pdf/p13.pdf.

Chaddha, Anmoi, and William J. Wilson. 2010. "Why We're Teaching 'The Wire' at Harvard." *Washington Post,* September 10. Accessed February 10, 2014. http://www.washingtonpost.com/wp-dyn/content/article/2010/09/10/AR2010091002676.html.

Chester, Barbara, Robert W. Robin, Mary P. Koss, Joyce Lopez, and David Goldman. 1994. "Grandmother Dishonored: Violence against Women by Male Partners in American Indian Communities." *Violence and Victims* 9, no. 3: 249–58.

Children's Defense Fund. 2012. "Cradle to Prison Pipeline Campaign." Accessed June 5, 2017. http://www.childrensdefense.org/programs-campaigns/cradle-to-prison-pipeline.

Chiricos, Ted, and Sarah Eschholz. 2009. "The Racial and Ethnic Typification of Crime and the Criminal Typification of Race and Ethnicity in Local Television News." *Journal of Research in Crime and Delinquency* 39, no. 4: 400–424.

Coates, Rodney D. 2004. "Critical Racial and Ethnic Studies: Profiling and Reparations." *American Behavioral Scientist* 47, no. 7: 873–78.

———, ed. 2011. *Covert Racism: Theories, Institutions, and Experiences.* Leiden, Netherlands: Brill.

Cohen, Patricia. 2010. "'Culture of Poverty' Makes a Comeback." *New York Times,* October 18, A1. Accessed June 5, 2017. http://www.nytimes.com/2010/10/18/us/18poverty.html?pagewanted=all.

Collins, Patricia Hill. 2000a. "Black Feminist Thought in the Matrix of Domination." In *Black Feminist Thought: Knowledge, Consciousness, and the Politics of Empowerment.* 2nd ed. New York: Routledge.

———. 2000b. "Mammies, Matriarchs, and Other Controlling Images." In *Black Feminist Thought: Knowledge, Consciousness, and the Politics of Empowerment.* 2nd ed. New York: Routledge.

———. 2004. *Black Sexual Politics: African Americans, Gender, and the New Racism.* New York: Routledge.

Colvin, Mark, Francis T. Cullen, and Thomas Vander Ven. 2002. "Coercion, Social Support, and Crime: An Emerging Theoretical Consensus." *Criminology* 40, no. 1: 19–42.

Cooper, Hannah L. F. 2015. "War on Drugs Policing and Police Brutality." *Substance Use and Misuse* 50, nos. 8–9: 1188–94.

Corley, Cheryl. 2011. "In Chicago, Stopping Crime before It Happens." *Morning Edition,* NPR, March 25. Accessed February 18, 2014. http://www.npr.org/2011/03/25/132633966/chicago-youth-program-aims-to-decrease-violence.

Cowan, Gloria. 2000. "Beliefs about the Causes of Four Types of Rape." *Sex Roles* 42, nos. 9–10: 807–23.

Davis, Angela. 1996. "Benign Neglect of Racism in the Criminal Justice System." *Michigan Law Review* 94, no. 6: 1660–86.

———. 1998. "Masked Racism: Reflections on the Prison Industrial Complex." *ColorLines,* Fall. Accessed July 12, 2014. http://colorlines.com/archives/1998/09/masked_racism_reflections_on_the_prison_industrial_complex.html.

———. 1999. *The Prison Industrial Complex.* Audiobook. Chico, CA: AK Press.

De Bow, J. D. B. (1851) 1967. *De Bow's Review of the Southern and Western States,* Vol. 11, *New Orleans.* New York: AMS Press. Accessed November 12, 2014. http://www.pbs.org/wgbh/aia/part4/4h3106t.html.

Demby, Gene. 2016. "Imagining a World without Prisons for Communities Defined by Them." *Code Switch,* NPR, September 20. Accessed September 27, 2016. http://www.npr.org/sections/codeswitch/2016/09/20/494248596/imagining-a-world-without-prisons-for-communities-defined-by-them.

DiLorenzo, Thomas J. 2010. "The Culture of Violence in the American West: Myth versus Reality." *Independent Review* (Fall). Accessed October 11, 2014. http://www.independent.org/publications/tir/article.asp?a=803.

Domestic Workers United and DataCenter. 2006. *Home Is Where the Work Is: Inside New York's Domestic Work Industry.* Brooklyn: Domestic Workers United/Oakland, CA: DataCenter. Accessed June 5, 2017. http://www.datacenter.org/wp-content/uploads/homeiswheretheworkis.pdf.

Donovan, Roxanne, and Michelle Williams. 2002. "Living at the Intersection: The Effects of Racism and Sexism on Black Rape Survivors." *Women and Therapy* 25, nos. 3–4: 95–105.

Du Bois, W. E. B. 1904. *Some Notes on Negro Crime, Particularly in Georgia.* Atlanta: Atlanta University Press. Accessed November 5, 2014. http://scua.library.umass.edu/digital/dubois/dubois9.pdf.

Dugdale, Richard Louis. 1891. *"The Jukes": A Study in Crime, Pauperism, Disease and Heredity.* New York: G. P. Putnam's Sons.

Durkheim, Émile. 1897. *Le Suicide.* Paris: Alcan.

Durr, Marlese. 2015. "What Is the Difference between Slave Patrols and Modern-Day Policing? Institutional Violence in a Community of Color." *Critical Sociology* 41, no. 6: 873–79.

Duru, Jeremi. N. 2004. "The Central Park Five, the Scottsboro Boys, and the Myth of the Bestial Black Man." *Cardozo Law Review* 25, no. 1315: 1–41.

Duster, Troy. 2004. "Selective Arrests, an Ever-Expanding DNA Forensic Database, and the Specter of an Early-Twenty-First-Century Equivalent of Phrenology." In *DNA and the Criminal Justice System: The Technology of Justice,* edited by David Lazer. Cambridge: MIT Press.

Egley, Arlen, Jr., James C. Howell, and Meena Harris. 2014. "Highlights of the 2012 National Youth Gang Survey." Juvenile Justice Fact Sheet, December. U.S. Department of Justice, Office of Juvenile Justice and Delinquency Prevention. Accessed November 28, 2016. https://www.ojjdp.gov/pubs/248025.pdf.

European Commission. 2016. "United against Hate Speech on the Web: Where Do We Stand? Speech by Commissioner Jourova at Conference with German Justice Minister Maas." Press release, September 26. Accessed September 27, 2016. https://www.neweurope.eu/press-release/united-against-hate-speech-on-the-web-where-do-we-stand-speech-by-commissioner-jourova-at-conference-with-german-justice-minister-maas.

Farrell, Ronald A., and Victoria Lynn Swigert. 1988. "General Introduction." In *Social Deviance,* 3rd ed., edited by Ronald A. Farrell and Victoria Lynn Swigert. Belmont, CA: Wadsworth.

Federal Bureau of Investigation. 2014. "Sixteen Juveniles Recovered in Joint Super Bowl Operation Targeting Underage Prostitution." Press release, February 4. Accessed February 14, 2014. http://www.fbi.gov/news/pressrel/press-releases/sixteen-juveniles-recovered-in-joint-super-bowl-operation-targeting-underage-prostitution.

———. 2015. "Latest Hate Crime Statistics Available." November 16. Accessed November 28, 2016. https://www.fbi.gov/news/stories/latest-hate-crime-statistics-available.

Fellner, Jamie. 2009. "Race, Drugs, and Law Enforcement in the United States." *Stanford Law and Policy Review* 20, no. 2: 257–92.

Fenning, Pamela, and Jennifer Rose. 2007. "Overrepresentation of African American Students in Exclusionary Discipline: The Role of School Policy." *Urban Education* 42, no. 6 (November): 536–59.

Fitzpatrick, Caroline, Tracie Barnett, and Linda S. Pagani. 2012. "Early Exposure to Media Violence and Later

Child Adjustment." *Journal of Developmental & Behavioral Pediatrics* 33, no. 4: 291–97.

Ford, Matt. 2017. "Jeff Sessions Reinvigorates the Drug War." *Atlantic,* May 12. Accessed June 21, 2017. https://www.theatlantic.com/politics/archive/2017/05/sessions-sentencing-memo/526029.

Foster, Holly, and John Hagan. 2009. "The Mass Incarceration of Parents in America: Issues of Race/Ethnicity, Collateral Damage to Children, and Prisoner Reentry." *Annals of the American Academy of Political and Social Science* 623: 179–94.

Friedrichs, David O. 2007. *Trusted Criminals: White Collar Crime in Contemporary Society.* 3rd ed. Belmont, CA: Thomson Wadsworth.

Gabrielson, Ryan, Ryann Grochowski Jones, and Eric Sagara. 2014. "Deadly Force, in Black and White." ProPublica, October 10. Accessed December 10, 2014. http://www.propublica.org/article/deadly-force-in-black-and-white.

Gardner, Joby. 2010. "Beyond 'Making It' or Not: Future Talk by Incarcerated Young Men." *Urban Education* 45, no. 1: 75–102.

Gardner, Trevor. 2004. "The Political Delinquent: Crime, Deviance, and Resistance in Black America." *Harvard Black Letter Law Journal* 20: 137–61.

Ginwright, Shawn, and Julio Cammarota. 2002. "New Terrain in Youth Development: The Promise of a Social Justice Approach." *Social Justice* 29, no. 4: 82–95.

Glasgow, Douglas G. 1980. *The Black Underclass.* New York: Vintage Books.

Goldberg, David Theo. 1993. "Modernity, Race, and Morality." *Cultural Critique* 24 (Spring): 193–227.

Goldfield, David. 2011. *America Aflame: How the Civil War Created a Nation.* New York: Bloomsbury.

Gonnerman, Jennifer. 2004. "Million-Dollar Blocks: The Neighborhood Costs of America's Prison Boom." *Village Voice,* November 16.

Gottfredson, Michael, and Travis Hirschi. 1990. *A General Theory of Crime*. Stanford, CA: Stanford University Press.

Gould, Stephen Jay. 1981. *The Mismeasure of Man.* New York: W. W. Norton.

Gray, Herman. 1995. *Watching Race: Television and the Struggle for "Blackness."* Minneapolis: University of Minnesota Press.

Greene, Helen Taylor, and Shaun L. Gabbidon. 2012. "Theoretical Perspectives on Race and Crime." In *Race and Crime: A Text/Reader,* 95–168. Thousand Oaks, CA: Sage.

Greene, Judith, and Patricia Allard. 2011. "Numbers Game: The Vicious Cycle of Incarceration in Mississippi's Criminal Justice System." American Civil Liberties Union of Mississippi, March. Accessed June 6, 2017. http://www.justicestrategies.org/sites/default/files/publications/DLRP_MississipppiReport%20Final%20Mar%202011.pdf.

Guardian. 2016. "The Counted: People Killed by Police in the U.S." Accessed September 27. https://www.theguardian.com/us-news/ng-interactive/2015/jun/01/the-counted-police-killings-us-database.

Gunning, Sandra. 1996. *Race, Rape, and Lynching: The Red Record of American Literature, 1890–1912.* New York: Oxford University Press.

Guo, Guang, Michael E. Roettger, and Tianji Chai. 2011. "The Integration of Genetic Propensities into Social-Control Models of Delinquency and Violence among Male Youths." *American Sociological Review* 73, no. 4: 543–68.

Gutiérrez, Ramón A. 1991. *When Jesus Came, the Corn Mothers Went Away: Marriage, Sexuality, and Power in New Mexico, 1500–1846.* Stanford, CA: Stanford University Press.

Hagan, John. 1994. *Crime and Disrepute*. Thousand Oaks, CA: Pine Forge Press.

Hagedorn, John M. 2008. *A World of Gangs: Armed Young Men and Gangsta Culture.* Minneapolis: University of Minnesota Press.

Harrell, Erika, Lynn Langton, Marcus Berzofsky, Lance Couzens, and Hope Smiley-McDonald. 2014. "Household Poverty and Nonfatal Violent Victimization, 2008–2012." Special Report, NCJ 248384. U.S. Department of Justice, Bureau of Justice Statistics, November. Accessed November 30, 2016. https://www.bjs.gov/content/pub/pdf/hpnvv0812.pdf.

Harris, Cheryl. 1993. "Whiteness as Property." *Harvard Law Review* 106: 1709–95.

Harris, Trudier. 1984. *Exorcising Blackness: Historical and Literary Lynching and Burning Rituals.*

Bloomington: Indiana University Press.

Hawkins, Darnell F. 2011. "Things Fall Apart: Revisiting Race and Ethnic Differences in Criminal Violence amidst a Crime Drop." *Race and Justice* 1, no. 1: 3–48.

Headley, Clevis. 2004. "Delegitimizing the Normativity of 'Whiteness': A Critical Africana Philosophical Study of the Metaphoricity of 'Whiteness.'" In *What White Looks Like: African American Philosophers on the Whiteness Question,* edited by George Yancy, 87–106. New York: Routledge.

Helo, Ari, and Peter Onuf. 2004. "Jefferson, Morality, and the Problem of Slavery." *William and Mary Quarterly,* 3rd ser., 60, no. 3 (July): 583–614.

Herrnstein, Richard J., and Charles Murray. 1994. *The Bell Curve.* New York: Free Press.

Higginbotham, A. Leon. 1978. *In the Matter of Color: Race and the American Legal Process.* New York: Oxford University Press.

Hindelang, Michael J. 1978. "Race and Involvement in Common Law Personal Crimes." *American Sociological Review* 43, no. 1 (February): 93–109.

Hines, Darlene Clark. 1989. "Rape and the Inner Lives of Black Women in the Middle West." *Signs* 14, no. 4: 912–20.

Hirschi, Travis, and Michael J. Hindelang. 1977. "Intelligence and Delinquency: A Revisionist Review." *American Sociological Review* 42, no. 4 (August): 571–87.

Horwitz, Sari. 2014. "New Law Offers Protection to Abused Native American Women." *Washington Post,* February 8. Accessed February 13, 2014. http://www.washingtonpost.com/world/national-security/new-law-offers-a-sliver-of-protection-to-abused-native-american-women/2014/02/08/0466d1ae-8f73-11e3-84e1-27626c5ef5fb_story.html.

Howell, James C., and John P. Moore. 2010. "History of Street Gangs in the United States." *National Gang Center Bulletin* 4: 1–25. Accessed November 28, 2016. https://www.nationalgangcenter.gov/content/documents/history-of-street-gangs.pdf.

Huff, Rodney, Christian Desilets, and John Kane. 2010. "The 2010 National Public Survey on White Collar Crime." National White Collar Crime Center. Accessed June 11, 2014. http://nw3c.org/docs/research/2010-national-public-survey-on-white-collar-crime.pdf?sfvrsn=6.

Hundley, Kris, Susan Taylor Martin, and Connie Humburg. 2012. "Florida 'Stand Your Ground' Law Yields Some Shocking Outcomes Depending on How Law Is Applied." *Tampa Bay Times,* June 1. Accessed February 17, 2014. http://www.tampabay.com/news/publicsafety/crime/florida-stand-your-ground-law-yields-some-shocking-outcomes-depending-on/1233133.

Independent Voter Network. 2012. "Gun Control: An International Comparison." July 25. Accessed March 9, 2014. http://ivn.us/2012/07/25/gun-control-an-international-comparison.

IndexMundi. 2016. "United States Demographic Profile 2016." Accessed June 5, 2017. http://www.indexmundi.com/united_states/demographics_profile.html.

Innocence Project. 2016. "DNA Exonerations in the United States." Accessed November 12, 2016. http://www.innocenceproject.org/dna-exonerations-in-the-united-states.

Iwamoto, Derik Kenji, and William Ming Liu. 2009. "Asian American Men and Asianized Attribution: Intersections of Masculinity, Race, and Sexuality." In *Asian American Psychology: Current Perspectives,* edited by Nita Tewari and Alvin Alvarez. New York: Taylor & Francis.

Jackson, Ronald. 2006. *Scripting the Black Masculine Body: Identity, Discourse, and Racial Politics in Popular Media.* Albany: State University of New York Press.

Jipquep, Marie-Claude, and Kathy Sanders-Phillips. 2003. "The Context of Violence for Children of Color: Violence in the Community and in the Media." *Journal of Negro Education* 72, no. 4: 379–95.

Johnson, Corey G. 2013. "Female Inmates Sterilized in California Prisons without Approval." Center for Investigative Reporting, July 7. Accessed February 11, 2014. http://cironline.org/reports/female-inmates-sterilized-california-prisons-without-approval-4917.

Jordan, Winthrop D. 1968. *White over Black: American Attitudes toward the Negro, 1550–1812.* Chapel Hill: University of North Carolina Press, for the Institute of Early American History and Culture.

Kansal, Tushar. 2005. *Racial Disparities in Sentencing:*

A Review of the Literature. Washington, DC: Sentencing Project.

Kozol, Jonathan. 1991. *Savage Inequalities: Children in America's Schools.* New York: Crown.

Kupchik, Aaron. 2006. *Judging Juveniles: Prosecuting Adolescents in Adult and Juvenile Courts.* New York: New York University Press.

Kutateladze, Besiki, Vanessa Lynn, and Edward Liang. 2012. "Do Race and Ethnicity Matter in Prosecution? A Review of Empirical Studies." Vera Institute of Justice, June. Accessed June 13, 2014. http://www.prisonpolicy.org/scans/vera/race-and-ethnicity-in-prosecution-first-edition.pdf.

Lee, Nella. 1993. "Differential Deviance and Social Control Mechanisms among Two Groups of Yup'ik Eskimo." *American Indian and Alaska Native Mental Health Research* 5, no. 2: 57–92.

Lee, Tony. 2013. "Sharpton Condemns 'Racist' Knockout Game." Breitbart, December 3. Accessed June 17, 2014. http://www.breitbart.com/Big-Journalism/2013/12/03/Sharpton-Condemns-Racist-Reprehensible-Knockout-Game-After-Pressure-from-Conservative-Media.

Leland, John, and Colin Moynihan. 2012. "Thousands March Silently to Protest Stop-and-Frisk Policies." *New York Times,* June 17. Accessed June 17, 2014. http://www.nytimes.com/2012/06/18/nyregion/thousands-march-silently-to-protest-stop-and-frisk-policies.html?nl=nyregion&emc=edit_ur_20120618.

Leonard, Ira M., and Christopher C. Leonard. 2003. "The Historiography of American Violence." *Homicide Studies* 7, no. 2 (May): 99–153.

Lewis, Oscar. 1961. *The Children of Sanchez: Autobiography of a Mexican Family.* New York: Random House.

———. 1966a. "The Culture of Poverty." *Scientific American,* October, 19–25.

———. 1966b. *La Vida: A Puerto Rican Family in the Culture of Poverty—San Juan and New York.* New York: Random House.

Liss-Schultz, Claudia. 2013. "'Orange Is the New Black': Taking Privilege to Task." *Ms. Magazine* (blog), July 17. Accessed February 10, 2014. http://msmagazine.com/blog/2013/07/17/orange-is-the-new-black-taking-privilege-to-task.

Massey, Douglas S., and Robert J. Sampson. 2009. "Moynihan Redux: Legacies and Lessons." *Annals of the American Academy of Political and Social Science* 621: 6–27.

Mauer, Marc. 2006. *Race to Incarcerate.* New York: Sentencing Project.

Maynard, Robyn. 2010. "Fighting Colonialism, Racism, and Imperialism: Fundamental to a Decent Feminism." *Canadian Dimension* 44, no. 6: 34–36.

McDevitt, Jack, Jack Levin, and Susan Bennett. 2002. "Hate Crime Offenders: An Expanded Typology." *Journal of Social Issues* 58, no. 2: 303–17.

McLaughlin, Eugene, and Tim Newburn, eds. 2010. *The SAGE Handbook of Criminological Theory.* Thousand Oaks, CA: Sage.

McVay, Doug, Vincent Schiraldi, and Jason Ziedenberg. 2004. "Treatment or Incarceration? National and State Findings on the Efficacy and Cost Savings of Drug Treatment versus Imprisonment." Policy Report, Justice Policy Institute, January. Accessed November 11, 2016. http://www.justicepolicy.org/uploads/justicepolicy/documents/04-01_rep_mdtreatmentorincarceration_ac-dp.pdf.

Mele, Christopher. 2016. "Veterans to Serve as 'Human Shields' for Dakota Pipeline Protesters." *New York Times,* November 29. Accessed December 21, 2016. http://www.nytimes.com/2016/11/29/us/veterans-to-serve-as-human-shields-for-pipeline-protesters.html?_r=0.

Merton, Robert K. (1938) 1993. "Social Structure and Anomie." In *Social Theory: The Multicultural Readings,* edited by Charles Lemert. Boulder, CO: Westview Press.

Messerschmidt, James W. 1993. *Masculinities and Crime: Critique and Reconceptualization of Theory.* Lanham, MD: Rowman & Littlefield.

———. 2012. *Gender, Heterosexuality, and Youth Violence: The Struggle for Recognition.* Lanham, MD: Rowman & Littlefield.

Messner, Steven F., and Richard Rosenfeld. 2001. *Crime and the American Dream.* 3rd ed. Belmont, CA: Wadsworth.

Miller, Fayneese, and Erica Foster. 2002. "Youths' Perceptions of Race, Class, and Language Bias in the Courts." *Journal of Negro Education* 71, no. 3 (Summer): 193–204.

Morrisette, P. J. 1994. "The Holocaust of First Nation

People: Residual Effects on Parenting and Treatment Implications." *Contemporary Family Therapy* 16, no. 5: 381–92.

Moynihan Daniel P. 1965. *The Negro Family: The Case for National Action.* Washington, DC: U.S. Department of Labor, Office of Policy Planning and Research.

Mulcare, Daniel. 2008. "Restricted Authority: Slavery Politics, Internal Improvements, and the Limitation of National Administrative Capacity." *Political Research Quarterly* 61, no. 4 (December): 671–85.

Mustard, David B. 2001. "Racial, Ethnic, and Gender Disparities in Sentencing: Evidence from the U.S. Federal Courts." *Journal of Law and Economics* 44: 285–314.

Mustufa, Asraa. 2011. "North Carolina Confronts the Ugly Past of Its Eugenics Law." *ColorLines,* June 15. Accessed June 6, 2017. http://colorlines.com/ archives/2011/06/north_ carolina_sterilization_victims_ to_share_stories.html.

Nagel, Joanne. 2000. "Ethnicity and Sexuality." *Annual Review of Sociology* 26: 107–33.

National Gang Center. 2012. "National Youth Gang Survey Analysis." Accessed February 14, 2014. http:// www.nationalgangcenter .gov/survey-analysis/ demographics.

National Gang Intelligence Center. 2011. "2011 National Gang Threat Assessment: Emerging Trends." Accessed February 17, 2014. http:// www.fbi.gov/stats-services/ publications/2011- national-gang-threat-

assessment/2011-national- gang-threat-assessment- emerging-trends.

National Sexual Violence Research Center. 2015. "SAAM 2015: An Overview on Campus Sexual Violence Prevention." Accessed June 21, 2017. http://www .nsvrc.org/publications/ nsvrc-publications-sexual- assault-awareness-month/ saam-2015-overview- campus-sexual.

Nettleton, Pamela Hill. 2011. "Domestic Violence in Men's and Women's Magazines: Women Are Guilty of Choosing the Wrong Men, Men Are Not Guilty of Hitting Women." *Women's Studies in Communication* 34, no. 2: 139–60.

Nevins, Rick. 2012. "Lead Poisoning and the Bell Curve." Unpublished working paper. Accessed February 11, 2014. http://www .ricknevin.com/uploads/ Nevin_Lead_Poisoning_and_ The_Bell_Curve.pdf.

New York Civil Liberties Union. 2012. "Stop-and-Frisk 2011." May 9. Accessed April 12, 2014. https://www .nyclu.org/sites/default/files/ publications/NYCLU_2011_ Stop-and-Frisk_Report.pdf.

Orcutt, James D. 1983. *Analyzing Deviance.* Homewood, IL: Dorsey Press.

O'Reilly, Bill. 2014. "What the Ferguson Protesters Accomplished." *The O'Reilly Factor,* Fox News, December 2. Accessed December 10, 2014. http://www.foxnews .com/transcript/2014/12/02/ bill-oreilly-what-ferguson- protesters-accomplished.

Osman, Eric. 2015. "Officials Reach Partial Settlement in DOJ Lawsuit against Arizona Sheriff." *NewsHour,* PBS,

July 17. Accessed November 17, 2016. http://www.pbs .org/newshour/rundown/ officials-reach-partial- settlement-doj-lawsuit- arizona-sheriff.

Pager, Devah. 2003. "The Mark of a Criminal Record." *American Journal of Sociology* 108, no. 5: 937–75.

Pager, Devah, and Hana Shepherd. 2008. "The Sociology of Discrimination: Racial Discrimination in Employment, Housing, Credit, and Consumer Markets." *Annual Review of Sociology* 34: 181–209.

Parker, Douglas. 2011. "Understanding and Eliminating Discrimination against Blacks." *Societies without Borders* 6, no. 3: 123–56.

Patrick, Leslie. 2010. "Crime and Punishment in Colonial America." In *Encyclopedia of American History,* Vol. 2, *Colonization and Settlement, 1608–1760,* rev. ed., edited by Billy G. Smith and Gary B. Nash. New York: Facts on File.

Pellow, David N. 2004. "The Politics of Illegal Dumping: An Environmental Justice Framework." *Qualitative Sociology* 27, no. 4: 511–25.

Perry, Barbara. 2001. *In the Name of Hate: Understanding Hate Crimes.* New York: Routledge.

Perry, Barbara, and Shahid Alvi. 2012. "'We Are All Vulnerable': The In Terrorem Effects of Hate Crimes." *International Review of Victimology* 18, no. 1: 57–71.

Petrosino, Carolyn. 1999. "Connecting the Past to the Future: Hate Crime in America." *Journal of Contemporary Criminal Justice* 15, no. 1: 22–47.

Phillips, Julie A. 2002. "White, Black, and Latino Homicide Rates: Why the Difference?" *Social Problems* 49, no. 3: 349–74.

Phillips, Scott. 2008. "Racial Disparities in the Capital of Capital Punishment." *Houston Law Review* 45, no. 3: 807–40.

Piquero, Nicole Leeper, Stephanie Carmichael, and Alex R. Piquero. 2007. "Research Note: Assessing the Perceived Seriousness of White-Collar and Street Crimes." *Crime & Delinquency* 54: 292–312.

Piquero, Nicole Leeper, and Miriam D. Sealock. 2010. "Race, Crime, and General Strain Theory." *Youth Violence and Juvenile Justice* 8, no. 3: 170–86.

Pitts, Leonard. 2011. "Media Coverage Does Pretty Young White Women No Favors." *National Memo,* December 4. Accessed October 13, 2013. http://www.nationalmemo .com/media-coverage-does-pretty-young-white-women-no-favors.

Porter, Henry. 2016. "God Save the United Kingdom." *Vanity Fair,* September. Accessed September 27, 2016. http://www.vanityfair.com/ news/2016/09/god-save-the-united-kingdom-brexit.

Praso, Sheridan. 2005. *Dragon Ladies, Geisha Girls, and Our Fantasies of the Exotic Orient.* New York: PublicAffairs.

President's Commission on Law Enforcement and Administration of Justice. 1968. *The Challenge of Crime in a Free Society.* Washington, DC: Government Printing Office.

Provine, Doris Marie. 2007. *Unequal under Law: Race in the War on Drugs.* Chicago: University of Chicago Press.

Pyrooz, David, Andrew M. Fox, and Scott H. Decker. 2010. "Racial and Ethnic Heterogeneity, Economic Disadvantage, and Gangs: A Macro-Level Study of Gang Membership in Urban America." *Justice Quarterly* 27, no. 6: 867–92.

Rankin, Seija. 2014. "The New Miss USA Wants Women to Start Fighting Off Attackers." Refinery29, June 9. Accessed June 10, 2014. http://www.refinery29 .com/2014/06/69239/miss-usa-2014-nia-sanchez.

Ratcliffe, Caroline, and Signe-Mary McKernan. 2012. "Child Poverty and Its Lasting Consequence." Low-Income Working Families Paper 21, Urban Institute, September. Accessed February 5, 2015. http://www.urban.org/ UploadedPDF/412659-Child-Poverty-and-Its-Lasting-Consequence-Paper.pdf.

Redfield, Horace V. 1880. *Homicide, North and South.* Philadelphia: Lippincott.

Rich, Michael, Elizabeth R. Woods, Elizabeth Goodman, S. Jean Emans, and Robert H. DuRant. 1998. "Aggressors or Victims: Gender and Race in Music Video Violence." *Pediatrics* 101 (ed. 4, pt. 1): 669–74.

Rickerd, Chris, and Joanne Lin. 2012. "U.S. House Votes Show Acceptance of Racial Profiling of Latinos, Minorities." Washington Markup (blog), American Civil Liberties Union, May 10. Accessed June 5, 2017. http://www.aclu.org/blog/ content/us-house-votes-show-acceptance-racial-profiling-Latinos-minorities.

Rios, Victor. 2006. "The Hyper-criminalization of Black and Latino Male Youth in the Era of Mass Incarceration." *Souls: A Critical Journal of Black Politics, Culture, and Society* 8, no. 2: 40–54.

Roberts, Sam. 2011. "Fewer Broken Windows and a Decline in Crime." City Room (blog), *New York Times,* February 23. Accessed January 20, 2014. http:// cityroom.blogs.nytimes .com/2011/02/23/fewer-broken-windows-and-a-decline-in-crime.

Robinson, Mathew, and Marian Williams. 2009. "The Myth of a Fair Criminal Justice System." *Justice Policy Journal* 6, no. 1 (Spring): 1–52.

Roman, John K. 2013. "Race, Justifiable Homicide, and Stand Your Ground Laws: Analysis of FBI Supplementary Homicide Report Data." Urban Institute, July. Accessed February 10, 2014. http://www.urban.org/ UploadedPDF/412873-stand-your-ground.pdf.

Rose, Brian. 2008. "The Wire." In *The Essential HBO Reader,* edited by Gary Edgerton and Jeffrey Jones. Lexington: University of Kentucky Press.

Rose, Nancy E. 2000. "Scapegoating Poor Women: An Analysis of Welfare Reform." *Journal of Economic Issues* 34, no. 1 (March): 143–57.

Sampson, Rana. 2002. "Acquaintance Rape of College Students." Problem-Oriented Guides for Police Series, No. 17. Washington, DC: U.S. Department of Justice, Office of Community Oriented Policing Services.

Sampson, Robert J., and W. Byron Groves. 1989. "Community Structure and Crime: Testing Social

Disorganization Theory." *American Journal of Sociology* 94, no. 4: 774–802.

Sampson, Robert J., Stephen W. Raudenbush, and Felton Earls. 1997. "Neighborhoods and Violent Crime: A Multilevel Study of Collective Efficacy." *Science* 227, no. 5328 (August 15): 918–24.

Sanger, Margaret. 1922. *The Pivot of Civilization*. New York: Brentano's.

Schnitzer, Vivianne. 2013. "Latinos Disproportionately Sterilized for Decades in California." *Michigan News,* May 29. Accessed February 9, 2014. http://www.ns.umich.edu/new/releases/21493-Latinos-disproportionately-sterilized-for-decades-in-california.

Scott, James C. 1985. *Weapons of the Weak: Everyday Forms of Resistance.* New Haven, CT: Yale University Press.

——. 1992. *Domination and the Arts of Resistance: Hidden Transcripts.* New Haven, CT: Yale University Press.

Sellin, Thorsten. 1938. "Culture Conflict and Crime." *American Journal of Sociology* 44, no. 1: 97–103.

Sentencing Project. 2005. "Women in the Criminal Justice System: An Overview." Accessed February 5, 2015. http://www.sentencingproject.org/doc/publications/womenincj_total.pdf.

Shaw, Clifford R. 1952. *Brothers in Crime.* Philadelphia: Albert Saifer.

Shaw, Clifford R., and Henry D. McKay. 1969. *Juvenile Delinquency and Urban Areas*. Chicago: University of Chicago Press.

Shover, Neal, and Andy Hochstetler. 2006. *Choosing White-Collar Crime.*

New York: Cambridge University Press.

Simon, David R. 2006. *Elite Deviance.* Boston: Pearson Education.

Snell, Tracy L. 2010. "Capital Punishment, 2009—Statistical Tables." NCJ 231676. U.S. Department of Justice, Bureau of Justice Statistics, December. Accessed February 9, 2014. https://www.bjs.gov/content/pub/pdf/cp09st.pdf.

Solomon, Akiba. 2012. "Why Native American Women Are Battling for Plan B." *ColorLines,* March 22. Accessed February 13, 2014. http://colorlines.com/archives/2012/03/on_july_29_2010_lisa.html.

Soss, Joe, Richard C. Fording, and Sandford D. Schram. 2011. *Disciplining the Poor: Neoliberal Paternalism and the Persistent Power of Race.* Chicago: University of Chicago Press.

Spohn, Cassia, and Dawn Beichner. 2000. "Is Preferential Treatment of Female Offenders a Thing of the Past? A Multisite Study of Gender, Race, and Imprisonment." *Criminal Justice Policy Review* 11: 149–84.

Stabile, Carol A. 2005. "'The Most Disgusting Objects of Both Sexes': Gender and Race in the Episodic Crime News of the 1930s." *Journalism* 6, no. 4: 403–21.

Stemen, Don. 2007. "Reconsidering Incarceration: New Directions for Reducing Crime." Vera Institute of Justice, January. Accessed February 2, 2014. http://www.vera.org/sites/default/files/resources/downloads/veraincarc_vFW2.pdf.

Stewart, Eric A., and Ronald L. Simons. 2009. "The Code

of the Street and African-American Adolescent Violence." Research in Brief, National Institute of Justice, February. Accessed June 5, 2017. https://www.ncjrs.gov/pdffiles1/nij/223509.pdf.

Starr, Sonja B. 2012. "Estimating Gender Disparities in Federal Criminal Cases." Law and Economics Working Paper 57, University of Michigan Law School, August 1. Accessed February 5, 2015. http://repository.law.umich.edu/cgi/viewcontent.cgi?article=1164&context=law_econ_current.

Stoughton, Seth. 2015. "Law Enforcement's 'Warrior' Problem." *Harvard Law Review* 128: 225–34.

Sudbury, Julia. 2002. "Celling Black Bodies: Black Women in the Global Prison Industrial Complex." *Feminist Review* 70: 57–74.

Sutherland, Edwin H. 1931. "Mental Deficiency and Crime." In *Social Attitudes,* edited by K. Young. New York: Henry Holt. Accessed June 5, 2017. http://www.brocku.ca/MeadProject/Young/1931/15_Sutherland.html.

——. 1940. "White Collar Criminality." *American Sociological Review* 5: 1–12.

——. 1949. *White Collar Crime.* New York: Dryden Press.

Swisher, Raymond R., and Maureen R. Waller. 2008. "Confining Fatherhood: Incarceration and Paternal Involvement among Nonresident White, African American, and Latino Fathers." *Journal of Family Issues* 29, no. 9: 1067–88.

Tapia, Michael. 2011. "Gang Membership and Race as Risk Factors for Juvenile Arrest." *Journal of Research* in Crime and Delinquency 48, no. 3: 364–95.

Terrill, William, and Michael D. Reisig. 2003. "Neighborhood Context and Police Use of Force." *Journal of Research in Crime and Delinquency* 40, no. 3: 291–321.

Thomas, William I. 1927. "The Behavior Pattern and the Situation." In *Papers and Proceedings of the Twenty-Second Annual Meeting of the American Sociological Society.* Chicago: University of Chicago Press.

Thomas, William I., and Dorothy Swaine Thomas. 1928. *The Child in America: Behavior Problems and Programs.* New York: Alfred A. Knopf.

Thompson, Jennifer. 2013. After Innocence: Exoneration in America. American Public Media. Accessed July 22, 2017. http://www.thestory .org/stories/2013-06/jennifer-thompson.

Tillery, Alvin B., Jr. 2009. "Tocqueville as Critical Race Theorist: Whiteness as Property, Interest Convergence, and the Limits of Jacksonian Democracy." *Political Research Quarterly* 62, no. 4 (December): 639–52.

Tjaden, Patricia, and Nancy Thoennes. 2000. *Extent, Nature, and Consequences of Intimate Partner Violence: Findings from the National Violence Against Women Survey.* NCJ 181867. Washington, DC: National Institute of Justice/Centers for Disease Control and Prevention. Accessed June 6, 2017. https://www.ncjrs .gov/pdffiles1/nij/181867.pdf.

Tonry, Michael. H. 1994. "Racial Politics, Racial Disparities, and the War on Crime." *Crime & Delinquency* 40, no. 4 (October): 474–94.

———. 1995. *Malign Neglect: Race, Crime, and Punishment in America.* New York: Oxford University Press.

Truman, Jennifer L., and Rachel E. Morgan. 2014. "Nonfatal Domestic Violence, 2003–2012." Special Report, NCJ 244697. U.S. Department of Justice, Bureau of Justice Statistics, April. Accessed June 10, 2014. https://www .bjs.gov/content/pub/pdf/ ndv0312.pdf.

Tulchin, Simon H. 1939. *Intelligence and Crime: A Study of Penitentiary and Reformatory Offenders.* Chicago: University of Chicago Press.

Unnever, James D., and Shaun L. Gabbidon. 2011. *A Theory of African American Offending: Race, Racism, and Crime.* New York: Routledge.

U.S. Department of Education, Civil Rights Division. 2014. "Civil Rights Data Collection—Data Snapshot: School." Issue Brief 1, March. Accessed June 13, 2014. http://www2.ed.gov/ about/offices/list/ocr/docs/ crdc-discipline-snapshot.pdf.

U.S. Department of Justice, Bureau of Justice Statistics. 1982–2001. *Sourcebook of Criminal Justice Statistics.* Washington, DC: Government Printing Office.

van de Rakt, Marieka, Joseph Murray, and Paul Nieuwbeerta. 2012. "The Long-Term Effects of Paternal Imprisonment on Criminal Trajectories of Children." *Journal of Research in Crime and Delinquency* 49, no. 1 (February): 81–109.

Wade, Lisa. 2013. "Framing Children's Deviance." Sociological Images, July 17. Accessed February 1, 2014.

http://thesocietypages .org/socimages/2013/07/17/ framing-childrens-deviance.

Warner, Margaret, Li Hui Chen, and Diane M. Makuc. 2009. "Increase in Fatal Poisonings Involving Opioid Analgesics in the United States, 1999–2006." NCHS Data Brief 22, National Center for Health Statistics, September. Accessed June 11, 2014. http://www.cdc.gov/nchs/ data/databriefs/db22.htm.

Washington, John. 2016. "At Least 24,000 Inmates Have Staged Coordinated Protests in Past Month." *The Nation,* October 14. Accessed November 30, 2016. https:// www.thenation.com/article/ at-least-24000-inmates-have-staged-coordinated-protests-in-the-past-month-why-have-you-not-heard-of-their-actions.

Watkins, S. Craig. 1998. *Representing: Hip Hop Culture and the Production of Black Cinema.* Chicago: University of Chicago Press.

Waymer, Damion. 2009. "Walking in Fear: An Autoethnographic Account of Media Framing of Inner-City Crime." *Journal of Communication Inquiry* 33, no. 2: 169–84.

Wayne, Jack. 1975. "Colonialism and Underdevelopment in Kogoma Region, Tanzania: A Social Structural View." *Canadian Review of Sociology and Anthropology* 12, no. 3: 316–43.

Weichselbaum, Simone. 2015. "The Problems with Policing the Police." Marshall Project, April 23. Accessed October 24, 2016. https://www .themarshallproject .org/2015/04/23/policing-the-police#.w3g6ycqRd.

Weisburd, David, Stanton Wheeler, Elin Waring, and

Nancy Bode. 1991. *Crimes of the Middle Classes: White-Collar Offenders in the Federal Courts.* New Haven, CT: Yale University Press.

Weitzer, Ronald. 2002. "Incidents of Police Misconduct and Public Opinion." *Journal of Criminal Justice* 30, no. 5: 397–408.

Western, Bruce. 2006. *Punishment and Inequality in America.* New York: Russell Sage Foundation.

Western, Bruce, and Becky Pettit. 2010. *Collateral Costs: Incarceration's Effect on Economic Mobility.* Washington, DC: Pew Charitable Trusts. Accessed January 15, 2014. http://www .pewtrusts.org/ uploadedFiles/ wwwpewtrustsorg/Reports/ Economic_Mobility/ Collateral%20Costs%20 FINAL.pdf.

Western, Bruce, and Christopher Wildman. 2009. "The Black Family and Mass Incarceration." *Annals of the American Academy of Political and Social Science* 621: 221–42.

Wheeler, Stanton, David Weisburd, Elin Waring, and Nancy Bode. 1988. "White Collar Crimes and Criminals." *American Criminal Law Review* 25: 331–57.

Widom, Cathy Spatz, and Linda M. Brzustowicz. 2006. "MAOA and the 'Cycle of Violence': Childhood Abuse and Neglect, MAOA Genotype, and Risk for Violent and Antisocial Behavior." *Biological Psychiatry* 60, no. 7: 684–89.

Wiggins, Jennifer. 1983. "Rape, Racism, and the Law." *Harvard Women's Law Journal* 6: 103–42.

Wilkinson, Deanna L., Chauncey C. Beaty, and Regina M. Lurry. 2009. "Youth Violence—Crime or Self-Help? Marginalized Urban Males' Perspectives on the Limited Efficacy of the Criminal Justice System to Stop Youth Violence." *Annals of the American Academy of Political and Social Science* 623: 25–38.

Williams, Timothy. 2012. "For Native American Women, Scourge of Rape, Rare Justice." *New York Times,* May 22. Accessed February 1, 2014. http://www .nytimes.com/2012/05/23/ us/native-americans-struggle-with-high-rate-of-rape. html?pagewanted=all.

Wilson, James Q., and George L. Kelling. 1982. "Broken Windows: The Police and Neighborhood Safety." *Atlantic Monthly,* March. Accessed February 1, 2014. http://www.manhattan-institute.org/pdf/_atlantic_ monthly-broken_windows.pdf.

Wilson, William Julius. 1987. *The Truly Disadvantaged: The Underclass and Public Policy.* Chicago: University of Chicago Press.

——. 1996. *When Work Disappears: The World of the New Urban Poor.* New York: Alfred A. Knopf.

Wirth, Louis. 1931. "Culture Conflict and Delinquency, I: Culture Conflict and Misconduct." *Social Forces* 9: 484–92.

Xu, Yiuli, Mora L. Fiedler, and Karl H. Flaming. 2015. "Discovering the Impact of Community Policing: The Broken Windows Thesis, Collective Efficacy, and Citizens' Judgment." *Journal of Research in Crime and Delinquency* 42, no. 2: 147–86.

Yaniv, Oren. 2011. "Court Rules That Cops Do Use Quotas; Woman Injured in 2006 Arrest Settles for $75,000." *New York Daily News,* February 19. Accessed February 20, 2014. http:// www.nydailynews.com/ news/crime/court-rules-cops-quotas-woman-injured-2006-arrest-settles-75-000-article-1.134856.

Yick, Alice G., and Jody Oomen-Early. 2008. "A 16-Year Examination of Domestic Violence among Asians and Asian Americans in the Empirical Knowledge Base: A Content Analysis." *Journal of Interpersonal Violence* 23, no. 8: 1075–94.

■ CHAPTER 8

Adams, Bert N., and R. A. Sydie. 2002. *Classical Sociological Theory.* Thousand Oaks, CA: Pine Forge Press.

Ager, Phillip. 2013. "The Persistence of De Facto Power: Elites and Economic Development in the U.S. South, 1840–1960." Working Paper 38, European Historical Society. Accessed February 17, 2017. http:// econpapers.repec.org/ RePEc:hes:wpaper:0038.

Alexander, James. 1994. "Vilfredo Pareto, Sociologist and Philosopher: Life, Work, and Impact of the Karl Marx of

Fascism." *Journal of Historical Review* 14, no. 5: 10–18.

Allen, Theodore W. 1997. *The Invention of the White Race: The Origin of Racial Oppression in Anglo-America.* New York: Verso Books.

——. 2012. *The Invention of the White Race: The Origin of Racial Oppression in Anglo-America.* Vol. 2. New York: Verso Books.

Ambrosio, Thomas. 2002. *Ethnic Identity Groups and U.S. Foreign Policy.* Westport, CT: Praeger.

American Council on Education. 2016. "ACE Survey Finds Increased Focus among College Presidents on Campus Racial Climate." Accessed March 18, 2016. http://www.acenet .edu/news-room/Pages/ ACE-Survey-Finds-Increased-Focus-Among-College-Presidents-on-Campus-Racial-Climate.aspx.

Arnwine, Barbara, and Marcia Johnson-Blanco. 2013. "Voting Rights at the Crossroads: The Supreme Court Decision in *Shelby* Is the Latest Challenge in the 'Unfinished March' to Full Black Access to the Ballot." Economic Policy Institute, October 25. Accessed October 30, 2013. http:// www.epi.org/publication/ voting-rights-crossroads-supreme-court-decision.

Badger, Emily. 2015. "Redlining: Still a Thing." *Washington Post,* May 28. Accessed February 22, 2017. https:// www.washingtonpost.com/ news/wonk/wp/2015/05/28/ evidence-that-banks-still-deny-black-borrowers-just-as-they-did-50-years-ago/?utm_term= .dbbc1c4a0709.

Balfour, Lawrie. 2005. "Representative Women: Slavery, Citizenship, and Feminist Theory in Du Bois's 'Damnation of Women.'" *Hypatia* 20, no. 3 (Summer): 127–48.

Bates, Karen Grigsby. 2017. "Race and Feminism: Women's March Recalls the Touchy History." *Code Switch,* NPR, January 21. Accessed June 22, 2017. http://www.npr.org/sections/ codeswitch/2017/01/ 21/510859909/race-and-feminism-womens-march-recalls-the-touchy-history.

Berlinger, Joshua, and James Griffiths. 2016. "Chinese Firm Apologizes after 'Racist' Detergent Ad." CNN, May 29. Accessed June 2, 2016. http:// www.cnn.com/2016/05/29/ asia/chinese-racist-detergent-ad-apology.

Blackwell, Maylei, and Nadine Nagber. 2002. "Intersectionality in an Era of Globalization: The Implications of the UN World Conference against Racism for Transnational Feminist Practices—A Conference Report." *Meridians: Feminism, Race, Transnationalism* 2, no. 2: 237–48.

Boghosian, Alison. 2015. "8 Important Social Movements on College Campuses." Fresh U, November 29. Accessed March 21, 2016. https://www.freshu.io/ alison-boghosian/social-movements-on-college-campuses.

Bonacich, Edna. 1973. "A Theory of Middleman Minorities." *American Sociological Review* 38 (October): 583–94.

Brands, H. W. 2006. *Andrew Jackson: His Life and Times.* New York: Anchor Books.

Breen, T. H. 1973. "A Changing Labor Force and Race Relations in Virginia 1660–1710." *Journal of Social History* 7, no. 1 (Autumn): 3–25.

Bronner, Ethan. 2013. "Workers Claim Race Bias as Farms Rely on Immigrants." *New York Times,* May 7. Accessed February 17, 2017. http://www.nytimes .com/2013/05/07/us/suit-cites-race-bias-in-farms-use-of-immigrants.html.

Burawoy, Michael. 2007. "Open Letter to Wright Mills." *Antipode* 40, no. 3: 365–75.

Burks, Mary Fair. 1990. "Trailblazers: Women in the Montgomery Boycott." in *Women in the Civil Rights Movement,* edited by Vicki L. Crawford, Jacqueline Anne Rouse, and Barbara Woods. Bloomington: Indiana University Press.

CBS News. 2016. "Students Stage 'Sanctuary Campus' Protests against Trump's Immigration Policy." November 19. Accessed December 19, 2016. http:// www.cbsnews.com/videos/ students-stage-sanctuary-campus-protests-against-trumps-immigration-policy.

Celarent, Barbara. 2010. "*Caste, Class, and Race* by Oliver Cromwell Cox." *American Journal of Sociology* 115, no. 5 (March): 1664–69.

Center for American Women and Politics. 2017. "Women of Color in Elective Office 2017." http://www.cawp .rutgers.edu/women-color-elective-office-2017.

Chancellor, Carl. 2011. "After Civil War, Blacks Fought for Rights for 100 Years." *USA Today,* April 11. Accessed February 21, 2017.

http://usatoday30.usatoday
.com/news/nation/2011-04-
11-civil-war-civil-rights_N.
htm.

Cieply, Michael, and Brooks
Barnes. 2016. "Why the Film
Academy's Diversity Push
Is Tougher Than It Thinks."
New York Times, February 5.
Accessed June 1, 2016. https://
www.nytimes.com/2016/02/06/
business/media/motion-picture-
academy-diversity-efforts-a-
risk-of-bias.html?mcubz=1&_
r=0.

Cockburn, Cynthia. 2004. *The
Line: Women, Partition and
the Gender Order in Cyprus.*
London: Zed Books.

Colvin, Claudette. 2016. "History:
Claudette Colvin." Congress
of Racial Equality. Accessed
February 20, 2017. http://
www.core-online.org/History/
colvin.htm.

Combahee River Collective. (1977)
2013. "A Black Feminist
Statement: The Combahee
River Collective." In *Feminist
Theory Reader: Local and
Global Perspectives,* edited
by Carole McCann and
Seung-kyung Kim. New York:
Routledge.

Cooper, Anna J. 1892. *A Voice
from the South.* Xenia, OH:
Aldine.

Cooper, Anna J. (1891–92) 2013.
"Woman versus the Indian."
In *The Voice of Anna Julia
Cooper,* edited by Charles
Lemert and Esme Bhan.
Lanham, MD: Rowman &
Littlefield.

Crenshaw, Kimberlé. 1991.
"Mapping the Margins:
Intersectionality, Identity Politics,
and Violence against Women
of Color." *Stanford Law Review*
43, no. 6: 1241–99.

Dahl, Robert A. 1961. *Who
Governs? Democracy and
Power in an American*

City. New Haven, CT: Yale
University Press.

DeConde, Alexander. 1992.
*Ethnicity, Race and American
Foreign Policy.* Lebanon,
NH: Northwestern University
Press.

Delgado, Richard. 2006. "The
Current Landscape of
Race: Old Targets, New
Opportunities." *Michigan Law
Review* 104, no. 6: 1269–86.

Diamond, Jeremy. 2016. "Russian
Hacking and the 2016
Election: What You Need
to Know." CNN, December
12. Accessed December 22,
2016. http://www.cnn
.com/2016/12/12/politics/
russian-hack-donald-trump-
2016-election.

Dietz, Mary G. 2002. *Turning
Operations; Feminism,
Arendt, and Politics.* New
York: Routledge.

Domhoff, G. William. 2005. "Social
Movements and Strategic
Nonviolence." Who Rules
America, March. Accessed
June 17, 2017. http://www2
.ucsc.edu/whorulesamerica/
change/science_nonviolence
.html.

Donnella, Leah. 2016. "The
Standing Rock Resistance
Is Unprecedented (It's
Also Centuries Old)."
Code Switch, NPR,
November 22. Accessed
December 12, 2016. http://
www.npr.org/sections/
codeswitch/2016/11/22/
502068751/the-standing-
rock-resistance-is-
unprecedented-it-s-also-
centuries-old.

Du Bois, W. E. B. 1903. *The Souls
of Black Folk.* Chicago.
A. C. McClurg.

———. 1918. "The Black
Man and the Unions."
TeachingAmericanHistory
.org, Ashbrook Center,

Ashland University. Accessed
February 22, 2013. http://
teachingamericanhistory.org/
library/document/the-black-
man-and-the-unions.

———. 1986. *Writings: The
Suppression of the African
Slave-Trade, The Souls of
Black Folk, Dusk of Dawn,
Essays.* Des Moines, IA:
Library of America.

———. (1933) 2000. "Marxism and
the Negro Problem." In *W.
E. B. Du Bois, 1919–1963:
The Fight for Equality and
the American Century,* edited
by David L. Lewis. London:
Macmillan.

Engerman, Stanley L., Richard
Sutch, and Gavin Wright.
2004. "Slavery." In *Historical
Statistics of the United
States, Millennial Edition,*
edited by Susan B. Carter,
Scott S. Gartner, Michael
Haine, Allan Olmstead,
Richard Sutch, and
Gavin Wright. New York:
Cambridge University Press.

Enten, Harry. 2016. "Young
Millennials Love Obama, but
Clinton Is Struggling to Win
Them Over." FiveThirtyEight,
September 12. Accessed
January 2, 2017. http://
fivethirtyeight.com/features/
young-millennials-love-
obama-but-clinton-is-
struggling-to-win-them-over.

Erlanger, Steven, and Stephen
Castle. 2016. "Britain
Grapples with Enduring
Questions of Religion and
Race." *New York Times,*
April 25. Accessed June 2,
2016. http://www.nytimes
.com/2016/04/26/world/
europe/britain-grapples-
with-enduring-questions-of-
religion-and-race.html.

Ewing, Walter. 2012. "Opportunity
and Exclusion: A Brief
History of U.S. Immigration

Policy." American Immigration Council, January 13. Accessed June 22, 2017. https://www.americanimmigrationcouncil.org/research/opportunity-and-exclusion-brief-history-us-immigration-policy.

Feagin, Joe R. 2010. *The White Racial Frame: Centuries of Racial Framing and Counter-framing.* New York: Routledge.

Flanagan, Maureen A. 2005. "Suffrage." In *Encyclopedia of Chicago.* Chicago: Chicago Historical Society. Accessed March 15, 2016. http://www.encyclopedia.chicagohistory.org/pages/1217.html.

Fogg-Davis, Hawley. 2003. "The Racial Retreat of Contemporary Political Theory." *Perspectives on Politics* 1, no. 3 (September): 555–64.

Foucault, Michel. 1984. "Truth and Power." In *The Foucault Reader,* edited by Paul Rabinow, 51–75. New York: Pantheon.

Fryer, Joe. 2016. "Muhammad Ali, 'the People's Champ.'" MSNBC, June 4. Accessed December 21, 2016. http://www.msnbc.com/msnbc-news/watch/ali-the-people-s-champ-699002435867.

Gajanan, Mahita. 2016. "Colin Kaepernick and a Brief History of Protest in Sports." *Time,* August 29. Accessed December 12, 2016. http://time.com/4470998/athletes-protest-colin-kaepernick.

Galenson, David W. 1984. "The Rise and Fall of Indentured Servitude in the Americas: An Economic Analysis." *Journal of Economic History* 44, no. 1: 1–26.

Giménez, Martha E. 1992. "U.S. Ethnic Politics." *Latin American Perspectives* 19, no. 4 (Fall): 7–17.

Goldberg, Milton M. "A Qualification of the Marginal Man Theory." *American Sociological Review* 6, no. 1: 52–58.

Goldstein, Joshua S., and Jon C. Pevehouse. 2009. *Principles of International Relations.* New York: Pearson/Longman

Gonyea, Don. 2012. "'Midwest Firewall' Helps Secure Obama Victory." *All Things Considered,* NPR, November 7. Accessed January 2, 2017. http://www.npr.org/2012/11/07/164631071/midwest-firewall-helps-secure-obama-victory.

Gottfried, Heidi. 2008. "Reflections on Intersectionality: Gender, Class, Race and Nation." *Gender Studies: Orchanomizu University Center for Gender Studies Annual Report* 11: 23–40. Accessed June 17, 2017. http://www.igs.ocha.ac.jp/igs/IGS_publication/journal/11/jenda_2_heidi.pdf.

Griffith, Erin. 2016. "The Black Lives Matter Founders Are among the World's Greatest Leaders." *Fortune,* March 24. Accessed June 2, 2016. http://fortune.com/2016/03/24/black-lives-matter-great-leaders.

Hersh, Eitan D., and Clayton Nall. 2015. "The Primacy of Race in the Geography of Income-Based Voting: New Evidence from Public Voting Records." *American Journal of Political Science* 60, no. 2: 289–303.

Higginbotham, Evelyn Brooks. 1992. "African-American Women's History and the Metalanguage of Race." *Signs* 17, no. 2 (Winter): 251–74.

Hochschild, Jennifer L. 2005. "Race and Class in Political Science." *Michigan Journal of Race and Law* 11, no. 1: 99–114.

Hochschild, Jennifer L., and Brenna M. Powell. 2008. "Racial Reorganization and the United States Census 1850–1930: Mulattoes, Half-Breeds, Mixed Parentage, Hindoos, and the Mexican Race." *American Political Development* 22, no. 1: 59–96.

Hutchings, Vincent L., and Nicholas A. Valentino. 2004. "The Centrality of Race in American Politics." *American Review of Political Science* 7: 383–408.

Jacobson, Matthew Frye. 2006. "More 'Trans,' Less 'National.'" *Journal of American Ethnic History* 25, no. 4: 66–84.

Jaschik, Scott. 2016. "Taking a Stand by Refusing to Stand." Inside Higher Ed, September 12. Accessed December 19, 2016. https://www.insidehighered.com/news/2016/09/12/debate-grows-over-national-anthem-college-events.

Jelten, Tom G. 2015. "The Immigration Act That Inadvertently Changed America." *Atlantic,* October. Accessed February 20, 2017. https://www.theatlantic.com/politics/archive/2015/10/immigration-act-1965/408409.

Kilgore, Ed. 2016. "Minor-Party Candidates Unlikely to Have Major Effect on the Presidential Race." *New York Magazine,* August 24. Accessed June 27, 2017. http://nymag.com/daily/intelligencer/2016/08/minor-party-candidates-wont-have-major-effect-on-race.html.

King, Desmond S., and Rogers M. Smith. 2008. "Strange Bedfellows? Polarized Politics? The Quest for Racial Equity in Contemporary America." *Political Research Quarterly* 61, no. 4 (December): 687–703.

King, Martin Luther, Jr. 1958. *Stride toward Freedom.* New York: HarperCollins

Knight, Nika. 2016. "The Power Is in Our Hands: Virginia Students Protest Coal Ash Dumping." Common Dreams, March 7. Accessed March 24, 2016. http://www.commondreams.org/news/2016/03/07/power-our-hands-virginia-students-protest-coal-ash-dumping.

Lam, Bourree. 2017. "Americans Feel More Confident about the Economy." *Atlantic,* March 31. Accessed June 21, 2017. https://www.theatlantic.com/business/archive/2017/03/americans-consumer-confidence/521574.

Lincoln, Abraham. 1862. "A Letter from President Lincoln: Reply to Horace Greeley. Slavery and the Union, the Restoration of the Union the Paramount Object." *New York Times,* August 24. Accessed February 21, 2017. http://www.nytimes.com/1862/08/24/news/letter-president-lincoln-reply-horace-greeley-slavery-union-restoration-union.html.

Lind, JoEllen, 2009. "Dominance and Democracy: The Legacy of Woman Suffrage for the Voting Right." *UCLA Women's Law Journal* 5: 104–216.

Ludwig, Mike. 2015. "How Much of Big Pharma's Massive Profits Are Used to Influence Politicians?" Truthout, September 30. Accessed April 26, 2017. http://www.truth-out.org/news/item/33010-how-much-of-big-pharma-s-massive-profits-are-used-to-influence-politicians.

Magid, Shaul. 2013. *American Post-Judaism: Identity and Renewal in a Postethnic Society.* Bloomington: Indiana University Press.

Marx, Karl. (1852) 1964. *The Eighteenth Brumaire of Louis Bonaparte.* New York: International Publishers.

Massey, Eli. 2016. "Meet the Rabbi Who Renounced Zionism and Embraced Palestinian Liberation." *In These Times,* June 1. Accessed June 2, 2016. http://inthesetimes.com/article/19105/rabbi-brant-rosen-tzedek-chicago-zionism-palestine.

Mayari, Sarena. 2015. "Intersectionality and Title VII: A Brief (Pre-)History." *Boston University Law Review* 95, no. 3: 713–32.

McElwee, Sean. 2016. "Race versus Class in the Democratic Coalition." *The Nation,* March 7. https://www.thenation.com/article/race-versus-class-in-the-democratic-coalition.

McLaughlin, James. 1891. "An Account of Sitting Bull's Death." Archives of the West, PBS. Accessed February 22, 2017. http://www.pbs.org/weta/thewest/resources/archives/eight/sbarrest.htm.

Melish, Joanne Pope. 1998. *Disowning Slavery: Gradual Emancipation and "Race" in New England, 1780–1960.* Ithaca, NY: Cornell University Press.

Miliband, Ralph. 1977. *Marxism and Politics.* Oxford: Oxford University Press.

Miller, Matt. 2016. "Here's Every Person and Business Boycotting North Carolina for Its LGBT Discrimination." *Esquire,* April 13. Accessed June 1, 2016. http://www.esquire.com/news-politics/news/a43931/north-carolina-anti-lgbt-law-boycott.

Miller, Robert J. 2006. "American Indians and the United States Constitution." Flash Point. Accessed February 20, 2017. http://www.flashpointmag.com/amindus.htm.

Mills, Wright C. 1956. *The Power Elite.* New York: Oxford University Press.

——. 1959. *The Sociological Imagination.* New York: Oxford University Press.

——. 1997. *The Racial Contract.* Ithaca, NY: Cornell University.

Mommsen, Wolfgang. 1984. *Max Weber and German Politics, 1890–1920.* Chicago: University of Chicago Press.

Morin, Rich. 2016. "Behind Trump's Win in Rural, White America: Women Joined Men in Backing Him." Fact Tank, Pew Research Center, November 17. Accessed January 15, 2017. http://www.pewresearch.org/fact-tank/2016/11/17/behind-trumps-win-in-rural-white-america-women-joined-men-in-backing-him.

Morris, Aldon. 2015. *The Scholar Denied: W. E. B. Du Bois and the Birth of Modern Sociology.* Berkeley: University of California Press.

Morrison, Toni. 1993. "On the Backs of Blacks." *Time,* December 2. Accessed March 21, 2016. http://content.time.com/time/magazine/article/0,9171,979736,00.html.

National Women's Law Center. 2015. "National Snapshot:

Poverty among Women and Families, 2014." Accessed June 1, 2015. http://nwlc .org/resources/national-snapshot-poverty-among-women-families-2014.

Nussbaum, Bruce. 2010. "Is What's Good for Corporate America Still Good for America?" *Harvard Business Review,* October 26. Accessed February 17, 2017. https://hbr.org/2010/10/is-whats-good-for-corporate-am.

O'Brien, Keith. 2016. "Inside the Protest That Stopped the Trump Rally." *Politico Magazine,* March. Accessed March 24, 2016. http://www .politico.com/magazine/ story/2016/03/donald-trump-chicago-protest-213728.

Omi, Michael, and Howard Winant. 2015. *Racial Formation in the United States.* 3rd ed. New York: Routledge.

Pearson, Allison. 2016. "Pale, Male and Stale: The Sorry State of the Oscars." *Telegraph,* January 18. Accessed May 29, 2016. http://www.telegraph .co.uk/culture/film/oscars/ 12108200/Pale-male-and-stale-the-sorry-state-of-the-Oscars.html.

Pew Research Center. 2014. "Millennials in Adulthood: Detached from Institutions, Networked with Friends." March. Accessed June 17, 2017. http://www .pewsocialtrends.org/ 2014/03/07/millennials-in-adulthood.

———. 2015. "A Deep Dive into Party Affiliation: Sharp Differences by Race, Gender, Generation, Education." April. Accessed December 9, 2016. http://www.people-press.org/2015/04/07/a-

deep-dive-into-party-affiliation.

Porter, Eric. 2010. *The Problem of the Future World: W. E. B. Du Bois and the Race Concept at Midcentury.* Durham, NC: Duke University Press.

Poulantzas, Nicos. 2008. *The Poulantzas Reader: Marxism, Law and the State.* Edited by James Martin. London: Verso Books.

Reed, Adolph, Jr. 2001. "Race and Class in the Work of Oliver Cromwell Cox." *Monthly Review,* February. Accessed December 9, 2016. http://monthlyreview .org/2001/02/01/race-and-class-in-the-work-of-oliver-cromwell-cox.

Rehmann, Jan. 2013. *Max Weber: Modernisation as Passive Revolution—A Gramscian Analysis.* Leiden, Netherlands: Brill.

Restifo, Salvatore J., Vincent J. Roscigno, and Zhenchao Qian. 2013. "Segmented Assimilation, Split Labor Markets, and Racial/Ethnic Inequality." *American Sociological Review* 78, no. 5: 897–924.

Robinson, Joanna. 2017. "Nominees Caution That the 'Oscars So White' Fight Isn't Over Yet." *Vanity Fair,* February. Accessed February 22, 2017. http:// www.vanityfair.com/ hollywood/2017/02/viola-davis-bafta-win-dev-patel-mahershala-ali-oscars-so-white-naomie-harris.

Roediger, David R. 2006. *Working Toward Whiteness: How America's Immigrants Became White: The Strange Journey from Ellis Island to the Suburbs.* New York: Basic Books.

———. 2007. *The Wages of Whiteness: Race and the*

Making of the American Working Class. Chicago: Haymarket Press.

Rojas, Rick. 2016. "In New York, Thousands Protest Officer Liang's Conviction." *New York Times,* Februaryy 21. Accessed June 2, 2016. http://www.nytimes .com/2016/02/21/nyregion/ in-new-york-thousands-protest-officer-liangs-conviction.html?_r=0.

Ross, Steven J. 2008. "A New Democratic Coalition." *Washington Independent,* August 22. Accessed June 2, 2016. http:// washingtonindependent .com/6/a-new-democratic-coalition.

Sacks, Karen Brodkin. 1989. "Toward a Unified Theory of Class, Race, and Gender." *American Ethnologists* 16, no. 3: 534–50.

Sherman, Shantella Y. "Chinese Defend Racist Ad." AFRO, June 1. Accessed June 2, 2016. http://afro .com/chinese-defend-racist-ad.

Smith, Charles E. 1966. "Negro-White Intermarriage: Forbidden Sexual Union." *Journal of Sex Research* 2, no. 3 (November): 169–77.

Tehranian, John. 2000. "Performing Whiteness: Naturalization Litigation and the Construction of Racial Identity in America." *Yale Law Journal* 109, no. 4: 817–48.

Torres, Andrea. 2016. "Black Miami Police Officers Protest Beyoncé Boycott." WPLG Local10.com, February 20. Accessed March 22, 2016. http://www.local10.com/ news/crime/black-miami-police-officers-protest-beyonc-boycott.

Tushnet, Mark V. 2003. "Segregation." In *Dictionary*

of American History, 3rd ed., edited by Stanley I. Kutler. New York: Scribner.

Tyson, Alec, and Shiva Maniam. 2016. "Behind Trump's Victory: Divisions by Race, Gender, Education." Fact Tank, Pew Research Center, November 9. Accessed June 17, 2017. http://www.pewresearch.org/fact-tank/2016/11/09/behind-trumps-victory-divisions-by-race-gender-education.

Uggen, Christopher, Ryan Larson, and Sarah Shannon. 2016. "6 Million Lost Voters: State-Level Estimates of Felony Disenfranchisement, 2016." Sentencing Project. Accessed February 24, 2017. http://www.sentencingproject.org/publications/6-million-lost-voters-state-level-estimates-felony-disenfran chisement-2016.

United Farm Workers of America. 2016. "The 1965–1970 Delano Grape Strike and Boycott." Accessed October 20, 2016. http://www.ufw.org/_board.php?mode=view&b_code=cc_his_research&b_no=10482.

Upchurch, Thomas Adams. 2004. Legislating Racism: The Billion Dollar Congress and the Birth of Jim Crow. Lexington: University Press of Kentucky.

Villarreal, Vezmin. 2016. "Nation's Largest Latino Civil Rights Group Joins LGBTs in N.C. Boycott." Advocate, May 18. Accessed May 31, 2016. http://www.advocate.com/transgender/2016/5/18/nations-largest-latino-civil-rights-group-joins-lgbts-nc-boycott.

Wagner, Alex. 2016. "Why Are Asian Americans Politically Invisible?" Atlantic, September. Accessed April 4, 2017. https://www.theatlantic.com/politics/archive/2016/09/why-dont-asians-count/498893.

Watson, Lori. 2010. "Toward a Feminist Theory of Justice: Political Liberalism and Feminist Method." Tulsa Law Review 46, no. 1: 35–44.

Weber, Max. 1947. Max Weber: The Theory of Social and Economic Organizations. Translated by A. M. Henderson and Talcott Parsons. New York: Free Press.

———. (1920) 1978. Economy and Society: An Outline of Interpretive Sociology. Berkeley: University of California Press.

Weeks, Daniel. 2014. "Why Are the Poor and Minorities Less Likely to Vote?" Atlantic, January. Accessed May 31, 2016. http://www.theatlantic.com/

politics/archive/2014/01/why-are-the-poor-and-minorities-less-likely-to-vote/282896.

Wellford, Rachel. 2014. "By the Numbers: Veterans in Congress." NewsHour, PBS, November 11. Accessed April 26, 2017. http://www.pbs.org/newshour/rundown/by-the-numbers-veterans-in-congress.

Wines, Michael. 2016. "Virginia's Governor Restores Voting Rights for 13,000 Ex-Felons." New York Times, August 23. Accessed February 24, 2017. https://www.nytimes.com/2016/08/23/us/virginia-governor-mcauliffe-voting-rights-felons.html?_r=1.

Woodard, Benjamin. 2016. "Meet Faith Spotted Eagle, Who Received One Washington State Elector's Presidential Vote." Seattle Times, December 19. Accessed December 21, 2016. http://www.seattletimes.com/seattle-news/politics/meet-faith-spotted-eagle-the-native-elder-voted-for-president-by-a-washington-state-elector.

Wright, J. Leitch. 1968. "A Note on the First Seminole War as Seen by the Indians, Negroes, and Their British Advisers." Journal of Southern History 34, no. 4: 565–75.

■ CHAPTER 9

Abrams, Jonathan. 2009. "Auriemma Says Perceptions of Stanford Based on Race." New York Times, December 18. Accessed September 13, 2013. http://thequad.blogs.nytimes.com/2009/04/04/auriemma-

says-perceptions-of-stanford-based-on-race/?_r=0.

Alamillo, José M. 2013. "Beyond the Latino Sports Hero: The Role of Sports in Creating Communities, Networks, and Identities." American Latino

Theme Study, National Park Service. Accessed April 10, 2013. http://www.nps.gov/Latino/Latinothemestudy/sports.htm.

Anderson, Eric. 2006. "Using the Master's Tools: Resisting

Colonization through Colonial Sports." *International Journal of the History of Sport* 23, no. 2: 247–66.

Andrews, David L., and Steven J. Jackson, eds. 2001. *Sports Stars: The Cultural Politics of Sporting Celebrity.* New York: Routledge.

Armstrong, Kevin. 2006. "Private Enterprise: When Private High Schools Court Top Athletes, Public Schools Usually Lose." *Sports Illustrated,* November 6. Accessed June 15, 2017. https://www.si.com/vault/2006/11/06/8393250/private-enterprise.

Aronson, Anne. 2012. "Dames in the Dirt: Women's Baseball before 1945." The National Pastime, Society for American Baseball. Accessed January 18, 2017. http://sabr.org/research/dames-dirt-womans-baseball-1945.

Bale, J. 1993. "The Spatial Development of the Modern Stadium." *International Review for the Sociology of Sport* 28, nos. 2–3: 121–31.

Billings, Andrew C., and James R. Angelini. 2007. "Packaging the Games for Viewer Consumption: Gender, Ethnicity, and Nationality in NBC's Coverage of the 2004 Summer Olympics." *Communication Quarterly* 55, no. 1: 95–111.

Billings, Andrew C., Michael L. Butterworth, and Paul D. Turman. 2012. *Communication and Sport: Surveying the Field.* Thousand Oaks, CA: Sage.

Birrell, Susan, and Mary G. McDonald. 2000. "Reading Sport, Articulating Power Lines." In *Reading Sport: Critical Essays on Power and Representation*, edited by Susan Birrell and Mary G. McDonald. Boston: Northeastern University Press.

Borish, Linda J. 2014. "Women in American Sport History." In *A Companion to American Sport History,* edited by Steven A. Riess. Chichester: John Wiley.

Brandt, M., and A. Carstens. 2011. "Visual Stereotyping of Women's Sports in the Sports Media." *South African Journal for Research in Sport, Education and Recreation* 33, no. 2: 1–16.

Brownell, Susan. 2008. "Bodies before the Boas, Sport before the Laughter Left." In *The 1904 Anthropology Days and Olympic Games: Sport, Race, and American Imperialism,* edited by Susan Brownell. Lincoln: University of Nebraska Press.

Bruening, Jennifer E. 2005. "Gender and Racial Analysis in Sport: Are All the Women White and All the Blacks Men?" *Quest* 53, no. 3: 330–49.

Buford, Kate. 2010. *Native American Son*. New York: Alfred A. Knopf.

Burgos, Adrian. 2007. *Playing America's Game: Baseball, Latinos, and the Color Line*. Berkeley: University of California Press.

Butterworth, Michael L. 2007. "Race in 'The Race': Mark McGwire, Sammy Sosa, and Heroic Constructions of Whiteness." *Critical Studies in Media and Communication* 24, no. 3: 228–44.

Cacabelos, Kevin. 2009. "High School Sports: Private vs. Public." Bleacher Report, January 20. Accessed December 16, 2013. http://bleacherreport.com/articles/113694-high-school-sports-private-vs-public.

Cameron, Christopher David Ruiz. 2012. "You Can't Win If You Don't Play: The Surprising Absence of Latino Athletes from College Sports." *Wake Forest Journal of Law and Policy* 2, no. 1: 227–46.

Carini, Robert M., and Jonetta D. Weber. 2015. "Female Anglers in a Predominantly Male Sport: Portrayals in Five Popular Fishing-Related Magazines." *International Review for the Sociology of Sport* 52, no. 1: 45–60.

Carrington, Ben. 2013. "The Critical Sociology of Race and Sport: The First Fifty Years." *Annual Review of Sociology* 39: 379–98.

Carroll, Bret E., ed. 2003. *American Masculinities: A Historical Encyclopedia.* Thousand Oaks, CA: Sage.

Carton, Andrew M., and Ashleigh Shelby Rosette. 2011. "Explaining Bias against Black Leaders: Integrating Theory on Information Processing and Goal-Based Stereotyping." *Academy of Management Journal* 54, no. 6: 1141–58.

Carty, Victoria. 2005. "Textual Portrayals of Female Athletes: Liberation or Nuanced Forms of Patriarchy?" *Frontiers* 26, no. 2: 132–55.

Ceron-Anaya, Hugo. 2010. "An Approach to the History of Golf: Business, Symbolic Capital, and Technologies of the Self." *Journal of Sport and Social Issues* 34, no. 3: 339–58.

Chappell, Bob. 2001. "Race, Ethnicity and Sport." In *The Sociology of Sport and Physical Education: An Introductory Reader,* edited by Anthony Laker. New York: Routledge Falmer.

Chidester, Phillip J. 2009. "'The Toy Store of Life': Myth, Sport and the Mediated Reconstruction of the American Hero in the Shadow of the September 11th Terrorist Attacks." *Southern Communication Journal* 74, no. 4: 352–72.

Childress, Sarah. 2014. "A Return to School Segregation in America?" *Frontline,* PBS, July 2. Accessed January 2, 2017. http://www .pbs.org/wgbh/frontline/ article/a-return-to-school-segregation-in-america.

Chu, Bryan. 2008. "Asian Americans Remain Rare in Men's College Basketball." *San Francisco Chronicle,* December 16. Accessed February 14, 2013. http:// www.sfgate.com/sports/ article/Asian-Americans-remain-rare-in-men-s-college-3258007. php#page-3.

Coakley, Jay. 2004. *Sports in Society: Issues and Controversies.* 8th ed. New York: McGraw-Hill.

Coelho, Daniel, Eduardo Pimenta, Izinara Rosse, Christiano Venerosa, Lenice K. Becker, Maria Raquel Santos Carvalho, Guilherme de Azambuja Pussieldi, and Emerson Silami Garcia. 2016. "The Alpha-Actinin-3 R577X Polymorphism and Physical Performance of Soccer Players." *Biology of Sport* 56, no. 3: 241–48.

Conchas, Gilberto Q. 2006. *The Color of Success: Race and High-Achieving Urban Youth.* New York: Teachers College Press.

Cooky, Cheryl, Michael A. Messner, and Robin H.

Hextrum. 2013. "Women Play Sport, but Not on TV: A Longitudinal Study of Television News Media." *Communication and Sport* 1, nos. 1–2: 1–28.

Cooley, Will. 2010. "'Vanilla Thrillas': Modern Boxing and White-Ethnic Masculinity." *Journal of Sport and Social Issues* 34, no. 4: 418–37.

Crawford, Russ. 2013. "America Plays: Sports in Colonial Times." In *American History through American Sports: From Colonial Lacrosse to Extreme Sports,* edited by Danielle Sarver Coombs and Bob Batchelor. Santa Barbara, CA: Praeger.

Crupi, Anthony. 2015. "Sports Now Accounts for 37% of Broadcast TV Ad Spending." *Advertising Age,* September 10. Accessed January 20, 2017. http://adage .com/article/media/sports-account-37-percent-all-tv-ad-dollars/300310.

Culin, Stuart. 1897–98. "American Indian Games." Presidential Address, American Folk-Lore Society. *Journal of American Folk-Lore* 11, no. 43 (October): 245–52.

Dangerfield, Whitney, and Allen Barra. 2012. "Before and After Title IX: Women in Sports." *New York Times Sunday Review,* June 16. Accessed January 15, 2014. http://www.nytimes.com/ interactive/2012/06/17/ opinion/sunday/ sundayreview-titleix-timeline .html?_r=0#/#time12_265.

Daniels, Bruce C. 1995. *Puritans at Play: Leisure and Recreation in Colonial New England.* New York: Palgrave Macmillan.

Dash, Barbara. 2003. "Jesse Owens, 1913–1980." Audio/

People in America, Voice of America. Accessed April 25, 2013. http://learningenglish .voanews.com/content/jesse-owens-1913—1980-he-was-once-the-fastest-runner-in-the-world-128523103/116594 .html.

Davis, Amira Rose. 2016. "No League of Their Own: Baseball, Black Women, and the Politics of Representation." *Radical History Review* 125: 74–96.

Davis, Angela. 1989. "Complexity, Activism, Optimism." *Feminist Review* 27, no. 1: 60–69.

Davis, Laurel R., and Othello Harris. 1999. "Race and Ethnicity in US Sports Media." In *Media Sport,* edited by Lawrence Wenner, 154–69. New York: Routledge.

Davis, Timothy. 2007. "Race and Sports in America. An Historical Overview." *Virginia Sports and Entertainment Law Journal* 7, no. 2: 291–311.

Day, Jacob C., and Steve McDonald. 2010. "Not So Fast, My Friend: Social Capital and the Race Disparity in Promotions among College Football Coaches." *Sociological Spectrum: Mid-South Sociological Association* 30, no. 2: 138–58.

Delaney, Tim. 2015. "The Functionalist Perspective on Sport." In *Routledge Handbook of the Sociology of Sport,* edited by Richard Giulianotti, 18–28. London: Routledge.

Delaney, Tim, and Tim Madigan. 2009. *The Sociology of Sports: An Introduction.* Jefferson, NC: McFarland.

Delsahut, Fabrice, and Thiuerry Terret. 2014. "First Nations

Women, Games, and Sport in Pre- and Post-Colonial America." *Women's History Review* 23, no. 6: 675–95.

Donnelly, Peter. 2008. "The Sociology of Sport." In *21st Century Sociology,* edited by Clifton D. Bryant and Dennis L. Peck. Thousand Oaks, CA: Sage.

Eagleman, Andrea M. 2011. "Stereotypes of Race and Nationality: A Qualitative Analysis of Sport Magazine Coverage of MLB Players." *Journal of Sport Management* 25: 156–68.

Ecker, Danny. 2017. "This Company Coaches Student Athletes on the Race to College." *Crain's Chicago Business*, February 10. Accessed March 1, 2017. http://www.chicagobusiness .com/article/20170210/ ISSUE01/170219980/this- company-coaches-student- athletes-on-the-race-to- college.

Edwards, Harry. 1970. *The Revolt of the Black Athlete.* New York: Free Press.

———. 2003. "The Sources of the Black Athlete's Superiority." In *Sport: Critical Concepts in Sociology,* edited by Eric Dunning and Malcolm Dominic. New York: Routledge.

Eisen, George. 1977. "Voyageurs, Black-Robes, Saints, and Indians." *Ethno History* 24, no. 3: 191–205.

———. 1994. "Introduction." In *Ethnicity and Sport in North American History and Culture,* edited by George Eisen and David K. Wiggins. Westport, CT: Praeger.

Eitzen, D. Stanley, and George H. Sage. 2003. "Sport, Social Stratification, and Social Mobility." In *Sociology of North American Sport,*

7th ed., edited by D. Stanley Eitzen and George H. Sage, 267–84. New York: McGraw-Hill.

Ellis, Carolyn Gaither, ed. 2003. *The Legend of Jocko: Hero of the American Revolution.* Chicago: Lefall.

Entine, Jon. 2000. *Taboo: Why Black Athletes Dominate Sports and Why We're Afraid to Talk about It.* New York: PublicAffairs.

Fields, Sarah K. 2008. "Title IX and African American Female Athletes." In *Sports and the Racial Divide: African American and Latino Experience in an Era of Change,* edited by Michael E. Lomax. Jackson: University Press of Mississippi.

Forbes. 2016. "The World's Highest-Paid Athletes." Accessed December 21, 2016. https://www .forbes.com/athletes/ list/#tab:overall.

Fox, John. 2006. "Students of the Game: Archaeologists Are Researching Ulama—Oldest Sport in the Americas." *Smithsonian,* April.

Freeman, Mike. 2013. "The Rooney Rule 10 Years Later: It's Worked . . . Usually, and We Still Need It." Bleacher Report, October 24. Accessed December 18, 2013. http://bleacherreport .com/articles/1822988-the- rooney-rule-10-years-later- its-worked-usually-and-we- still-need-it.

Gaines, Cork. 2012. "The Highest-Paid Players in the NFL." Business Insider, September 27. Accessed February 19, 2013. http://www .businessinsider.com/the-25- highest-paid-players-in-the- nfl-2012-9?op=1.

———. 2016. "The 25 Schools That Make the Most Money in College Sports." Business Insider, October 13. Accessed January 20, 2017. http://www.businessinsider .com/schools-most-revenue- college-sports-2016-10.

Gane-McCalla, Casey. 2009. "Athletic Blacks vs. Smart Whites: Why Sports Stereotypes Are Wrong." Huffington Post, May 20. Accessed December 18, 2013. http://www .huffingtonpost.com/casey- ganemccalla/athletic-Blacks- vs-smart_b_187386.html.

Gasparini, William, and Aurélie Cometti, eds. 2010. *Sport Facing the Test of Cultural Diversity.* Strasbourg: Council of Europe Publishing. Accessed March 10, 2015. http://www.coe.int/t/DG4/ EPAS/resources/6718%20 Sport%20facing%20 cultural%20diversity%20 assemble.pdf.

Gems, Gerald R. 2001. "Welfare Capitalism and Blue-Collar Sport: The Legacy of Labor Unrest." *Rethinking History* 5, no. 1: 43–58.

Gems, Gerald R., Linda J. Borish, and Gertrud Pfister. 2008. *Sports in American History: From Colonization to Globalization.* Champaign, IL: Human Kinetics.

Gems, Gerald R., and Gertrud Pfister. 2009. *Understanding American Sports.* New York: Routledge.

Gil-White, Francisco. 2004. "Resurrecting Racism: The Modern Attack on Black People Using Phony Science." Historical and Investigative Research. Accessed April 3, 2013. http://www.hirhome.com/rr/ rrintro.htm.

Giulianotti, Richard. 2016. *Sport: A Critical Sociology.* 2nd ed. Malden, MA: Polity Press.

Goldsmith, Pat António. 2003. "Race Relations and Racial Patterns in School Sports Participation." *Sociology of Sport Journal* 20, no. 2: 147–71.

Gonzalez, Christopher. 2016. "Latina/os and the American Sports Landscape." In *The Routledge Companion to Latina/o Popular Culture,* edited by Frederick Luis Aldama, 334–44. New York: Routledge.

Gorn, Elliot J. (1989) 2010. *The Manly Art: Bare-Knuckle Prize Fighting in America.* Ithaca, NY: Cornell University Press.

Graves, Joseph, Jr. 2003. "Interview with Joseph Graves, Jr." *Race—The Power of an Illusion,* PBS. Accessed April 3, 2013. http://www.pbs.org/race/000_About/002_04-background-01-06.htm.

Grundy, Pamela. 2000. "From Amazons to Glamazons: The Rise and Fall of North Carolina Women's Basketball, 1920–1960." *Journal of American History* 87, no. 1: 112–46.

Guth, Lisa M., and Stephen M. Roth. 2013. "Genetic Influence on Athletic Performance." *Current Opinion in Pediatrics* 25, no. 6: 653–58.

Hall, Ronald E. 2002. "The Bell Curve: Implications for the Performance of Black/White Athletes." *Social Science Journal* 39, no. 1: 113–18.

Hargreaves, Jennifer. 1994. *Sporting Females: Critical Issues in the History and Sociology of Women's Sports.* New York: Taylor & Francis.

Harper, Shaun R. 2016. "Black Male Student-Athletes and Racial Inequities in NCAA Division I College Sports: 2016 Edition." Center for the Study of Race and Equity in Education, University of Pennsylvania. Accessed June 27, 2017. http://www.gse.upenn.edu/equity/sites/gse.upenn.edu.equity/files/publications/Harper_Sports_2016.pdf.

Harper, Shaun R., Collin D. Williams, and Horatio W. Blackman. 2013. "Black Male Student-Athletes and Racial Inequities in NCAA Division I College Sports." Center for the Study of Race and Equity in Education, University of Pennsylvania. Accessed February 19, 2013. https://www.gse.upenn.edu/equity/sites/gse.upenn.edu.equity/files/publications/Harper_Williams_and_Blackman_%282013%29.pdf.

Harris, Othello. 2000. "African Americans." In *Encyclopedia of Ethnicity and Sports in the United States,* edited by George B. Kirsch, Othello Harris, and Claire E. Nolte. Westport, CT: Greenwood Press.

Hart, Marie M. 1976. "Stigma and Prestige: The All-American Choice." In *Sport in the Socio-cultural Process,* 2nd ed., edited by Marie M. Hart, 176–82. Dubuque, IA: William C. Brown.

Hine, Chris. 2016. "Meet the First Openly Gay Professional Baseball Player." *Esquire,* June 24. Accessed January 17, 2017. http://www.esquire.com/news-politics/a45822/david-denson-gay-baseball-player.

Hoenig, Chris. 2014. "The Measure of Diversity That Only One U.S. Pro Sport Meets." DiversityInc, July 16. Accessed March 11, 2015. http://www.diversityinc.com/news/measure-diversity-one-u-s-pro-sport-meets.

Hofstede, Gert Jan, Frank Dignum, Rui Prada, Jillian Student, and Loïs Vanhée. 2015. "Gender Differences: The Role of Nature, Nurture, Social Identity and Self-Organization." In *Multi-Agent-Based Simulation XV: International Workshop, MABS 2014,* edited by Francisco Grimaldo and Emma Norling. Berlin: Springer.

Hunt, Thomas. 2006. "American Sport Policy and the Cultural Cold War: The Lyndon B. Johnson Presidential Years." *Journal of Sport History* 33, no. 3: 273–97.

Hurt, Douglas A. 2005. "Dialed In? Geographic Expansion and Regional Identity in NASCAR's Nextel Cup Series." *Southeastern Geographer* 45: 120–37.

Hylton, Kevin. 2010. "How a Turn to Critical Race Theory Can Contribute to Our Understanding of 'Race,' Racism, and Anti-racism in Sport." *International Review for the Sociology of Sport* 45, no. 3: 335–54.

Iannotta, Joah G., and Mary Jo Kane. 2002. "Sexual Stories as Resistance Narratives in Women's Sports: Reconceptualizing Identity Performance." *Sociology of Sport Journal* 19: 347–69.

Ingen, Cathy van. 2003. "Geographies of Gender, Sexuality and Race." *International Review of Sport* 38: 2001–16.

Ingersoll, Keith, Edmund J. Malesky, and Sebastian M.

Saiegh. 2013. "Heterogeneity and Group Performance: Evaluating the Effect of Cultural Diversity in the World's Top Soccer League." Social Science Research Network. Accessed June 18, 2017. https://papers .ssrn.com/sol3/papers.cfm? abstract_id=2333289.

Jarvie, G., and I. Reid. 1997. "Race Relations, Sociology of Sport and the New Politics of Race and Racism." *Leisure Studies* 16: 211–19.

Kahn, Lawrence M., and Malav Shaw. 2005. "Race, Compensation and Contract Length in the NBA: 2001–2002." *Industrial Relations* 34, no. 3: 444–62.

Kamphoff, Cindra S., and Diane L. Gill. 2013. "Issues of Exclusion and Discrimination in the Coaching Profession." In *Routledge Handbook of Sports Coaching,* edited by Paul Potroc, Wade Gilbert, and Jim Denison. New York: Routledge.

Kay, Aaron C., Martin V. Day, Mark P. Zanna, and A. David Nussbaum. 2013. "The Insidious (and Ironic) Effects of Positive Stereotypes." *Journal of Experimental Social Psychology* 49, no. 2: 287–91.

Keating, Peter. 2011. "Importance of an Athlete's Background." ESPN, July 17. Accessed January 19, 2017. http:// www.espn.com/espn/story/_/ id/6777581/importance-athlete-background-making-nba.

Kendall, Diane Elizabeth. 2008. *Members Only: Elite Clubs and the Process of Exclusion.* Lanham, MD: Rowman & Littlefield.

Kerr, Ian B. 2010. "The Myth of Racial Superiority in Sports."

Hilltop Review (Spring). Accessed March 24, 2013. http://scholarworks.wmich .edu/hilltopreview/vol4/ iss1/4/

Kessel, Anna. 2014. "PFA: Just 4% of Backroom Jobs in Football Go to Ethnic Minorities." *Guardian,* November 1. Accessed March 10, 2015. http:// www.theguardian.com/ football/2014/nov/01/pfa-backroom-jobs-football-ethnic-minorities.

Killion, Ann. 2013. "Paying to Play Is New Normal for Youth Athletes." *San Francisco Chronicle,* October 18. Accessed March 11, 2015. http://www.sfgate.com/ sports/article/Paying-to-play-is-new-normal-for-youth-athletes-4902034.php.

Kimmel, Michael S. 2005. *The History of Men: Essays on the History of American and British Masculinities.* Albany: State University of New York Press.

King, Nicelma, Ella R. Madsen, Marc Braverman, Carole Paterson, and Antronette K. Yancey. 2008. "Career Decision-Making: Perspectives of Low-Income Urban Youth." *Spaces for Difference* 1, no. 1: 21–41.

Kirsch, George B. 2003. *Baseball in Blue and Gray: The National Pastime during the Civil War.* Princeton, NJ: Princeton University Press.

Kirwan, W. E., and R. G. Turner. 2010. "Changing the Game: Athletics Spending in an Academic Context." *Trusteeship* 18, no. 5: 8–13. Accessed February 10, 2013. http://agb.org/ trusteeship/2010/ septemberoctober/changing-

game-athletics-spending-academic-context.

Kleinknecht, Merl F. 2017. "Blacks in 19th Century Organized Baseball." Society for American Baseball Research. Accessed January 18, 2017. http://research.sabr.org/journals/ Blacks-in-19th-c-baseball.

Knight, Jennifer L., and Traci A. Giuliano. 2001. "He's a Laker, She's a Looker: The Consequences of Gender-Stereotypical Portrayals of Male and Female Athletes by the Print Media." *Sex Roles* 45, nos. 3–4: 217–29.

Kusz, Kyle. 2007. *Revolt of the White Athlete: Race, Media and the Emergence of Extreme Athletes in America.* New York: Peter Lang.

Kutz, Steven. 2016. "NFL Took in $13 Billion in Revenue Last Season." Market Watch, July 1. Accessed January 12, 2017. http://www .marketwatch.com/story/ the-nfl-made-13-billion-last-season-see-how-it-stacks-up-against-other-leagues-2016-07-01.

LaFrance, Adrienne. 2014. "How the Bicycle Paved the Way for Women's Rights." *Atlantic,* June. Accessed January 18, 2017. http:// www.theatlantic.com/ technology/archive/2014/06/ the-technology-craze-of-the-1890s-that-forever-changed-womens-rights/373535.

Lapchick, Richard E. 2008. "Sense of Urgency to Address Colleges' Lack of Diversity." *Street and Smith's Sport Business Journal* 11, no. 41: 34. Accessed April 11, 2013. http://www .sportsbusinessdaily.com/ Journal/Issues/2008/12/ 20081222/Opinion/ Sense-Of-Urgency-

Needed-To-Address-Colleges-Lack-Of-Diversity.aspx?hl=Lapchick&sc=0.

———. 2010. "The 2010 Racial and Gender Report Card: College Sport." Institute for Diversity and Ethics in Sport, University of Central Florida. Accessed April 18, 2013. http://www.tidesport.org/RGRC/2010/2010_College_RGRC_FINAL.pdf.

———. 2012. "The 2012 Racial and Gender Report Card: Major League Baseball." Institute for Diversity and Ethics in Sport, University of Central Florida. Accessed April 4, 2013. http://nebula.wsimg.com/c338db497f95b8758669c703c9e60de1?AccessKeyId=DAC3A56D8FB782449D2A&disposition=0&alloworigin=1.

———. 2014. "The 2014 Racial and Gender Report Card: College Sport." Institute for Diversity and Ethics in Sport, University of Central Florida. Accessed March 10, 2015. http://www.tidesport.org/2014%20College%20Sport%20Racial%20&%20Gender%20Report%20Card.pdf.

———. 2015. "The 2015 Racial and Gender Report Card: College Sport." Institute for Diversity and Ethics in Sport, University of Central Florida. Accessed October 21, 2016. http://nebula.wsimg.com/5050ddee56f2fcc884660e4a03297317?AccessKeyId=DAC3A56D8FB782449D2A&disposition=0&alloworigin=1.

———. 2016. "The 2015 Racial and Gender Report Card: National Basketball Association." Institute for Diversity and Ethics in Sport, University of Central Florida.

Accessed January 17, 2017. http://nebula.wsimg.com/b9943b418cddb15b914afb9d18b62e16?AccessKeyId=DAC3A56D8FB782449D2A&disposition=0&alloworigin=1.

Lavigne, Paula. 2016. "Rich Get Richer in College Sports as Poorer Schools Struggle to Keep Up." ESPN, September 6. Accessed January 12, 2017. http://www.espn.com/espn/otl/story/_/id/17447429/power-5-conference-schools-made-6-billion-last-year-gap-haves-nots-grows.

LeCompte, Mary Lou. 1985. "The Hispanic Influence on the History of Rodeo, 1823–1922." *Journal of Sport History* 12, no. 1: 21–38.

Levine, Peter. 1992. *Ellis Island to Ebbets Field: Sport and the American Jewish Experience.* New York: Oxford University Press.

Lipsyte, Robert, and Peter Levine. 1995. *Idols of the Game: A Sporting History of the American Century.* Atlanta: Turner.

Lomax, Michael E. 2002. "Revisiting the Revolt of the Black Athlete: Harry Edwards and the Making of the New African American Sport Studies." *Journal of Sport History* 29, no. 3: 469–80.

Macri, Kenneth J. 2012. "Not Just a Game: Sport and Society in the United States." *Inquiries* 4, no. 8. Accessed January 17, 2017. http://www.inquiriesjournal.com/articles/676/not-just-a-game-sport-and-society-in-the-united-states.

Malesky, Edmund J., and Sebastian M. Saiegh. 2014. "Diversity Is Good for Team Performance in Soccer." *Washington Post,* June 2.

Accessed January 19, 2017. https://www.washingtonpost.com/news/monkey-cage/wp/2014/06/02/diversity-is-good-for-team-performance-in-soccer/?utm_term=.acdebe0253f7.

Manning, Sarah Sunshine. 2016. "Love and Rez Ball, State Titles, and Community Hope." Indian Country Today, March 1. Accessed January 12, 2017. https://indiancountrymedianetwork.com/culture/sports/manning-love-and-rez-ball-state-titles-and-community-hope.

Martel, Brett. 2013. "Cardinals' Schimmel Sisters Demonstrate Their 'Rez Ball.'" *Star Tribune,* April 9. Accessed April 12, 2013. http://www.startribune.com/printarticle/?id=202056991.

McCook, Walt Sehnert. 2004. "The Sad Story of the Great Jim Thorpe." *McCook Daily Gazette,* August 27. Accessed January 18, 2013. http://news.google.com/newspapers?nid=1933&dat=20040827&id=fiMgAAAAIBAJ&sjid=aGkFAAAAIBAJ&pg=1312,6864072.

McDonald, Mary G. 2012. "The Whiteness of Sport Media/Scholarship." In *Examining Identity in Sports Media,* edited by Heather L. Hundley and Andrew C. Billings. Thousand Oaks, CA: Sage.

McKenzie, Sheena. 2013. "The Forgotten Godfathers of Black American Sport." CNN, February 22. Accessed April 15, 2013. http://edition.cnn.com/2013/02/22/sport/Black-jockeys-horse-racing-sports-stars.

Meyers, Donald W. 2016. "Former College Basketball Stars Give Advice to Wapato Students."

Yakima Herald, November 26. Accessed January 11, 2017. http://www.yakimaherald.com/news/education/former-college-basketball-stars-give-advice-to-wapato-students/article_05794564-b6c0-11e6-aaee-ef35c0d13f39.html.

Mincy, Ronald B., ed. 2006. *Black Males Left Behind.* Washington, DC: Urban Institute Press.

Mitchell, Elmer. 1922a. "Racial Traits in Athletics." *American Physical Education Review* 27, no. 4: 147–52.

———. 1922b. "Racial Traits in Athletics." *American Physical Education Review* 27, no. 5: 197–206.

Mormimo, Gary Ross. 1982. "The Playing Fields of St. Louis: Italian Immigrants and Sports, 1925–1941." *Journal of Sport History* 9, no. 2: 5–19.

Murphy, Elizabeth. 2016. "Beyond X's and O's: What Female Coaches Are Saying about Gender Bias in Women's College Sports." Women's Sport Foundation, June 1. Accessed January 18, 2017. https://www.womenssportsfoundation.org/education/beyond-xs-and-os-what-female-coaches-are-saying-about-gender-bias-in-womens-college-sports.

Myler, Patrick. 2012. *Fight of the Century: Joe Louis Vs. Max Schmeling.* New York: Arcade.

Myre, Greg. 2016. "U.S. Women Are the Biggest Winners at the Rio Olympics." NPR, August 21. Accessed January 19, 2017. http://www.npr.org/sections/thetorch/2016/08/21/490818961/u-s-women-are-the-biggest-winners-in-rio-olympics.

National College Players Association. 2016. "The Price of Poverty in Big Time College Sport." Accessed January 19, 2017. http://www.ncpanow.org/research/study-the-price-of-poverty-in-big-time-college-sport.

National Collegiate Athletic Association. 2011. "Trends in Graduation-Success Rates and Federal Graduation Rates at NCAA Division I Institutions." Accessed January 18, 2013. http://www.ncaa.org/sites/default/files/GSR%2Band%2BFed%2BTrends%2B2013_Final_1.pdf.

———. 2014. *Student-Athlete Participation: 1981–1982–2013–14.* Indianapolis: NCAA. Accessed October 27, 2016. http://www.ncaapublications.com/productdownloads/PR1314.pdf.

———. 2017. "Estimated Probability of Competing in Professional Athletics." Accessed June 23, 2017. http://www.ncaa.org/about/resources/research/estimated-probability-competing-professional-athletics.

Nelson, Amy K. 2013. "Women in Sports: Fight the Power Outage." The Hairpin, November 12. Accessed January 27, 2014. http://thehairpin.com/2013/11/women-in-sports-fight-the-power-outage.

Palmer, Matthew C., and Randall H. Hing. 2006. "Has Salary Discrimination Really Disappeared from Major League Baseball?" *Eastern Economic Journal* 32, no. 2: 285–97.

Parkes, Pamela. 2014. "Boxing: When a Freed Slave Fought a Sporting Star." BBC News, June 22. Accessed January 18, 2017. http://www.bbc.com/news/uk-england-bristol-27632884.

Peltz, James F., and Samantha Masunaga. 2016. "Why Sporting Goods Retailers Are Fumbling." *Los Angeles Times,* April 19. Accessed January 20, 2017. http://www.latimes.com/business/la-fi-sport-chalet-problems-20160419-story.html.

Pember, Mary Annette. 2007. "'Rezball' Gains NCAA Certification Thanks to Native American Basketball Invitational (NABI)." *Diverse Issues in Higher Education,* April 10. Accessed April 12, 2012. http://diverseeducation.com/article/7221.

Pennington, Bill. 2006. "Breaking a Barrier 60 Years before Robinson," *New York Times,* July 26. Accessed April 17, 2013. http://www.nytimes.com/2006/07/27/sports/27hall.html.

Plunkett Research. 2012. "Sports Industry Overview." Accessed January 13, 2013. http://www.plunkettresearch.com/sports-recreation-leisure-market-research/industry-statistics.

Pope, Steven W. 1993. "Negotiating the 'Folk Highway' of the Nation: Sport, Public Culture, and America Identity, 1870–1940." *Journal of Social History* 27, no. 2: 327–40.

———. 2006. "Decentering 'Race' and (Re)presenting 'Black' Performance in Sport History: Basketball and Jazz in American Culture, 1920–1950." In *Deconstructing Sport History: A Postmodern Analysis,* edited by Murray

G. Phillips. Albany: State University of New York Press.

Rader, Benjamin G. 1977. "The Quest for Subcommunities and the Rise of American Sport." *American Quarterly* 29, no. 4: 355–69.

———. 1996. *American Sports: From the Age of Folk Games to the Age of Spectators.* 3rd ed. Englewood Cliffs, NJ: Prentice Hall.

Rhoden, William. 2007. "The Unpleasant Reality for Women in Sports." *New York Times,* April 9. Accessed January 20, 2013. http://www .nytimes.com/2007/04/09/ sports/09rhoden. html?mcubz=1.

———. 2012. "Black and White Women Far from Equal under Title IX." *New York Times,* June 10. Accessed January 20, 2013. http://www .nytimes.com/2012/06/11/ sports/title-ix-has-not-given- Black-female-athletes-equal- opportunity.html.

Riess, Steven A. 1990. "The New Sport History." *Reviews in American History* 18, no. 3: 311–25.

Rigalado, Samuel O. 1992. "Sport and Community in California's Japanese American 'Yamato Colony,' 1930–1945." *Journal of Sport History* 19, no. 2: 130–43.

Ripley, Amanda. 2013. "The Case against High-School Sports." *Atlantic,* October. Accessed December 12, 2013. http:// www.theatlantic.com/ magazine/archive/2013/10/ the-case-against-high- school-sports/309447.

Robeson, Paul. 1978. *Paul Robeson Speaks: Writings, Speeches, and Interviews.* New York: Citadel Press.

Robinson, Manie. 2017. "Community, Competition Builds SEC Women's Hoops Brand." Greenville Online, February 25. Accessed March 1, 2017. http://www .greenvilleonline.com/story/ sports/college/2017/02/25/ sec-womens-basketball- tournament-dawn- staley/98307078.

Sabo, Don, and Phil Veliz. 2008. *Go Out and Play: Youth Sports in America.* East Meadow, NY: Women's Sports Foundation.

Sage, George H. 1990. *Power and Ideology in American Sport.* Champaign, IL: Human Kinetics.

———. 2007. "Introduction." In *Diversity and Social Justice in College Sports,* edited by Dana D. Brooks and Ronald C. Altouse. Morgantown, WV: Fitness Information Technology.

Sage, George H., and D. Stanley Eitzen, eds. 2015. *Sociology of North American Sport.* 10th ed. New York: Oxford University Press.

Sando, Mike. 2016. "Rooney Rule in Reverse: Minority Coaching Hires Have Stalled." ESPN, July 19. Accessed January 2, 2017. http://www.espn.com/ nfl/story/_/id/17101097/ staggering-numbers-show- nfl-minority-coaching-failure- rooney-rule-tony-dungy.

Schmidt, Hans C. 2013. "Women, Sports, and Journalism: Examining the Limited Role of Women in Student Newspaper Sports Reporting." *Communication and Sport* 1, no. 3: 246–68.

Schwartz, Larry. 2005. "Owens Pierced a Myth." Sports Century, ESPN. Accessed April 23, 2013. http://espn .go.com/sportscentury/ features/00016393. html.

Scraton, Sheila, and Anne Flintoff. 2013. "Gender, Feminist Theory, and Sport." In *A Companion to Sport,* edited by David L. Andrews and Ben Carrington. London: Blackwell.

Shakib, Sohaila, and Phillip Veliz. 2012. "Race, Sport and Social Support: A Comparison between African American and White Youths' Perceptions of Social Support for Sport Participation." *International Review for the Sociology of Sport* 48, no. 3: 295–317.

Shulman, James L., and William G. Bowen. 2001. *The Game of Life: College Sports and Educational Values.* Princeton, NJ: Princeton University Press

Smith, Barbara. 2000. "Introduction." In *Home Girls: A Black Feminist Anthology,* edited by Barbara Smith, xxi–lviii. New Brunswick, NJ: Rutgers University Press.

Smith, Earl, and Angela J. Hattery. 2006. "Hey Stud: Race, Sex, and Sports." *Sexuality & Culture* 10, no. 2: 3–32.

Starn, Orin. 2006. "Caddying for the Dalai Lama: Golf, Heritage Tourism, and the Pinehurst Resort." *South Atlantic Quarterly* 105, no. 2: 447–63.

Stein, Rob. 2011. "Genetic Testing for Sports Genes Courts Controversy." *Washington Post,* May 18. Accessed January 12, 2017. https:// www.washingtonpost.com/ national/genetic-testing- for-sports-genes-courts- controversy/2011/05/09/ AFkTuV6G_story.html.

Stephens-Davidowitz, Seth. 2013. "In the N.B.A., ZIP Code Matters." *New York Times,* November 2. Accessed March 1, 2017. http://www.nytimes.com/2013/11/03/opinion/sunday/in-the-nba-zip-code-matters.html.

Talleu, Clotilde. 2011. "Access for Girls and Women to Sport Practices." Council of Europe, September. Accessed March 10, 2015. http://www.coe.int/t/DG4/EPAS/Publications/Handbook_2%20_Gender_equality_in_sport.pdf.

Tanewasha, Patti. 2013. "That's All I Do Is Play Rez Ball." Native News Network. Accessed July 5, 2013. http://www.nativenewsnetwork.com/thats-all-i-do-is-play-rez-ball.html.

Thomas, Isiah, and Na'ilah Suad Nasir. 2013. "Black Males, Athletes and Academic Achievement." Huffington Post, May 7. Accessed January 20, 2104. http://www.huffingtonpost.com/isiah-thomas/Black-males-athletes-and-_b_3232989.html.

Thompson, Derek. 2014. "Which Sports Have the Whitest/Richest/Oldest Fans?" *Atlantic,* February 10. Accessed June 23, 2017. https://www.theatlantic.com/business/archive/2014/02/which-sports-have-the-whitest-richest-oldest-fans/283626.

Thorn, John. 2011. *Baseball in the Garden of Eden: The Secret History of the Early Game.* New York: Simon & Schuster.

TitleIX.info. n.d. "Athletics under Title IX." Accessed January 15, 2014. http://www.titleix.info/10-key-areas-of-title-ix/athletics.aspx.

Totalsportek2. 2016. "Biggest Athlete Endorsement Deals in Sports History." Accessed January 20, 2017. http://www.totalsportek.com/money/biggest-endorsement-deals-sports-history.

Vidal, Juan. 2016. "Why Does American Sports Have a Latino Problem?" *Rolling Stone,* September 16. Accessed December 12, 2016. http://www.rollingstone.com/sports/news/why-does-american-sports-have-a-latino-problem-w440069.

Wallace, Kelly. 2015. "The Real March Madness: When Will Women's Teams Get Equal Buzz?" CNN, March 30. Accessed January 18, 2017. http://www.cnn.com/2015/03/30/living/feat-march-madness-womens-sports-attention-money-men.

Washington, Robert E., and David Karen. 2001. "Sport and Society." *American Review of Sociology* 27: 187–219.

Weiss, Maureen R. 2016. "Old Wine in a New Bottle: Historical Reflections on Sport as a Context for Youth Development." In *Positive Youth Development through Sport,* 2nd ed., edited by Nicholas L. Holt, 7–20. London: Routledge.

Westfall, Leah. 2011. "Athletic Scholarships—Who Gets Them and How Many Are There?" Fastweb, July 15. Accessed December 22, 2016. http://www.fastweb.com/student-news/articles/athletic-scholarships-who-gets-them-and-how-many-are-there.

Wiggins, David K. 1989. "'Great Speed but Little Stamina': The Historical Debate over Black Athletic Superiority." *Journal of Sport History* 16, no. 2: 158–85.

Wigginton, Russell T. 2006. *The Strange Career of the Black Athlete: African Americans and Sports.* Westport, CT: Praeger.

Wilner, Barry. 2013. "NFL Rooney Rule Broken, Say Black Ex-Coaches." Huffington Post, January 31. Accessed April 2, 2013. http://www.huffingtonpost.com/2013/01/31/nfl-rooney-rule-broken-say-Black-ex-coaches_n_2594344.html.

Winslow, Barbara. 2012. "The Impact of Title IX." History Now. Accessed March 1, 2017. https://www.gilderlehrman.org/history-by-era/seventies/essays/impact-title-ix.

Women's Sports Foundation. 2017. "Factors Influencing Girls' Participation in Sports." Accessed March 1, 2017. https://www.womenssportsfoundation.org/support-us/do-you-know-the-factors-influencing-girls-participation-in-sports.

Yep, Kathleen S. 2009. *Outside the Paint: When Basketball Ruled at the Chinese Playground.* Philadelphia: Temple University Press.

Zirin, David. 2000. *A People's History of Sports in the United States: 250 Years of Politics, Protests, People, and Play.* New York: New Press.

■ CHAPTER 10

Abdel-Malek, Anouar. 1981. *Social Dialectics: Nation and Revolution.* Albany: State University of New York Press.

Alvarez, Lizette. 2009. "More Americans Joining Military as Jobs Dwindle." *New York Times,* January 18. Accessed May 10, 2017. http://www.nytimes.com/2009/01/19/us/19recruits.html.

Amadeo, Kimberly. 2017. "War on Terror Facts, Costs and Timeline." The Balance, May 26. Accessed June 18, 2017. https://www.thebalance.com/war-on-terror-facts-costs-timeline-3306300.

Ashe, Samuel A'Courte. 1908. *History of North Carolina: From 1584 to 1783.* Greensboro, NC: Charles L. Van Noppen.

Asturias, Lani. 2008. "Navajo Code Talkers." In *Encyclopedia of Bilingual Education,* edited by Josué M. González. Thousand Oaks, CA: Sage.

Aziz, Sahar. 2012. "Racial Profiling by Law Enforcement Is Poisoning Muslim Americans' Trust." *Guardian,* February 21. Accessed May 11, 2017. https://www.theguardian.com/commentisfree/cifamerica/2012/feb/21/racial-profiling-law-enforcement-muslim-americans.

Bachman, Jerald G., David R. Segal, Peter Freedman-Dolan, and Patrick M. O'Malley. 2000. "Who Chooses Military Service? Correlates of Propensity and Enlistment in the U.S. Armed Forces." *Military Psychology* 12: 1–30.

Bailey, Beth. 2009. *America's Army: Making the All-Volunteer Force.* Cambridge, MA: Harvard University Press.

Baker, Mike. 2013. "Costs of US Wars Linger for Over 100 Years." Associated Press, March 19. Accessed March 25, 2014. http://bigstory.ap.org/article/ap-costs-us-wars-linger-over-100-years.

Baofu, Peter. 2014. "Racism and Inferiority Complex in Japan's Current Foreign Policy towards China." *Foreign Policy Journal* 15. Accessed May11, 2017. https://www.foreignpolicyjournal.com/2014/07/22/racism-and-inferiority-complex-in-japans-current-foreign-policy-towards-china.

Barry, Catherine N. 2013. "New Americans in Our Nation's Military: A Proud Tradition and Hopeful Future." Center for American Progress, November 8. Accessed September 3, 2015. https://www.americanprogress.org/issues/immigration/report/2013/11/08/79116/new-americans-in-our-nations-military.

Barry, Jennifer L. 2013. "A Few Good (Wo)men: Gender Inclusion in the United States Military." *Journal of International Affairs,* November 19. Accessed September 1, 2015. http://jia.sipa.columbia.edu/online-articles/few-good-women-gender-inclusion-united-states-military.

Batalova, Jeanne. 2008. "Immigrants in the U.S. Armed Forces." Migration Policy Institute, May 15. Accessed April 20, 2013. http://www.migrationinformation.org/USFocus/display.cfm?id=683.

Best, James D. 2012. *Principled Action: Lessons from the Origins of the American Republic.* Tucson, AZ: Wheatmark.

Bettelheim, Bruno, and Morris Janowitz. 1949. "Ethnic Tolerance: A Function of Social and Personal Control." *American Journal of Sociology* 55, no. 2: 137–47.

Binkin, Martin. 1993. *Who Will Fight the Next War?* Washington, DC: Brookings Institution Press.

Bird, J. B. 2008. "Rebellion: John Horse and the Black Seminoles, the First Black Rebels to Beat American Slavery." Accessed November 21, 2015. http://www.johnhorse.com/index.html.

Blanton, DeAnne, and Lauren M. Cook. 2002. *They Fought Like Demons: Women Soldiers in the Civil War.* Baton Rouge: Louisiana State University Press.

Booth, Bradford, William W. Faulk, David R. Segal, and Mady Wechsler Segal. 2000. "The Impact of Military Presence in Local Labor Markets on the Employment of Women." *Gender & Society* 14: 318–32.

Booth, Bradford, and David R. Segal. 2005. "Bringing the Soldiers Back In: Implications of Inclusion of Military Personnel for Labor Market Research on Race, Class and Gender." *Race, Gender & Class* 12, no. 1: 34–57.

Bottomore, Tom P. 1981. "A Marxist Consideration of Durkheim." *Social Forces* 59, no. 4: 902–17.

Brady, Kyle R. 2017. "Beware the Limits of Hard Power in 2017." *Small Wars Journal,* May 6. Accessed May 10, 2017. http://smallwarsjournal.com/jrnl/art/beware-the-limits-of-hard-power-in-2017.

Bray, Chris. 2016. *Court Martial: How Military Justice Has Shaped America from the Revolution to 9/11.* New York: W. W. Norton.

Brooks, Rebecca Beatrice. 2011. "The Boston Massacre." History of Massachusetts, November 10. Accessed June 26, 2017. http://historyofmassachusetts.org/the-boston-massacre.

Burk, James. 2001. "The Military's Presence in American Society, 1950–2000." In *Soldiers and Civilians: The Civil–Military Gap and American National Security,* edited by P. D. Feaver and R. H. Kohn. Cambridge: MIT Press.

Callaway, Colin G. 1995. *The American Revolution in Indian Country: Crisis and Diversity in Native American Communities.* Cambridge: Cambridge University Press.

Calvin, Mathew J. 2015. *Aiming for Pensacola: Fugitive Slaves on the Atlantic and Southern Frontiers.* Cambridge, MA: Harvard University Press.

Cardoso, Fernando H. 2001. *Charting a New Course: The Politics of Globalization and Social Transformation.* Lanham, MD: Rowman & Littlefield.

Center on Budget and Policy Priorities. 2016. "Policy Basics: Where Do Our Federal Tax Dollars Go?" March 4. Accessed January 25, 2017. http://www.cbpp.org/research/federal-budget/policy-basics-where-do-our-federal-tax-dollars-go.

Chretien, Jean-Paul, David L. Blazes, Rodney K. Coldren, Michael D. Lewis, Jariyanart Gaywee, Khunakorn Kana, et al. 2007. "The Importance of Militaries from Developing Countries in Global Infectious Disease Surveillance." *Bulletin of the World Health Organization* 85, no. 3: 174–80.

Chu, Thai Q., Mark D. Seery, Whitney A. Ence, E. Alison Holman, and Roxane Silver. 2006. "Ethnicity and Gender in the Face of a Terrorist Attack: A National Longitudinal Study of Immediate Responses and Outcomes Two Years after September 11." *Basic and Applied Social Psychology* 28, no. 4: 291–301.

Coates, Charles Hunter, and Roland J. Pellegrin. 1965. *Military Sociology: A Study of American Military Institutions and Military Life.* University Park, MD: Social Science Press.

Cockerham, William. 2003. "The Military Institution." In *Handbook of Symbolic Interactionism,* edited by Larry T. Reynolds and Nancy J. Herman-Kinney, 491–510. Lanham, MD: Rowman & Littlefield.

Codinha, Alessandra. 2017. "American Women in the Military." *Vogue,* March 8. Accessed May 5, 2017. http://www.vogue.com/projects/13528881/american-women-in-the-military-female-soldiers.

Coffey, David. 1998. "African Americans in the Vietnam War." In *Encyclopedia of the Vietnam War: A Political, Social, and Military History,* edited by Spencer C. Tucker. Santa Barbara, CA: ABC-CLO.

Cole, Juan. 2011. "Islamophobia and American Foreign Policy Rhetoric: The Bush Years and After." In *Islamophobia: The Challenge of Pluralism in the 21st Century,* edited by John L. Esposito and Ibrahim Kalin, 127–42. Oxford: Oxford University Press.

Converse, Elliott V. III, Daniel K. Gibran, John A. Cash, Robert K. Griffith Jr., and Richard H. Kohn. 1997. *The Exclusion of Black Soldiers from the Medal of Honor in World War II.* Jefferson, NC: McFarland.

Crigger, Megan, and Laura Santhanam. 2015. "How Many Americans Have Died in U.S. Wars?" *NewsHour,* PBS, May 24. Accessed February 2, 2017. http://www.pbs.org/newshour/updates/many-americans-died-u-s-wars.

Crow, Jeffrey J. 1992. "'Liberty to slaves': The Black Response." *Tar Heel Junior Historian* 32, no. 1: 19–22. Accessed March 24, 2014. http://www.learnnc.org/lp/editions/nchist-revolution/1917.

Defense Manpower Data Center. 2017. "Armed Forces Strength Figures." Accessed March 31, 2017. https://www.dmdc.osd.mil/appj/dwp/dwp_reports.jsp.

DeSilver, Drew. 2013. "Most Members of Congress Have Little Direct Military Experience." Fact Tank, Pew Research Center, September 4. Accessed June 26, 2017. http://www.pewresearch.org/fact-tank/2013/09/04/members-of-congress-have-little-direct-military-experience.

Donaldson, Gary. 1991. *The History of African Americans in the Military: Double V.* Malabar, FL: Krieger.

Doyle, Don H. 2015. "The Civil War Was Won by Immigrant Soldiers." *Time,* June 29. Accessed May 11, 2017. http://time.com/3940428/civil-war-immigrant-soldiers.

Drabble, John. 2004. "To Ensure Domestic Tranquility: The FBI, COINTELPRO-WHITE HATE and Political Discourse, 1964–1971." *Journal of American Studies* 38, no. 2: 297–328.

Duster, Troy. 2013. "Merit Scholars, the Military, and Affirmative Action." The Conversation (blog), *Chronicle of Higher Education,* January 23. Accessed June 26, 2017. http://www.chronicle.com/blogs/conversation/2013/01/23/merit-scholars-the-military-and-affirmative-action.

Eikenberry, Karl W. 2013. "Reassessing the All-Volunteer Force." *Washington Quarterly* 36: 7–24.

Eloe, Cynthia. 2014. "The Recruiter and the Skeptic: A Critical Feminist Approach to Military Studies." *Critical Military Studies* 1, no. 1: 3–10.

Feimster, Crystal N. 2013. "Rape and Justice in the Civil War." Opinionator (blog), *New York Times,* April 25. Accessed June 26, 2017. https://opinionator.blogs.nytimes.com/2013/04/25/rape-and-justice-in-the-civil-war.

Ferling, John. 2010. "Myths of the American Revolution." *Smithsonian Magazine,* January. Accessed June 26, 2017. http://www.smithsonianmag.com/history/myths-of-the-american-revolution-10941835.

Ferran, Lee, and Randy Kreider. 2015. "Selling the 'Fantasy': Why Young Western Women Would Join ISIS." ABC News, February 20. Accessed September 9, 2015. http://abcnews.go.com/International/young-women-join-isis/story?id=29112401.

Figley, Charles, Barbara L. Pitts, Paula Chapman, and Christine Elnitsky. 2015. "Female Combat Medics." In *Women at War,* edited by Elspeth Cameron Ritchie and Anne L. Naclerio. New York: Oxford University Press.

Finucane, Melissa L., Paul Slovic, C. K. Mertz, James Flynn, and Theresa A. Satterfield. 2000. "Gender, Race, and Perceived Risk: The 'White Male' Effect." *Health, Risk & Society* 2, no. 2: 159–72.

Fixico, Donald. 2008. "A Native Nations Perspective on the War of 1812." *The War of 1812,* PBS. Accessed November 21, 2016. http://www.pbs.org/wned/war-of-1812/essays/native-nations-perspective.

Foubert, John D., and Ryan C. Masin. 2012. "Effects of the Men's Program on U.S. Army Soldiers' Intentions to Commit and Willingness to Intervene to Prevent Rape: A Pretest–Posttest Study." *Violence and Victims* 27, no. 6: 911–21.

Foucault, Michel. 1977. *Discipline and Punish: The Birth of the Prison.* London: Routledge.

———. 2008. *The Birth of Biopolitics: Lectures at the Collège de France, 1978–1979.* Translated by Graham Burchell; edited by Michel Senellart. Basingstoke: Palgrave Macmillan.

Fox, Lauren. 2012. "U.S. Government Still Pays Two Civil War Pensions." *U.S. News & World Report,* February 9. Accessed March 25, 2014. http://www.usnews.com/news/blogs/washington-whispers/2012/02/09/us-government-still-pays-two-civil-war-pensions.

Frederique, Nadine. 2009. "Cointelpro and Covert Operations." In *Encyclopedia of Race and Crime,* edited by Helen Taylor Greene and Shaun L. Gabbidon. Thousand Oaks, CA: Sage.

Freking, Kevin. 2013. "Military Sexual Assault Victims Seek Help from Veterans Affairs." Huffington Post, May 20. Accessed April 20, 2013. http://www.huffingtonpost.com/2013/05/20/military-sexual-assault_n_3306295.html?utm_hp_ref=politics.

Galbraith, John Kenneth. 1967. *The New Industrial State.* Princeton, NJ: Princeton University Press.

Galea, S., J. Ahern, H. Resnick, D. Kilpatrick, M. Bucuvalas, J. Gold, and D. Vlahov. 2002. "Psychological Sequelae of the September 11 Terrorist Attacks in New York City." *New England Journal of Medicine* 346: 982–87.

Giddens, Anthony. 1984. *The Constitution of Society: Outline of the Theory of Structuration.* Berkeley: University of California Press.

Gifford, Brian. 2005. "Combat Casualties and Race: What Can We Learn from the 2003–2004 Iraq Conflict?" *Armed Forces & Society* 31, no. 2: 201–25.

Gonzalez, Gilbert G. 2013. *Guest Workers or Colonized Labor? Mexican Labor Migration to the United States.* Boulder, CO: Paradigm.

Hafetz, Jonathan. 2011. "Targeted Killing and the 'War on Terror.'" Al Jazeera, October 19. Accessed May 11, 2017. https://www.globalpolicy.org/war-on-terrorism/50878-targeted-killing-and-the-war-on-terror.html?itemid=id#609.

Harlow, Roxana, and Lauren Dundes. 2004. "'United' We Stand: Responses to the September 11 Attacks in Black and White." *Sociological Perspectives* 47, no. 4: 439–64.

Hoh, Matthew P. 2009. "Resignation Letter to Ambassador Nancy J. Powell." September 10. Accessed August 10, 2015. http://www.washingtonpost.com/wp-srv/hp/ssi/wpc/ResignationLetter.pdf.

Homan, Timothy R., and Eric Pianin. 2014. "The Military Gateway to the Middle Class Is Vanishing." *The Week,* March 6. Accessed June 27, 2017. http://theweek.com/articles/449697/military-gateway-middle-class-vanishing.

Honey, Maureen. 2007. "African American Women in World War II." History Now. Accessed February 10, 2017. https://www.gilderlehrman.org/history-by-era/world-war-ii/essays/african-american-women-world-war-ii.

Hosek, S. D., P. Tiemeyer, M. R. Kilburn, D. A. Strong, S. Duckworth, and R. Ray. 2001. *Minority and Gender Differences in Officer Career Progression.* Mr-1184-OSD.

Santa Monica, CA: RAND Corporation.

Huntington, Samuel P. 1957. *The Soldier and the State: The Theory and Politics of Civil-Military Relations.* Cambridge, MA: Harvard University Press.

Ingraham, Christopher. 2015. "Anti-Muslim Hate Crimes Are Still Five Times More Common Today than before 9/11." *Washington Post,* February 11. Accessed May 11, 2017. https://www.washingtonpost.com/news/wonk/wp/2015/02/11/anti-muslim-hate-crimes-are-still-five-times-more-common-today-than-before-911/?utm_term=.8cab17fe31ed.

Janowitz, Morris. 1957. "Military Elites and the Study of War." *Conflict Resolution* 1, no. 1: 9–18.

———. 1960. *The Professional Soldier: A Social and Political Portrait.* New York: Free Press.

———. 1967. "American Democracy and Military Service." *Transaction* 4, no. 3: 5–11.

———. 1973. "The Social Demography of the All-Volunteer Armed Forces." *Annals of the American Academy of Political and Social Science* 306: 86–93.

Kane, Tim. 2006. "Who Are the Recruits? The Demographic Characteristics of U.S. Military Enlistment, 2003–2005." Heritage Foundation Center for Data Analysis, October. Accessed April 20, 2013. http://www.heritage.org/research/reports/2006/10/who-are-the-recruits-the-demographic-characteristics-of-us-military-enlistment-2003-2005.

Keith, Jeanette. 2000. "The Politics of Southern Draft Resistance, 1917–1918: Class, Race, and Conscription in the Rural South." *Journal of American History* 87, no. 4: 1335–61.

Kelty, Meredith Kleykam, and David R. Segal. 2010. "The Military and the Transition to Adulthood." *Future of Children* 1, no. 1: 181–207.

Kent, Alexander. 2015. "The Most Expensive Wars in U.S. History." *USA Today,* May 24. Accessed February 8, 2017. http://www.usatoday.com/story/news/nation/2015/05/24/24-7-wall-st-expensive-wars/27795049.

Kestnbaum, Meyer. 2009. "The Sociology of War and the Military." *Annual Review of Sociology* 35: 235–54.

Kohn, Richard. 1981. "The Social History of the American Soldier: A Review and Prospectus for Research." *American Historical Review* 86, no. 3: 553–76.

Krauss, Clifford. 1986. "Revolution in Central America?" *Foreign Affairs* 65, no. 3: 564–81.

Lanning, Michael L. 2000. *African Americans in the Revolutionary War.* New York: Kensington.

Lawrence, Quil. 2016. "Service Members, Not Citizens: Meet the Veterans Who Have Been Deported." *Morning Edition,* NPR, January 13. Accessed May 10, 2017. http://www.npr.org/2016/01/13/462372040/service-members-not-citizens-meet-the-veterans-who-have-been-deported.

Lee, Chang-Hun. 2008. *Violent Military Crimes: A Comparative Study on*

Violent Crimes Committed by U.S. Army Personnel. Saarbrücken: Müller Aktiengesellschaft.

———. 2010. "Institutionalized Hegemonic Masculinity and Rape by United States Army Personnel in South Korea: A Perspective on Military Subculture." *Asian Criminology* 5: 11–25.

Lender, Mark Edward. 2016. *The War for American Independence: A Reference Guide.* Santa Barbara, CA: ABC-CLIO.

Lin, Patrick. 2010. "Robots, Ethics and War." Center for Internet and Society, December 15. Accessed January 27, 2017. http://cyberlaw.stanford.edu/blog/2010/12/robots-ethics-war.

Lutz, Catherine. 2002. "Making War at Home in the United States: Militarization and the Current Crisis." *American Anthropologist* 104, no. 3: 723–35.

———. 2008. "Who Joins the Military? A Look at Race, Class, and Immigration Status." *Journal of Political and Military Sociology* 36, no. 2: 167–88.

MacKenzie, Debora. 2011. "British Used Bioweapon in US War of Independence." *New Scientist,* August 19. Accessed February 2, 2017. https://www.newscientist.com/blogs/shortsharpscience/2011/08/george-washington-biowarrior.html.

Martin, Paul Kawika. 2015. "Is There an Alternative to War with ISIS?" MSNBC, February 12. Accessed May 11, 2017. http://www.msnbc.com/msnbc/alternative-war-isis.

McCarthy, Niall. 2017. "Most Terrorists in the U.S. since 9/11 Have Been American Citizens or Legal Residents." *Forbes,* January 31. Accessed February 13, 2017. http://www.forbes.com/sites/niallmccarthy/2017/01/31/most-terrorists-in-the-u-s-since-911-have-been-american-citizens-or-legal-residents-infographic/#6e28894482c6.

Military Leadership Diversity Commission. 2010a. "Recent Officer Promotion Rates by Race, Ethnicity, and Gender." Issue Paper 45, Promotion, June. Accessed April 13, 2013. http://diversity.defense.gov/Portals/51/Documents/Resources/Commission/docs/Issue%20Papers/Paper%2045%20-%20Officer%20Promotion%20by%20Race%20Ethnicity%20and%20Gender.pdf.

———. 2010b. "Reenlistment Rates across the Services by Gender and Race/Ethnicity." Issue Paper 31, Retention, April. Accessed April 13, 2013. http://diversity.defense.gov/Portals/51/Documents/Resources/Commission/docs/Issue%20Papers/Paper%2031%20-%20Reenlistment%20Rates%20Across%20the%20Services.pdf.

Moore, Brenda L. 1991. "African American Women in the U.S. Military." *Armed Forces & Society* 17: 363–84.

———. 2003. *Serving Our Country: Japanese American Women in the Military during World War II.* New Brunswick, NJ: Rutgers University Press.

Moskos, Charles C. 1966. "Racial Integration in the Armed Forces." *American Journal of Sociology* 72, no. 2: 132–48.

———. 1970. *The American Enlisted Man: The Rank and File in Today's Military.* New York: Russell Sage Foundation.

———. 1979. "The All-Volunteer Force." *Wilson Quarterly* 3, no. 2: 131–41.

———. 1988. *A Call to Civic Service: National Service for Country and Community.* New York: Free Press.

———. 1993. "Citizens' Army to Social Laboratory." *Wilson Quarterly* 17, no. 1: 83–94.

Moskos, Charles C., and John Sibley Butler. 1996. *All That We Can Be: Black Leadership and Racial Integration the Army Way.* New York: Basic Books.

Moskos, Charles C., John Sibley Butler, Alan Ned Sabrosky, and Alvin J. Schexnider. 1980. "Symposium: Race and the United States Military." *Armed Forces & Society* 6, no. 4: 586–613.

National Archives. 2016. "Statistical Information about Casualties of the Vietnam War." Accessed February 8, 2017. https://www.archives.gov/research/military/vietnam-war/casualty-statistics.html#category.

National Coalition for Homeless Veterans. 2017. "FAQ about Homeless Veterans." Accessed February 8, 2017. http://nchv.org/index.php/news/media/background_and_statistics.

National Park Service. 2010. "Forgotten Warriors: Fort Scott National Historic Site." Accessed May 11, 2017. https://www.nps.gov/articles/forgotten-warriors.htm.

Ogan, Christine, Lars Wilnat, Rosemary Pennington, and Manaf Bashir. 2013. "The Rise of Anti-Muslim

Prejudice: Media and Islamophobia in Europe and the United States." *International Communication Gazette* 76, no. 1: 27–46.

O'Keefe, Ed. 2013. "Congress Approves Reforms to Address Sexual Assault, Rape in Military." *Washington Post,* December 19. Accessed April 4, 2014. http://www.washingtonpost.com/politics/congress-poised-to-approve-reforms-to-address-sexual-assault-rape-in-military/2013/12/19/bbd34afa-68c9-11e3-a0b9-249bbb34602c_story.html.

Olivas, Michael A. 2008. "The 'Trial of the Century' That Never Was: Staff Sgt. Marcario García, the Congressional Medal of Honor, and the Oasis Café." *Indiana Law Journal* 83, no. 4: 1391–1403.

Oropeza, Lorena. 2005. *¡Raza Si! ¡Guerra No! Chicano Protest and Patriotism during the Viet Nam War Era.* Berkeley: University of California Press.

Panagopoulos, Costas. 2009. "The Polls–Trends: Arab and Muslim Americans and Islam in the Aftermath of 9/11." *Public Opinion Quarterly* 70, no. 4: 608–24.

Park, Robert E. 1941. "The Social Function of War: Observations and Notes." *American Journal of Sociology* 46, no. 4: 551–70.

Patten, Eileen, and Kim Parker. 2011. "Women in the Military: Growing Share, Distinctive Profile." Pew Research Center, December 22. Accessed April 13, 2013. http://www.pewsocialtrends.org/2011/12/22/women-in-the-u-s-military-growing-share-distinctive-profile.

Perret, Geoffrey. 1989. *A Country Made by War: From the Revolution to Vietnam—The Story of America's Rise to Power.* New York: Random House.

Platt, Melissa, and Carolyn B. Allard. 2011. "Military Sexual Trauma: Current Knowledge and Future Directions." *Journal of Trauma and Dissociation* 12, no. 3: 213–15.

Powers, Rod. 2016. "Immigrants in the US Armed Forces." The Balance, September 8. Accessed May 10, 2017. https://www.thebalance.com/immigrants-in-the-us-armed-forces-3353965.

Rasdal, Dave. 2012. "Six Brothers Give Ultimate Sacrifice in Civil War." *Gazette,* February 14. Accessed March 14, 2014. http://thegazette.com/2012/02/14/six-brothers-give-ultimate-sacrifice-in-civil-war.

Ray, Celeste. 2007. *The New Encyclopedia of Southern Culture,* Vol. 6, *Ethnicity.* Chapel Hill: University of North Carolina Press.

Rhoades-Piotti, Tiffany. 2017. "Ann Simpson Davis." In *Women in American History: A Social, Political, and Cultural Encyclopedia and Document Collection,* edited by Peg A. Lamphier and Rosanne Welch. Santa Barbara, CA: ABC-CLIO.

Rockman, Seth. 2009. *Scraping By: Wage Labor, Slavery, and Survival in Early Baltimore.* Baltimore: Johns Hopkins University Press.

Rostker, Bernard D., Susan D. Hosek, and Mary E. Vaina. 2011. "Gays in the Military: Eventually, New Facts Conquer Old Taboos." *Rand Review* (Spring). Accessed April 4, 2014. http://www.rand.org/pubs/periodicals/rand-review/issues/2011/spring/gays.html.

Roth-Douquet, Kathy, and Frank Schaeffer. 2006. *AWOL: The Unexcused Absence of America's Upper Classes from Military Service—and How it Hurts Our Country.* New York: HarperCollins.

Rothkopf, David, and Kristin Lord. 2013. "The Alternative to War." *Foreign Policy,* October 3. Accessed May 11, 2017. http://foreignpolicy.com/2013/10/03/the-alternative-to-war.

Sadler, Anne G., Brenda M. Booth, Brian L. Cook, and Bradley N. Doebbeling. 2003. "Factors Associated with Women's Risks of Rape in the Military Environment." *American Journal of Industrial Medicine* 43: 262–73.

Sandford, Victoria. 2003. "Learning to Kill by Proxy: Colombian Paramilitaries and the Legacy of Central American Death Squads, Contras, and Civil Patrols." *Social Justice* 30, no. 3: 63–81.

Segal, David R. 2008. "Military Sociology." In *21st Century Sociology,* edited by Clifton D. Bryant and Dennis L. Peck. Thousand Oaks, CA: Sage.

Segal, Mady Wechsler, and David R. Segal. 2007. "Latinos Claim Larger Share of U.S Military Personnel." Population Reference Bureau, October. Accessed September 3, 2015. http://www.prb.org/Publications/Articles/2007/HispanicsUSMilitary.aspx.

Segal, Mady Wechsler, Meridith Hill Thanner, and David R. Segal. 2007. "Hispanic and African American Men and

Women in the Military: Trends in Representation." *Race, Gender & Class* 14, nos. 3–4: 48–64.

Shaw, Jessica Marmor. 2016. "Is America's Military the No. 1 Fighting Force in the World—or Not?" Market Watch, February 20. Accessed May 5, 2017. http://www .marketwatch.com/story/ is-america-the-no-1-military-in-the-world-or-not-2016-02-20.

Sicard, Sarah. 2016. "How Affirmative Action Works at West Point." Task & Purpose, July 19. Accessed May 12, 2017. http://taskandpurpose .com/race-factors-west-point-admissions.

Snider, Don M., and Gayle L. Watkins. 2002. *The Future of the Army Profession.* New York: McGraw-Hill.

Stouffer, Samuel A., Edward A. Suchman, Leland C. DeVinney, Shirley A. Star, and Robin M. Williams, Jr. 1949. *The American Soldier.* 2 vols. Princeton, NJ: Princeton University Press.

Stout, Harry S. 2009. "Review Essay: Religion, War, and the Meaning of America." *Religion and American Culture* 19, no. 2: 275–89.

Straw, Joseph. 2014. "Obama Awards Medal of Honor—the Military's Highest Decoration for Bravery—to 24 Veterans across Three Wars Who Were Originally Overlooked Due to Their Race." *New York Daily News,* March 19. Accessed March 24, 2014. http://www .nydailynews.com/news/ politics/president-obama-award-medals-honor-tuesday-article-1.1725488.

Stutzman, Maureen. 2009. "Rape in the American Civil War: Race, Class, and Gender

in the Case of Harriet McKinley and Perry Pierson." *Transcending Silence* (Spring). Accessed April 23, 2013. http://www .albany.edu/womensstudies/ journal/2009/stutzman.html.

Sullivan, Kevin, and Mary Jordan. 2004. "In Central America, Reagan Remains a Polarizing Figure." *Washington Post,* June 9. Accessed May 24, 2013. http://www .washingtonpost.com/ wp-dyn/articles/A29546-2004Jun9.html.

Talbot, Richard P., and Jon T. Oplinger. 2014. "Social Stratification and Ethnic Mobilization: U.S. Military Deaths in Southeast Asia." *Race, Gender & Class* 21, nos. 1–2: 195–210.

Taylor, Adam, and Laris Karklis. 2016. "This Remarkable Chart Shows How U.S. Spending Dwarfs the Rest of the World." *Washington Post,* February 9. Accessed January 25, 2017. https://www .washingtonpost.com/news/ worldviews/wp/2016/02/09/ this-remarkable-chart-shows-how-u-s-defense-spending-dwarfs-the-rest-of-the-world/?utm_ term=.490065b114b7.

Timm, Annette F. 2010. *The Politics of Fertility in Twentieth-Century Berlin.* Cambridge: Cambridge University Press.

Tucker, Phillip. 1992. "John Horse: Forgotten African-American Leader of the Second Seminole War." *Journal of Negro History* 77, no. 2: 74–83.

U.S. Department of Defense. 2014. *Population Representation in the Military Services: Fiscal Year 2014 Summary Report.*

Washington, DC: Office of the Under Secretary of Defense, Personnel and Readiness. Accessed June 18, 2017. http://www .people.mil/Portals/56/ Documents/2014%20 Summary.pdf?ver=2016-09-14-154051-563.

U.S. Department of Veterans Affairs. 2017. "America's Wars." Accessed May 11, 2017. https://www.va.gov/ opa/publications/factsheets/ fs_americas_wars.pdf.

Vecchio, R. P., and R. C. Bullis. 2001. "Moderators of the Influence of Supervisor–Subordinate Similarity on Subordinate Outcomes." *Journal of Applied Psychology* 86: 884–96.

Vine, David. 2014. "America Still Has Hundreds of Military Bases Worldwide. Have They Made Us Any Safer?" *Mother Jones,* November. Accessed August 12, 2015. http:// www.motherjones.com/ politics/2014/11/america-still-has-hundreds-military-bases-worldwide-have-they-made-us-any-safer.

Warshauer, Mathew. 2007. "Andrew Jackson and the Constitution." History Now. Accessed April 20, 2017. https://www.gilderlehrman .org/history-by-era/age-jackson/essays/andrew-jackson-and-constitution.

Weber, Max. 1978. *Economy and Society.* Translated and edited by Guenther Roth and Claus Wittich. Berkeley: University of California Press.

———. 1991. "Bureaucracy." In *From Max Weber: Essays in Sociology,* translated and edited by H. H. Gerth and C. Wright Mills, 196–244. London: Routledge.

Weinstein, Adam. 2012. "Nobody Puts Tammy Duckworth

in a Corner." *Mother Jones,* August. Accessed March 19, 2014. http://www.motherjones.com/politics/2012/08/tammy-duckworth-versus-joe-walsh-congress.

Williams, Irene, and Kunsook Bernstein. 2012. "Military Sexual Trauma among U.S. Female Veterans." *Archives of Psychiatric Nursing* 25, no. 2: 138–47.

Williams, Rudi. 2000. "21 Asian American World War II Vets to Get Medal of Honor." Armed Forces Press Service, May 19. Accessed April 20, 2013. http://www.defense.gov/news/newsarticle.aspx?id=45192.

Wunderle, William D. 2006. *Through the Lens of Cultural Awareness: A Primer for US Armed Forces Deploying to Arab and Middle Eastern Countries.* Fort Leavenworth, KS: Combat Studies Institute Press. Accessed August 10, 2015. http://usacac.army.mil/cac2/cgsc/carl/download/csipubs/wunderle.pdf.

Wynn, Neil A. 2010. *The African American Experience during World War II.* Lanham, MD: Rowman & Littlefield.

Zinn, Howard. 2003. *A People's History of the United States.* New York: New Press.

Racial and Ethnic Categories Have Changed Over the Past 220 Years

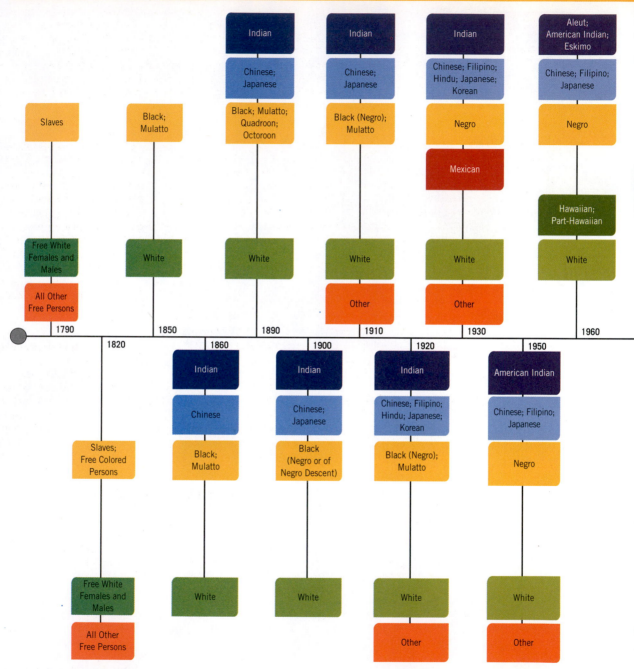

1790: Slaves; Free White Females and Males; All Other Free Persons

1850: Black; Mulatto; White

1890: Indian; Chinese, Japanese; Black, Mulatto, Quadroon, Octoroon; White

1910: Indian; Chinese, Japanese; Black (Negro), Mulatto; White; Other

1930: Indian; Chinese, Filipino, Hindu, Japanese, Korean; Negro; Mexican; White; Other

1960: Aleut, American Indian, Eskimo; Chinese, Filipino, Japanese; Negro; Hawaiian, Part-Hawaiian; White

1820: Slaves; Free Colored Persons; Free White Females and Males; All Other Free Persons

1860: Indian; Chinese; Black, Mulatto; White

1900: Indian; Chinese, Japanese; Black (Negro or of Negro Descent); White

1920: Indian; Chinese, Filipino, Hindu, Japanese, Korean; Black (Negro), Mulatto; White; Other

1950: American Indian; Chinese, Filipino, Japanese; Negro; White; Other

Source: U.S. Census Bureau, "Measuring Race and Ethnicity across the Decades: 1790–2010," http://www.census.gov/population/race/data/MREAD_1790_2010.html.